Globalization and Maritime Power

Globalization and Maritime Power

edited by Sam J. Tangredi

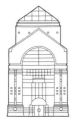

NATIONAL DEFENSE UNIVERSITY PRESS
WASHINGTON, D.C.
2002

Library of Congress Cataloging-in-Publication Data

Globalization and maritime power/edited by Sam J. Tangredi.
     p.cm.
Includes bibliographical references and index.
    ISBN 1–57906–060–9
    1. United States. Navy. 2. Globalization. 3. Sea-power. 4. Navies. 5. Shipping. 6. Security, International. 7. World politics—21st Century. I. Tangredi, Sam J.
    VA50.G58 2002
    359′.03′0973—dc21

2002151078

First Printing, December 2002

NDU Press publications are sold by the U.S. Government Printing Office. For ordering information, call (202) 512-1800 or write to the Superintendent of Documents, U.S. Government Printing Office, Mail Stop: SSOP, Washington, D.C. 20402. For GPO publications on-line access their Web site at: http://www.access.gpo/su_docs/sale.html.

For current publications of the Institute for National Strategic Studies, consult the National Defense University Web site at http://www.ndu.edu.

To the men, women, and children who died as a result of the terrorist attacks on September 11, 2001—in the World Trade Center, in the Pentagon, on the airliners, and in the subsequent campaign in Afghanistan—including the sailors and naval officers of the Navy Command Center and the Strategy and Concepts Branch of the Office of the Chief of Naval Operations. Many of the contributors to this volume previously served in the Strategy and Concepts Branch or had a professional relationship with its members.

Contents

Part V—Globalization and Force Structure

Illustrations

Preface

Vice Admiral Paul G. Gaffney II, USN
President, National Defense University

In 1998, the Institute for National Strategic Studies at the National Defense University was asked to conduct a major study of the effects of globalization on America's national security. The results of the study were published as *The Global Century: Globalization and National Security*, a two-volume book and associated summary report, both of which have received acclaim. Over 50 experts from a wide range of fields contributed to the effort. Sponsored by the Department of the Navy, *The Global Century* contained a section addressing the future of military and naval power in a globalizing world; however, the majority of the study concentrated on the causes of globalization and the ensuing political, economic, cultural, and societal effects.

Following in the wake of the original project, the volume you now hold takes the study to a deeper, more specific level of analysis. *Globalization and Maritime Power* focuses on the direct impact of globalization on naval forces and maritime aspects of commerce and international relations. It seeks to translate the general knowledge that we have learned about the phenomenon of globalization into the language of strategy and defense policy. It is both deductive and inductive in its approach—using general knowledge of globalization to deduce its impact on the maritime world, and using inductive reasoning in applying those maritime impacts to the overall fabric of defense planning. Its intent is to provide our national security leaders with analyses that can be directly applied to some of the problems and issues that we will face in the future security environment.

Many of the ideas presented in this book were discussed and debated in a series of colloquia held at the National Defense University and were part of a dialogue with other analytical organizations, principally the Center for Naval Analyses and the Center for Strategic and International Studies. Particular effort was made to elicit contributions from a broad range of experts with diverse sets of experiences and perspectives. The institutional affiliations of individual authors vary from the Department of the Navy to the Joint Staff to intelligence agencies to our sister war colleges to civilian universities. Of course, the views presented herein are those of the authors and do not necessarily reflect the official position of any of these agencies.

Although the focal points of *Globalization and Maritime Power* are naval and maritime, its spirit is very joint. It approaches its assessment of maritime power as a part of our overall joint military capabilities. Moreover, its treatment of such effects of globalization as terrorism and transnational threats contains lessons of value for all involved in national security decisionmaking, including agencies outside the Department of Defense.

Acknowledgments

This volume is the product of a research project on the maritime implications of globalization sponsored by the Department of the Navy and carried out by the Institute for National Strategic Studies (INSS) at the National Defense University (NDU). While not intended to be "the third volume" of the previous INSS study, *The Global Century: Globalization and National Security*, it fits closely with the themes of that earlier work and greatly benefits from previous insights. The earlier work was the brainchild of former Under Secretary of the Navy Jerry MacArthur Hultin, who also deserves credit for inspiring this continuation. Current Under Secretary of the Navy Susan Livingstone also provided encouragement. The continuation of the project was due to the unflagging support of former Deputy Under Secretary of the Navy Charles Nemfakos, who recently retired after over 30 years of Federal service. Many individuals on Mr. Nemfakos' staff made contributions, most notably Captain Kenneth Milhoan, USN, and Captain Kip Nicely, USN, who served as project supervisors on the Navy's end. Rear Admiral Stephen G. Smith, USN, Director, Office of Program Appraisal, Office of the Secretary of the Navy, also provided guidance for the overall project.

Under the leadership of NDU President Vice Admiral Paul G. Gaffney II, USN, the project was supervised at INSS by Stephen J. Flanagan, NDU Vice President and Director of INSS, and James A. Schear, INSS Director of Research. Richard L. Kugler, INSS distinguished research fellow, and Ellen L. Frost, visiting fellow at the Institute for International Economics—who were the editors of *The Global Century*—provided sound advice and assistance. Kimberley L. Thachuk, INSS scholar and one of the chapter authors, graciously consented to manage the project budget during the transition from the earlier work and was a participant in many of the key decisions about the project. Deborah Jefferson of INSS also performed financial management, along with Captain Donald D. Mosser, USN (Ret.), INSS dean of administration. Administrative support was provided along the way by INSS senior military fellow Captain Jerry Faber, USN, Linda B. Vaughn, Brenda D. Bennett, and Crystal Crump.

Robert A. Silano's team at NDU Press did the technical editing and publication management. All members of the press participated, including William R. Bode, George C. Maerz, Lisa M. Yambrick, and Jeffrey D. Smotherman.

Esther A. Bacon of INSS deserves vast credit for keeping this project afloat. As analyst, research associate, colloquium coordinator, and keen observer of the humorous ironies that befall such projects, she made valuable contributions on a daily basis—while performing a host of tasks for her many other bosses.

As editor, I am indebted to all the chapter authors, as well as the many participants in our colloquium series who provided commentary, discussion, and feedback. Many, many people provided advice and support. On a personal level, I am grateful to my parents, Sam and Anna Tangredi, for strongly encouraging me to write extensively during my formative years, and especially to the one who encouraged, inspired, and strengthened me throughout the editing of this volume—my lovely and insightful wife, Reverend Deborah L.H. Mariya.

Introduction

Sam J. Tangredi

Globalization has altered the dynamics.... We have to respond to that.

—President-elect George W. Bush, January 16, 2001

Prior to September 11, 2001, most Americans viewed globalization as primarily—perhaps exclusively—an economic phenomenon.[1] The economic evidence—rapidly shifting flows of world capital, expansion of overseas markets and investments, the global connections of e-commerce and the Internet, as examples—seemed readily apparent, even if some critics viewed *globalization* itself as an ill-defined term. But appropriately defined or not, the concept of globalization had already achieved considerable stature, causing corporate boards and shareholders to thirst after presumably growing international markets, Internet junkies to claim their own transnational community, and antiglobalization protestors to smash municipal trash cans from Seattle to Washington.

Although a number of studies suggested that globalization held profound national security implications—*The Global Century: Globalization and National Security* among others—these implications were largely confined to debates that might be considered esoteric by those outside the defense intellectual community.[2] The above quotation by President Bush actually referred to a question of how to integrate concerns about economic globalization into the national security decisionmaking process—the answer to which did not seem to be as pressing a problem in early 2001.[3] Publicists of globalization, such as journalist Thomas Friedman, did point to the "hidden fist" of U.S. military power as being critical for providing the global security necessary for the flourishing of democracy and free markets.[4] But even his (relatively few) cautionary comments seemed to be drowned out by the exuberant trumpeting of a world in which geo-economics had replaced geopolitics.[5] Friedman himself put forward "the Golden Arches Theory of Conflict Prevention," arguing that economic globalization had made interstate war nearly impossible, or as he put it, "No two countries that both had McDonald's had fought a war against each other since each got its McDonald's."[6]

Friedman later had to modify his theory in light of the North Atlantic Treaty Organization (NATO) bombing of targets in Serbia in support of autonomy for Kosovo (he did exempt civil wars from the theory—which could arguably cover the NATO action),[7] but the idea that globalization, economic interdependence and development, the spread of democratic governance, and the potential for the development of a global-cosmopolitan culture would combine to make for a more peaceful world was becoming quite widespread. Dissident voices, such as Benjamin Barber and Samuel Huntington, warned of a coming "clash of civilizations" when the effects of globalization began to face resistance from the self-established defenders of more traditional cultures.[8] But the prevailing sentiment—fueled by buoyant financial markets and the tremendous valuation of emerging high-tech companies worldwide—remained quite optimistic in its assumption that economic prosperity, albeit uneven, precluded the level of interstate (and, by implication, intrastate) violence that marked the 20th century.[9]

As the expression goes, what a difference a day makes. The terrorist attacks of September 11 and the subsequent anthrax scare succeeded in doing what even the most riotous of antiglobalization protestors could not do—make evident the dangerous "dark side" of globalization to the American and, indeed, world public. In contrast, the equitability and ecological concerns of the anti-World Trade Organization protestors seemed almost petty.[10] Here was a demonstrated clear, present, and immediate danger: terrorists originating in Southwest Asia, but living and training in Western Europe and North America, had used the non-military tools of global communications, efficient air transportation, borderless financial transactions, and the rights and freedom of movement afforded by democratic governance (even to non-citizens) to kill thousands of people and strike at the symbolic hearts of American and global commerce and defense. All of these tools have been identified as attributes of late 20th-/21st-century globalization. In other worlds, the very assets expected to help usher in a more global, peaceful age were used as weapons of mass "disruption." As a U.S. Department of State official recently noted, "even the most benign evidence of globalization—the cell phone—begins to look rather sinister."[11]

Of course, the September 11 terrorists also violated—to use an understatement—principles that have come to be known as international or global norms. Beyond the question of their status as legal combatants, they flouted the most critical element of the international law of war by deliberately targeting civilians—civilians of all ages and nationalities, perhaps even some sympathetic to their putative cause. Their supposed cause is actually antiglobalization in nature, based on a radical, isolated interpretation of the Islamic religion—an interpretation that was considered extreme by Muslims even in the 19th century. Here we have a tangle of the "dark" (destructive) and "light" (constructive) sides of globalization: terrorists violating globalized norms in fighting against the effects of globalization, using the tools of globalization, purportedly for a religion with global aspirations.

Clearly, this dark side of globalization is a national security threat to the United States. The United States has responded to September 11 by launching a global war on terrorism using all of its national security tools—international diplomacy, law enforcement, economic power, intelligence agencies, and joint military forces. Yet global terrorism is but one of a number of national security threats stemming from the effects of globalization. Other dangers may not be as evident but may have significant effects on American security as well. Likewise, operations against global terrorists are but one of a number of military missions that may be necessary to protect America's security and provide support for the constructive or beneficial aspects of globalization.

Nature of this Volume

Globalization and Maritime Power is an attempt to respond to President George W. Bush's task to investigate means of integrating the issues of globalization into the national security decisionmaking process. Its deliberately narrow focus is the examination of the effects of globalization on one particular area of political and economic activity—the maritime realm—and on one specific component of the joint military forces of the United States—the operation of naval forces.[12] As indicated in the Foreword, this volume is intended to identify insights from previous studies of globalization that may have direct or indirect applicability to naval planning and overall defense policy. It is a continuation of an earlier study sponsored by the Under Secretary of the Navy and conducted in the Institute for National Strategic Studies at the National Defense University. As noted, the previous research was published as *The Global Century* and represents a wide-ranging effort to come to grips with the national security implications of globalization. One of the implications identified was indeed the impact of global terrorism as a prime transnational threat. But there are other implications, including some that directly (as well as indirectly) affect U.S. naval forces.

Globalization and Maritime Power attempts to bring these theoretical insights to a level of analysis that is one step closer to that of actual defense policymaking. From this perspective, the ideas offered by the chapter authors constitute a sort of "news you can use" for decisionmakers involved in determining the future of America's naval and maritime power. It is an effort at *applied scholarship*, in the same sense that *applied physics* is differentiated from the study of theoretical physics. Each chapter is guided by three practical questions: what is the impact of globalization on this specific naval or maritime activity; what are the effects of maritime forces on this related aspect of globalization; and what are the alternatives for policy?

Though coordinated by theme, each chapter is an individual effort to examine a small piece of the overall mosaic that constitutes contemporary globalization. Like any mosaic, the relationship between a particular piece and the overall design may be unclear until the observer steps back and examines the whole.

The current volume was conceived and produced in an environment of intellectual freedom afforded by the Nation's premiere academic institution of the U.S. Armed Forces. There is no tension between academic freedom and institutional responsibilities, but—naturally enough—it is biased toward the view that the national security of the United States and the lives and prosperity of Americans should be protected.[13] The volume can also be considered American-centric in nature—all the authors are Americans. However, many have previously studied and written on non-American perspectives of security. For this reason, it does not claim to be a comprehensive study of all aspects of globalization from all possible perspectives.

It does, however, represent a deliberate attempt at diverse perspectives. Diversity is a much-overused term, but in this case the institutional affiliations of the authors range from Joint Staff to service staff, from the Department of Defense (DOD) to intelligence agency, from war colleges to civilian universities, from civilian think-tank to Federal contractor. The specialties of the authors also range from economics to history to international relations to naval and joint warfare. Several of the chapters contain differing conclusions and are juxtaposed in a manner so as to create debates on particular topics—most notably the importance of geopolitics and on the nature of the antiaccess or area denial threat. None of the chapters are meant to be parochial in a service sense; the intent is to present naval and maritime forces as but one important component of America's overall military power. At the same time, many of the insights and issues identified are applicable to other components, services, and government agencies.

What Is Globalization?

The inevitable opening question of any such assessment is, *what exactly is meant by globalization?*

Some may see globalization as an ill-defined term, with a myriad of potentially conflicting definitions. Yet its use is becoming ubiquitous; it is hard to turn on the news without hearing the word used at least once.

For the purposes of this volume, *globalization* is defined in two complementary ways. As a phenomenon, globalization is defined as a substantial (some would say unprecedented or exponential) "expansion of cross-border networks and flows."[14] Such flows may include the creation of a global financial market, expansion of democratic governance, or the increasing ubiquity of the Internet and other forms of communications via modern information technology.

Ellen Frost describes globalization as a long-term process leading to "globality—a more interconnected world system in which interdependent networks and flows surmount traditional boundaries (or make them irrelevant)."[15] Jan Aart Scholte—who has probably done more agonizing over a proper definition for globalization than any other scholar—uses the term *superterritoriality* to describe the same concept.[16] (In contrast, chapter 3 of this volume argues that the degree by which traditional boundaries are surmounted is rather small.) But Frost and Scholte, like other careful scholars, are quick to point out that globalization is a relative term, referring to "relative deterritorialization."[17] Scholte admits that "Territory still matters in the contemporary globalizing world . . . globalization (as an increasing transcendence of territorial space) can also be linked to processes of *reterritorialization* such as localization and regionalization."[18] The concept of the relative nature of globalization is also captured in perhaps the simplest definition, from John Baylis and Steven Smith: "By globalization we simply mean the process of increasing interconnectedness between societies such that events in one part of the world more and more have effects on peoples and societies far away."[19] Although DOD has yet to formulate an official definition for globalization, the Defense Science Board provides one very close to Baylis and Smith: "the integration of the political, economic, and cultural activities of geographically and/or nationally separated peoples."[20]

Most scholars see previous eras of globalization (notably in the years prior to World War I) but view the contemporary flavor as being unique due to the "revolution in information technology, accompanied by the spread of personal computers and the instant availability of information."[21] This revolution in information technology has a much-discussed counterpart—the *revolution in military affairs.*[22] But whether contemporary globalization represents a historically unprecedented state of world affairs, it must be admitted that it does seem to lead to a fundamentally different international system than existed during or immediately following the Cold War.

This leads to the second, complementary definition: globalization as the dominant element of the current security environment. Globalization can be seen as the defining aspect of the current post–post-Cold War international system, and therefore, an appropriate title for the system itself. The attributes of this contemporary international system—such as coalition-building against global terrorism or the cascading effects of regional economic crises in Asia or elsewhere—appear clearly entwined with the globalization phenomenon.

Both globalization as process and as system imply significant and ongoing changes in the international security environment—and suggest the need for new responses to these changes.

Globalization Effects on Maritime Forces

These changes in international security may be most evident in the direct and indirect effects of globalization on the maritime environment and on the military forces that operate in and from the maritime environment. Such changes become readily apparent due to the nature of the maritime world: through the historical evolution of international law, the oceans have effectively been *globalized* for over a century—that is, their use as what Alfred Thayer Mahan would call "the great common" has been open to all nations with the desire, access, and resources to master it. (A discussion of this historical evolution is found in chapter 12.) The maritime world can also be seen as a primary source—in recent parlance, a *root cause*—of globalization because it is the medium by which 90 percent of world trade (when measured by weight and volume) is transported. Without the method of oceanic trade, the barriers to global commerce would be insurmountable, and the history of the world would have been vastly different. E-commerce and the Internet may be the symbols of the most modern version of globalization, but historically the symbols have been the ever-increasing size and speed of ships and the shrinking cost of commercial transport. Ultimately, the open ocean is still the prime medium and symbol of globalization—for the *thoughts* transmitted along the Internet must be translated into *products*, which must in turn be transported to far markets. Even the financial flows that might travel along the wires and fiber-optic cables of today's information network have the eventual purpose of producing goods that are sold and consumed. If these goods are to be sold and consumed in somewhere other than a localized, domestic market, they are likely to be transported by sea.

The nature of the maritime environment as *great common* also bears a striking similarity to the perceived nature of modern economic globalization—particularly as identified by globalization's discontents. The participants with the *access* and *resources* benefit the most, even as all nations benefit to some degree. Developed economies appear to have benefited more from globalization than the least developed economies—leading to questions of structural inequity. Likewise, those nations—sea power states—who have maintained the most powerful navies and/or most efficient shipping systems appear to have benefited the most from the oceanic common, even as subsequent benefits can be identified in all nations, including the landlocked.

Effects on the maritime environment have very practical—though easily ignored—consequences for U.S. national security and economic well-being. That over 90 percent of international trade travels by sea is a fact taken for granted; the dependence of the global economy on maritime transport is hardly remarked upon because, like oxygen, its existence is primarily evident in its absence. Most would agree that seaborne trade is the linchpin of global economic development—development that is ultimately fueled by the transfer of raw materials from sources of supply to manufacturing centers to markets. It is also acknowledged that, although the transfer of investment and financial services can be done by electronic means and personnel and light products can be transferred by air, the most practical and lowest-cost method of transferring durable goods is by water. Clearly, any substantial interference on seaborne commerce would thus have a severe effect on the global economy, including its leading national economy—that of the United States. But few can contemplate a drastic disruption or absence of such a critical economic element.

This is also true from a national security perspective. First is the paradox that even with the world's dominant navy, our maritime borders appear to have become more porous in the era of modern globalization. The United States has been the dominant power of a peaceful continent surrounded by the world's two largest oceans. Within the last 100 years, potential opponents have been unable to deploy their forces to the continental United States; even modest American naval power—when combined with transoceanic distance—has been sufficient since 1812 to keep the world's great powers at bay. Although vulnerable to potential ballistic missile attack, the vast size of U.S. territory and its distance from sources of attack (other than the strategic forces of the former-Soviet Union) enable American military forces to be oriented toward a power-projection role far outside the confines of North America. Since the end of the Cold War and the collapse of Soviet naval pretensions, the global dominance of the United States has become greater than ever before. Yet our coastlines and harbors are largely undefended—by choice. Relatively open borders mean more efficient international trade, a true economic advantage. At the same time, the naval and military power of the United States is such that no other state—the waning nuclear power of Russia exempted—could make a militarily significant attack on the continental United States.

The result is that—until recently—there was relatively little interest in increasing port and coastal security beyond what an underfunded Coast Guard, along with the Border Patrol, Customs Service, and the Immigration and Naturalization Service were already doing in the effort to inspect a portion of incoming maritime traffic—thereby, in theory, deterring potential threats. (See chapter 23 concerning the efforts of the U.S. Coast Guard.) Only the smallest of hostile forces could possibly penetrate the maritime borders. Such forces would not have been deemed militarily significant—that is, until September 11, 2001, demonstrated the effect that such small forces could have on the civilian population. Now the *strong naval power but undefended coast* paradox has become very evident.

But there is a second element to this globalization paradox. As the ease of transportation, which is an element of modern globalization, makes the defense of our sea frontiers more important, globalization also makes actions in the more remote regions of the world even more important to Americans and their economy. The linkage between economic growth and foreign trade increases American dependence on the oceans that physically connect it to these remote regions as well as the importance of control over the connecting ocean areas. This control is the forte of our globally deployed naval forces. Arguably, a direct effect of globalization has been to make the power and effectiveness of naval forces even more important than before. It is not simply a question of retaining the access to trade and resources; America's ability to sustain its influence over events in remote regions has become more maritime dependent—witness recent operations in Afghanistan in which aircraft carrier-based air power conducted the majority of tactical strikes because of a lack of access to nearby land bases.

As will be explored in greater detail in chapter 1, there are at least seven categories of direct effects of globalization on the maritime environment and maritime/naval forces. These include:

1. *A global security environment characterized by an increase in nonstate and transnational threats to U.S. security.* The most obvious of such nonstate threats is global terrorism. However, other threats include global crime, drug trafficking, illegal arms transfers, illegal migrations, and international corruption. America's borders appear porous to certain of these threats. At the same time, all of these threats pose the potential for destabilization of the remote regions with which the U.S. economy is increasingly linked. Both vulnerabilities to and protections from these threats have maritime components. Some transnational threats, such as piracy, are almost exclusively maritime in nature.

2. *Increasing maritime traffic and trade.* Since tangible international trade is dependent on maritime transport, an increase in trade due to or as a means of globalization would naturally result in a corresponding increase in maritime traffic. Estimates of this increase vary; however, according to a U.S. Department of Transportation report issued in February 2000, global ocean-borne commerce is expected to grow 3 to 4 percent annually into the foreseeable future. Increased maritime traffic raises concerns about the safety of sea lines of communications (SLOCs) and of transit through chokepoints—both from a safety of navigation and environmental protection perspective and from a national security perspective. In the light of the global terrorist threat, the security of the maritime transit lanes as well as the ports servicing international trade have become very serious concerns—concerns that were deemed almost inconsequential in the immediate post-Cold War years.[23] As presented in chapter 9, there are good reasons to see SLOCs and chokepoints as scarce resources requiring increased protection.

3. *Increasing American concerns about economic security.* These formerly submerged concerns have both specific and general elements. Specific concerns go hand in hand with the physical and indirect effects of increasing nonstate and transnational threats. Can the U.S. economy weather successive terrorist shocks? The events of September 11 have been identified as deepening the chances of recession. What would happen to the economy if there were severe attacks against economic infrastructure, such as the Internet and global communication? Other concerns are related to the

increase in maritime traffic and trade in light of threats posed by global terrorism. What about attacks on transportation hubs or utilities? (Chapter 7 details the increasing global dependence on a few super-sized *hub* ports.) Are the sea lines and straits that pass through international trade secure? General concerns include the question of whether the United States is gaining economic benefit from its current spending of defense, or whether such spending is a dangerous drag on an overburdened economy. Given that some increase in spending is needed for homeland security in the face of terrorist threats, is the rest of the defense budget—particularly that for forward-deployed naval forces—being well spent? Are our defense industries being affected by globalization, and what are the effects on the economy as well as security? Is our environment—including the oceans—being imperiled by economic globalization? Whether these concerns are valid, they have obviously increased due to public perceptions of globalization.

4. *Greater likelihood of U.S. military presence and intervention in locations not previously considered of vital interest, including regions in which maritime forces must provide the initial—and sometimes exclusive—means of applying joint military power.* The interconnectedness of modern globalization, as noted by Baylis and Smith, is manifest in the cascading effects of regional conflicts. Intervention to prevent the globalization of such conflicts might take the form of peacekeeping, logistical support for local forces, or direct assault. As in Afghanistan—which, ironically, is completely land-locked—the significant portion of the initial forces are likely to be supported from a seabase composed of carrier battlegroups and amphibious ready groups. The Bush administration has expressed some skepticism about the effectiveness of peacekeeping and the need for U.S. involvement in several of the longer-term peacekeeping operations. However, the events of September 11 and the broad range of U.S. national interests suggest the assignment of even greater resources to the future contingencies in which the United States chooses to become involved.

5. *New, unpredicted effects on alliances and coalition-formation and their maritime components.* During the Cold War, alliance behavior was relatively predictable: there was an overshadowing threat that made close cooperation essential throughout NATO and its Pacific partners. Soviet control was repressive over the Warsaw Pact and what are now independent republics in Europe and Asia, but, again, predictable in ways that are not true of these regions today. With the overwhelming Soviet threat removed, old alliances take on new characteristics. Traditional allies, such as France—a nation whose 20th-century survival twice hinged on U.S. involvement in world conflicts—suggest that U.S. "hyperpower" in the globalizing world has become disturbing. Unlikely allies, such as former Soviet republics, have become supportive of U.S. military presence in their region. Coalition-building—such as the coalition supporting U.S. counterterrorist actions—requires differing approaches and tools.

One of these tools is naval cooperation, long a mainstay of NATO interoperability and the defense relationship with Japan. The use of naval cooperation and the peace-time engagement of U.S. maritime forces may need to take on new characteristics. In certain regions, such as the Western Pacific, naval engagement may become the dom-inant, and in some cases sole, form of military-to-military cooperation with coali-tion partners. In a globalized world, U.S. naval forward presence—the peacetime posture of U.S. naval forces—may take on a revitalized role as an agent for political and economic stability. This naval component of U.S. overseas military presence has unique, and sometimes controversial, characteristics, which become even more ap-parent under globalization.

6. *A global security environment characterized by the proliferation of information technology and high-technology sensors and systems.* This is an indisputable feature of military globalization and a premise of proponents of the concept of an ongoing *rev-olution in military affairs.* Information technology is obviously becoming more ubiq-uitous, and much of it has military application—particularly in command and con-trol and battle management. The proliferation of commercial technology brings with it new forms of military-applicable sensors and intelligence, surveillance, and recon-naissance techniques. For example, satellite imagery has become commercialized. The global positioning system, originally designed for military navigation, is now the prime commercial global locating system, used to track shipments and direct trans-portation—both at sea and on land. The implications of the information technology (IT) explosion go far beyond the commercial effects that characterize economic glob-alization. IT and advanced sensors may not yet be able to "lift the fog of war," but the use of commercial off-the-shelf systems greatly enhances the military capabilities of many potential opponents—including global terrorists.

7. *A global security environment characterized by the proliferation of advanced weapons systems and development of* antiaccess *or* area denial *strategies by potential op-ponents, facilitated by the proliferation of high-technology information systems and sen-sors described above.* The proliferation of advanced weapons systems, such as nuclear, chemical, and biological systems, as well as increasing numbers of ballistic missiles, has become a popular concern. Moving beyond the availability of these weapons, their integration with IT and advanced sensors to create advanced antiaccess or area denial systems may represent the true globalization of high-tech military power.

It is possible to identify other effects of globalization that may impact the mar-itime world or categorize the effects described in a much different fashion. However, these seven effects seem an appropriate starting point to examine the implications of globalization for maritime power and to provide the underlying framework for the chapters that follow.

Figure 1. **Effects of Globalization on Maritime Power**

1. Increasing nonstate and transnational threats to U.S. security

---

2. Increasing maritime traffic and trade

---

3. Increasing American concerns about economic security

---

4. Military (including naval/maritime) presence and intervention in locations not previously considered of vital interest

---

5. New, unpredicted effects on alliances and coalition-formation and their maritime components

---

6. Proliferation of information technology and high-technology sensors and systems

---

7. Proliferation of advanced weapons systems and development of *anti-access* or *area denial* strategies by potential

---

Figure 1 lists these seven effects of globalization on maritime power that are the intellectual framework for this volume.

The Chapters

As mentioned, the following chapters are intended to capture a diversity of viewpoints. But, at the same time, they are organized for a cascading flow of interlinked—perhaps we should say *internetted*—topics and ideas. The sections are organized in terms of the globalization effects described above, with the individual chapters examining related topics in a flow from more general observations to more specific examinations and recommendations.

The first chapter sets the stage for the discussion by providing an overview of the theoretical relationship between naval forces and 21st-century globalization. It discusses the seven direct effects in greater detail. It also identifies the thus-far little-explored relationship between sea power and globalization, a relationship that, perhaps, has not been seriously examined since the later works of the great prophet of sea power, Alfred Thayer Mahan. This relationship was previously identified in chapters in *The Global Century* and has recently begun to appear in professional literature.[24]

This is followed by the first major part, "Globalization and the Security Environment." In this part, chapter 2 attempts to characterize the globalized security environment, analyzing the elements contributing to the seven direct effects. Much of this effort capitalizes on the research of the recent Commission on National Security/21st Century (Hart-Rudman Commission), as well as other sources. One of the primary characteristics that defines this new security environment is the rise of nonstate and transnational threats to security (effect 1). Other aspects include the global proliferation of advanced information systems and sensors (effect 6) and potential proliferation of antiaccess or area denial weaponry (effect 7). In the spirit of open scholarly discourse, chapter 3 challenges its predecessor's view of globalization as the prime characteristic of the security environment, arguing that traditional geopolitics still reigns. Chapter 4 focuses directly on nonstate and transnational threats to U.S. security (effect 1), defining these threats and offering insights into the role of maritime/naval forces in combating them. Chapter 5 plunges into the most pressing nonstate threat of global terrorism by assessing the strategies behind global terrorist groups—specifically al Qaeda—and discusses what naval forces could potentially provide in the counterterrorism struggle. One of the capabilities that naval forces can provide in this and other struggles is a relatively secure, legally sanctioned, sovereign maritime forward presence within regions of concern. All the chapters of part one (to a greater or lesser degree) support the contention that globalization entails a greater likelihood of U.S. military intervention in such regions and locations not previously considered of vital interest (effect 4)—Afghanistan being but one example.

Chapter 6 leads off the next part on "Economic Issues and Maritime Strategy" by attempting a rigorous econometric examination of the forward-presence role of naval forces in terms of their effects on globalization as reflected in commodity and stock markets. It extracts key elements of the most ambitious research effort to date in quantifying and estimating the economic benefits of naval forward presence in a world of interconnected markets and financial flows. Current results may be more suggestive than conclusive; however, they appear to point to an intriguing and vibrant area for continuing inquiry—one that should be of considerable interest to the overall study of economic globalization and to those concerned about economic security (effect 3). Chapter 7 incorporates the element of increased maritime traffic and trade (effect 2) into the economic security concerns by examining global dependency on a small number of megaports or hub ports. Chapter 8 continues this combined examination of effect 2 and effect 3 through an investigation of potential threats to SLOCs and chokepoints. In doing so, chapter 8 raises the concern of ecological degradation that has become a major feature of the public debate on globalization, arguing that threats to national and economic security need not be deliberate—but that even resource threats might merit naval involvement. This chapter characterizes SLOCs and chokepoints as scarce resources. But the ecological effects of economic globalization, specifically global warming, may alter the future locations of SLOCs and chokepoints. Chapter 8 identifies several maritime regions, including the Arctic seas, where ecological changes wrought by economic globalization may have impacts on both international trade and national security. As a case study of these impacts, chapter 9 examines the potential consequences of ice-free Arctic seas in detail.

Continuing the "Economic Issues and Maritime Strategy" part, chapter 10 returns to the question of the economic impact (and necessity) of naval forward presence in a region of current concern, Asia-Pacific. The 2001 DOD *Quadrennial Defense Review Report* identifies a policy shift in American defense policy, from a Eurocentric focus to increased emphasis on potential security threats in Asia-Pacific. Chapter 10 explains the need for such a shift through its examination of the energy needs of the existing and emerging Asian economic powers—notably China. According to forecasts, perhaps more than 50 percent of Mideast oil production will be directed to the Asia-Pacific region, much of it traveling by tankers through such chokepoints as the Strait of Hormuz (between Iran and Oman) and the Strait of Malacca (between Indonesia, Thailand, Malaysia, and Singapore). This and the potential for interstate and intrastate conflict in an "arc of crises" running from the Middle East to Northwest Asia suggest a continuing and increasing role for the U.S. Navy—the world's last global navy—and the U.S. Marine Corps and other maritime forces in maintaining the peace and stability if that region is to share in the benefits of economic globalization.

Chapter 11 shifts gears and examines yet another aspect in national and economic security, the globalization (real or predicted) of U.S. defense industries. Such a defense industrial globalization might have both direct effects on America's ability to conduct autonomous military actions and indirect effects that fan the proliferation of military-directed or dual-use information systems (effect 6) and advanced weapons (effect 7). Appropriate for a volume on globalization and maritime power, the second half of chapter 11 narrows its focus to shipbuilding.

Chapter 12 leads off the part on "International Politics and Maritime Alliances and Coalitions" through an examination of the international law of the sea, which allows for naval forward presence at the same time it prohibits piracy, unlawful acts of war at sea, and maritime terrorism. (Chapter 12 does, however, conclude that international law, by itself, can do little to prevent global terrorism.) Chapter 13 examines the issue of globalization and maritime security from the perspective of the European Union (somewhat balancing the Asia-Pacific tilt of chapter 10), including the effects on alliances, such as NATO, and coalitions (effect 5). Chapter 14 takes the perspective of all the allied and friendly navies (which currently include almost all of the world's navies, except those of Iran, North Korea, Cuba, and China) and argues for the need to develop a multinational naval doctrine that would allow them to integrate their defense efforts even more closely with the U.S. Navy (and U.S. Coast Guard).[25] Such a multinational naval doctrine would be symbolic of an operational "globalization" of navies and could potentially forge quite a number of new alliances and coalitions centered on maritime security (effect 5).

Concluding this part, chapter 15 returns to the issue of naval forward presence in terms of the overall trends in joint U.S. military overseas presence. Given that naval presence may have economic security effects, does it conform to the desires of current DOD leadership, particularly as expressed in the *Quadrennial Defense Review Report*? Does it play a major role in stabilizing military alliances and coalitions (effect 5)? Chapter 15 concludes that it does satisfy both accounts but may require alterations in deployment policy and force structure to keep pace with globalization effects (such as effects 6 and 7).

Part four, "Globalization and Naval Operations," assesses all the globalization effects on the individual warfare areas of contemporary naval operations. Chapter 16 provides an entry to operational concept development through an examination of the emerging concept of *effects-based operations*. This chapter argues that a policy of deterrence centered on conventional effects-based capabilities is the most appropriate defense posture in a globalized world and could shore up the deterrence effects that naval forward presence is assumed to generate. Chapter 17 begins the individual assessments of the *more traditional* categories of naval operations with a look at current and future undersea warfare. Chapter 18 examines the future of naval aviation, including both strike warfare and maritime patrol. The role of surface warfare under globalization is discussed in chapter 19. Chapter 20 focuses on mine warfare, considered one of the most perniciously globalized areas of antiaccess weapons proliferation (effect 7). Naval mine warfare is perhaps the cheapest of all area denial strategies, putting it in reach of even the most limited of national defense budgets. Chapter 21 looks at amphibious and naval expeditionary warfare, an element of maritime capabilities that—along with naval strike warfare—is frequently called up to enable the projection of American military power into the crises-prone remote regions that appear to be increasingly important to global security (effect 4).

Chapter 22 looks directly at the effects of globalization on the U.S. Marine Corps, in sustained expeditionary warfare ashore as well as forcible-entry amphibious operations. As a response to the effects of the globalized security environment, chapter 22 advocates a new form of operational organization: expeditionary maneuver brigades. Chapter 23 broadens the part from naval to maritime by examining the expanding post-September 11 role of the U.S. Coast Guard, both in homeland security and deployed operations. This chapter advocates the increased use of the Coast Guard in conducting more aspects of the military-to-military *engagement* with nations that lack the resources or have no intention of developing an oceangoing *blue water* navy. Such engagements are presumed to enhance the beneficial nature of the globalization phenomenon and enhance alliance and coalition building in the post–post-Cold War world (effect 5). Chapter 24 focuses on another aspect of homeland defense—the development of a national missile defense (NMD)—and assesses the future role that the U.S. Navy could play in an integrated NMD system.

The final part, "Globalization and Force Structure," is the most prescriptive in nature, seeking to make more detailed recommendations on how maritime forces could best *transform* themselves to deal effectively with the security issues generated by globalization. Chapters 25 and 26 tackle head-on the issue of information technology and antiaccess weapons proliferation (effects 6 and 7) but come up with significantly different conclusions. Chapter 25 postulates that the ability to continue extensive forward presence may prove problematic in light of *anti-navies* and antiaccess or area denial systems and strategies designed to deny U.S. naval reach into the coastal or littoral regions of potential opponents. A potential solution to maintaining robust U.S. power projection capabilities in the face of proliferating antiaccess weaponry would be to transform the current U.S. Navy into two distinct forces: a relatively light and expendable forward-presence navy designed as a trip-wire to reassure allies of U.S. military commitment to their defense, and a power-projection navy—working in consonance with joint long-range strike forces—that could be kept safely outside the reach of antiaccess systems (possibly 1,000 nautical miles or more) and be gradually moved forward while conducting effects-based or attrition warfare against the enemy.

Examining the actual global procurement of potential antiaccess weapons systems, chapter 26 suggests that the antiaccess threat is greatly overstated and need not require a radical transformation in naval force structure. In that case, a more evolutionary pace of technological development and experimentation may suffice to enable so-called legacy systems to project combat power effectively against a prepared, entrenched opponent.

Working with some of the same assumptions as chapter 25 about the decreasing survivability of the legacy Navy, chapter 27 puts forward a set of specific propositions on how U.S. naval forces should be structured and organized to operate effectively under the conditions of contemporary globalization. Chapter 27 also challenges some of the traditional views discussed in chapters 6, 10, and 15 as to the actual effects of naval forward presence in a globalized world. This chapter views forward presence as having some moderate success in reassuring allies and maintaining coalitions (dealing with effect 5) but sees it as rarely, if ever, deterring the outbreak of an actual regional crisis or conflict (dealing with the ultimate results of effects 6 and 7). In this view, it is the effectiveness of naval peacetime operations that has been overstated, not the antiaccess threat.

More in tune with the chapter 26 view of evolving (versus exponential) challenges, chapter 28 proposes a new naval operational architecture to ensure U.S. naval predominance in future combat. *Operational architecture* is a term in current use in DOD to describe the manner in which military units can be organized, equipped, and trained to achieve greatest tactical efficiency. (Operational architecture is often used to refer exclusively to combinations of information technologies; however, a broader definition is adopted here.) The focus is not on the question of exactly which systems should be procured, but how existing and future systems can be combined to achieve best effects—what some might call a synergetic *system of systems*.[26]

Chapter 29 attempts to put all the previous force structure proposals (and some additional ones) in context by describing the difference in expectation America has of its naval forces before and after September 11. In this approach (particularly in sync with chapters 4, 5, and 6), the terrorist attack is the true introduction to the security threats of globalization, making obsolete some of the assumptions under which naval forces—and the entire maritime environment—previously operated. While solutions may be premature, radical changes are seen as looming over the horizon—changes that are needed if the United States is truly to use its maritime power to influence positively the outcome of 21st-century globalization. Chapter 30 reinforces this view by calling on naval professionals to change their modes of thinking to grasp the implications of the identified (and unforeseen) effects of globalization.

The volume ends with a brief conclusion and bibliography of sources. The purpose of both is to encourage further, even more detailed research and discussion on related issues.

Invitation to Continuing Participation

The research detailed in these pages is but an introduction to the potential for fruitful investigation into this critical element of American national security, as well as to the overall study of globalization. It is our belief that scholars and students of globalization have not yet begun to recognize the importance that sea power, among other maritime elements, has in the globalization process.[27] Similarly, many defense analysts do not yet grasp the elements of globalization that have such a profound impact on future defense planning. The chapters in this volume constitute an invitation for a broadened debate on the topic of globalization, national security, and the future roles, missions, force structure, and organization of maritime forces.

None of the chapters that follow claim to be complete, definitive examinations of their chosen topics. However, collectively they provide an effective baseline from which more detailed and analytical research could proceed.

In an effort to start such a dialogue, the chapter authors join me in inviting the readers to analyze, debate, and challenge their conclusions. Welcome aboard the study of globalization and maritime power as issues in our continuing quest for global security.

Notes

[1] For example, see the approach of Jeffrey D. Sachs in discussing globalization in a professional military journal: Sachs, "The Geography of Economic Development," *Naval War College Review* 53, no. 4 (Autumn 2000), 93–105.

[2] Others include Andrew J. Bacevich, "Policing Utopia: The Military Imperative of Globalization," *The National Interest*, no. 56 (Summer 1999), 5–13; Thomas P.M. Barnett and Henry H. Gaffney, Jr., "Globalization Gets a

Bodyguard," U.S. Naval Institute *Proceedings* 127, no. 11 (November 2001), 50–53; Paul Bracken, "The Second Nuclear Age," *Foreign Affairs* (January/February 2000), 146–157; Jean Marie Guehenno, "The Impact of Globalisation on Strategy," *Survival* (Winter 1998/1999), 5–19; Thomas Keaney, "Globalization, National Security and the Role of the Military," *SAISphere* [electronic version], Winter 2000, accessed at <www.sais-jhu.edu/pubs/saisphere/winter00/indexkk.html>; Michael Renner, "Alternative Futures in War and Conflict," *Naval War College Review* 53, no. 4 (Autumn 2000), 45–56; Kenneth N. Waltz, "Globalization and American Power," *The National Interest*, no. 59 (Spring 2000), 46–56.

[3] "Security Council's New Role," *The New York Times*, January 16, 2001, A10.

[4] Thomas L. Friedman, *The Lexus and the Olive Tree*, rev. ed. (New York: Anchor Books, 2000), 464–468.

[5] One of the first to state this boldly was Edward N. Luttwak, "From Geopolitics to Geo-Economics," *The National Interest*, no. 20 (Summer 1990), 17–23.

[6] Friedman, 248.

[7] Thomas L. Friedman, "Was Kosovo World War III?" *The New York Times*, July 2, 1999, A17.

[8] See Benjamin R. Barber, *Jihad Versus McWorld* (New York: Times Books, 1996); Samuel P. Huntington, *The Clash of Civilizations and the Remaking of World Order*, 2d ed. (New York: Touchstone Books, 1997).

[9] It has become a scholarly trend to view the 20th century as an *age of global conflict*, and indeed World Wars I and II were fought on a vast scale and with great destructiveness. But whether conflict was more endemic to the 20th century than preceding eras is unclear. The 20th century also contained long periods of relative peace, and some scholars of globalization seem to be using the age of global conflict argument primarily to castigate nationalism for creating a "global war system"—a system that will presumably fall away with the demise of the nation-state. See representative discussion in David Held, Anthony McGrew, David Goldblatt, and Jonathan Perraton, *Global Transformations: Politics, Economics and Culture* (Stanford, CA: Stanford University Press, 1999), 87–148.

[10] A sentiment captured in Steven Pearlstein, "Globalization Regaining Impetus," *The Washington Post*, December 7, 2001, A12–A13.

[11] Remarks by Richard N. Haass, Department of State director of policy planning at Strategic Assessment Group Conference, *The United States in the Third World Century: How Much Will Demographics Stress Geopolitics?* Wilmington, DE, November 14, 2001.

[12] Strictly speaking, the term *naval forces* does not include the U.S. Coast Guard in peacetime. Properly, the term to describe all of the elements discussed in this volume is *maritime power*, hence the title. But it must be admitted that the significant portion of the book concentrates on the U.S. Navy and U.S. Marine Corps.

[13] This volume is grounded in the philosophy that there is no such thing as *value-free* research in the social sciences but that scholars should strive to be *value-explicit*. This as a critical distinction was highlighted in the recent work of James N. Rosenau, *Turbulence in World Politics: A Theory of Change and Continuity* (Princeton, NJ: Princeton University Press, 1990), 33–34. All the contributors to this volume are personally committed to American security—some with their lives and careers.

[14] Ellen L. Frost, "Globalization and National Security: A Strategic Agenda," in *The Global Century: Globalization and National Security*, ed. Richard Kugler and Ellen L. Frost (Washington, DC: National Defense University Press, 2000), 37.

[15] Ibid.

[16] Jan Aart Scholte, *Globalization: A Critical Introduction* (New York: St. Martin's Press, 2000), 42.

[17] Ibid.

[18] Ibid. Frost refers to this as *subglobal globalization*. Frost, 39–41.

[19] John Baylis and Steve Smith, eds., *The Globalization of World Politics* (Oxford: Oxford University Press, 1997), 7.

[20] U.S. Office of the Secretary of Defense, Defense Science Board Task Force on Globalization and Security, *Report of the Task Force on Globalization and Security* (December 1999), 1. Also cited in Frost.

[21] Frost, 38.

[22] The literature on the revolution in military affairs (RMA) is extensive; however, for definitions and discussion of RMA by original proponents, see Eliot A. Cohen, "A Revolution in Warfare," *Foreign Affairs* (March/April 1996), 37–54; James R. FitzSimonds and Jan M. van Tol, "Revolutions in Military Affairs," *Joint Force Quarterly* (Spring 1994), 24–31; and Andrew F. Krepinevich, "Calvary to Computer: The Patterns of Military Revolutions," *The National Interest*, no. 37 (Fall 1994), 30–42. A more skeptical discussion that is supportive of transformation is Michael E. O'Hanlon, "Can

High Technology Bring U.S. Troops Home?" *Foreign Policy* (Winter 1998–1999), 72–86; and further developed in O'Hanlon, *Technological Change and the Future of Warfare* (Washington, DC: The Brookings Institution Press, 2000).

[23] See, for example, the views expressed in several sources cited in chapter 8—particularly John H. Noer and David Gregory, *Chokepoints: Maritime Economic Concerns in Southeast Asia* (Washington, DC: National Defense University Press, 1996)—which implies that the closure of individual chokepoints, such as the Strait of Malacca, have but a marginal effect on overall world trade.

[24] See Sam J. Tangredi, "Security from the Oceans," in *The Global Century*, 471–492. Implications are further developed in Sam J. Tangredi, "Beyond the Sea and Jointness," U.S. Naval Institute *Proceedings* 127, no. 9 (September 2001), 60–63.

[25] In the case of many smaller coastal navies (essentially coast guards), training and integrated operations are more appropriately done with the U.S. Coast Guard, which periodically deploys its vessels to foreign waters specifically for the purpose of such "engagement."

[26] For a military perspective of the *systems of systems* concept, see William A. Owens with Edward Offley, *Lifting the Fog of War* (New York: Farrar, Straus and Giroux, 2000), 98–102, 224–225.

[27] As noted in chapter 1, a broad definition of sea power would describe much of the activities discussed in this volume, including maritime trade and exploitation of ocean resources, as well as naval power. In recent years, however, sea power has become frequently seen as a parochial term—a concept justifying the positions of the U.S. Navy and U.S. Marine Corps in DOD budget decisions. With this connotation in mind, the term *maritime power* was chosen for use throughout this volume as an alternative to sea power. Maritime power should be properly thought of as including other elements of U.S. joint military forces—the U.S. Army and U.S. Air Force—which also conduct operations or are dependent on transport in the maritime environment. For a discussion of a modern, broad definition for sea power, see Sam J. Tangredi, "Sea Power—Theory and Practice," in *Strategy in the Contemporary World*, ed. John Baylis, James Wirtz, Eliot Cohen, and Colin S. Gray (New York: Oxford University Press, 2002), 111–136.

Globalization and Maritime Power

Chapter 1

Globalization and Sea Power: Overview and Context

Sam J. Tangredi

Globalization can . . . be defined as the intensification of worldwide social relations which link distant localities in such a way that local happenings are shaped by events occurring many miles away and vice versa.[1]

Globalization entails an accelerating rate and/or higher level of economic interaction between nation-states and national economies.[2]

[Globalization is] the inexorable integration of markets, nation-states, and technologies to a degree never witnessed before—in a way that is enabling individuals, corporations and nation-states to reach around the world farther, faster, deeper and cheaper than ever before.[3]

This, with the vast increase in rapidity of communication, has multiplied and strengthened the bonds knitting the interests of nations to one another, till the whole now forms an articulated system, not only of prodigious size and activity, but of an excessive sensitiveness, unequalled in former ages.[4]

W hich of the above quotations is *not* a description of globalization circa 2002? Even experts on globalization are likely to consider all four as accurate depictions of the widely discussed economic phenomenon of the 21st century. Contemporary globalization *does* appear to link local events to international effects, to be fueled by continuing advancements in the speed of communications, to be characterized by an accelerating rate of international economic and social relations, and to

Captain Sam J. Tangredi, USN, is senior military fellow in the Institute for National Strategic Studies at the National Defense University. Previously he served as head of the Strategy and Concepts Branch, Office of the Chief of Naval Operations. His numerous articles and chapters on defense strategy and international relations have won nine literary awards, including the U.S. Naval Institute's prestigious Arleigh Burke Prize. A graduate of the U.S. Naval Academy and a distinguished graduate of the Naval Postgraduate School, he earned a Ph.D. in international relations from the University of Southern California.

result in an articulated system in which more and more activities are extremely sensitive to occurrences in distant nations. Many experts emphasize the fact that today's globalization is occurring at a degree unequalled to similar trends in the past.

Thus, it might come as a surprise to point out that the last quotation appeared in an American journal in 1902 and was written by a then-popular historian who would be uncharitably described by later scholars as a nationalist, jingoist, and imperialist. The author was U.S. Navy Captain Alfred Thayer Mahan, known to both supporters and detractors as the father of the concept of sea power.[5]

Therein lies an initial clue to the little-explored relationship between sea power—or in the unifying terminology of this volume, *maritime power*—and globalization. The similarity between the intrinsic elements of the concept of sea power as popularized by Mahan—accelerated communications and international trade, multinational use of a "global common," reduction in the security and sovereignty of (certain) nation-states—and the recognized components of the modern version of globalization seems almost uncanny. But this similarity, as pointed out in the Introduction, is not a coincidence. If, as many scholars contend, modern globalization is but the continuation of a process that began contemporaneously with the development of nation-states,[6] the dominant facilitator of the process of globalization has always been the sea. As argued later (in chapter 12), the human ability to navigate successfully across the vast oceans was *the* historical turning point that enabled higher levels of international trade (and profit) to spark the evolutionary trend toward economic globalization. Ocean navigation is unique in that it represents the initial means by which humans were able to use routinely a fluid medium that could not be normally inhabited as a primary means for communication and commerce.[7] Fast-forwarding to today, the development of the Internet and e-commerce—which observers like Thomas Friedman consider the defining characteristic of the modern version of globalization[8]—represents a step similar to ocean navigation: the Internet is a new fluid medium that humans cannot physically inhabit but can use for communications and commerce.

As the primary military element of sea/maritime power, naval forces—and specifically the naval forces of the world's dominant political and economic power, the United States—contribute to the international security function of protecting the mediums and markets critical to this increasing international exchange known as globalization. Indeed, the very nature of navies appears to make their protective role uniquely attuned to the new-era dynamics created by globalization. This is as true in 2002 as it was in 1902. Moreover, because the U.S. Navy is the sole global navy in existence today, it plays a vitally important role in ensuring the favorable outcome of the current globalization process. In that sense, the Navy and its traditional partner, the U.S. Marine Corps, are both globalized and globalizing forces.

What Is Sea Power?

To understand the linkage between sea power and globalization, one must first unlearn the popular characterization that sea power (and the work of Mahan) is exclusively about war at sea. The term *sea power* is not exclusively synonymous with naval warfare. It is a much broader concept that entails at least four elements: the control of international trade and commerce; the usage and control of ocean resources; the operations of navies in war; and the use of navies and maritime economic power as instruments of diplomacy, deterrence, and political influence in time of peace. Unlike the concepts of land power or air power, which are generally defined only in military terms, sea power can never be quite separated from its geo-economic purposes. Navies may be the obvious armed element of sea power. However, maritime shipping, seaport operations, undersea resources (such as oil), fisheries, and other forms of commerce and communications through fluid mediums can all be seen as integral to a nation's sea power.

Mahan himself often seemed confused about the most appropriate definition for sea power; his writings focus largely on the "clash of interests" created by the desire of nations to possess a "disproportionate share" of the "sea commerce upon which the wealth and strength of countries was clearly seen."[9] From this perspective, he concluded, "the history of Sea Power is largely, though by no means solely, a narrative of contests between nations, of mutual rivalries, of violence frequently culminating in war ... largely a military history."[10] Yet he routinely described sea power in terms of characteristics that fall outside of the military realm.

Mahan identifies six characteristics as "principal conditions affecting the sea power of nations": geographic position, physical conformation (including natural resources and climate), extent of territory, population, character of the people, and character of the government.[11] Modern naval historians have updated and reformulated the list, and a recent depiction includes economic strength, technological prowess, sociopolitical culture (as "first order" conditions), and geographic position, dependence on maritime trade and sea resources, and government policy and perception (as "second order" conditions).[12] Whether first or second order, all of the characteristics cited contribute to a vibrant, powerful economy and hence play a role as a potential participant in the beneficial aspects of globalization. In short, the characteristics that, in Mahan's words, tend "to make people great upon the sea, or by the sea"[13] are the same characteristics that make a people economically powerful overall and—theoretically—willing participants in the globalization process. Thus, our first conclusion is that sea power and the ability to participate in and benefit from globalization share common characteristics.

In a broad sense, *modern sea power* can be defined as the combination of a nation-state's capacity for international maritime commerce and utilization of oceanic resources, with its ability to project military power *into* the sea, for the purposes of sea and area control over commerce and conflict, and *from* the sea, in order to influence events on land by means of naval forces.[14] As noted, this broad concept is often challenged by a more narrow view of sea power as "a military concept, that form of military power that is deployed at or from the sea."[15]

Globalization Begins at Sea

From a historical perspective, the linkage between sea power and economic power is indeed obvious. Beyond sharing defining characteristics, sea power is a facilitator of economic power, and the quest for economic power is, in turn, a motivator for the development of sea power. Some have defined the era of pre-World War I colonialism as an earlier period of globalization—sort of a *globalization by force*. Critics have charged sea power (and Mahan specifically) as being both a symptom and progenitor of imperialism.[16] No one denies the linkage between seaborne commerce and global economic development, although some have questioned the cumulative effect of naval expenditures and national economies.[17] But in the confusion of interpreting the details, few have truly grasped the continuing truth of Sir Walter Raleigh's dictum, "Whosoever commands the sea commands the trade; whoever commands the trade of the world commands the riches of the world, and consequently the world itself."[18]

Those who would find Raleigh's words a bit too Elizabethan (or grandiose) for the reality of today's economic system would do well to consider the synergy between four facts of the contemporary world. The first is that over 70 percent of the world's surface is covered by ocean. Second is that over 90 percent of international trade, when measured in weight and volume, travels by water. This includes most of the world's raw materials.[19] Third is that the majority of the world's major cities and urban populations lie within 200 kilometers of a coastline. Fourth is that international law provides for freedom of the seas in which any nation can use the open ocean for purposes of trade or defense without infringement on another's sovereignty, subject to international agreements on pollution and exploitation of resources.

These four facts have remained fairly constant throughout the last century and appear to likely remain so throughout this one. When placed in context, it is evident that the seas have been a major factor in the history of human economic and industrial development—and the history of war. In that sense, our second conclusion is that the historical impact of the sea in the pursuit of wealth and the development of a global economy has been as a facilitator or driver of globalization.

But the fact that sea power is ultimately about global trade and that globalization is based on the effects of global (presumably free) trade do not capture yet another similarity between the workings of the global market in a capitalist economy and the acquisition of dominant sea power in a competitive international political system. As noted in the introduction, the sea is relatively free for the use of all states (and even nonstate actors), but it also remains a self-help system. Its use is most beneficial to those actors who have the resources (and desire) to use it effectively, either for the harvesting of resources or for international trade. For example, the fact that the most modern cargo ships require expensive unloading facilities (discussed in detail in chapter 7) limits the number of ports that receive the greatest portions of world trade. To develop such a hub port requires an expenditure of private or public resources that would prove unaffordable to economically lesser developed states. Lesser developed states may indeed benefit from the increase in world trade that hub ports facilitate, but it is likely that the owners of the hub ports initially benefit more.

Likewise, the international law of the sea may provide for equal access to trade and resources, but the means to defend such access against interdiction ultimately lie in the possession of an effective navy. To build such a navy—particularly one that can operate globally—requires a level of state resources that is within the reach only of great powers. Enforcement of the freedom of the seas (against the threat of closure) by a global navy benefits all members of the international economic system. But in terms of sovereignty and freedom of action, the possessor of that global navy would appear to gain more leverage. Our third conclusion is that access to the sea is a metaphor for access to the global economy, both functioning in similar marketplace fashion with a linkage between resources invested and results.

In that sense, access to the sea can be thought of as the perfect economic market model. All parties involved benefit from an efficient market that allows free access and supply to match demand, but the profits to all parties in an efficient market are not equal. Those with better or more desirable products (facilitated by greater knowledge or production resources) make greater profits than those whose products are less desirable. Freedom of the seas as codified in international law allows benefits to be awarded in similar fashion—which drives the historical quest of nations for naval power.

Naval Power and the Global Economy

The importance of a navy rests on twin pillars: its ability to affect events on land and its ability to control use of the sea. The importance of the first ability has evolved with technology as naval weapon systems have continually increased their reach. The importance of the second has continually increased with the world's growing dependence on international trade and ocean resources. If, in a globalized economic system, we are all more dependent on international trade, then naval power becomes more important to all.[20]

Even as accelerated globalization appears to have made naval power as an element of sea power more important to the workings of the global economy, the number of truly global navies has shrunk to one: that of the United States. Largely this has been the result of historical circumstances—the Cold War victory of democratic capitalism. The collapse of the Soviet Union ended the global naval competition that pitted the United States and other North Atlantic Treaty Organization (NATO) navies, along with other allies, against the expanding Soviet Navy. With this Western victory and the fact that the United States intended to keep a superpower-sized navy, there seemed little political reason for nations satisfied with the evolution of the international system to maintain much of an oceangoing navy at all.

This historical circumstance allowed previous security issues to recede and economic concerns to emerge—which is in itself why economic globalization became the prime issue of the post-Cold War international system. And, beyond the disappearance of the immediate security threat, the most obvious reason for the demise of navies is economic: navies require tremendous resources. The main economic inhibitors are the costs of maintaining the logistic capabilities required by an oceangoing fleet and of acquiring the modern naval technology to make such a fleet combat credible in the modern world. Most nations simply cannot or do not want to afford it, particularly if their focus is on competing in the globalizing economy. When combined with the general lack of a naval threat to the security of most nations, the motivation to afford a global oceangoing navy disappears. The result is that the U.S. Navy can be considered a *globalized*, as well as a global, navy. In essence, it is no longer solely the U.S. Navy; it has become the world's navy—delivering the security of access function across the entire world system. It is this security of access function that represents the primary contribution of naval power (as an element of sea power) to peacetime globalization. During periods of conflict, this access function allows the United States (and the globalized world) to project power into contested and otherwise inaccessible regions.

From Global to Globalized Navy

By protecting access to this open market to all those who accept international law, the U.S. Navy performs a common security function on a global basis. In reality, it provides the protocols and security structure of the "maritime Internet," which, in terms of international trade in goods, remains the ultimate Internetted exchange.

Arguably, everyone "uses" the U.S. Navy. With the exception of the "states formerly known as rogues," global terrorists, and (at least rhetorically) the Chinese Communist Party, no one expects any harm from the U.S. Navy. Japan, which remains potentially America's number one economic rival, even allows the Navy to homeport both a carrier battlegroup and an amphibious ready group in its own port cities—and pays for the infrastructure to do so. When building its own ships, Japan routinely licenses technology used by the U.S. Navy. Russia, with a military still often suspicious of the West, has conducted post-Cold War exercises with NATO and U.S. naval forces. The Navy is welcomed in ports around the globe, and the forward naval presence of

U.S. warships is readily accepted—if not always articulated—by most nations as a sound policy for maintaining regional security.

U.S. naval forces are frequently called upon to provide restabilization during periods of potential or real crisis. This is true of land forces as well, but the principle of freedom of the seas provides a unique advantage to navies; they can operate during peacetime in an environment close to the location of the crisis without infringing on the sovereignty of any other state. Thus, the United States can send its naval forces into the Taiwan Strait to defuse a brewing China-Taiwan crisis without infringing the sovereignty of either China or Taiwan. It can even maintain a forward presence there after the crisis is over without any legitimate legal challenge. In this way, naval forces can provide for a stabilizing or calming effect on international markets that might be adversely affected by impending regional crises.

Of course, freedom of the seas can be said to benefit the dominant sea power—the United States—in ways similar to how critics (and even proponents) see globalization as benefiting the dominant economic power. As a globalized service, the U.S. Navy can—within certain limits—determine the location, timing, and procedures of the world's maritime exchanges, as well as control access to land regions. This represents an omnipresent influence of U.S. sea power on the global economy and the overall globalization process. The United States simultaneously operates major fleets in the Mediterranean, Arabian Sea, and Western Pacific, and it has individual ships and squadrons in almost every major locale. U.S. naval presence influences not only economic commerce but also the new-era geopolitics of regions in stabilizing ways. One's view of this situation reflects one's overall view of the role of the United States as the stabilizing influence (read, sole superpower) of the international system. Right now, the majority of international political actors and the entirety of the global economic system value the stabilizing role to a degree that appears obvious but is difficult to measure (although chapter 6 reports on attempts to measure it.)

Like the U.S. dollar in international commerce and the use of the English language in the development of information technology, the U.S. Navy has become the benchmark and dominant standard for all things naval.

Participant in Globalizing Functions

In addition to being a globalized navy, the U.S. Navy facilitates at least four key globalization functions. First, it provides the world standards for naval operations. Second, it conducts direct interactions—such as combined training and exercises—with almost every other national fleet. Such interactions, which the U.S. Department of Defense (DOD) previously referred to as *engagement* but now falling under the term *security cooperation*, are expected to promote the existing and future policies of the engagement and enlargement of global democracy.[21] Third, it carries out the long-term mission of naval forward presence (that is, the continual deployment of naval forces to potential regions of crisis to provide stability and deter hostilities). Fourth, it provides naval weapons technology to selected foreign navies—a globalization, so to speak, of naval power. All of these functions contribute in important ways to the expansion of cross-border networks and flows.

Since the end of World War II, the U.S. Navy has replaced the British Royal Navy in providing the world standards for naval operations. With the exception of Russia, China, and states formerly known as rogues, such as Iran and North Korea, almost all national navies use concepts of operations and procedures derived from or similar to those of the U.S. Navy. This ensures a considerable degree of interoperability. Even those navies that do not have the technology to establish electronic links with U.S. tactical information networks are generally well versed in *Allied Tactical Publication 1*, the NATO signal book for naval operations. The signals and tactics of the United States and NATO have become global; they are used to facilitate naval communications and tactics throughout the world.

This degree of interoperability is solidified and enhanced by combined exercises and operational training around the globe. The U.S. Navy routinely conducts combined exercises and operations, as well as policy discussions, with almost every other fleet. Operations range from the highly integrated NATO Standing Naval Forces Atlantic and Standing Naval Forces Mediterranean; to frequent exercises with Latin American and Asian navies and with that of Australia; to passing exercises with friendly coastal navies; to occasional exercises with Black Sea navies, including that of Russia. A biannual seminar, the International Seapower Symposium, brings high-level representatives from almost every naval staff—including those of Russia and China—to the U.S. Naval War College in Newport, Rhode Island, for discussions of naval policies. The location is familiar because many of the flag officers of the world's navies are graduates of the Naval War College. Bilateral talks between the Chief of Naval Operations' staff and its foreign counterparts are also routine.

As a primary mission of U.S. naval forces in peacetime, forward presence—the continual deployment of naval forces to potential regions of crisis—places the U.S. Navy in the forefront of the proverbial global security market. (Chapter 15 discusses the presence function from a joint perspective and in the context of the 2001 DOD *Quadrennial Defense Review Report*.) Like the best of global corporations, the Navy maintains representatives in the immediate vicinity of its significant customers. Not a day goes by in which U.S. naval forces cannot strike in some fashion at the forces of Saddam Hussein, ethnic cleansers, international terrorists, or maritime drug traffickers, to name but a few potential threats to global and U.S. security. Most international decisionmakers express their support (privately, if not publicly) for the

Navy to continue performing this regional deterrence and stability function.[22] This is a de facto globalization of a common concept of deterrence and security.

Finally, the U.S. Navy provides naval weapons and technology to selected foreign navies or develops systems jointly with allies, and it includes foreign weapon systems on board some of its own ships and aircraft. A few examples of the former include the AEGIS air defense system outfitted on destroyers of the Japanese Maritime Self-Defense Force, and the Cooperative Engagement Capability under development with the United Kingdom; examples of the latter include the German-American rolling air-frame missile ship self-defense weapon, unmanned aerial vehicle prototype systems from Canada and Israel, and the Italian OTO Melara 76-millimeter gun on U.S. FFG–7 class ships.[23] This exchange of systems, which the United States dominates by virtue of its robust defense industrial sector, increases the level of global naval interoperability.[24]

Effects of Globalization on the U.S. Naval Force

Globalized and globalizing, U.S. naval forces—like all American maritime assets—are directly affected by the overall trends in globalization. The multidimensional aspects of naval power (and sea power itself) magnify these effects. Modern navies operate not only on the surface of the ocean but also in the depths below it and the air above it, and they project power both individually and jointly onto land and into space and cyberspace. Ultimately, sea power has an inseparable connection with air power, although that is not necessarily an understanding with which independence-minded theorists of the strategic bombing concept of air power might agree.[25] The multidimensional aspect of naval warfare is illustrated by the range of different naval platforms (ships, submarines, aircraft) and weapon systems (sea mines, guns, torpedoes, cruise missiles) specialized for use in particular maritime environments. Although a platform or system may prove decisive in one environment—such as the dominance of the aircraft carrier and its air wing in long-range open ocean combat—no one platform is necessarily dominant in all aspects of naval warfare. Even the nuclear-powered submarine, with its advantages of undersea stealth and relatively unlimited energy source, is at a disadvantage in shallow water or in conducting operations that expose it to surface attack. U.S. Marine Corps and other naval expeditionary forces add a littoral land warfare focus. The point is that different components of multidimensional naval forces may be affected differently by the various trends of globalization—which is why later chapters in this volume examine the effect of globalization of the individual components in some detail.

Globalization is also a multidimensional and *multidirectional* process. Numerous globalization trends have a direct operational impact on the U.S. Navy of today and will have implications for future naval policy and force structure. As identified in the introduction, seven of these trends are increasing nonstate and transnational threats to U.S. security; increasing maritime traffic and trade; increasing American concerns about economic security; military (including naval/maritime) presence and intervention in locations not previously considered of vital interest; new, unpredicted effects on alliances and coalition-formation and their maritime components; proliferation of information technology and high-technology sensors and systems; and proliferation of advanced weapon systems and development of antiaccess or area denial strategies by potential opponents.

Development of Nonstate and Transnational Threats

The term *nonstate threat* is used to denote a threat to national security that is not directly planned or organized by a nation-state. Today, the foremost among these threats are acts of global terrorism, particularly those carried out without direct sponsorship by a rogue state. (An act of terrorism identified as sponsored directly by a rogue state could be considered an act of war, that is, a threat by another nation-state.) However, there is a loosely defined spectrum of nonstate threats, increasing in intensity from humanitarian disasters to mass migrations, to piracy, to computer network attack (hacking), to organized international crime and drug trafficking, to terrorism with conventional weaponry, to terrorism with weapons of mass destruction (WMD). Along this spectrum, terrorist WMD use is the threat of greatest possible concern, although one with the lowest likelihood.[26]

The term *transnational threat* indicates a threat to national security (presumably a *nonstate threat*) that is not confined within the boundaries of any one state. The National Defense Panel of 1997 referred to such activities as transnational threats—with the implication that such threats could be subject to potential multinational control. Indeed, the panel report states, "Transnational challenges and threats, by definition, reside in more than one country and require a multi-partner response."[27] A simpler definition states, "transnational threats include terrorism, drug trafficking and other international crime, and illegal trade in fissile materials and other dangerous substances."[28]

Whichever term is preferred, it has become evident that the tools of globalization facilitate the cross-border movement of individuals and financial flows involved in crime or terrorism. Transnational threats will be discussed in detail in chapter 4, but it should be pointed out that the term *nonstate* can also include international organizations, nongovernmental organizations (NGOs), multinational corporations, and multinational interest groups, the increase of which is frequently cited as evidence for globalization and the reduction of state sovereignty. Of course, that is not to imply that the activities of such entities are seen as threats to the security of nation-states; however, their actions can sometimes be interpreted in such a fashion.[29]

On issues in which popular opinion is at odds with governmental policy, it is recognized that NGOs can galvanize opinion to change national policies or even affect international policies by promoting a degree of discomfort for a certain state. This level of influence is also taken as evidence of political globalization. A prime example in maritime affairs is the Greenpeace-led campaign to change Japanese or Russian policy toward whaling and toward the creation of an international/global moratorium. On the other hand, even the most aggressive issue-oriented NGOs have found limits to their ability to challenge national sovereignty. When a Greenpeace chapter attempted to prevent the U.S. Navy from conducting an underwater test launching of submarine launched ballistic missiles by positioning a vessel in the launch area, [30] they were rammed, towed, and arrested without a flutter in popular opinion.[31]

Other NGOs—from commercial maritime associations to arms control lobby groups—have significant potential to affect maritime affairs. These hardly constitute threats, but terrorist groups such as al Qaeda can also be considered NGOs.[32] The bombing of the USS *Cole* in Aden harbor has been attributed to al Qaeda, and naval units of many coalition partners have been involved in the interdiction of possible al Qaeda members fleeing via the Indian Ocean. In addition to this deadly NGO, almost all of the transnational threats mentioned above have a maritime component.

Some have argued that nation-states are as vulnerable to transnational threats as the choices they make—such as for greater commercial dependence on the Internet or for wider ranging free trade agreements—require or permit them to be. Others argue that globalization effectively removes any such freedom of choice.[33] As a commercial phenomenon, globalization has tied the economies of advanced states tighter together, but it is still unclear what the effects of a severe downturn (along the line of the Great Depression of the 1930s rather than the recession of 2001–2002) in the global economy might be on the process of globalization itself. Individually, some states will choose greater degrees of autarky than others, cutting their vulnerability to certain nonstate threats. For example, states that erect significant physical barriers to immigration will be less vulnerable to the effects of mass migrations than those that do not. Such barriers often involve action by naval forces (which will be addressed in chapter 4).

The U.S. Commission on National Security/21st Century has identified the evolutionary nature of nonstate threats through the juxtaposition of two of their findings. The growth of nonstate and transnational threats is acknowledged by the observation that "All borders will be more porous; some will bend and some will break." But at the same time, the resilience of the nation-state in retaining its role as primary international actor is recognized by the finding that "The sovereignty of states will come under pressure, but will endure."[34] Yet such endurance will obviously require action.

Increases in Maritime Trade and Traffic

A key effect of economic globalization is the continuing increase in maritime trade and traffic. While the new economy that helps fuel globalization is knowledge-based, the fact is that knowledge needs to be transformed into goods and services. These goods and services need to be transported internationally. While personnel may travel by air, most goods can travel economically only by sea. If globalization indeed results in an increase of world trade and cross-border networks and flows, it will necessarily result in an increase in maritime traffic.

At the same time, ongoing trends could make maritime trade more vulnerable to disruption. As discussed in chapter 7, modernization of maritime off-load and on-load is being consolidated in a handful of *megaports* or hub ports such as Rotterdam, Singapore, Kobe, Vancouver, and Long Beach. The impact of future crises near these megaports—or the sea lines of commerce leading to them—will have a greater overall effect on international trade than it had in the past, when there were many more ports open to the most modern ships. Obviously, this increases the potential workload of the Navy and Coast Guard in providing the maritime security function, whether against bellicose states or against piracy and international crime.

The impact of a global navy and a "national fleet" of U.S. Navy and Coast Guard vessels[35] is directly related not only to its workload but also to the perception of stability that it brings to the international environment. This argues that the requirement for naval forward presence—naval forces operating within the regions of potential crises—will become even more important under continuing globalization. Indeed, the demand for forward presence forces could increase sharply with an increase in the number of small-scale contingencies (SSCs) and peace enforcement and peacekeeping operations in which the United States and its military become involved.

Emerging Concerns about Economic Security

The proliferation of WMD, potential threats to commerce, potential denial of access, and erupting national conflicts have created emerging concerns about U.S. economic security. Homeland security, rarely a topic of popular discussion prior to September 11, 2001, has been of increasing interest to political, business, and economic leaders. Of particular concern is the potential for terrorist use of chemical or biological weapons on U.S. soil. While the effects on individuals are frightening to contemplate, there are also concerns as to what impact the very existence of such an ever-increasing threat may have on U.S. prosperity. Can the United States be truly open to the beneficial aspects of cross-border networks and flows without becoming more vulnerable to terrorist and hacker attacks on individuals, infrastructure, and computer networks? At the same time, there are emerging concerns as to whether U.S. or multinational businesses operating overseas can be protected against what appears to be a increasingly chaotic world filled with WMD-capable terrorists, disgruntled ethnic groups, and increasingly sophisticated international criminal groups. Demands for increased homeland and overseas protection could have significant impact on naval forces. These demands are discussed in numerous chapters in this volume and particularly in chapters 17 through 23.

Presence and Involvement in Locations Not Previously Considered of Vital Interest

In their foreign policies of engagement and humanitarian intervention, the post-Cold War administrations of George H.W. Bush and William Clinton greatly increased U.S. military involvement in many world crises. Supporters of these policies argue that the end of the Cold War lifted the lid off many national and ethnic conflicts and that the United States can make positive steps to contain and reduce them. Opponents argue that such conflicts have been steady throughout history and that U.S. involvement, while worthy and effective in certain cases, is akin to bailing water from the sea. Whatever position dominates, one effect of globalization is to make it appear that such crises have greater effects on the rest of the world than they did in the past. Thus, there is a perception that the increase in cross-border networks and flows necessitates international involvement in the internal crises of far-off nations, to include such supposedly smaller-scale contingencies as NATO bombing of Serbian forces and peace enforcement and peacekeeping in a variety of locales.

Although much of the actual stability operations/peace enforcement and peacekeeping involves ground forces, strong support from air and sea is often a prerequisite. As a part of the Department of the Navy, the Marine Corps is a naval service, thereby bringing direct naval involvement to day-to-day peacekeeping on the ground. The Clinton administration also increased the use of sea-based force in such peacetime SSCs, even using sea-launched Tomahawk land attack missiles to strike terrorist targets in landlocked countries. Such actions now appear as precursors to the more extensive use of naval power in Operation *Enduring Freedom* (counterterrorism). Additionally, naval forces have direct involvement in enforcing international sanctions, such as those against illegal maritime traffic with Iraq and the southern no-fly zone. If globalization continues to increase, along with the perception that such missions are a vital American responsibility, the Navy operational tempo may continue to increase. This would have a significant impact on the numbers and types of naval forces required for such contingencies.

U.S. Navy and Marine forces, of course, will also continue to play important roles in defense strategy for waging major regional wars. The Marines provide about 25 percent of the Nation's active duty ground forces. Together, the Navy and Marines generate about 40 percent of the Nation's tactical air power, including the capacity for precision strikes. Often, the Navy and Marines will be among the first U.S. forces to converge on the scene of a war, where they will play an important role in halting enemy attacks to provide time for larger U.S. forces to deploy to the scene. Once the

U.S. buildup is complete, they will contribute importantly to counterattack plans and ultimate victory. Should some future conflicts be primarily maritime events, their role will be even larger.

Maritime Components of Alliance and Coalition Formation

The tight Western alliance systems that were the hallmark of the Cold War have retained much of their structures, but they have had to transition from their original purposes—containment of the Soviet Union—to other, less encompassing issues. Some argue that NATO has exceeded expectations in this regard, gaining members from the former Warsaw Pact. However, issues such as Balkan peacekeeping are, in reality, indirect threats to the Alliance and therefore do not provoke an immediate, unitary response. For issues outside of the traditional regional interests of Western Europe, Japan, and Australia, the United States has had to forge new coalitions of the willing (for example, in order to prosecute Operation *Desert Storm* or the campaign against al Qaeda). This does not mean that traditional American allies are likely to choose not to join in such coalitions, only that the process of alliance and coalition formation has changed.

Globalization—bringing its wealth of economic and political issues and concerns—has transformed what were previously seen as merely distracting concerns into political disputes among long-standing allies, even as it makes the same states economically interdependent. Economic interdependence magnifies the effects of such disputes at the same time that the lack of a pressing security threat makes the United States less likely to forego economic concerns for alliance unity (the so-called free rider effect). Such concerns inevitably affect the maritime aspects of alliances. These effects include more than burdensharing; they involve agreements on interoperability, access to training areas and live-fire ranges, and the imposition of ever-increasing environmental restrictions on naval activities. Disputes include the sale of military technology to nonallies, with the United States expressing concerns about the sale of European systems to China and Middle Eastern states (such as satellite imagery), and European allies feeling discomfort on U.S. matériel support for Taiwan (such as the pledge to provide diesel submarines). Negotiations over overseas basing rights have become more complex and contested.

Commitment of military forces to U.S.-led interventions outside of NATO or the Western Pacific becomes a matter for debate for states that do not perceive the same level of threat as Americans. To a considerable extent, it has been easier for many to commit naval forces rather than ground troops to such efforts as the campaign against the Taliban. Naval forces from France, Japan, and Germany—among others—have been included in the coalition effort to prevent the flight of al Qaeda members by sea. This creates both new opportunities and new challenges for naval cooperation. Integration of less-capable coalition ships in a way that provides for meaningful participation without adding an additional burden on U.S. logistics requires considerable planning and imagination. Political considerations in allowing for coalition participation may outweigh limited contributions to military effectiveness. Economic concerns may add limitations to the where and when of coalition participation. Rules of engagement (ROE) may vary between coalition units. Chapter 14 discusses the role that multinational naval doctrine might play in standardizing ROE and facilitating maritime coalitions.

Overall, the effects of globalization add complexity to commitments that were presumed throughout the Cold War. Chapter 13 discusses this complexity from a European perspective. At the same time, the freedom of the seas environment may encourage naval cooperation while roadblocks exist on other issues.

Proliferation of Information Systems and Sensors

Another likely effect of economic globalization is a continuing increase in the capability and proliferation of high-speed information systems and remote sensors. Of particular concern to naval forces is the increasing availability of commercial satellite imagery, as well as satellite communications and navigation systems. Satellite imagery is the key element in military reconnaissance and targeting. Satellite navigation systems allow for accurate attacks. Space-based communication systems are more difficult to jam and allow communications between units in difficult operating terrain, including urban terrain.

As part of a revolution in military affairs, many sources claim or imply that naval forces will be more detectable in the future because of the proliferation of space-based imagery. Transformation advocates within the defense analysis community have argued that surface vessels have become vulnerable to detection and strike by antiaccess weapons, particularly in littoral regions, and are no longer viable warfighting platforms. This argument is challenged by sources pointing out the inability of most potential opponents to strike moving targets, particularly at sea.[36] An additional debate concerns the continued use of commercial satellite imagery, navigation, and communications during actual hostilities. The availability of such information to potential opponents of the United States during time of war remains doubtful.[37] But whatever the actually survivability of U.S. surface ships may be, the reality of commercial targeting data becoming widely available is of considerable concern and is a globalization trend that should be taken into consideration in naval planning.

Additionally, as a recent study notes:

the diffusion of information age technologies has eroded American technological supremacy especially in areas of weapons production. As technologies have spread through transnational corporations and new communications mediums such as the World Wide Web, states and other potential adversaries have found it easier to pursue asymmetric military strategies to counter U.S. and western military power.[38]

This spread of asymmetric strategies and system can be referred to as *antiaccess weapons proliferation.*

Antiaccess Weapons Proliferation

A key trend is the proliferation of advanced weapon systems and sensors, particularly to the few nations—mostly states formerly (and now informally) known as rogues—that might seek to challenge U.S. military power. Although the United States does share military technology with selected nations, advanced technology from the former Soviet Union (some of it in continued Russian production, and some of it surplus) has also emerged on the world market.[39]

The technology being marketed includes weapons that the Soviet Union would not export to other Warsaw Pact states during the Cold War.[40] Also, the end of the immediate Cold War threat has prompted several Western states to seek aggressively new markets for their weapon technologies—markets they might have previously pursued with caution. The cost of developing modern military technology has become so high that many individual nations—even well-developed economic powers—need to pursue foreign arms sales to be able to start technological development on systems designed for their own defense.

The proliferation of advanced military systems—such as intelligence, surveillance and reconnaissance sensors, ballistic and cruise missiles, submarines, sea mines, and WMD—parallels the intellectual proliferation of a post-Gulf War operational concept on how to defeat U.S. forces, known as antiaccess or area denial strategy. This strategy recognizes the difficulty in defeating U.S. power projection forces after they have entered the region of conflict and are ready for combat. Instead of fighting U.S. forces on a regional battlefield (where the results might be similar to those of the Gulf War), the potential opponent could attempt to prevent U.S. forces from entering the region at all. In the logic of the antiaccess approach, a potential opponent would initially seek to destroy any forward-based U.S. forces stationed in the region, and then seek to block U.S. maritime and air forces from entering and bringing troops into regional littoral waters and territory by massive attrition attacks using the proliferated weapons systems.[41]

According to this construct, if there were threats to U.S. naval operations, they would come from asymmetrical weapon systems designed to deny U.S. passage through maritime chokepoints or Navy ability to conduct operations near land.[42] The Office of the Secretary of Defense publication *Proliferation: Threat and Response* reports the steady proliferation of such weapons as ballistic missiles, cruise missiles, diesel-electric submarines, sophisticated naval mines, and fast patrol craft.[43]

Under current trends, the U.S. Navy may not have to face another globalized navy in the future, but it may have to face globalized antiaccess weapons. In an antiaccess scenario, with regional land bases capable of supporting U.S. forces destroyed and littoral access denied, the opponent may have effectively extended its defenses out to the entry points of its region. The United States could find itself in the position of having to undertake potentially costly forcible entry operations against a range of high-technology weaponry. Even in this war of attrition, it is likely that the United States would eventually breech the antiaccess defenses, both through naval operations and the use of standoff weapons stationed outside the region or in the continental United States.

However, the real goal of an antiaccess strategy is to convince the United States and its allies or coalition partners that the cost of penetration is simply too high.[44] Hostilities could thereby be ended via a diplomatic agreement that, in effect, grants the regional power its wartime objectives. Such an agreement might be encouraged by international organizations that traditionally advocate negotiated peace. In these ways, an adversary whose military forces are inferior to those of the United States might still be able to attain its political objectives notwithstanding the opposition of U.S. forces. This holds the potential for transforming wars—their nature, their prosecution, and their end states—in the era of globalization.

Conclusion: Considerations Governing Disposition of Future Naval Forces

The existence of a relationship between the modern phenomenon of globalization and the concept of sea power is evident. The extent of that relationship requires additional analysis, but at least four major conclusions can be drawn. First, the concept of effective sea power and the ability to participate in and benefit from globalization share common characteristics. Second, the sea (and the control of it) has played a significant role in the historical development of international trade, global economy, and globalization. Third, the use of the sea and development of sea power appears to be a metaphor—and potentially a research model—for certain aspects of the globalization phenomenon. Finally, distinct effects of globalization on sea power, particularly naval power, can be detected (of which seven provide a starting point for this study).

The overarching questions concerning naval forces and globalization revolve around whether today's U.S. Navy and Marine Corps—and the Coast Guard—are configured so as to be able to deal with the challenges just described. Do they need to make significant changes to support the beneficial aspects of globalization or protect us from hazardous trends? If globalization is a continuing phenomenon, how should naval forces adapt? Are future Department of the Navy programs designed to deal with the anticipated trends in globalization? Are other platforms, platform mixes, and operational concepts needed? How joint do naval forces need to be, and how much jointness is needed to deal with the maritime effects of globalization?

Linking naval force structure requirements directly to the globalization process requires considerable analysis. Force structure choices are presumably based on the anticipated threat and related military requirements. Current U.S. naval force structure is also tied to the requirements of a robust policy of naval forward presence. Globalization, as it is currently construed, is a recent and not fully understood phenomenon. Nonetheless, it is possible to suggest how current, planned, and proposed naval systems might fit in a globalized world. More importantly, the seven globalization effects discussed in this chapter provide a framework for which programs can be evaluated. Appropriate questions concern the versatility of proposed future systems: whether they can be utilized in the interdiction of transnational threats, are rapidly deployable to unexpected locations for use in varying intensities of conditions, and justified in terms of economic security concerns; whether they would promote interoperability with current and unanticipated allies and coalition members and retain their capabilities throughout the steady proliferation of information systems and sensors; and how they would perform in an expanding antiaccess environment.

In the *Quadrennial Defense Review Report* of 2001, the Bush administration indicated its desire to move to a *capabilities-based approach* to defense, which it defines as a model focused "more on how an adversary might fight than who the adversary might be and where a war might occur."[45] Including the seven globalization effects in the methodology of future requirement assessment would prove helpful in developing such a capabilities-based approach. And where the basis for concrete suggestions may be lacking, at the very least questions for future analysis can be posed. Such would be a method of which Captain Mahan, with his desire to analyze the underlying principles of current history, would have undoubtedly approved.

Notes

[1] Anthony Giddens, director, London School of Economics, 1990, accessed at <http://www.ihizittau.de/bwl/studienablauf/b2/begriffsdefinitionen.ppt>.

[2] Gerald Epstein and Richard Polin, Political Economy Research Institute, University of Massachusetts, 1998, accessed at <http://www.ihizittau.de/bwl/studienablauf/b2/begriffsdefinitionen.ppt>.

[3] Thomas L. Friedman, *The Lexus and the Olive Tree* (New York: Anchor, 1999), 7–8.

[4] Alfred Thayer Mahan, "Considerations Governing the Disposition of Navies," *National Review*, July 1902, 701–719, in *Mahan on Naval Strategy*, ed. John B. Hattendorf (Annapolis, MD: Naval Institute Press, 1991), 284.

[5] A succinct critical treatment of Mahan is Phillip A. Crowl, "Alfred Thayer Mahan: The Naval Historian," in *Makers of Modern Strategy*, ed. Peter Paret (Princeton, NJ: Princeton University Press, 1986), 444–477. Efforts to defend and rehabilitate the image of Mahan among scholars are found throughout the works of Jon Tetsuro Sumida, particularly *Inventing Grand Strategy and Teaching Command: The Classic Works of Alfred Thayer Mahan Reconsidered* (Baltimore: Johns Hopkins University Press, 1997).

[6] A main premise of David Held, Anthony McGrew, David Goldblatt, and Jonathan Perraton, *Global Transformations: Politics, Economics and Culture* (Stanford: Stanford University Press, 1999), especially 16–21, 32–87.

[7] It has been argued elsewhere that control over such activities defines what constitutes a navy (as opposed to armies). See Sam J. Tangredi, "Beyond the Sea and Jointness," U.S. Naval Institute *Proceedings* 127, no. 9 (September 2001), 60–63.

[8] Friedman, xviii.

[9] Alfred Thayer Mahan, *The Influence of Sea Power Upon History 1660–1783* (Boston: Little, Brown, 1890), 1, in Hattendorf, 1.

[10] Ibid.

[11] Ibid., 25–61.

[12] Eric Grove, *The Future of Sea Power* (Annapolis, MD: Naval Institute Press, 1990), 229–232.

[13] Mahan, *The Influence of Sea Power Upon History 1660–1783*, 1.

[14] See further discussion in Sam J. Tangredi, "Sea Power—Theory and Practice," in *Strategy in the Contemporary World*, ed. John Baylis, James Wirtz, Eliot Cohen, and Colin S. Gray (New York: Oxford University Press, 2002), 111–136.

[15] Grove, 3.

[16] For example, Walter LaFeber, *The New Empire: An Interpretation of American Expansionism, 1860–1898* (Ithaca, NY: Cornell University Press, 1963), 85–101. Also see discussion in Crowl, 462–469.

[17] Which is the premise of Paul M. Kennedy, *The Rise and Fall of British Naval Mastery* (London: Ashfield Press, 1976), and (on military expenditures overall) Kennedy, *The Rise and Fall of the Great Powers* (New York: Random House, 1987).

[18] Sir Walter Raleigh, *Historie of the Worlde*, 1616, quoted in Robert D. Heinl, *Dictionary of Military and Naval Quotations* (Annapolis, MD: Naval Institute Press, 1966), 288.

[19] To put seaborne commerce in perspective, a medium-sized oceangoing cargo vessel carries tonnage on one voyage approximately equivalent to that carried by 300 of the largest cargo-carrying aircraft.

[20] Even in Mahan's day, there was considerable debate on the relationship between naval power and economic dominance. For example, Sir Norman Angell (author of the historically controversial book *The Great Illusion*) argued that "England's unquestioned naval predominance . . . has given England no privilege not freely possessed by the commerce of all nations." See Norman Angell, *The World's Highway: Some Notes on America's Relation to Sea Power and Non-Military Sanctions For the Law of Nations* (New York: George H. Doran Company, 1915), 3. Today critics point out that the largest number of merchant ships is registered in Liberia and Panama, hardly naval powers. Setting aside the fact that those two nations are merely flags of convenience for owners residing elsewhere, the advantage of naval power is the assurance of market access in the face of potential threats and—if necessary—the closure of access to all others. This does not give a direct market advantage to U.S. trade goods over those of other states—it simply ensures that such a market can exist unhindered by violence. Sir Angell accepted as much, noting that *command of the seas* means "that the state obtaining it can carry on its maritime commerce without interruption or with only slight interruption from the armed ships of the enemy" (120–121).

[21] *Engagement* and *enlargement* were terms used in the Clinton administration to describe measures used to reinforce America's traditional support for democratic regimes elsewhere. Although the current Bush administration does not use these terms in articulating a formal policy, America's support for democratic governance internationally remains relatively constant. Indeed the post–Cold War resurgence in intellectual support for expanding democracy worldwide originated in the later years of the Reagan and Bush administrations.

[22] See discussion in Sally Newman, "Political and Economic Implications of Global Naval Presence," in *Naval Forward Presence: Present Status, Future Prospects* (Washington, DC: Center for Strategic and International Studies, 1997), 48–50.

[23] A brief discussion of joint development programs is George K. Hamilton, "Foreign Cooperation Is Essential for Force Protection," U.S. Naval Institute *Proceedings* 125, no. 7 (July 1999), 44–45.

[24] However, critics charge that the U.S. Navy does not do enough to increase the exchange of technology by buying promising non-U.S. developed systems, particularly as U.S. allies appear to be falling behind in military technology and interoperability.

[25] Naval strategists have always viewed aviation as an essential component of sea power. Historically, this is a legacy of World War II, in which the aircraft carrier replaced the battleship as the capital ship of fleets. Today, this view is evident most strongly in the composition of the U.S. Navy, in which there are more officers and sailors assigned to aviation commands than to surface ships or submarines. Almost 40 percent of the Navy is involved in naval aviation activities, a much larger percentage than other world navies but indicative of a common sea and air linkage.

[26] A short, balanced assessment of this possibility is the Congressional Research Service Report to Congress 97–75 ENR by Zachary S. Davis, *Weapons of Mass Destruction: New Terrorist Threat?* (Washington, DC: Congressional Research Service, January 8, 1997). A more recent and lengthier official source is Advisory Panel to Assess Domestic Response Capabilities for Terrorism Involving Weapons of Mass Destruction, *First Annual Report: Assessing the Threat* (Washington, DC: RAND, December 15, 1999). A list of recent sources on the topic of catastrophic terrorism can be found in U.S. Commission on National Security/21st Century, *New World Coming: American Security in the 21st Century*, September 15, 1999, as fn. 95, 48. An argument that "superterrorism" is unlikely and that measures taken to prevent it may be counterproductive is made in Ehud Sprinzak, "The Great Superterrorism Scare," *Foreign Policy* (Fall 1998), 110–119.

[27] National Defense Panel, *Transforming Defense: National Security in the 21st Century* (Washington, DC: Department of Defense, December 1997), 16–17. The panel was chartered by the Secretary of Defense (at the prompting of Congress) to provide alternatives to the Quadrennial Defense Review of 1997 and reflected Congressional concern over defense transformation. This need for a multipartner response creates distinctions between the National Defense Panel report, other definitions of transnational threats, and those sources using the *nonstate threats* term. Although nonstate threats may cross boundaries, it is not assumed that a multinational response is the sole means of defense. Additionally, the term *transnational threats* can also be applied to dangers that are generated through nation-state action such as mass migrations prompted by genocide. The subtle difference between the two terms creates a degree of analytical confusion when comparing sources.

[28] The White House, *A National Security Strategy for a New Century* (Washington, DC: The White House, December 1999), 14.

[29] Such interpretations vary according to philosophical views of the world system. See discussion in Sam J. Tangredi, *All Possible Wars? Toward A Consensus View of the Future Security Environment* (Washington, DC: National Defense University Press, 2000), 58–63.

[30] "Ship Rams Greenpeace; Sub Unleashes Trident 2," *San Diego Union Tribune*, December 5, 1989, A10; Jeffrey Schmalz, "After Skirmish with Protestors, Navy Tests Missile," *The New York Times*, December 5, 1989, A1. On public reaction, see "Greenpeace's Risky Tactics," *St. Louis Post-Dispatch*, December 7, 1989, A35.

[31] Likewise, Greenpeace's opposition to the deployment of U.S. forces to the Persian Gulf in support of Operations *Desert Shield* and *Desert Storm* caused such a significant loss in U.S. contributions that a number of local chapters quickly backed away from that position.

[32] This argument is made in Moises Naim, "Al Qaeda, the NGO," *Foreign Policy* (March/April 2002), 99–100.

[33] Thomas L. Friedman refers to this effect as "the golden straitjacket." See Friedman, 101–111.

[34] U.S. Commission on National Security/21st Century, 142.

[35] On the "national fleet" concept, see Thomas Fargo and Ernest Riutta, "A 'National Fleet' for America," *U.S. Naval Institute Proceedings* 125, no. 4 (April 1999), 48–51; and Bruce Stubbs, "Whither the National Fleet?" *U.S. Naval Institute Proceedings* 127, no. 5 (May 2001), 72–73.

[36] See discussion of this debate in Sam J. Tangredi, "The Fall and Rise of Naval Forward Presence," *U.S. Naval Institute Proceedings* 126, no. 5 (May 2000), 29–32.

[37] See discussion in Tangredi, *All Possible Wars?* 65–68.

[38] Peter Dombrowski et al., "National Security Policies from the Dombrowski Scenario," unpublished paper, Naval War College, January 30, 2002, 5.

[39] Additionally, numerous Western European nations—notably Sweden, France, and Italy—sell advanced naval systems. China is the original source for many weapons that emerge in the hands of "states formerly known as rogues." North Korea has a reengineer and reexport network with other states, such as Iran.

[40] A primary example is the SS–N–22 Sunburn (Russian name *Moskit*) antiship cruise missile, which was considered one of the most potent ship killers of the Cold War. According to reports, the United States had attempted in the mid-1990s to buy the entire former Soviet inventory of 841 Sunburn missiles from Russia before they could reach

the global market. The attempt failed. See discussion in Norman Friedman, *World Naval Weapons Systems 1997–1998* (Annapolis, MD: Naval Institute Press, 1997), 243–244.

[41] The term *asymmetrical* includes weapons designed to attack U.S. weaknesses and take advantage of the geographical features of the region, such as straits and narrow passages. From the naval perspective, these weapons can be considered asymmetrical because the U.S. Navy is largely configured for open-ocean operations. But historically, use of such weapons or their antecedents might be considered a *normal* aspect of naval warfare in narrow seas. An excellent study of the historical and environmental factors influencing near-shore naval operations is Milan N. Vego, *Naval Strategy and Operations in Narrow Seas* (Portland, OR: Frank Cass Publishers, 1999).

[42] A good discussion can be found in Tim Sloth Joergensen, "U.S. Navy Operations in Littoral Waters: 2000 and Beyond," *Naval War College Review* 51, no. 2 (Spring 1998), 20–29.

[43] Detailed in Office of Naval Intelligence, *Challenges to Naval Expeditionary Warfare* (Washington, DC: Office of Naval Intelligence, 1997).

[44] For discussions on antiaccess, see Thomas G. Mahnken, "America's Next War," *The Washington Quarterly* (Summer 1993), 171–184; and Mahnken, "Deny U.S. Access?" U.S. Naval Institute *Proceedings* 124, no. 9 (September 1998), 36–39.

[45] Department of Defense, *Quadrennial Defense Review Report* (Washington, DC: Department of Defense, 2001), 13.

Part I

Globalization and the Security Environment

Chapter 2

Characteristics and Requirements of the Evolving Security Environment

Frank G. Hoffman and Sam J. Tangredi

And there will be other ways and means which no one can foresee at present, since war is certainly not of those things which follow a fixed pattern; instead it usually makes its own conditions in which one has to adapt oneself to changing situations.[1]

—Thucydides

Neither our security environment nor our understanding of the complex interactions inherent to conflict are constant. As Thucydides pointed out 2 millennia ago—and as sadly reinforced by the events of September 11, 2001—the future is often unforeseeable and frequently violent. There are immutable elements to war: its clash of human wills, political basis, and dramatic unpredictability. But the physical characteristics of conflict and the demands placed on the military component of any strategy are always evolving. Today is no different. Globalization has accelerated changes in the ways and means of conflict and may yet instill enough fear and disruption to generate new ends for war itself.

Since war is "certainly not of those things which follow a fixed pattern," our approach to thinking about it cannot remain rigid or inflexible. New strategic goals and security interests must be advanced when opportunities arise or protected when

---

Frank G. Hoffman served on the professional staff of the U.S. Commission on National Security/21st Century (the Hart-Rudman Commission) from 1998–2001 and participated in drafting all three commission reports, including their futures assessment *New World Coming*. He is a lieutenant colonel in the U.S. Marine Corps Reserve. Sam J. Tangredi is the author of *All Possible Wars? Toward a Consensus View of the Future Security Environment, 2001–2025* (Washington, DC: National Defense University Press, 2000).

threatened. The new threats that emerge may be only dimly recognized at first or may be the unintended consequences of previous actions.

Need for Continuous Evaluation and Adaptability

For a global power with far-ranging interests like the United States, a constant evaluation of ends and means is in order. In short, the methods of advancing and protecting the interests of the United States must adapt themselves, as Thucydides suggests, to changing situations. In this respect, our current global campaign against terrorism and reemphasis on homeland security are natural, appropriate adaptations in policy. But to be effective, there must be concurrent adaptation in the means and institutions needed to carry out the policy.

History records distinct advantages to those adaptive institutions that anticipate and boldly incorporate new concepts, structures, and innovative technologies that respond to these altered circumstances. But history also offers a litany of examples about outmoded capabilities and complacency bred of success and arrogance. Often, the most successful institutions face the hardest time adapting, their previous fortune blinding them to altered circumstances.[2] A major shock or failure may be the only means of forcing change. Such historical warnings should serve to spur American military leaders to critically examine fundamental assumptions, standing organizational constructs, and operational paradigms for their continued utility and relevance in today's turbulent era. Whether the tragedies of September 11 can be considered failures is irrelevant, but they do point to the need for critical examination.

The 21st century, a global century, offers vast opportunities and pernicious problems.[3] If history is any guide at all, naval forces along with all other aspects of national power will continue to have critical responsibilities in support of American strategic interests. This chapter explores the elements of globalization that will continue to affect the future security environment, including political, economic and technological trends, and resulting impacts on defense policy.

The Security Environment

Geopolitics: Power in Flux. In the Cold War's aftermath, several commentators trumpeted today's "unipolar moment."[4] There is little doubt that America's military power and economic clout today is impressive. However, while current dominance is a given, its continuation will be contested. Political history is largely defined by a struggle for dominance. The unipolarity of today's international system could well prove to be a short-lived, transitory phenomenon, as it masks many political, economic, and military trends that could undermine American power and security. The relative uncertainty of potentially seismic changes in geopolitical competition is a major complicating factor in national security planning and thus in sizing and shaping our military component.

Both history and current trends point toward greater plurality in the international system. Power, measured in real terms, is becoming widely distributed among many more countries, groups, and players. Since 1990, more than 40 nation-states have joined the United Nations, and the number of nongovernmental groups has exploded into the hundreds of thousands. In the next decade, traditional nation-states, ethnic groups, and even individuals will wield both political and military power. The appearance and potential effectiveness of such nonstate power will be magnified by global media; witness the influence of an exiled religious extremist hiding in the mountains of the world's poorest and least globalized region.

In the economic dimension, nation-states no longer control their own currencies, and they may not even control their own finances and economies. They are subject to rapidly shifting capital investment funds, which one commentator calls the Electronic Herd.[5] Political, economic, and technological changes are altering what constitutes national power, and industrial age measures of mass and natural resources are growing less relevant. National power is thus measured in different and less absolute or nonlinear terms.[6] More and more, small players on the world stage—international terrorists being the most obvious example—will yield inordinate power, more evidence of nonlinearity.

Today's unipolar or "hyperpower" experience will not last forever. While a competitive superpower on the scale of the United States is considered less probable, a more multipolar system will probably evolve over the next several decades. From the commanding heights it now dominates, America's relative power could decline gradually over the next 25 years.[7] The causes of this readjustment will vary, from political change to technological advances and economic adaptation. A number of scenarios can be postulated that constitute contradictory power transitions that sharply alter the aggregate position of the United States and its allies. In this regard, the United States might find itself in the same position as Great Britain in the 19th century. Britain adapted early and seized most of the benefits of the industrial revolution but ultimately failed to adjust as other powers and new technologies emerged.[8]

Sources of Challenge. The relative decline of American power can come from power fluxes in multiple directions. Rising powers such as China represent one such example. China's economic transformation could produce a gross domestic product half as big as that of the United States.[9] Its regional interests, rising energy needs, and internal political cohesion could all sharply alter the status of the geopolitical competition. India is another large, populous, and technically agile state whose aggregate national power could grow.[10] It is feasible, although unlikely, that the evolutionary integration in Europe could produce a European Union whose economic competition constitutes a substantial threat to U.S. interests.[11] A coalition of radicalized Islamist states can also be contemplated, whose energies might be directed toward confronting the West.

Relative decline or new threats can also come from fragmentation and collapse. The collapse of the U.S. economy is very unlikely, but the continued decline of Japan's economic fortunes could alter U.S. relationships in Asia. Russian decline appears very likely, very deep, and very darkening.[12] The disintegration of Russia could also create destabilizing impacts, including the loss of control over significant amounts of dangerous materials. In the wrong hands, such materials could substantially threaten U.S. forces and interests. Equally dangerous, if China's leadership fails to successfully adapt its political and economic systems to meet demands for employment and growth, its devolution might regenerate ideological conflict or give rise to an extreme form of nationalism that could foment significant challenges for itself and others.

Disintegration of other populous states, such as Pakistan or Indonesia, may not be as direct a threat to U.S. security but would send a shock wave through the globalized system and would directly threaten other U.S. friends and allies.

Wholly unpredictable are a number of permutations of states whose balancing and bandwagoning could produce coalitions to counteract American interests. Such alliances may already be emerging, although there are inherent contradictions within some of the potential anti-American coalitions.[13]

Globalization's Discontents. Globalization, shorthand for the interdependence of political and economic systems, has generated an economic transformation and a degree of convergence in today's international community. Politically, liberal democracies seem ascendant. Concomitantly, free market economies are steadily increasing and increasingly interdependent. Globalization is even generating what looks to be a convergence toward Western culture. To some, the defining characteristic of the age is integration, an interwoven degree of connectedness generated by trade and information technology. The world is moving past the divisive walls of the Cold War to the unifying networked webs of political, economic, and social interaction.[14]

But globalization generates both discontents and polarities, producing both winners and losers. It is far more than an economic phenomena, generating sharp social and political changes.[15] There are forces of both integration and fragmentation at work all around the planet. Global dynamics are causing distress about cultures, values, jobs, and governance. This distress is captured by the term *globalocalization.*[16] The word captures contrasting benefits and losses from globalization. Globalization generates great tensions between forces of change and stability. As James Rosenau puts it, "The simultaneity of the good and the bad, the integrative and the disintegrative, and the coherent and the incoherent are at the heart of global affairs today."[17] The term *fragmegration* captures this pervasive tension and the confluence of forces pushing and pulling today's world.

Already a backlash and resentment of both globalization and America is clearly palpable—and growing. One level of this spectrum is reflected in the protest movement that stalks the various meetings of the World Trade Organization, International Monetary Fund, and World Bank. The other, more sinister and dangerous level is exhibited in the terrorist acts purportedly committed in the name of the Islamic world. Arguably, Osama bin Laden's war is against the effects of globalization rather than any deliberate Western policy.[18] Globalization also abets a loss of sovereignty and accountability at the state level, which stresses governments and generates crises of authority. States are weakened from above, within, and below as a result of globalization's many faces.[19] The pluralism of international organizations and the bewildering array of unseen economic and political forces at work lessen the confidence of some populations in their governments and lead them to seek other groups for identity, support, and security.

The impact of these fragmegrative forces is not yet clear, but the world is being divided into "haves" and "have nots"—those who benefit from and those who have no stake in or receive no benefit from a globalized world. The divisions occur among states but also within states and cultures. In an age of extreme power and knowledge gaps, income disparities, and health deficits, the potential for an angry reaction exists.[20] The means to translate this sense of rage into violence will be more available, as we see in the next part.

Technological Diffusion. Today, the most profound technological development has been the revolution in information technology (IT). To many, the information age represents the most significant development since the industrial revolution. The world will encounter more benefits from IT and in other areas of science and technology over the next 2 decades. New applications and continued convergence of information technology products will arise and become quickly assimilated, at least by certain societies.

The rate of diffusion may be greater than anticipated since demand is high and rates of assimilation appear to be accelerating.[21] New IT developments require minimal infrastructure, which will only reinforce the diffusion of modern communications in developing areas of the world. Continued diffusion will also empower nonstate actors—whether benevolent or malevolent.

But the next decade will probably witness a new wave of technologically driven change. Biotechnology will emerge as the source of the next wave of innovation and sociopolitical challenge. One the one hand, great advances are anticipated, as illustrated by the mapping of deoxyribonucleic acid. On the other hand, great fears are engendered, as with the continuing potential for terrorist attacks with anthrax or other biological agents. The coming biotech age will benefit (or suffer, if results are weaponized) from advances in computer processing, which will radically accelerate the diffusion of biotech research. A continuing series of autocatalytic revolutions in information technology, biotechnology, materials science, and nanotechnology will generate a quantum leap in new research and investments. Undoubtedly, such developments will prove to be disruptive technologies with unknown consequences.[22]

Because the fields and applications that biotechnology can help are so fundamental to the world economy (food, medicine, cosmetics, pharmaceuticals, health services, and environmental remediation), the biotech revolution's impacts will be sharper, steeper, and deeper than those of information technology. We can expect an enormous advance in science with great benefit to humanity, but we have already seen and may continue to see individuals and groups who will abuse their access to this technology. The dark side of the biotech revolution contains consequences that are potentially catastrophic and make the current anthrax scare seem as innocuous as a mild cold.[23]

Weapons of mass destruction (WMD) and their related technologies (some of which are biotech) probably will continue to proliferate. The proliferation of WMD will alter the dynamics of conflict and potentially further escalate small conflicts to larger regional (or even intercontinental) wars. In contrast, the availability of WMD could motivate states and others to revert to more indirect forms of conflict, including state-sponsored terrorism, to avoid direct combat—although this is something the global campaign against terrorism is designed to prevent. Suspicions about WMD proliferation, however, undoubtedly will trigger preemptive conflicts or spur other states to become proliferants to build deterrent forces to hold their neighbors at bay. Even as Russian and American nuclear arsenals are reduced, other states—as evidenced by India and Pakistan—may seek their own share of the *ultimate* deterrent.

Conflict and Military Revolutions. No evaluation of the emerging security environment would be complete without consideration of the impacts of political, economic, and technological change on the nature and character of conflict. Given the discussion to this point, the potential for military revolution—discontinuous leaps in military effectiveness—should be readily apparent. The advent of new technologies and different military applications has major implications for strategists, since the development of new systems and combinations of new technologies generates possibilities that may radically alter the balance of power in some regions and obviate existing strategies and operational advantages.[24] New technologies offer distinct advantages to both military and business organizations that can effectively transition their doctrine, hardware, and organizational structures.[25]

Those nations and military forces that can harness new ideas and make the transitions needed to fundamentally transform themselves will enjoy distinct advantages. The current situation is still fraught with uncertainty, but enough illumination exists to suggest that substantial change in the way industrial age military forces operate is in the offing. The exact nature of the transformation of the military and its adoption of new concepts, force structures, and operating platforms is not completely clear but strongly suggests aggressive exploration.[26]

The risk of war between major developed countries appears to be of low probability, but it cannot be ignored entirely. War might be less productive, but it is not an obsolete means of political interaction, no matter how much we dream for it. The international community will witness numerous other forms of conflicts ranging from minor internal or civil wars to less frequent but highly disruptive regional interstate wars.[27] Combat can take the form of terrorist attacks against civilian populations; in fact, much of the conflict in the developing world already takes that form.[28]

Conflict could arise from various rivalries in Asia, or it could emanate from ancient confrontations of the Middle East. Energy and water disputes may further increase the possibility of future conflict as some areas face continued unfilled requirements.[29] Long-term demographic trends point to increased instability from urban areas as well as resource shortfalls. The lethality of interstate wars could grow substantially, driven by the availability of WMD, longer-range missile delivery systems, and other technologies.[30]

Internal conflicts stemming from religious, ethnic, economic, or political disputes will continue and may even increase in number.[31] Failures to stem this tide of misery could further heighten instability and conflict. For the next decade, the most frequent source of instability will be intrastate conflicts. Such internal conflicts will also become increasingly more lethal as a result of both the strong political enmities and resource conflicts unleashed during this era and the higher availability of more destructive weapons and deadly technology. Such conflicts will be violent and emotionally charged, making them extremely difficult to terminate, leaving massive human displacements, disease, and other flotsam in their wake. They also may not be remedied by the investment in high-technology weapon systems that are optimized for great power conflict.[32]

Asymmetric Warfare. The United States has already had its first taste of asymmetric warfare in the form of hijacked aircraft striking symbolic buildings. However, such asymmetric attacks are not necessarily solely within the provenance of terrorism. Against military targets, they hold considerable tactical logic. Future adversaries will recognize the overwhelming military superiority of the United States in conventional terms and seek techniques and technologies that will deter or deflect American intervention. Instead of resigning themselves to expensive losses or subordination, they will try to avoid or minimize U.S. strengths and exploit perceived weaknesses. U.S. opponents—state and nonstate actors—will not want to engage the American military on its terms.[33] Pitting strength against weakness is a fundamental aspect of warfare throughout history, but options will exist for adversaries to think beyond asymmetries at the tactical or operational level of war. These will include forms of conflict inconsistent with traditional approaches of the Western way of warfare or the codified laws of war.[34]

Asymmetric capabilities need not be a very costly proposition for countries, given increased access to technology, information systems, and resources. Present and potential adversaries will continue to pursue these capabilities against U.S. forces and interests abroad as well as on U.S. soil.[35]

The proliferation of both weapons of mass destruction and their delivery systems has been rising for the last decade.[36] Nonproliferation regimes seem to be fragmenting, and proliferation of advanced unconventional weapons appears contagious. Most of this proliferation is oriented toward regional threats and serves as a deterrent. However, the diffusion of dangerous technologies fuels expenditures and breeds too much exposure to potential use in crisis. Missiles capable of delivering WMD or conventional payloads with great precision against fixed targets will be available. Key nodes for transportation and theater reception at major air and sea ports, logistics bases, and facilities will increasingly be at risk, vastly complicating U.S. power projection operations.[37]

Simultaneously, the nature of globalization and its accompanying technical diffusion will permit highly diverse transnational networks or groups to expand in influence and lethality. Failed states or "states of despair" could elect to revert to terrorism or become inadvertent or deliberate hosts—as we have seen in Afghanistan.[38] Terrorist tactics will continue to advance in sophistication and focus on achieving mass casualties. Conventional attacks will continue to be more probable, but highly lethal means will be sought and eventually used. As President George W. Bush has frequently maintained, only a long-term, sustained campaign would appear to hold success against the potential for continued, increasingly lethal terrorist attacks.

Summary: Hypercompetition. America will live in an unpredictable world dominated not by its own hyperpower, but by hypercompetition (perception of zero-sum competition in the economic marketplace), vulnerability, and substantial uncertainty.[39] It is a world that classic realists will readily recognize.[40] Despite any of the beneficial effects of globalization, the international arena itself has not changed. It is still anarchic, highly competitive, and based on power politics. The balance of power is still paramount to security, although national power may be more difficult to measure. The threat posed by rising anti-status-quo powers, as well as dying states, represents the greatest threat to stability and order. However, the nonlinear opportunities afforded by the dynamics of globalization only exacerbate the competition by providing minor players the capacity to act globally on a scale heretofore reserved for major state actors. In particular, some nonstate actors can acquire means of competition in the military sense that have usually been associated only with major powers.

Violent tensions will be an ever-present force in a hypercompetitive world. The prospects for violence are inherent in the contradictions of today's global environment, as one student of international tension puts it:

> We are entering a bifurcated world. Part of the world is inhabited by Hegel's and Fukuyama's Last Man, healthy, well fed, and pampered by technology. The other, larger part is inhabited by Hobbes' First Man, condemned to a life that is poor, nasty, brutish, and short.[41]

The effects of globalization will challenge both parts of this world. The Last Man will survive and perhaps even master it; the First Man will not. The resentment of Hobbes' First Man could inflame and empower more hatreds than ever before. Thus, Samuel Huntington's thesis that future conflict will be along cultural lines is partly correct. Some cultures and civilizations will thrive and prosper, others will try to merely survive. Others will succumb, not to the clash of civilizations but to the crash of globalization. But their demise will not be with a whimper. Huntington correctly points out that conflicts borne of this crash will "more frequent, more sustained, and more violent."[42]

As the unipolar moment fades away, the world will revert to traditional power dynamics with untraditional players. This is a world far different than the stability of the Cold War, a world of constant conflict and "nasty little wars."[43] But, excepting the effects of technology and the inclusion of new actors, it may not be all that different than humanity's pre-Cold War experience—for good or for ill.

Implications for U.S. Strategy and Military Capabilities

The contradictions of the globalized environment that are illustrated by Fukuyama's Last Man and Hobbes' First are apparent in elite attitudes toward the U.S. military. As described by one commentator, even among those most optimistic about the human condition:

> We are envisioning . . . an era marked by both an increasing integration of societies and a need for greater commitment of military forces. This might seem an inherent contradiction, but it is possible nevertheless.[44]

How to deal with the contradictions of globalization and resulting threats to national security is the most critical question of the 21st century's first decade. An examination of the military implications of this postulated security environment leads to a series of policy recommendations that can be concisely summarized as follows:

- Strategic integration, operational fusion, and adaptive interagency structures are needed. National security strategy will require a tighter fusion of military, diplomatic, economic, and informational components in both peacetime planning and actual operations.[45] National security organizations will need to work together more frequently at all levels from strategic planning to tactical execution overseas. At the operational level, interagency and military organizations will of necessity be polymorphic—adaptable, flatter, and modular in response to their external environment.

■ Homeland security is first. Defense planners and decisionmakers can no longer assume that strategic power will keep the U.S. homeland safe from attack. Homeland security will become a factor in designing U.S. overseas military responses in a way that it has not been in recent decades.

■ Prevention is preferred over response. Conflict prevention and stability operations will be increasingly more important to preclude or contain crises and state failures. This is an era of complex contingencies, limited by scope but not by complexity or potentially dire consequences.[46]

■ Managing chaos may be the best possible result. Preserving stability may prove to be too rigid and too costly as a strategic goal. Managing or controlling chaos in such a way as to mitigate costs may have to suffice.[47] In conducting humanitarian interventions, attempts to build or rebuild multiethnic societies will likely prove grandiose; only reducing the level of violence and suffering may be achievable.

■ Developing coalitions and partnerships will be the initial requirement. Building and maintaining relationships with friends and allies over a host of interrelated interests will remain critical. The developed world will have to deal constructively with the management of change and resentment in those areas that fail to adapt. Coalitions and various temporary multiactor arrangements with nonstate entities will spring up in reaction to events.[48]

■ Responses against asymmetric threats will require sustained campaigns. American military advantage in conventional war remains too great to be challenged by most, particularly nonstate, actors. Asymmetric strategies and systems will be used; it will be difficult to clearly identify the beginning or end of a conflict. Victory will often require a sustained campaign that combines short periods of high-technology warfighting with long periods of special operations and guerrilla-style warfare, with even longer periods of diplomatic maneuvering and nation building. The current campaign in Afghanistan may become a model for modern war. Conversely, the United States may sometimes be forced to use more decisive, less discriminate force to achieve rapid results.

■ Plans need to hedge against strategic surprise. It will be increasingly difficult to anticipate developments and interactions due to the accelerating nature of social, political, economic, and technological changes. Intelligence, properly analyzed and distributed, will be a precious commodity, and surprises will be more frequent. Strategic warning will be ambiguous.[49]

- Decision/response cycles need to be reduced. Strategic, operational, and tactical decisions will have to be made faster in networked environment to match fast-paced operations, and often without adequate information or intelligence.[50] Fear of failure or unintended consequences cannot be allowed to paralyze action; paralysis itself will constitute failure.

- Force design will need to emphasize flexibility and speed. Military force design will stress greater flexibility, versatility, responsiveness, speed, and reach, and highly discriminate force usage. This will require combinations of lethal and less than lethal means. Versatility and credible military power remain more useful than narrowly specialized forces. The Nation still requires a decisive war-winning capability to deter aggression, but some dedicated forces should be designed to provide highly responsive, middleweight forces that can be lethal and sustained at a distance. Such forces should be fully prepared to operate within an austere environment.

- Force structure will center on adaptive joint forces. Force design and planning will have to anticipate or build in the capacity to prepare for asymmetric and nonlinear counterresponses from a variety of antagonists. [51] This reinforces the need for flexible and adaptive units and the seamless integration of various components into a joint force.[52] American military planners will have to be more flexible about unconventional warfighting than the linear mindset represented by *Joint Vision 2020*.[53]

- Forward/overseas presence will need to be more flexible in composition and activities. Force deployment patterns will not be as routine as during the Cold War. Forward presence will be costly but invaluable, shifting rather than fixed, depending on the needs of the moment. They will be "neither positional or continental."[54] Our efforts in Central Asia show how difficult it is to gain political access; we might operate without reliance on host nation support. But at the same time, overseas presence resource requirements will compete against homeland security requirements. Premiums will need to be paid for military assets with capabilities to perform well in both missions.

- Force employment will become increasingly complex. The context for force employment will be part of the complexity of complex contingencies, focused on the littorals and in extensive urban environments.[55] Indirect approaches for dealing with the challenges of urban combat are illusory.[56] The proliferation of WMD and delivery systems must be addressed in both force design and operations. In addition to active defensive measures, greater operational mobility, dispersion, force protection, and decontamination will be required. This combination suggests a heavy reliance upon maritime and naval expeditionary forces.[57]

■ People remain the most critical requirement. Higher-quality personnel and training will be needed to address the complexity of modern security operations, which place severe demands on the mental agility and ingenuity of military personnel. Despite the surge of patriotism and interest in military/public service following the September 11 attacks, it is unclear whether—in a future of possible disincentives—the Armed Forces can rely solely on volunteers to provide critical skills. A serious examination and public debate on the benefits and costs of instituting universal military, public, and community service are in order.[58]

Conclusions

Our perspective of the future from the year 2002 is considerably different than it was in 1992. Even then, the outline of increasing globalization was evident; however, it seemed largely a beneficial outline. The fall of the Soviet empire and loosening of client states presaged a worldwide expansion in democratic governance. The crushing coalition victory in Operation *Desert Storm* seemed to herald a new world order in which aggression and international violence would be senseless and rare. Strong countries would defend and assist the weak. Capitalist markets expanded, and the tide appeared ready to lift all boats. But such transformations are never smooth and never seem to match our idealistic views.

As the 1990s continued, it became more apparent that not every society or culture shared these idealistic views. Opposition to globalization—often propelled by fear, illogic, or misinformation—grew. But this opposition still appeared manageable through explanation, dialogue, and negotiated social, economic, and ecological safeguards. Few would suspect that opposition to globalization—masked by expressions of religion or nationalism—would lead to brutal, ferocious attacks of international terrorism.[59] Few would also recognize the resilience of international power politics in the face of internetted economics and culture.

The resulting security environment is more anarchic, perhaps more traditional, than expected. Globalization has magnified human behaviors that lead more to war than to peace. When combined with the dark side of human ingenuity and the advance of technology, these behaviors suggest the prudence of dynamic, relentless, but tailored military planning and preparation on our part. Increasing the equality of benefits may reduce some of the motivations for violence, but clearly not all. Force will remain a necessary instrument.

In assessing globalization, if—metaphorically speaking—all boats rise with the tide, we should be prepared to find both warships and pirate ships hiding among the world's ostensibly peaceful commercial fleet.

Notes

[1] Robert R. Strassler and Victor Davis Hanson, *The Landmark Thucydides: A Comprehensive Guide to the Peloponesian War* (New York: Free Press, 1996), 106.

[2] Clayton M. Christensen, *The Innovator's Dilemma: When New Technologies Cause Great Firms to Fail* (Cambridge, MA: Harvard Business School, 1997).

[3] Richard L. Kugler and Ellen L. Frost, eds., *The Global Century: Globalization and National Security* (Washington, DC: National Defense University Press, 2001). (Hereafter referred to as *Global Century*.)

[4] For example, Charles Krauthammer, "The Unipolar Moment," *Foreign Affairs* (February 1991), 24–25.

[5] Thomas L. Friedman, *The Lexus and the Olive Tree* (New York: Anchor, 1999), 12, 93–114.

[6] Ashley J. Tellis, Janice Bially, Christopher Layne, Melissa McPherson, and Jerry Sollinger, *Measuring National Power in the Postindustrial* Age (Washington, DC: RAND, 2000).

[7] This domination reflects the fact that the Cold War was indeed a stupendous victory for the West and the United States in particular. This theme is laced throughout Norman Friedman, *The Fifty-Year War: Conflict and Strategy in the Cold War* (Annapolis, MD: Naval Institute Press, 1999).

[8] Regarding British failures to adapt to the telegraph and chemical industries, see Howard Bloom, *The Lucifer Principle: A Scientific Expedition into the Forces of History* (New York: Atlantic Monthly Press, 1995).

[9] Brzezinski argues that "China will not be emerging as a global power in the foreseeable future. Even in the most unlikely circumstance of continued rapid economic growth, China will not be top-ranked in any of these domains for many decades to come." Zbigniew Brzezinski, *The Strategic Triad: Living with China, Europe and Russia* (Washington, DC: Center for Strategic and International Studies, 2001), 6.

[10] On China and India, see U.S. Commission on National Security/21st Century, *New World Coming: American Security in the 21st Century: Supporting Research and Analysis* (Washington, DC: Government Printing Office, 1999), 71–91.

[11] In this regard, Fred Bergsten warns, "The United States and the European Union are on the brink of a major trade and economic conflict," in "America's Two Front Economic Conflict," *Foreign Affairs* (March/April 2001), 17.

[12] Brzezinski notes that Russia's gross domestic product (GDP) is one-tenth of the United States, half of India's, and still declining. He estimates that Russian GDP will be 2 percent of world GDP by 2015 (*The Strategic Triad*, 57–58).

[13] Henry Chu and Richard C. Paddock, "Russia Looks to China as an Ally Amid West's Ire," *Los Angeles Times*, December 8, 1999, 1; "Herding Pariahs: Russia's Dangerous Games," February 8, 2000, accessed at <www.stratfor.com>; Susan Glasser, "Russian, Iran Renew Alliance Meant to Boost Arms Trade," *The Washington Post*, March 13, 2001, A14. An argument against a possible Russia-China coalition is in Jennifer Anderson, *The Limits to Sino-Russian Strategic Partnership*, International Institute for Strategic Studies Adelphi Paper 315 (Oxford: Oxford University Press, December 1997).

[14] Friedman, 8.

[15] However, the argument that globalization is all about monetary expansions can be found in Michael Pettis, "Will Globalization Go Bankrupt?" *Foreign Policy* (September/October 2001), 52–59.

[16] This term describes the local impact of seemingly unrelated political and economic events taking place globally. E.J. Dionne, Jr., "The "Glocalization" Problem," *The Washington Post*, June 6, 2000, A27. See also Friedman, 295.

[17] James N. Rosenau, "Stability, Stasis and Change: A *Fragmegrating* World," in *Global Century*, 127–154.

[18] Thomas P.M. Barnett, "Globalization is Tested," U.S. Naval Institute *Proceedings* 127, no. 10 (October 2001), 57; Kurt M. Campbell, "Globalization at War," *The Washington Post*, October 22, 2001, A19.

[19] Michael Howard, *The Invention of Peace: Reflections on War and International Order* (New Haven: Yale University Press, 2000), 96–101.

[20] Friedman's assessment is echoed by Richard L. Kugler, who notes, "What globalization likely will produce is not a homogeneous zone of prospering happy capitalists, but instead a diverse pattern of winners, losers, and canoe paddlers: i.e., countries struggling to stay afloat." Kugler's comment accessed at <www.ndu.edu/inss/spa/1kugler.html>.

[21] Peter Brimelow, "The Silent Boom," *Forbes Magazine*, July 7, 1997, 170–171.

[22] Clayton Christensen has used the term "disruptive technologies" to describe new and transformative developments in commercial applications, but for political and social impacts, see Clayton Christensen, Thomas Craig, and Stuart Hart, "The Great Disruption," *Foreign Affairs* (March/April 2001), 80–95.

[23] For the most dramatic concerns see Bill Joy, "Why the Future Doesn't Need Us," *Wired*, April 2000, 238–262. On the potential for bioterrorist attacks on food supplies (and a response plan), see Henry S. Parker, *Agricultural Bioterrorism: A Federal Strategy to Meet the Threat* (Washington, DC: National Defense University Press, 2002).

[24] Lonnie Henley, "The RMA After Next," *Parameters* 29, no. 4 (Winter 1999–2000), 46–57, and Thomas K. Adams, "Radical Destabilizing Effects of New Technologies," *Parameters* 28, no. 3 (Autumn 1998), 99–111.

[25] Andrew F. Krepinevich, "From Cavalry to Computers: The Pattern of Military Revolutions," *The National Interest* (Fall 1994), 30–42.

[26] Steven Kosiak, Andrew F. Krepinevich, and Michael Vickers, *A Strategy for a Long Peace* (Washington, DC: Center for Strategic and Budgetary Assessments, January 2001).

[27] Michael E. O'Hanlon, "Coming Conflicts: Interstate War in the New Millenium," *Harvard International Review* (Summer 2001), 42–46. O'Hanlon provides a concise and logical review of potential flashpoints and causes of conflict, including potential conflict over resources.

[28] See the prolific writings of Ralph Peters, particularly *Fighting for the Future: Will America Triumph?* (Mechanicsburg, PA: Stackpole Books, 1999), 32–48.

[29] National Intelligence Council, *Global Trends 2015* (Washington, DC: Government Printing Office, January 2001), 20–23; and Michael Klare, "The New Geography of Conflict," *Foreign Affairs* (May/June 2001), 49–61.

[30] Others argue that modern technology makes war less lethal for noncombatants. For a discussion of this debate, see Sam J. Tangredi, *All Possible Wars? Toward a Consensus View of the Future Security Environment, 2001–2025* (Washington, DC: National Defense University Press, 2000), 97–100.

[31] A conclusion shared by the U.S. Commission on National Security and the Central Intelligence Agency. See *New World Coming*, 46–47, and *Global Trends 2015*, 8.

[32] Charles J. Dunlap, Jr., "How We Lost the High Tech War of 2007," *The Weekly Standard*, January 29, 1996, 22–28.

[33] For a superb study, see Kenneth F. McKenzie, Jr., *The Revenge of the Melians: Asymmetric Threats and the 2001 QDR* (Washington, DC: National Defense University Press, 2000).

[34] Dunlap, 22–28; see also Charles J. Dunlap, "21st Century Land Warfare: Four Dangerous Myths," *Parameters* 27, no. 3 (Autumn 1997), 27–37; Peters, 44–48.

[35] For a disturbing study of the homeland security problem, see Richard Falkenrath, Robert D. Newman, and Bradley A. Thayer, *America's Achilles' Heel: NBC Terrorism and Covert Attack* (Cambridge, MA: MIT Press, 1998).

[36] See the biennial Department of Defense report, *Proliferation: Threat and Response* (January 2001); accessed at <www.defenselink.mil/pubs>.

[37] A key conclusion of the National Defense Panel, *Transforming Defense: National Security in the 21st Century* (Washington, DC: 1997), 22. See also Tangredi, *All Possible Wars?* 73–82.

[38] Thomas L. Friedman, "Altered States," *The New York Times*, October 1, 2000, A17.

[39] Arguably, this world is still less dangerous than it was at the height of the Cold War, when huge nuclear arsenals were targeted on civilian populations.

[40] Robert D. Kaplan, *The Coming Anarchy: Shattering the Dreams of the Post Cold War* (New York: Random House, 2000), xi; Kenneth N. Waltz, "Structural Realism after the Cold War," *International Security* 25, no.1 (Summer 2000), 5–41.

[41] Kaplan, 24.

[42] Samuel P. Huntington, "The Clash of Civilizations," *Foreign Affairs* (Summer 1993), 22–60.

[43] Ralph Peters, "Constant Conflict," *Parameters* 27, no. 2 (Summer 1997), 4–14. See also Anatol Lieven, "Nasty Little Wars," *The National Interest* (Winter 2000–2001), 65–76.

[44] Thomas Keaney, "Globalization, National Security and the Role of the Military," *SAISphere* (Winter 2000), accessed at <www.sais-jhu.edu/pubs/saisphere/winter00/indexkk.html>.

[45] Jonathan T. Howe, "A Global Agenda for Foreign and Defense Policy," *Global Century*, 189, and U. S. Commission on National Security/21st Century, *Seeking A National Strategy* (Washington, DC: Government Printing Office, September 2000), 16.

[46] This is the main argument of Ashton B. Carter and William J. Perry, *Preventive Defense: A New Security Strategy for America* (Washington, DC: Brookings, 1999). See also Howe, 189; Ellen L. Frost, "Globalization and National

Security: A Strategic Agenda," in *Global Century*, 56; and Harlan K. Ullman, "Influencing Events Ashore," in *Global Century*, 502.

[47] Richard L. Kugler, "Controlling Chaos: New Axial Strategic Principles," in *Global Century*, 101.

[48] For an historical argument for a more institutionalized approach to post-war order, see G. John Ikenberry, *After Victory: Institutions, Strategic Restraint, and the Rebuilding of Order after Major Wars* (Princeton, NJ: Princeton University Press, 2001).

[49] Anthony H. Cordesman, "The Military in a New Era: Living with Complexity," in *Global Century*, 399. See also *New World Coming: Supporting Research and Analysis*, 55.

[50] Howe, 188.

[51] For discussion of the effects of nonlinearity, see Robert Jervis, *Systems Effects: Complexity in Political and Social Life* (Princeton: Princeton University Press, 1997).

[52] Howe, 192. For a strong argument on joint forces, see William A. Owens with Edward Offley, *Lifting the Fog of War* (New York: Farrar, Straus and Giroux, 2000).

[53] Cordesman, 419.

[54] Richard L. Kugler, "Future U.S. Defense Strategy," in *Global Century*, 365. On naval presence, see Sam J. Tangredi, "The Fall and Rise of Naval Forward Presence," U.S. Naval Institute *Proceedings* 126, no. 5 (May 2000). For an assessment of forward presence and "shaping," see Edward Rhodes, et al., "Forward Presence and Engagement: Historical Insights into the Problem of 'Shaping,'" *Naval War College Review* (Winter 2000), 25–61.

[55] This runs against the prevailing Powell Doctrine, which reflects the U.S. Armed Forces' reluctance to address unconventional conflict or complex contingencies where American military strengths cannot be employed without constraints. This is a major theme of F. G. Hoffman, *Decisive Force: A New American Way of War* (Westport, CT: Praeger, 1996).

[56] For an indirect approach see Robert H. Scales, Jr., "The Indirect Approach: How U.S. Military Forces Can Avoid the Pitfalls of Future Urban Warfare," *Armed Forces Journal International* (October 1998), 68–74. Such an approach does not support U.S. political objectives and appears to ignore the "CNN effect" or temporal limitations to modern crises.

[57] Kugler, "Future U.S. Defense Strategy," in *Global Century*, 367. See also Paul Bracken, *Fire in the East: The Rise of Asian Military Power and the Second Nuclear Age* (New York: HarperCollins, 1999).

[58] A need recently argued in John McCain and Evan Bayh, "A New Start for National Service," *The New York Times*, November 6, 2001, A23.

[59] One exception was Benjamin R. Barber, *Jihad vs. McWorld: How Globalism and Tribalism are Reshaping the World* (New York: Houghton Mifflin, 1996).

Chapter 3

Geopolitics versus Globalization

Douglas E. Streusand

In the company of such contemporary buzzwords as *globalization*, the word *geopolitics* seems an anachronism. It brings to mind the era of coaling stations and colonization or the nightmare of Nazi expansionism, not the turbulent and complex realities of our time. One observer, Brian Blouet, goes so far as to define the two concepts as polar opposites in policy: "Geopolitical policies seek to establish national or imperial control over space and the resources, routeways, industrial capacity and population the territory contains," but "[g]lobalization is the opening of national space to the free flow of goods, capital, and ideas. Globalization removes obstructions to movement and creates conditions in which international trade in goods and services can expand."[1] This chapter denies the opposition between geopolitics and globalization, both as historical forces and as policy alternatives. It contends that the era of globalization has not ended the need for geopolitical analysis and that the policy imperatives that geopolitical analysis generates do not contradict the principles of globalization.

Despite the absence of a coherent global threat such as the Axis powers or the Soviet Union, and the development of significant nonstate adversaries like al Qaeda, geopolitical analysis offers vital insights for development of U.S. grand strategy, military strategy, and military forces for the coming decades.

This chapter has four parts: a brief exposition of the concept and principles of geopolitics, a review of the notion of globalization, an examination of the arguments that geopolitical analysis is no longer relevant and does not fit contemporary realities, and several suggested insights that geopolitics offers for American policy.

What Is Geopolitics?

Geopolitics has a simple definition but a series of complex and controversial connotations. Geoffrey Parker defines it as "the study of international relations from a

Dr. Douglas E. Streusand is a professor at American Military University and is founding director of the Global Strategy Seminar and guest lecturer at the Institute of World Politics. He has taught at the University of Maryland and The Johns Hopkins University and is author of *The Formation of the Mughal Empire* (New York: Oxford University Press, 1990) and several articles and reviews.

spatial or geographic perspective."[2] Some writers, including Thomas Friedman, the most fluent and influential student of globalization, use the term not for an academic discipline or a particular approach to international politics but for the reality of power politics, the striving of state against state for power, wealth, and influence.[3] This broad usage strips the term of its focus on geographic factors. In contrast, the seminal authors on geopolitics, such as Rudolph Kjellen, Friedrich Ratzel, and Halford Mackinder, propound geographic determinism in world politics. Mackinder's oft-quoted dictum expresses this determinism:

- Who rules East Europe commands the Heartland
- Who rules the Heartland commands the World Island
- Who rules the World Island commands the World[4]

Mackinder intended this epigram as prediction and as policy guidance for the Allied negotiators at the Versailles conference. Unlike much of academic political science, geopolitics has always addressed policy issues. During World War II and the Cold War, numerous authors, most notably Mackinder, Nicholas Spykman, Robert Strausz-Hupé, and Colin Gray, described the geographic underpinnings of Western grand strategy.[5] All these geopolitical thinkers have a common theme: the prevention of the emergence of a global hegemon. All believed that any single power capable of dominating Eurasia would become one. Though George Kennan and the other architects of containment did not acknowledge the debt explicitly, the doctrine of containment reflected the views of Mackinder and Spykman.[6] Since the end of the Cold War, several thinkers, notably Saul Cohen and Mackubin Owens, have sought to define the geopolitics of the contemporary era.[7] The idea of geopolitical analysis does not, however, require either determinism or a set of permanent geographic definitions, such as *the Heartland*.

Each era has its own geopolitics. The discipline of geography, after all, encompasses political, social, cultural, and economic factors as well as spatial and topographic ones.[8] Because populations, economies, and cultures change, geopolitical patterns change.

The Geopolitics of Globalization

A much newer word than geopolitics, globalization also has a more variable definition. Thomas Friedman describes globalization as "the defining international system" of the time, comparable in significance to the Cold War between 1945 and 1991. The Cold War meant global division and bipolar competition between ponderous adversaries; globalization means global integration and dynamic competition among a changing array of rivals. The military stalemate between the United States and the Soviet Union during the Cold War meant a divided world; the status of the United States as the sole superpower forms the foundation of globalization.[9] Stephen Flanagan and Ellen Frost both define globalization as a process. Flanagan calls it a "long-term process of change. . . . The central features of globalization are the rapid, growing, and uneven cross-border flow of goods, services, people, money, technology, information, ideas, culture, crime, and weapons."[10] Frost adds that globalization implies a transition toward "'globality,' a more interconnected world system in which independent networks and flows surmount traditional boundaries (or make them irrelevant)." The surmounting of traditional boundaries implies a transformation in the concept of sovereignty.[11] Frost contends that globalization has transformed the strategic environment radically. She calls for a "globalization-infused strategy," the protection and fostering of U.S. interests by shaping globalization.[12] This assertion implies that globalization has made geopolitics irrelevant; Frost excludes geography from the "holistic" thinking that she advocates in the formation of national security policy:

> cross-disciplinary analysis informed by all aspects of globalization including not only commercial, financial, technological, military, political, environmental and social aspects, but also cultural, religious, psychological, educational, and historical perspectives.[13]

Frost does not assert that globalization has already produced a world free of conflict but says that "external threats have increasingly assumed transnational forms."[14]

It is notable that the sober and insightful survey of the future security environment presented in chapter 2 of this volume appears to reflect no such profound alteration in that environment (beyond the rise and fall of individual actors, both state and nonstate). The authors contend that the "world will revert to traditional power dynamics with untraditional players," that "internetted economics and culture" have not squelched the "resilience of international power politics" in "a world that classic realists will readily recognize." This vision of the "globalized" world differs from the world of the classic realists, however, because it does not include a geopolitical dimension. As Mackubin Owens points outs, most, though not all, realists incorporate geopolitics in some form into their doctrine.[15] Though Hoffman and Tangredi do not deny the possibility of conflict among states, they emphasize the probability of asymmetric warfare and terrorism, more likely to involve "highly diverse transnational networks" than states. Friedman, writing well before September 11, 2001, characterizes this type of threat effectively:

> The greatest danger that the United States faces today is from Super-empowered individuals who hate America more than ever because of globalization and who do something about it on their own, more than ever, thanks to globalization.[16]

The current war against al Qaeda lends credence to the perspectives of Hoffman, Tangredi, and Frost. Since the September 11 attacks, the United States has assembled and led a coalition that includes, albeit at different levels of commitment, all the major military and economic powers of the world, against a transnational network. Al Qaeda controlled the Taliban government of Afghanistan and has (or at least had) other state connections but no territorial identity or coherence. The reality of nonspatial global conflict, however, does not automatically mean an end to spatial conflict.

Globalization and Conflict

The belief that globalization has made interstate conflict highly unlikely rests on three propositions: that economic interdependence among states has made war too costly to contemplate; that cultural and interpersonal interaction will reduce the misperceptions and misunderstandings that have produced conflict in the past; and that the spread of democracy and the changes in governance necessary for states to participate in the global system will produce open, honest, and representative governments unlikely to fight each other. Each proposition has merit; each has its limitations. Before evaluating the propositions, we must consider the standard of proof for such an evaluation. Because the stakes at hand are the highest—the national security of the United States and global order—and because the propositions contend that a fundamental change in the nature of human affairs has occurred, the propositions must meet the highest possible standard of proof. Like guilt in a criminal case, the irrelevance of geopolitics must be proven beyond doubt to become a standing assumption of national security policy.

As Friedman contends, the argument that commerce should produce peace is nothing new.[17] The Baron de Montesquieu contended that "peace is the natural effect of trade. Two nations which traffic with each other become reciprocally dependent."[18] Norman Angell repeats this argument: "The capitalist has no country, and he knows that arms and conquests and juggling frontiers serve no ends of his and may well defeat them."[19] The clear-eyed sage of the 18th century and the doomed prophet of peace of the early 20th each wrote shortly before a war that set new standards for violence and waste. Friedman contends that Montesquieu and Angell argue correctly that the value of commerce raises the economic cost of war but err in assuming that that cost would end war. He himself does not contend that it will, but that "today's version of globalization significantly raises the costs of countries using war as a means to pursue honor, react to fears, or advance their interests." But "people are still attached to their culture, their language, and a place called home. And they will sing for home, cry for home, fight for home, and die for home. Which is why globalization does not, and will not, end geopolitics."[20]

Friedman's remarks refer to Thucydides' list of "three of the strongest motives, fear, honor, and interest."[21] He might more effectively have argued that because globalization has made war obviously more costly, that governments will rarely find it in their interests to fight even for honor or out of fear. If commerce and capitalism militate against war, foreign direct investment—ownership of assets in the territory of potential adversaries—does even more so. Friedman himself considers this change only a matter of probability; he does not believe that globalization as a system will prevent conflict by itself. His argument alone creates sufficient doubt to leave the first proposition unproven.

The second proposition, that cultural and personal interaction will reduce misperceptions and misunderstandings that lead to conflict, appears convincing at first glance, but not in the light of history. There was no misunderstanding or lack of acquaintance between Athens and Sparta. The governing elites of the European powers who made the decisions to go war in 1914 knew each other well. Globalization's increase in the cross-border flow of information does not inevitably mean a growth in mutual understanding and amity. In the words of Michael Vlahos, "What is important is not the rate of flow, but how it is received; and all must pass culture-customs through highly controlled ports of entry."[22] Samuel Huntington's contention that cultural conflict will dominate the future challenges the second proposition.[23] Huntington wrote before globalization became a buzzword; today, cultural conflict takes the form of, or at least is interpreted as, opposition to globalization rather than conflict between cultures.

Opposition to globalization is a cross-cultural, transnational phenomenon. Friedman calls the opponents fundamentalists; he speaks of the "backlash of all those millions of people who detest the way globalization homogenizes people . . . brings strangers into your home with strange ways, erases the distinctiveness of cultures, and mercilessly uproots the olive trees that locate and anchor you in your world."[24] Scott Macdonald uses the term *Neo-Luddites*, emphasizing opposition to modernity in general rather than to Western or American culture specifically.[25] Whatever the designation, the opponents of modernity constitute the main nonspatial threat to global order and to the United States. Not all of them are religious extremists, or to use alternative language, cultural particularists; the opponents of global capitalism, animal rights extremists, and environmental extremists also fit into the category.

All these positions have widespread appeal throughout much of the world and will not go away, but such groups have rarely been able to gain and hold political power. The Islamic Republic of Iran, the short-lived Taliban regime in most of Afghanistan, and the embattled National Islamic Front government in the Sudan, which has shown some signs of turning away from Islamism, come to mind.[26] The Bharatiya Janata Party, which has governed India in coalition since 1998, is a Hindu extremist organization in origin and partisan ideology but has not governed as one.[27] Although neither the Taliban nor the National Islamic Front government were able to unify their countries and the Islamic Revolution in Iran took place under truly unique circumstances, the possibility clearly exists that antimodern movements may take power in major states and form a spatial, and thus geopolitical, threat.[28] This possibility ends the validity of the second proposition as an argument against the need for geopolitical strategy. In all probability, however, antimodernist movements will remain in the nonspatial shadows, capable of doing enormous harm (as al Qaeda has done) but not of governing. They will find allies in criminals, grand and petty (as argued in chapter 4), and will take advantage of governmental failures, as the Taliban did in Afghanistan. Robert Kaplan describes a "bifurcated world," in which sophisticated wealth confronts brutal poverty; the combination of antimodernism and crime makes that the poor side dangerous to the wealthy.[29]

The third proposition, that the spread of open and representative government will end war, dates back at least to Immanuel Kant. His *Perpetual Peace: A Philosophical Proposal* contends that because the transnational ties among peoples outweigh national loyalties, there would be no motivation for war if citizens rather than monarchs governed.[30] This idea has a long history, but Michael Howard offers a withering response to it:

> Democracies from France at the end of the eighteenth century to the United States in the middle of the twentieth, have failed to live up to the expectations of eighteenth-century liberal thinkers. On the contrary, they have displayed a bellicose passion reminiscent of the worst of the Wars of Religion. . . . [T]heir ignorance of foreign politics make them suspicious and xenophobe, prone to paranoia, and passionately vindictive in proportion to the shattering of their peaceful ideals.[31]

Howard's rhetoric may be excessive, but his point is hard to dispute. Moreover, democracy does not necessarily equal open, representative government. J.L. Talmon's distinction between Anglo-Saxon representative democracy and continental totalitarian democracy, though controversial to say the least, also suggests that the spread of democracy does not necessarily mean a benign future.[32]

A Grand Strategy for Globalization?

The unproven status of the three propositions means that we cannot assume that globalization processes themselves will keep peace. The United States must rely on traditional statecraft, including geopolitics, to maintain security and preserve peace. Indeed, Friedman himself contends globalization depends on geopolitics, rather than making it obsolete. Both Friedman and Frost assert that the process of globalization began in the 19th century. Steamships and railways provided reliable long-distance transportation over water and land at a far lower cost than previously; the telegraph, with transoceanic cables, offered rapid global communication. These developments created global financial and commodities markets and permitted an unprecedented degree of economic specialization. The cutting-edge technologies of the 19th century, analog though they were, established globalization. Microchips, fiber optics, and communications satellites are only refinements. This first era of globalization coincided with the Pax Britannica. The technical and institutional advances of the industrial revolution made European expansion possible. Britain's balance of power policy did not prevent conflict among major European powers, but it did prevent extended struggles from disrupting the process of global integration. Similarly, British financial and military power supported the development of the international legal and financial standards necessary for integrated commerce.[33]

In the current era of globalization, the United States has done what Britain did in the 19th century. In a sense, this era of globalization began with containment. George Kennan, describing in 1985 the doctrine he had outlined 4 decades earlier, makes no reference whatsoever to geopolitics.[34] But the doctrine clearly rested on geopolitical ground:

> [I]ndustry was the key ingredient of power, and the United States controlled most of the centers of industry. There were five such centers in the world: the United States, Britain, West Germany, Japan, and the Soviet Union. The United States and its future allies constituted four of the centers, the Soviet Union just one. Containment meant confining the Soviet Union to that one.[35]

Three years before Kennan's 1946 telegram, Spykman gave the lecture that became his last major work. He presented the geopolitical imperative in an epigram of his own: "Who controls the Rimland rules Eurasia; who rules Eurasia rules the world." He depicts World War II, then at its height, as "a war for control of the rimland littoral of Europe and Asia." Looking to the future, he contends, "the safety and independence of this country can be preserved only by a foreign policy that will make it impossible for the Eurasian land mass to harbor an overwhelmingly dominant power in Europe and the Far East."[36] Kennan's containment corresponds to Spykman's admonition, which meant keeping most of the major economic powers integrated into an American-dominated political and economic structure. The success of containment, the end of the Cold War, permitted the expansion of that system to include the entire world. Geopolitics thus underlay the policies that made globalization possible.

The role of geopolitics in the formation of the global order that permitted the current phase of globalization does not mean that globalization necessarily requires a geopolitical substructure to continue. But to assume that it does not would require the same assumptions that are necessary to prove that national security policy can depend on globalization rather than traditional means—deterrence and defense—to ensure the safety of the United States. We have already seen that those assumptions are at best unproven and thus unreliable. Friedman argues that "the globalization system cannot hold together without an activist and generous American foreign policy."[37] If the grand strategies, British and then American, that underlay the evolution of globalization both had geopolitical roots, we may prudently assume that the next grand strategy should as well.

This realization is more profound than it appears. It eliminates the polarity between globalization and geopolitics and the hard distinction between a "globalization-infused strategy" and a conventional grand strategy. A distinction certainly exists, since a significant school of thought holds that globalization itself threatens the interests of the United States.[38] But in practice, the measures taken to protect American security foster globalization and vice versa.

What guidance, then, does spatial analysis of the world offer for grand strategy in the coming decades? Much has changed in the five and a half decades since the idea of containment took shape, but much remains the same. Industry—which includes, after all, the production of software in all its ramifications as well as hardware—and the resources necessary to support it remain the foundation of both wealth and power. Both industry and resources are distributed unevenly through the world. That unevenness forms the root of the geopolitical component of grand strategy.

Of the 5 great centers of industry in 1946, only North America remains unaltered. Though the future of European integration remains uncertain, from a broad spatial perspective Britain, Germany, and the other industrial powers of Europe have coalesced into the European Union. Eleven of the world's 25 largest economies are located in Europe west of Russia. Of the other 14, 3 are in North America (including Mexico, which had the 11th largest economy in the world in 2000), 8 in Asia and the Pacific Rim, and 2 in Latin America. Russia and Turkey are the odd men out.[39] Gross national product figures do not, of course, tell the whole story. Examination of the rates of growth in output and population draws attention to Asia and the Pacific Rim. The Population Reference Bureau projects a 9-percent decrease in the population of Europe, including Russia and Ukraine, by 2050. Of the 11 European states among the 25 largest economies, 6 are projected to shrink. In contrast, the Bureau predicts that only one Asian country, Japan, will lose population between now and 2050. The other large Asian economies are projected to grow significantly in population. China, after decades of population control efforts, will grow only 8 percent between 2001 and 2050; India, growing by 58 percent, will surpass China in population. Though some of the Pacific Rim countries, such as South Korea, will grow slowly (5 percent), others, such as Singapore (151 percent) and Malaysia (94 percent), will soar.[40]

For several decades, the notion of overpopulation as an ecological danger has led most observers to neglect the strategic value of a large and growing population. Today, the correlation between population and military power is certainly less direct than in the past because the size of military forces matters less than their technical sophistication. But it is still difficult to imagine that countries with shrinking populations will be able to retain their political and economic power.[41] Russia's demographic prospects, even more than its economic and environmental woes, make its future as even a regional power dubious; its population is projected to shrink by 14 percent by 2050. Demographic realities compel us to focus on Asia and the Pacific Rim.

Whatever its origin, the term *Pacific Rim* resembles Nicholas Spykman's term *Rimland*. Spykman drew attention to the importance of the outer tier of the Eurasian land mass. His definition of Rimland includes Europe, Anatolia, the Arabian Peninsula, the Iranian plateau, the Indian subcontinent, Southeast Asia, China (the Huang-He and Chang Jiang valleys), and the Korean Peninsula. In Spykman's terms, the policy of containment prevented the continental Eurasian power from dominating the Rimland, and thus the world. It began in Europe because Europe had the greatest economic potential in the postwar years and was most vulnerable to Soviet power. Colin Gray describes the North Atlantic Treaty Organization (NATO) as "organizing the Rimland."[42] Although there was no comparable comprehensive organization in the Pacific, the bilateral U.S. relationships with the Republic of Korea, Japan, the Republic of China, the Philippines, and eventually the Association of Southeast Asian Nations served the same purpose. There was less need for formal military arrangements because neither the Soviet Union nor China could project power at sea. Ultimately, the Seventh Fleet and forward-deployed U.S. air and ground forces organized the Pacific Rim.

Rise of a Regional Hegemon

The collapse of the Soviet Union and the separation of Ukraine and the Central Asian republics from Russia make the emergence of a Eurasian power, as Mackinder and Spykman envision one, unlikely in the coming decades. But even a regional hegemon could disrupt the global balance of power. China, a Rimland state in the Spykman universe, has the potential to become a regional hegemon in East Asia and the Pacific Rim. Spykman's Rimland does not include the offshore islands, such as Indonesia, the Philippines, Taiwan, and Japan, but they clearly form a rim. Mackinder's and Spykman's principle of preventing an inland power from dominating its outer rim and becoming a regional hegemon applies in this case. As Ross Munro and Richard Bernstein state:

> [T]he central issue for the United States and its Asian allies and friends is whether an increasingly powerful China is going to dominate Asia, as its leaders intend, or whether the United States, working primarily with Japan, can counterbalance China's emergence to great-power and eventually to super-power status. That issue will be resolved on Asia's eastern rim—in the band of territory that begins in the

Russian Far East and continues through the Korean peninsula, Japan, and Taiwan and probably the Philippines and Indonesia as well.[43]

As in Europe during the Cold War, domination would not require a conquest. If China gained sufficient leverage over the Pacific Rim countries to control their political and economic policies, as the Soviets did in Finland, it would become an effective hegemon without the overt use of force. China's proximity and huge population give it major advantages over the United States in the Pacific Rim. Tokyo is 4,000 miles further from San Francisco than from Shanghai. China does not require forward bases or intercontinental aircraft and missiles to project power in the Pacific Rim. As China's population becomes wealthier, it will become a larger market for the Pacific Rim economies and will gain leverage as a result. These advantages create the fundamental strategic problem in Asia for the United States.

The Cold War offers a useful analogy. Although the Soviet Union extended from the Baltic to the Pacific, it was oriented toward Europe. Europe's industrial capability was far more valuable and accessible to the Soviet Union than any other possible conquest. Like China in East Asia, the Soviet Union had the advantages of mass and proximity. The United States overcame those advantages through nuclear deterrence and basing U.S. forces in Europe. On the Pacific Rim, there is no major land frontier. The Taiwan Strait has replaced the Fulda Gap. This fact has two obvious corollaries. First, there can be no doubt that from a strictly geopolitical perspective without reference to any historical, political, or cultural considerations, having an independent Taiwan on poor terms with mainland China serves the interests of the United States. A Taiwan under Chinese control would put China astride the sea lines of communication of Japan and South Korea. Second, the task of counterbalancing Chinese power and influence must depend primarily on maritime forces, including air and space assets, rather than ground forces.

To explain a complex sequence of events in a few words, NATO succeeded because of the linkage between conventional forces on the ground in Europe and the American nuclear deterrent. This linkage, which included the forward deployment of U.S. ground forces, formed the keystone of the arch of containment. Will such an arch succeed in the 21st century? More concretely put, will the Pacific Rim countries regard the threat of American retaliation as sufficient to protect them from the threat of Chinese nuclear weapons? Or will the possibility of Chinese nuclear attack on American cities make the Pacific Rim countries doubt the reliability of American guarantees against the possibility of Chinese aggression, even when American forces are present? The answer to this question must determine much of U.S. grand strategy in the coming decades, and not only in the Pacific. A definitive answer will of course be possible only in retrospect; a systematic examination is beyond the scope of this chapter. There is, however, substantial doubt that the strategic linkage that worked in NATO will work in the Pacific Rim. Europeans often doubted that an American President would place his cities at risk to defend Berlin or Paris; Asians are even more likely to be doubtful. Ballistic missile defenses, for both the continental United States and the Pacific Rim countries, would make U.S. commitments to support and protect the Pacific Rim countries from China far more credible. From the perspective of global geopolitics, this requirement creates the primary justification for ballistic missile defenses for the United States in the coming decades, even though a ballistic missile attack from a rogue state or nonstate entity appears more likely than an attack from China. (Implications for a naval role in missile defense are discussed in chapter 24.)

Oil as the Driving Imperative

All the world's industrial economies depend on fossil fuels, especially petroleum. Because petroleum is a fungible commodity—as is pointed out in chapter 6—there is a single world market in it. All oil consumers depend on all oil producers, regardless of where they actually obtain their oil. And the world oil market, of course, means the Persian Gulf region, with almost two-thirds of the world's reserves.[44] As is extensively detailed in chapter 10, because both population and economic output will grow far more rapidly in Asia than in the rest of the world in the coming decades, energy consumption will grow fastest there. According to the Energy Information Administration (EIA), Asia (not including the Middle East) currently consumes nearly 100 quadrillion British thermal units of energy, roughly as much as the United States does. By 2020, Asian energy consumption will double, while U.S. consumption will increase by only 25 percent. This increase in consumption will include all sources of energy, but only the increase in petroleum and natural gas consumption will have a geopolitical impact. Asia is nearly self-sufficient in coal but imports huge amounts of oil and natural gas. Asian oil imports will increase by about 12 million barrels a day by 2020, roughly doubling current imports. Asia will become the primary market from Persian Gulf petroleum, supplanting Europe and North America. EIA projects that Asian consumption of natural gas will increase from 9.6 trillion cubic feet in 1999 to 26.6 trillion cubic feet in 2020. Most of that supply will have to come from outside the region, either from the Middle East or from Russia and Central Asia. Asia, in the EIA categories, includes both China and the Pacific Rim. As also concluded in chapter 10, the Asian dependence on energy supplies from outside the region creates a geopolitical opportunity for the United States.[45]

At present, the United States guarantees free and safe access to petroleum and natural gas from the Persian Gulf through our presence in the Persian Gulf and our unchallenged global maritime supremacy. For this reason, Asia, including China, depends on the United States, not merely on the actual sellers of the petroleum and natural gas, for its energy and thus for its economic prosperity and growth. The leverage of energy access control can counterbalance the leverage of China's size and proximity on the Pacific Rim. It also offers significant leverage over China itself. From this perspective, the U.S. commitments in the Persian Gulf and Indian Ocean protect not only our own energy supplies but also our status as a global power. Since we are currently engaged in a war against Osama bin Laden, who claims the American presence in Saudi Arabia as the principle justification for his hostility, there is no doubt that the U.S. presence in the Gulf brings painfully expensive baggage. But it is an essential component of the maintenance of global order. According to Thomas P.M. Barnett, "Our forward presence [in East Asia] both reassures local governments and obviates their need for larger military hedges."[46] But this statement does not go far enough, in two senses. First, our guarantee of energy access, not merely our forward presence on the Pacific Rim itself, provides that reassurance. Second, the reassurance must counterbalance China's size, proximity, and growing military and economic power.

Balancing Disruptive Regional Hegemons

Looking at the Pacific Rim geopolitically draws attention to Vietnam. Vietnam has the seventh largest population in Asia (after China, India, Indonesia, Pakistan, Bangladesh, and Japan), a long history of antipathy toward China, and a pivotal position. History and ideology aside, the United States and Vietnam have common concerns neither country can ignore.

China is not the only emerging regional hegemon in Asia. The United States began to take India seriously as a strategic power only after the 1998 nuclear tests, but there is good reason to do so. India's population, already over a billion, is growing far faster than China's (by 58 percent from 2001 to 2050, as opposed to China's 8 percent) and India will pass China in population before 2050. Although India's economy is growing more slowly than China's, both overall and in industrial output, it has made enormous economic strides in the last decade, especially in software exports. Extraordinary regional disparities within the country obscure pockets of rapid growth.[47] Since the end of the Cold War, and especially since September 11, many observers and policymakers have regarded the United States and India as natural partners, both democracies, both confronting Islamist terrorism, both concerned about the growth of Chinese power and influence. The countries have these things in common, and the potential for cooperation certainly exists. India's support for the U.S. decision to deploy ballistic missile defenses and cooperation since September 11 shows that a new era of relations has begun.[48] But India's agenda for cooperation includes a call for American recognition of India's "strategic interests not just in South Asia, but along an arc from the Suez Canal to the Straits of Malacca." Though entirely rational from the Indian perspective, this proposition clashes with the American geopolitical imperative to retain control—the ability to use and to deny use—of the sea line of communications between the Middle East and East Asia. [49] Beyond this substantive point of tension, many Indians view the United States with considerable suspicion. The Hindu nationalist movement (in which the ruling Bharatiya Janata Party has its roots), though eager to make the United States an ally against Islam, does not love the United States.[50]

Conclusions

Though cursory and incomplete, this inquiry has drawn some clear conclusions for American national security policy.[51] It demonstrates, most importantly, that despite the manifestation of intense nonspatial/nonlinear threats, American grand strategy cannot assume that the era of spatial threats, and thus of geopolitics, has ended. Looking at the coming decades through a geopolitical lens requires that we focus on Asia, especially the Pacific Rim, because of the combination of growing population and growing economic capacity in that region. Even though the Pacific Rim countries have not yet become as productive, either in absolute terms or per capita, as the leading economies of Western Europe, their continued growth gives them greater weight in the shaping of the global future. With Russia's economic and demographic decline and massive loss of territory, Europe no longer faces a potential hegemon on its eastern frontier, at least not for a generation. Europe's aging and, over the next 50 years, shrinking population makes the Continent an unlikely hegemon, even if European integration proceeds apace.

The dynamism and uncertainty of the prospects of Asia, especially the Pacific Rim, give it the greatest weight in the future of the world. It must receive similar weight in the grand strategy of the United States. To prevent China from Finlandizing the Pacific Rim, the United States must counterbalance the leverage China has in the region because of its proximity and size. To borrow Gray's words, the United States must organize the Pacific Rim as we did the Rimland during the Cold War. But it must do so, in all probability, without the benefit of an overall alliance like NATO, and probably in most cases without bilateral treaties beyond those that already exist with Japan, the Republic of Korea, and Australia. For this reason, the existing bases in the region, in South Korea, Japan, Okinawa, Guam, and Diego Garcia, are extremely important. The unfortunate loss of the bases in the Philippines makes the task significantly harder.[52] The paucity of bases puts a premium on forces capable of operating without them: long-range bombers and maritime forces, the same assets that have made the operations against al Qaeda and the Taliban possible. Ballistic missile defense—for both the United States and the Pacific Rim countries—will be necessary to offset the threat of Chinese theater ballistic missiles and make a U.S. response to the possibility of Chinese aggression credible in the face of the Chinese intercontinental ballistic missile threat to the continental United States. Such defenses, as well as conventional military operations, require space assets; the extreme importance of space assets will require positive space control, and perhaps space denial as well.

This partial sketch of a grand strategy appears far from the world of globalization, focused on the potential for conflict rather than the prospect of cooperation and interdependence. But if a geopolitically oriented grand strategy functions to prevent conflict in the most rapidly growing regions of the world, it will in fact foster, not impede, globalization. In this sense, there is no opposition between globalization and geopolitics.

Notes

[1] Brian Blouet, *Globalization and Geopolitics* (London: Reaktion Books, 2001), 1.

[2] Geoffrey Parker, *Geopolitics: Past, Present, and Future* (London: Pinter, 1998), 5. This Geoffrey Parker, author of a series of books on geopolitics, is not the same man as the distinguished military historian.

[3] Thomas L. Friedman, *The Lexus and the Olive Tree*, rev. ed. (New York: Anchor Books, 2000), 250.

[4] Parker, 10–43, 98–118. Parker quotes Mackinder's dictum on 105; it originally appeared in Halford Mackinder, *Democratic Ideas and Reality* (London: Henry Holt, 1919). National Defense University Press published a reprint of MacKinder's great work in 1996 with an introduction by Stephen V. Mladineo. The dictum appears in that edition on page 106.

[5] Parker, 95–139. For specific examples of this literature other than Mackinder, see Nicholas Spykman, *The Geography of Peace* (New York: Harcourt Brace, 1944); Robert Strausz-Hupé, *Geopolitics: The Struggle for Space and Power* (New York: Harcourt Brace, 1942); Colin S. Gray, *The Geopolitics of the Nuclear Era: Heartland, Rimlands, and the Technological Revolution* (New York: Crane, Russak, 1977), and Colin S. Gray, *The Geopolitics of Superpower* (Lexington: University of Kentucky Press, 1988).

[6] Gray, *Geopolitics of Superpower*, 4.

[7] Saul B. Cohen, "Geopolitics in the New World Era: A New Perspective on an Old Discipline," in *Reordering the World: Geopolitical Perspectives on the 21st Century*, 2d ed., ed. George J. Demko and William B. Wood (Boulder: Westview Press, 1999), 40–68; and Mackubin Thomas Owens, "In Defense of Classical Geopolitics," *Naval War College Review* (Autumn 1999), 59–77.

[8] On the reach of geography, see William B. Wood and George J. Demko, "Introduction: Political Geography for the Next Millennium," in Demko and Wood, 3–4.

[9] Friedman, 7–14; the quote is from page 7.

[10] Stephen Flanagan, "Meeting the Challenges of the Global Century," in *Global Century: Globalization and National Security*, ed. Richard L. Kugler and Ellen Frost (Washington, DC: National Defense University Press, 2001), 9.

[11] Ellen L. Frost, "Globalization and National Security," in *Global Century*, 37.

[12] Ibid., 36.

[13] Ibid.

[14] Ibid., 57.

[15] Owens, 3, 12.

[16] Friedman, 398; the discussion of super-empowered individuals continues to page 405.

[17] Ibid., 249–250.

[18] Charles de Secondat, Baron de Montesquieu, *Spirit of Laws*, trans. Thomas Nugent, rev. J.V. Prichard, vol. 35 of *The Great Books of the Western World*, ed. Mortimer Adler (Chicago: Encyclopedia Britannica, 1990), 146.

[19] Norman Angell, *The Great Illusion* (London: W. Heinemann, 1913), 309, quoted in Michael Howard, *War and the Liberal Conscience* (New Brunswick, NJ: Rutgers University Press, 1986), 70.

[20] Friedman, 250.

[21] Robert R. Strassler and Victor Davis Hanson, *The Landmark Thucydides: A Comprehensive Guide to the Peloponnesian War* (New York: Free Press, 1996), 43.

[22] U.S. Department of State, Foreign Service Institute, Center for the Study of Foreign Affairs, *Thinking About World Change* (Washington, DC, 1990), 123. Page 2 of the report indicates that Vlahos drafted the report; page 3 lists the 40 individuals who participated in the working group that produced it.

[23] Samuel P. Huntington, *The Clash of Civilizations and the Remaking of World Order* (New York: Simon and Schuster, 1996).

[24] Friedman, 344; he discusses the backlash against globalization on pages 327–347. On fundamentalism as a cross-cultural phenomenon, see Bruce B. Lawrence, *Defenders of God: The Fundamentalist Revolts Against the Modern Age* (San Francisco: Harper and Row, 1989).

[25] Scott B. Macdonald, "The New Bad Guys: Exploring the Parameters of the Violent New World Order," in *Gray Area Phenomena: Confronting the New World Disorder,* ed. Max G. Manwaring (Boulder: Westview Press, 1993), 38.

[26] For a brief explanation of the National Islamic Front's rise and fall from power, see "Turabi Down But Not Out," *The Economist* (August 17, 2000).

[27] On the history of the Bharatiya Janata Party, see Yogendra Malik and V.B. Singh, *Hindus Nationalists in India: Rise of the Bharatiya Janata Party* (Boulder: Westview Press, 1994).

[28] I find no single account of the Iranian Revolution satisfactory, but several give a sense of the uniqueness of the circumstances: Mohsen M. Milani, *The Making of Iran's Islamic Revolution: From Monarchy to Islamic Republic* (Boulder: Westview Press, 1988); Jerrold M. Green, *Revolution in Iran: The Politics of Countermobilization* (New York: Praeger, 1982); Gholam R. Afkhami, *The Iranian Revolution: Thanatos on a National Scale* (Washington, DC: Middle East Institute, 1985).

[29] Robert D. Kaplan, *The Coming Anarchy: Shattering the Dreams of the Post Cold War* (New York: Vintage, 2000), 24. The essay "The Coming Anarchy," from which the quotation comes, was originally published in *The Atlantic Monthly* in 1994. The essay as a whole supports the argument made in this paragraph.

[30] Immanuel Kant, *Perpetual Peace: A Philosophical Essay,* trans. M. Campbell Smith (New York: Garland, 1972).

[31] Howard, 137.

[32] J.L. Talmon, *Origins of Totalitarian Democracy* (New York: Norton, 1970); see also Claes G. Ryn, *The New Jacobinism: Can Democracy Survive* (Washington, DC: National Humanities Institute, 1991).

[33] Friedman, xvi–xviii, 467–468; Frost, "Globalization," 38–39. Frost does not discuss the British role and emphasizes the "significant, relentless, and irreversible difference in kind" between contemporary globalization and its predecessor. She recognizes the reality of the earlier globalization nonetheless.

[34] George F. Kennan, "The Origins of Containment," in *Containment: Concept and Policy,* ed. Terry L. Deibel and John Lewis Gaddis (Washington, DC: National Defense University Press, 1985), 23–31.

[35] Steven W. Hook and John Spanier, *American Foreign Policy Since World War II,* 15th ed. (Washington, DC: Congressional Quarterly Press, 2000), 44. See also Gray, 4–5.

[36] Nicholas Spykman, *The Geography of the Peace,* ed. Helen R. Nicholl, introduction by Frederick Sherwood Dunn (New York: Harcourt, Brace and Company, 1944), 43–44, 45, 58–60.

[37] Friedman, 467–468.

[38] See, for example, Alan Tonelson, *The Race to the Bottom: Why a Worldwide Worker Surplus and Uncontrolled Free Trade Are Sinking American Living Standards* (Boulder: Westview Press, 2000); and Pat Buchanan, *The Great Betrayal: How American Sovereignty and Social Justice Are Being Sacrificed to the Gods of the Global Economy* (New York: Little, Brown and Company, 1998).

[39] 2000 gross national product in current dollars accessed at <http: www.scaruffi.com/politics/gnp.html>.

[40] This reference, and all subsequent from the Population Reference Bureau's *World Population Data Sheet,* accessed at <www.prb.org/Content/NavigationMenu/Other/2001_World_Population_Data_Sheet.html>.

[41] For an antique but extremely valuable discussion of population from a strategic perspective, see Robert Strausz-Hupé, "Population as an Element of National Power," in *Foundations of National Power: Readings in World Politics and American Security,* 2d ed., ed. Harold and Margaret Sprout (New York: Van Nostrand, 1951), 111–116. The essay is an excerpt from Strausz-Hupé's *The Balance of Tomorrow* (New York: Putnam, 1945).

[42] Gray, 75.

[43] Richard Bernstein and Ross H. Munro, *The Coming Conflict with China* (New York: Random House, 1998), vii.

[44] Energy Information Administration, International Energy Annual 1999, accessed at <www.eia.doe.gov/emeu/iea/table91.html>.

[45] All energy production and consumption projects are from the Department of Energy, Energy Information Administration, *International Energy Outlook 2001*, DOE/EIA-0484 (2001), accessed at <www.eia.doe.gov/oiaf/ ieo/index.html>. Chapter 10 of this volume by Thomas P.M. Barnett interprets the EIA figures in the Asian context. Barnett's work provided much of the inspiration for my own chapter.

[46] Thomas P.M. Barnett, "Asia: The Military-Market Link," U.S. Naval Institute *Proceedings* 128, no. 1 (January 2002), 55.

[47] For a convenient survey of recent developments in the Indian economy, see "Survey: Indian Economy, The Plot Thickens," *The Economist* (May 31, 2001).

[48] See, for example, Rahul Bedi, "Bush Clears Sale of 20 Military Items to India," *Jane's Defence Weekly* (February 13, 2002), 3.

[49] Former Indian Minister of External Affairs Jaswant Singh has articulated four principles of cooperation with the United States, summarized in the Center for Strategic and International Studies *South Asia Monitor* as follows: "First, India sees itself as a powerful individual player in international politics. Second, it seeks a positive and equal relationship with the United States, not a traditional alliance. Third, India wants the United States to take account of its strategic interests not just in South Asia, but along an arc from the Suez Canal to the Straits of Malacca. Fourth, India will continue to buy most of its military hardware from Russia . . . Implicit in this outline is a fifth principle: that India would prefer a multipolar world to a bipolar or unipolar one." From *South Asia Monitor* 34 (June 1, 2001).

[50] For an example of Hindu nationalist suspicion of the United States, see, "What Hindus Should Do–Part I," accessed at <www.hinduunity.org/articles/hindutva/ whathindusshould1.html>. According to the site: "America learnt a big lesson from the Vietnam war: do not fight directly on the alien soil; rather wreck it from within as it did in the case of Russia. It is trying to disintegrate India through a long-term conspiracy. America is not a friend of India, and wants India to remain limited by the size of American designs by all means." Friedman describes a conversation in which an Indian teenager told a group of visiting academics: "China is our biggest neighbor and we had a war with China, but China stands up for weaker nations and we have no problem with China [but the United States is] a bully, it elbows everybody and thinks only of itself" (Friedman, 391).

[51] Part of the incompleteness, of course, consists of the failure to discuss Latin American and sub-Saharan Africa at all. I do not address these regions because of the extraordinary unlikelihood that they could produce a dangerous regional hegemon, not because I consider them unimportant from other perspectives. See Owens, 9; Cohen, 52–53.

[52] Drew A. Bennett, "Military Presence in Asia is Key," U.S. Naval Institute *Proceedings* 128, no. 1 (January 2002), 57–60. Some would view U.S. support for Philippine counterterrorism as reestablishing a "base" in the Philippines.

Chapter 4

Transnational Threats and Maritime Responses

Kimberley L. Thachuk and Sam J. Tangredi

Transnational threats are activities perpetrated by nonstate actors that not only transcend national borders but also have global impact. Yet—at least prior to September 11, 2001—they seemed easy to overlook because they are so varied in nature and scope. Further, their effects are obscured by the fact that many are somewhat insidious with gradual and long-term consequences rather than immediate ones. With the exception of global terrorism, most transnational threats clearly have a lower overall profile in global security considerations than do big-power geopolitics, regional wars, and weapons of mass destruction (WMD) proliferation. But while some transnational threats are not direct threats to U.S. national security, they are threats to the U.S. economy and the quality of life of its citizens and therefore threaten U.S. national interests. The combined effect of transnational threats such as drug, military hardware, and human trafficking, piracy, and acts of terrorism—along with their critical enablers, corruption and money laundering—cannot be overlooked for their seriously damaging long-term consequences for global political and economic stability and thus for U.S. security.

All transnational threats are not the result of contemporary globalization. Indeed, most of the underlying activities—such as smuggling, corruption, and uncontrolled migrations—have occurred throughout history. Many have been enduring concerns for national governments. But globalization has increased both the range and effects of these activities by providing the physical means to transcend even the most surveilled borders and to move across ever-increasing distances. At the same time, the

Kimberley L. Thachuk is a senior fellow in the Institute for National Strategic Studies at the National Defense University, where her research focus is on countering terrorism and international crime, particularly in the Latin American region. She has lectured throughout the National Defense University and at the Inter-American Defense College and is also an adjunct professor at George Washington University. Captain Sam J. Tangredi's operational experience includes participation in maritime counterdrug and United Nations sanctions-enforcement operations in the Atlantic, Pacific, and Indian Oceans, and the Persian Gulf.

increasing globalization of national economies now means that the effects of these threats on any one country (based on the level of integration with the global economy) can have devastating effects on all.

The U.S. Government dedicates considerable resources to combating transnational threats but usually deals with each threat individually or in a *stovepipe* fashion. This is not an optimal approach. Not only are resources potentially wasted by duplication of overhead functions, but also it inhibits the flow of information, lessons learned, and best practices across the teams and agencies that focus on individual threats.

With that in mind, this chapter begins by identifying and analyzing transnational threats according to collective categories. The value of this method will be to uncover some of their common traits and therefore discover the vulnerabilities they share. Further, many international criminal groups have begun to diversify their activities, and hence, a law enforcement organization that directs its limited resources and energy at fighting drug trafficking might be tempted to overlook a parallel activity—such as trafficking of human migrants—that is being conducted by the same group or one that has a relationship with that group. Such related criminal groups often employ the same routes, launder their money using the same schemes, and conduct multiple parallel activities. Overlooking or simply passing the information to an agency that deals with a different, parallel threat does not provide for a synergistic use of countercrime resources. Also, many lessons have already been learned in combating some of the threats. These lessons might successfully be used if applied to other threats. The solution is to analyze and understand transnational threats in terms of collective categories and to organize to deal with them in a collective fashion.

Following the analysis of these threats, the chapter suggests ways in which maritime forces might be used, in coordination with other agencies, to combat them. This effort is not to imply that naval and other maritime forces would be capable of taking the primary role against any specific threat, nor to suggest that collectively these threats be the sole focus of naval operations. But it is meant to point to the fact that in a globalized world in which *traditional* major theater wars have become increasingly rare, it makes sense to use America's overwhelming maritime power to deter or defeat our most likely and insidious enemy: the cumulative effects of transnational threats. In effect, that is what we are now doing in conducting a war against global terrorism. Maritime roles in combating terrorism will be discussed in detail in the following chapters. This chapter examines the aspect of terrorism in general but focuses primarily on the parallel transnational threats that facilitate some of the activities of the terrorist networks.

In the context of the future security environment outlined by chapter 2, the transnational threats discussed can be viewed as part of the asymmetric challenge to U.S. and global security but also as a *backlash* of a sort against the beneficial aspects of globalization—the aspects that promise to mitigate the environments in which transnational threats can flourish. It should also be noted that many of the technological advances postulated in chapter 2 can be used to further transnational criminal activities.

The Actors

Transnational threats originate primarily from two types of nonstate actors: terrorist groups and organized criminal groups. Both groups can be classified as international criminals because they commit acts that are prohibited by most domestic laws, international criminal laws, and international agreements. While the actors themselves are often conceived of as the *threats*, it perhaps more accurate to state that their *actions* are what constitute the threats.

In previous decades, terrorists were viewed largely as directed by foreign governments and focused on a particular set of political motivations. This made them easier to identify and monitor. While some terrorist groups still benefit from state sponsorship, many of today's terrorist groups have not only lost their more comprehensible ideals but also are increasingly turning to smuggling and other criminal activities to fund their operations. For their part, organized crime groups were considered domestic law enforcement concerns until fairly recently. However, as their activities have increasingly become more international in scope and perhaps more intense, the recognition that they pose threats to national security has gradually developed. Certainly this is the case for drug trafficking, the smuggling of military hardware, money laundering, market manipulation and other financial fraud, international prostitution rings and the smuggling of aliens, and the smuggling of contraband. Further, there are numerous links between the two types of actors that, while mostly ad hoc, are increasing as the line between terrorist motivations and criminal enterprise become gradually blurred.

While these criminal groups are ever more transnational in scope, they still have to conduct their operations from within sovereign states. But globalization has facilitated their activities with modern communications systems, technology, and rapid travel. They now have considerable coercive political and economic leverage from largely unknown vantage points in cyberspace. The use of electronic transfers, unfettered Internet access, and high-tech communications equipment such as encryption devices, cellular phones, and satellites has permitted international criminals increasingly to commit faceless crimes that erode states' authority and to develop vast virtual networks that span multiple regions. While these activities can take place anywhere, criminals find it much easier to operate from states that are either unwilling or unable to detect and disrupt their activities. Countries that have weak institutions of justice and traditions of corruption and personalized rule are faced with a myriad of economic and governance issues, making them unable to designate resources for countering international crime and susceptible to the financial benefits that the latter can bring. They thus suffer from a certain degree of collapse and are unable to govern effectively. As a result, increasingly weak states have become safe havens for criminal groups to conduct international operations with virtual impunity.

Some scholars speculate that countries such as Russia and China will begin to sponsor criminal activities for profit, thereby providing crime groups the political support that they need to operate unfettered. While this remains to be seen, the truth is that the larger criminal groups are very difficult to control. They often undertake campaigns of corruption and extortion against governments to safeguard their operations or resort to armed opposition in alliance with other armed groups. In countries such as Colombia and Russia, the attempts to bring organized criminal groups to justice have met with little success. As their activities become increasingly transnational, criminal groups will not only be more difficult to apprehend, but also beleaguered governments may use jurisdictional arguments to avoid addressing the problem. That is, much of the criminal activity is dependent on demand in other countries, and thus—as the impact of the crimes are felt elsewhere—some states feel it is not incumbent on them to be the ones that must not only attempt to apprehend and try criminals but also pay the economic and social costs for such an endeavor.

The Facilitators

The two main factors that sustain criminal actors' ability to continue operations are their reliance on the corruptibility of officials and the ability to launder the proceeds of their criminal activity.

Corruption. Corruption is the main vehicle, and likely the most socially damaging activity, by which criminal groups achieve their aims. To protect their business interests, organized crime has engaged in large-scale subornation rackets that help to grease the wheels of illicit commerce. Such campaigns often involve the use of bribery, graft, collusion, and/or extortion of officials and political leaders in numerous countries simultaneously. One of the more dire consequences of corruption has been that organized crime has infested and virtually overrun entire criminal justice systems in some states. This formula efficiently and effectively attacks the very order of society by paying off or threatening officials to alter charges, change court rulings, lose evidence, and not try cases at all. From there, criminal largesse is distributed among members of political parties and the various offices of government as well as the staffs and politicians of local administrations in an attempt to alter policy considerations.

Money Laundering. The purpose of money laundering is to lower the risk of being connected with the crimes from which the money derived and, further, to allow international criminals to integrate operations in the legitimate business world. The fact that somewhere between $300 billion and $500 billion are laundered annually means that international criminals are exploiting significant weaknesses in international financial systems.[1] Illicit capital can be moved through several different countries in one day to disguise its origins and to confuse authorities. Further, the sheer volume and complexity of such transactions, which might have averaged a few hours to complete, usually requires a year of investigation to uncover. Thus, not only do such vast sums of money bankroll illicit transactions of all forms, but they also practically guarantee anonymity and bolster the ability of organized crime groups to be ruthless with impunity.

The Threats

For the purpose of analysis and organized response, transnational threats can be broken down into three collective or functional categories: *smuggling, trafficking, and piracy*, which are functionally dependent on the transportation of illicit or stolen goods or the interdiction of legally transported goods; *acts of terrorism*, which are functionally dependent on the acquisition of weapons (both primitive and complex) by nonstate actors; and *nascent ecological/social threats*, which involve nonstate activities that may not necessarily be under the control of an organized group that benefits from them in any fashion. An obvious relationship between these parallel activities can be discerned: for example, smuggling allows for the transport of weapons acquired by terrorist groups into a target country. Likewise, the trafficking in illegal human migrants can inadvertently spread the nascent transnational threat of infectious diseases.

Smuggling, Trafficking, and Piracy

Drug Trafficking. The illegal narcotics business is estimated to be the second largest industry in the world, meeting the demand of between three and four percent of the world's population.[2] The glut of profits that flow from it not only rivals the gross national product of many countries but also is sufficient to undermine legitimate commerce and countries' balance of payments, monetary systems, and international bank cooperation. Such sums have enabled drug traffickers to become increasingly adept at suborning, undermining, and threatening entire governments and thereby to elude law enforcement efforts and continue their activities with relative freedom.

Trafficking in Military Hardware. Much of the world's small arms trade is conducted illicitly.[3] With the end of the Cold War, a number of countries desperate for foreign exchange are selling their large stockpiles of machineguns, rocket launchers, grenade launchers, ammunition, and explosives on the black market. Theft of military hardware and/or the corruption of the officials guarding the stockpiles also account for many of the components available for sale to buyers from insurgent and terrorist groups.

Military hardware and drugs are often exchanged by a number of criminal groups depending on their needs. The net result is that the proliferation of small arms perpetuates situations of civil unrest and encourages militancy rather than negotiated settlements of violence. Populations and governments alike are often held hostage to armed insurgents, which ultimately results in both weakened democracies and regional instability. Conversely, what began as a political revolution in Albania in 1990 was transformed into criminal enterprise in Kosovo and elsewhere after the 1996 economic collapse and the plundering of the national arsenals. Seeing the opportunity presented by the approximately 1 million pilfered small weapons, organized crime quickly developed a network of small arms sales, using previously established drug trafficking routes and contacts, that extended throughout Europe and to the Middle East and the United States.[4]

Smuggling and Trafficking of Humans. The global traffic in humans has become the fastest growing criminal business in the world.[5] It is often a more attractive business prospect than other highly profitable enterprises such as narcotics and smuggling of military hardware, as it does not require technical expertise or a distribution network. Further, in many countries, the penalties for trafficking in persons are significantly lower than they are for narcotics, for example (which in states such as Malaysia carries the death penalty). The illegal immigrants make payment prior to departure, and the smugglers have no obligation to return the money if the operation is a failure.

The darker aspect of this trade involves the abduction or fraudulent recruitment of women and children for the purposes of the sex industry, domestic servitude, and sweatshop labor, which means that the activity both contravenes international criminal law and is a human rights issue. This activity is usually conducted in concert with other criminal enterprises such as extortion campaigns, racketeering, money laundering, the subornation of public officials in both the target state and the country of origin, and gambling rings. For example, the Wah Ching, an Asian organized crime group, not only smuggles Asian women for the purposes of prostitution but also is engaged in loan sharking and drug trafficking. Such an operation involves conspiracy, forgery of official documents such as passports and visas and even social security numbers, and mail and wire fraud.

Piracy. Piracy has made an alarming comeback in Indonesia, Bangladesh, the Malacca Straits, the South China Sea, India, Ecuador, and the Red Sea, with a reported 469 attacks in 2000.[6] Most pirate attacks are perpetrated by organized criminal groups among whose number are experienced sailors. While many incidents likely go unreported, ships are attacked while at anchor as well as at sea. Most often, the target is a container ship carrying valuable cargo. Often, the entire ship along with its cargo is taken after its crew has been killed or set adrift. The cargo is then sold using false documents, and the ship is sometimes painted and given a fake registration and its identification numbers changed so that it too may be sold. (Piracy is discussed in greater detail in chapter 8.)

Acts of Terrorism

Terrorist activities are discussed in detail in chapter 5. Discussed below are two of the emerging *means* that facilitate the conduct of terrorist activities on a transnational scale.

Biological, Chemical, and Nuclear Proliferation. Biological weapons use living or viral organisms or the toxins produced by them to kill or incapacitate members of an opponent's population. Toxins cause death within minutes or hours, while bacteria and viruses usually require an incubation period of at least 24 hours before symptoms appear. Chemical weapons comprise such agents as nerve, sarin, and cyanide gases and other toxic industrial chemicals such as chlorine. The proliferation of both chemical and biological weapons has increased since the termination of chemical/biological programs in a number of countries, most significantly the former Soviet Union.

With the economies of the states of the former Soviet Union tenuous, some stockpiles of nuclear materials are also at risk of being smuggled to terrorist groups for quick profits. The number of smuggling cases involving highly enriched uranium and plutonium to date has been limited, but security is lax at the over 1,000 nuclear facilities that store these materials. To date, there have been 14 confirmed seizures totaling 15.3 kilograms of weapons-grade uranium at various levels of enrichment and 368.8 grams of plutonium—fortunately, far less than what is necessary for a nuclear weapon.[7] Borders are also porous, and nuclear materials are difficult to detect. These problems allow for the possibility that sufficient nuclear materials will eventually fall into the hands of terrorists, although it must be noted that highly specialized knowledge is required to successfully cause mass casualties using all three forms of weapons.[8] Unfortunately, countless unemployed scientists from the former Soviet Union have such expertise.

Cyberthreats. In most states, the once fairly independent five main pillars of critical infrastructure—financial institutions, transportation, communications systems, electric power, and oil and gas supply—are now, as a result of vast technical advances in the past few decades, almost completely automated as well as interconnected. This presents a great target of vulnerability for terrorists to threaten many states' individual national security as well as to possibly destabilize entire countries and regions.

The easily accessible Internet is the greatest source of vulnerability in this regard. Not only can criminal groups successfully commit a number of faceless crimes and launder the proceeds largely anonymously, they also can launch cyberattacks against government, business, and social infrastructures that can take weeks or months to trace. Issues of jurisdiction then arise. Because criminals are so adept at weaving the attacks through a variety of countries, the fear of being apprehended and eventually tried is minimal. It would not be in the best interests of organized crime to target Internet and communications infrastructures, which serve their business interests, but not so for terrorists. Terrorists bent on causing mass disruption and misery might stage cyberattacks on any of the five main critical infrastructure nodes with potentially drastic consequences.

Nascent Environmental/Social Threats

Infectious Diseases. Despite tremendous public health progress during the 20th century, numerous infectious conditions have grown harder to control, and some 30 new infectious diseases have emerged in the last few decades, such as Ebola and a number of hemorrhagic fevers. Increased global travel, the deployment of armed forces overseas, changes in human behavior and diet, changes in land-use patterns, the breakdown of public health systems due to war or economic decline, microbial adaptation and resistance to antibiotics, climatic changes, and accelerated world trade have all exacerbated the spread of infectious diseases.

Infectious diseases also pose obstacles to U.S. efforts to help countries develop and may have the effect of destabilizing entire regions as is the case with the acquired immune deficiency syndrome/human immunodeficiency virus epidemic in sub-Saharan Africa. The World Health Organization reports that infectious diseases like malaria and tuberculosis account for approximately half of all premature deaths in the world and nearly two-thirds of deaths among children under 5 years of age.[9]

Environmental Threats (including resource depletion). Understanding that environmental problems are a security threat is somewhat difficult in terms of the more traditional definitions of national security. Easier to understand might be the fact that the political and ideological questions that dominate the international agenda are being increasingly linked to environmental problems and resource scarcity. Such issues as population growth and mass migrations are often linked to inadequate natural resources such as potable water. These demographic shifts, in turn, place demands on other regions for resources and often lead to conflict and social unrest.

While there are a number of cases of resource scarcity and environmental degradation that may pose long-term security threats, the example of water is perhaps the most illustrative. In recent decades, the watersheds of some of the largest rivers such as the Ganges, Nile, Colorado, and Yangtze have been severely polluted or overused to the point that little of their flow now reaches the sea. The number of people worldwide without sufficient access to potable water now stands at approximately 1.2 billion.[10] Because great volumes of water are required to irrigate land, the pressures of increased population (translated into demand for food) will create great competition for that resource. Security issues will only increase as competition mounts between states to provide water for their populations. Turkey, Syria, and Iraq, for example, all share the Tigris-Euphrates River, while India and Pakistan share the Ganges. Sudan, Ethiopia, and Egypt share the Nile River in what Boutros Boutros-Ghali warned would be the cause for the "next war in [the] region."

Mass Human Migration. Humanitarian crises and disasters, ethnic cleansing, and wars and insurgencies have also become opportunities for organized crime. Smugglers have found that desperate people fleeing their states are an easy target. The illegal boat services between Albania and Italy in the early 1990s, for example, soon extended to smuggling of Kurds and migrants from South Asia, Eastern Europe, and many African states.

At least 22 million people worldwide are currently displaced by war, violence, and human rights violations. Of those, 12 million are refugees, and the remainder are internally displaced. The problem has been further complicated by the recent involvement of warlords, militia, child soldiers, foreign mercenaries, and other maverick groups who are flagrant violators of humanitarian norms.

Naval Responses

Smuggling, Trafficking, and Piracy

Drug Trafficking. For the past 20 years, the U.S. Navy has had a well-defined support role in drug interdiction. With the perception that *posse comitatus* laws prevent direct law enforcement by naval units, U.S. Navy vessels and aircraft have served as surveillance platforms, as well as adjunct forces assigned to the U.S. Coast Guard—a law enforcement agency—through the command mechanism of two standing Joint Inter-Agency [antidrug] Task Forces (JIATFs), one operating on the east coast and one on the west.[11] Each JIATF, commanded by a Coast Guard flag officer, controls the maritime drug enforcement activities in its area by coordinating the efforts of U.S. Coast Guard, U.S. Navy, Drug Enforcement Agency (DEA), other Federal agencies, and sometimes the U.S. Marine Corps and other armed services. While other Federal agencies focus on local ground interdiction, JIATFs focus primarily on sea and air smuggling. U.S. naval ships and aircraft are routinely "chopped" (assigned) to JIATFs for counterdrug operations lasting from days to months. Often these operations are performed during the inter-deployment training cycle while the unit is preparing for its *real* overseas deployment to the Western Pacific or Persian Gulf. During the Cold War and immediately afterward, selected ships whose capabilities were perceived by the Navy leadership as dwindling in respect to an increasingly sophisticated potential wartime threat were assigned to counterdrug operations as their prime operational deployment. However, this is now done infrequently due both to the shrinkage of the

U.S. naval fleet after Operation *Desert Storm* (from over 560 ships to 316) and the decommissioning of vessels considered less capable to face front-line threats.

Naval counterdrug activities include both deployments to the Caribbean and off the coasts of Latin American countries, particularly Colombia, and operations within the normal fleet exercise areas off the coasts of the United States. Operations include monitoring both airspace and sea by radar and reporting the operational picture to the JIATF so that law enforcement units could be directed to further investigate suspicious activity, as well as actual boarding and searches of suspicious vessels in both U.S. and international waters. Often the U.S. Navy vessels involved carry a small Coast Guard law enforcement detachment (LEDET) of 5 to 6 members to train and direct naval personnel in these boardings. In the case of counterdrug activities in U.S. waters—where the U.S. Navy does not have law enforcement authority—Coast Guard personnel lead the actual boarding and the Naval warship hoists the Coast Guard flag onto its signal halyard in a fashion observable by the target vessel (even illuminating the Coast Guard flag at night). If an arrest is to be made, the Coast Guard LEDET personnel conduct it. On the high seas, international law allows for direct U.S. Navy apprehension of drug trafficking suspects for further turnover to local law enforcement authorities (in the United States or, by previous agreement, to another country).

Other naval and Coast Guard personnel, along with Army Special Forces and Air Force support, participate in training counterdrug forces of foreign militaries, from the maintenance of military equipment to the techniques of interdiction. These efforts are complementary to the extensive law enforcement and intelligence training provided by other U.S. agencies.

But even with such relatively extensive participation, there is always tension involved in naval support for the counterdrug operations. It is not the tension of *posse comitatus*—despite the public musings of civil libertarians—since many of the concerns about militarizing law enforcement have been or can be satisfactorily addressed. Rather, it is the tension between counterdrug operations and the training and preparations for major warfare operations. Counterdrug operations are usually seen as a competitor (for time and resources) to warfighting training. From this perspective, the more time a military unit spends on counterdrug operations, the less time it is spending on preparing for major war—since the skills for both are perceived as largely exclusive.

To what extent should preparations for major war be sacrificed to fulfill the counterdrug mission? Answers to that question are largely premised on one's expectations of the future. Many would argue that a major regional or theater war is unlikely, while the threat of drug trafficking is immediate and very evident. Since it would be logical for military forces to focus on the immediate rather than the unlikely, putting significant time and resources toward counterdrug operations makes sense—in fact, such logic argues for putting more resources toward the problem until drug trafficking is significantly curtailed (to a level that it is more easily managed by law enforcement agencies). But the opposite viewpoint, based on the premise that the whole point of having military forces is to deter wars and fight them if necessary, argues that counterdrug operation must be secondary to warfighting training and in fact should be conducted by non-frontline units or during gaps in the usual deployment training cycle.

However, naval crews operating in the counterdrug missions utilize the same general surveillance, reconnaissance, seamanship, and targeting skills that they would employ in actual combat. With the exception of actual weapons release, counterdrug operations can be seen as excellent real-world training for individual crews. From this perspective, the mission enhances rather than takes away from predeployment readiness. This both creates a different perception between the U.S. Navy and U.S. Army as to what activities contribute to force readiness and contributes to a lesser degree of reluctance to involve naval units in the drug enforcement effort at sea (and in the air).

Viewing transnational threats as national security issues rather than simply law enforcement issues argues for the significant involvement of national security forces— that is, military forces—to counter these threats. In the Pentagon, this was not a popular conclusion before September 11. But, ironically, the launching of the current counterterrorism campaign has reduced the percentage of military assets assigned to counterdrug operations. The Coast Guard has reported a significant shift of assets away from drug interdiction and to other aspects of homeland defense, particularly port security.[12] However, this trend may later reverse with greater recognition of how much terrorist funding is received via drug trafficking.

From a functional standpoint, the role of naval forces in counterdrug operations falls under three general categories: detection, interdiction, and deterrence/channeling. Used in a surveillance mode, naval units can detect potential trafficking vessels and aircraft, providing intelligence or real-time information to law enforcement agencies. This can often be done within the normal training areas of the fleet, such as Fleet Operating Area Southern California, which sits astride (or close to) a potential drug smuggling route. Detection of potential targets (which would include potential smugglers) is a normal part of at-sea training. In contrast, actual interdiction requires the specific assignment of naval units, usually at the expense of other missions. But the global forward presence that is the normal feature of the naval deployment cycle—no matter what the actual mission being conducted—can be thought of as providing a deterrent or channeling effect on overt drug trafficking at sea, forcing smugglers into narrower corridors that can be more effectively patrolled by police or drug enforcement agencies.

Trafficking in Military Hardware. Interdiction of illegal military weapons transfers is primarily the result of international sanctions brought against an outlawed
movement or rogue regime. Any state has the legal authority to interdict illegal
weapons entering its own territorial waters, whether headed to insurgents or criminal
organizations. Indeed, modern international law requires states to interdict weapons
bound for terrorist organizations that may be passing through their sovereign territory, whether or not the particular receiving group poses an internal threat (as opposed to simply a threat to another state). Such action would be considered part of na-
tional/international law enforcement even if military forces are used for the task.
Seizure of a freighter carrying weapons to Palestinian groups is a recent example.[13] But
much of the trafficking in military hardware transits the open seas, where international law normally allows for the free flow of trade—military goods included.

The interdiction of weapons to Iraq and the former Republic of Yugoslavia has
been a part of sanctions regimes imposed by United Nations (UN) resolution.[14] The
point of such sanctions is to deny weapons to states that are conducting aggression (or
are threatening to) or are carrying out a brutal civil conflict that could be characterized by war crimes. In other circumstances, blockading weapons bound for a legitimate government would itself be considered an act of war. The legality of interdiction
is bound to treaty enforcement or to UN action. Prior to the founding of the United
Nations, interdiction of trafficking in military hardware also relied on international
cooperation (primarily by the major powers), although such efforts—such as the
League of Nations sanctions during the Spanish Civil War—seemed at best partially
effective.[15] Effectiveness, even today, is largely determined by the overwhelming
strength of the force conducting the interdiction—which today means that the U.S.
Navy or the collective naval forces of the North Atlantic Treaty Organization (NATO)
are the prime enforcers of international sanctions. The U.S. and NATO navies use the
term *maritime interception operations* (MIOs) to describe these activities.

Under UN sanctions or international treaty enforcement, any state may seize
weapons (or other contraband) bound for a sanctioned state or materials whose
transfer violates international treaty—such as the transfer of nuclear weapons material in contradiction to the nonproliferation or weapons control regimes. The
seized shipment is subject to confiscation or destruction and the transport vessel
subject to disposition (such as forfeiture or fine) at an assigned admiralty court. In
the case of Iraqi sanctions, the U.S. and allied/coalition navies maintain a tight
blockade of contraband trafficking both in and out of Iraq (including oil and dates,
as well as weapons). All vessels transiting the northern Persian Gulf are subject to
search. Those carrying contraband to or from Iraq are seized and turned over to admiralty courts in the United Arab Emirates (although critics have charged that these
courts have been arbitrary and have functioned merely as a "tax" on smugglers).

However, smugglers have used Iranian territorial waters to avoid the blockade. The United States routinely deploys two to five warships as a Mid-East force to conduct sanctions enforcement, bolstered by additional capabilities from forward-deployed carrier battlegroups operating in the region. Traditionally, destroyers and frigates have carried out the interdiction operations; however, since 1997, amphibious warships have also been assigned to the task. Additionally, marines and Navy sea/air/land (SEAL) troops deployed on the amphibious warships have been specifically trained for conducting takedowns of vessels that refuse to stop to be boarded and searched.

The role of naval forces in counterweapons smuggling also falls under the three general categories of detection, interdiction, and deterrence/channeling. Sources suggest there is considerable public support for the use of force in preventing the smuggling of nuclear materials and other potential weapons of mass destruction; this should be considered the highest priority in the prevention of weapons smuggling and leads to a fourth naval role: direct action. Direct action (the direct use of force) is also appropriate for the prevention of weapons shipments by terrorists.

Smuggling and Trafficking of Humans. The suppression of smuggling was the founding mission of the U.S. Revenue Marine, the forerunner of the U.S. Coast Guard. Historically, naval forces have supported this mission wherever possible, even when it was not viewed as a primary task. Smuggling has been considered a law enforcement issue, with naval and other military forces supporting civil authorities when requested. Naval forces encountering potential smuggling would take appropriate action as the circumstances require; most frequently this means promptly alerting civilian law enforcement agencies or the Coast Guard.

Interdicting the trafficking of humans, however, actually is a traditional mission of the U.S. Navy. In the 1820s, Congress made international slave trading by American flag vessels an act of piracy and thereby punishable by death (this act was later repealed).[16] U.S. naval warships were expected to enforce this prohibition, although the general agreement of that time was that naval personnel would only board and inspect vessels of their own flag, which effectively allowed for slave trade smuggling by foreign ships.[17] In 1843, an Africa squadron was established specifically to suppress the slave trade by U.S. flagged vessels; it was joined in this effort by warships assigned to station off Brazil.[18]

Since the abolition of slavery in the United States, interdiction of human trafficking has become a secondary concern to naval forces and has rarely in itself been an assigned mission. Interdiction of trafficking on the high seas has been the result of inspections and boarding directed at other contraband (that is, drugs) or as the result of the UN sanctions enforcement regime. However, it is a continually significant mission for the U.S. Coast Guard in its law enforcement role in protection of U.S. maritime borders. Volume of traffic has focused Coast Guard attention on boat people from

Haiti and Cuba and on smuggling in vessels from Asia. Since smuggling and human trafficking are still considered law enforcement issues, the role of naval forces today involves detection, interdiction, and deterrence/channeling.

Piracy. Suppression of piracy is a more obvious naval tradition, but one (like the suppression of the slave trade) associated with an era long past. Until relatively recently, the press had little interest in the routine piratical attacks being carried out at poorly policed locations such as the Malacca Straits. Recent attention has focused on the apparent increase in ferocity of such attacks and the use of automatic and heavier weapons by pirates. Since piracy is considered by international law to be an attack on the global community, all naval forces are empowered to take action wherever piracy is encountered.

However, current debate revolves around the issue of whether U.S. and allied naval forces or the U.S. Coast Guard should be specifically assigned to patrol for and protect merchant traffic against attack in remote waters rather than simply carrying out such functions (and providing a deterrent) when available or as part of other forward-deployed missions.[19] Patrolling against piracy is essentially a police function and is heavily resource-dependent in order to provide complete security. Like the number of cops on the beat in a city, the number of vessels and aircraft assigned has a direct effect in the suppression of nautical crime. The U.S. Navy has been reluctant to take the lead in counterpiracy, since that mission is seen as siphoning resources away from the primary missions of deterring war and conducting combat operations.[20] Police and private protection measures are perceived as being more cost-effective. Whether public concerns will increase the perceived importance of the counterpiracy mission and what effect that would have on the size, structure, and deployment patterns of the U.S. fleet remains to be seen.

Although there are suggested linkages between piracy and global terrorist activities, international law defines piracy as being very distinct from terrorism—which complicates the legal aspect of linking counterpiracy to the overall counterterrorism effort.[21]

Acts of Terrorism

Naval and other military roles in the war on terrorism will be discussed in detail in chapter 5. However, suppression of biological, chemical, and nuclear proliferation and cyberthreats are two aspects of counterterrorism that could benefit directly from naval interdiction efforts.

Biological, Chemical, and Nuclear Proliferation. Military roles in defending America against weapons of mass destruction are obvious. The Bush administration emphasis on developing a national missile defense (NMD) and theater ballistic missile defense (TBMD) is a primary indication of the seriousness with which this threat is perceived (see chapter 24). However, the extent of the military role in counterproliferation *prior* to the conduct of or potential for an actual attack is fiercely debated. Key defense officials during the Clinton administration suggested that military preemption might be an acceptable response to WMD proliferation—particularly by a rogue state or criminal enterprise to a terrorist group. Indeed, the attack using naval launched cruise missiles against a suspected Sudanese chemical/biological weapons plant in 1998 was just such a use of naval forces. The term *counterproliferation* has been defined as actions involving military forces, as opposed to *nonproliferation*, which relies on diplomatic means.

Cyberthreats. Defense against cyberthreats is considered a joint military and interagency activity. Of the military services, the U.S. Air Force has concentrated the most resources toward the effort, with the former U.S. Space Command (now combined into U.S. Strategic Command) taking the lead in computer network defense (CND) operations. More controversial efforts involve the development of computer network attack (CNA) capabilities. Naval forces have considerable information technology expertise and can play a substantial role in these joint activities. Some have suggested that the "fluid nature" of the infosphere is such that naval forces should devote the resources necessary to take a leading role in CND/CNA.[22] Public perception of the threat will also play a factor in the overall military resources devoted to all aspects of infrastructure protection.

Nascent Environmental/Social Threats

By definition, *nascent threats* are those toward which military responses have not been directed or against which force is not the most effective response. However, naval forces have historically played a secondary role in responding, generally through the capabilities of specialized services.

Infectious Diseases. Historically, the military role in defending against infectious diseases has been through research. Prompted by the exposure of troops in Latin America during the early 20th century, noted U.S. Army doctor Major Walter Reed discovered the source of yellow fever. Navy doctors have made similar—though perhaps not as famous—medical discoveries. With organized and rigorous hygiene standards and inoculation programs, military and naval forces have had considerable success in protecting deployed service members from infectious diseases, which ultimately protects the overall U.S population from being infected by returning service members.

Military efforts to develop vaccines and protective regimens against biological weapons have become well known and, in some cases, controversial. No one doubts the seriousness of the military-led effort in developing protection of both service members and the American public against biological weapons. The results of this effort would logically improve protection against non-weaponized infectious diseases as well.

As a part of ongoing operations, naval and other military medical units routinely provide inoculations and assistance in lesser developed countries to the population encountered by U.S. forces. Naval units such as the hospital ship USNS *Comfort* have conducted extensive assistance programs in conflict areas such as Haiti.

Yet all of these efforts are byproducts of other military missions and are dwarfed by nonmilitary governmental and civilian efforts to provide protection against infectious diseases. Ultimately, the primary naval role is to support this effort, lead (along with other joint forces) the research and development of defenses against weaponized diseases, and provide support for security and personnel control to National Guard forces in event of a pandemic. It is hard to conceive of the potential for direct application of military force against this threat, with the exception of the elimination of chemical and biological weapons and laboratories or in responding to a deliberate biological attack.

Environmental Threats (including resource depletion). Many environmental activists would consider naval operations themselves to be environmental threats. Ships are either nuclear powered or fossil fuel-driven, and as with any human interaction with nature, there is always the chance of environmental accidents. Nongovernmental organization (NGOs)—most notably Greenpeace—protested the participation of naval units in Operation *Desert Storm* under the "logic" that any war (or in this case, response to war) represents an environmental disaster. This sentiment was drowned out by Saddam Hussein's deliberate strategy of environmental damage (oil well fires and oil pipeline spillage into the Persian Gulf), and it has became quite evident to even the greenest of activists that a lack of response to armed aggression leads to far worse disasters for the human environment. The terrorist attacks on the World Trade Towers and the Pentagon underscored this realization. However, disputes over the effect of low frequency sonar on marine mammals and the potential for open-ocean whale strikes by transiting warships still characterize the collision between security and environmental interests—which, in turn, has effects on the scope of permissible naval training in peacetime. Obviously, the first role of naval forces in the face of environmental threats must be good stewardship of resources and routine prevention of any deliberate or accidental environmental damage while conducting operations. The prime combat role would be the use of force against regimes that would use ecological damage as a weapon in wartime.

As a byproduct of its peacetime operations, naval forces have provided routine research support for scientists involved in studying ecological damage, particularly in the Arctic and Antarctic or other areas difficult for civilian infrastructure to reach.[23] U.S. Navy oceanographers—a specialized community in the Naval Service—have themselves conducted considerable oceanographic and meteorological research involving environmental issues, and Department of the Navy civilian scientists supported by Arctic submarine operations have taken the lead on environmental research in the Arctic seas.[24] (See the extensive discussion in chapter 9.) Such research can perform an early warning function concerning growing ecological threats in the environments in which naval forces operate.

Resource scarcity—particularly access to water rights—as a source of conflict among lesser developed countries is a potential aspect of globalization effect 4 (military and naval/maritime intervention in locations not previously considered of vital interest), which could necessitate the use of naval forces for peace enforcement/peacekeeping functions (or even direct actions).

Mass Human Migration. Primary response to mass human migration at sea belongs by law to the U.S. Coast Guard, and, as noted, the Coast Guard expended considerable resources in handling the periodic waves of boat people from Cuba and Haiti.[25] U.S. naval vessels and aircraft have supported this mission when available. Along with other members of U.S. joint forces, sailors and marines have been used in support of humanitarian and peacekeeping missions in areas of mass human migrations, such as Rwanda. The Marine Corps has had considerable experience in protecting the personnel of humanitarian NGOs in dealing with such crises; infrastructure is often provided by U.S. Naval Construction Battalions and medical assistance by the U.S. Naval Medical, Dental, Nurse, and Medical Service Corps. Navy chaplains have often assisted in counseling, morale, and religious support to refugees and those involved in humanitarian aid. It is difficult, however, to envision a primary (as opposed to support) role for naval forces in countering mass human migrations.

Force Structure Requirements

Questions regarding the extent to which naval forces should be utilized to counter transnational threats inevitably involve force structure decisions. This is mainly because countering transnational threats—piracy, for example—is numbers-intensive in terms of platforms and personnel. To patrol all areas potentially threatened by piracy, ships and aircraft must be diverted from other deployment areas or missions, or there needs to be a substantial (some would say unaffordable) increase in the U.S. fleet. This is true for the U.S. Coast Guard as well, whose prime focus has become homeland security, not the interdiction of transnational threats at their source.

It has been stated that transnational threats require multinational responses, which might imply that greater interoperability with foreign naval forces might eliminate the need for a larger number of U.S. ships and aircraft. Foreign navies—notably British, Dutch, and French ships—have indeed taken greater roles in Caribbean counterdrug operations, allowing U.S. assets to focus on counterterrorism missions. At the same time, other allied navies (including naval forces from Germany and Japan) have helped in counterterrorism patrols in the Indian Ocean.[26] However, world naval strength has been shrinking precipitously since the end of the Cold War, and most navies would require considerable budget increases to achieve truly effective interoperability with U.S. naval forces. Dealing with transnational threats in a manner that is significantly different from today's use of multipurpose forward naval presence (in which responses to transnational threats are but one among numerous missions, and generally not the priority) inevitably requires an increase in naval force structure. The promise of greater network-centricity of platforms might mitigate this somewhat—but would not necessarily affect the deterrence of transnational threats, which appears to require a *cop on the beat* approach.

A force structure increase to deal specifically with transnational threats might *not* be completely unaffordable, however. This is because dealing with such threats may not require as sophisticated, well armed, or large units as would high-technology warfighting. Aircraft carriers, AEGIS cruisers and destroyers, and nuclear attack submarines would be most effective in almost every conceivable detection, interdiction, and deterrence/channeling role, but much smaller, less costly units could perform these missions adequately. Countering transnational threats would seem a likely mission for the proposed littoral combat ship or the Coast Guard's *Deepwater* project platform.[27] However, this raises the question of creating a two-tiered Navy in which a substantial portion of the fleets would be perceived as unsuited for high-end warfighting, particularly in an antiaccess environment (see discussion in chapter 25). This is a force structure solution toward which the U.S. Navy leadership has been opposed since the early 1990s.[28]

Another implication of an increase in maritime transnational threats is the need for an increase in maritime patrol aircraft. With the end of the Cold War and near-collapse of the Russian submarine force, U.S. Navy maritime patrol squadrons (flying the P–3 *Orion*) took perhaps the greatest force structure cut of any naval community. Choosing a replacement aircraft for the venerable P–3 has been a much lower priority for naval aviation than acquiring the F/A–18E/F carrier-based strike aircraft (see discussion in chapter 18). However, maritime patrol aircraft, which have great range and much greater speed than surface ships, would appear to be among the most useful assets in tactical detection and surveillance of transnational threats. Focusing on transnational threats may require a reprioritization in naval aviation force structure in order to make more maritime patrol assets available.

But, at least initially, force structure changes may not be as important as systems acquisition. If, in fact, the primary naval roles in countering transnational threats fall under the categories of detection, interdiction, and deterrence/channeling, as well as interagency support, the top acquisition priority would be the development of an interagency-capable tactical data information system that could produce a common operational picture for all agencies and units involved.

Development of a common operational picture has been mastered to some extent in counterdrug operations on the JIATF level. However, the ability to transfer data between and beyond naval forces has barely scratched the surface of the current information revolution. In order to harness this revolution, the Department of the Navy has focused on acquisition of the cooperative engagement capability (CEC) system under development by The Johns Hopkins Advanced Physics Laboratory and Raytheon Corporation. CEC promises to be a great improvement in the effective integration of tactical data among naval units—although some critics claim that competing systems such as the tactical component network are even more promising.[29] The British Royal Navy has committed to support the development of CEC and utilize it as their data network—a milestone for allied interoperability. U.S. Air Force sources have also suggested that CEC may be a system of significance for their operations.[30] However, there has thus far been no agreement on the integrated development of a joint forces common operating picture, a limitation that has perhaps the greatest impact to practical interagency responses to the emerging transnational threats. A logical first step in defeating transnational threats remains the development of a real-time, interagency-accessible common operational picture.

Conclusions

Because transnational threats are both symptoms and causes of a number of underlying problems, a better understanding of them as they pertain to national security is of utmost importance. One of the main strategic challenges facing the United States will be to preempt these threats rather than react to them incrementally. As the literature on crisis decisionmaking amply demonstrates, under conditions of adverse circumstances or crisis, public policy tends to be made disjointedly and badly. Important and often irreversible decisions are made during crises that can be portentous to the future of a country. Hence, in order to avoid this contingency, the U.S. Government faces an incentive to make a concerted effort to proactively address transnational threats.

Suitable coordination and adequate resources will be key in this effort—hence the need for a common operational picture. Coping with these threats in the regions in which nonstate criminal actors base their operations will be important, but as these threats are a global phenomenon, transit and target states must be included in the planning and implementation phases. Integrated multilateral cooperation for finding global solutions to global problems will be crucial. In the United States, interagency cooperation will continue to be valuable with increased sharing of information and areas of responsibility. The Department of Defense may gain a more important role, perhaps to the point of pursuing new missions and purposes that lie outside its traditional domain or taking a greater lead in interagency responses (including leading the development of a common interagency operational picture).

Naval forces are particularly critical in protection against transnational threats during the actual transit of dangerous goods, much of which is conducted by sea. Trafficking in drugs, weapons, and illegal migrants all have major sea components, and MIOs founded on effective intelligence information remain a front line of protection.[31] Terrorists have also used the sea for transit in persons and weapons—currently coalition naval forces are conducting intercept operations in the North Arabian Sea and Indian Ocean to prevent the flight of al Qaeda fighters from Pakistan. Piracy is primarily a seagoing threat, with navies and coast guards as the prime suppressant. Since many transnational threats can approach the United States only by or over the sea, naval forces would also be feeding tactical information throughout interagency information networks, including proposed port security information systems. Naval forces—operating under the freedom of the seas—may be the most unobtrusive means of detecting and surveilling transnational threats beyond what is available to our satellites. Likewise, they may be the most effective first responders in situations where preemption or retribution is warranted.

Arguably, the U.S. Navy and U.S. Marine Corps were created in 1794 for the specific purpose of countering what were then transnational threats (such as Barbary piracy). The future world of globalization may find the naval services returning to their operational roots.[32]

Notes

[1] "Money Laundering and Financial Crimes," in *International Narcotics Control Strategy Report* (Washington, DC: Bureau for International Narcotics and Law Enforcement Affairs, March 1999), 1.

[2] For recent trends, see United Nations Office for Drug Control and Crime Prevention, *Global Illicit Drug Trends 2000* (Vienna: United Nations International Drug Control Programme, 2000).

[3] *International Crime Control Strategy* (Washington, DC: The White House, May 1998), 21.

[4] *International Crime Threat Assessment* (Washington, DC: U.S. Government Interagency Working Group, 2000), 32.

[5] See, for example, U.S. National Intelligence Council, *Growing Global Migration and its Implications for the United States* (Washington, DC: National Intelligence Council, March 2001).

[6] International Chamber of Commerce, Crime Services, *Weekly Piracy Report*, May 22–28, 2001, 1.

[7] *International Crime Threat Assessment*, 32.

[8] In Senate testimony, Secretary of Defense Donald H. Rumsfeld stated that terrorists will "inevitably" obtain weapons of mass destruction. See Bill Miller and Christine Haughney, "Nation Left Jittery By Latest Series of Terror Warnings," *The Washington Post*, May 22, 2002, A1.

[9] See Gro Harlem Brundtland, "Global Health Challenges and the Question of Sovereignty," paper presented at the Academic Council on the United Nations System, June 16–18, 2000.

[10] Richard E. Benedick, "Human Population and Environmental Stresses in the Twenty-first Century," *Environmental Change & Security Project Report No. 6* (Summer 2000), 11.

[11] Recent interpretations on U.S. *posse comitatus* laws suggest that they were originally intended to restrict the actions of the Federal army, and that—in consonance with the fact that the Constitution directs that Congress raise armies when necessary but to maintain a navy—such laws do not have an actual legal effect on the U.S. Navy and

Marine Corps. Steven J. Tomisek argues that " The specific provisions of the Posse Comitatus Act (U.S. Code, Title 18, Section 1385) are applied to the Navy and Marine Corps as a matter of DOD policy," not as a matter of law. See Tomisek, *Homeland Security: The New Role for Defense*, Strategic Forum 189 (Washington, DC: National Defense University Press, February 2002), note 4.

[12] Tim Johnson, "Drug-Policing Efforts May Suffer," *Miami Herald*, October 18, 2001; "Coast Guard Sharpens Mission: After Sept. 11, Drug Interception is Virtually Eliminated as National Security Becomes Concern," *Baltimore Sun*, October 17, 2001. On earlier concerns following the Peruvian shoot-down of the missionaries' plane, see Anthony Boadle, "Senators Worry Pentagon May Retreat in Drug War," Reuters, May 15, 2001, accessed at <http://www.dailynews.yahoo.com/h/nm/20010515/pl/drugs_usa_pentagon_dc_1.htm>.

[13] See details in "Arms Seizure Backfires, Wounds Israel," January 8, 2002, accessed at <http://www.stratfor.com/MEAF/commentary/0201082120.htm>.

[14] Currently the best published study on the law and practice of maritime interception under UN resolutions is Lois E. Fielding, *Maritime Interception and U.N. Sanctions* (Bethesda, MD: Austin and Winfield, Publishers, 1997).

[15] For an excellent recent summary, see Adam B. Siegel, "International Naval Cooperation during the Spanish Civil War," *Joint Force Quarterly* (Autumn/Winter 2001–2002), 82–90.

[16] Kenneth J. Hagan, *This People's Navy: The Making of American Sea Power* (New York: The Free Press, 1991), 154.

[17] John B. Hattendorf, "The Nineteenth Century Forward Stations," unpublished paper prepared for the U.S. Navy Forward Presence Bicentennial Symposium, Center for Naval Analyses, Alexandria, VA, June 21, 2001, 17.

[18] Assessment of the effectiveness of this effort is mixed. The best short summary is chapter 4 of Peter Duignan and L.H. Gann, *The United States and Africa: A History* (New York: Cambridge University Press, 1984), 32–40, which is a generally positive assessment. A more negative assessment is found in W.E.B. DuBois, *The Suppression of the African Slave-Trade to the United States 1638–1870* (Boston: Harvard University Press, 1896, reprinted Williamstown, MA: Corner House Publishers, 1970), 160–193.

[19] On U.S. Coast Guard role, see Dean Visser, "U.S. Helping Asia Combat Sea Piracy," Associated Press, July 5, 2001, accessed at <http://wire.ap.org/public_pages/WirePortal.pcgi/ us_portal.html>.

[20] However, since September 11, at least 2 U.S. Navy warships—diverted from Persian Gulf deployments—have been assigned to escort vessels through the Straits of Malacca. See William H. McNeil, "Navy on Lookout For Pirates in Indonesia," *Navy Times*, January 24, 2002, 10.

[21] See discussion of this distinction in chapter 8 of this book and in *Maritime Terrorism and International Law*, ed. Natalino Ronzitti (Boston: Martinus Nijhoff/Kluwer Academic Publishers, 1990).

[22] See Sam J. Tangredi, "Space is an Ocean," U.S. Naval Institute *Proceedings* 125, no. 1 (January 1999), 52–53; and Tangredi, "Beyond the Sea and Jointness," U.S. Naval Institute *Proceedings* 127, no. 9 (September 2001), 60–63.

[23] Though in recent years much of this support—particularly in the Antarctic—has been contracted to civilian firms as cost-saving measures.

[24] The leading personality in the field of arctic undersea research was long-serving Department of Navy scientist Dr. Waldo K. Lyon, who ran the world's only arctic submarine laboratory. See Richard Boyle, "Waldo Lyon: A Legacy of Dedication," *Submarine Review*, July 1998, 115–117; and CAPT George B. Newton, USN (Ret.), Chairman, U.S. Arctic Research Commission, "Don't Forget the Arctic," *Submarine Review*, April 2001, 91–100.

[25] A primary issue in this effort is whether the migrants are refugees from oppressive governments and therefore deserving of asylum and refugee status, or whether they are simply seeking greater economic opportunity through illegal migration.

[26] Marc Lacey, "Hunting For Elusive Terrorists Off Somalia's Coast," *The New York Times*, April 2, 2002, A13. In fact, the U.S. Government requested in late April 2002 that the German Navy assume command of the coalition task force operating off the Horn of Africa. See Michael Nitz, "Germany to take command of task force," *Jane's Defence Weekly*, May 22, 2002.

[27] Implied in Tom Canahute, "U.S. Coast Guard Tweaks Requirements For Deepwater Program," *Defense News*, December 17, 2001. See discussion of interdiction platform requirements in chapter 20.

[28] Note also the concern of Coast Guard officers as reflected in Michael R. Kelley, "The Shoal Water of Homeland Defense," U.S. Naval Institute *Proceedings* 128, no. 5 (May 2002), 65–70.

[29] See Greg Schneider, "Scuttled By the Process: Navy Likes Md. Firm's Ideas for Battle System—but Won't Use Them," *The Washington Post*, August 29, 2001, E1; Terry C. Pierce, "Sunk Costs Sinks Innovation," U.S. Naval Institute *Proceedings* 128, no. 5 (May 2002), 32–35.

[30] "U.S. Air Force to Test Navy's CEC," *Jane's Defence Weekly*, August 1, 2001, 6.

[31] Lois Fielding notes: "The maritime interception itself is one of the best examples of the creative ideas fashioned by the forces of the immediate post-Cold War period. It is flexible, limited, controlled, and humanitarian. The maritime interception is an assertion of the rule of law in an age of law." Fielding, 338.

[32] According to Lt. Cmdr. Pamela Warnken, a U.S. Navy spokesman in Singapore, "Fighting piracy is nothing new to the U.S. Navy, which was formed in the 19th century to battle marauders who pillaged merchant ships off North Africa's notorious Barbary Coast. Here it is 200 years later and we're in the same situation in the Straits of Malacca." From Visser, "U.S. Helping Asia Combat Sea Piracy," Associated Press, July 5, 2001.

Chapter 5

Global Terrorism, Strategy, and Naval Forces

Randall G. Bowdish

We're at war. There has been an act of war declared upon America by terrorists, and we will respond accordingly.

—George W. Bush, September 15, 2001

Globalization has enabled tremendous prosperity for America. However, a backlash against globalization is growing, not only within the United States but around the world as well. While globalization has enabled expanded economic opportunities, it has also had disruptive societal effects. Whether real or imagined, many believe that it threatens industries, jobs, living standards, and imposes unwanted societal values upon them. The United States is viewed as the champion of globalization, making it a target for groups intent on ending globalization through both peaceful and violent means.[1]

In the age of globalization, the U.S. Navy is the global navy. Operating at the frontiers of freedom, it not only defends American interests abroad but also maintains the world's sealanes for global trade. Naval forward presence both places our naval forces at risk of global terrorism and, at the same time, positions them well to lead the fight against it.

Naval forces are not strangers to global terrorists. The bombing of the Marine barracks in Beirut, Lebanon, on October 23, 1983, in which 241 marines were lost; the hijacking of TWA Flight 847 on June 14, 1985, during which Petty Officer Robert Stetham, a Navy Construction Battalion sailor, was murdered; and most recently, the

Commander Randall G. Bowdish, USN, is a faculty member of the USMC Command and Staff College. A surface warfare officer, he most recently commanded the USS *Simpson*. Previously he served as strategic planner on the Joint Staff, and in the Strategy and Concepts Branch of the U.S. Navy staff, where he was responsible for drafting a long-range naval vision. He dedicates this chapter to the World Trade Center and Pentagon victims, particularly Captain Gerald DeConto, USN, former commanding officer of the USS *Simpson*, killed in the September 11 terrorist attack on the Pentagon.

bombing of the USS *Cole* on October 12, 2000, in which 17 shipmates were killed, were tragic acts of terrorism conducted against forward-deployed naval forces tasked with maintaining peace and stability in a troubled world. On the other hand, the August 20, 1998, Navy Tomahawk strikes against a terrorist training camp in Afghanistan and a chemical weapons facility in Sudan in retaliation for the U.S. Embassy bombings in Kenya and Tanzania indicate one way naval forces can be employed in countering global terrorism.

The terrorist attack on the World Trade Center and Pentagon on September 11 marked the beginning of a new era in the fight against global terrorism. President Bush declared war against terrorism, dictating a strategic shift from a diplomatic/police action to war.[2] It will be a difficult war against an elusive enemy. It is a war that must draw from the full complement of American power—to include diplomatic, economic, military, and nontraditional means—coupled with respective elements of coalition power. It requires out-of-the-box thinking and innovative solutions to difficult problems. With all of that, to be effective, it must be based upon sound strategy. As the Nation crafts and refines its new strategy in the war against terrorism, the Navy, too, must develop a maritime component of that strategy. Maritime strategy must dovetail into and support national and joint military strategy, while also dictating unique naval capabilities to be brought to bear against the enemy. The precursor to the development of strategy is understanding the threat.

The Threat

Know the enemy and know yourself; in a hundred battles you will never be in peril.

—Sun Tzu, *The Art of War*

Global Terrorism

Terrorism has been around since the dawn of warfare. It is defined as "the calculated use of unlawful violence or threat of unlawful violence to inculcate fear; intended to coerce or to intimidate governments or societies in the pursuit of goals that are generally political, religious, or ideological."[3] It is a tactic of psychology and violence, used by the weak against the strong, to achieve disproportionate ends via otherwise modest means of violence, through the leverage of fear.

Although terrorism has been around for ages, global terrorism is a relatively modern phenomenon. Transnational and multiethnic, it is international in scope, with terrorists representing all walks of life, poor to rich, third world to first world, illiterate to educated. Ironically, the same mechanisms that have fueled globalization have also enabled terrorism on a global scale. Global financial transactions underwrite terrorist acts around the world. Cross-continent, networked communications, whether

Table 5–1. **Components of Global Terrorism**

Component	Characterized by	Directed against
Physical act	Violent destruction and casualties	Symbols and constituents of enemy (tens to thousands)
Psychological impact	Media reach, strength of rhetoric and images to influence behavior	Center of gravity (millions to billions)

Internet, conventional or cellular phone, interconnect transnational terrorists in near-real and real time. Most importantly, a global media spread their message of terror instantaneously around the world on an unprecedented scale—a scale that grows larger each year. Paradoxically, global terrorists employ the very *means* of globalization to destroy the *process* of globalization.

As shown in table 5–1, global terrorism comprises two components, the physical act and the psychological impact. The physical act consists of destructive acts of violence directed against the people and symbols of the enemy. But the physical act of violence is an intermediary act against the real target, the *center of gravity*. As defined by Carl von Clausewitz, the center of gravity is "the hub of all power and movement, on which everything depends . . . the point at which all our energies should be directed." Whether by design or happenstance, global terrorists adhere to this most fundamental tenet of warfare, deriving results far greater than their numbers and capabilities warrant. They understand how to propagate their message through the global media to deliver maximum psychological impact against the enemy center of gravity.

Terrorists

The Department of State currently designates 28 groups as foreign terrorist organizations (FTOs).[4] To be designated as an FTO, an organization must be foreign, it must engage in terrorist activity as defined in Section 212 (a)(3)(B) of the Immigration and Nationality Act, and its activities must threaten the security of U.S. nationals or the national security (national defense, foreign relations, or the economic interests) of the United States. There are two special classes of FTOs: state-sponsored and loosely affiliated extremists. The distinctions are important because the ways for countering each (discussed later) are very different.

State-sponsored FTOs are backed by a state in pursuit of its national objectives, such as influencing policy of targeted nations or organizations. Seven nations currently are designated as state sponsors of terrorism: Cuba, Iran, Iraq, Libya, North Korea, Sudan, and Syria. The same seven states have remained on the list since 1993.

Although Afghanistan has not been designated a state sponsor of terrorism, it nonetheless remains a hotbed for terrorists. Sanctions were imposed against the Taliban on November 15, 1999, by Security Council Resolution 1267 calling for the Taliban to turn over Osama bin Laden. With the exception of Afghanistan, all of these nations border the sea.

Perhaps as a result of diplomatic success in reducing state-sponsored terrorism, a particularly virulent class of global terrorism known as loosely affiliated extremism is on the rise. Known for their operation outside of state sponsorship, uncompromising, radical objectives, and focus on producing maximum destruction and casualties, loosely affiliated extremist terrorists operate from small, often transnational/multiethnic cells, to conduct spectacular acts of terrorism.

The Department of State tracks FTOs, discerning their background, aims, composition, activities, location, area of operation, and sources of external aid—all useful information in the development of strategies against terrorism. An example of this information is shown in table 5–2 for al Qaeda.[5] From this information and other sources, defense analysts can determine the terrorists' strategy, enabling them to devise a strategy to combat terrorism.

Strategy

Determine the enemy's plans and you will know which strategy will be successful and which will not.
—Sun Tzu, *The Art of War*

The words of Sun Tzu, written over 2,000 years ago, are as germane today as they were in his era. It is first necessary to discern the strategies of global terrorists prior to developing U.S. strategy. This is important for two reasons: to deny them their objectives and to ensure U.S. strategy does not unwittingly contribute to theirs.

Simple in concept yet difficult in construction, it is strategy that links *ends* with *means*. Through strategy, limited resources are employed to obtain the objective. Although there are commonalties between FTO objectives, they are different enough that a reconstruction of each FTO strategy will be required to develop countering strategies.

Terrorist Strategy

Table 5–3 illustrates how analysis can be used to determine the al Qaeda strategy. Its stated ends are well known through publication via mass media. Although taking an enemy's stated objectives on face value opens one to the risk of deception, in the case of al Qaeda, its terrorist acts are in consonance with its stated ends. The means available to al Qaeda appear rather limited on the surface, when considering the group's small numbers and limited capabilities. However, global access through the

Table 5–2. **al Qaeda**

Aliases	al Qaeda, "the Base," the Islamic Army, the World Islamic Front for Jihad against Jews and Crusaders, the Islamic Army for the Liberation of the Holy Places, the Osama bin Laden Network, the Osama bin Laden Organization, Islamic Salvation Foundation, the Group for the Preservation of the Holy Sites
Description	Established by Osama bin Laden about 1990 to bring together Arabs who fought in Afghanistan against the Soviet invasion. Helped finance, recruit, transport, and train Sunni Islamic extremists for the Afghan resistance. Current goal is to "reestablish the Muslim State" throughout the world. Works with allied Islamic extremist groups to overthrow regimes it deems "non-Islamic" and remove Westerners from Muslim countries. Issued statement under banner of "The World Islamic Front for Jihad against Jews and Crusaders" in February 1998, saying it was the duty of all Muslims to kill U.S. citizens, civilian or military, and their allies everywhere.
Activities	Conducted the bombings of the U.S. Embassies in Nairobi, Kenya, and Dar Es Salaam, Tanzania, on August 7, 1998, which killed at least 301 persons and injured more than 5,000 others. Claims to have shot down U.S. helicopters and killed U.S. servicemen in Somalia in 1993 and to have conducted 3 bombings targeted against the U.S. troop presence in Aden, Yemen, in December 1992. Linked to plans for attempted terrorist operations, including the assassination of Pope John Paul II during his visit to Manila in late 1994; simultaneous bombings of the U.S. and Israeli embassies in Manila and other Asian capitals in late 1994; the midair bombing of a dozen U.S. trans-Pacific flights in 1995; and a plan to kill President William Clinton during a visit to the Philippines in early 1995. Conducted airline hijack/suicide crashes into the World Trade Center and the Pentagon on September 11, 2001, which killed over 2,000 persons. Continues to train, finance, and provide logistic support to terrorist groups that support these goals.
Strength	May have from several hundred to several thousand members. Also serves as the core of a loose umbrella organization that includes many Sunni Islamic extremist groups, including factions of the Egyptian Islamic Jihad, Gama'at al-Islamiyya, and Harakat ul-Mujahidin.
Location/Area of Operation	The Embassy bombings in Nairobi and Dar es Salaam underscore al Qaeda's global reach. Bin Laden and his key lieutenants reside in Afghanistan, and the group maintains terrorist training camps there.
External Aid	Bin Laden, son of a billionaire Saudi family, is said to have inherited around $300 million that he uses to finance the group. Al Qaeda also maintains moneymaking businesses, collects donations from like-minded supporters, and illicitly siphons funds from donations to Muslim charitable organizations.

Table 5–3. **al Qaeda Strategy**

Ends	"Reestablish the Muslim State" throughout the world
	Overthrow regimes it deems "non-Islamic"
	Remove Westerners from Muslim countries
	Kill U.S. citizens, civilian or military, and their allies everywhere
	Jihad
Means	Innovative explosive devices and conventional weapons
	Several hundred to several thousand ideologically committed, well-financed and trained transnational terrorists working in nearly independent cells
	Global access through communications and the media
Strengths	Core group totally committed and willing to die for cause
	Capable of patient, methodical secret planning
	Have support within Arab regions
	Covert, largely able to move freely in Western world
	Decentralized command, insulated cells—complicates breaking the network
	Leverages the media to obtain large-scale psychological effects through small-scale acts of violence
Weaknesses	Inferior in numbers and capabilities, must fight asymmetrically
	Does not have easy access to weapons of mass destruction
	Operatives must act covertly to avoid detection
	Decentralized command, insulated cells—destroy nodes and fragment the organization
	Operatives require financial support—vulnerable to financial tracking
	Operatives require training support—vulnerable to compromise
al Qaeda Center of Gravity	al Qaeda leadership
Perceived U.S. Center of Gravity	Will of the people
	American people
	Arouse people to force Government to bring troops home
	Stir a movement among people for violent action against Muslim world
	Muslim people
	Arouse Muslim people to force own governments to oust U.S. presence; stir a movement among Muslim people for jihad
Strategy	Through catastrophic and spectacular terrorist acts against American civilian and military targets, provoke quid pro quo reprisals, resulting in escalation to war, followed by U.S. withdrawal from the region
Assumptions	Global media will be drawn to news of the catastrophe
	The United States will react violently
	Images of bloodied Muslims will stir Muslim people to violence
	Images of bloodied Americans will stir the American people to violence and escalation
Risks	The United States will obtain proof of sponsorship
	Terrorists will be caught prior to executing plans
	The United States will not react violently
	The global media will not transmit images of death and destruction
	The United States will not disengage from global presence
	The Muslim world will not support them
	The Muslim world will suffer catastrophic casualties and destruction

media adds an entirely new dimension to its means. Large-scale acts of terrorism have historically drawn the global media, providing global terrorists with much more powerful means than their limited resources otherwise allow.

Through evaluation of al Qaeda's stated ends, the center of gravity can be deduced. The people, both American and Muslim, are the targets—on the one hand, to stir sentiment for a war between the two ideologies and, secondly, to move their respective governments to eliminate American presence in Muslim countries. When viewed from the prism of stated ends and available means, the al Qaeda strategy logically links the two together.

A number of key assumptions, however, dictate the success or failure of the al Qaeda strategy. First and foremost, the group must accomplish a terrorist act that produces a large enough number of casualties and/or destruction to be "newsworthy." Second, the horrific images of death and destruction will drive Americans to react violently. Third, this violent action will, in turn, lead to large-scale, bloody images of Muslim injuries, death, and destruction. Fourth, a quid pro quo escalation of responses will result.

The al Qaeda strategy is fraught with risk. Successful terrorist acts may actually sow the seeds of the group's own demise. With each successful act of terrorism, the United States will devote more resources to countering al Qaeda, to include the capture or elimination of all its members. The United States may not react violently, denying the terrorists the media images of bloodied Muslims that they covet. Another option (albeit an unlikely one) is that rather than withdrawing from the Muslim world, the United States might be invited to provide more help to assist Muslim governments in eliminating the anarchist threat posed by terrorists. Worse, the Muslim people may reject the twisted ideology of radical Islamic extremists and withdraw their support for, and tolerance of, al Qaeda and other FTOs.

Similar strategic assessments should be made for all FTOs. An analysis of each respective strategy will yield individual countering strategies. Additionally, an analysis of all terrorist strategies will yield commonalties and patterns that will be important in the formulation of American grand strategy to root out terrorism altogether.

American Grand Strategy

Grand strategy is the highest form of strategy. It brings together all elements of a nation's power—diplomatic, economic, and military—to bear on the attainment of national objectives in a coherent, integrated fashion.

The principal goal in the war against global terrorism is to *eradicate terrorism*. While very simple to state, it will prove enormously difficult, if not altogether impossible, to achieve this end. In the process of eradicating terrorism, it will also be important to *deny terrorists their objectives*. But it will not be enough to just combat or limit

Figure 5–1. **Strategic Framework**

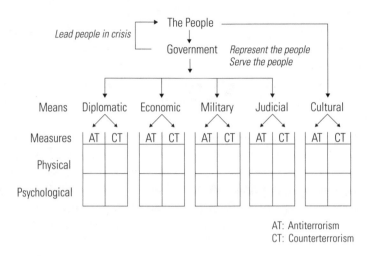

AT: Antiterrorism
CT: Counterterrorism

terrorism, for any and all acts of terrorism are unacceptable. Given that global terrorism strikes at the very heart of America, threatening its citizenry, critical infrastructure, and economic well being, it is in the vital interests of the United States to stamp it out completely.

Strategic Approach

Given that global terrorism is a different type of conflict, it also requires a different strategic approach. There are four principals to the strategic approach: that global terrorism must be fought on two fronts; that different sets of offensive and defensive measures are required on each front; that nontraditional means of power are required; and that support of the American people must be maintained. A diagram of the strategic framework, discussed below, is shown in figure 5–1.

Fundamental to the development of a grand strategy against global terrorism is an understanding that *it will be a two-front war.* A front is defined as "the most forward battle line." Globalization and the information age require us to think of fronts in a different way, beyond mere geographic boundaries, to include the battle lines fought through the media. As previously discussed, global terrorism has two components, the physical and the psychological. The physical front exists not only where physical acts of violence occur, but also where terrorists and their supporters reside, train, and otherwise operate. The psychological front exists at the interface between the terrorist message—propagated through mass media—and the minds and wills of the people. The psychological war is fought on the information battlefield, with terrorist rhetoric and images aimed at the psyche of the people and organizational leadership. It is war fought both directly, through carefully aimed messages from leaders launched across the media, and indirectly, by proxy, with reporters, pundits, and analysts adding their views while also carrying forward the terrorists' message. A grand strategy to eradicate global terrorism and deny terrorists their objectives must address both the physical and psychological fronts.

The strategic approach must also address *defensive and offensive measures* against terrorism. These measures, known respectively as antiterrorism and counterterrorism,[6] will be very different altogether along the two fronts. Collectively, they must work in consonance with one another, both physically and psychologically, across the entire spectrum of national means.

While traditional diplomatic, economic, and military means are still needed, *nontraditional means of national and international power will also be required to combat global terrorism.* Judicial measures have already been employed in both domestic law and law enforcement, but they must become better connected to allow for greater interagency cooperation. The same also needs to occur in international law and between international law enforcement agencies. Cultural means must be developed in order to defend the public on the psychological front.

The foundation for the strategic approach is the support of the American people. Democratic governments represent the people to serve the people. In times of crisis, democratic governments also lead the people. The power of the United States is based upon the strength of the American people—without their support, any action to eradicate terrorism is doomed to failure.

Table 5–4 depicts both the offensive and defensive, physical and psychological objectives that need to be distributed between governmental and nongovernmental entities to achieve the ends of eradicating terrorism and, in the interim, denying terrorists their objectives. Because of the push-pull relationship between the two fronts, where physical measures can impact psychological, and vice versa, it is important to deconflict measures that may have unintended consequences along the other front.

For example, special forces might be assigned to neutralize a terrorist cell. If these forces were to get into a firefight with the terrorists and video was obtained and later released that depicted Muslims killed by Americans, the results could be very damaging. A tactical victory on the physical front involving tens of people would result in an operational defeat on the psychological front as viewed by millions to billions! A small band of terrorists would be eliminated, contributing to the stated end, but the terrorist objective would gain mightily because of the antagonizing of the Muslim world, potentially providing terrorists with more recruits, more support, and more bad will toward the West.

Table 5–4. **Deconflicting Two Fronts: Dual Approaches to Eradicate Terrorism and Deny Terrorist Objectives**

	Antiterrorism	Counterterrorism
Physical	Reduce the vulnerability of individuals and infrastructure to terrorist acts Deny terrorists entry to the United States	Deny terrorists sanctuary Harsh penalties/imprisonment of supporters Conduct covert "snatch and drag" operations against terrorists that: ⌐
Psychological	Deny terrorists operational information Educate public, media, entertainers, and leadership about psychological warfare and enemy objectives on the psychological front—do not censor the media! Keep allies and coalition informed—present a united front	Eliminate/capture terrorists Prevent antagonizing news and images of local bloodshed Deter further acts and support for terrorism via publication of harsh punishment of those apprehended Counter terrorist misinformation, deception, and false prophecy with the truth Give guidance to, and sustain morale of, those fighting terrorism in media-denied area

The Psychological Front

While operations on the physical front are well understood, operations on the psychological front are fraught with not only the danger of unintended consequences, but also uncontrollability and severe backlash.

Terrorism in the 21st century will be forever linked to the images of the fall of the World Trade Towers, images the terrorists actively sought to achieve. These images are indelibly etched on the psyche of this generation. However, in the aftermath of the tragedy, a countering image—a picture of three firefighters raising the American flag at the site of the World Trade Center ruins—rallied American patriotism and resolution. The first image intended to induce terror in support of al Qaeda objectives; the second, a spontaneous picture of patriotic heroes in action, illustrates the complexity of image control on the psychological front. Images from the September 11 attack may have inadvertently sown the seeds of terrorist defeat by galvanizing governments and people of all faiths throughout the world against them, rather than contributing to any of their objectives.

Governments face a particularly daunting dilemma on the psychological front. Countering psychological manipulation, whether by terrorists or other enemies, is a vexing problem, particularly given the power and reach of television. Not only must government expose terrorist propaganda as it surfaces, it also must protect influential American leaders, broadcasters, and entertainers from succumbing to its spell, as well. For example, during the Vietnam War, actress Jane Fonda was manipulated by communist propaganda to the point that she openly assisted the communists. During her visit to North Vietnam, she mounted the gunner's seat of a communist Vietnamese antiaircraft gun. While she did not shoot down any American planes, the image was still damaging, buttressing the spirits of the North Vietnamese while hurting morale of American fighting men and women. Eighteen years later, in an interview with Barbara Walters, she would apologize for allowing herself to be duped as a propaganda vehicle:

> I would like to say something, not just to Vietnam veterans in New England, but to men who were in Vietnam, who I hurt, or whose pain I caused to deepen because of things that I said or did. I was trying to help end the killing and the war, but there were times when I was thoughtless and careless about it and I'm . . . very sorry that I hurt them. And I want to apologize to them and their families.

Attempts to censor the free press to control the psychological front have met with resistance since the Vietnam War. However, this resistance is not necessarily reflected in the attitude of the American public. According to journalist Howard Kurtz of *The Washington Post*:

> During the Vietnam War, journalists had free rein to accompany U.S. troops, and military leaders blamed that unfettered coverage for helping turn the country against the war. In the Persian Gulf War, the Pentagon slapped severe restrictions on the press, even censoring some dispatches, and made it all but impossible for journalists to accompany U.S. forces during the brief ground war. The public clearly sided with the first Bush administration. Nearly eight in 10 Americans in a 1991 Times Mirror poll supported the Pentagon's restrictions on journalists, and 60 percent said there should be more limits.[7]

Yet there is an understanding among some journalists that the media must tread carefully on the psychological front. In the same article about journalistic limits on information in the aftermath of the September 11 tragedy, Kurtz noted an e-mail to a *Washington Post* reporter that stated, "Criticism of the administration at this critical time is more than unpatriotic—to the extent it undermines our national confidence and political will to proceed, it gives comfort to the enemy."[8]

Americans are more tolerant of operational security and the need to withhold information that may put the lives of military members at risk. They still want to know the truth—something a just and righteous government should always endeavor to provide them. Yet one man's truth can appears as another man's propaganda. In the absence of any information from the government, the media will still fill the information void, airing and publishing the best guesses of pundits, journalists—even the enemy.

Deception, which can be used to mislead an adversary, will also chip away at the people's trust and confidence in their government. Acts of deception reduce government credibility. Nonetheless, Americans will tolerate deception on occasion, when the stakes are deemed worth it. General Norman Schwarzkopf's "left hook" maneuver during Operation *Desert Storm* was masked by the deception that coalition forces would conduct a frontal attack directly into the Iraqi defenses in Kuwait, engaging in a battle of attrition rather than maneuver. Americans did not question the deception, as the limited casualties were well worth it, and exact knowledge of the attack plan did not seem necessary for a public understanding of U.S. policy.

As the previous discussion indicates, the United States must tread carefully on the psychological front in the war against global terrorism. A particularly awkward problem in crafting a psychological strategy against global terrorism is how to address radical Islam. Perverted in its twisting of the Islamic faith, radical Islam provides global terrorists with both a powerful recruiting tool and a means to get otherwise rational men to willingly give up their lives for the cause. For example, found in the belongings of Mohamed Atta, one of the leaders of the September 11 acts of terrorism, was "a five-page handwritten document in Arabic that includes Islamic prayers, instructions for a last night of life," described by Bob Woodward of *The Washington Post* as "a cross between a chilling spiritual exhortation aimed at the hijackers and an operational mission checklist."[9]

In a country based upon freedom of religion, the U.S. Government is largely devoid of options to counter this weapon. While President Bush has been able to tap Islamic scholars for intellectual tools in speeches against radical Islam,[10] that is about the limit of democratic government bounds in the world of religion. For example, Italian Prime Minister Silvio Berlusconi made an apparently damaging assertion that Western civilization is superior to Islam and suggested that he hopes the West conquers Islamic civilization.[11] The backlash was immediate, when "Muslims around the world . . . demanded an apology from Prime Minister Silvio Berlusconi and the European Union recoiled with horror."[12]

Cultural leaders who do not have a government affiliation are best suited to handle the province of culture and religion. Words of wisdom have risen spontaneously from leaders in American culture. A heartening example was the September 21 telethon conducted by entertainment superstars that raised $150 million for victims.[13] Muhammad Ali, one of the world's most famous followers of Islam, stated in the show (seen by nearly 60 million viewers):

I've been a Muslim for 20 years, and I'm against killing, violence—and all Muslims are against it . . . Islam is peace, against killing, murder, and the terrorist. The people that do it in the name of Islam are wrong. And if I had a chance, I'd do something about it.[14]

In summary, the U.S. Government must take the moral high ground at the strategic level on the psychological front. It must take a strategic approach that maintains its credibility with truth when it can speak, silence when it cannot. Terrorist misinformation, lies, and propaganda must be publicly exposed. The public, media, entertainers, and other key cultural leaders should be educated about psychological warfare to prevent them from being unwittingly duped. A united international front must be built against global terrorism, with every overture of unity made public. Provocative criticism of Muslims in general and Islam specifically must be prevented. Images of bloodied Muslims, even though they are terrorists, must be forestalled through covert snatch-and-drag operations, in which video opportunities are limited and prisoners and casualties are evacuated from the battlefield. Censorship should be limited to that required by operational necessity. Government guidance must publicly buttress morale, not only of those engaged in the war against global terrorism, but also those witness to and potentially victim of its indiscriminate acts of violence and global psychological impact.

The Physical Front

The United States must seize the strategic initiative against global terrorism on the physical front. Prior to the World Trade Center/Pentagon attack, the United States countered terrorism through a diplomatic/judicial approach. This approach was reflected in U.S. policy goals, described by the Department of State:

Through international and domestic legislation and strengthened law enforcement, the United States seeks to limit the room in which terrorists can move, plan, raise funds, and operate. Our goal is to eliminate terrorist safehavens, dry up their sources of revenue, break up their cells, disrupt their movements, and criminalize their behavior.[15]

The Department of State engages terrorism diplomatically, directly and indirectly, through policy aimed at designated terrorist organizations and state sponsors of terrorism. Designated terrorist organizations, of which the State Department currently lists 28, are addressed through policy that:

makes members and representatives of those groups ineligible for U.S. visas and subject to exclusion from the United States. U.S. financial institutions are required to block the funds of those groups and of their agents and to report the blocking action to the U.S. Department of the Treasury. Additionally, it is a criminal offense for U.S. persons or persons within U.S. jurisdiction knowingly to provide material support or resources to such groups.[16]

Secondly, the United States enlists sanctions against nations designated as state sponsors of terrorism in order to isolate them from the international community. The intent is to drain the swamps where terrorists seek refuge. The seven nations designated as state sponsors of terrorism are Cuba, Iran, Iraq, Libya, North Korea, Sudan, and Syria.[17]

Acts of terror are deemed crimes, and crime is dealt with in the judicial system. The Federal Bureau of Investigation, the lead organization against terrorism committed in the United States, not only must meet the judicial system's significant burden of proof requirements, but ironically, also must safeguard terrorists' rights in the course of investigation:

> Terrorists are arrested and convicted under existing criminal statutes. All suspected terrorists placed under arrest are provided access to legal counsel and normal judicial procedure, including Fifth Amendment guarantees.[18]

This peacetime, judicial approach came at a steep price—it placed the United States on the strategic defensive against terrorism. Terrorists were afforded the freedom to reconnoiter the landscape for weakness. Terrorists picked the time and place of their attacks. Terrorists were able to mass covertly, in very small windows of time, limiting their vulnerability. On the other hand, the United States was forced to attempt the impossible—to build strong defenses everywhere, and remain strong all the time—in a legalistic, Maginot Line approach.

A *war* on terrorism, however, would seemingly unshackle the Government, enabling it to let loose "the big dog" and utilize military means of fighting terrorism, along with diplomatic, economic, judicial, and cultural means. In war, the military is not bound by the onerous burden of proof that confronts diplomatic and judicial means of combating terrorism. Once an adversary is declared hostile, the military can engage enemy combatants, which are defined as "all members of the regularly organized armed forces[19] of a party to the conflict, as well as irregular forces who are under responsible command and subject to internal military discipline, carry their arms openly, and otherwise distinguish themselves clearly from the civilian population."[20] The problem with terrorists, however, is that they do not carry their arms openly or otherwise distinguish themselves from the civilian population. They pose as noncombatants, an unlawful deception in war known as *perfidy*, punishable as a war crime. Global terrorists care little about perfidy and war crimes, in the same vein as rebel forces in modern insurgencies.

This presents a problem on the military side of the physical front. Military history provides many lessons on how to counter an insurgency, a cousin of global terrorism.

The Israel/Palestine experience, the United States experience in Vietnam, and the British experience in Northern Ireland provide valuable, hard-earned lessons on how and how not to combat global terrorism.

Counterinsurgency has been conducted through both attrition and maneuver approaches. According to Gavin Bulloch, a British counterinsurgency expert, the attrition approach has a storied past, with generally poor results.[21] Military dominated attrition campaigns have largely proven to be ineffectual, except in instances where military operations were subordinate to the overall political effort.

Israel, a predominantly Jewish nation bordered by several Muslim nations, faces a much clearer and present terrorist danger, both internally and across its borders. The Israelis have taken an attrition approach to their counterinsurgency/counterterrorism campaign, reflected in former Israeli Prime Minister Benjamin Netanyahu's statement before the U.S. House Government Reform Committee:

> To win this war, we have to fight on many fronts. Well, the most obvious one is direct military action against the terrorists themselves. Israel's policy of preemptively striking at those who seek to murder its people is, I believe, better understood today and requires no further elaboration.[22]

The United States experience in Vietnam was largely an attrition approach to counterinsurgency. However, the United States did attempt a pacification strategy designed to win the "hearts and minds" of the people during the early period of the war. The Marines instituted a Combined Action Platoon (CAP) program in 1965, based upon previous success with the concept in Haiti, Nicaragua, and Santo Domingo earlier in the century. The CAP units consisted of 15-man rifle squads, all volunteers, trained in Vietnamese language, culture, and customs. Tasked initially with establishing village security in hamlets within the Marine area of operations, the long-term CAP mission was to destroy the National Liberation Front infrastructure, organize intelligence networks, and train the local Vietnamese militia known as the Popular Forces. The CAPs were successful but eventually were discontinued due to a lack of top-level support. General Victor Krulak, the senior Marine champion of the CAP program, was unable to persuade General William Westmoreland and President Lyndon Johnson to pursue the pacification strategy across Vietnam. The Marines then fell in with the Army's attrition-based strategy.[23]

British counterinsurgency doctrine is based upon maneuver warfare, in which one strives to attack the enemy's "system" from a position of advantage rather than head on through cumulative destruction of every component in the enemy arsenal.[24] Nonetheless, Bulloch recognizes that:

> Physical destruction of the enemy still has an important role to play. A degree of attrition will be necessary, but the number of insurgents killed should be no more

than is absolutely necessary to achieve success. Commanders should seek "soft" methods of destroying the enemy; by arrest, physical isolation, or subversion, for example. The use of the minimum necessary force is a well-proven counterinsurgency lesson. In an era of intense media intrusiveness—one in which legality, from domestic and international viewpoints, will become ever more important—sound judgment and close control will need to be exercised over the degree of physical destruction which it is possible, necessary, or desirable to inflict. For example, the killing of a teenage gunman could be justifiable in military terms, but its possible effect on his community could jeopardize a potentially far more significant though less spectacular Hearts and Minds operation.[25]

Taking the strategic initiative will mean going after global terrorists where they live, train, and operate, forcing global terrorists on the defensive. What has worked well in counterinsurgencies may not work in countering global terrorism. Countering global terrorism differs markedly from counterinsurgency in that military forces may not have the legitimacy of working within their own territory. Military forces may have to be inserted into the potentially hostile territory of states that sponsor terrorism. A conundrum exists in that any land-based forces staged overseas to *attack* terrorism must also *defend* against terrorism. They are, at once, *a risk to* the terrorists but *at risk from* the terrorists as well. Worse, their very presence on the sovereign territory of a predominantly Muslim nation may go farther to exacerbate anti-Western sentiment on the psychological front.

Plainly, declaring war on global terrorism does not unleash "the big dog" at all. While it adds the military to the mix of means that decisionmakers have available to combat global terrorism, it also raises the stakes, introducing a Pandora's Box of unintentional consequences. Decisionmakers must weigh the risks of introducing military forces with the benefits, chief of which is the means to take the battle to the enemy.

The war on global terrorism will be a war of maneuver. The strategy must be crafted such that measures implemented on the physical front work in harmony with psychological measures. Tactical engagements will have to be planned with an eye toward operational and strategic implications. Maximum effort must be focused on eliminating the terrorist center of gravity—its leadership, without fueling more terrorism by lionizing their martyrdom.

Finding the terrorist center of gravity may prove to be the most difficult aspect in the war against global terrorism. Localizing and fixing the position of terrorist leadership will demand a plethora of intelligence and law enforcement resources. Military intelligence must work seamlessly with not only U.S. interagency intelligence sources but international ones as well. Domestic and international law enforcement agencies must also be integrated into the overall intelligence effort. Individually, one agency might hold a key piece of the intelligence puzzle that, although seemingly insignificant at the micro level, provides the critical detail needed at the macro level to solve the terrorist network.

Seizing the initiative against global terrorism will require a broad, international, interagency effort, unprecedented in liaison, communication, and sharing of information. Bureaucratic rivalries must be shelved. Political agendas must be put aside. Military forces must be added to and integrated with diplomatic, economic, judicial, and cultural means in a coherent strategy that criminalizes terrorism and its support, eliminates or captures terrorists, denies them sanctuary, and dries up their support on the physical front. Internationally, allies and coalition partners will have to commit to the strategy and keep the pressure on in an unrelenting pursuit of global terrorists, allowing no reprieve or sanctuary. Most importantly, America, as the sole remaining superpower and leader of the free world, must remain engaged and stay the course.

Naval Forces

If a man does not know to what port he is steering, no wind is favorable.

—Seneca, 4 BCE–65 CE

The U.S. Navy and Marine Corps have always responded to the needs of the nation by evolving within the bounds of resources and national will to meet the threat. In the beginning, our forefathers established the Navy and Marine Corps to protect the American coast and to raid commerce. The Barbary pirates provided a need for a fleet that could enforce respect for U.S. interests, especially trade and shipping. After the War of 1812, naval forces were used as an instrument of foreign policy, showing the flag around the world as foreign trade was expanded and the seas were cleared of pirates and slavers. Blockade operations and riverine campaigns during the Civil War required naval forces to command the seas and provide direct support for land operations. During World War II, naval forces projected force inland from the seas in amphibious and carrier operations. The Navy once again evolved during the Cold War to provide the Nation with a strategic nuclear deterrence capability.[26]

The September 11 strike on the World Trade Center and Pentagon provided impetus for naval forces to add yet another function, to conduct counterterrorism operations and defend the homeland. Although the current naval vision, ... *From the Sea*, updated with *Forward ... From the Sea*, is still legitimate in its focus on littoral operations, it will require an update to include the function of countering terrorism and defending the homeland. Combating global terrorism will entail an expanded role for naval forces in both conventional and nonconventional ways.

As discussed previously, the United States must seize the strategic initiative from global terrorists and root them out from their hiding places throughout the world. To do this, the United States must project power far from the shores of America into the terrorists' backyard. Naval power projection capability provides a menu of means to reach terrorists. Cruise missiles, launched from submarines and surface ships, can reach terrorist strongholds hundreds of miles inland. Precision-guided munitions can similarly be utilized from carrier-based aircraft. Marines can attack terrorist camps close to the beach. Navy SEALS can either attack or "snatch and drag" terrorists covertly, from the sea, air, or land. Many naval capabilities that traditionally support power projection also contribute in other ways to the fight against terrorism. Cryptologic capability and signals intelligence not only directly support naval power projection, but they also fuse into the overall intelligence network.

The utilization of naval forces in counterterrorism offers an advantage over land-based forces. Any land-based forces sent overseas to attack terrorists will concurrently be at risk of attack from terrorists. Sea-based naval forces, on the other hand, can operate at sea, over the horizon and out of sight of terrorists, indefinitely. The blue-water mobility of naval forces allows them an element of inherent force protection.[27] More importantly, naval forces can move stealthily to the point of launch, mounting surprise attacks against the enemy.

The Marine Corps is poised to take full advantage of seabasing through the conduct of expeditionary maneuver warfare. Over the past decade, the Marines have refined their operational concepts of operational maneuver from the sea and ship to objective maneuver to the threshold of reality. With the full-scale fielding of such equipment as the LPD 17 class of ship, the advanced amphibious assault vehicle, and the MV–22 Osprey, the Navy and Marine Corps team will take advantage of the stealth, mobility, and operational reach afforded operations from the sea, to deny global terrorists sanctuary in the littorals.

Naval forces should consider adding a few areas to their list of extensive capabilities, given the advantages described above. In order to extend the advantage of seabasing to joint forces, the Navy should consider building two new classes of ships. The first would be a new joint command and control class of ship,[28] designed to host a joint task force (JTF) commander. The ship should be configured to support not only the JTF commander and his staff but also interagency personnel, knowledgeable in the offerings of their agencies with the connectivity means to coordinate with them. Included in the command and control warfare suite would be a joint psychological operations capability. Given the importance of winning the war on the psychological front, the Navy should seriously consider hosting a robust capability in this area.[29] Additionally, the addition of linguistic personnel expert in various Arabic dialects should be pursued to support psychological operations, intelligence, and cryptologic missions.

Second, the Navy should consider a joint special operations class of ship, either an altered LPD 17 or a new ship of similar design. This class of ship would host Special

Forces and be equipped with helicopters and the tilt-rotor V–22 Osprey for vertical operations. Likewise it could accommodate small boats or SEAL delivery vehicles from the well deck for submerged or surface operations. It should also be tailored to support the *Cyclone*-class coastal patrol boat, to include nesting, refueling, rearmament, resupply, and rest and relaxation for special forces. A joint special operations class of ship could accommodate adaptive joint force packaging,[30] with forces tailored for the specific counterterrorism mission.[31]

Although naval forces possess the endurance to stay at sea indefinitely, it is hard on the sailors and marines to stay on a ship for an entire 6-month deployment. Subsequently, ships must make overseas port calls, during which they are as vulnerable as land-based forces. The Navy learned a host of antiterrorism lessons from the USS *Cole* tragedy and has implemented many procedures to prevent another such occurrence. Still, there is much to be done. Ships simply do not have the resources to check out a port prior to entry. Navy fleet support infrastructure must be beefed up to include port security fly-away teams. Fly-away teams from the numbered fleets should be tasked with clearing a port for entry and ensuring adequate force protection prior to the arrival of U.S. Navy ships and submarines to foreign ports. All surface ships should be upgraded with the phalanx surface mode to the Mk 15 Phalanx Close-In Weapon System (CIWS).[32] This upgrade provides an electro-optical day/night detection capability, enabling CIWS to engage surface and slow-moving air targets at an astounding rate of very accurate fire, providing ships with the means to thwart even the most determined overt terrorist attack.

Conclusion

The global terrorist threat is a clear and present danger to all Americans. The Navy and Marine Corps team offers the Nation a global maneuver force, well suited to taking the fight to the enemy. To meet and defeat global terrorism, however, the U.S. Navy and Marine Corps team will have to evolve to provide the Nation with contributory capabilities to deny terrorists their objectives and, ultimately, to eradicate global terrorism altogether. Naval forces must align with other means of national power in a coherent, integrated strategy that combats terrorism on both the physical and psychological fronts.

In the age of globalization, sound strategy, rather than the winds of which Seneca wrote, dictates the course to take once the destination is known. There is no greater duty for a nation's military than protecting its citizens abroad and at home. May the Navy and Marine Corps team plot the right course to reach this most important of all ports.

Notes

[1] See discussion in Frank Carlucci, Robert Hunter, and Zalmay Khalilzad, *Taking Charge: A Bipartisan Report to the President Elect on Foreign Policy and National Security—Discussion Papers* MR1306/1–RC (Santa Monica, CA: RAND, 2000), 9–11.

[2] Prior to the September 11, 2001, attacks on the World Trade Center and Pentagon, the Department of State was the lead agency against terrorism outside the United States, while the Department of Justice led the effort against terrorism within the United States.

[3] U.S. Department of Defense, Joint Publication 1–02, *Department of Defense Dictionary of Military and Associated Terms* (Washington, DC: Department of Defense, April 12, 2001).

[4] U.S. Department of State, *Foreign Terrorist Organizations*, Designations by Secretary of State Madeleine K. Albright, 1999 Report Index, October 8, 1999, accessed at <http://www.state.gov/www/global/terrorism/fto_1999.html>.

[5] From U.S. Department of State *Background Information on Foreign Terrorist Organizations*, October 8, 1999.

[6] U.S. Joint Chiefs of Staff, Joint Publication 3–07.2, *Joint Tactics, Techniques and Procedures for Antiterrorism* (Washington, DC: Department of Defense, March 17, 1998), I–1.

[7] Howard Kurtz, "Journalists Worry About Limits on Information, Access," *The Washington Post*, September 24, 2001, A5.

[8] Ibid.

[9] Bob Woodward, "In Hijacker's Bags, a Call to Planning, Prayer, and Death," *The Washington Post*, September 28, 2001, A1.

[10] Dana Milbank, "Professor Shapes Bush Rhetoric," *The Washington Post*, September 26, 2001, A6.

[11] Associated Press, "Italian Leader Says West Can 'Conquer' Islam," *The Washington Post*, September 27, 2001, A15.

[12] Crispian Balmer, "Muslims Call Italian's Take on Islam 'Racist'," *The Washington Post*, September 28, 2001, A26.

[13] ABCNews.com, "Stars Raise $150 Million," September 25, 2001, accessed at <http://more.abcnews.go.com/sections/entertainment/DailyNews/tribute010925.html>.

[14] "Telethon Audience is Bigger Than Bush's," *Los Angeles Times*, September 23, 2001, accessed at <http://www.latimes.com/news/nationworld/nation/la-092301tele.story>.

[15] U.S. Department of State, *Patterns of Global Terrorism: 1999* (Washington, DC: Department of State, April 2000), 1.

[16] Ibid., 4.

[17] Ibid., 2.

[18] U.S. Department of Justice, Counterterrorism Threat Assessment and Warning Unit, Counterterrorism Division, Federal Bureau of Investigation, *Terrorism in the United States, 1999*, i.

[19] Exempted are medical personnel, chaplains, civil defense personnel, and members of the armed forces who have acquired civil defense status.

[20] See U.S. Navy, NWP 7, *The Commander's Handbook on the Law of Naval Operations*, chapter 5, accessed at <http://www.cpf.navy.mil/pages/legal/NWP%201–14/NWPCH5.htm>.

[21] Gavin Bulloch, "Military Doctrine and Counterinsurgency: A British Perspective," *Parameters* 26, no. 2 (Summer 1996), 4–16.

[22] Statement by Former Prime Minister Benjamin Netanyahu, Hearing of the U.S. House Government Reform Committee, *Preparing For The War On Terrorism: Understanding The Nature And Dimensions Of The Threat*, Washington, DC, September 20, 2001.

[23] Peter Brush, "The War's 'Constructive Component'," *Vietnam*, February 1997, Web version accessed at <www.shss.montclair,edu/english/furr/pbvietnam0297.html >; Max Boot, "Vietnam's Lessons on How to Fight Globo-Guerrillas," *Wall Street Journal*, October, 2, 2001, A18.

[24] U.S. Marine Corps, MCDP 1, *Warfighting* (Washington, DC: Department of the Navy, June 20, 1997), 37.

[25] Bulloch, 4–16.

[26] See John Chase, "The Function of the Navy," U.S. Naval Institute *Proceedings* (October 1969), 27–33, for a discussion on the functions of the Navy, and Peter M. Swartz, "Classic Roles and Future Challenges: The Navy After Next,"

in *Strategic Transformations and Naval Power in the 21st Century,* ed. Pelham G. Boyer and Robert S. Wood (Newport, RI: Naval War College Press 1998), 273–305, for an updated version.

[27] Critics have suggested that the bombing of the USS *Cole* indicates that naval forces are as vulnerable as land-based overseas presence to terrorist attack. However, the *Cole* was in Aden harbor primarily for the diplomatic purpose of engagement; she could have been scheduled to refuel at sea.

[28] See Christopher E. Brown, The 'Q' Transition," U.S. Naval Institute *Proceedings* 123, no. 2 (February 1997), 57–61, for a discussion on the functionality that a command and control ship should contain. Another argument for a joint ship is Sam J. Tangredi, "A Ship for All Reasons," U.S. Naval Institute *Proceedings* 125, no. 9 (September 1999), 92–95.

[29] Randall G. Bowdish, "Psychological Operations . . . From the Sea," U.S. Naval Institute *Proceedings* 124, no. 2 (February 1998), 70–72. See also Bowdish, "Information Age Psychological Operations," *Military Review* (December 1998/January-February 1999), 29–37.

[30] See Paul David Miller, "A New Mission for Atlantic Command," *Joint Force Quarterly* (Summer 1993), 80–87, for a discussion on adaptive joint force packaging.

[31] As of mid-October 2001, the aircraft carrier USS *Kitty Hawk* was operating in a similar role, precipitating a debate on the appropriateness of aircraft carriers as special operations platforms.

[32] U.S. Navy, Deputy Chief of Naval Operations, *Vision . . . Presence . . . Power, A Program Guide to the U.S. Navy—2000 Edition.*

Part II

Economic Issues and Maritime Strategy

Chapter 6

Market Effects of Naval Presence in a Globalized World: A Research Summary

Robert E. Looney

W hat are the economic benefits of the peacetime operations of the U.S. Navy? Over the years, that has been one of the more elusive questions posed to and by the Navy. Today's phenomenon of globalization makes the question even more pertinent, and this initial question can be extended to ask: What is the impact of these economic benefits on globalization? Since naval forward presence (also known as forward engagement or, simply, naval presence) is the dominant mission of peacetime naval operations, a starting point would be the examination of the economic benefits to the United States and allied countries provided by U.S. naval forward presence. Forward presence is presumed to enable timely crisis response. But while most authorities on the subject contend that these benefits are significant, their measurement has always been fraught with conceptual and computational difficulties. The greatest difficulty has always involved developing a convincing counterfactual—what would the state of affairs have been in the absence of forward deployed naval forces?

The purpose of this chapter is to provide a taste of the research being conducted at the Naval Postgraduate School in identifying and measuring the economic benefits of naval forward presence. This chapter briefly summarizes two previous studies that

Robert E. Looney is professor of national security affairs at the Naval Postgraduate School. An economist, he is the author of numerous studies on the oil-based economies of the Arabian Gulf region. This chapter is based on the report "Economic Impact of Naval Forward Presence: Benefits, Linkage, and Future Prospects as Modified by Trends in Globalization" by Robert Looney, David Schrady, and Douglas Porch (Monterey, CA: Naval Postgraduate School, December 2001). It also summarizes the results of two previous studies conducted at the Naval Postgraduate School: Ron Brown, Siriphong Lawphongpanich, Robert Looney, Daniel Moran, David Schrady, James Wirtz, and David Yost, "Forward Engagement Requirements for U.S. Naval Forces: New Analytical Approaches" (July 1997) and Robert Looney and David Shrady, "Estimating Economic Benefits of Naval Forward Presence" (September 2000).

identify the levels of economic benefit and provides details of a third, more recent study that attempts to tie the benefits of forward presence to the globalization phenomenon (as reflected in the collective impact on groups of countries with differing levels of economic globalization). The chapter does not attempt to replicate the methodology of the first two studies and argue their merit—indeed, that has been done elsewhere.[1] Readers interested in challenging the validity of our findings on the levels of economic benefits to the United States and its allies (reflected in oil futures and market indices) achieved by forward presence are referred to the two study reports themselves. Rather, this chapter introduces the argument that: the greater the level of integration into the global economy for any state, the greater is the beneficial impact of U.S. naval forward presence on its economy.[2]

Development of a Methodology: Effects on Oil Futures

The issue of how to quantify the economic benefits of naval forward presence came to the fore in preparing for the Congressionally mandated 1997 Quadrennial Defense Review (QDR). Early in that process, Navy leaders asked if the economic benefits of forward engaged naval forces could be quantified and thereby communicated to policymakers. Until this point, the only evidence of such benefits was anecdotal.[3] At that time the Naval Postgraduate School was asked to develop new methodologies directed toward the quantification of these benefits.

In our initial study of this issue (1997), we developed a methodology focused on the effects of naval forward engagement and crisis response on world oil prices, as reflected by oil futures markets.[4] Using a vector autoregression econometric model,[5] this approach linked the oil price effects associated with naval forward engagement and crisis response to changes in major economic indicators.

This methodology was then applied to three cases of naval forward engagement and crisis response: the opening stages of Operation *Desert Shield* (1990 Gulf War); the Iraq-Kuwait border incident of October 1994; and the January 1987 Gulf shipping crisis (reflagging of Kuwaiti tankers and defense of other shipping during the Iran-Iraq war). These crises varied in terms of the military threat posed to U.S. and allied interests, oil market conditions, business cycles, and the general world economic climate. But a clear trend emerged from the analysis of each incident. When oil futures markets become aware of naval forward engagement/crisis response, oil prices decline.

By stabilizing and lowering prices in oil futures markets during these crises, naval forward presence provided significant benefits to the U.S. economy. These benefits can be measured in terms of dollar losses that would have occurred in the absence of timely crisis response facilitated by naval presence. Conservative estimates (all in 1997 dollars) indicate that naval crisis response in the opening stages of *Desert Storm* provided $55.22 billion worth of economic benefits (in terms of gross domestic product

[GDP]) to the United States. Similarly, naval forward engagement during the 1994 Iraq-Kuwait border incident yielded $7.13 billion in benefits, while naval forward engagement during the 1987 Gulf shipping crisis produced $5.01 billion in benefits. Naval forward engagement and crisis response had a positive impact not only on the U.S. economy but also on the economies of America's allies. Naval crisis response in the opening stages of *Desert Storm* alone is likely to have provided up to an $86.8 billion increase in world income (in terms of GDP).

Several major findings emerged from the initial study:

■ Most important, it is possible to develop procedures to quantitatively measure some of the economic impacts of naval forward presence.

■ Economic impacts can be measured in terms of dollar cost savings and/or additional dollar resources available to the economy.

■ These economic impacts can be significant. They may also persist over a fairly long time period and across the economies of a large number of U.S. allies.

■ While these initial estimates of the economic benefits associated with naval forward presence may appear high, it is also apparent that they actually underestimate the complete benefits associated with crisis response—one simply cannot put a hard figure on the total benefits from avoidance of the crises prevented by the forward presence of the Navy.

The 1997 study concluded that economic benefits associated with naval forward engagement in the Gulf region would most likely outweigh the actual financial costs associated with these operations. Given the nature of oil markets and the volatility of the region, it is safe to assume that naval forward engagement probably would continue to yield significant economic gains in the future.

Methodological Issues

The main difficulties in estimating the economic benefits derived from naval forward presence and crisis response are in establishing a credible counterfactual argument and a meaningful measure of impact. Specifically, what would have been the state of the U.S. economy if naval forces had not responded to the crisis at hand? Given that naval forces did respond, what is the relevant measure to capture the economic impact associated with this response?

Both problems are fraught with a number of conceptual issues that need to be resolved before the calculation of economic benefits can be undertaken. First, by their nature, crises tend to have a negative impact on markets and economic activity. Forward engaged naval forces are often the first to respond to a crisis, and their arrival on scene usually has a stabilizing political influence. The stabilizing influence extends to economic activity as well. Oil appears to be the most tractable vehicle for analyzing the economic benefit of naval forward presence and crisis response. Because oil is essential to nearly all economic activity in the industrialized world, price movements of that commodity in reaction to world events provide a useful index of the overall economic impact of international crises and of the response of naval forces to them.

Second, it is essential to select an index capable of reflecting the market's interpretation of the severity of a crisis as well as the degree to which trader confidence is restored following the response of naval forces to a crisis. Because oil futures prices provide more information than spot prices, the first study uses futures prices to explore the effect of naval forward presence and crisis response. Oil futures markets serve as an efficient substitute for the bulk storage of oil. Instead of stockpiling oil reserves, futures markets such as the New York Mercantile Exchange allow companies to purchase contracts to buy or sell oil at some future time. These contracts are transacted for individual months in the future. Traders base their offers on the best economic, political, and military information available to them at the time the contract is traded. As a result, futures prices are considered to be the most unbiased estimate of the likely spot or daily price of oil when the contracted delivery date actually arrives.[6]

Of course, one still has great difficulty in arguing convincingly that changes in oil prices or other key economic variables during a period of crisis were due in large part to the movement of naval forces from forward presence positions. Even though a clear pattern seemed to exist between crisis response and oil price movement in our earlier cases in the Gulf, the strongest arguments making this link had to rely largely on the process of elimination; that is, no other credible events could have produced the observed pattern of oil prices.

A way to overcome this difficulty is to examine effects on other markets concerned with safety of supplies, access to raw materials, and future economic conditions. With increased globalization and the increased interlinking of markets, it is clear that naval actions are likely to affect exchange rates, share values, and a whole host of related commodity indexes. Associated movements in these markets are also likely to affect the U.S. economy. Specifically, associated movements in one or more of these markets may enhance the positive impacts of naval actions or, conversely, offset the oil-derived benefits. For example, although naval crisis response often lowers oil prices, it may simultaneously weaken the yen, providing Japanese exporters with a competitive edge in the U.S. market. Subsequently, increased imports and associated loss of jobs could conceivably offset all of the benefits derived from lower oil prices.

Beyond the Gulf: Association between Naval Events and Markets

With the methodological issues in mind, a second study (2000) was undertaken to address the limitations of the first, while at the same time strengthening and extending our basic methodology. The new elements included the use of a highly objective statistical analysis (cointegration, error correction) capable of quantifying the short- and long-run impacts of naval movements on oil prices;[7] and the analysis of new cases of naval forward presence/crisis response. Cases were selected to provide our sample with greater geographical diversity and market impact. In addition, care was taken to assure that these cases involved primarily naval units, with at best limited participation from the other services. Four new cases were selected:

- The Taiwan Strait crisis (1996) was selected because of its importance and also the fact that it did not appear to involve oil markets.
- Operation *Desert Strike* (1996) was chosen to see if a crisis of very short duration involving naval forces was capable of altering oil markets in a manner that resulted in a significant impact on the U. S. economy.
- Operation *Desert Fox* (1998) was selected because it represents a case where there was great uncertainty in oil markets concerning both Iraq's intentions and the consequences of naval actions.
- Libyan operations (1986) were chosen because they represented a time in which oil markets were first developing sophisticated forward markets. They also represent a case close to Europe and thus possible links to exchange and share markets.

The core task for this major extension of our earlier model was to design a method for statistically linking naval actions and other events to price movements in key markets. As noted above, our earlier study made this key connection largely through the process of elimination. In the second study, formal event analysis provides a true statistical test of the association of naval actions and markets. It can also be used for hypothesis testing. Specific questions were asked throughout the study: Do naval actions increase market uncertainty, or do they provide a stabilizing impact? Do naval actions produce only a transitory movement in market prices, or are these actions responsible for longer run adjustments in these markets? If the latter is the case, the credibility of the forward market analysis outlined above is strengthened in that the consequences of naval actions are not confined to the short-run up-and-down fluctuations of spot prices. Instead, these actions actually set in motion a whole series of economic adjustments that, taken as a whole, provide significant economic benefits.

While oil markets were the one constant throughout the cases, several other markets were affected by naval actions. These include: the dollar/yen exchange rate, the Commodity Research Bureau commodity index, the Goldman-Sachs commodity index, the Standard and Poor 100, the Nikkei 100, the Hang-Seng, and the New York Stock Exchange composite index. In each case involving oil or commodity markets, naval events reduced the price from what it would have been in the absence of forward presence/crisis response. In the case of share markets and the dollar/yen exchange rate, prices were higher than they would have been if naval forces had not been present.

In affecting these markets, naval events were shown to produce a short-run (overnight) effect in the directions noted above. More important, the analysis found that the impact of naval events on these markets lingers for a significant time, altering prices for a period of time that allows for significant benefits to the United States economy. These benefits were considerable, with each operation yielding well over $1 billion of added GDP to the U.S. economy.

Assessing Future Effects: Oil Price Shocks as Measures of Globalization

The conclusions noted above can be the basis for assessing future economic impacts associated with naval forward presence/crisis response. But can we predict in advance the general magnitude of economic benefits accruing from similar operations? What methods are best to do this? What factors need to be taken into account? How might these change with the evolution of globalization and increased economic integration? Will these changes in the international economic environment likely strengthen or weaken the positive economic impacts associated with naval forward presence/crisis response?

Addressing these issues requires us to develop an integrated framework for assessing the consequences of globalization on the market forces associated with naval forward presence/crisis response. Here we need to draw heavily on the rapidly expanding literature on globalization, integrating it with our quantitative findings on economic benefits. Focus is on the key linkages between naval forward presence, oil prices, and globalization. Has globalization over time strengthened or weakened this link? What elements of globalization have been most important in this regard? Are these trends likely to continue into the foreseeable future?

In our third study (2001), the linkages between naval forward presence/crisis response and oil prices are examined in the context of changes in the global economy and the various dimensions of globalization. An operational procedure is developed to measure the various facets of globalization and track their movements over time. Next, the magnitude of oil price shocks' effect on domestic economies is shown to depend critically on the global environment in which they occur. Several groups of countries are identified by the manner in which oil shocks reduce their national incomes. Because of trends in globalization, the first group of advanced countries—including the United States—has become more vulnerable over time to oil price shocks. That is, oil shocks of a given magnitude have tended over time to produce greater and greater reductions in GDP. The second group of countries, consisting largely of the top layer of developing countries led by Mexico, South Africa, and South Korea—is also affected by globalization, but to a lesser extent. While GDP is still reduced by oil price shocks in these countries, globalization appears to have been less of a factor.

In short, the main finding of the third study is that naval forward presence plays an increasingly important role in stabilizing the economies of the advanced industrial nations. Other parts of the world also benefit, although trends in globalization suggest that, for them, the economic gains that accrue from naval forward presence are of a lower magnitude.

Categorizing Globalization

Current debates over the relative merits of globalization provide some insight into the manner in which market price modifications brought about by naval forward presence impact on the economies in different parts of the world. In a recent article, Nobel Prize winner Amartya Sen of Cambridge University provides some basic answers to several of the key elements of this debate—answers that have relevance to the changing economic impact of naval forward presence. Sen maintains:

- Globalization is not new, nor is it just Westernization: Over thousands of years, globalization has progressed through travel, trade, migration, spread of cultural influences and dissemination of knowledge and understanding (including science and technology).
- Globalization is not in itself a folly. It has enriched the world scientifically and culturally and benefited many people economically as well. In this regard, modern technologies as well as economic interrelations have been influential.
- The use of the market economy can produce different outcomes. Specifically, the market economy can generate many different results, depending on how physical resources are distributed, how human resources are developed, what rules prevail, and so on in all these spheres, and the state and the society have roles, within a country and in the world.
- The world has changed since the Bretton Woods agreement. The current economic, financial, and political architecture of the world (including the World Bank, the International Monetary Fund, and other institutions) was largely set up in the 1940s, following the Bretton Woods Conference in 1944. The implication is that the current system does not have institutions that are responsive to many of the changed economic circumstances, and, as such, many parts of the world are not well served by the current system.[8]

Sen suggests that various parts of the world have evolved somewhat differently over the last several decades and, as a result, possess economic environments that respond quite differently to various types of external shocks. The main problem for assessing the economic consequences of naval forward presence is, therefore, one of deriving an operational classification of these environments.

In this regard, Jeffrey Sachs provides a good starting point for grouping countries in terms of their interaction with the global economy.[9] Although Sachs' paper was written to provide a framework for examining the consequences of globalization for the growth potential of various parts of the world, it develops an initial country classification scheme that appears appropriate for the assessment of the manner in which naval forward presence market links, such as oil market price movements, produce a differential impact on domestic economies. As a first approximation to the world's different economic environments, Sachs develops five main groupings (table 6–1).

Endogenous growth countries. These countries are experiencing the process of self-sustaining increases in income generated mainly by technological innovation. Innovation raises national income, which in turn stimulates further innovation in a positive feedback process.[10] For this group of countries, globalization should be a major spur to innovation by increasing the extent of the market. It may also concentrate innovative activity if it creates a more integrated global labor market for scientists and engineers who are then likely to aggregate in the highly innovative core economies. Most proxies of innovative activity (patents, research and development expenditures, and numbers of scientific publications) suggest a huge spurt in such activities in the 1990s. The rapid growth of labor productivity in the United States since the early 1990s also supports the notion of a surge in innovation in line with the increasing globalization of the world economy.

On the other hand, it is not obvious that globalization is reducing or increasing this group's vulnerability to oil price shocks. The standard answer is that information-based economies use less oil per unit of GDP and, therefore, are becoming less dependent on imported energy. For example, in the case of the United States during the 1970s, oil products accounted for almost 9 percent of GDP.[11] Today, the figure is about 3 percent. More efficient car engines are one explanation. Another is the steady shift of the American economy to knowledge-driven activities. Also, the endogenous growth countries' flexibility and abilities to shift to alternative sources of energy in the short run presumably aid in minimizing the economic impact produced by oil price shocks. However, a good case could be made that increased globalization has created a greatly expanded set of macroeconomic linkages between these and many nonendogenous group countries who may be becoming more vulnerable to oil price shocks as they speed up industrialization. An oil-shock-induced recession in these countries could feed back to the endogenous countries, seriously affecting their economies through declining export sales. Ultimately, then, the net impact of oil price movements on the endogenous countries can only be assessed through empirical testing. But if these countries are indeed more vulnerable to oil shocks, the market stability-inducing effects of naval forward presence become more important to them.

Table 6–1. **Initial Categorization of Countries According to Globalization and Growth Mechanism**

Endogenous Growth	Catching up	Primary Producer	Malthusian	Isolated Economies
Australia	Bangladesh	Algeria	Afghanistan	Armenia
Austria	Bulgaria	Angola	Benin	Azerbaijan
Belgium	China	Bolivia	Botswana	Belarus
Canada	Dominican Republic	Cameroon	Burkina Faso	Kazakhstan
Denmark	Hungary	Chile	Cambodia	Kyrgyzstan
Finland	Indonesia	Congo	Central African	Moldova
France	Jamaica	Costa Rica	Republic	Turkmenistan
Germany	Malaysia	Côte d'Ivoire	Chad	Uzbekistan
Hong Kong	Mauritius	Ecuador	Congo, DR	
Ireland	Mexico	Gambia	Eritrea	
Israel	Mongolia	Ghana	Ethopia	
Italy	Nicaragua	Guinea Bissau	Gabon	
Japan	Oman	Honduras	Guatemala	
Korea	Philippines	Kenya	Haiti	
Netherlands	Poland	Kuwait	Iraq	
New Zealand	Portugal	Mauritania	Jordan	
Norway	Romania	Mozambique	Laos	
Singapore	Spain	Nigeria	Lesotho	
Sweden	Sri Lanka	Papua New	Liberia	
Switzerland	Thailand	Guinea	Mali	
Taiwan	Tunisia	Saudi Arabia	Namibia	
United Kingdom	Turkey	Sierra Leone	Nepal	
United States	Vietnam	Syria	Niger	
		Tanzania	Pakistan	
		Togo	Paraguay	
		Trinidad	Rwanda	
		Uganda	Somalia	
		United Arab	Sudan	
		Emirates	Tajikistan	
		Venezuela	Zambia	
		Yemen		
		Zimbabwe		

Source: Jeffrey D. Sachs, "Globalization and Patterns of Economic Development," *Weltwirtschaftliches Archiv* 136, no. 4 (2000), 583. Of note is the absence of Russia in the above list.

Catching-up growth countries. This group of countries—starting with a lower level of technology and income (the "follower")—is in the process of narrowing the income gap with the higher technology and richer countries (the "leader") through a process of technological diffusion and capital flows from leader to follower.

While all countries enjoy some benefit from the technological growth of the leading countries, the rate at which technology diffuses from leader to follower differs sharply around the world. A region that is geographically isolated, for example, is much less likely to benefit from technological diffusion.

Two kinds of countries appear to be winners in the race in absorbing technologies from abroad. Countries with successful export-promotion policies, such as Korea and Taiwan, have earned the foreign exchange necessary to import technologies from abroad. Also, countries that have been able to attract large flows of foreign direct investment have similarly been able to upgrade technologies with particular success.

There is little doubt that successful catching-up growth involves a positive feedback process between technological diffusion and human capital accumulation. Initially, human capital is low in the laggard economy, and technologies are rudimentary. The country may achieve some modest inflow of technology by attracting labor-intensive export-oriented foreign direct investment—for example, labor-intensive assembly operations in export processing zones. These simple assembly operations generate income, some modest skills, and the resources to invest in improved education. The combination of rising skill levels and rising educational attainment leads to an upgrading of the foreign investment facilities.

As with the endogenous countries, it is impossible to say much a priori about the manner in which increased globalization is affecting the net effects on these countries produced by an oil shock. On the one hand, increased globalization has accelerated the long-term growth path of these countries (as illustrated in table 6–2), suggesting that they may be operating at close to full potential and thus be more vulnerable to oil price increases. On the other hand, with increased diversification, these economies may be able to shift to alternative sources of energy, thus avoiding the full brunt of the external shocks. Finally, as in the case of the endogenous growth countries, oil price shocks may impact indirectly through slowing the growth of major external markets. The matter must ultimately be resolved through empirical testing and simulation.

Resource-based growth. Resource-based growth describes the process whereby an economy experiences cycles of per capita income mainly as the result of resource booms and busts. In fact, it has often been noted in recent years that natural-resource-rich economies have faired particularly badly (see table 6–2), especially in comparison to many of the resource-scare economies. Even oil booms may have an adverse effect on oil-producing countries through the Dutch Disease mechanisms—overvalued exchange rate, increased domestic inflation, and a shift to nontrade activities.[12] However,

Table 6–2. **Characteristics of Countries According to Growth/Globalization Categories**

Country Types	Number of countries	Population (total for group in millions)	GNP per capita (US$ basis)	Annual growth of GNP per capita 1990–1999	Percentage of population in temperate ecozones	Percentage of population within 100 km of the sea
Endogenous growth countries	23	844	20,400	2.1	76	69
Catching-up growth countries	23	2,063	5,599	2.7	28	59
Primary commodity producers	32	465	3,694	0.0	9	44
Malthusian countries	31	466	1,782	-0.3	4	19
Isolated economies	8	74	2,372	na	14	0

Source: Jeffrey D. Sachs, "Globalization and Patterns of Economic Development," *Weltwirtschaftliches Archiv* 136, no. 4 (2000), 584.

given the Dutch Disease effect is a longer-term phenomenon, it is probably safe to conclude that at least in the case of oil producers' increased globalization, the short-run effect of an oil price increase would be positive. Given their rigidity and lack of diversification, non-oil-producing countries would most likely have declines in their incomes during periods of oil price shocks, especially with globalization increasing their dependence on foreign markets.

Malthusian decline. Malthusian decline is a process of falling per capita income caused by population pressures that outstrip the carrying capacity of the local economy—particularly in circumstances in which the country is neither innovating nor successfully adopting technologies from abroad. These countries appear to be experiencing a long-term decline in living standards that transcends the effects of terms-of-trade shocks of cyclical phenomena. Sub-Saharan Africa is the most disturbing case of an impoverished region suffering outright declines in living standards. Somewhat less dramatically, the Andean region seems also to be stocked with stagnant or even falling living standards. Given the economic structure of this group of countries, it is probably safe to assume that any trends in globalization would increase their vulnerability to oil price shocks.

Economic isolation. Economic isolation is a phenomenon of economic stagnation that results from an economy's physical or policy-induced isolation from world markets. The main problem with the landlocked countries is that their geographical isolation sharply hinders international trade. In terms of increased globalization, foreign investors in particular do not view these impoverished nations as effective platforms for export-oriented foreign direct investment. Thus these countries are typically unable to attract the kind of assembly operations in garments, electronics, footwear, and other sectors that have been important steppingstones to economic development in more favorably located economies. Foreign investors come, if at all, only to exploit primary commodities with a high value per unit weight—such as oil and gas, diamonds, and metals—since such commodities can be profitably exploited even when transport costs are high. Without the diversification and flexibility needed to modify oil price shocks, one must conclude that these countries, unless hydrocarbon producers themselves, are very vulnerable to developments in the international oil market.

Summary. The point of identifying distinctive national economies categorized by similar characteristics is the development of a hypothesis: it is reasonable to expect that most or all countries in a particular group would be affected in a roughly similar manner by external oil shocks. Behavior following oil price shocks, of course, is our tool for analyzing the stabilizing effects of naval forward presence.

Building on this hypothesis, the next step is the development of an operational method for quantifying these country groupings and, when necessary, reclassifying countries to better reflect a common underlying set of global economic forces. The point of this analysis is to help assess the manner in which globalization has altered the structure of these countries over time with regard to making them more or less vulnerable to oil price shocks. Given the trends in globalization, this provides a rough tool to examine the question of which countries are benefiting more from naval forward presence and to what extent. Which are less affected by naval presence, and by how much?

Quantifying Globalization

One of the main hindrances to a meaningful assessment of the manner in which increased globalization affects the economic benefits associated with naval forward presence is that the term *globalization* remains vague, meaning different things to different people and groups. Currently, a consensus appears to be forming that globalization—whether economic, political, cultural, or environmental—is defined by increasing levels of interdependence over vast distances. However, a study by A.T. Kearny, Inc., notes few researchers have undertaken the task of actually trying to measure those levels of interdependency.[13] "For instance, how do we determine the extent to which a country has become embedded within the global economy? How do we demonstrate that globalization is racing ahead, rather than just limping along?"[14] The lack of a clear, precise definition underlies many of the current arguments and debates over the extent of globalization and the manner that phenomenon is changing the structure of national economies. As the Kearney study notes: "Without the means to quantify the extent of globalization, any meaningful evolution of its effects will remain elusive."[15] Foreign policy scholar James Rosenau has also outlined many of the benefits and conceptual problems of devising a meaningful operational definition of globalization.[16]

Previous attempts at quantification. The Kearney approach is to reverse-engineer globalization and break it down into component parts. On a country-by-country basis, Kearney quantifies the levels of personal contact across national borders by combining data on international travel, international phone calls, and cross-border remittances and other transfers. The A.T. Kearney/*Foreign Policy* globalization index charts the World Wide Web by assessing not only its growing numbers of users but also the number of Internet hosts and secure servers through which they communicate, find information, and conduct business transactions.

The Kearney globalization index also measures economic integration; it tracks the movements of goods and services by examining the changing share of international trade in each country's economy; and it measures the permeability of national borders through the convergence of domestic and international prices. The index also tracks the movements of money by tabulating inward and outward direct foreign investment and portfolio capital flows, as well as income payments and receipts.

As the Kearney study notes, much of the conventional wisdom cherished by both champions and critics of globalization collapses under the weight of hard data—beliefs ranging from the pace and scale of global integration and the characteristics of the digital divide to the impact of globalization on income inequality, democratization, and corruption.

But while the Kearney index is a step in the right direction, it still suffers from many of the problems associated with index construction. Several fundamental problems are the choice of which measures to include in the index, the ability of these measures to be compared across countries, and the choice of which system of weights to use to combine the various measures into a final summary index. Clearly each possible (arbitrary) weighting system will provide a somewhat different picture as to the extent of globalization in any particular country. The Kearney study does not treat these issues, but they need to be addressed before the index can provide any new meaningful insights to the globalization process.[17]

A new approach to quantification. One way to get around this problem is to compile an extensive data set of the most widely used economic statistics and measures of world trade, such as capital flows and economic integration. Many of these measures will overlap and thus be redundant. Using factor analysis, however, the main dimensions of global diversity can be identified.

More specifically, the basic assumption of factor analysis is that a limited number or underlying dimensions (factors) can be used to explain complex phenomena. The resulting data reduction produces a limited number of independent (uncorrelated) composite measures. In the current example, measures such as value added per unit of capital, value added per laborer, value added per firm, and so on could provide a composite index of productivity or relative efficiency in factor usage. One advantage of indexes formed in this manner is that it avoids the problem of selecting one measure of efficiency—such as value added per worker—over other logical alternatives.

As an initial step in exploratory data analysis, factor analysis has three objectives: to study the correlations of a large number of variables by clustering the variables into factors such that variables within each factor are highly correlated; to interpret each factor according to the variables belonging to it; and to summarize many variables by a few factors.

The usual factor analysis model expresses each variable as a function of the factors common to several variables and a factor unique to the variable:

$$z_j = a_{j1}F_1 + a_{j2}F_2 + \ldots + a_{jm}F_m + U_j$$

where
z_j = the jth standardized variable
m = the number of factors *common* to all the variables
U_j = the factor unique to variable z_j
a_{ji} = *factor loadings*

The number of factors, m, should be small, and the contribution of the unique factors should also be small. The individual factor loadings, a_{ji}, for each variable should be either very large or very small so each variable is associated with a minimal number of factors.

To the extent that this factor analysis model is appropriate for the problem at hand, the objectives noted above can be achieved. Variables with high loadings on a factor tend to be highly correlated with each other, and variables that do not have the same loading patterns tend to be less highly correlated. Each factor is interpreted according to the magnitudes of the loadings associated with it.

Perhaps more important for the problem at hand, the original variables can be replaced by the factors with little loss of information. Each case (firm) receives a score for each factor; these *factor scores* can be computed as:

$$F_i = b_{i1}z_1 + b_{i2}z_2 + \ldots b_{ip}z_p$$

where b_{ij} are the *factor score coefficients*. Factor scores are in turn used in the discriminate analysis that follows. In general, these factor scores have less error and are therefore more reliable measures than the original variables. The scores express the degree to which each case possesses the quality or property that the factor describes. The factor scores have a mean of zero and standard deviation of one.

Operationally, the computations of factors and factor scores for each country are obtained through a principal components procedure. The data used in the analysis of our third study was taken from the annual World Bank World Development Indicators[18] and include:

- Domestic absorption (percentage of GDP)
- Domestic credit provided by banking sector (percentage of GDP)
- Expenditure, total (percentage of GDP)
- Trade (percentage of GDP)
- Trade (percentage of goods GDP)
- Imports of goods and services (percentage of GDP)
- Financing from abroad (percentage of GDP)
- Foreign direct investment, net inflows (percentage of GDP)
- Exports of goods and services (percentage of GDP)
- Domestic financing, total (percentage of GDP)
- Gross private capital flows (percentage of GDP, purchasing power parity [PPP])
- Telephone mainlines (per 1,000 people)
- Gross foreign direct investment (percentage of GDP, PPP)
- GDP growth (annual percentage)
- Import growth (annual percentage)
- Exports of goods and services (annual percentage growth)
- Sub-Saharan dummy
- Small country dummy
- Oil dummy
- Revised country classification

Quantified dimensions of globalization. While the exact composition of factors varied slightly from year to year over the analysis period (1985–1997), the 20 variables generally produced 5 main dimensions or factors:

Structural openness depicts the degree of national economic integration into the world economy. Operationally, this comprises the share of imports and exports as a percentage of GDP. The variables comprising structural openness do not change much over time, and this usually is the first factor to be extracted from the data set.

- *General globalization* (for lack of a better term) incorporates those variables that load on Sachs' country grouping dimension (table 6–1). The third study also expands Sachs' list of countries to include several additions, such as Brazil. The number of variables loading on this factor increases considerably over time, with the factor incorporating an increasingly diverse set of global indices. The third study makes clear that globalization affects each of the different country groupings in unique ways and that globalization is an ongoing process.

- *Finance* comprises both domestic and foreign components—for example, foreign direct investment and financing from abroad.

- *Growth/trade expansion* includes both external and internal measures of economic expansion. The main variables that make up this factor are import and export growth and overall GDP growth. GDP growth usually, but not always, is highly correlated with the measures of trade expansion.

- *Global structure* comprises several structural variables that take into account unique country characteristics identified in the literature. For example, the literature suggests that the sub-Saharan African countries may have a unique set of factors that sets them apart from other developing countries.[19] To take this potential factor into account, a variable (SUBAF) was created that gives a score of zero to the non-African countries and one to the African nations.

Researchers also contend that small countries, with much narrower resource bases and smaller domestic markets, are at a disadvantage in comparison to their larger counterparts.[20] To take this effect into account, the third study utilizes a unique variable with a value of one assigned to the smaller nations (usually those with a population less than 5 million), and a zero for the larger countries.

Finally, another body of literature stresses the unique structure of the oil economies.[21] This factor is taken into account with a final variable entitled *oil*, which assigns a value of one to the oil economies and a zero to non-oil nations.

Revised factor scores and country groupings. Because Sachs' classification was intended to examine the growth potential of a large group of countries, his country groupings may not be ideal for the identification of differential impacts on unique economic environments stemming from oil price shocks. Also, Sachs' classification scheme appears to be static. There is little evidence of movement between groups and no precise indication of the circumstances under which movement might take place. In the case of economic environments, we would expect discernable shifting between groups as countries and their economic policies evolve.

To overcome these limitations, the third study used the following procedure (illustrated as figure 6–1).[22] First, for each individual year examined, a factor analysis was undertaken using the 20 variables noted above. In the case of 1995, 54 countries had complete data observations for this period and were retained in the analysis.[23] The 20-variable data set was comprised of 5 main dimension or factors (based on the constraint of an eigen value [characteristic root value] of one or greater).

Sachs' country classification term was included in the second factor along with gross private capital flows, export share in GDP, and gross foreign direct investment. These variables differed significantly by country grouping. The country factor scores on each dimension are based on a scale with a mean of zero. Positive numbers indicate

Figure 6–1. **Globalization and Country Economic Environments**

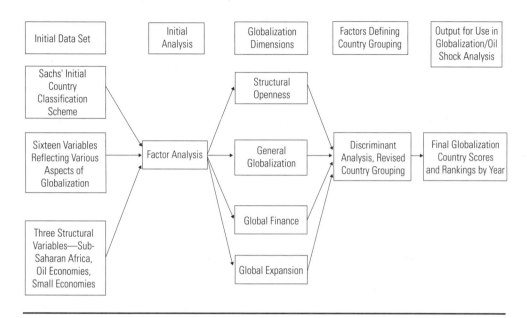

above-normal attainment of a particular factor or global dimension, while negative values indicate that the country/group is below average in attainment of that dimension. For example, in 1995 the trade patterns of the United States accounted for a considerably smaller share of GDP than the sample norm. The United States was even well below the norm of the endogenous growth countries (group 1 of table 6–1). The United States was considerably above the sample average for its attainment of general globalization (dimension 2) but again considerably below the norm for endogenous growth countries. The United States was, however, slightly above the norm for global financial flows. Finally, the country had above-average growth during this period, again somewhat above that of the endogenous growth countries.

Second, using the country factor scores from this step, a discriminant analysis was undertaken to assign a new set of country groupings. The five main dimensions of globalization noted above were weighted in reassigning countries to one of the five groups originally developed by Sachs. For the sample year of 1995, two dimensions, general globalization and trade expansion, were statistically significant in separating the sample countries into five main groupings. Of the original country classifications, 71.7 percent remained in their initial groups, with the remainder assigned to new groups. For example, Korea had only an 8.3 percent chance of being an endogenous growth (group 1) country but a 90.3 percent chance of correctly falling into the catching-up group (group 2). The point of the second step is to tailor the Sachs country classification scheme into a more dynamic analysis that can account for continuing globalization effects (that is, changes over time).[24]

The third step entailed redefining the country classification variable from the results of the second step. Here, the factor analysis was rerun to generate a new set of factor scores, more reflective of each country's position in the total sample and in its assigned group.[25]

Finally, using these scores, a new discriminate analysis found that the factors of general globalization and global expansion were statistically significant in assigning countries to the five group model. On this basis, the probability of correct placement in one of the five groups was 92.6 percent, with all of the endogenous growth (group 1) countries correctly placed. This last step provides the country groupings and factor scores used in the oil price impact analysis. The analysis was undertaken for 1977, 1980, 1983, and each year for the period 1985–1997.

Globalization and the Strength of Oil Shocks

The revised factor scores or globalization dimensions for each country are a key element for assessing the manner in which oil price shocks have been modified over time by changes in the world economy. Using the United States as an example, the link between oil price shocks and globalization is outlined in figure 6–2.

As a starting point, a macroeconomic model was constructed for each of the 19 countries examined. In the case of the U.S. economy, the model consisted of three endogenous macroeconomic variables (gross capital formation, government consumption, and exports [all at constant dollar prices]) and three exogenous variables (Japanese constant price GDP, the dollar exchange rate, and world oil prices). A first set of simulations for each year (1985–1997) was made using the historical values for oil prices. A second set of simulations was made assuming a 10 percent increase in the price of oil for each base year. The net impact on GDP was then calculated by subtracting the simulations incorporating oil price shocks from the historical series. Oil shock impacts were calculated for the shock year and 2 subsequent years. Finally, the resulting oil shocks were put through a regression analysis on the various globalization dimensions to assess the role that changes in a country's level of globalization might have had in modifying the manner in which oil prices altered that country's GDP.

Based on these findings, implications were drawn (figure 6–3) for the likely future role of naval forward presence/crisis response. For example, if the size of oil price shocks increases over time for a particular country, then naval forward presence, by limiting the rise of oil prices, would play an increasingly important role in stabilizing that country's GDP. On the other hand, if the dimensions of globalization lessened the

Figure 6–2. **Globalization Impact on Oil Price Shocks (U.S.)**

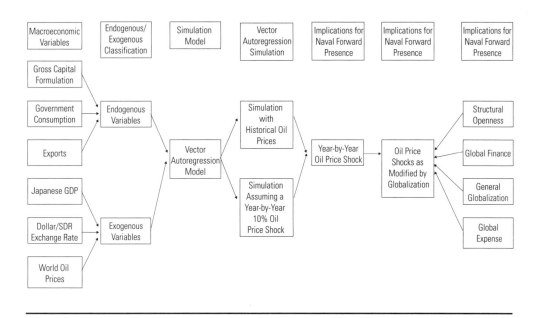

loss in GDP associated with oil price shocks, then naval forward presence would de-cline in importance in providing economic benefits to that country.

Economic Impact of Naval Forward Presence on America

Using the framework developed above, a sample of 19 countries (including the United States) was analyzed to determine the changing strength of oil price shocks. Based on the results, a number of generalizations can be drawn concerning the likely future economic role played by naval forward presence.

Patterns of globalization. The United States is far and away the world's leading economic power. Its GDP totaled $9.3 trillion in 1999; assuming international pur-chasing power parity, this was 3 times the size of Japan's output, 4.8 times the size of Germany's, and almost 7 times the size of the United Kingdom's. Although the volume of its exports and imports exceeds that of any other country, the value of the U.S. ex-ternal sector as a percentage of its GDP is comparatively low. Exports of goods and services accounted for less than 11 percent of GDP in 1999, considerably less than the European Union's 25 to 29 percent in recent years.[26]

As noted earlier, our approach focuses largely on 1985 to 1997, a period when many argue that the process of globalization began to significantly affect the world's

Figure 6–3. **Implications of Globalization for Naval Forward Presence**

VAR Macroeconomic Simulations	Over Time Global Modification Factors	Impact on Oil Price Shocks	Changing Strength of Oil Price Shocks	Implications

Structural Openness

Year-by-Year 10% Oil Price Shocks

Global Finance

General Globalization

Global Expansion

Modified Oil Price Shocks

Group 1 Countries

Group 2 Countries

Oil Producers

Economic Strength of Naval Forward Presence/Crisis Response

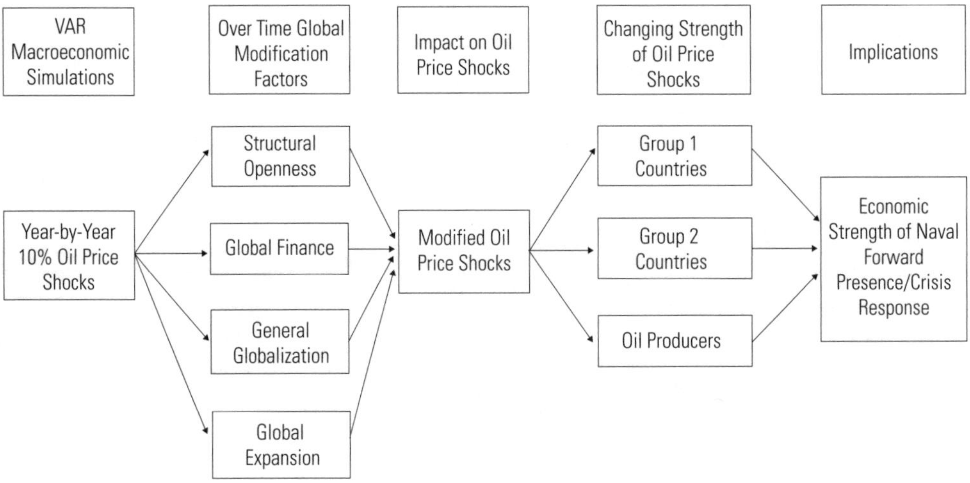

leading economies. This provides a framework for examining a large sample of countries in such a manner that their various unique patterns of globalization could be identified and then examined as possible contributing factors to the differing impacts of oil price shocks on national economies. This in turn would contribute to identifying those countries most likely to benefit from naval forward presence/crisis response.

With these goals in mind, the factor/discriminant analysis of U. S. globalization found some significant differences between the U.S. economy and the overall norm for the endogenous growth (group 1) countries. Table 6–3 reports the factor scores on the globalization dimensions for the United States, along with the comparative scores for the overall endogenous growth (group 1) and catching-up (group 2) countries.[27] From the results, three patterns can be identified: U.S. structural openness dimension scores are considerably below the group average which suggest that trade plays less of a role in the American economy than for other advanced industrial nations; the U.S. general globalization dimension is also somewhat below the group norm; and U.S. financial globalization and growth in the world market are above the pattern typically found in other advanced countries.

Recent patterns of U.S. globalization (as in the other endogenous growth/group 1 countries) have been characterized by a rapid increase in the general globalization dimension (illustrated by figure 6–4). Contrary to popular belief, the United States has not

Table 6–3. **Dimensions of Globalization: Factor Scores, 1988–1996**

Year		Structural Openness	General Globalization	Financial Globalization	Global Growth
1988	U.S.	-1.305	1.367	0.023	0.773
	Group 1	-0.190	1.166	-0.081	0.116
	Group 2	0.112	-0.290	-0.080	0.690
1989	U.S.	-1.109	1.238	-0.104	-0.078
	Group 1	0.004	1.669	-0.119	-0.103
	Group 2	-0.056	-0.292	-0.102	0.148
1990	U.S.	-1.031	0.615	-1.114	0.143
	Group 1	-0.024	1.387	-0.722	-0.109
	Group 2	-0.027	-0.481	-0.600	0.037
1991	U.S.	-1.116	1.185	-0.003	-0.108
	Group 1	-0.066	1.423	-0.200	-0.208
	Group 2	0.069	0.161	0.116	0.132
1992	U.S.	-1.229	1.007	-0.041	0.280
	Group 1	-0.142	1.504	-0.067	-0.269
	Group 2	0.257	0.043	-0.182	0.306
1993	U.S.	-1.159	0.876	0.054	0.247
	Group 1	-0.180	1.399	0.407	-0.182
	Group 2	0.381	0.102	-0.285	0.074
1994	U.S.	-1.342	0.968	0.590	0.036
	Group 1	-0.156	1.541	0.244	-0.223
	Group 2	0.325	0.110	-0.071	0.146
1995	U.S.	-1.278	1.134	0.074	0.214
	Group 1	-0.294	1.618	-0.023	-0.208
	Group 2	0.096	-0.117	-0.294	0.706
1996	U.S.	-1.115	1.213	-0.160	0.217
	Group 1	-0.326	1.724	-0.239	-0.106
	Group 2	0.159	-0.034	-0.341	0.140
1997	U.S.	-1.146	2.124	0.024	0.316
	Group 1	-0.694	2.538	0.079	-0.159
	Group 2	0.461	0.028	-0.558	0.100
Average	U.S.	-1.183	1.173	-0.066	0.204
	Group 1	-0.207	1.597	-0.072	-0.145
	Group 2	0.178	-0.077	-0.240	0.248

Figure 6–4. **Patterns of U.S. Globalization**

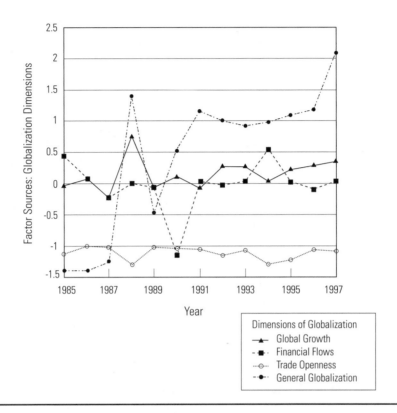

dramatically increased its position relative to other countries with regard to the other dimensions of globalization—particularly global openness, financial flows, or
expansion in the global economy. This finding is consistent with recent conclusions by
Robert Dunn.[28] While Dunn's main conclusion is that the U.S. economy is far from
being completely globalized, our findings suggest that, at least with regard to the general globalization dimension, significant movement has been made in that direction.

Globalization and oil price shocks. With regard to the impact of oil price shocks
on its economy, the United States has the normal pattern of a positive sign (indicated
in table 6–4) associated with increased levels of general globalization. Over time, and
everything else being equal, oil price shocks have been stronger because of globalization, and there has been a significant increase in the amount of GDP loss associated
with oil price shocks (illustrated in figures 6–5 and 6–6).

Table 6–4. **Summary of Oil Shock Impact Analysis (U.S.)**

	Globalization Dimensions			
Period of Impact	**General Globalization**	**Structural Openness**	**Financial Globalization**	**Global Growth**
Cumulative				
Impact Year	+	ins	ins	ins
Impact Year + 1	+	ins	ins	ins
Impact Year + 2	+	ins	ins	ins
Cumulative % GDP				
Impact Year	+	ins	ins	ins
Impact Year + 1	+	ins	ins	ins
Impact Year + 2	+	ins	ins	ins
Yearly				
Impact Year	+	ins	ins	ins
Impact Year + 1	+	ins	ins	ins
Impact Year + 2	+	ins	ins	ins

Notes: Group 1 Country. U.S. data used in the analysis. + indicates a factor increasing the strength of oil price increases in affecting gross domestic product (GDP); ins = statistically insignificant at the 95% level. - indicates a factor weakening the strength of oil price increases in affecting GDP.

Implications for naval forward presence. The above finding suggests that in the absence of offsetting effects produced by the other dimensions of globalization, future naval forward presence should be increasingly important to the U.S. economy by dampening oil price increases caused by destabilizing events.

Economic Impact of Naval Forward Presence on Other Countries

A similar analysis was undertaken in the third study for 18 additional countries whose selection was largely dictated by the available data. Here, the analysis found clear linkage between the globalization-defined country groupings and the manner in which oil shocks affect their economies (illustrated in table 6–5). Over time, and contrary to popular opinion, endogenous growth (group 1) countries have become more vulnerable to oil price shocks. The oil shock-driven loss in income as a percent of GDP has increased gradually over time and in line with the process of globalization. In other words, a 10 percent increase in the price of oil today would cause greater reductions in national income than it would in previous years. For endogenous growth countries (advanced economies), general globalization and structural openness have been the factors

Figure 6–5. **Yearly Oil Shock Impact (U.S.)**

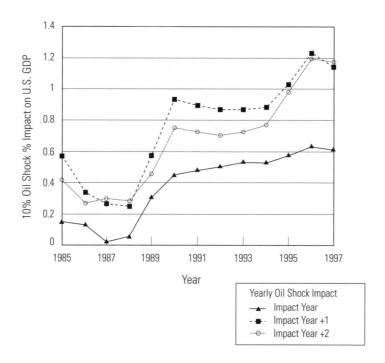

most responsible for the increased severity of oil shocks. Neither of these factors is easily controlled by governments without considerable damage to economic growth. Changes in the factors of financial globalization and in the global growth dimension of globalization have played a much smaller role.[29] In fact, increases in these factors have made some countries less vulnerable and others more vulnerable—with no clear patterns emerging from these aspects of globalization.

Because naval forward presence/crisis response tends to suppress oil shocks and return prices to their equilibrium levels, the role of such naval activities should be of increasing benefit to all endogenous growth countries, as well as all industrialized countries seeking to enter that category. With the likely continuation of global trends, naval forward presence/crisis response should play an even greater positive role for global economic stability in the foreseeable future.

Of course, this economic stability may not benefit individual oil-producing states. The two oil economies included in the study, Mexico and Norway, would likely experience declines in income associated with forward deployed naval operations—

Figure 6–6. **Cumulative Oil Shock Impact (U.S.)**

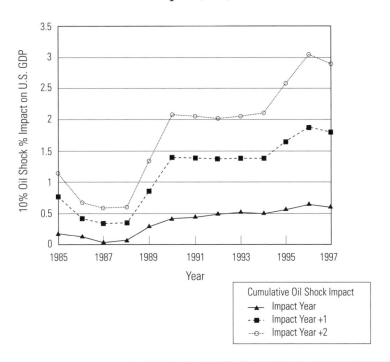

even as such operations benefit their national security interests. On the other hand, movements in globalization have resulted in Norway obtaining diminishing economic gains from oil price shocks, while Mexico's gains have stabilized rather than increased.

A very different globalization/oil shock pattern characterizes the catching-up countries (group 2). Over time, increases in the factor of general globalization have lessened the impact of oil price shocks on these countries, while trends in the financial dimension have worked to increase their severity. The net effect is that countries such as the Philippines, Portugal, and South Africa have experienced a gradual increase in the severity of oil price shocks. In Korea's case, the forces of globalization have appeared to neutralize each other. But the net effect has still been a rather constant loss in national income associated with oil price shocks. Given these patterns, naval forward presence/crisis response should continue to play an important role (but a less critical role than for group 1 countries) in stabilizing the national economies of group 2 countries.

Table 6–5. **Summary of Oil Shock Impact Analysis**

	Globalization Dimension Impact				Oil Shock Strength Over Time	Naval Forward Presence
	General Globalization	Structural Openness	Financial Globalization	Global Growth		
Group 1 Countries						
United States	+				+	++
Australia	+	+	+		(-)	++
Austria	+	+	(-)		+	++
Canada	+			+	+	++
Finland	+	+	+	(-)	+	++
France	+				+	++
Germany	+	+		+	+	++
Italy	+				+	++
Netherlands	+	+	?	+	+	++
Sweden	+	+	(-)	(-)	+	++
United Kingdom	+				+	++
Japan	+		(-)		+	+
Spain	+	+	(-)	(-)	=	+
Group 2 Countries						
Korea	(-)	+	+	(-)	=	+
Philippines	(-)	(-)	+		+	+
Portugal	(-)			(-)	+	+
South Africa	(-)		+	+	+	+
Oil Countries						
Mexico (Group 2)	(-)	(-)			=	(-)
Norway (Group 1)	(-)	(-)	+	(-)	(-)	(-)

Summary and Conclusions

The findings of all three Naval Postgraduate School studies (1997, 2000, 2001), combined with anticipated trends in globalization, suggest that the Navy's forward presence is more than likely to produce economic benefits to the United States and the other major industrial economies in the years to come. Increased integration of markets should aid in transmitting the Navy's stabilizing effect on markets.

Figure 6–7 conceptualizes and summarizes the effect of naval forward presence as a factor in our refined globalization model.

It is likely that increased world trade and increased economic growth associated with globalization will place a growing demand on oil supplies—creating, in turn, the

Figure 6–7. **Globalization and the Economic Strength of Naval Forward Presence**

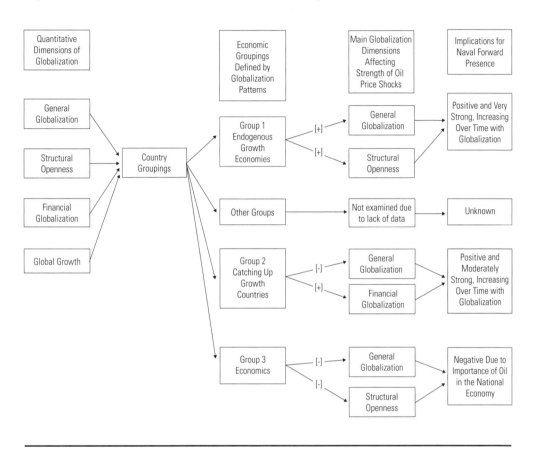

chance of more volatile oil shocks associated with crises around the world. Statistical evidence indicates that endogenous growth countries (such as the United States) sustain the greatest economic damage when oil price shocks occur. These are also the countries that fuel overall global economic growth. That fact, in itself, increases the positive economic impact of naval forces during forward-deployed naval operations. Similar arguments can be made for the effects on the share and foreign exchange markets.

Summing up, the third study's findings confirm and reinforce our original findings as to the significant and positive economic impacts associated with naval forward presence and crisis response. We have now examined seven cases and in each found benefits of at least $1 billion (over $50 billion in the Gulf War) to the U. S. economy. The third study's categorization of globalization and assessment of globalization factors indicate that, with regard to globalization, naval actions are seen to complement the positive impact that increased globalization has had on the American economy. In addition, it is argued that naval forward presence and crisis response tended to strengthen the process of globalization by providing stability and security for markets. Increased integration of markets should aid in transmitting the Navy's stabilizing effect on markets, while naval presence should aid in speeding up the process of globalization, which in and of itself is providing significant benefits to the American economy.

The statistical findings presented by the series of studies confirm many of the educated guesses made in earlier assessments concerning the links between naval actions, markets, and the U.S. economy. Likely changes in the various facets of globalization should strengthen the economic impacts of naval forward presence and crisis response. In turn, the stability provided by naval forward presence should assure continued deepening of the globalization process. This would set up a virtuous or self-replicating cycle that would reinforce itself over time.

Notes

[1] For example, see discussions in Sally Newman, "Political and Economic Implications of Global Naval Presence," in Dan Goure and Dewey Mauldin, *Naval Forward Presence: Present Status, Future Prospects* (Washington, DC: Center for Strategic and International Studies, November 1997), 47–59; and Sam J. Tangredi, "The Fall and Rise of Naval Forward Presence," U.S. Naval Institute *Proceedings* 126, no. 5 (May 2000), 29–32.

[2] This assumes the accuracy of the argument that the U.S. Navy has become "the global navy" (with benefits to the overall international community) identified in chapter 1.

[3] Anecdotal studies include: System Planning Corporation, *Political and Economic Implications of Global Naval Presence*, Report for the Office of the Deputy Chief of Naval Operations, September 30, 1996; Sally Newman, "Political and Economic Implications of Global Naval Presence;" and various papers produced by Kapos Associates, Inc. A suggestive editorial is "Oil Prices and the Navy," *The Washington Post*, May 4, 1988, 22.

[4] Summarized in Robert E. Looney, David A. Schrady, and Ronald L. Brown, "Estimating the Economic Benefits of Forward-Engaged Naval Forces," *Interfaces* (July 2001), 74–86.

[5] C. Sims, "Large Scale Econometric Models," *Econometrica* (January 1980), 1–48

[6] Anthony E. Boop and George M. Lady, "A Comparison of Petroleum Futures versus Spot Prices as Predictors of Prices in the Future," *Energy Economics* (October 1991), 274–282.

[7] M. Hashem Pesaran and Bahram Pesaran, *Working With Microfit 4.0: Interactive Econometric Analysis* (Cambridge: Camfit Data, 1997).

[8] Amartya Sen, "If It's Fair, It's Good: 10 Truths About Globalization," *International Herald Tribune*, July 14, 2001.

[9] Jeffrey Sachs, "Globalization and Patterns of Economic Development" *Weltwirtschaftliches Archiv* 136, no. 4 (2001).

[10] Robert Lucas, "On the Mechanics of Economic Development," *Journal of Monetary Economics* (July 1988), 3–42; Paul Romer, "Endogenous Technical Change," *Journal of Political Economy* (October 1990), s71–s102; Paul Romer, "Increasing Returns and Long Run Growth," *Journal of Political Economy* (October 1986), 1002–1037.

[11] Irwin Stelzer, "Oil Loses Power to Drive Boom off Course," *London Times*, January 23, 2000.

[12] Robert E. Looney, "Oil Revenues and the Dutch Disease in Saudi Arabia: Differential Impacts on Sectoral Growth," *Canadian Journal of Development Studies* 11, no. 1 (1990), 119–133.

[13] A.T. Kearney, Inc./*Foreign Policy* Magazine, "Measuring Globalization," *Foreign Policy* (January/February 2001), 56–65.

[14] Ibid., 56.

[15] Ibid.

[16] James Rosenau, "The Dynamics of Globalization: Toward an Operational Formulation," *Security Dialogue* (September 1996), 247–262.

[17] For other problems associated with the Kearney index, see Ben Lockwood, *A Note on the Robustness of the Kearney*/Foreign Policy *Globalization Index*, GSR, University of Warwick Working Paper No. 79.01, August 2001.

[18] World Bank, *World Development Indicators, 2000* (Washington, DC: World Bank, 2000).

[19] D. Bloom and Jeffrey Sachs, "Geography, Democracy, and Economic Growth in Africa," *Brookings Papers on Economic Activity*, no.2 (Washington, DC: The Brookings Institution, 1998), 207–289.

[20] Robert E. Looney, "The Viability of Arab Gulf Industrial Development: The Relative Importance of Linkages versus Size Effects," *Economia Internazionale* (July/August 1991), 228–243.

[21] Robert E. Looney, "Real or Illusionary Growth in an Oil Based Economy: Government Expenditures and Private Sector Investment in Saudi Arabia," *World Development* (September 1992), 1367–1376.

[22] An illustrative example using 1995 as a typical year is presented in annex D of Robert E. Looney, David Schrady, and Douglas Porch, *Economic Impact of Naval Forward Presence: Benefits, Linkage, and Future Prospects as Modified by Trends in Globalization* (Monterey, CA: Naval Postgraduate School, December 2001), 199–219.

[23] Ibid., 199.

[24] Ibid., 217.

[25] Ibid., 209.

[26] Ibid., 121–124, contains a discussion of the effects of the *new economy* on overall U.S. economic conditions.

[27] These factor scores are, in effect, an index formed from the weighted average of the most important elements entering into a dimension. They have a mean of zero, with positive numbers indicating an above average attainment of the country/group on that dimension. Negative scores are indicative of below average attainment of that dimension.

[28] Robert M. Dunn, Jr., "Has the U.S. Economy Really Been Globalized?" *Washington Quarterly* (Winter 2001), 53–64.

[29] The two group 1 exceptions are Spain and Japan, where financial flows have lessened somewhat the severity of oil price shocks. Nonetheless, oil price shocks still inflict considerable economic losses on these countries assuring an important role for naval crisis response.

Chapter 7

Globalization of Maritime Commerce: The Rise of Hub Ports

Daniel Y. Coulter

In an era of economic globalization, ports are evolving from being traditional interfaces between land and sea to providers of complete logistics networks. The momentum of this trend is creating a port shakeout, leading to the development of a sharply delineated hierarchy on a global scale. Ports are being increasingly differentiated by their ability to handle the latest generation of container ships coming on stream. With the trend toward even bigger container ships, fewer ports are becoming capable of handling them. As a result, the flexibility of the world seaborne trade flow is becoming increasingly constricted—particularly in the event of a natural or man-made crisis or disturbance.

While the emergence of the hub-and-spoke networks in the container liner industry in the past decade has been widely noted in shipping literature, much less has been written about the underlying maritime security implications of hub ports. With respect to vulnerabilities in seaborne trade flows, we are accustomed to thinking in terms of chokepoints, which are heavily defined by physical geography. Examples that come to mind are the Strait of Hormuz, Suez Canal, and South China Sea (the issue of chokepoint vulnerability is dealt with extensively in chapter 8). But an even more potentially disruptive effect resides within hub ports such as Singapore and Rotterdam, which possess similar attributes of a chokepoint, since they "collect" numerous trades at a single concentrated point; hence, the name "hub port."

The difference between the two lies in the response mechanisms in a disruption scenario. In the case of chokepoints, ships may deviate around an obstacle, and the business inventory cycles can adjust accordingly, since the amount of extra transit times can be calculated with a high degree of certainty. With hub ports, the effect is

---

Daniel Y. Coulter is an analyst working for the U.S. Department of Defense (DOD) in Washington, DC. Since 1991, Mr. Coulter has worked on a variety of DOD projects involving maritime security issues and has lectured and published extensively on maritime security, international trade, and naval issues.

both cascading and chaotic, since ships in a hub-and-spoke network adhere to a stringent and fixed sailing schedule. This, in turn, makes the necessary adjustments in inventory cycles more difficult to formulate quickly and effectively.

Introduction of Containerization

Since the first container ship crossed the Atlantic in May 1966, world trade has come to be dominated by containerized freight. The ubiquitous container now accounts for 60 percent of the world's trade by value and is expected to reach 70 percent by 2010. The container's success has been due to its ease of handling and the protection it offers against damage and theft.[1] One crane operator can load and unload cargoes that would have taken an army of dockworkers in the 1950s. Port turnaround times of vessels have been reduced from 3 weeks to less than 24 hours.[2] This greater efficiency has dramatically reduced the cost of shipping. Before the arrival of the container, the cost of sea freight was typically 5 to 10 percent of the value of the retail price. Now a $6,000 motorcycle can be shipped on an intercontinental journey for $85, 1.5 percent of its value, and a $1 can of beer for one cent.[3]

World trade and globalization have been facilitated by containerization, as evidenced by four significant trends:

Shift from ocean carrier to total logistics system. The carriers' strategy has shifted from a port-to-port to a door-to-door focus. The container made this shift possible by virtue of its interchangeability among the various modes of transport (road, rail, sea), giving birth to the term *intermodalism.* Containers packed with goods at the point of production can be transported over water and land without ever being opened until they reach their point of sale of final destination, creating a secure, seamless flow of goods from the manufacturer to the retailer.

Greater concentration of trade flows. The worldwide spread of containerization has led traditional commodities such as raw cotton, sugar, wood pulp, waste paper, raw timber, and even grain to become increasingly containerized. Consequently, once-specialized trade flows carrying specific commodities to ports with general cargo-handling facilities are gradually merging to form a steady stream of containers to ports equipped only to handle containers. For bulk commodities such as iron ore, coal, and crude oil, there is less concentration due to geographical diversity of supplies.

Globalization of production facilities. Manufacturing is becoming a process of bringing together and assembling raw materials, parts, and semi-finished products from all over the world. Only final assembly adjustments are carried out in local markets. To imagine the scale of this complexity, consider as an example the automotive giant, Ford:

Ford owns 154 factories worldwide. Of these, 58 are "vehicle operations" plants, which make tools/dies, fabricate body frames and stampings, and actually assemble vehicles. Then there are 55 "powertrain plants" making castings, forgings, transmissions, chassis, and engines. A further 41 plants make "automotive components," i.e., body trim, glass, fuel systems, electronics, climate control equipment, and plastic items. Then there are another 30 joint-venture plants (mainly Asia) making a whole range of items. Many of these plants' outputs must be moved to other plants as the production processes progress. In addition, the plethora of "vendor" components—brought in from outside suppliers—have to get to where they are needed.[4]

The rise of supply chain management as a discipline. With the container offering visibility in the cargo pipeline, the constant need to reduce inventory investment and speed products to the market has prompted companies to focus on supply logistics in their quest for a competitive edge. Future emphasis will center on consumers choosing to view how a product gets delivered as an actual part of what they are buying, based on the theory that as goods move faster, then the logistics directly affect the value, and overall buyer appeal rises. In this instance, speed and selection can become more important than price. As a consequence, many companies are shifting logistics strategies from "operational effectiveness" to one of customer "value maximization."[5]

Emergence of Megaships in Ocean Shipping

The ocean shipping industry today focuses on pursuing greater economies of scale to generate lower unit costs per ton or container moved. This is certainly true of the container liner industry, where the term *mega* is de rigueur. In their quest for dominance, major shipping lines are ordering megaships of 6,000 twenty-foot equivalent unit (TEU) capacity and greater in efforts to leverage their enormous economies of scale and force their smaller competitors to either be swallowed or relegated to marginal/niche trades. (Twenty-foot equivalent unit is the standard measurement of size [length] for the container shipping industry. Although containers are available in a variety of sizes, capacity is typically calculated in TEUs.)

These megaships are chiefly employed on the high-volume or mainline trade routes, and they call principally at hub ports equipped to handle them. These hub ports are dubbed *megaports* for their ability to handle these monster ships. Such ports must meet the following criteria: minimum quay length of 330 meters (m); minimum draft of 15m without tidal windows; and minimum crane outreach of 48m. The ports that qualify will then need to ensure fast turnaround times for these ships or risk losing the alliances and the many associated feeder connections. For ports not selected by the major shipping lines, the choice will then be to either invest heavily in an attempt to gain hub status or seek their market serving niche or feeder trades that typically employ ships less than 4,000–TEU capacity.

This mega phenomenon is sparking a coalescence of power, which is dividing the container world via ports along the lines of volume, strength, and reach. With plans on the drawing board for container ships up to 18,000–TEU capacity, the port shakeout is far from settled. What is clear is that there will be an inverse relationship between the size of the ship and the availability of suitable ports to handle it. The price of admission to the exclusive hub club will not be principally determined by geography factors, but rather by the amount of capital investments and politics. Dredging for deeper draft, ordering the latest generation of cranes, and expanding the land available for port development not only require huge sums of capital but also deft navigation of the political and environmental approval process.

The fate of ports worldwide is also being determined by the development of hub-and-spoke service networks. Such a network allows the ocean carriers to serve smaller markets where volumes do not warrant direct calls; reduce container repositioning costs by giving carriers multiloading opportunities and enhanced utilization of main-line vessels; eliminate duplicated ports of call for those carriers with multiple service strings; and negotiate a volume contract that can make the cost of the whole voyage, including its feeder connections, more competitive.[6]

The Hub Port as Weak Link

The vulnerabilities of just-in-time (JIT) logistics to disruption and its subsequent economic impact are well known. Consider the impact of the 17-day strike in March 1996 by a local United Auto Workers union at 2 Delphi Chassis Systems brake plants in Dayton, Ohio. The strike virtually shut down General Motors, halting production lines at 22 of its 29 assembly plants in the United States and Canada. More than 75,000 workers were without paychecks at parts and assembly plants from Chihuahua, Mexico, to Lordstown, Ohio, to Oshawa, Ontario.[7] The strike lasted long enough to shave a half a percentage point off the growth in Canada's gross domestic product (GDP) in the first quarter of 1996.[8]

It also provided a particularly instructive comment by David Andrea, director of forecasting at AutoPacific, an auto marketing firm, who said, "There just isn't the slack in the [JIT] system to keep assembly plants running for 2 to 3 weeks anymore."[9]

Indeed, like the Dayton brake plant and the oil refineries, the hub port constitutes a weak link in the global transport chain. The great Hanshin earthquake that destroyed the Japanese port of Kobe on January 17, 1995, provides an excellent case study. At the time of the earthquake, Kobe was Japan's biggest international trade hub and a major production and logistics center. It handled 25 percent of all trade from Asian countries going to North America and Europe,[10] and some 30 percent of Japan's maritime transport network was concentrated there.[11] The port accounted for 17.8 percent and 14.5 percent of Japan's total exports and imports, respectively, by value in yen.[12] The Kansai region, which includes Kobe, accounted for 20 percent of Japan's GDP[13] and for half of the world's supply of flat-panel displays found in personal computers.[14]

The global impact of the earthquake was best described by the headline that appeared 4 days later on the front page of *The New York Times*: "Quake in Japan: Kobe Earthquake Disrupts the Flow of Global Trade."[15] The article noted that the "effects of the quake, which made the port unserviceable, were being felt in many parts of the world, with companies in Japan and the United States having to hold back goods. The closing of the port and uncertainty of finding alternate routes had a domino effect."[16]

Yet the worst fears of the closure of Kobe paralyzing global trade did not materialize. The Japanese ports of Osaka, Nagoya, Tokyo, and Yokohama and the regional ports of Pusan, South Korea, and Kaohsiung, Taiwan, were able to handle the diversion of the ships en route to Kobe. The global impact was mitigated by the fact that a large part of Kobe's business involved the transshipment of containers. Since the container-handling infrastructure was relatively standardized in most Japanese ports and throughout the Pacific Rim, the diversion of container ships was accomplished with relative ease and with minimal delays. The location of transshipment was dependent not on the physical infrastructure, but rather on pricing and service.

All that changed, however, with the introduction of 6,000–TEU containerships. The 6,000–TEU number is significant since neither this specific ship designator nor the container cranes to handle these behemoths were in existence before the Kobe earthquake. The first 6,000–TEU ship did not enter service until a year later in January 1996, and the first cranes specifically designed to handle them were on the drawing board when the earthquake struck. The introduction of the 6,000–TEU ships has since forced the ocean carriers into a race to "outsize" their competitors by ordering ever larger sizes of containerships. As of 2001, the biggest container ship can handle 7,400 TEUs.

The carriers have discovered that bigger is beautiful when it comes to cost savings. In comparison to two 4,000–TEU ships, a single 8,000–TEU ship requires less capital expenditure for new building and offers up to 20 percent savings in annual operating costs. The prospect of such savings has prompted Ocean Shipping Consultants (OSC) to declare in a recent report that "8,000–TEU ships will be dominant in all trades by 2010."[17]

Since the OSC prediction in 1997, the goal post has shifted to 18,000–TEU ships, dubbed the Malacca-max containership. As the name suggests, these container ships will reach the limits of the draft in the Malacca Straits, which is the key artery for the Asia-Europe container trades. They are currently on the drawing board, but the team responsible for the Malacca concept—Professor Niko Wijnolst, chairman of the Dutch

Maritime Network foundation and former member of the marine engineering faculty at the respected Delft University of Technology, and Marco Scholtens, a Delft student of naval architecture—argues persuasively in its publication, "Malacca-Max(2): Container Shipping Network Economy," that such super ships will be a commercial reality far sooner than anyone anticipates.[18]

The significance of this statement is that as the more popular these behemoths become, the fewer ports there will be to handle them. For example, there are only four ports on the Atlantic side of North America—Halifax, Nova Scotia; Freeport, Bahamas; Hampton Roads, Virginia; and Charleston, South Carolina—that can handle the latest generation of container ships on order. Yet only two of the ports (Halifax and Freeport) can handle ships greater than (>) 6,000 TEUs when they are fully loaded. Thus, the flexibility of ships and trade to divert would not be as elastic as it was at the time of the Kobe earthquake. Not only are there significantly fewer ports capable of meeting the criteria of handling > 6,000–TEU ships, but also they are spread around the globe. This means that the loss of a hub port halfway around the world creates a cascading effect, since the > 6,000–TEU ships represent the linchpin of a fixed and regular delivery schedule on a global basis.

Linkage beyond Hub Ports

The vulnerability of the global economy to hub port disruption is best described by analogy to a cybermap of the world's Internet coverage. Such a map would consist of a network of spindly wires converging in key nodes in the cyberuniverse, similar to the hub-and-spoke network of the airline industries and the one emerging in the ocean container shipping networks. In December 2000, an accidental cut to the world's longest sub-sea cable system in the Strait of Malacca, allegedly caused by an unspecified "marine contact," brought chaos to Web links in Australia, Singapore, and Indonesia, and users in the United States, Europe, and elsewhere trying to connect with them. Losses through business interruption ran into the millions of dollars daily before repairs could be completed. During the emergency, telecommunications were able to reroute Web traffic to another sub-sea cable, but the cascading effect of the rerouting slowed down the speed of Internet connections worldwide.[19]

Now consider the world's busiest container handling port, Hong Kong, where a vessel arrives or departs every 1.2 minutes, one TEU is handled every 2 seconds, and one passenger arrives or leaves by ferry every 2 seconds.[20] Imagine the ensuing chaos to world container movements if the port of Hong Kong was crippled either accidentally or by more sinister means. The severity of the business losses would, of course, depend to a large degree on how quickly the other regional ports could absorb Hong Kong's transshipment business and how quickly the manufacturers can adjust their production schedules.

But the crippling of the port need not be through the destruction of physical assets—it can also occur through the disruption of the information systems controlling port flow. Only a sophisticated information network management system can allow the port of Hong Kong to manage the volumes and complexity of handling different cargoes all at once. If an event similar to the damage to the sub-sea cable were to occur in Hong Kong's information system, significant disruption to the port's activities would occur until repair.

This points to the growing linkage between Internetted information systems and hub port operations. As the hub ports grow bigger, even more information needs to be processed and disseminated. This makes the hub ports—and the entire maritime shipping structure—even more vulnerable to disruption of the information network itself.

Conclusion

With the global port shakeout under way, the eventual winners in the hub port sweepstakes may engender significant maritime security implications. Similar to the chokepoint concept, the hub port represents a vulnerable link in the chain of the free and orderly flow of maritime commerce. However, it differs from a chokepoint in several important respects:

- Unike in the case of chokepoints, ships beyond a certain size cannot circumvent hub ports; they have to unload and load cargoes.
- Hub ports deal with matters of sovereignty as opposed to "freedom of navigation" and "innocent passage" in strategic waterways or maritime chokepoints.
- Business inventory cycles are much more susceptible to disruption from a hub port than a chokepoint.
- The economic consequences from the loss of a hub port are much more unpredictable and immediate than from a chokepoint closure; and the threats to focal points are both electronic and physical, whereas only the latter applies to chokepoints.

These differences are further described in *Chokepoints: Maritime Economic Concerns in Southeast Asia,* a study conducted by the Center for Naval Analyses in 1996.[21] The analysis notes that if all the straits, including Malacca, Sunda, Lombok, Makassar, and the South China Sea, were closed and the ships diverted around Australia, the extra steaming costs would amount to roughly $8 billion per year based on 1993 seaborne trade flows. In sharp contrast, the same study estimated that the global economic impact from a closure of the port of Singapore alone could easily exceed $200 billion per year from disruptions to inventory and production cycles.

This disparity suggests the need for a change in strategic thinking concerning maritime security. For example, what role do navies play in defending a port against transnational threats that do not possess traditional naval attributes, such as those described in chapter 4? All of those threats have a potential impact on hub port activity. What role do navies play in cyberattacks on a port? Who is responsible for the security of landside facilities in the port? Why continue to invest in power projection capabilities at the expense of homeland defense mission?

All of those are policy issues that require in-depth analysis. But there are several preliminary suggestions that may be offered concerning our responses to the hub port phenomenon and its implications for security. First, it may be in our interest to use Federal dollars to construct (or at least encourage the development of) a series of dispersed > 6,000–TEU handling facilities. The growth of vessel size and the development of hub ports are the result of the search for efficiencies and profit by private businesses competing in a fierce shipping market. Attempts to prohibit these developments by U.S. Government legislation would inevitable place U.S. commerce at a grave disadvantage. But the development of alternative, perhaps standby, facilities that could be activated in case of hub port disruption would be in keeping with our Nation's new emphasis on homeport security. Such facilities would not be intended to replace all of the capabilities of commercially developed hub ports but would provide redundancies that would be essential to our economy and security in a crisis. Likely locations for such alternative facilities might be naval bases scheduled for downsizing or decommissioning. In 1998, for example, Maersk Shipping Lines considered the defunct Naval Air Station Quonset Point, Rhode Island, as a possible candidate for its U.S. East Coast megahub operations, which eventually went to the Port of New York/New Jersey.

Second, port protection should be viewed as a joint and interagency effort, not simply as the province of the U.S. Coast Guard (or potentially naval units). Cyberprotection of port operations should be included in our joint efforts for computer network defense (CND) for critical infrastructure. This task may be best assigned to the forthcoming Department of Homeland Security (DHS), but the Department of Defense is also developing joint CND assets. Physical protection of the landsides of our ports might be assigned to National Guard units on a regular basis or to some other force the DHS might create. Most important is that we take steps to enhance the existing (and sometimes weak) private security that currently exists.

Third, there must be a general recognition that naval assets—when called upon— should be capable of playing a significant role in the protection of U.S. ports and commerce at home, and not simply an offensive role from a forward presence posture. This is more a question of mindset and planning than of asset allocation. Any naval role would be as a supplement to U.S. Coast Guard or other port protection agencies—but if plans and training efforts are not developed, the ad hoc nature of current naval participation will not be sufficient to significantly enhance homeland security.

In the aftermath of September 11, the answers to these and other issues pertaining to maritime security have taken on new sense of urgency and will not go away any time soon. They require an institutional awareness of the potential for even greater terrorist attacks and a paradigm shift in how we handle the security of maritime trade. Only will such an awareness lead to a multifaceted and multilayered approach to the maritime and general security of global trade and economic development.

Notes

[1] As noted in chapter 4, the use of containers to smuggle weapons, drugs, and illegal migrants, as well as terrorists' bombs or weapons of mass destruction, has been recognized as a major homeland security threat. See, for example, Richard Owen and Daniel McGrory, "Business-Class Suspect Caught in Container," *The Times* (London), October 26, 2001.

[2] Charles Batchelor, "Choppy Waters Ahead: Declining Returns on Container Operations are Behind Recent Spate of Mergers," *The Financial Times*, April 25, 1997, 21.

[3] Ibid.

[4] John Critchon, "Ford—the Global Shipping Shopper," *Containerisation International* (February 1997), 33.

[5] *Intermodal Asia* (Summer 1997), 49.

[6] *Containerisation International* (June 1997), 43.

[7] Michael Clements, "GM Strike Snowballs: Local Labor Dispute Out of Control," *USA Today*, March 14, 1996, B1.

[8] Bertrand Marotte, "GM Strike Will Be Brutal for Economy," *Vancouver Sun*, October 4, 1996, D6.

[9] Clements.

[10] Florence Chong, "Kobe's Dogged Hop, Step, and Jump," *Business Times*, July 14, 1995, 6.

[11] Ibid., 2.

[12] *The Nikkei Weekly*, February 20, 1995, 3.

[13] EQE, *The January 17, 1995 Kobe Earthquake: An EQE Summary Report*, April 1995, accessed at <www.eqe.com/publications/kobe/economic.htm>.

[14] Craig Heaps, Cable News Network, January 24, 1995, transcript #721–1.

[15] Agis Salpukas, "Quake in Japan: Commerce: Kobe Earthquake Disrupts the Flow of Global Trade," *The New York Times*, January 21, 1995, 1.

[16] Ibid., 1.

[17] "Mega Boxships Loom: Ships of 13,000 TEU Possible," *Fairplay*, July 10, 1997, 38.

[18] Niko Wijnolst, "Malacca-Max-2," *Lloyd's List*, November 28, 2000, 7.

[19] James Brewer, "Internet: Malacca Break Reveals New Web of Demands," *Lloyd's List*, December 5, 2000, 2.

[20] "Hong Kong Retains Top Box Slot," *Fairplay*, January 11, 2001, 11.

[21] John H. Noer and David Gregory, *Chokepoints: Maritime Economic Concerns in Southeast Asia* (Washington, DC: National Defense University Press, 1996).

Chapter 8

Sea Lane Security and U.S. Maritime Trade: Chokepoints as Scarce Resources

Donna J. Nincic

D uring the 1970s and 1980s, there was considerable concern over the security of the world's sea lanes of communication (SLOCs)[1] and their attendant chokepoints, which were considered vulnerable to Soviet threats. For example, sea lanes in the eastern Mediterranean, Red Sea, and Indian Ocean were within range of Soviet Backfire bombers based in southern Afghanistan.[2] Similarly, Moscow's desire to acquire military facilities in Mozambique was interpreted in part as a desire to control the Mozambique Channel, a chokepoint on the critical East Africa/Western Europe–United States mineral trading route.[3] Concerns were not limited to this part of the world. In the Caribbean Sea, the fear was that the Soviets, in conjunction with Latin American allies in the region, could present a direct military threat to U.S. shipping routes in the Gulf of Mexico and could interdict key supplies at times of crisis.[4] Thus, at the height of the Cold War, there were worries that armed conflict could occur due to Soviet threats to freedom of navigation through key strategic SLOCs and chokepoints.

Concern over sea lane and chokepoint security has abated considerably since the end of the Cold War. Nevertheless, because of the globalization of the world economy and the corresponding dependence of a greater number of nations on foreign trade, the security of global maritime trade remains as critical as ever. Now, however, the threats to maritime chokepoints stem less from direct attack than from indirect threats

Donna J. Nincic is assistant professor of economics and politics at the California State University Maritime Academy, Vallejo, California. She previously taught at the University of California, Davis, and currently serves as a member of the Advisory Board of MAST (Maritime Anti-Terrorist Security Team), a private firm that advises the shipping industry on piracy and other security threats. Her latest publication is "From Sea-Lanes to Global Cities: The Policy Relevance of Political Geography," in *Being Useful: Policy Relevance and International Relations Theory*, ed. Miroslav Nincic and Joseph Lepgold (Ann Arbor: University of Michigan Press, 2000).

such as piracy, collisions, and regional instability, all of which could reduce their utility to ocean-borne trade. When taken together, these indirect threats to a natural resource—the SLOC chokepoints—can impede passage through maritime trade routes or make them economically scarce and subject them to a greater likelihood of conflict. Thus, the current threats to global sea trade routes and their implications for U.S. trade and national security are best grasped when chokepoints are viewed as increasingly scarce *natural resources.*

Resource Scarcity, Conflict, and Sea Lanes

In the 1960s, concern about the natural environment led to recognition of the limits imposed by nature on human ambitions. A first wave of writing warned of the dangers of environmental degradation and advocated policies to avoid catastrophe, but it did not explicitly link environmental concerns to national security. In recent years, the concept of *environmental security* has evolved to merge these two areas. While this concept may refer to the application of security theories to environmental issues[5] or the environmental deterioration resulting from conflict or war,[6] it has typically come to refer to the conflict that can result from scarcities of natural resources stemming from population and/or economic growth.

This latter approach is most closely associated with the work of Thomas Homer-Dixon, whose *Project on Environmental Change and Acute Conflict* has highlighted the relationship between population growth, which leads to environmental degradation—particularly of nonrenewable resources—and ethnic and regional violence in developing countries.[7] For example, farmland deterioration in Bangladesh, leading to migrations into neighboring India, subsequently led to a violent insurgency in the 1980s between the original Buddhist and Christian population and the Hindu migrants.[8] Similarly, disputes over access to the fertile farmland along the Senegal River led to an explosion of ethnic violence between blacks and Moors in Senegal and Mauritania in 1989.

Other authors have written on the relationship between resource scarcity and conflict as well. Nazli Choucri and Robert North were among the first to establish a relationship between growth, resource scarcity, and conflict. In *Nations in Conflict*, they suggest that natural resource scarcities within a country may provoke wars with other countries over access to alternate supplies of that resource.[9] Arthur Westing also noted that over one dozen 20th-century wars—including those not particularly noted as "resource wars"—often had a resource scarcity component to them.[10] According to his argument, both World War I and World War II were concerned in part with access to oil, iron, and other minerals. More recently, the Falklands conflict between Britain and Argentina was as much about control over the rich fish and oil reserves around the islands as it was about historical sovereignty claims. While emphases may differ among each of these and other authors, all argue that resources that are both economically important and scarce can produce conflict between the nations and groups that need and/or use them. Additionally, most authors tie resource scarcity directly to the twin processes of population growth and economic growth.

There is some debate, however, on whether issues of environmental degradation can or should be considered matters of national security. Typically, this is suggested because of a belief that environmental degradation is so acute and serious as to threaten the conditions for human life and that because national security by definition implies the protection of human life, environmental degradation must become a security issue. The threat from, and protection against, acid rain or deforestation, for example, is considered on par with protection against invasion or terrorist attacks. Responses to environmental degradation, therefore, span a continuum from viewing the problem within a national security paradigm to military action to address either the ecological damage or its consequences. In the first instance, imposing a national security framework on the issue is believed to increase the likelihood that resources will be devoted to the objective and the problems resolved. If political leaders and the public believed, for example, that meeting the challenge of the deterioration of the ozone layer is as important as meeting the Soviet challenge was during the Cold War, greater funding would probably be devoted to the problem. In the second instance, it is believed that many problems of environmental deterioration will elicit a military response to prevent more bloodshed in the future. It may be increasingly necessary to militarize environmental politics—in some cases of migrations provoked by deteriorated farmland, for example—to prevent ethnic conflict in the future between the indigenous and migrant populations. While some may disagree with this perspective, it is clear that some natural resources are generally considered so economically vital as to make them national security issues. Oil is the prime example here.

However, other economically important resources not typically considered "natural resources" can be considered scarce and capable of provoking conflict: specifically, the chokepoints of the world's maritime trade routes.[11] The world's SLOCs and chokepoints are vital to the world economy, especially to an increasingly globalized economy. Maritime transport still remains the most inexpensive means of transporting bulk goods; consequently, over 80 percent of the world's trade involves ocean transit.[12] In the United States, more than 95 percent of all foreign commerce is maritime, flowing through more than 300 deep draft ports.[13] And international trade is projected to reach 2 billion tons within the next 20 years—twice today's levels.

While there are hundreds of chokepoints of regional and local economic importance, fewer than two dozen lie on the world's international maritime trade routes (see figure 8–1), endowing them with global economic significance. Of these, nearly half

Figure 8–1. **World Vital Chokepoints**

Eastern Mediterranean and Persian Gulf	Eastern Pacific	Europe	Africa	The Americas
Bosporus	Strait of Malacca	Great Belt	Mozambique Channel	Panama Canal
Dardanelles	Sunda Strait	Kiel Canal		Cabot Strait
Suez Canal	Lombok Strait	Dover Strait		Florida Straits
Strait of Hormuz	Luzon Strait	Strait of Gibraltar		Yucatan Channel
Bab-el Mandab	Singapore Strait			Windward Passage
	Makassar Strait			Mona Passage

are vulnerable to a form of stress or threat that could make them economically scarce resources. As such, they may become a source of conflict between nations.

Sea Lanes as Scarce Resources

The security of maritime trade hinges on the conception of sea lanes and chokepoints as scarce resources. Resource scarcities are typically characterized as *absolute* (the resource is nonrenewable) or *relative*; that is, "limited with respect to human wants and needs"[14] (some scholars refer to these as Malthusian and Ricardian scarcities, respectively), but what all definitions have in common is that resource scarcity reflects the forces of supply and demand. In other words, scarcity of a resource implies that the quantity available and/or accessible falls short of effective demand. A resource is scarce when its supply is threatened: either the resource is nonrenewable or it is being used up too quickly to renew itself. Scarcity also exists when there is an increase in demand for the resource and, for whatever reason (typically because the supply of the good is fixed or diminishing and it has few, if any, substitutes), the market cannot set the price high enough to regulate the demand for the resource (the resource is price-inelastic).

Fixed Supply

Even at the end of the 20th century, most of the world's goods continue to be traded by ship. Despite technological advances in transportation systems, prevailing winds, as well as ocean currents and predominant weather patterns, still determine the safest and most efficient trade routes. Certain parts of the oceans are off-limits during certain times of the year due to the threat of waves of severe destructive force. Zones of violent wave activity exist in the Atlantic and North Pacific during the winter, primarily between latitudes 50° and 60°N (including the British Isles and North Sea countries), and in the corresponding latitudes during the summer in the southern ocean (affecting the increasingly used Cape Horn and Strait of Magellan routes). Similarly, ships transiting the Indian Ocean, the tropical southwest Pacific, the West Indies, and the China Sea during the monsoon season may also encounter waves of destructive force sufficient to damage or sink even a modern merchant vessel.

For these reasons, the world's ocean trading routes have remained relatively fixed for centuries, and few have been added to regular use. There are only a few exceptions: as ship design and technology have allowed for larger, faster, and stronger ships, some shippers have become more willing to transit their fleets through increasingly dangerous waters. For example, the Cape of Good Hope (around southern Africa), the Straits of Magellan and Cape Horn (around South America), and, to a lesser extent, the Northwest Passage across North America are now routinely used most months of the year.

Another factor unrelated to the physical nature of the ocean that discourages the addition of new trade routes is the extremely high cost of creating manmade routes where none existed before. Projects such as the Panama and Suez Canals are not likely to be replicated in the future. One notable exception involves the oil trade, where pipelines are increasingly replacing shipping. This is the preferred option for many oil producers in the new oil fields around the Caspian Sea. Instead of shipping through the already congested Turkish Straits, producers would rather expand the existing network of pipelines to bypass the Straits altogether. Similarly, the Suez Canal and the Strait of Hormuz have lost some of their traffic to pipelines in recent years. For nonoil and gas trade, however, the available supply of SLOCs and chokepoints must be considered reasonably fixed. With the addition of the Cape Horn, Cape of Good Hope, Northwest Passage, and Strait of Magellan routes, very few areas of the ocean are left where it is feasible or necessary to add new trade routes.

Increased Demand

On the demand side, chokepoints can also be considered scarce resources because of the growing volume of global maritime trade. Pressure on existing SLOCs is increasing because more nations than ever now belong to the global capitalist trading system, and most of the world's international trade moves by ship. More trading nations mean more shipping nations, which, in turn, mean more ships on the world's sea lanes and transiting global chokepoints. According to the United Nations Conference on Trade and Development (UNCTAD):

> Strong growth in the demand for dry bulk cargoes will help world seaborne trade grow by an estimated 3.8% this year [1997], to a record 4.94bn tones. . . . [UNCTAD] expects dry bulk cargoes to grow by 5.1%. . . . [S]eaborne trade grew by 2.3% in 1996.[15]

Figure 8–2. **U.S. Foreign Waterborne Trade, 1980–1999 (million metric tons)**

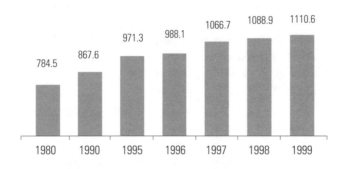

In the United States, foreign waterborne commerce increased by 41.6 percent between 1980 and 1999, as can be seen in figure 8–2.

While maritime trade has grown worldwide, nowhere is increased demand more evident than in Asia. Since coastal areas achieve faster growth than do inland areas, even in the same country,[16] exports from this region are moving primarily by ship throughout the region's extensive access to ocean sea lanes and inland waterways. Dependence on shipping in this part of the world is intensified by a scarce land and air transport infrastructure for large-scale trade. Rapid economic growth in the world's coastal areas places an increased demand on SLOCs and chokepoints. What was true in Adam Smith's time remains true today: despite technological advances in rail, road, and air transport, sea-based trade remains the most cost-effective means of international trade.[17] Consequently, merchant shipping tonnage has doubled in the western Pacific in recent years,[18] and maritime traffic on the United States–Asia dry bulk cargo routes is expected to double in the next century.[19]

Other chokepoints are also under stress due to increased demand. The Panama Canal is currently described as "clogged due to heavy use by ships,"[20] and demand is only expected to increase in the future. The canal, already operating at full capacity, is anticipating an 18.5 percent rise in traffic by 2010 and a 48 percent rise (from current levels) by the middle of the century. A planned $1 billion program to boost capacity by 20 percent will only take care of short-term needs.[21] Additionally, the special pressures placed on those SLOCs and chokepoints feeding the Middle East oil trade must be considered. The U.S. Department of Energy anticipates that world demand for oil will grow by 44 percent between 1995 and 2015, with most of the increase being met

Figure 8–3. **Resource Scarcity Summary: Increased Demand**

SLOC/Chokepoint	Importance to the United States	Demand
Turkish Straits	Black Sea and Caspian Sea Oil	1996: 123 ships/day 1997: 137 ships/day
Strait of Malacca	Asian/Oil Trade	2000: 200+ ships/day
Sunda Strait	Asian/Oil Trade	3,500/year
Lombok/Makassar Straits	Asian/Oil Trade	3,900/year
Singapore Strait	Asian/Oil Trade	1997: 200 ships/day
Strait of Hormuz	Global Oil Trade	1997: 60 ships/day
Panama Canal	U.S. East Coast-Asia, West Coast-Europe Trade	1997: 37 ships/day 2010: 44 ships/day 2050: 55 ships/day

by the Persian Gulf nations.[22] As will be discussed in detail in chapter 10, much of this oil will be flowing to the Far East through chokepoints.

Decreased/Threatened Supply: Physical Constraints

Chokepoints are affected both by decreased supply and increased demand. While the physical supply of them is, for all practical purposes, fixed, and there are few current, economically viable, substitutes, the *effective* supply—that is, *availability*—is threatened by a number of factors (piracy, physical degradation, and the like) that may reduce or restrict their availability. Threats to supply can take two forms: physical constraints that restrict passage and actions by states or nonstate actors that threaten or restrict free passage through the chokepoint.

The geographical characteristics of many of the world's chokepoints present increasing problems to global maritime traffic, and the greater numbers of ships using these transit points magnify many of their physical limitations. The problem is two-fold: the physical characteristics of some chokepoints, combined with the increased size (length, width, and draft) of new merchant ships, have rendered a few chokepoints impassable. At the same time, the geography of some chokepoints, combined with both the increased size of new ships and increased traffic, has increased the likelihood of accident and environmental damage. While problems in their own right, accidents and environmental damage may also require temporary closing of, or at least restricted access to, a chokepoint.

Many chokepoints are extremely narrow, often only a mile or two at their narrowest point. Some are so narrow (the Turkish Straits, for example) that they have to be closed to two-way traffic when the largest ships are in transit, because their breadth requires the simultaneous use of both the inbound and outbound traffic lanes when they negotiate turns. In other cases, navigation difficulties of the larger ships through the narrowest straits are compounded by attendant tide, current, and wind extremes. In still other cases, depth is the paramount issue, as silt begins to accumulate in the narrow passageways.

Depth is a serious issue for the Suez Canal as ships, especially oil tankers, have become considerably larger over time.[23] Traffic through the Suez Canal fell by 9.4 percent in 1995 over 1994 levels and by 8 percent during the first half of 1996.[24] In an effort to lure back lost traffic, the Suez Canal Authority (SCA) has frozen canal tolls at 1994 levels,[25] has agreed to consider extending existing bulk carrier rebates for longer periods (an act intended to attract ships that would otherwise use the Cape route),[26] and is seeking an agreement with its main competitor, the Sumed (Suez-Mediterranean) pipeline, to prohibit any tanker small enough to transit the canal from using the pipeline.[27] Despite the SCA attempts to lure back lost traffic, the canal still cannot handle the world's largest oil tankers. The fully laden very large crude carriers require transit depths of 68 to 70 feet; current dredging operations will attain a depth of only 62 feet by the year 2000.[28]

Depth is also a serious issue for the Panama Canal. Currently, the canal can only accommodate ships up to 65,000 tons, meaning that the new megaships of 150,000 tons, with correspondingly deeper draft, have to use the longer, and more dangerous, Cape Horn or Strait of Magellan routes or avoid the canal trade altogether. While these "post-Panamax" ships currently comprise only 8 percent of the world fleet, they are expected to account for 30 percent of it within the next 30 years.[29] During the 1997–1998 El Niño event, draft restrictions were particularly severe. In normal years, maximum allowable draft in the canal is 12.04 meters. During the El Niño, which resulted in drought conditions in the canal zone, the maximum allowable draft had to be lowered to as little as 10.52 meters.[30]

Accidents are an increased concern in many chokepoints as near-misses or actual collisions or groundings highlight the dangers of ever-larger ships carrying cargoes that could create an environmental or human disaster if an accident should occur. We are all familiar with oil spills caused by human error in navigationally challenging situations, but these are not the only dangers that exist. Many ships carry chemicals that, if released, could result in great loss of life. A close call occurred in the narrow entrance to the San Francisco Bay when a tanker carrying lethal liquefied anhydrous ammonia lost steering and threatened to collide with the Golden Gate Bridge. Attempts to regain

Figure 8–4. **Resource Scarcity Summary: Physical Constraints**

SLOC/Chokepoint	Importance to the United States	Physical Constraints
Suez Canal	Red Sea Trade	Silting, Depth
Panama	Coast-to-Coast	Aging Infrastructure, Depth Width

control of the ship, which were ultimately successful, were complicated by the fact that the 561-foot tanker had little room to maneuver in the narrow shipping channel.[31]

Another problem area is the Turkish Straits, due to the recent development of the Caspian Sea oil fields. The early oil from these fields will pass through the Bosporus and Dardanelles from the Caspian Sea to the Black Sea by pipeline, through the Sea of Marmara, and out into the Mediterranean by ship, adding to an already near-capacity flow of traffic through the Straits. Turkey has expressed strong environmental concerns about any increase in shipping traffic, citing its fear of increases in collisions and major oil spills. These worries are not without foundation: between 1988 and 1994, the number of collisions increased dramatically, including a major oil spill in 1994 that burned for a week in the narrow Straits.[32] In 1996, Turkish Energy Minister Nusnu Dogan said that the amount of oil transited through the Bosporus could be raised safely by only an additional 20 percent. More than that could mean closing the strait to two-way sea traffic for 8 hours "almost every day."[33]

Decreased/Threatened Supply: State Challenges to Free Passage

The behavior of a handful of nations has threatened free passage through some of the world's chokepoints. Those most affected include the straits in and bordering the South China Sea; the Strait of Hormuz in the Persian Gulf; and the Turkish straits of the Bosporus and the Dardanelles. In each case, littoral powers have undertaken or threatened actions that—sometimes inadvertently—have threatened free passage. State challenges to free passage are of two forms: disputed state claims and state military actions.

Disputed State Claims

Unhindered navigation is currently or has been recently disputed in three sea lanes of concern to the United States: the Northwest Passage, the Turkish Straits, and in Indonesia. In the Northwest Passage, national security and future oil trade are at stake. In the case of Turkey, the trade—especially the oil trade—of our European trading partners is affected. In the case of Indonesia, safe and efficient passage through the arch-ipelagic straits is of vital national security importance for the United States.

The Northwest Passage. The Northwest Passage is the long-sought-for trade route into the Arctic Circle above Canada. Accessed from the Davis Strait on the East and the Bering Strait on the West, it passes through waters that are ice-bound for much of the year. Although it was first navigated successfully by ship in 1906 by the Norwegian ex-plorer Roald Amundson, it was not until 1969 that the first commercial vessel—Hum-ble Oil Company's *Manhattan,* a refitted tanker specially strengthened for ice condi-tions—made its way, with the additional assistance of two ice breakers, through the passage. Between 1942 and 1998, about 50 successful transits were made of the North-west Passage, about half of which were by icebreakers.

The *Manhattan* voyage sparked the beginning of a dispute between the United States and Canada over the sovereignty of the Northwest Passage. In May 1969, Ottawa informed the United States that Canada was claiming, among other things, the Arctic waters as national terrain. The United States believes the passage through the channels of the Canadian Arctic archipelago is an international strait. As such, it challenges Canada's understanding that the passage is part of Canadian internal waters.

At issue is the degree to which Canada can assert control over the passage. If, in-deed, the passage is part of Canadian internal waters, full Canadian sovereignty ob-tains: Canada can require states to request permission to transit the passage, and Ot-tawa can impose environmental restrictions on its use. However, if the passage is declared an international strait—the U.S. position—Canada can impose only limited restrictions on the innocent passage[34] of ships using the strait.[35]

The dispute took on new importance in 1985, with the voyage of the U.S. Coast Guard icebreaker *Polar Sea* through the passage.[36] Until the sailing of the *Manhattan,* U.S. interests in the passage had been essentially strategic. Canada had long been con-sidered a first line of defense from the Soviet Union, primarily as part of an early warn-ing system for protection against the threat of Soviet nuclear ballistic submarines (only icebreakers and nuclear submarines can transit the passage unaided). The *Manhattan* voyage shifted the focus to the economic viability of the passage as a trade route for Alaskan oil; the *Polar Sea* transit shifted the focus back to U.S. security.

The argument could be made that as long as commercial traffic requires the as-sistance of icebreakers, the Northwest Passage is unlikely to become a viable commer-cial route, thus making the dispute purely academic. However, a final note is in order. Global warming is occurring to such a degree in Arctic waters that, with the polar ice cap melting, commercial ships may start using the Arctic route instead of going through the Panama Canal—a shortcut of more than 4,000 nautical miles.[37] While the route is not expected to be entirely ice-free, advances in oil tankers, such as double hulling, make it feasible to consider transit without icebreaker assistance. Furthermore, the rise in oil prices makes the production of Alaskan oil more feasible and, when oil production in the North Sea winds down, the passage could become important for oil exports to Europe.[38] This scenario is examined in considerable detail in chapter 9.

Clearly, Washington has not desired an overt conflict with Canada; the intent has always been to play down the dispute and "agree to disagree." Nevertheless, the concerns—most actively voiced by the U.S. Defense Department—have been about the international precedent that might be established were any agreement reached that recognized Canadian claims. If Canada were able to limit transit passage on the grounds of national sovereignty or environmental conservation, then other coastal states with straits of national security importance to the United States (such as Indonesia and the Philippines) might be able to do the same.

The Turkish Straits. The Turkish Straits—the Bosporus and the Dardanelles, anchoring either end of the Sea of Marmara—are historically among the strategically most important straits in the world. Connecting the Black Sea with the Mediterranean, they provide Russia and many of the former Soviet republics with the only warm-water access to the rest of the world. With the increased importance of the Caspian Sea oil, the Straits become even more vital, as they provide at the moment the only viable means of transporting the oil to the rest of the world.[39]

The Turkish Straits are currently operating at capacity. By some estimates, it is three times busier than the Suez Canal and four times busier than the Panama Canal.[40] This has led the Turkish government to seek means of restricting and/or controlling the passage of ships through the Straits; in 2001, Turkish Foreign Minister Ismail Cem announced that Turkey intended to levy substantial tolls on oil passing through the Bosporus.[41] This poses a significant challenge to international law; the Straits are an international waterway, covered by international treaty and law and, as such, can have only limited passage restrictions placed on them. While states are allowed to impose restrictions on international waterways for environmental reasons, some fear Turkey's proposed toll scheme is a way to gain control over the lucrative Caspian oil trade. If this were to occur, and as more oil comes from the former Soviet Union, the Bosporus could become a strategic chokepoint comparable to the Strait of Hormuz.

The Russians are particularly opposed to any further Turkish attempts to restrict passage through the Straits. When the Straits are closed to two-way traffic to allow for the passage of ships in excess of 150 meters in length, ships must wait at the entrance to the Bosporus for the Straits to reopen. As it is, two-way traffic was suspended for 1,550 hours in 1997, forcing delays for some 3,774 ships.[42] The Russians are concerned at the extent of the wait and are trying to change the International Maritime Organization ruling that granted Turkey the right to impose a traffic separation scheme in the Straits. Russia's position is that as the Bosporus and Dardanelles are an international strait, no restrictions should be allowed.

An argument can be made in support of the Turkish position that congestion has reached a point in the Straits where environmental and human disasters become a significant risk. Between 1988 and 1992, 155 collisions occurred in the Straits. With so much of the Straits traffic comprised of oil, the threat of environmental damage is significant. For example, in 1994 the Greek Cypriot tanker *Nassia* collided with another ship in the Straits. Thirty seamen were killed, and 20,000 tons of oil were spilled into the Straits, creating a slick that burned for 5 days.[43] Major spills plus the routine release of contaminated ballast water has contributed to a decline in fishing levels in the region to one-sixtieth of their former levels.[44]

The United States currently has no formal position on the Turkish Straits dispute, but this may change as Caspian oil becomes increasingly important. With oil reserves estimated at the size of those of Kuwait, U.S. firms are responsible for much of the Caspian oil exploration and extraction. It then becomes critical to ensure that the oil gets to market safely and securely. It should be noted that the United States has opposed one of the more favored plans for Caspian oil transportation, which would allow the oil to bypass the Straits altogether: a series of pipelines through Iran to the Persian Gulf. This means that for the foreseeable future, Caspian oil will be transited through the Straits. Any attempt to affect significantly the flow of oil would raise serious concerns—as in the case of the Northwest Passage—about transit rights in other critical chokepoints and waterways of the world.

Indonesia. In 1996, Indonesia announced that it intended to restrict military and commercial shipping to three lanes running through the archipelago (the Sunda Strait between Sumatra and Java, the Lombok Strait between the islands of Bali and Lombok, and through the Moluccan Sea). Access to the critical Strait of Malacca was to be restricted. The United States lodged an "angry protest" with the Suharto government, as Indonesia's actions would keep U.S. naval forces out of the sea lane that runs between Java, Sumatra, and Borneo, thereby hindering the movement of its naval forces in a crisis.[45] The immediate crisis was resolved, but concerns remain. For example, in fall 1997, the U.S. aircraft carrier *Nimitz* was deployed in Asia; at the same time, the crisis over United Nations (UN) inspections in Iraq was beginning to intensify, and the Clinton administration decided it needed quickly to position a credible military threat in the Persian Gulf. With guaranteed navigation rights, the *Nimitz* was allowed to sail through the South China Sea, through the Strait of Malacca, off the coast of India, and then up to the Gulf. Without these rights, it would have had to have circumvented Australia to remain in international waters at all times, adding some 5,800 nautical miles and 15 days to the trip (assuming a speed of 15 knots). Additionally, restrictions on transit through Malacca would add millions of dollars to the cost of shipping between Australia and Japan.

State Military Actions

Wars have been justified by maritime trade route security concerns on several occasions since the end of World War II. In 1956, when Egyptian President Gamal Nasser nationalized the Suez Canal, British and French troops, along with Israel, invaded the Canal Zone. U.S. President Dwight Eisenhower pressured Britain, France, and Israel into agreeing to a cease-fire and eventual withdrawal from Egypt. The war itself lasted only a week, and invading forces were withdrawn within the month. Suez was again the scene of conflict in 1967. Having excluded Israeli ships from the Suez Canal since May 1948, Egypt's Nasser blockaded the Gulf of Aqaba in 1967, Israel's only access to the Red Sea. Israel responded, resulting in the Six-Day War. On June 6, 1967, Egypt closed the Suez Canal and broke relations with the United States. UN Resolution 242, passed in its aftermath to lay down the principles for Middle East peace, had as one of its conditions free navigation for all ships through international waterways such as the Suez Canal. However, the canal remained closed for the next 15 years due to continued military skirmishes in the canal region.

During the Iran-Iraq war of the 1980s, military actions between the warring parties threatened the passage of tankers through the Persian Gulf and the Strait of Hormuz. Iran's threats to disrupt oil tanker traffic led Kuwait to seek protection from the Soviet Union, an overture that dramatically raised the stakes for the United States. At the urging of the Department of State and the Pentagon, the United States undertook the reflagging of 11 Kuwaiti oil tankers and provided a naval escort for their transit through the Strait of Hormuz.

A final example of military action to keep a vital sea lane open occurred with the U.S. military intervention in Panama. Guillermo Endara was elected to the presidency in May 1989, but General Manuel Noriega, who was considered threatening to U.S. interests in the region, annulled the elections. While the primary objective of Operation *Just Cause* in December 1989 was to restore Endara to power and to remove Noriega, a secondary objective was to keep the canal open. Noriega had, on more than one occasion, threatened to close the canal by sinking several ships in it.

Currently, military actions—large, visible naval buildups—are of concern in two areas: the South China Sea and the Persian Gulf/Strait of Hormuz.

The South China Sea. Concerns arise largely because of China's claim, in 1992, to 95 percent of the South China Sea as its territorial waters.[46] Contrary to international law, which recognizes only a 12-nautical-mile territorial sea plus a 200-mile exclusive economic zone, this area extends up to 1,000 miles from the Chinese mainland and includes Japan and the Philippines within Beijing's security range. This area also includes the Spratly, Paracel, and Senkaku island chains, which China claims as its own and which are contested in varying degrees by six other states: Taiwan, the Philippines, Indonesia, Vietnam, Brunei, and Malaysia. The Philippines, Malaysia, and Brunei claim specific parts of the South China Sea, while China, Taiwan, and Vietnam claim all of its islands, islets, and reefs. In addition, China and the Philippines have staked a claim to many of the submerged features as well (most of the reefs, cays, and shoals are under water much of the year.)[47] The disputes over the Spratly Islands—230 islands, islets, and reefs comprising a mere 3.1 square miles of entirely uninhabitable land—are the most worrisome as they lay directly in the path of shipping lanes that converge on the Indonesian Straits. These vital sea lanes transport oil from the Middle East to Japan and the west coast of the United States. Approximately one quarter of the world's total shipping trade passes through this contested area every year.[48]

China has backed its claims with armed force on more than one occasion. In March 1988, Vietnamese and Chinese forces clashed, resulting in the deaths of 72 people, the loss of 2 Vietnamese ships, and the occupation by China of 6 islands.[49] A more recent example is its brief military standoff with the Philippines in 1995 over Mischief Reef in the Spratlys. China has also engaged in a number of large and sometimes bellicose military exercises, such as those that coincided with the presidential elections in Taiwan in March 1996 when Beijing engaged in live-fire wargames off the southeast coast near the Taiwan Strait involving more than 10 warships and as many aircraft dropping bombs.

China's contentions with Indonesia—the world's largest natural gas exporter—over the Natunas Islands is particularly troubling. In dispute since 1993, when China published a map showing "historic claims" to the islands, the Natunas are rich in oil and natural gas. In September 1996, the Indonesian military conducted its most extensive wargames in 4 years on the islands; the location was chosen to carry the message that "the Natunas belong to Indonesia."[50]

China's perceived ambitions are not the only concern in the South China Seas. In July 1997, Singapore increased the number of its armed vessels patrolling the South China Sea with the intent of securing the area's sea lanes. The addition of two navy patrol vessels was justified on the grounds that "freedom of navigation through the Malacca and Singapore Straits as well as the South China Sea is fundamental to the continued survival and prosperity of Singapore," in the words of the Minister for Foreign Affairs and Law, Shanmugam Jayakumar.[51]

In none of these incidents has merchant shipping been the direct target of state actions. Rather, the worry is that were a regional territorial dispute to escalate, merchant shipping would have to be detoured—for reasons of safety—around the zone of conflict. This loss, even temporarily, of some of the world's most important shipping lanes would disrupt trade, extend transit schedules significantly, and result in higher prices. At the same time, were a conflict to occur, merchant ships bound for an adversary's territory could be intercepted, harassed, or worse.

The Strait of Hormuz. The Strait of Hormuz, by far the world's most critical oil chokepoint, lies at the entrance to the Persian Gulf. Over 14 million barrels of oil pass through the Strait each day. At its narrowest, the Strait consists of two 1-mile-wide channels for inbound and outbound tanker traffic, as well as a 2-mile-wide buffer zone. Closure of the Strait could require the use of longer alternate routes, if available, at increased transportation costs.[52] The most serious concerns in the region center around Iran and Iraq, Iran being considered the greatest long-term threat to U.S. interests in the region because of its strategic position at the entrance to the strait, controlling access between the Persian Gulf and the rest of the world. In early 1995, Iran deployed some 6,000 troops and heavy weapons on Abu Musa (also claimed by the United Arab Emirates) and other islands at the entrance to the strait. At the time, then-Secretary of Defense William Perry said that the deployment, which also included antiship Silkworm missiles and air defense missiles, "can only be regarded as a potential threat to shipping in the area."[53]

Passage through Hormuz is an issue of concern several times a year when Iran holds its wargames at the mouth of the Gulf. In April 1996, the Iranian Navy conducted a series of naval maneuvers that had the effect of slowing ship traffic through the Strait of Hormuz. The action intimidated oil tanker owners "into holding their ships back from potentially risky passages through [the] Strait, thus temporarily raising spot oil prices and helping fuel the dramatic 'week of hell' price drop in U.S. capital markets."[54] (According to chapter 6, this incident was an example of the market effects of a lack of naval presence.)

Freedom of Navigation Program

In 1992, the U.S. Navy and Marine Corps detailed a new strategy in a white paper entitled . . . *From the Sea* (rearticulated in 1994 by a follow-on paper, *Forward . . . From the Sea*). This strategy is based on power projection and crisis response in littoral regions. The new doctrine recognizes that, for the foreseeable future, naval control of the sea is not likely to be challenged; rather, the threats that the Navy will be called upon to counter are expected to be regional, not global, and the potential opponents will be diverse, potentially dispersed, and individually far less powerful than the former Soviet Union. Rather than blue-water sea control, the new concept calls for control over littoral areas and support of land activities through integrated operations with the Marine Corps, Army, and Air Force.

The strategy calls for the U.S. Navy to operate more actively in coastal zones— precisely the area that is being used most intensively and the area to which states are making increased claims. An emphasis of the new U.S. littoral focus has been to ensure that other states recognize the legal right of all to operate freely in international waters and respect the navigational provisions of the United Nations Convention on the Law of the Sea (UNCLOS) III. This is critical for U.S. naval—as well as commercial—mobility through the world's sea lanes and is directly tied to the rise of regional threats and the need to respond quickly to these threats as they arise. Because of this consideration, the U.S. Navy has been charged with the Freedom of Navigation program, introduced during the Jimmy Carter presidency. The objective of the program has been to ensure that all states recognize the legal right to operate freely in international waters and respect the navigation provisions of UNCLOS III. Since 1979, U.S. military ships and aircraft have asserted navigational rights against excessive claims of more than 35 countries, at the rate of 30 to 40 per year.

Decreased/Threatened Supply: Nonstate Challenges to Free Passage

As explained in chapter 4, nonstate actors increasingly challenge the sovereignty of states and their ability to have an effect on international affairs. While the state remains the predominant actor on the world stage, nonstate actors—especially those whose actions defy the norms and values of the international community—will play an increasingly significant role.[55] Nonstate actors "undermine law and order, and . . . create conditions conducive to instability and conflict." For commercial traffic through chokepoints and SLOCs, pirates and maritime terrorists are the primary concerns. Unlike nation-states, pirates and terrorists will not attempt to resolve their differences through diplomatic means, using "violence and intimidation" to undermine states and the international system.[56]

Maritime Piracy

Threats to merchant shipping from piracy are a serious, if little-known, problem and have been on the rise worldwide since the early 1990s.[57] The international shipping industry regards several key areas of the world's oceans as particularly at risk from attacks by pirates. In Asia, these include the Singapore Strait, Indonesian, Vietnamese, and Philippine waters and, to a lesser extent, the whole of the South China Sea. Other risk areas comprise West Africa—especially from Mauritania to Angola—and the eastern coast of South America, as well as occasional occurrences off the Horn of Africa, East Africa, Sri Lanka, India, and Bangladesh. Brazil, Colombia, and Venezuela are highlighted in South America, with attacks also occurring in Mexico in Latin America and the Caribbean. Somalia is of special concern, and mariners are routinely warned to transit at least 50 miles from the coast to avoid attack. Pirate attacks are increasing throughout the entire Caribbean Sea, with attacks on shipping often aimed at seizing vessels for use in drug trafficking.[58] Additional attacks have been reported in the Mediterranean and Black Seas. Most of the attacks in Asia and the

Figure 8–5. **Number of Reported Pirate Attacks Worldwide, 1994–2000**

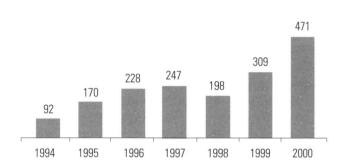

Caribbean occurred while the ships or yachts were in transit; the majority of the remainder were reported in territorial waters, while the ships were at anchor or berthed.

The United Nations Convention on the High Seas (1958) and Convention on the Law of the Sea (1982) define *maritime piracy* as "an attack mounted for private ends on a ship, involving violence, illegal detention of persons or property, or the theft of destruction of goods" that is "directed on the high seas or in a place outside the jurisdiction of any state." Inside territorial waters, the laws of littoral states determine what actions constitute piracy, and most subsume piracy under offense categories such as murder, assault, robbery, or theft. However, the International Maritime Bureau (IMB), an offshoot of the International Chamber of Commerce, has adopted a practical, rather than legal, definition of piracy within a largely commercial frame of reference. The IMB definition refers simply to "any act of boarding any vessel with the intent to commit theft or other crime and with the capability to use force in furtherance of the act." It is thus wider than the UN definition and ignores questions of jurisdiction. For our purposes, the majority of pirate attacks could simply be described as "armed robbery at sea" or the intent to commit such an act.

While data on pirate attacks is difficult to obtain,[59] the cost of pirate attacks is estimated at $16 billion a year,[60] and evidence suggests that these attacks are increasing.[61] The number of incidents of piracy and armed robbery against ships reported to the International Maritime Organization was 228 in 1996, a rise of 96 over the figure for 1995. Since 1984, 968 such acts have been reported.[62]

The typical pirate attack occurs at night and generally lasts no more than 15 or 20 minutes. A small number of individuals tend to be involved, with an average of 4 to 6 persons, although numbers over 30 have been reported. The pirates generally board the vessel by coming alongside in small high-speed boats and using grappling hooks. The pirates are armed typically with knives, but crowbars and bayonets also have been used successfully. Guns are becoming more common, with the result of a steep rise in casualties in recent years. Pirates killed 72 seamen in 2000, up from 3 reported deaths in 1999.[63]

While most pirates are lightly armed bands of outlaws, there is some concern that states are complicit, if not overt, participants in the piracy. For example, in the early 1990s, Russian ships made allegations of piracy against the Chinese Coast Guard regarding irregular searches and seizures. China's People's Liberation Army (PLA) Navy has been implicated as well. Recent reports describe documented attacks on a number of ships on the high seas that were boarded by personnel from military gunboats bearing the markings of the PLA Navy, with the pirates dressed in PLA Navy uniforms. While piracy is certainly not condoned officially in China's regional maritime security forces, the temptation to participate in it or to turn a blind eye to it in exchange for kickbacks or bribes appears to be very strong.[64]

A successful response to an attack is complicated by the fact that the threat is usually from a rogue element within the state and not from the state itself. Delicate jurisdictional issues arise regarding sovereignty and must be carefully balanced. This said, dealing with pirate attacks has three components: detection, deterrence, and response. Detection is generally regarded as the responsibility of the ship itself; if the ship can spot the pirates before the attack occurs, the pirates lose the element of surprise, greatly mitigating the likelihood of attack. As Tom Keller, director of public affairs for MAST (Maritime Anti-Terrorist Security Team, a California-based security organization) states:

> If it's in daylight time, you bring your people up to the deck and they stand there and they watch. They take some pictures. A lot of times they don't even need to brandish a firearm. . . . The bad guys are going to see that, and they're going to say, "Well, maybe, I'm not going to take this guy, because it would be too difficult." The energy to get the target at that point exceeds the gains from getting it.[65]

To this extent, the responsibility for deterrence has generally been thought to lie with the ship as well. Having a vigilant crew, standing good watch (most pirates have boarded the ship before the crew is aware they are alongside), or maintaining on-board armed security personnel have been the usual means of deterring pirate attacks. This, however, may be changing. As the number and violence of pirate attacks increase, shipping companies may find themselves increasingly unable to deal with the situation on their own. Furthermore, as the typical pirate is more often a member of a large organized crime syndicate than a "down-on-his-luck local,"[66] and as governments in whose waters these attacks have occurred have been unable to deal effectively with them,[67] an international role in deterrence and response becomes more likely. To this end, the U.S. Coast Guard has offered its expertise in the fight against maritime piracy in Southeast Asia, citing similarities to the U.S. battle against drug smuggling.[68] In an interview with *The Shipping Times*, then-Coast Guard Commandant Admiral James Loy said:

> In the "old days" if something happened on the high seas, every effort would be made to trace it back to the nation state. . . . But nowadays there are so many of what I will call transnational threats on the horizon that it is a very difficult challenge for international law enforcement to deal with them. . . . [T]he kind of things we've learned from drug law enforcement activities in the Caribbean . . . might be formative towards a helpful solution . . . based on international collaboration.[69]

Maritime Terrorism

Maritime terrorism is functionally different from maritime piracy. Pirate attacks occur for economic gain; terrorist attacks occur for political or social gain. The U.S. Department of State defines *terrorism* as "premeditated, politically motivated violence perpetrated against noncombatant targets by sub-national groups or clandestine agents, usually intended to influence an audience."[70] While no official definition of maritime terrorism exists, in 1988 the Rome Convention for the Suppression of Unlawful Acts Against the Safety of Maritime Navigation was open to international signatories.[71] Although sidestepping a formal definition, the convention states its deep concern "about the world-wide escalation of acts of terrorism in all its forms" and is directed against any person who "seizes or exercises control over a ship by force . . . performs an act of violence against a person on board . . . or destroys or seriously damages maritime navigation facilities," no matter the motive.[72]

In the post-September 11 world, three forms of maritime terrorism are of particular concern: an attack on an individual ship, the hijacking of a ship carrying dangerous materials, and the use of a ship as a weapon to attack port or land facilities.

Terrorist attacks on ships—passenger, commercial, and military—are not new. From the hijacking of the Portuguese-flagged passenger vessel *Santa Maria* in 1961, to the 1985 hijacking of the *Achille Lauro*,[73] to the 2000 attack on the USS *Cole*,[74] attacks on individual vessels have been cause for increased concern. Since the September 11 attacks, this concern has increased. Iran and Libya are reported to have provided diver and underwater training to terrorist groups based in the Middle East.[75] Other terrorist groups also have developed a maritime attack capability. The Sri Lankan Tamil Sea Tigers, for example, have conducted multiple maritime terrorist attacks. Two of the most recent of these attacks occurred in October 2001 when a Tamil Tiger suicide boat hit the oil tanker *MV Silk Pride* off northern Sri Lanka, setting the ship on fire[76] and in October 2002 when a suspected al Qaeda suicide boat detonated alongside the French tanker *Limburg* off Yemen. The Philippine-based Abu Sayyang group has also committed a number of terrorist attacks at sea. In the future, cruise ships are expected to be particularly vulnerable to maritime terrorism.

One of the greatest concerns regarding maritime terrorism stems from the transport of nuclear material at sea. Twenty-two countries possess or control a worldwide estimated total of 1,000 metric tons of separated plutonium in various forms for use in both military and civilian applications.[77] The strategic value of plutonium gives rise to fear that nuclear terrorists might hijack ships carrying nuclear materials. Such ships could be used for blackmail, where terrorists threaten to blow up the ship unless their demands are met.

An example of this concern occurred in the mid-1980s.[78] Japan, due to its lack of oil and other energy resources, has relied increasingly on nuclear energy for its energy needs. Much of the plutonium for its reactors comes from Europe and is transited by ship. In 1984, the United States and environmental groups expressed great concern when an unescorted Japanese cargo vessel carrying 253 kilograms of reprocessed plutonium applied for a permit to transit the Panama Canal; passage was approved only after provision was made for armed naval escort. A 1988 bilateral agreement now requires Japan to get approval from the U.S. Government for any plan to transfer reprocessed plutonium from Europe.

A future concern is that ships will be used as weapons against port or land facilities. Either ships will be used for the transit of hazardous material that could be transmitted into a country or they will themselves be used as weapons against ports or harbors. Regarding the former, much has been made of the fact that only some two percent of all containers entering the United States on ships are currently inspected.[79] While no current evidence of culpability exists, these containers could be used to transmit anything from anthrax or other biological agents to chemical agents into the United States or into any other nation.

The use of a ship as a weapon, in the manner of the World Trade Center and Pentagon attacks, is a troubling scenario. While this has never occurred, accidents or near-accidents in certain parts of the world suggest how devastating a purposeful attack could be. For example, if a ship carrying liquid petroleum gas were to explode in the Turkish Straits, scientists estimate the impact would be the same as an 11.0 earthquake on the Richter scale:[80] "it will threaten the whole of Istanbul like an atomic bomb, and it can also reach 50 kilometers in diameter."[81]

Maritime security experts say that any one of the tens of thousands of containers entering U.S. ports on a daily basis could conceal "a weapon of mass destruction aimed at the heart of America."[82] Of particular concern are tankers loaded with liquefied natural gas or a nuclear device hidden on a container ship. In the wake of the

September 11 attacks, Boston Mayor Thomas Menino asked a U.S. Federal court to ban liquefied natural gas tankers from the city's port, saying there was no adequate plan to cope with any explosion.[83] A nuclear device need not be particularly sophisticated: Clifford Beal, editor of *Jane's Defence Weekly*, said that enriched uranium wrapped around a conventional explosive could be used "to deadly effect."[84]

The problems of combating terrorism resemble those of combating piracy— identifying a priori those who intend to commit such acts and bringing to justice those responsible for such attacks. Additionally, as maritime terrorist attacks—just as maritime pirate attacks—are overwhelmingly likely to occur in a nation's territorial waters (the UN definition of piracy notwithstanding), there remain significant sovereignty and jurisdictional problems with responding to foreign attacks. Effective response will require international coordination of coastal states and cooperative regional regimes to respond to and deter piracy and maritime terrorist attacks.

In the case of attacks against U.S. ports or in U.S. territorial waters, the problem will be twofold: manpower and economics. With only two percent of containers currently inspected in U.S. ports, significant delays will certainly obtain if a greater percentage of containers is to be inspected. These delays will add (perhaps meaningfully) to transportation costs and may even create serious transportation bottlenecks. Additionally, the U.S. Coast Guard, currently charged with port security, is facing significant manpower shortages. Since the September 11 attacks, the Coast Guard expanded its missions to include port patrols, cargo and passenger ship escorts under bridges, and even service as air marshals aboard U.S. commercial flights. To meet these new demands, the Coast Guard has had to call up about one-third of its 6,000 reservists and has had to expand the use of the 35,000 volunteer members of the Coast Guard Auxiliary. Even so, other critical functions, such as search and rescue and drug interdiction, have suffered.[85]

Decreased/Threatened Supply: Summary

Figure 8–6 summarizes the importance to the United States and current security threats for SLOCS whose transits are being challenged.

Sea Lane Security: Conclusions

Resource scarcity has many components. It arises from increased demand or insufficient or threatened supply when economically viable substitutes are few or lacking altogether. At the same time, the supply remains relatively fixed and, with the exception of oil transport via pipeline, few affordable alternatives exist that have not already been put in place. Demand on global sea lanes is increasing, since more of the world's nations than ever are part of the global capitalist trading economy. The majority of this increasing global trade moves by ship through ocean sea lanes and

Figure 8–6. **Resource Scarcity Summary: Security Threats**

SLOC/Chokepoint	Importance to the United States	Security Threat
South China Sea	Asian/Oil Trade	China's territorial disputes over Spratly Islands; piracy
Strait of Hormuz	Access to Persian Gulf	Iran's military buildup
Strait of Malacca	Asian/Oil Trade	Arbitrary closure by Indonesian government; piracy
Singapore Strait	Asian/Oil Trade	Piracy
Caribbean Sea	U.S. Gulf and Oil Trade	Piracy
Gulf of Paria	U.S. Oil Trade	Territorial dispute between Venezuela and Trinidad and Tobago

chokepoints. Supply threats are twofold: *physical threats* posed by the geographical placement, size, and shape of the chokepoint, and *security constraints* from either state or nonstate actors that threaten a ship's ability to use a passage.

Many threats and concerns face the sea lanes and chokepoints that the United States depends on for its international trade. They can be understood not only by the source of the threat—increased demand and supply threats such as physical constraints, disputed state claims, state aggression, and nonstate actors—but also by the solutions they imply. Within the broad objective of preserving national, international, and global trade security, responses include: *diplomacy*, *policing* measures concerned with the maintenance of law and order at sea, and when necessary, active *military* responses.

Little can be done to reduce demand on the world's sea lanes of communication or their attendant physical constraints in the near future. For demand to reduce, alternate means of transportation would have to be provided. Although this is possible—much could be done to develop the road and rail infrastructure throughout Asia, for example—it is unlikely to occur to a significant extent to alleviate pressure on maritime transportation routes. Similarly, there is little that can be done to mitigate the physical constraints facing key chokepoints and trade routes; while the Panama and Suez Canals could be deepened and widened, capitalization is insufficient to make this certain. Alleviating the physical constraints on the natural maritime chokepoints, even if it were technologically feasible, would almost certainly be under-capitalized as well. Lastly, as has been discussed, the addition of any new trade routes—barring the Cape Horn, Strait of Magellan, and Northwest Passage routes—is not likely to occur.

In each of the cases of disputed state claims (Canada and the Northwest Passage, the Turkish Straits and Indonesia and the Strait of Malacca), the conflict occurred with a state considered friendly to the United States. At no time did any of these disputes threaten to escalate beyond the measures of active diplomacy. Additionally, in each of these examples, a case could be made that the littoral states attempted to impose restrictions for the purposes of environmental conservation or maritime safety. The Arctic is a fragile and unique ecosystem, particularly vulnerable to pollution and oil spills. The Turkish Straits have witnessed excessive traffic congestion, pollution, and maritime accidents. The Indonesian Straits are among the most crowded in the world, and collisions and groundings are routine. Nonetheless, it is vital to U.S. and global commerce that these sea lanes remain open with minimal state restrictions and interference. Active diplomacy is the best means of resolving the concerns of the littoral states and global maritime trade.

Potential threats to sea lane trade security from states typically will require policing measures. Currently, the states most worrisome to maritime trade are China, with its ambition to exert its control throughout the South China Sea, and Iran, with its control of the Strait of Hormuz. While each threat should be taken seriously, China and Iran would stand to suffer as much as anyone were hostilities to obtain. As will be discussed in chapter 10, if maritime trade was threatened in the South China Sea and traffic became diverted, China would stand to lose its lifeline to Middle Eastern oil. With almost no domestic oil of its own, China depends on the free transit of shipping through the South China Sea. Furthermore, China is fast developing on the strength of its ability to export; were this ability threatened, the Chinese economy might experience significant contractions.

The case is similar for Iran: While it may have the ability to close the Strait of Hormuz, Tehran would end up as one of the greatest losers. Some 90 percent of Iran's foreign exchange earnings come from oil and, consequently, from safe and secure access through the Persian Gulf. This said, states have been known to act against their own interests in the past. Consequently, the U.S. Navy must continue to enforce the Freedom of Navigation Acts by maintaining a significant blue water presence in those parts of the world critical to maritime trade.

Threats from nonstate actors—essentially pirates and terrorists—imply a direct attack on U.S. interests and will be best met by means of active defense. Pirates and terrorists are rarely amenable to negotiations, and they must be prevented and deterred by force. However, as most pirate and terrorist attacks occur in the territorial waters of another state, it is problematic to speak of a unilateral U.S. military response. Regional rapid reaction capabilities, such as those already under way in Asia, must be promoted, and the United States must be an active participant. Currently, the U.S. Department of State and Coast Guard participate in regional seminars and workshops on piracy and armed robbery in Asia. While a start, this is insufficient. Actions must be taken to create the conditions in known pirate areas for the pirates to be apprehended, tried and convicted, and punished for their crimes. For example, the U.S. Coast Guard can provide training to its foreign counterparts, and economic assistance can be linked to aggressive pursuit of maritime crime.

Viewing sea lanes and chokepoints as scarce resources has two important functions. First, it provides a constant reminder that conflict can obtain when a vital economic resource is threatened. That most of the world's critical ocean arteries are under some kind of threat or stress means that we must be alert to the possibility of conflict, armed or otherwise, over safe and secure access. Second, viewing sea lanes and chokepoints as scarce resources provides a framework for a policy response best suited to each existing threat.

Notes

[1] As suggested in chapter 1, in modern terms SLOCs might properly be conceived as sea lines of commerce. Although the traditional and military term remains sea *lines* of communication (SLOCs), the civilian maritime community frequently refers to such zones of transit as sea *lanes* of communication. To combine the commercial perspective with the imperative to defend maritime commerce using military forces, the author deliberately chooses *sea lanes of communication* and the acronym *SLOC* for use throughout this chapter.

[2] Miroslav Nincic, *How War Might Spread to Europe* (London: Taylor and Francis, 1985), 18.

[3] Ibid.

[4] A major theme of Michael C. Desch, *When the Third World Matters: Latin America and United States Grand Strategy* (Baltimore: Johns Hopkins University Press, 1993).

[5] This is to say that the ecological balance has some features reminiscent of a "balance of terror." This approach emphasizes the need to "deescalate" from the environmental "brink," noting that the desired outcome cannot be achieved unilaterally, but only through compatible choices made by all.

[6] Here we note issues such as the Iraqi destruction of the Kuwaiti oil fields during the Gulf War; land mines rendering farmland essentially nonarable; and the dumping of military nuclear waste at sea.

[7] See, particularly, Thomas F. Homer-Dixon, "On the Threshold: Environmental Changes As Causes of Acute Conflict," *International Security* 16, no. 2 (Fall 1991), 76–116; and Thomas F. Homer-Dixon, "Environmental Scarcities and Violent Conflict: Evidence from Cases," *International Security* 19, no. 1 (Summer 1994), 5–40.

[8] Homer-Dixon, "Environmental Scarcities," 21–23.

[9] Nazli Choucri and Robert North, *Nations in Conflict: National Growth and International Violence* (San Francisco: Freeman, 1975), 283–284.

[10] Arthur H. Westing, *Global Resources and International Conflict: Environmental Factors in Strategic Policy and Action* (Oxford: Oxford University Press, 1986).

[11] While ships can, in theory, travel anywhere on the world's oceans, the most efficient means of getting from one point to another by sea have remained fairly constant for more than 100 years. In spite of technological advances in transportation systems, prevailing winds, as well as ocean currents and predominant weather patterns, determine the safest and most efficient maritime trade routes, or sea lanes of communication/commerce (SLOCs). A chokepoint is a narrow strait or passage on a SLOC through an isthmus (the Panama Canal), a group of islands (the Straits of Malacca), or between two continental shores (the Bosporus and Dardanelles). Chokepoints can be vulnerable due to natural hazards (shallow depth or dangerous shoals, for example), or the danger of collision can increase due to "bottlenecking" and increased congestion. Furthermore, because they are, by definition, proximate to land and to land-based means of military power, they are at risk of being closed or threatened by an unfriendly state.

[12] Independent World Commission on the Oceans, *The Ocean, our Future. . . . The Report of the Independent World Commission on the Oceans* (Cambridge: Cambridge University Press, 1998), 186.

[13] "Marine Transportation Policy," National Governors Association, accessed at <www.nga.org/nga/legislative-Update/1,1169,C_POLICY_POSITION^D_490,00.html>.

[14] Edward B. Barbier, *Economics, Natural-Resource Scarcity and Development: Conventional and Alternative Views* (London: Earthscan Publications Limited, 1989), x.

[15] "Dry Bulk Volumes Grow," *Hong Kong Shipping News International*, no. 27 (November 10, 1997), n.p.

[16] Jeffrey Sachs, "The Limits of Convergence: Nature, Nurture, and Growth," *The Economist* (June 14, 1997), 19.

[17] Ibid.

[18] John R. Anderson, "Multi-National Naval Cooperation into the 21st Century," Halifax Maritime Symposium (Halifax, Nova Scotia: May 22–23, 1996).

[19] Paul de Bendern, "Booming World Trade Threatens Panama Canal Status," Reuters, September 23, 1997.

[20] Ibid.

[21] Ibid.

[22] Richard N. Cooper, "The Gulf Bottleneck: Middle East Stability and World Oil Supply," *Harvard International Review* 19, no. 3 (Summer 1997), 20–21.

[23] Ironically, the problem is of its own making. The canal was closed between 1967 and 1982 due to the Arab-Israeli conflict. The extended closure of the Suez Canal further encouraged the use of supertankers (very large crude carriers), developed in the 1960s, which are too large to use the Suez Canal but which offer cost-effective transportation for the Cape of Good Hope route around southern Africa.

[24] U.S. Department of Energy, Energy Information Administration, "Egypt," accessed at <http://www.eia.doe.gov/emeu/international/egypt.html>.

[25] Ibid.

[26] "Suez Authority to Rethink Bulker Rebates," *Hong Kong Shipping News International*, no. 18 (September 8, 1997).

[27] U.S. Department of Energy, "Egypt."

[28] Ibid.

[29] de Bendern.

[30] "More Panama Canal Draft Reductions Loom," *Hong Kong Shipping News International*, no. 50 (May 11, 1998).

[31] "Piloting: Chemical-laden Tanker's Hair-Raising Close Call at the Golden Gate," *Marine Watch Institute*, accessed at <http://www.marinewatch.com>.

[32] U.S. Department of Energy, Energy Information Administration, "Turkey," accessed at <http://www.eia.doe.gov/emeu/international/turkey.html>.

[33] Ercan Ersoy, "Chevron Talks Straits, Pipeline with Turkey," *Turkish Daily News*, May 17, 1996, 1.

[34] The right of innocent passage, one of the fundamental tenets in the International Law of the Sea, states that all ships enjoy the right of passage through another state's territorial sea, as long as that passage is continuous and expeditious, and as long as it is not prejudicial to the peace, good order, or security of the coastal state. "Commentary—the 1982 United Nations Convention on the Law of the Sea and the agreement on implementation of part XI (Law of the Sea Convention)," *U.S. Department of State Dispatch* 6, supp–1 (February 1995), 5.

[35] To assert their respective positions, Canada granted the *Manhattan* transit permission, even though the United States refused to request it.

[36] In spring 1985, the *Polar Sea*, based in Seattle, was unexpectedly required to resupply the U.S. airbase in Thule, Greenland. The *Polar Sea* could have been sent through the Panama Canal, but this would have allowed insufficient time to return back through the canal to the western Arctic to complete its assigned western mission.

[37] Ruth Walker, "Arctic Thaw Opening Up Lucrative Shipping Route," *The Christian Science Monitor*, June 7, 2000, 1.

[38] Ibid.

[39] While the Straits do not connect to the Caspian Sea, which is landlocked, a series of pipelines transits the oil from the Caspian to ports on the Black Sea, where it is put on ships and then moves through the Straits into the Mediterranean.

[40] "State Minister Mirzaoglu Says Maritime Traffic Capacity in Turkish Straits Has Reached Its Limits," *Turkish Maritime Pilot's Association*, March 28, 2001, accessed at <http://www.turkishpilots.org>.

[41] "Turkey Threatens to Tax Oil Shipped Through Bosporus Straits," accessed at <http://www.stratfor.com>.

[42] Jolyon Naegele, "Turkey: Caspian Oil Presents Challenge to the Straits," Radio Free Europe/Radio Liberty, June 23, 1998, accessed at <http://www.rferl.org>.

[43] U.S. Department of Energy, Energy Information Administration, "Turkey: Environmental Issues," accessed at <http://www.eia.doe.gov/emeu/cabs/turkenv.html>.

[44] Ibid.

[45] Russell Skelton, "Jakarta Shipping Plan Sparks Anger," and "Passage Limits Raise Nations' Ire," *Sydney Morning Herald*, June 5, 1996.

[46] Anderson.

[47] William J. Dobson and M. Taylor Fravel, "Red Herring Hegemon: China in the South China Sea," *Current History* 96, no. 611 (September 1997), 258.

[48] Joe Havely, "World: Asia-Pacific Analysis: Flashpoint Spratly," BBC News On-line, February 14, 1999.

[49] Dobson and Fravel, 258.

[50] Maria Ressa, "Indonesian War Games on Oil-Rich Island Sends Message," CNN, September 22, 1996, accessed at <http://cnn.com/WORLD/9609/22/indonesia/index.html>.

[51] "Singapore Adds Two Navy Patrol Vessels," Reuters, July 19, 1997.

[52] U.S. Department of Energy, Energy Information Administration, "Chokepoints," accessed at <http://www.eia.doe.gov/emeu/international/petroleu.html>.

[53] "New U.S. Fleet Defies Iran's Terror," *Minnesota Daily Online*, April 22, 1996, accessed at <http://www.daily.umn.edu/daily/1996/04/22/editorial_opiniions/ofleet.col/index.html>.

[54] "Iran Ends Naval Exercises: Oil Shipments Resume Through Strait of Hormuz," *Digital News Network*, April 14, 1996, accessed at http://www.pres96.com/nwi10s5.htm.

[55] See for example, U. S. Coast Guard, *Threats and Challenges to Maritime Security 2020*, II–18, on "noncivil" actors, accessed at <http://www.uscg.mil/deepwater>.

[56] Ibid., II–18, II–20.

[57] Jon Vagg, "Rough Seas? Contemporary Piracy in South East Asia," *British Journal of Criminology* (Winter 1995), 63–80.

[58] Ibid.

[59] There is no single, universally accepted set of data on pirate attacks. Many organizations keep figures, and the figures do not always agree. Furthermore, the number of pirate attacks worldwide is considered to be significantly underreported for a number of reasons. First, ship captains are reluctant to file attack reports as it can delay their passages and/or result in a problematic reputation; crews are unwilling to sail with captains who have been the victims of crime. Second, insurance rates are likely rise as pirate attacks are seen to increase; thus, shipowners often prefer that the attacks not be reported.

[60] Stephanie Mann, "Maritime piracy increasing dramatically," *VOA News*, July 8, 2001. Notwithstanding the reasons cited above for underreporting, some of the increase in the number of attacks is believed to be due to greater numbers of incidents being reported.

[61] David N. Kellerman, *Worldwide Maritime Piracy*, Special Ops Associates, June 1999; International Maritime Organization, Maritime Safety Committee, "Dramatic Increase in Piracy and Armed Robbery," May 2001.

[62] International Maritime Organization, "Draft bulk carrier safety regulations agreed by Maritime Safety Committee," briefing at the Maritime Safety Committee meeting, June 9, 1997.

[63] Mann.

[64] Dana R. Dillon, "Piracy in Asia: A Growing Barrier to Maritime Trade," The Heritage Foundation, June 22, 2000, accessed at <http://www.heritage.org/library/backgrounder/bg1379.html>.

[65] Mann.

[66] Ibid.

[67] Kellerman.

[68] "U.S. Coast Guard Offers Help in Fight Against Piracy," June 5, 2001, Deutsche Presse-Agentur.

[69] Ibid.

[70] Accessed at <http://www.state.gov>. *Noncombatant* refers to civilians and to military personnel not armed or not on duty.

[71] The best source on the Rome Convention is *Maritime Terrorism and International Law,* ed. Natalino Ronzitti (Boston: Martinus Nijhoff/Kluwer Academic Publishers, 1990).

[72] Ronzitti, 141–144.

[73] The hijacking of the *Achille Lauro* was a prime motivation for calling the Rome Convention.

[74] The Rome Convention excludes warships from its provisions.

[75] U.S. Coast Guard, *Threats and Challenges to Maritime Security 2020,* reports that open sources indicate that the Lebanese Hizbollah and the Popular Front for the Liberation of Palestine are conducting maritime training at various sites. See II–27.

[76] "Tamil Suicide Boat Rams Oil Tanker," BBC News Online, October 30, 2001.

[77] James Broadus and Raphael V. Vartanov, eds., *The Oceans and Environmental Security: Shared U.S. and Russian Perspectives* (Washington, DC: Island Press, 1994), 140.

[78] Ibid.

[79] Pete Harrison, "Container Ships Could Be Used as Bombs by Terrorists," *The Irish Examiner,* October 30, 2001.

[80] Yüksel Inan, "The Current Regime of the Turkish Straits," *Perceptions: Journal of International Affairs* 6, no.1 (March-May 2001), accessed at <http://www.mfa.gov.tr/grupa/percept/VI-1/default.htm>.

[81] Naegele.

[82] Harrison.

[83] Ibid.

[84] Ibid.

[85] Ken Coons, "Coast Guard Stretches to Expand Mission," October 4, 2001, accessed at <http://www.seafood.com>.

Chapter 9

Economic and Strategic Implications of Ice-Free Arctic Seas

Jessie C. Carman

One of the principal public concerns about the globalization process is environmental degradation resulting in climatic changes. Aside from a multitude of effects on agriculture and human health, such changes hold other direct national security implications. Global climate predictions forecast the largest temperature change to be in the Arctic, and preliminary observations support the magnitude of Arctic change. National strategic scenario documents occasionally touch on global climate change as it pertains to such issues as disease, agriculture, or water availability; however, they do not perceive the impact of an Arctic change. A reduction of Arctic ice will open Arctic sea routes to commercial shipping and fishing and Arctic regions to economic hydrocarbon removal, producing significant global strategic implications. Impediments to Arctic development arise from the Russian economic situation, bipolar military security issues, Law of the Sea issues, physical infrastructure, and the risk of environmental damage. These and other impacts of this major change are worthy of consideration in long-range U.S. policy and force planning. This chapter details such a climate change scenario from a military planning perceptive, making recommendations for an appropriate naval response.[1]

Commander Jessie C. Carman, USN, is a naval oceanographer currently serving as the staff meteorologist and oceanographer for Commander Fifth Fleet in Bahrain. She has previously served as the department head for the Models and Data Department of the Fleet Numerical Meteorology and Oceanographic Center, Monterey, California. She has additionally served as meteorologist and oceanographer with aviation and submarine units and in USS *Bataan* (LHD–5), and she earned a Ph.D. in applied physics (oceanography and underwater acoustics) from Harvard University as a Secretary of the Navy Graduate Fellow in Oceanography. She would like to thank Jan Breemer of the Naval Postgraduate School for his comments on the original draft of this chapter.

Projection of Arctic Climate

An increasing accumulation of scientific evidence supports projections that Arctic ice will be dramatically reduced or possibly disappear during part of the summer as soon as 2050. The evidence comes from a variety of sources, such as changes in ice thickness as reported by U.S. and British submarines,[2] satellite measurements of ice coverage, and climate modeling. Conservative estimates calculate a 12- to 40-percent reduction in summer ice extent has already occurred.[3] Commercially viable Arctic sea lanes are anticipated to be opened for part of the year well before 2050, which could make the Arctic Ocean a major global trade route.[4] The transit of the Northwest Passage by the Royal Canadian Mounted Police patrol ship *St. Roch II* in August 2000 without encountering ice supports this prediction.[5] Additionally, technological progress in shipping indicates that the hydrocarbon industry will not wait for sea lanes to open for exploitation.[6] Obviously, these trends have the potential to profoundly alter the international geopolitical and economic environment.

Current Intergovernmental Panel on Climate Change climate projections call for a global average temperature increase that ranges from 1.4 to 5.8° C over the next century. This temperature increase will be greater for areas over land than over water and greater in polar than in temperate regions. In particular, the projected increase for the northern high-latitude winter exceeds the projected average global increase by 40 percent. The projected Arctic warming is highly seasonal, with an increase by mid-century in summer temperature of only 1 to 2° C but of 8 to 9° C in winter. The variability in predictions is almost as large as the warming itself, with variabilities ranging from 1 to 2° C in summer to 5 to 6° C in winter.[7]

An increase in global average water vapor concentration and precipitation by about 1 centimeter per month is projected to accompany this prediction, although the variability in precipitation predictions is wider than the variability in temperature predictions.[8] Nevertheless, all projections hold that changes will be manifested first and with greatest magnitude in polar regions.

These temperature and precipitation projections translate into summer and winter Arctic weather conditions that remain harsh. A more ice-free ocean or longer ice-free season would lead to an increase in heat and moisture transfer from the ocean into the Arctic air, producing more low cloudiness, poorer visibility, freezing mist, and drizzle. These conditions would also contribute to more localized low pressure formation and hence increasing precipitation and high wind events.[9] Freezing precipitation accompanied by high winds and seas implies significant ship superstructure and aircraft icing.

Exact ice conditions cannot be predicted, considering the range of variability in the climate conditions. However, model runs conducted by the Geophysical Fluid Dynamics Laboratory at the National Oceanographic and Atmospheric Administration show considerable loss of ice along the Arctic borders, although these results should be considered as suggestive for further research rather than as predictions of specific conditions. As ice coverage decreases, ice advection with wind and currents will cause considerable movement in non-landlocked ice, resulting in transit passages opening and closing on a scale of days.[10]

Review of National Scenario/Strategy Documents

Long-range geostrategic trend projections by different Federal agencies share a feature that is common in expert predictions:[11] the issues of the day tend to frame our thoughts, and the underlying assumptions that are the important issues of the present are assumed to retain their importance in the future. Our traditional map projections do us a psychological disservice, creating the impression that the Arctic Ocean is extremely large and at the edge of the economically powerful world. Without a sea-ice barrier to maritime communications, the Arctic Ocean becomes an internal ocean less than four times larger than the Mediterranean, a traditional highway of commerce.[12]

The National Intelligence Council's *Global Trends 2015* identified key drivers and critical uncertainties for the period through 2015. Early in this time period, many of the changes will remain small, but effects should become apparent by its end in 2015, particularly since the largest changes are predicted for Arctic regions. The ice-free Northwest Passage transit of the *St. Roch II* in 2000 confirms that such changes are already occurring. *Global Trends 2015* identified one key driver of the geostrategic environment as "natural resources and environment." However, the document restricted its view to issues of food production and water scarcities. Climate discussions touched on some water and health-related issues but made no mention of the Arctic. Regarding global warming, only polar ice melting, sea level rise, and an increasing frequency of major storms are mentioned.[13]

Another geostrategic driver cited was energy resources. These were projected to remain concentrated in the Persian Gulf region, the Atlantic Basin, and to a lesser extent, the Caspian region and Central Asia.[14] The report mentioned only that technological applications are opening remote and environmentally hostile areas to petroleum production.[15] *Global Trends 2015* went on to cite the possibility of "global energy supplies suffering a disruption" as a key uncertainty.[16] The likelihood of this uncertainty could grow if changes progress as discussed below.

The National Defense Panel report *Transforming Defense: National Security in the 21st Century* addressed the period 2010 to 2020 but made no mention of any climate issues in its extrapolation of geopolitical, social-demographic, economic, or technological trends. It hypothesized four plausible alternative world futures, essentially permutations of current social and political circumstances. However, the natural environment was not considered even to the limited extent it was in *Global Trends 2015.*[17]

The Report of the United States Commission on National Security/21st Century, *New World Coming*, projected global scenarios to 2025. The document predicted that the national security of all advanced states will be increasingly affected by the vulnerabilities of the evolving global economic infrastructure and that energy will continue to have a major strategic significance.[18] However, the document made no mention of Arctic trade routes and their potential significance for the economic infrastructure or the implications of access to Arctic energy sources for national strategy.[19]

In sum, most of the various national geostrategic scenario documents show some awareness that climate change will have an effect on the international strategic environment but do not address the possible implications of an Arctic Ocean open to transit.

Strategic Importance of the Arctic Ocean

The Arctic Ocean is an enclosed basin surrounded on all sides by technologically advanced countries with significant natural resources. It follows that an ice-free Arctic passage would provide for direct access to natural resources and hence enhanced opportunities for trade to those coastal areas. Additionally, routes through the Arctic dramatically shorten transit distances between existing commercial regions and trade centers.

Trans-Arctic trade. Trade routes through the Arctic translate into significant decreases in transit distances between the globe's economic centers. For instance, the Northern Sea Route between Europe and East Asia is 40 percent shorter through the Arctic than through the Suez Canal. The over-the-top route will be primarily of interest for trade between Europe and the Far East, between Europe and the west coast of the United States, and between the Far East and the east coast of the United States.

One assessment estimates that the Northwest Passage could be open for navigation for most of the year within 10 to 20 years.[20] This route will almost certainly spur an increase in trade between opposite coasts of major continents.

Ice-breaking currently makes Arctic navigation expensive. With a decrease in ice, some ice-breaking programs may be cut back, but interannual variability in ice thickness and location will prevent its elimination altogether. Ironically, the demand for newly available routes may be such they will need to be kept open longer, at either end of the summer season, thus driving up the cost again.[21]

Fishing industry. Increased access to polar waters will greatly affect the fishing industry. In polar regions, the number of dominant fish species is small. The poleward expansion of bordering species might produce better yields for temperate species, but some cold-water species are very sensitive to temperature change in their spawning grounds. These might be destroyed by changes in water properties, making prediction of future fishing stocks difficult.[22] As troubled fishing stocks continue to dwindle, increasing pressure on fishery resources in the North Pacific and North Atlantic may cause the fishing industry to "push the limits" and attempt to exploit the Arctic sooner than natural conditions permit. Naval and Coast Guard rescues of fishing vessels caught in ice may become routine long before sea ice degradation allows extensive civil transport through the Arctic Ocean.[23]

Hydrocarbons. In the past decade, the gas and oil industries have shown serious interest in using the Northern Sea Route with ice-capable tankers even before practical ice-free use of the route becomes available. The Finnish company Kvaerner-Masa Shipyards has developed an effective propeller and hull design, with which the tanker *Uikku* has passed her 5-year survey;[24] *Uikku* and her sister ship *Lunni* have operated on the Northern Sea Route since 1993.[25] Fortum Shipping has ordered new double-acting tankers from Sumitomo Heavy Industries in Japan for delivery in 2002. Built to Finnish/Swedish specifications, these ships will enable year-round operations in the Pechora Sea.[26] Lukoil added ice-capable tankers to its fleet after acquiring Murmansk Shipping Company.[27] Gazprom and the Norwegian companies Statoil and Norsk Hydro were active in the southeast Pechora Sea in summer 1998. These developments have already prompted the statement that the "legendary Northern Sea Route is losing its Russian appearance."[28] The implication is that foreign (non-Russian) shipping is already moving to open and develop the Northern Sea Route for resource access and trade.

Siberia's huge oil and natural gas resource reserves are the reason for economic pressure to open the Northern Sea Route. Reserves are estimated to be comparable to those in the Middle East.[29] Oil amounts are estimated at over 10.5 billion tons in Tyumen Oblast and Krasnoyarsk Kray alone, of which 5.5 percent has been exploited.[30] Extraction of resources on land is already feasible from an engineering standpoint; the difficulty is getting materials out economically. Current infrastructures place severe restrictions on transporting oil from these regions, because of the aging Russian pipeline system (under control of the Russian state company Transneft) and the limited handling capacity at sea ports on the Baltic and Black Seas. At this time, there is no way to transport Siberian oil to the Russian Far East, but given that Asia will be a primary energy customer in the early part of this century, there will be a strong impetus to create an export route toward the east.[31] (Increasing Asian requirements for oil are discussed in detail in chapter 10.) Local and consortium projects to pipe oil to ports on the Northern Sea Route and ship it out are under development, creating a transportation infrastructure more under control of the investors and, incidentally, opening up new oil and trade markets both eastward and westward.[32]

In short, the hydrocarbon industries are already moving to exploit Arctic regions through new technologies and consortium projects. Climate change will make their task easier and more economical. An interesting sequela to this newly available source of energy is that, when economically feasible, the resources will all be the property of technologically developed countries with diversified economic bases, which are already major consumers of resources (in contrast to the supply monocultures of the Middle East). This change could dramatically alter the balance of trade with other resource-producing countries. An influx of currency would greatly help Russia to overcome its economic woes, although infrastructure and health problems will suboptimize economic benefit in the immediate future.[33]

Increased access for the hydrocarbon industry will occur in conjunction with increased fishing activity and trade possibilities, all of which could act together to promote dramatic development if policies are implemented to foster that development in a sustainable fashion.

Impediments to Arctic Development

Great potential clearly exists for economic development when Arctic coastal waters open up. However, several impediments will make development more difficult or uneven.

Russian economic situation. A key impediment is Russia's economic situation. The Russian North has been painfully affected by the post-Soviet transition of the country because the area's former state-owned, nearly monoculture economy has been incapable of self-regulation. Economic woes have triggered a massive emigration; state programs and funding have been insufficient to mitigate the crisis. [34] However, international cooperation in the Northern Sea Route is part of current Russian economic strategy; the country is working with Conoco, Amoco, Exxon, and Texaco in a joint venture to extract petroleum deposits from the Barents and Timano-Pechora basins.[35] The principal need is for transport systems to link the Arctic region with other parts of Russia and overseas partners. One problem decreasing the economic competitiveness of the Northern Sea Route has been ice-breaking fees.[36] However, as the need for ice breaking decreases, such fees should be lessened or discontinued. Additional foreign investment in Arctic commercial ships, both foreign and Russian-flag, and in ports and associated infrastructure will be necessary for the Northern Sea Route to flourish.[37]

Bipolar security issues. Political perceptions of the Arctic sea routes may be another problem. These perceptions are a legacy of the Cold War-era bipolar security paradigm. Moreover, the underlying assumptions have little validity.[38] During the U.S.-Soviet standoff, control of Arctic sea routes was thought crucial for surveillance, ballistic missile submarine (SSBN) stationing, and as a communications link for

Russian Navy interfleet transfers. Examination of these points shows they are not robust. The Northern Sea Route is not important for surveillance, as any classified information obtained visually from a ship's deck is more likely available via satellite.[39] As a station for SSBNs, the Northern Sea Route is too shallow, except in extremely constricted locations (submerged chasms), which are poor tactical choices.[40] As a route for interfleet transfer of Russian Navy ships, the Northern Sea Route has been hazardous: Russian ships are constructed with thin hulls for speed; during the Cold War, one in three suffered damage due to ice during transit and one in five naval transfers spent the winter ice-bound in Arctic waters.[41]

In contrast to the sea routes, the strategic importance of the marginal ice zone and open ocean is much greater; as the open waters become more benign, their use may increase, driving an increase in naval interactions.[42] Therefore, as ice retreats, the Arctic will witness an increase in surface naval activity over subsurface activity. From a post-Soviet Russian point of view, the true importance of the Northern Sea Route should be not military but economic. This importance has grown as many temperate ports that were part of the former Soviet Union were lost to the new republics.[43]

Law of the Sea issues. Another impediment to Arctic development may be diplomatic and turns on different interpretations of the 1982 United Nations Convention on the Law of the Sea (UNCLOS III) issues. UNCLOS III defines various terms for legally establishing a country's maritime territory. The baseline is the line from which the outer limits of the territorial sea and other coastal state zones, including the contiguous zone and exclusive economic zone, are measured. UNCLOS III also defines permissible points for locating baselines around indented coastlines, fringing islands, and bays.

In the case of Russia, there are discrepancies between Russia's declared Arctic baselines and the traditional criteria. For instance, Russia draws baselines connecting Novaya Zemlya and Vaigach Islands to the mainland, rendering the straits between (connecting the Barents and Kara Seas) to be internal waters. These islands are only arguably "fringing islands" and do not form a screen masking a large proportion of the coast from the sea. However, several other countries draw baselines having large degrees of deviation from the general direction of the coast or lying large distances from the coast.[44] Similar and more detailed analyses can be made for Russian baselines joining Severnaya Zemlya and Novosibirskiye Ostrova to the mainland. Additionally, some areas of the mainland coastline have baselines drawn that fail to meet UNCLOS III requirements for enclosing bays or determining points to establish baselines.[45] However, Russia has moderate support for its position in state practice, for some 12 states have enclosed failed juridical bays and some 14 states have located basepoints at sea. Additionally, Russian claims have been largely unopposed; only the United States has protested.[46] U.S. legal positions regarding these straits are based more on perceptions of the straits' strategic importance than on their legal relevance; thus, a stand on this issue could cause more difficulties than it is worth.[47] Although the waters enclosed by these baselines can arguably be claimed as internal waters, if they could not previously have been considered as internal waters, the right of innocent passage exists. It must be noted that Russian claims only impact transits of limited numbers of straits; exclusive economic zone issues and control of resources are unaffected.

The Canadian attitude toward sovereignty over Arctic waters is tangled. Ottawa's positions have not developed consistently with time, showing an ad hoc policy on Arctic archipelagic waters motivated largely by reaction to U.S. actions and to public perceptions.[48] As a maritime nation and one concerned about international precedent, the United States has taken the position that the waters north of the Canadian landmass are "international straits" through which freedom of navigation prevails.[49] The Canadian position has developed over the years in an uneven path, with Canada finally claiming the waters to be internal in 1985 by declaring straight baselines around the archipelago.[50]

In 1988 the Arctic Cooperation Agreement between Canada and the United States declared that navigation by U.S. icebreakers within those waters claimed to be internal by Canada would be undertaken with Canadian consent; the agreement did not address the status of the waters.[51] The agreement temporarily stabilized the situation, but it only addressed icebreakers under the assumption that any commercial vessel would require the assistance of at least one icebreaker.[52] As climate conditions change, this assumption may be invalid, and the situation may become uncertain again.

Physical infrastructure. Another impediment to economic development in the Arctic is the physical infrastructure—or rather, its lack. Arctic travel depends on ice roads in winter and water routes in summer.[53] These roads are fragile and at risk with climate change. Widespread loss of permafrost will trigger erosion or subsidence of ice-rich landscapes. Liquefaction of the thawed layer will result in mudflows on slopes in terrain that is poorly drained. Building roads on transient landscape will be problematic. Additionally, with earlier snowmelt and with more precipitation falling as rain than as snow, the seasonality of river flows will change; since many such rivers are north-flowing, cross several climate zones, and will carry a heavier load of sediments, predictions of river trafficability or bridge requirements are further complicated.[54] Thus transportation of goods and people will be uncertain, and engineering solutions will become a major challenge.

Environmental issues. Spills will present a major difficulty to resource exploitation in the Arctic. For various reasons, oil spills present a greater problem to the Arctic environment than to temperate areas.[55] While several sources contribute to the Arctic load of hydrocarbon contamination (marine shipping, burning of fossil fuels, long-range transport, natural oil seeps), oil and gas development is the major cause of contamination.[56] Accidental oil spills and chronic releases from poorly maintained pipelines and ships are the greatest threat. The Russian pipelines are old, lack safety valves, and are constantly plagued by leaks. Oil is often left flowing while repairs are made because losing oil is less expensive than building a bypass and stopping the flow might cause the oil in the pipeline to solidify.[57]

Based on statistics outside of the Arctic, the probability of spills over the production period of specified Arctic petroleum reserves can be estimated. In the Beaufort and Chukchi Seas, there is a probability of 0.58 to 0.99 of between 1 and 8 spills equal to or larger than 1,000 barrels. Spills exceeding 10,000 barrels have an estimated probability between 0.24 and 0.92.[58]

Tanker spills present the largest shipping pollution risk; most incidents occur at terminals where tankers load or unload. Most damage is usually localized to the immediate area around the port.[59]

Many legal instruments are already in place to address this issue—for example, UNCLOS III, the International Convention for the Prevention of Pollution from Ships (MARPOL 73/78), and the London Convention of 1972;[60] compliance is another problem when enforcement capability is limited.[61]

Thus, for all the real benefits to be gained with increased Arctic development, there will also be risks and problems to manage. Many of these problems could act as triggers for international incidents.

Impacts on Non-Arctic Regions

During the early part of the 21st century, the impact of global warming will be less visible in other parts of the world than in the Arctic, since the climate change "signal" is largest in the Arctic, and the more dramatic changes will be seen later in the century. The environment and infrastructures of various world regions will be stressed in different ways.[62] Two key problems will be reduced water availability due to salt water incursions into ground water, and increased concentrations of sewage waste and industrial effluents due to a projected drop of water level in dams and rivers.[63] These changes could lead to an increase in water politics internationally.[64]

In addition to these general pressures, most of the Arctic changes described so far will likely have negative consequences for the Middle East. Much of the Western motivation to support local regimes can be summed up in one word: oil. If—or when— effective competitors for providing resources arise, Middle Eastern regimes will have less Western support. This could mean, in turn, that existing demographic problems, social unrest, religious and ideological extremism, and terrorism already occurring will become more acute. Most Middle East regimes are change-resistant, buoyed by continuing energy revenues, and will likely find it difficult to make necessary reforms to change these trends.[65]

The emergence of Arctic oil sources could decrease long-term dependence on Middle East sources, but due to the impediments discussed above, the shift in primary source will not occur overnight but will involve a transition period in which Middle East sources are still important but of decreasing criticality. This stress could trigger one of the *Global Trends 2015* key uncertainties, by producing conflict among key energy-producing states, sustained internal instability in two or more major energy-producing states, or major terrorist actions leading to such a disruption.[66] Such instability could drive shippers to choose Arctic routes not only for their shorter length but also for their greater safety.

New Theater of Operations

The inexorable changes in the Arctic will have dramatic impacts on the international environment, and the United States should position itself carefully to benefit responsibly. Planning for external policy issues should emphasize diplomatic and economic options so long as minimal military support requirements are met.

Rather than allowing legalistic intergovernmental conflicts to determine the tone of international relations, the United States should pursue a leadership role in external policies to promote effective, responsible, and sustainable development of Arctic trade. This changing world picture will involve enough difficult issues as to require strong leadership with a long-term global perspective.

The government should promote strong intergovernmental ties through participation in such efforts as the Arctic Council and its subsidiary organizations. Through these organizations issues can be addressed that affect wide regions. By actively promoting a view for the Arctic based less on territorial sovereignty and more on overlapping and interpenetrating authority in economic, political, cultural, and environmental affairs,[67] some of the sovereignty issues discussed above can be seen in a larger perspective. Policies should emphasize sustainable development, emergency preparedness and response, and conservation issues in the face of a changing climate.

For instance, increased traffic will require an increase in policing, rescue, and environmental needs to enforce existing legal requirements. Canadian funding for Arctic patrols is insufficient to meet an increased demand; the maritime forces have no capability to operate in the north.[68] Past funding efforts, such as the Polar-8 icebreaker program and fixed underwater surveillance systems, were cancelled in 1990 and 1996 respectively.[69] A collective security agreement could allow U.S. assistance for some events; due to sovereignty sensitivities the specific events in which the United States would assist could be limited by agreement to search and rescue, vessel rescue, pollution incidents, or similar activities.

The United States should actively participate in the development of unified and international ship standards specifically addressing polar ships, to strengthen polar ship safety and enhance protection of polar marine environments. Canadian and Russian experience with "Canadian Arctic Pollution Prevention Regulations" and "Regulations for Navigation on the Seaways of the Northern Sea Route" respectively provide a major body of experience.[70]

The United States should promote coalitions with the European Union and Eastern Pacific countries to support trade, which will benefit from shorter routes.

The economic effects of changing resource availability and trade will particularly hurt the Middle East. This change could lead to an increase in religious or ethnic resentment, activism, and organized terrorism as the only means of fighting. Economic aid and diplomacy to help these countries adapt to changing circumstances could mitigate the effects; the United States should additionally maintain an alert posture to ensure the protection of its interests against potential threats.

Old Mission in a New Region

The above-described policies will incur some force requirements, particularly for maritime patrol in the Arctic. Protection of SLOCs does appear in various strategy documents; this naval obligation will extend to a new region with a harsh environment. Additionally, protection and ice rescue of fishing vessels, tankers, and cargo ships will add to Coast Guard obligations.

We are currently unprepared for such obligations, as current warships do not have ice strengthening; it must be factored into future designs, in particular to protect bow-mounted sonar domes and arrays.[71] When planning such designs, we should assume likely operation of surface warships in the Arctic could be in an area of "first-year" ice, less than one meter thick, covering no more than 60 percent of the total area of operations. In this situation, American Bureau of Shipping rules require strengthening of the bow and stern areas.[72] U.S. Naval ships do not meet such requirements; to have any ships capable of meeting these requirements, long planning times must be factored in. The U.S. Coast Guard has three icebreakers, the USCGC *Polar Sea* and USCGC *Polar Star*, built in the 1970s[73] and the USCGC *Healy*, built in 1997.[74] These assets will be insufficient to meet realistic patrol requirements.

This new operational region involves primarily a presence mission. As noted in chapter 15, a force planning methodology based on analyzing threat-based major regional contingency scenarios tends to underestimate the military forces required for overseas presence.[75] Using the interests-to-military-tasks methodology, a key political interest within the Arctic will be protection of SLOCs and an unimpeded flow of oil at fair market value. The military objective associated with this political interest is "protection of shipping." To support this objective, a force must be capable of air defense/superiority; littoral undersea warfare; strike/surface fire; intelligence/surveillance/command, control, and communications; escort operations; maritime interdiction operations;

mine countermeasures; and gas/oil platform operations. The force required for this objective includes five surface combatants (three Aegis), two mine countermeasures ships, and supporting surveillance and logistics assets.[76] Coast Guard maritime security cutters could be an alternative to some of these ships, to fill the gap between U.S. Navy destroyers and patrol boats. Such assets would also permit integration of U.S. Coast Guard maritime security experience into the Navy force or would conduct maritime-intercept tasks, coastal patrol duties, or environmental defense activity with less impact on political sensitivities. All of these assets must be capable of operating in an Arctic environment without needing assistance themselves, able to conduct flight operations in conditions of heavy aircraft and superstructure icing and occasional heavy fog. There must additionally be sufficient resources to permit rotation of forces in the region.

Concurrently with physical resources, support for missions in these areas must be planned and programmed. Northern basing, probably in Alaska, would help logistical support. Not only logistics and training but also operational environmental support for operations under harsh Arctic conditions must be prepared for. Operational support, however, is an easy problem relative to the financial outlays involved in ship, aircraft, weapon, sensor, and logistic support.

While these issues involve increases in naval resource requirements, opening Arctic sea lanes will also shorten U.S. interfleet transfers just as it shortens merchant routes. Since carriers and large-deck amphibious ships are too big to transit the Panama Canal, they currently travel around Cape Horn when transferring from one coast to the other. As a comparison, the route from Norfolk to Yokosuka via the Northwest Passage is roughly half the distance via Cape Horn; the route from Norfolk to San Diego via the Northwest Passage is roughly two-thirds the distance via Cape Horn. As an additional benefit, a ship making such a transfer could conduct its "protection of shipping" mission in transit.

Planning Considerations and New Scenarios

Current scenario-planning documents reflect a historical mindset, assuming that the only effect of the Arctic on global politics is from a Cold War security standpoint and that the only effects of global warming are the environmental stresses (which are, in fact, projected to be significant). The report *Transforming Defense—National Security in the 21st Century* identifies geopolitical and economic trends for the period 2010 to 2020, but none of the above.[77] The Clinton administration National Security Strategy committed the United States to supporting freedom of navigation/overflight and mentions environmental and health initiatives.[78] Its section on integrated regional approaches discusses different world regions from the point of view of security and promoting prosperity; however, the Arctic was not one of the regions discussed.[79]

Consequently, the National Military Strategy mentions freedom of navigation[80] and *Joint Vision 2020* projects changing transportation, communications, and information technology,[81] but neither registers that these missions will occur in new environments. The assessments and recommendations in these documents describe valid issues that will undoubtedly affect the world in the next 20 to 25 years; the documents simply miss a change that could transform the global geopolitical balance.

This silence is a symptom of the apparent invisibility of Arctic issues in national security policy. No longer seized by a Soviet threat, the United States perceives no substantial interests specific to the Arctic.[82] The trend presently occurring is unrecognized, in spite of early indications such as ice-free summertime passages and the petroleum industry's preparations to open shipping through the North whether or not open sea routes appear. Thus, in dealing with international cooperation regarding management of Arctic waters, the United States is not playing the leadership role it could and should.[83]

While these force-planning recommendations may appear slanted toward maritime rather than joint forces, it must be realized that the current topic is a "new" ocean basin with all that implies. This is a presence mission like others; expanding the area required will impact deployment coverage, while expanding the environment will drive platform capabilities. One may ask why we need to extend our capabilities to the environmentally harsh but relatively peaceful Arctic environment. However, incidents tend to arise overnight, and the impediments discussed above could provide ample potential triggers; let an economically important region produce an incident to which the nation is materially incapable of responding, and we will find ourselves forced to accept an undesirable political or economic outcome.

This chapter has concentrated on a basically peaceful vision of Arctic opening. The presence of technologically capable nations along the Arctic rim does, however, raise the possibility of a peer competitor intent on aggressively confronting U.S. interests within the time frame included here. The interests-to-military-tasks methodology yields the force required to meet the military task of "credible U.S. naval combat force in situ"; that force is a carrier battlegroup and an amphibious ready group with embarked special-operations-capable Marine expeditionary unit and supporting forces.[84] Forces again must be capable of operating in an Arctic environment without needing assistance themselves, able to conduct combat operations in the harsh Arctic environment, and with sufficient resources to permit rotation of forces. Hopefully the United States can exert sufficient diplomatic and economic leadership to minimize this possibility.

The resource planning implications of these changes are considerable, and the large range of variability remaining in the climate projections for this century means a wide range of scenarios to plan/program for. Further research to more closely quantify the rate of ice thinning is necessary to narrow the climate predictions and permit more timely planning of programs requiring long lead time for acquisition. In the meanwhile, defense and foreign planning scenarios should reflect the possibility that a *globalized* ice-free Arctic Sea could become a region of economic and political conflict.

Notes

[1] The climate changes discussed in this chapter are among the many documented and projected by the Intergovernmental Panel on Climate Change (IPCC), but rather than address all the impacts of climate change, this discussion focuses on how the Arctic changes will affect global political and economic issues. Warming in the Arctic will have dramatic effects on the lives of local peoples as well as local flora and fauna; however, external geopolitical and economic forces may arguably drive more change in the Arctic than climate does. This chapter does not address climate mitigation policies, as their implementation is part of a decisionmaking process separate from the military force planning process.

[2] D. A. Rothrock, Y. Yu, and G. A. Maykut, "Thinning of the Arctic Sea-Ice Cover," *Geophysical Research Letters* (December 1, 1999), 3469–3472; P. Wadhams, and N. Davis, "Further Evidence of Ice Thinning in the Arctic Ocean," *Geophysical Research Letters* (December 15, 2000), 3973–3975.

[3] G. W. Brass, ed., *The Arctic Ocean and Climate Change: A Scenario for the U.S. Navy, U.S. Arctic Research Commission Special Report* (Arlington, VA: U.S. Arctic Research Commission, 2001), 7; Institute of Ocean Sciences, Sidney, B.C., "Is Arctic Sea Ice Rapidly Vanishing?" accessed at <http://www.sci.pac.dfo-mpo.gc.ca/osap/projects/jpod/projects/arc_thin/thin1.htm>.

[4] Intergovernmental Panel on Climate Change (IPCC), *Special Report, The Regional Impacts of Climate Change: An Assessment of Vulnerability, Summary for Policymakers*, November 1997, 8.

[5] James Brooke, "Through the Northwest Passage in a Month, Ice-Free," *The New York Times,* September 5, 2000, A3.

[6] "Opening up the Northern Sea Route," *The Naval Architect* (November 2000), 6–8.

[7] IPCC Working Group 1, *Contribution to the Third Assessment Report of the IPCC, Climate Change, 2001: The Scientific Basis (Draft), Summary for Policymakers,* January 21, 2001, 8, available at <http://www.ipcc.ch/pub/spm22–01.pdf>; IPCC Working Group 2, *Contribution to the Third Assessment Report of the IPCC, Climate Change 2001: Impacts, Adaptation, and Vulnerability (Draft), Summary for Policymakers,* February 19, 2001, 1, accessed at <http://www.ipcc.ch/pub/wg2SPMFinal.pdf>. Climate effects due to unexpected events like climate-change-induced marine current changes have not been considered, as they cannot be predicted at present. (See IPCC, *Special Report, The Regional Impacts of Climate Change: An Assessment of Vulnerability, Summary for Policymakers,* 1, accessed at <http://www.grida.no/climate/ipcc/regional/501htm>.) Most models show a weakening of the ocean thermohaline (temperature-salt, or "conveyor belt") circulation leading to a reduction of heat transport into high latitudes of the northern hemisphere; however, even models in which the thermohaline circulation weakens still show a warming over Europe due to increased greenhouse gases. Current projections using climate models do not exhibit a complete shutdown of the thermohaline circulation by 2100. (See IPCC Working Group 1, 10.)

[8] Brass, 5.

[9] Ibid., 8.

[10] Wieslaw Maslowski, Naval Postgraduate School, personal communication, December 28, 2000. With this ice melt predicted, a sea level rise of 0.09 to 0.88 meters is expected by 2100. (See IPCC Working Group 2, 1.) This range includes thermal expansion of the oceans as well as expected melting of ice caps; melting of floating ice will not alter sea levels.

[11] United States Commission on National Security/21st Century, *New World Coming: American Security in the 21st Century, Study Addendum* (Washington, DC: Government Printing Office, September 15, 1999), 4.

[12] National Geographic Society, *National Geographic Atlas of the World,* 7th ed. (Willard, OH: R.R. Donnelley and Sons, 1999), 135.

[13] National Intelligence Council, *Global Trends 2015: A Dialog about the Future with Nongovernment Experts,* NIC 2000–02 (Washington, DC: Government Printing Office, December 2000), 32.

[14] Ibid., 9.

[15] Ibid., 28.

[16] Ibid., 39.

[17] National Defense Panel, *Transforming Defense: National Security in the 21st Century*, December 1997, accessed at <http://www.dtic.mil/ndp/FullDoc2/pdf>.

[18] United States Commission on National Security/21st Century, *New World Coming: American Security in the 21st Century, Major Themes and Implications, Phase I Report on the Emerging Global Security Environment for the First Quarter of the 21st Century* (Washington, DC: Government Printing Office, September 15, 1999), 4–5.

[19] United States Commission on National Security/21st Century, *Seeking a National Strategy: A Concept for Preserving Security and Promoting Freedom, Phase II Report on a U.S. National Security Strategy for the 21st Century* (Washington, DC: Government Printing Office, April 2000).

[20] Canadian Directorate of Defense, *Arctic Capabilities Study*, June 2000, accessed at <http://12.1.239.251/arctic/Arctic%20Study%20Final%20-%20Canada1.htm>, 6.

[21] IPCC, *Special Report: The Regional Impacts of Climate Change: An Assessment of Vulnerability*, November 1997, accessed at <http://www.grida.no/climate/ipcc/regional/054.htm>.

[22] IPCC, *Special Report: The Regional Impacts of Climate Change: An Assessment of Vulnerability*, November 1997, accessed at <http://www.grida.no/climate/ipcc/regional/053.htm>.

[23] Brass, 11.

[24] "Opening Up the Northern Sea Route," 6–8.

[25] Lawson W. Brigham, "The Northern Sea Route, 1998," *Polar Record* 36 (2000), 19–24.

[26] "Opening Up the Northern Sea Route," 6–8.

[27] Ibid.

[28] Brigham, 19–24.

[29] "Opening Up the Northern Sea Route," 6.

[30] Valery Kryukov, Valery Shmat, and Arild Moe, "West Siberian Oil and the Northern Sea Route: Current Situation and Future Potential," *Polar Geography* 19 (1995), 234.

[31] Kryukov, Shmat, and Moe, 228; United States Commission on National Security/21st Century, 79.

[32] Kryukov, Shmat, and Moe, 230–232.

[33] Murray Feshbach, "Dead Souls," *The Atlantic Monthly* (February 1999), 26–27.

[34] Alexander G. Granberg, "The Northern Sea Route: Trends and Prospects of Commercial Use," *Ocean and Coastal Management* 41 (1998), 183–184 and 198.

[35] Ibid., 200.

[36] Ibid., 200–201.

[37] Lawson Brigham, "The Northern Sea Route: Soviet Legacy and Uncertain Future," *British East-West Journal* (September 1998), 3–4.

[38] R. Douglas Brubaker, and Willy Østreng, "The Northern Sea Route Regime: Exquisite Superpower Subterfuge?" *Ocean Development & International Law* 30, no. 4 (October–December 1999), 323.

[39] Ibid., 310.

[40] Ibid., 306.

[41] Ibid., 305.

[42] Ibid., 310.

[43] Ibid., 303; Granberg, 182.

[44] R. Douglas Brubaker, "The Legal Status of the Russian Baselines in the Arctic," *Ocean Development & International Law* 30, no. 4 (October–December 1999), 209–210.

[45] Ibid., 213–217.

[46] Ibid., 218.

[47] Brubaker and Østreng, 323.

[48] Rob Huebert, "Polar vision or tunnel vision: the making of Canadian Arctic waters policy," *Marine Policy* 19, 1995, 343.

[49] Elizabeth B. Elliot-Meisel, "Still Unresolved after Fifty Years: The Northwest Passage in Canadian-American Relations, 1946–1998," *American Review of Canadian Studies* 29, no. 3 (Autumn 1999), 409. See also Donald R. Rothwell,

"The Canadian-U.S. Northwest Passage Dispute: A Reassessment," *Cornell International Law Journal* 26, no. 2 (Spring 1993), 347.

[50] In 1969, the SS *Manhattan* with a small cargo of oil was deliberately sent through the passage by its owners to demonstrate that an icebreaking bulk carrier was capable of year-round sailings between Alaska and the east coast of the United States. At the time of the passage, Canada had not asserted any sovereignty claim over the archipelago's waters other than a 3-mile territorial sea; consequently, most of the passage fell under the regime of high seas navigation. Although the *Manhattan* carried a Canadian government representative and was accompanied by a Canadian Coast Guard vessel, public controversy over this voyage caused Canada to implement the Arctic Waters Pollution Act, extend its territorial sea from 3 to 12 nautical miles, and withdraw its acceptance of compulsory jurisdiction of the International Court of Justice (ICJ) for matters regarding Canada's Arctic jurisdiction (Rothwell, 339–340). In 1985, the United States sent the USCGC *Polar Sea* through the passage, informing Canada and carrying two Canadian Coast Guard captains as "invited observers" but not asking official permission. After this voyage and the media controversy it generated, Canada declared straight baselines around the archipelago, withdrew its reservation to the ICJ, and called for construction of the Polar Class 8 icebreakers (ibid., 344). This declaration made all enclosed waters "internal" and provided for enforcement. Legal support exists for both the U.S. and Canadian positions (ibid., 345). The 1988 Arctic Cooperation Agreement between Canada and the United States provided for both states to facilitate and develop cooperative measures for icebreaker navigation in their respective Arctic waters, for both states to take advantage of their icebreaker navigation to share research information, and for navigation by U.S. icebreakers within waters claimed by Canada to be internal to be undertaken with the consent of Canada (ibid., 353–360). Then the Polar Class 8 icebreakers were cancelled in 1990 in part as a result of the 1988 Arctic Cooperation Agreement (Huebert, 356).

[51] Rothwell, 345.

[52] Huebert, 360.

[53] Granberg, 176.

[54] IPCC, *Special Report: The Regional Impacts of Climate Change: An Assessment of Vulnerability*, November, 1997, accessed at <http://www.grida.no/climate/ipcc/regional/048.htm>; Brass, 10.

[55] The Arctic environment responds differently than extra-Arctic regions to oil spills. The ice provides surfaces both above and below the water where oil can be trapped. The undersurface of ice can be very rough, with large pockets in which the oil can remain for as long as the ice stays solid. Some of the oil may become encapsulated and move with the ice. Thus, on the edge of the multi-year pack ice, oil can move about 150 kilometers per month in winter. Oil encapsulated in ice will not break down but will appear essentially unweathered at the surface when the ice starts to melt (Arctic Council/Arctic Monitoring and Assessment Programme, *Arctic Pollution Issues: A State of the Arctic Environment Report*, June 1997, 8, accessed at <http://www.amap.no/assess/soaer10.htm>). Degradation and cleaning by bacteria and fungi that use hydrocarbons as an energy source proceeds slowly due to the short season in which temperatures are high enough for bacteria and fungi to be active. Natural cleaning after a spill may therefore take decades rather than years (ibid., 14). Lack of equipment and methods to contain oil and to clean ice-infested areas increases the potential threat from oil spills in the Arctic (ibid., 8).

[56] Arctic Council/Arctic Monitoring and Assessment Programme.

[57] Ibid.

[58] Ibid.

[59] Ibid.

[60] Arctic Council/Protection of the Arctic Marine Environment, *Arctic Environmental Protection Strategy: Arctic Offshore Oil & Gas Guidelines*, June 13, 1997, 4.

[61] Arctic Council/Arctic Monitoring and Assessment Programme.

[62] IPCC, *Special Report, The Regional Impacts of Climate Change: An Assessment of Vulnerability, Summary for Policymakers*; United States Commission on National Security/21st Century, *New World Coming, Supporting Research and Analysis to the Phase I Report*, 58–115; National Intelligence Council, 60–82.

[63] IPCC, *Special Report, The Regional Impacts of Climate Change: An Assessment of Vulnerability, Summary for Policymakers*, 6.

[64] Robert D. Kaplan, "The Coming Anarchy," in *Strategy and Force Planning*, 3d ed., compiled by Strategy and Force Planning Faculty (Newport: Naval War College Press, 2000), 398–399.

[65] National Intelligence Council, 16.

[66] Ibid., 39.

[67] Franklyn Griffiths, "The Northwest Passage in Transit," *International Journal* 54, no. 2 (Spring 1999), 196.

[68] Canadian Directorate of Defense, 18.

[69] Elliot-Meisel, 417.

[70] Lawson W. Brigham, "An International Polar Navigation Code for the Twenty-First Century," *Polar Record* (1997), 283–284.

[71] Brass, 14.

[72] Ibid., 13–14.

[73] U.S. Coast Guard, "Polar Class Icebreakers (WAGB)," accessed at <http://www.uscg.mil/datasheet/icepolr.htm>.

[74] U.S. Coast Guard, "USCGC Healy," accessed at <http://www.uscg.mil/pacarea/healy/>.

[75] Philip A. Dur, "Presence: Forward, Ready, Engaged," in *Strategy and Force Planning*, 473.

[76] Ibid., 475.

[77] National Defense Panel, 5–7.

[78] White House, *A National Security Strategy for a New Century* (Washington, DC: The White House, December 1999), 12–13.

[79] Ibid., 29–47.

[80] Chairman of the Joint Chiefs of Staff, *Shape, Respond, Prepare Now: A Military Strategy for a New Era* (Washington, DC: Department of Defense, 1997), 29.

[81] Chairman, Joint Chiefs of Staff, *Joint Vision 2020*, June, 2000, 4.

[82] Franklyn Griffiths, "Environment in the U.S. Security Debate: The Case of the Missing Arctic Waters," *Environmental Change and Security Project Report*, Spring 1997, 22, accessed at <http://ecsp.si.edu/pdf/Report3a.pdf>.

[83] Ibid., 21.

[84] Dur, 474.

Chapter 10

Asia's Energy Future: The Military-Market Link

Thomas P.M. Barnett

G lobalization has resulted in the expansion of market capitalism throughout much of the world, particularly in East Asia.[1] Even China, with its recent entry into the World Trade Organization, appears poised to open its markets and unleash its commercial potential. China could be the world's largest auto market by 2020, increasing the oil needs of its enormous population by 40 percent. Obviously, this would have significant effects on the already-globalized energy market. In light of these global effects, both the Pentagon and Wall Street must understand their interrelationship: economic and political stability are crucial to reducing energy market risk.

As is evident in chapter 6, the Department of Navy is continuing its effort to enunciate the presumed linkage between the Navy's worldwide operations and the progressive unfolding of economic globalization. The goal is nothing less than the Holy Grail of naval presence arguments: proof positive that ship numbers—especially aircraft carriers—matter to international stability.[2] Some of this analytic effort will be rightly dismissed as pouring old wine into new bottles because many "Navy-as-the-glue-of-globalization" formulations sound an awful lot like the old bromides about the "Navy as the glue of Asia." Nice work if you can get it, but given the relative lack of naval crisis response in East Asia since the end of the Vietnam War, it is a hard story to sell. Simply put, once the Shah of Iran fell in 1979, U.S. naval crisis response activity quickly became concentrated on Southwest Asia—a pattern that continues to this day.[3] As far as "proving" the utility of naval presence, East Asia has long remained the dog that did not bark.

Thomas P.M. Barnett is professor and senior strategic researcher at the Naval War College. He directed the NewRulesSet.Project, an effort to draw new "maps" of power and influence in the world economy through collaboration with financial corporations such as Cantor Fitzgerald. Currently, he is serving as the assistant for strategic futures in the recently formed Office of Force Transformation within the Office of the Secretary of Defense. His articles appear with frequency in the U.S. Naval Institute *Proceedings*, and an abbreviated version of this chapter appeared in the January 2002 issue. The author would like to thank Bradd Hayes and Rear Admiral Michael McDevitt, USN (Ret.), for their comments on the original draft.

But all that is about to change, if you believe the stunning Department of Energy projections of growing Asian energy consumption over the next 20 years.[4] Not only do a lot of bad things have to not happen over the next 2 decades, but also a lot of good things must occur in both East Asia and the Middle East—and across all paths in between—to ensure the region's much-anticipated economic maturation will actually occur. In short, if you want a Pacific Century, you will need a U.S. Pacific Fleet—strong in numbers and forward deployed.

Asian Energy: A Globalization Decalogue

For several years, a Naval War College project (NewRuleSets.Project) on how globalization alters definitions of international security has provided considerable opportunity for an examination of the views of Wall Street executives, as well as of regional security experts (both military and civilian), on Asia's future economic and political development.[5] The following decalogue (summarized in table 10–1) distills the essential rule sets our project has identified concerning Asia's energy future:[6]

Global energy market has the necessary resources

Asia as a whole currently uses about as much energy as the United States, or about 100 quadrillion British thermal units.[7] By 2020, however, Asia will roughly double its energy consumption, while U.S. consumption will rise just more than 25 percent. Asia's plus-ups are significant no matter what the energy category, as evidenced in the following current estimates:

- oil consumption to increase by roughly 88 percent
- natural gas by 191 percent
- coal by 97 percent
- nuclear power by 87 percent when Japan is included, but 178 percent for the rest
- hydroelectric and other renewables by 109 percent.

This is a genuine changing of the guard in the global marketplace—a shifting of the world's "demand center." Today, North America accounts for just under a third of the world's energy consumption, with Asia second at 24 percent. But within one generation, those two regions will swap both global rankings and percentage shares. In short, Asia becomes the world's center of gravity for energy flows, giving it virtually the same market clout as the North Atlantic Treaty Organization countries—or North America and Western Europe combined.

The good news is that there's plenty of fossil fuel to go around. Confirmed oil reserves have jumped almost two-thirds over the past 20 years, according to the Department of Energy, while natural gas reserves have roughly doubled. Meanwhile, our best estimates on coal say we have enough for the next 2 centuries. So supply is not the

Table 10–1. **Asia's Energy Future: A Decalogue**

1	Global energy market has the necessary resources
2	But no stability, no market
3	No growth, no stability
4	No resources, no growth
5	No infrastructure, no resources
6	No money, no infrastructure
7	No rules, no money
8	No security, no rules
9	No (benign) Leviathan, no security
10	No U.S. Navy, no (benign) Leviathan

issue, and neither is demand, leaving only the question of moving the energy from those who have it to those who need it—and therein lies the rub.

But no stability, no market

Asia comes close to self-sufficiency only in coal, with Australia, China, India, and Indonesia the big producers. All told, Asia self-supplies on coal to the tune of 97 percent, a standard it will maintain through 2020. That is important, because virtually all of the global growth in coal use over the next generation will happen in Asia, mostly in just China and India.

Natural gas is a far different story. In 2001, Asia will used around 10 trillion cubic feet, with Japan, South Korea, and Taiwan representing the lion's share of consumption. The three of them already buy virtually all of the region's currently available methane (for example, from Australia, Brunei, Indonesia, and Malaysia). The trick is this: Asia's demand for natural gas skyrockets to perhaps 25 trillion cubic feet by 2020, with the majority of the increase occurring outside of that trio. So if those three countries already buy what is available in-region, that means the rest of Asia will have to go elsewhere—namely, the former Soviet Union (Russia with 33 percent of the world total) and the Middle East (Iran with 16 percent). This is what futurists might call an historical inevitability.

Finally, even though oil will decline as a percentage share in every major Asian economy over the coming years, absolute demand will grow by leaps and bounds. Asia currently burns about as much oil as the United States, or roughly 20 million barrels/day (mbd). Since oil is mostly about transportation nowadays, and Asia is looking at a quintupling of its car fleet by 2020, there is a huge swag placed on this projection.

The latest Department of Energy forecast is roughly 36 mbd, but even that means Asia as a whole has to import an additional 12 mbd from out of region, or close to double what it imports today from the Persian Gulf region.[8]

Asia already buys roughly two-thirds of all the oil produced in the Persian Gulf, and by 2010 that share will rise to approximately 75 percent.[9] Meanwhile, the West's share of Gulf oil will drop from just under a quarter today to just over a tenth in 2010. The strategic upshot is that the two most anti-Western corners of the globe are inexorably coming together over energy and money over the coming years. Increasingly, the Middle East becomes dependent on economic stability in Asia, and Asia on political-military stability in the Gulf. If either side of that equation fails, the energy market is put at risk.

No growth, no stability

All this predicted growth engenders social expectations. In other words, Asia's developing societies have been placed on consumption trajectories that are nothing short of revolutionary. As a middle class develops in these countries (small as a percentage but enormous as an absolute number), a significant portion of the global population is being rapidly promoted from an 18th- or 19th-century lifestyle into a 20th- or even 21st-century consumption pattern—and they will get used to it pretty darn fast.

Moreover, if Thomas Friedman's "electronic herd" of international investors decides to take it all away one afternoon in a flurry of currency attacks and capital flight, the struggling segment of the population that suddenly finds itself expelled from the would-be middle class is likely to get upset. This is basically what happened in Indonesia following the tumultuous events of the Asian Flu of 1997–1998. Huge portions of Indonesia's economy had experienced rapid development in the preceding generation, only to see it disappear virtually one fickle market day.

Yes, some good resulted; Suharto's crony capitalism collapsed, but with it went much of the country's emerging middle class. Now, as the country disintegrates into pockets of chaos, the machetes are flying as disoriented villagers work nightly to dispatch the "sorcerers" and "black ninjas" purported to be behind this continuing economic decline. In short, Indonesia loses its growth trajectory and suddenly finds itself transported back in time several centuries.[10]

No resources, no growth

Asia cannot grow without a huge influx of out-of-area energy resources. The quintupling of cars is impressive enough, when you consider that General Motors predicts China will indeed be the world's largest car market in 2020.[11] But even more stunning is the three-fold increase in electricity consumption, which will be generated mostly by coal and—increasingly—natural gas. Put those two together, and we are talking about an Asia that must open up to the outside world to a degree unprecedented in modern history. Or to put it in another way, Asia's choice of energy will largely determine its attitude on globalization. China is the classic example here.

One can think of China's decisions about its pattern of energy consumption as a choice between the past (coal), the present (oil), and the future (methane, or natural gas). If China chooses to remain, as much as possible, in the "past" with coal, this decision will essentially delay its full-fledged absorption into the global economy. This is clearly the path of least resistance for Beijing, and there lies the temptation, for the perception of autonomy afforded by coal allows China to:

- remain more opaque to outside scrutiny
- retain more control over its energy future
- continue the more easily directed top-down path of extensive growth (that is, more inputs versus more productivity).

If China chooses to move—as much as possible—into the "future" with natural gas, this decision will speed up its full-fledged absorption into the global economy. This is obviously a far more difficult path, because it:

- opens the country to greater interdependency with the outside world
- forces more transparency upon its financial systems
- asks it to trade control for calculated risk (nothing is guaranteed in the free market)
- demands a far greater push for intensive-style economic growth.

The bigger point, however, is this: neither China nor Asia as a whole can develop without opening to the outside world economically, and energy is the essential driving force in this process.

No infrastructure, no resources

Asia's infrastructure requirements over the next 2 decades will be unprecedented in human history. Simply put, never have so many people developed an economy at such a rapid pace in such a concentrated chunk of global real estate. This rough doubling of energy consumption will place extraordinary demands on the environment. The combination of rapid rises in energy consumption, population, urbanization, and water usage (especially for agriculture) will further damage an already battered regional ecosystem, creating great political pressures on national governments—both from within and outside—to limit the pollution associated with energy production.

Cleaner cars and more mass transportation are important, but even more so is the choice of how all that electricity is to be generated. Asia will attempt to grow its nuclear and renewables capacity to the fullest extent possible, but as a combined share of total energy production (that is, 10 percent), these categories will not grow—even as they double in absolute amounts to keep pace with economic development. The story is roughly the same with coal, which stands at just over 40 percent of total energy production now and still will in the year 2020. The real shift in Asia's energy profile comes in oil and natural gas, with the former declining from roughly 40 percent to 30 percent, and the latter basically doubling from 10 to 20 percent.

This 275 percent increase in the absolute amount of methane energy employed across the region highlights the story-within-the-story of Asia's energy future: the push for energy is really a push for infrastructure. Regarding natural gas, this infrastructure comes in three forms:

■ For the near term, the vast majority of natural gas that flows into Asia will arrive in a liquid form on ships. That means port facilities on both ends of the conduit, plus liquidification plants on the supplier's end and regasification plants on the buyer's end.

■ Over the longer haul, pipelines become the answer to meet the rising demand— both by land (for example, Kazakstan-to-China, Russia-to-China) and sea (Russia-to-Japan, Iran-to-India).

■ Finally, there is the domestic infrastructure required to pipe all that gas to the final consumers.

None of this comes cheaply, and as the recent history of regional electricity development makes clear, lots of outside money is required.[12]

No money, no infrastructure

Foreign direct investment (FDI) is the most significant scenario variable for Asia's energy future. Energy infrastructure requirements could easily top $1 trillion by 2020, according to many estimates. Such numbers will overwhelm the region's ability to self-finance, and that means Asia will have to open up its energy generation and distribution markets to far more joint or foreign ownership—a touchy subject, as former global energy giant Enron's experience in India demonstrated.[13]

Right now, Asian states invest in one another to a very high degree, as many developing regional economies funnel upward of 90 percent of their external capital investments into their neighbors. But their combined resources are very limited compared to the West. A good estimate of Asia's current outward stock—meaning the cumulative value—of foreign direct investment would be roughly $750 billion. In contrast, the United States and the European Union—even when one discounts intra-European investments—control roughly three times that amount of capital.[14]

Until now, Asia has relied on intra-Asian FDI for almost two-thirds of its cross-border capital needs, keeping the West at a certain distance in the mergers and acquisition trade. But this will have to change for Asia's ambitious energy future to unfold according to plan. On an annual basis, the European Union and the United States routinely account for over 80 percent of all cross-border direct investment flows, far outdistancing their combined share of global gross domestic product, which sits as just under 60 percent.[15] These two economic giants mostly invest in one another (and Europe in itself), creating an unbreakable trans-Atlantic bond. So if it seems inevitable that Asia must turn to the former Soviet Union and the Middle East for energy in the coming decades (the energy triad), it is just as inevitable that it must turn to the West for the money to finance this trade (the capital triad).

No rules, no money

Many on Wall Street voice the opinion that Asia has not sufficiently "cleaned up its act" as a result of the 1997–1998 financial crisis. The buzzword here is *transparency*, which refers primarily to internationally accepted accounting practices in the financial and corporate sectors. This is a huge challenge for Asia to overcome in terms of attracting the necessary foreign direct investment for future energy needs. Simply put, institutional investors need to feel confident in their ability to get a long-term return *of* investment and not just a short-term return *on* investment, and that sort of confidence comes only with the firm rule of law.

Another problem with Asia's energy investment climate is the current mix of private-sector investments and public-sector decisionmaking—in effect, too many bureaucrats with too much of other people's money. In most Asian economies, the government still plays far too large a role as far as Western financiers are concerned. For the most part, Wall Street likes to see monopolies build networks but prefers them to be run by market forces once they are operational—their version of having a cake and eating it too. But so long as rule sets lag behind, the rise of private-sector market makers is delayed, for firm rules of play are required before deregulation of state-run energy markets can proceed.

Viewed from this angle, it might be said that the greatest long-term threat to Asia's energy security is internal: its own proclivities for crony capitalism. Whether it is called *Asian values*, *capitalism with Chinese characteristics*, or *globalization on our terms*, all Asian claims to a particular brand of capitalism are ultimately self-defeating. In sum, money has to behave in Asia just like it does in the West if the region hopes to attract the investment necessary to secure its energy future.

No security, no rules

Foreign direct investment does not occur in a vacuum. Long-term certainty is the greatest attraction a country can offer to outside investors, whereas war and political-military instability (especially leftist revolutions) are the best methods to scare them away. Not surprisingly, the strongest FDI bonds exist between the three main pillars of the Cold War's trilateral alliance structure: the United States, Western Europe, and Japan.

This triad controls 80 percent of the world's stock in foreign direct investment, keeping two-thirds of that total invested in one another. That means the other 90 percent of the global population has to get by on the remaining half of global FDI capital available. In a nutshell, investment follows the flag far more than trade. For example, the United States does about a third of its trade with Western Europe and Japan but concentrates closer to a half of its FDI in these two markets.[16]

Developing Asia, in contrast, readily presents a handful of potential and/or existing security trouble spots that could negatively impact the region's FDI climate in significant ways:

- India-Pakistan nuclear standoff
- Indonesia's disarray
- The Korean situation (especially the North's nuclear/missile programs and/or "imminent collapse")
- China-Taiwan
- Overlapping sovereignty claims in the South China Sea.

Bluntly stated, Asia is still a place where military conflict could dramatically alter the FDI landscape, unlike a Europe where the conflict in the former Yugoslavia had a negligible impact on economic integration and investment flows.

No (benign) Leviathan, no security

Many international experts agree that Asia's current security situation belongs more to what Thomas Friedman calls the "olive tree" world, where backward tribes fight over little bits of land, even as its rising economic powerhouses clearly join the "Lexus" world, producing many of the global economy's best high-end technology products.[17] Lacking Europe's crucible-like history of 20th-century warfare, as well as its currently robust regional security alliances, Asia remains the one place in the world where direct great power warfare seems possible over the next generation. This becomes especially true as previously authoritarian states experience greater amounts of political pluralism, typically the most dangerous time for interstate wars.[18]

In this region where the concepts of *spheres of influence* and *security dilemma* are still valid, there remains a viable long-term market for the services of an outside Leviathan—namely, the United States. In a part of the world where numerous states are still technically at war (dating back more than half a century), the United States enjoys healthier security relationships with virtually every government than any two governments there enjoy with one another. While it is easy to deride the notion of a "four-star foreign policy," there is little doubt that the combatant commander of U.S. Pacific

Command plays a special—even unique—role in working the security arrangements that underpin the region's strong record of structural stability over the past quarter century (basically, since Vietnam was reunified).[19]

And if there was no U.S. military presence, then what? How comfortable could Japan be with China? Taiwan with China? South Korea with North Korea? India with Pakistan? India with China? Vietnam with China? The list goes on and on. Simply put, the U.S. military occupies both a physical and a fiscal space in Asia: our forward presence both reassures local governments and obviates their need for larger military hedges. Our presence is a moneymaker on two fronts: local governments spend less on defense and more on development (the ultimate defense), and FDI is encouraged, however subtly.

No U.S. Navy, no (benign) Leviathan

As noted earlier, what Asia needs in terms of future energy requirements is entirely available either in-region (for example, coal) or from the central portion of the Eurasian landmass (gas and oil from the Persian Gulf, Central Asia, and Russia). These distances are all feasibly conquered by pipelines, and most of the involved sea lines of communication lie within the reach of the region's naval forces—for good or ill.

Meanwhile, the West, which has come to rely less and less on Persian Gulf oil, is likewise becoming more regionally focused in its energy trade patterns. The United States, for example, imports more energy supplies from Canada than any other nation, and gets the bulk of its imported oil from North and South America.

None of these statements are meant to suggest that East-versus-West energy blocs are forming. In reality, the regionalization of energy trade occurs *precisely* because the commodities in question are behaving more and more as one would expect of a globally traded, highly fungible good. If price determines all, then reducing transportation distance makes sense.

In the end, all this regionalization comes about because the energy trade is no longer confined to the sort of strategic bilateral relationships of the Cold War era, so the new rules of energy are nothing more than that sector's joining up with the global marketplace and losing its special status as a strategic asset.

Having said all that, the U.S. Government—and the U.S. Navy in particular—faces a far more complex strategic environment in the 21st century, whether or not it yet realizes the change: our national security interests in the Persian Gulf, while increasingly important for the *global* economy, no longer hold the same immediate importance to our *national* economy.

In effect, U.S. naval presence in Asia is becoming far less an expression of our nation's forward presence than our exporting of security to the global marketplace. In that regard, we truly do move into the Leviathan category, for the product we provide is increasingly a collective good less directly tied to our particularistic national interests and far more intimately wrapped up with our global responsibilities.

And in the end, this is a pretty good deal. We trade little pieces of paper (our currency, in the form of a trade deficit) for Asia's amazing array of products and services. We are smart enough to know this is a patently unfair deal—unless we offer something of great value along with those little pieces of paper. That product is a strong U.S. Pacific Fleet, which squares the transaction quite nicely.

Understanding the Military-Market Connection

The collapse of the Soviet bloc and its longstanding challenge (or rejection) of the Western economic rule set made possible—really for the first time in human history—a truly global rule set for how military power buttresses and enables economic growth and stability.

How so? For the first time in human history, we have a true global military Leviathan in the form of the U.S. military, and no peer competitor in sight—not even a coherent alternative economic philosophy (although one clearly brews in the antiglobalization protests that started with Seattle). This unparalleled moment in global history both allows and compels the United States to better understand the national security-market nexus, in large part because of its complete reversal of the priority from that of the Cold War era. During the strategic standoff with the Soviet Union, economic might was seen as supporting military power, but now that situation has been turned on its head: to the extent that the military matters, it matters because of the stabilization role it can play in the global economy.

How do we define this yin-yang relationship between the military and business worlds? First, we speak of stability, which flows from national security, and then we speak of transparency, which is both demanded and engendered by free markets. These two underlying pillars form the basis of the single global rule set that now essentially defines the era of globalization.

Within those two pillars, the United States clearly plays a crucial role:

- The U.S. Government, through the U.S. military, supplies the lion's share of system stability through its Leviathan-like status as the world's sole military superpower.
- The U.S. financial markets, which lead the way in fostering the emergence of a truly global equities market that will inevitably operate all day, every day, play the leading role in spreading the gospel of transparency—any country's best defense against the sort of financial currency crises that have periodically erupted over the last decade (Mexico 1994, Asia 1997, Russia 1998, Brazil 1999, Turkey 2001).

As such, it is essential that these two worlds—the Pentagon and Wall Street—come to better understand their interrelationships across the global economy. Uncovering and comprehending this fundamental relationship is especially important because—the vast majority of the time—the security and financial communities operate in oblivious indifference to one another.

One is tempted to counter, "So what? They don't need to be aware of one another on a day-to-day basis." And in a basic sense, that is true. But if you consider the rise of system perturbations as a new form of international security threat, and if you understand that many of these perturbations first appear in the form of financial crises that can engender serious subnational violence (for example, Indonesia today), then perhaps this connectivity seems more pertinent. Ultimately, the global economy operates on trust, which is based on certainty, which in turn comes from the effective processing of risk.

In the end, the national security and financial establishments are in the same fundamental business: the effective assessment and mitigation of international risk. For the military, it is the risk of conflict and the disruption of normal life by large-scale violence, while in the financial world, it is the risk of bankruptcy (insolvency) and the disruption of normal business by large-scale panics or meltdowns.

Invariably, these two problem sets merge in the historical process that is economic globalization, so understanding the military-market connection is not just good business, it is good national security strategy. Osama bin Laden understood this connection when he selected the World Trade Center and the Pentagon as his targets. We ignore his logic at our peril.

Notes

[1] For the purposes of this article, the author defines Asia as extending from Afghanistan to Japan, but not including Australia and New Zealand (Oceania), although he identifies Australia as an in-region supplier of energy (coal and natural gas) due to its proximity.

[2] For a good example of this sort of work, see Thomas P.M. Barnett and Linda D. Lancaster, *Answering the 9–1–1 Call: U.S. Military and Naval Crisis Response Activity, 1977–1991* (Center for Naval Analyses Information Memorandum 229, August 1992).

[3] For the best analysis on this subject, see Henry H. Gaffney, Jr., et al., *U.S. Naval Responses to Situations, 1970–1999* (Center for Naval Analyses Research Memorandum D0002763.A2/Final, December 2000).

[4] See the Energy Information Administration's *International Energy Outlook 2000: With Projections to 2020*, DOE/EIA–0484 (2000), March 2000, accessed at <www.eia.doe.gov/oiaf/ieo/index.html>.

[5] The NewRuleSets.Project was a multi-year research effort designed to explore how globalization and the rise of the New Economy are altering the basic "rules of the road" in the international security environment, with special reference to how these changes may redefine the U.S. Navy's historic role as security enabler of America's commercial network ties with the world. The project was hosted by the online securities broker-dealer firm, eSpeed (an affiliate of Cantor Fitzgerald LP), and involved personnel from the Decision Strategies Department of the Center for Naval Warfare Studies. Adm. William Flanagan, USN (Ret.), and Philip Ginsberg of Cantor Fitzgerald (then-senior managing director and executive vice president, respectively) served as informal advisers to the project, actively participating in all planning and design. The joint Wall Street-Naval War College workshops in the series involved energy, environmental

issues and foreign direct investment in Asia. All research products relating to this effort can be found at <www.nwc.navy.mil/newrulesets>.

[6] All the energy data presented in the decalogue, unless otherwise specified, comes from the Department of Energy's *International Energy Outlook 2001*.

[7] A good rule of thumb for thinking about a quadrillion British thermal units (Btus) is that you can take the annual number for a region and divide it by two, giving you the rough equivalent in millions of barrels of oil per day the region would need to burn if it was achieving that entire energy amount by oil alone. For example, North America used about 110 quadrillion Btus in 1997, so that would equate to approximately 55 million barrels a day (mbd) of oil if that entire amount was achieved by oil alone. For point of comparison, note that the United States currently uses about 20 mbd, importing roughly half that number.

[8] For an excellent exploration of this, see Daniel Yergin, Dennis Eklof, and Jefferson Edwards, "Fueling Asia's Recovery," *Foreign Affairs* 77, no. 2 (March/April 1998), 34–50.

[9] The Middle East currently accounts for roughly 90 percent of all Asian oil imports; on this see Fereidun Fesharaki, "Energy and Asian Security Nexus," *Journal of International Affairs* 53, no. 1 (Fall 1999), 97.

[10] For a frightening description of this situation, see Nicholas D. Kristof's chapter, "Search for the Sorceror," in *Thunder from the East: Portrait of a Rising Asia*, ed. Kristof and Sheryl WuDunn (New York: Alfred A. Knopf, 2000), 5–23.

[11] Cited in Clay Chandler, "GM's China Bet Hits Snag: WTO (Car Shoppers Await Discount From Trade Deal)," *The Washington Post*, May 10, 2000, E1.

[12] See "Foreign Investment in the Electricity Sectors of Asia and South America," in *International Energy Outlook 2001*, 120–21.

[13] For a good description of Enron's difficulties in the Indian electricity market, see Celia W. Dugger, "High-Stakes Showdown: Enron's Right Over Power Plant Reverberates Beyond India," *The New York Times*, March 20, 2001, C1.

[14] These figures are derived from United Nations Conference on Trade and Development (UNCTAD), *World Investment Report 2000*.

[15] In contrast, Asia accounts for less than 10 percent of global foreign direct investment flows, even though its gross domestic product share sits at 25 percent.

[16] Estimates based on the figures taken from UNCTAD, *World Investment Review* and CIA, *World Factbook*, various years.

[17] See Thomas L. Friedman, *The Lexus And The Olive Tree: Understanding Globalization* (New York: Farrar, Strauss and Giroux, 1999).

[18] On this subject, see the data analysis by Edward D. Mansfield and Jack Snyder, "Democratization and War," *Foreign Affairs* 74, no. 3 (May/June 1995), 79–97.

[19] For an excellent exploration of this concept, see Dana Priest, "A Four-Star Foreign Policy? U.S. Commanders Wield Rising Clout, Autonomy," *The Washington Post*, September 28, 2000, A1. See also the second and third articles in the series (September 29–30).

Chapter 11

The Globalization of the Defense Sector? Naval Industrial Cases and Issues

Peter Dombrowski

Numerous authors have noted the importance of globalization for national security affairs, yet globalization remains a highly contested concept. Political scientists, economists, and historians have all sought to pin down the nature of globalization with little success. Many argue that whatever the historical antecedents of globalization, the current period represents a new watershed in international economic relations. As Robert Gilpin explains, proponents of the globalization thesis claim that "a quantum change in human affairs has taken place as the flow of large quantities of trade, investment and technologies across national borders has expanded from a trickle to a flood."[1] The financial services sector, biotechnologies, information services, and a host of other industries show increasing evidence that globalization is occurring or has occurred over the past 20 years.

The same cannot be said for the defense industrial sector. Although recent studies have pronounced that defense sector globalization presents a major challenge to U.S. national security, the evidence is more anecdotal than overwhelming.[2] Arguments tend toward prescription—advocating that officials facilitate globalization[3] or that they take steps to halt globalization's progress—or explaining, in theory, what globalization will mean for defense policy and military affairs.[4] In each case, globalization of

Peter Dombrowski is associate professor in the strategic research department of the U.S. Naval War College, where he is working on a major study of "Military Transformation and Defense Industry After Next." Previously he was associate professor of political science at Iowa State University. He is the author of *Policy Responses to the Globalization of American Banks* (Pittsburgh: University of Pittsburgh Press, 1996), as well as articles in numerous journals. He also serves as the co-editor of *International Studies Quarterly* and as the president of the International Political Economy Section of the International Studies Association. The author would like to acknowledge the influence of Andrew Ross and Eugene Gholz on his thinking about defense industrial globalization.

the defense sector is taken as a given.[5] Yet, as Judith Reppy has argued, discussions of defense industrial globalization are "still largely prospective."[6]

This chapter explores the issue of defense sector globalization with particular attention to those industries producing naval weapon systems. First, it analyzes the relationship between economic globalization and the cross-border activities of defense firms. Second, it discusses the current state of the transnational defense industry. Third, it offers three alternative perspectives on the globalization thesis—Americanization, internationalization, and regionalization/regionalism—and concludes that the defense sector is actually experiencing a moderate amount of regionalism. Finally, it examines an aspect of defense industry globalization that is most specific to the U.S. Navy—shipbuilding.

The (Il)Logic of Defense Industrial Globalization

In many respects, the logic underlying the overall process of economic globalization does not support its application to the defense industrial sector. Economic globalization is motivated by market logic. Firms seek profits wherever they might find them, at home or abroad. States acquiesce to and/or encourage globalization because private markets stimulate economic growth and increase national wealth. Anything that impedes open markets reduces opportunities for growth. In sectors where globalization has progressed the farthest—finance, for example—the last three decades have witnessed a gradual reduction of state controls over cross-border economic activity.

By contrast, defense industries are almost entirely creatures of states. States are the primary consumers of defense products, especially modern, high-technology weapon systems. Without government procurement defense industries would not survive. Recognizing this, states either own defense firms in toto, are significant shareholders in defense firms, or provide a range of subsidies and incentives to firms undertaking defense production. Defense firms find it difficult to survive as independent, stand-alone companies or as divisions within mixed commercial-defense enterprises. Historically, states have constrained the ability of defense industries to operate across national borders through a variety of mechanisms including export control laws.

Despite this, many analysts believe that the logic driving economic globalization applies to defense industries—for both theoretical and empirical reasons. On the theoretical side, it is argued that in a liberal world economy, no economic phenomena—much less an entire industry—is immune from the effects of globalization. The pressure to seek new markets, cut costs, and share technology pushes firms to globalization even if they are primarily engaged in producing weapon systems.[7] Globalization is facilitated by information-age technology systems that make it increasingly difficult for countries or firms to pursue independent, much less autarkic, economic policies in any industry. To resists the trend of globalization is to ensure technological backwardness, rising prices, and reduced productivity. By this reasoning, a country that does not allow its firms to expand internationally is doomed to lose future arms races to more open, nimbler competitors. "Thus in the name of self-sufficiency and security of supply, countries have long protected their defense industries against foreign competition whenever possible, even when the result is higher costs or less advanced equipment."[8]

Empirically, changes clearly are afoot in the world's defense industry. According to Ann Markusen, "Arms manufacturers are following the lead of their commercial counterparts and going global, pursuing transnational mergers and alliances and establishing design, production, and market operations abroad."[9] By Markusen's account, even the most potent symbols of American military superiority, such as the F–16, are filled with components produced abroad.[10] Although the producer of record might be an American-based firm such as Boeing, the various subcontractors and vendors assembled by Boeing to help manufacture the jet fighter often produce or buy components overseas.[11]

But in actuality, defense industrial globalization is more of a mirage than a reality. Across all three principal dimensions of economic globalization—trade, investment, and technology diffusion—there are reasons to doubt that the defense sector will follow other sectors such as the automobile or electronics industries, much less service industries such as banking, finance and transportation, on the road toward globalization.

Serious impediments remain to higher levels of cross-border defense related trade, investment, and technology flows. First, economic and political impediments to defense exports—from limited demand to concerns about regional instability and proliferation—continue to restrict trade in defense products and services. No matter how much the defense industry would like a freer hand to peddle its wares overseas, there are legitimate concerns from the national security perspectives of individual states. Second, cross-border investments, with some significant exceptions, often generate security concerns in host-nation governments—including, and perhaps especially, in the United States. Even if we accept declinist arguments about the future of the nation-state, most governments continue to believe that maintaining control over basic weapon production facilities is prudent. Third, advanced military-specific technologies in the United States and elsewhere are largely the product of public investment; few governments want to share the public patrimony with close allies much less with countries that qualify merely as *potential* allies or friends. Even dual-use technologies are subject to this logic, as indicated by the 2001 imbroglio over the sale of an American firm, Silicon Valley Group, Inc., to the Dutch firm of ASM Lithography Holding NV. As news accounts report, the United States is "concerned that SVG's lithography technology—used to make lenses for spy satellites and other high-tech equipment—will be shared by the Dutch firm with potentially hostile countries such as China."[12]

In sum, then, there are logical reasons to suspect that the alleged globalization of defense industries is either not as extensive as some analysts assume or is taking a different shape than the globalization processes under way in other industries.

Alternatives to Defense Industry Globalization?

If globalization seems implausible, the question then remains: What are we to make of the observable changes in the world defense industrial sector? Significant changes in the ways in which defense firms operate are clearly afoot. Moreover, if the advocates of defense sector globalization, both from industry and from inside various national governments, have their way, remaining impediments to cross-border defense trade, investment, and technological diffusion will soon be removed. Firms will then be freer to pursue global strategies based in firm-level strategies. What then?

Americanization. One answer is that, to date, the world has witnessed the Americanization of the defense sector.[13] By such logic it will see more of the same over the next decade as the United States increases defense spending in response to the war on terror and the DOD desire to achieve the "military after next." The U.S. defense market—in terms of research and development (R&D) and procurement spending—remains by far the world's largest. Given the size of the U.S. defense budget, foreign firms are at least as likely to seek to enter the U.S. market as American firms are to seek access to overseas markets. Companies such as BAE Systems and Rolls Royce may now be trying to do just that with their acquisition of smaller U.S. firms. Some analysts even predict that a European firm such as BAE may soon try to purchase or merge with an American prime contractor. Political opposition to such maneuvers can be expected, however, with some charging that foreign acquisitions "eat the technological seed corn" upon which American military superiority is based.[14]

Americanization is driven by more than the simple size of American defense budgets, however. It also reflects the dominance of American arms in the international marketplace. Since the end of the Cold War, the United States has increased its lead over competitors as the largest exporter of arms and other military equipment. Even as Russia, France, and other countries seek to promote arms sales by their own national champions, there is little reason to believe that they will supplant the United States as the leading arms supplier any time soon. The United States uses foreign military sales as a key component of its national security strategy; other governments buy American, at least in part, for the purpose of remaining interoperable with U.S. forces. American weapon systems, although relatively expensive, remain among the most sophisticated and prestigious in the world.

Internationalization. A second possibility is internationalization. Although this term is sometimes used as a synonym for globalization, it implies a state-to-state dynamic rather than the borderless, private-sector-dominated dynamic associated with most versions of globalization. Given, as we shall see, the importance of state decisionmaking in promoting the cross-border activities of defense firms, internationalization is an appealing alternative explanation to the globalization thesis. Yet it remains inadequate because it implies that the process spreads evenly across the entire world economy and system of states. Nothing could be further from the truth. Increased cross-border relationships among defense industrial concerns are geographically limited. They do not extend to huge swathes of the globe—from South America to Africa, for example. Even those regions that have historically participated in defense industrial production are today less active in the international arms market. East Europe and the former Soviet republics have been reduced to niche players with few pretensions to competing at the same level as their North American and West European counterparts.[15] Russia, although it has enjoyed a resurgence in arms sales over the past 2 or 3 years, sells largely to former client states or to countries that remain outside of the U.S. orbit by choice (India and China, for example) or because of imposed sanctions.[16]

Regionalism/Regionalization. The other main contender is the concept of regionalism. Sophisticated treatments of regionalism stress the need to distinguish "between regionalization, which refers to the regional concentration of economic flows, and regionalism . . . a political process characterized by economic policy cooperation and coordination among countries."[17] One way to look at this issue is to see that market processes drive regionalism, and that individual firms cross national borders in pursuit of markets, market share, and profits. Regionalization, like internationalization, is driven by the calculations of government and officials. By removing impediments to trade and investment in the defense sector, governments encourage defense firms to do business with key allies or cooperate with firms home-based in the territory of friends and allies. More actively, governments may even offer various incentives for firms to collaborate with foreign competitors and to sell arms to key allies.

In some respects, regionalism is not incompatible with globalization because, however defined, globalization is an uneven process. Not all countries in all regions are, or will be, fully integrated into the international arms market. A number of states critical to global and regional security remain largely outside the global marketplace in general, much less the market for arms sold by American and European firms. Thus, China, Iraq, Russia, and North Korea, to name the most prominent examples, are not full participants in cross-border arms sales or investment except—sometimes— among themselves. When they do take part in cross-border transactions, it is largely to purchase advanced technologies abroad that they cannot develop indigenously or to avoid arms control regimes or United Nations-imposed sanctions.

Others, like the former communist countries of Central and Eastern Europe and most of the former Soviet republics, have decreased their participation in international defense markets. Several Central and Eastern European countries have decided to concentrate development efforts in other economic areas and to buy much of the equipment needed to modernize their forces from the West. If they hope to achieve membership in Western security institutions such as the North Atlantic Treaty Organization (NATO) and achieve reasonable levels of interoperability, they cannot remain autarkic in arms production. For the most part, globalization for such regions will consist largely of imports and limited licensing agreements to produce lower-end systems and components. The potential for globalization is also limited by the fiscal constraints under which these countries operate.

Most regions participate in globalization largely as niche and regional players. With the exception of some commercial off-the-shelf components and subsystems that are included in major weapon systems, few expect that these left-behind areas will ever participate in the "globalization of defense industries" with regard to first-generation weapon systems. Even European firms often occupy niches far from the cutting edge. German, Dutch, and Italian expertise in designing diesel submarines, while impressive, hardly represents the apex of undersea technologies (see chapter 17). Often niche players emerge because their own strategic needs have forced them to invest in areas that eventually become desirable to the wider international community. Israel, for example, has played a significant role in developing unmanned aerial vehicles (UAVs) because of its need for tactical and operational intelligence and the paucity of national space-based intelligence, surveillance, and reconnaissance capabilities.

The most significant arena of defense industrial regionalism lies within the North Atlantic community. Like the United States, Europe experienced a wave of mergers and acquisitions in the 1990s, albeit somewhat later than the American process. To date, the result has been a more regionalized European defense industry.

The European Union has sought to rationalize procurement strategies by allowing for the consolidation of national champions into supranational regional champions. Thus EADS, BAE Systems, Thales, and Finmeccanica have emerged as the "big four" producers of defense equipment within the continent. To some extent, each of these firms is multinational—R&D and production facilities are spread across multiple European countries and, to a lesser extent, non-European countries such as the United States. It should be noted that, as in the United States, formal firm-level identification actually overstates the level of diversity within the European defense industry. Europe's big four actually collaborate and cooperate as often as they compete; Alberto Lina, the chief operating officer of Finmeccanica, estimates that nearly 45 percent of the total revenues of the big four result from civil and military joint ventures.[18] They are increasingly entangled in a complex web of partnerships, licensing agreements, joint ventures, and other forms of collaboration.[19] One consequence of these European mergers is that the largest firms, EADS and BAE Systems, are now large enough that they may be able to compete with the largest U.S. defense firms in certain areas of the defense market.[20]

According to Mattias Axelson, "each [EADS, BAE Systems, and Thales] has the sales and breadth of capabilities that are comparable to the leading U.S. defense companies and each is based on a complex network of cross-border ownership and joint ventures."[21] EADS has gone on record as saying that it will pursue American business, in direct competition with the major American firms, in an aggressive fashion. EADS co-chief executive officers Phillipe Camus and Rainer Hertrich argue that their firm can increase competition in the American market, solve interoperability problems within NATO, and reduce costs on both sides of the Atlantic by pooling development and production.[22] Moreover, EADS and the other European defense firms even enjoy some competitive advantages over their American rivals: less restrictive export regulations and lower levels of corporate debt, for example.

For these reasons, it has been predicted that the next logical step is a creation of a more tightly integrated trans-Atlantic defense industrial base.[23] But there is a paradox. Officially, NATO allies remain committed to meeting interoperability problems and equipment shortfalls with a strategy centered on the Defense Capabilities Initiative (DCI). But unofficially—and at the level of domestic and regional politics—what NATO countries view themselves as committed to is much less clear. As Alexander Moens observes, "European governments buy relatively little from other European defense industries . . . the 'new' European giants would not really compete with U.S. giants in the key European defence markets but with previous national citadels."[24]

Most Western European governments aggressively seek to secure a share of the overall procurement, capture R&D expenditures, and sustain those remaining national champions. Moreover, the fact remains that both at the individual country level and in the aggregate, defense procurement and R&D spending in Europe remains relatively small compared to U.S. spending.

Some analysts already see evidence that in the trans-Atlantic region, cross-border cooperation among national defense firms is occurring at an unprecedented rate. Firms such as Northrop Grumman and EADS have pursued numerous partnerships, including the Alliance Ground Surveillance system and Euro Hawk UAV.[25] Political pressures from defense industries, as well as legislators mindful of local employment, have encouraged policymakers to loosen the bonds restricting cross-border transactions among defense industrial concerns, at least within NATO. Thus, the Defense Trade Security Initiatives seek to allow greater cooperation with key American allies. Further, in the latter half of the administration of President Clinton and now in the George W. Bush administration, calls for defense industrial reforms often include provisions for allowing, if not encouraging, defense industrial globalization. This, in practice, usually means greater economic integration among firms serving the Western alliance. How far such initiatives progress remains to be seen. Many political impediments will have to be overcome before more significant trans-Atlantic regionalism—such as the acquisition of (or merger with) an American prime by a European conglomerate or vice versa—makes regionalism a reality.

Naval Implications of Defense Industry Regionalism

The U.S. Navy is affected by general developments in the overall defense industrial sector. As such, globalization or the other potential trends such as regionalism will affect Navy acquisition programs across the board. However, the remainder of this chapter will focus on the one component of the defense industrial base that is Navy unique: shipbuilding. As will be argued, this most Navy-specific area of the defense industrial sector is even less susceptible to globalization or regionalism than the other defense sectors.

Across the globe, naval shipbuilding represents one of the most protected segments of the defense marketplace and one of the least globalized industries. The United States is not an exception to this generalization; if anything, it may represent an extreme example. However, before considering the possible effects of globalization on naval construction in the United States, it is important to understand the general relationship between warship construction and commercial shipbuilding within the United States, as well as the contrast between the U.S. shipbuilding industry in general and shipbuilding in other parts of the world.

Commercial market share. Commercial shipbuilding in the United States remains uncompetitive in global markets. As of June 2000, the United States controlled just 1 percent of the world's market for newly constructed commercial vessels over 1,000 gross tons, a figure that ranks the United States tenth in the world behind South Korea and Japan, among others. Overall, less than 2 percent of the American shipbuilding revenue comes from exports. Many factors account for the American shipbuilding industry's position in world markets, including low productivity, high prices, and technological problems. Industry proponents also note that many international competitors protect and subsidize their shipbuilders.[26]

The relative weakness of the U.S. commercial shipbuilding industry matters insofar as the private sector provides a foundation for naval construction. At least in theory, a healthy commercial shipbuilding sector would be a source of innovation (in new technologies as well as in manufacturing processes), trained labor, and, perhaps, investment capital. Under current conditions, this relationship between naval and commercial shipbuilding is almost reversed. The U.S. Government (through the resources of the Navy, the Defense Advanced Research Projects Agency, and other departments) provides the impetus for innovation, seeks to ensure a supply of skilled professionals, and underwrites much of the industries' capital investment.

Naval trade. The U.S. naval shipbuilding industry has not broken into international markets for warships as much as might be supposed, given the pressure for profits and the competitive advantage American shipyards would appear to have in naval warfare systems. One reason underlying this failure is "that foreign navies do not require the types and configurations of vessels built for the U.S. Navy."[27] With the decline of the Soviet-era navy (now parceled out among Russia and Ukraine), few countries aspires to maintain large, global blue-water fleets; those that do so, including France and Great Britain, build their own warships.[28] American shipyards do, however, continue to pursue, sometimes successfully, contracts to build mid-sized naval vessels such as corvettes and frigates. Further, the United States continues to sell older or surplus vessels abroad such as *Oliver Hazard Perry*–class frigates to customers such as Turkey and Taiwan. Usually such sales include contractor services for engineering, repairs, training, and other purposes, thereby providing a much-needed source of revenue for the American naval industry.[29] However, the larger profit margins that could be obtained through the sale of very large (and sophisticated) combatants, such as aircraft carriers, amphibious assault ships, or cruisers, are not realized.

As for American imports of naval warships, this is the "third rail" of U.S. naval procurement policy: when proposed or even discussed within the national security community, the Congress—spurred on by the shipbuilding lobby—quickly rallies against such proposals. In 2000, for example, the American Shipbuilding Association (ASA), an industry lobby group, helped rally opposition to proposed legislation that reportedly "would have waived the U.S.-build laws for combat support ships, and allow the Navy to purchase these ships from foreign shipyards."[30] While ASA expressed its concerns to then-Secretary of Defense William Cohen, several members of Congress "moved quickly to kill the legislative proposal," and union officials questioned the economic patriotism of the Pentagon. Whether substantial cost savings could be achieved, allowing foreign shipbuilders into the American naval market would presumably encourage reciprocity and perhaps fuel further technological advances. Yet despite the gains that might be achieved through this legislation, there is little reason to believe the United States will purchase foreign-built naval vessels in the near future.

Trade in the components and systems that comprise warships is nearly as stunted. Foreign sourcing accounts for only 4 percent of the materials purchased by American shipbuilders—including both commercial and naval construction. Moreover, there are strong indications that the percentage of foreign-sourced materials that enter into American warships is much lower than in commercial vessels.

In some areas of potential international demand, the American naval domestic industrial base has atrophied, largely because the U.S. Navy no longer purchases those items. Conventionally powered (diesel) submarine construction may represent a paradigmatic case where certain engineering skills and trades have been lost to the United States. The last diesel submarine was built for the U.S. Navy in 1959. Some analysts have argued that without expensive investments, the United States—the world's leader in the construction of nuclear submarines—is no longer able to build conventionally powered submarines quickly and efficiently. Australia's struggle to build *Collins*-class submarines points to the difficulties that the United States might face if it decides to fulfill its promise to Taiwan through renewed domestic production.[31] Northrop Grumman seems undeterred, however, following its acquisition of Newport News Shipbuilding in 2001. In recent reports, company spokesmen claim that Newport News has the "capacity, the capability and the interest" to compete for prospective Taiwanese diesel submarine contracts.[32] Proof of this assertion will come when, and if, Newport News bids for the contracts, the Taiwanese government accepts or rejects the bid, and the diesel submarines are actually built and become operational.

Although the United States no longer appears to require the capability to build diesel submarines for its own navy, numerous friends and allies (including, for example, Germany and Japan) maintain this capacity. Several geopolitical revivals such as Russia also have had success selling their diesel models in international markets. In the wider context of U.S. national security policy, this shortfall has two implications. First, because it cannot produce some systems itself, the United States must approach third parties to supply American client states. In some circumstance, third parties may not be willing to accede to the U.S. request, no matter who is paying or how much, because they have their own foreign policy objectives. In the case of selling diesel submarines to the Taiwanese, potential suppliers appear to be dissuaded by the potential reaction by China. The People's Republic has made it clear that it will take strong actions against any firm and country that does business with Taiwan.

Second, the difficulties faced by the United States in fulfilling its promise to Taiwan pale in comparison to lost opportunities to supply "the emerging market for non-nuclear submarines."[33] Analysts predict that global demand for nonnuclear submarines will increase over the coming decades as a high percentage of existing submarines reach the end of their service lives. After all, nonnuclear submarines allow nations to use undersea warfare at relatively low cost. Prospects for the United States to reenter the market successfully appear dim, regardless of Northrop Grumman's plans, as 12 nations already design, build, and export nonnuclear submarines, while at least 4 more countries build under licensing agreements.

At the opposite end of the spectrum, the U.S. defense industrial base provides the Nation with naval systems that are not otherwise available from foreign suppliers. American aircraft carriers, for example, are not, strictly speaking, equivalent to British, French, or even Russian (Soviet-era) ships. They are larger, faster, and capable of carrying more aircraft. Few would seriously propose selling supercarriers abroad; but even if the U.S. Government was willing to allow such sales, the market for such products—as previously noted—would be limited. However, small deck conventional carriers remain a different story. Recent reports suggest that demand is growing, especially in East Asia.[34] But since the United States does not buy such ships, the U.S. defense industrial base has been unwilling to make the investments necessary to compete in this international market.

In sum, with regard to import and export of ships and specialized naval systems more generally, American participation in global markets appears limited with the possible exception of second-hand ships sold after they have completed their service with the U.S. Navy.

Innovation. One of the cherished notions of those who are convinced that globalization matters for the defense industrial base is that the commercial sector is "out-innovating" the defense sector. In some areas, this observation seems to be borne out. Commercial R&D in the information technology sector, for example, now vastly outstrips defense sector investment. In the international shipbuilding sector, commercial R&D investments for such things as process engineering exceed public sector investments. Unfortunately, this investment-driven innovation in the shipbuilding sector resides largely in other countries such as Japan, South Korea, and China. Given the predominance of commercial shipbuilding globally and America's relative backwardness in commercial shipbuilding, this might appear to represent a challenge to American naval shipbuilding leadership. Most American producers of warships seem fated to use high-cost, inefficient manufacturing processes and pass the higher bills to the U.S. Government.

The Navy has taken steps to explore promising technologies developed elsewhere in the world. A case in point is the high-speed vessel *Joint Venture* (HSV–XI), an Australian-made catamaran that can operate at high speeds and in shallow waters. *Joint Venture* is a follow-on to HMAS *Jervis Bay*, a high-speed ferry leased by the Royal Australian Navy for operations in East Timor. Under the Army's High-Speed Vessel program, the United States has leased *Joint Venture* from the Australian firm Incat, which converted it from a commercial vessel to a theater logistics vessel in Hobart. Incat then contracted with the Bollinger Shipyard, a U.S. shipbuilder that operates facilities in Louisiana and Texas, to support the high-speed catamaran during its one-year charter.[35] In a similar fashion, the Marine Corps is leasing the *Westpac Express*, a 331-foot ferry, in a joint venture between the Australian shipyard Austal Limited and another Gulf Coast shipyard, Bender Shipbuilding and Repair.[36]

The HMS *Triton* represents another model for the future—collaborative development between the United States and an ally, this time Great Britain. Such collaborative development offers the possibility of sharing R&D costs and combining technical capabilities to produce a more innovative product than might have been otherwise possible. In addition, if ultimately satisfactory to both parties, it could provide for a larger production run since, presumably, both partners will have a stake in procuring offspring of the developmental model.

A question arises as to whether these strategies of accessing ship technologies from abroad are sustainable. Leading high-technology vessels from joint ventures between foreign and American shipyards is one thing; entering into a large-scale procurement relationship is another. Political and economic disputes about prospective divisions of labor, not to mention questions of industrial security, may lie ahead if the naval services decide that high-speed vessels designed and built by foreign firms are necessary to field the future fleet. However, from a technology standpoint, this strategy may be desirable—at least in the short run. The services and American partner shipyards can gain access to technologies that might otherwise require prohibitive domestic investments.

From a broader perspective, the innovations represented by the *Joint Venture* and HMS *Triton* are indeed the product of competition—by foreign governments and shipyards seeking niches in international markets and competitive advantages in battle. As the high-speed vessels produced by Incat and Austal suggest, one potential source of competition for the "big six" U.S. defense corporations is in international naval shipbuilding. It is no secret that the American shipbuilding industry lags behind major international competitors in a number of areas, including small ship design and manufacturing technology. In theory, the United States could farm out production of all or part of its naval ships—at the very least, the construction of hulls—to the most technologically advanced shipyards in Europe and Asia. But as discussed above, political and security concerns virtually preclude such possibilities, even, it appears, on a small scale. Such international competition is unlikely given the political considerations of jobs and technological costs. On the security side, many officials and Congressional leaders are already concerned with safeguarding secrets in domestic industrial facilities. It is difficult, if not impossible, to imagine such concerns not arising with foreign purchases, particularly if maintenance and support requirements allow foreign access to increasing portions of the U.S. defense industrial base.

The American naval shipbuilding industry may yet experience changes that increase the influx of innovation into the sector from abroad, or that introduce more competition into the sector within the United States. For example, some analysts argue that the hull is perhaps the least important part of the ship. What goes inside the ship—power plants, weapon systems, electronic suites, communications systems, sensors and the like—are the most sophisticated components of ships. Arguably, they present tremendous integration problems for shipbuilders and perhaps should be left to defense primes who are in the business of integration. By this logic, it makes little sense for Newport News or Electric Boat to maintain in-house integration capabilities. Indeed, as subsidiaries of larger holding companies—Northrop Grumman and General Dynamics respectively—they benefit from the internal systems integration capabilities of other divisions with their parent firms.

Could a foreign prime such as BAE Systems or EADS acquire a smaller shipyard and use it as means to enter into competition with the U.S. big six?[37] In an era where it appears that smaller, faster, and lighter are gaining attention with naval and defense analysts advocating transformation, perhaps second-tier shipyards could reenter the markets for U.S. warships. Current research into this area remains mixed. Although shipbuilders such as the Australian firm Austal clearly would like to break into the U.S. naval market and have entered into joint ventures to do so, many smaller yards appear uninterested in emerging naval markets. Some shipyards such as San Diego-based National Steel and Shipbuilding Company, recently purchased by General Dynamics, see their niche as building lower-end transports rather than surface combatants. They apparently believe that the size of the prospective market, the erosion of their own capabilities, and the costs of reacquiring lost capabilities are prohibitive. They have little desire to help build the "Navy after next" except within the narrow parameters that they already participate. Others, such as Todd Pacific Shipyards in Seattle, appear to have little interest building warships at all—despite their long and storied relationship with the U.S. Navy.[38]

Could commercial shipyards abroad, especially those controlled by adversaries or potential adversaries, acquire the naval systems and systems integration capabilities to challenge the supremacy of American warships? Although it seems highly unlikely that this would occur on a grand scale, the possibility of niche competitors arising—fueled by countries seeking asymmetric responses to the American revolution in military affairs—may be possible. As highly respected analyst John Battilega argues:

> there are several countries, and several defense companies, who have targeted the systems integration function as a competitive niche area and offer those services globally. Systems-integration-for-hire will be a characteristic of the diffused armaments world.[39]

Investment/Production. The United States produces the most successful warships in the world and has done so at least since the beginning of World War II. It produces a wider range of technologically sophisticated warships than any of its allies, friends, enemies, or potential adversaries. Current plans to recapitalize the fleet, even if undertaken in an austere budget environment, will continue to strengthen American naval leadership. Although some nations produce highly capable warships in niche areas (Russia's *Sovremenny*-class destroyers, for example), no nation currently plans to build ships to match future-generation destroyers (DD[X] program), much less the next generation CVX aircraft carrier. American naval planners call for the next-generation warships to push already state-of-the-art naval technologies still further to achieve gains in propulsion, manning, communications, stealth, and lethality.

Joint ventures, teaming, and licensing arrangements that would allow the U.S. Government and American shipbuilders to develop cooperative relationships with foreign yards are feasible. Cooperation between U.S. and international shipbuilders are as likely to involve yards such as Bender and Bollinger as the big six, thereby potentially broadening the shipbuilding landscape.

Beyond traditional shipbuilding. Admittedly, thinking of the naval industrial base solely in terms of shipbuilding is an anachronism. Modern navies such as that of the United States rely only partly on ships to project power and perform the traditional functions of a maritime power. The U.S. Navy buys items from data processing systems to aircraft that draw upon the entire range of defense industries. As a consequence, the preceding analysis of the changing nature of the American naval shipbuilding industry in a globalizing and/or regionalizing world may miss important developments relevant to the future of the naval industrial base. Changes in the aircraft industry, for example, including the long-term implications of the recent down-select decision on the Joint Strike Fighter, will almost certainly affect the evolution of American naval aviation (see chapter 18). For another example, the emergence of UAVs and other unmanned vehicles of all sorts may allow smaller American firms or even foreign firms to play a larger role in U.S. acquisition programs in the coming years. From this perspective, assessing the state of the naval industrial base in the face of globalization (or Americanization, internationalization, and regionalism, for that matter) will require further analysis of issues beyond traditional shipbuilding.

Conclusion

Naval shipbuilding is clearly not undergoing a process of globalization, at least as conventionally understood. It may eventually undergo regionalization or regionalism (if prodded to do so by government authorities), but—at least to date—this appears possible only within the confines of the European Union or, perhaps, on a bilateral basis with close American allies such as Australia. But it still seems unlikely to occur on a grand scale, even across the Atlantic.

This finding reflects both general trends within the overall defense industrial sector and the conflict of logic that underlies arguments about defense sector globalization. What some analysts have referred to as defense globalization is largely a trans-Atlantic phenomena pursued by profit-seeking defense firms in North America and Europe. It is also largely a product of the fitful efforts of public officials in the United State and the European NATO member states to improve NATO interoperability and to strengthen political and economic relationships that have weakened since the end of the

Cold War. In the shipbuilding sectors more specifically, even these modest efforts on the part of firms and governments have foundered on the politics of producing ships. Large facilities employing large numbers of highly skilled workers and dealing with technologically sensitive systems are simply not clear candidates for the types of laissez-faire policies that have allowed other industries to globalize over the last 3 decades.

However, this conclusion does not preclude that naval shipbuilding may regionalize in the future as the larger defense conglomerates seek larger shares of all phases and all types of weapon systems production. In the trans-Atlantic region, longstanding security ties and a commonality of interests on a global scale may lead to more cooperation among defense industries and a reduction in the number of state-to-state barriers. The current war on terrorism, which has featured close cooperation in the North Atlantic region, may even provide an opportunity for regionalism, if not globalization.[40] As discussed above, this process has already begun for larger defense primes, especially on the European side, as firms such as BAE seek a share of growing American defense procurement budgets.

It should be noted again that powerful political forces are allied against further integration and that the strength of future ties will require a greater exercise of political will on both sides of the Atlantic. For this to happen, considerable trust will be required. The United States and its partners must be able to share technologies, profits, and costs without focusing exclusively on the dangers of technological diffusion or the local economic impact of further industry rationalization.

Even if trans-Atlantic regionalism succeeds, it remains to be seen whether it will eventually serve as a model for other regions such the Pacific Rim or Southeast Asia. Proponents of defense industrial integration need to remember that relations with Asian friends and allies have rarely achieved the level of intimacy and institutionalization that have characterized U.S.-European relations. Where the trans-Atlantic region has NATO and the European Union, the two most successful regional organizations in history, the Pacific Rim has the Association of Southeast Asian Nations and now Asia Pacific Economic Cooperation, two organizations whose promise has rarely been matched by real progress.

In the end, regionalization and regionalism may be better approaches to understanding the changing nature of the global economy with regard to defense industries and naval weapon systems. And—for the most part—the only area of the world economy that is approaching a more integrated system is in the Euro-Atlantic region. But this should be comforting for American and European national security analysts. The specter of globalization applied to defense industries is scary: a vision of technological diffusion, arms races, unbridled sales, lost technical superiority, and, ultimately, the creation of fertile ground for more arms races. In contrast, regionalization promises a future that is quite familiar and indeed manageable through existing policy instruments and institutional arrangements (including NATO and longstanding European Union–U.S. ties). For further integration, political and military leaders will have ample opportunity to weigh risk and benefits while negotiating with stakeholders over the nature and extent of globalization to be allowed in the coming years.

Notes

[1] Robert Gilpin and Jean Millis Gilpin, *The Challenge of Global Capitalism: The World Economy in the 21st Century* (Princeton, NJ: Princeton University Press, 2000), 19.

[2] For a variety of perspectives, see *The Global Century: Globalization and National Security*, ed. Richard L. Kugler and Ellen L. Frost (Washington, DC: National Defense University Press, 2001).

[3] See Office of the Under Secretary of Defense for Acquisition and Security, Defense Science Board, *Final Report of the Defense Science Board Task Force on Globalization and Security* (Washington, DC, December 1999), especially, 47–48. For a private sector perspective, see DFI International, *A Blueprint for Action*, report from the AIAA Defense Reform 2001 Conference (Washington, DC, February 14–15, 2001), 36–37.

[4] Mattias Axelson with Andrew James, *The Defense Industry and Globalization*, FOA–R–00–01698–179–SE (Stockholm: Division of Defence Analysis, Defence Research Establishment, December 2000).

[5] For a contrasting view, see Andrew L. Ross, "Defense Industrial Globalization: Contrarian Observations," prepared for an Atlantic Council Conference on Defense Industry Globalization (Washington, DC, November 16, 2001).

[6] Judith Reppy, "Conceptualizing the Role of Defense Industries in National Systems of Innovation," in *The Place of the Defense Industry in National Systems of Innovation*, ed. Judith Reppy, Occasional Paper no. 25 (Ithaca, NY: Cornell University Peace Studies Program, April 2000), 9.

[7] On the hows and whys of firm-level efforts to globalize, see Axelson, 19–21.

[8] Reppy, 8.

[9] Ann Markusen, "The Rise of World Weapons," *Foreign Policy* 114 (Spring 1999), 40.

[10] Ibid., 43.

[11] Concerns about the globalization of second-tier firms that supply components to primes and first-tier arms manufacturers as well as directly to governments deserve serious attention. Richard Bitzinger, for example, suggests that a global arms industry is emerging, structured along a "hub and spoke model" in which "a few large first-tier firms operating at the center" with "lines of outsourced production extending out to second tier states on the periphery." Given space limits for this chapter, the "globalization" of second-tier defense suppliers will not be systematically examined here. See Richard Bitzinger, "Twilight of the Demigods: The Dilemma Facing Second-Tier Arms-Producing Countries in the Post-Cold War Era," unpublished manuscript based on the author's forthcoming book, *Putting the Future Behind Them: The Failed Dreams and Lowered Expectations of Second-Tier Arms Producing Countries in the 21st Century.*

[12] Glenn R. Simpson, "Treasury Interpretation of Law Lets Bush Delay Taking Sides in Dutch-U.S. Merger," *The Wall Street Journal*, April 27, 2001, A20. See also Glenn R. Simpson, "Pentagon Moves to Postpone Dutch Deal for Silicon Valley Group," *The Wall Street Journal*, March 8, 2001, B6.

[13] John Lovering, "The Defense Industry as the Paradigmatic Case of 'Actually Existing Globalization,'" in Judith Reppy, ed., 13–24.

[14] For an example of this type of reasoning, see Frank J. Gaffney, Jr., "Defense Fire Sale Redux," *The Washington Times*, April 3, 2001, 15.

[15] For an overview of developments and future prospects in these regions, see Alan Smith and Michael Meese with Hartmut Spieker, *Defense Economics: Reform, Restructuring, Realignment*, a report of the George C. Marshall European Center for Security Studies, accessed at <http://www.marshallcenter.org/Conference%20Center/Conference%20Reports.htm>.

[16] On current Russian defense exports, see Aleksey Nikolskiy, "Russia has Overtaken France in Military-Technical Cooperation," *Moscow Vedemosti*, January 14, 2002 (FBIS translated text, document ID: CEP20020114000328).

[17] Edward D. Mansfield and Helen Milner, "The New Wave of Regionalism," *International Organization* 53, no. 3 (Summer 1999), 591.

[18] Alberto Lina, "Joint Ventures," briefing at the Globalization of the Defense Industry Conference, The Royal Institute of International Affairs (London, England, January 30, 2001), slide 6.

[19] See "Western European Industry Ownership Jigsaw Puzzle," *Defence Systems Daily*, accessed at <http://defence-data/current/pagerip1.htm>.

[20] Philip Finnegan, "Defense News Top 1000: Europeans Make Great Strides Against U.S. Megafirms," *Defense News*, August 7, 2000, 1.

[21] Axelson, 35.

[22] Vago Muradian, "Camus Hopes EADS Can Crack U.S. Defense Market Within Four Years," *Defense Daily*, April 23, 2001, 8.

[23] For a sophisticated argument as to why more cross-national mergers will not occur, see Eugene Gholz, "The Political Economy of Cross-Border Defense Industry Mergers," unpublished manuscript, March 2000.

[24] Alexander Moens with Rafal Domisiewicz, *European and North American Trends in Defence Industry: Problems and Prospects of a Cross Atlantic Defence Market* (Ottawa: Department of Foreign Affairs and International Trade, April 2001), 23.

[25] Robert P. Haffa, Jr., "Globalization, the War on Terrorism, and the U.S. Defense Industry," paper prepared for an Atlantic Council Conference on Defense Industry Globalization (Washington, DC, November 16, 2001), 14.

[26] A major theme of U.S. Department of Commerce, *National Security Assessment of the U.S. Shipbuilding and Repair Industry* (Washington, DC: U.S. Department of Commerce, May 2001).

[27] Ibid., 27.

[28] The lack of global interest in blue-water fleets is a key theme of Sam J. Tangredi, "Beyond the Sea and Jointness," U.S. Naval Institute *Proceedings* 127, no. 9 (September 2001), 60–63.

[29] For a recent example, see "Possible Sale of Perry Class Frigates to Turkey," *Defense Systems Daily*, January 25, 2002.

[30] "Pentagon Proposal for Foreign Build Navy Ships is Killed," *American Shipbuilder* (October 2000), 2, accessed at <http://www.americanshipbuilding.com/news-oct00.htm>.

[31] Lee Willett, "Global Submarines," accessed at <http://global-defence.com/subs.html>.

[32] Michael Fabey, "Northrop to Bid on Subs for Taiwan: NNS Yard's Expertise Gives it an Advantage," *Newport News Daily Press*, January 24, 2002, A1.

[33] Joshua Corless, "Fresh Approach to Submarine Upgrades," accessed at <http://www.global-defence.com/99/seasys/sea1.htm>.

[34] Damon Bristow, "Weighing the Balance of Power: Aircraft Acquisition on the Up in East Asia," accessed at <http://www.global-defence.com/99/1998/SeaSystems/weigh.htm>.

[35]Frank Wolfe, "Marine Officials Ride Austr alian-Built High Speed Vessel," *Defense Daily,* November 20, 2001, 4.

[36] "Marines Getting Good Results with Australian High Speed Vessel," *Inside the Navy*, October 15, 2001, 9.

[37] The *big six* of American defense companies refers to Lockheed Martin, McDonnell Douglas, Boeing, General Dynamics, Northrup-Grumman, and Raytheon. However, post-Cold War mergers and acquisitions periodically threaten to shift this lineup. Other companies such as General Electric still do substantial military business.

[38] On the aspirations of NASSCO and Todd Pacific, information was obtained through author interviews throughout 2001.

[39] John A. Battilega, *Transformation in Defense Markets and Industries: Implications for the Future of Warfare, Volume 1: The Emerging Global Armament Systems and the Future of Warfare*, prepared for the National Intelligence Council and the Office of the Secretary of Defense (Net Assessment) (Greenwood Village, CO: SAIC, February 1, 2001), 5. See also 29–30 and details in Battilega et al., *Volume 3: Country Studies*. Battilega's work (four volumes) is the most extensive study on the trends of post-Cold War global defense market that is currently available to researchers.

[40] Haffa makes a similar argument in "Globalization, the War on Terrorism, and the U.S. Defense Industry," although he does not make the distinction between globalization and regionalism as argued in this chapter.

Part III

International Politics and Maritime Alliances and Coalitions

Chapter 12

The International Law of the Sea in a Globalized World

Daniel Moran

Sensible people have long recognized the incongruity of the claim that Christopher Columbus discovered America, already home to perhaps a million souls at the time of his arrival. It is less widely recalled that Columbus did not mean to discover anything. He thought he knew where he was going and, famously, did not quite realize he had not gotten there. His motives, and those of his royal patrons, were more commercial than scientific. Columbus set out not to uncover new lands but to demonstrate the feasibility of transoceanic travel. It was this achievement, and not his accidental encounter with an unsuspected continent, that proved transformative. Three centuries later, Adam Smith, the evangelist of modern capitalism, would declare the voyages of Columbus and his successors to be the greatest events in the history of the world, a sentiment that has resonated among recent students of what is now called *globalization*.[1] Although it is not a point of view to be accepted uncritically, the fact remains that the inhabitants of the Americas were descended from Asian migrants who arrived on foot via a since-vanished land bridge across the Bering Strait. When Columbus sailed, neither they nor any other major human population had reached its present position on the globe by transiting the high seas.[2] Afterward, this would begin to change.

The Age of Discovery and Maritime Order

Columbus's success presented his contemporaries with two sets of problems, the first scientific, technical, and organizational; the second legal and political. The conversion of the world's oceans from an impassable barrier into what Alfred Thayer

Daniel Moran is professor of international history and strategic theory in the Department of National Security Affairs at the Naval Postgraduate School in Monterey, California. He is also a fellow of the Hoover Institution on War, Revolution, and Peace at Stanford University. His most recent work includes *Wars of National Liberation* (London: Cassell, 2001) and *The People in Arms: Military Myth and National Mobilization since the French Revolution* (New York: Cambridge University Press, 2002).

Mahan would call a "great common" required centuries of effort in the development of ships capable of withstanding the rigors of ocean voyages, new means of accurate navigation on the open seas (a puzzle that had only just been solved when Smith wrote), and a shore-based infrastructure capable of sustaining the new merchant fleets and the navies that protected them. Most histories of sea power take these achievements as their central theme.

Our interest, however, lies with the second set of problems, those having to do with the development of legal and political norms governing the use of sea and with their role in shaping *globalization*, an expression that requires some preliminary comment, since its meaning is dependent upon context. A recent collection of essays on the subject distinguished between economic, social, cultural, environmental, and military globalization, while noting that additional categories—political, scientific, linguistic, and so on—were possible.[3] Among economists, the group that has subjected the concept to the most rigorous scrutiny, the term refers to the tendency of prices and other measures of economic activity to converge around global norms.[4] Others employ it more generally to refer to the increasing speed and efficiency with which information, material goods, and money move about the planet, a process driven mainly by new technologies.[5]

For our purposes, however, the essential thing is to note that, as presently understood, globalization in all its forms refers to processes that increasingly operate independently not just of physical distance but also of nationality and the power of the state. It is this aspect that defines its relationship to international law and to our particular concern, which is the law of the sea.

That relationship is less harmonious than might be imagined, though there is a case to be made for what might be called mutual enablement—that is, that international legal rules are conducive to the globalization of trade and social intercourse, and vice versa. As abstract propositions, both international law (a body of theory and doctrine) and globalization (a social and technological practice) share a common impulse toward moderating, if not suborning, the authority of state governments. International law introduces order and due process into the metaphoric space that separates sovereign polities, a space that would seem to be a natural zone of expansion for globalizing economic, social, and cultural forces. Conversely, much of the political resistance to globalization is tinged with concern about its legal consequences: that it will create too much new international law, thus undermining the sovereignty of national governments; or that it will not create enough, and so expose the citizen to the unchecked influence of supranational institutions like the World Bank, the World Trade Organization, or the International Monetary Fund.

Without commenting on the merits of these concerns, it must be emphasized that they rest to some extent upon a misapprehension of what international law is. It is not global law, which is to say it is not the legal expression, even in theory, of the interests of a global civil society.[6] Should such a law become necessary in the future as a consequence of the changes globalization brings, it would require a wholesale re-constitution of the international legal system, which is an expression and creature of the sovereign states that are its subjects. International law, whether operating within the quasi-anarchical states system that prevailed before World War I or within con-federated structures like the League of Nations or the United Nations (UN), exists to legitimize certain forms of state power—above all those concerned with self-de-fense—and to define and coordinate reciprocal relationships among sovereignties, whose autonomy, authority, and equality are taken for granted.

One consequence of the early voyages of discovery was that they provided a sharp impetus for reflection upon these matters. The commercial possibilities of trans-oceanic trade were apparent even before Columbus made his voyage. To realize those possibilities, however, it was equally obvious that the high seas, once their navigability had been proven, could not simply be left as a zone of lawlessness, where each could prey without scruple upon all. At first, the effort to impose a maritime order took the form of schemes to extend the sovereign jurisdictions of the main maritime powers, a natural impulse given the decentralized and competitive nature of the European states' system, but by no means a universal one. The Chinese, who had sent fleets of treasure junks as far as the east coast of Africa before Columbus was born, made no attempt to devise a legal regime for the waters they traversed or the new lands they saw and ulti-mately abandoned their voyages of exploration on the grounds that the novelties they disclosed were of little practical use.

Among Europeans, however, the proposition that a coastal community had the right to control the water adjacent to it had been proverbial since ancient times and was now extended literally to the ends of the earth. In 1494, Spain and Portugal, with the encouragement of the Pope, divided the world's oceans between them along a line in the mid-Atlantic. Other maritime powers followed suit. For most of the 17th cen-tury, what would today be called the territorial sea of the British Isles was held by the English crown to extend to the shores of Scandinavia, thus fully encompassing the pu-tative national waters of the Danes. Genoa, Tuscany, the Ottoman Empire, the Venet-ian Republic, and the Papacy itself all advanced similarly extensive claims. Even on the most optimistic interpretation, there was reason to believe that when the principle of sovereignty was extended to the high seas, it ceased to be an antidote to anarchy and became an expression of it.

This was so because the pretensions of European princes to rule the oceans were entirely fanciful. On the high seas, the space between sovereignties, which interna-tional law seeks to organize, is not metaphorical. It is real. It is also vast and inhos-pitable to extended human habitation. When, in 1702, a Dutch jurist proposed that the "maritime marches" of a state be limited to waters within the range of cannon fired from the shore—a distance subsequently reckoned to be 3 miles—he was merely affirming the common-sense limits of the possible at the time; though, it would take another century or so before the practice of confining territorial claims to a narrow coastal belt became widely accepted.[7]

Credit for developing the theoretical framework for a maritime regime based upon freedom rather than extended sovereignty belongs to another Dutchman, Hugo Grotius, the preeminent figure in the history of early modern international law. In 1604, the Dutch East India Company asked Grotius to prepare a brief defending the actions of a Dutch admiral who had seized a Portuguese merchantman in the Strait of Malacca. Although Portugal and the Netherlands were at peace when the seizure occurred, Grotius argued in a work entitled *De Jure Praedae* ("On the Law of Prize and Booty") that the Dutch admiral was justified because of the impropriety of Portuguese claims to exclusive trading rights in the East Indies. Five years later, one section of this brief was published as book under the title *Mare Liberum* ("The Freedom of the Seas"), in which it was argued that the seas must be open to all.

Grotius' originality as a legal theorist lay in his claim that states, like individuals, were bound by natural law—that is, rules and principles independent of historical practice and divine revelation (although compatible with the latter) but rooted in the inherent logic of facts. As far as the ocean was concerned, the essential facts were its ubiquity, immensity, and fecundity. In contrast to the land, from which benefit could be derived only by possession, the sea represented an inconsumable, self-renewing resource, whose political subdivision was contrary to nature. From this, two principles and a stipulation followed: that the high seas could not be appropriated by individuals or states; that any use of the sea by one state must leave it available for use by others; and that both provisions must apply during peace and war, except for belligerents, whose goods were lawful prize for each other.[8]

Law of the Sea and the Law of War

Although Grotius' work acquired great prestige among scholars and political theorists,[9] its impact on the maritime law of preindustrial Europe had more to do with his analysis of belligerent rights than with his broader doctrine of freedom of the seas. Claims to sovereignty over the high seas faded during the 18th century less because of the power of ideas than because most of the countries that advanced them—Portugal, Spain, and the states of the Mediterranean littoral—lost out in the military and economic competition of the day; while Britain, one of the winners and an early advocate of closed seas, changed its mind after 1688, when the House of Orange replaced the Stuarts on the English throne, thus tempering Britain's longstanding trade rivalry with the Netherlands.[10] The retreat of sovereignty did not, however, entail any alteration in the prevailing economic attitude known as *mercantilism*, which regarded commerce, piracy, and warfare as, if not synonymous, then as points on a single continuum of international rivalry; and which measured economic success in terms of the accumulation of assets by the state, rather than by growth in trade volume, productivity, and so on.

In such circumstances, maritime law could amount to little more than a codicil of the law of war, by which the taking of prize and booty was organized to general advantage. This is not to suggest that the law of the sea was of no account in the Age of Sail. On the contrary: Clausewitz's peremptory dismissal of international law as a restraint upon the conduct of war,[11] which must have struck the soldiers of his day as mere common sense, would have seemed absurd to the sailors, whose professional lives proceeded among a dense web of prize courts, Orders in Council, Navigation Acts, letters of marque, and a host of treaties and licenses by which the rights to trade and plunder were parceled out.

Grotius and his successors contributed to the construction and management of this web by injecting it with theoretical integrity, in the form of what became known as the Old Rule of prizes. It held, in the words of one authoritative statement, that:

- the Goods of an Enemy, on Board the Ship of a Friend, may be taken
- that the lawful Goods of a Friend, on board the Ship of an Enemy, ought to be restored
- that Contraband Goods, going to the Enemy, tho' the Property of a Friend, may be taken as Prize; because supplying the enemy, with what enables him better to carry on the War, is a departure from Neutrality.[12]

The Old Rule afforded belligerent warships the right to stop, search, and demand explanations from any merchant vessel they encountered—a hard system for those in the carrying trade, who could be hauled before a prize court upon any pretext of irregularity in their papers or cargo. Yet given the alternative, which was piratical mayhem, this rough-and-ready practice afforded essential, if modest, protection to transoceanic commerce.

Toward a World Economy

The result was a steady expansion of world trade, which grew by just over 1 percent per annum during the 3 centuries following Columbus' voyage—in aggregate a 20-fold expansion, despite the fact that, for most of this period, warfare was endemic among the major maritime states.[13] A similarly dramatic transformation is apparent in the cultural outlook of European elites. Those who had access to the goods and knowledge that global commerce brought to Europe learned to think of themselves not as members of a world community by any means, but at least as the preeminent inhabitants of a planet whose farthest reaches offered scope for their ambitions.

Grotius himself regarded the ubiquity of the oceans as proof that God intended all the nations of the world to be in contact with each other, so that each might profit from the special talents and resources of the others.[14]

Nevertheless, the enthusiasm that some scholars have shown for the proposition that globalization, as presently experienced, antedates the industrial era is not supported by a close analysis of how long-distance maritime trade actually worked. It was, first of all, almost entirely the business of state-chartered monopolies—the Dutch East India Company is an example—that operated in cooperation with their respective national navies. The resulting trading patterns did not resemble a network but were confined to noncompetitive goods of high value relative to their bulk. Europeans imported spices, tea, coffee, silk, gold, and sugar, which were rare or nonexistent on the continent, and exported silver, wool, and linen to Asia. Only goods for which there was no local competition could command prices high enough to cover the costs of transoceanic transportation. This in turn meant that while the interruption of overseas trade in wartime might adversely affect the finances of a state that depended upon it for cash, it had no impact upon the broader society, which neither produced nor consumed the categories of goods involved.

True economic globalization, as measured by a combination of trade expansion, price convergence, and competition between imported and domestic goods, dates from the dismantling of mercantilism in the decades following the Napoleonic wars. Two general sets of factors contributed to the demolition. First, and most important, were improvements in transportation technology. The advent of railroads lowered the cost of overland transportation—historically an order of magnitude more expensive than moving the same goods over water—which expanded the market for products arriving from overseas and also increased the feasibility of producing low-margin primary commodities for export. The cost advantages of railroads were compounded by those of oceangoing steamships. The cost per ton of transoceanic trade did no better than hold its own (and probably rose) over the 17th and 18th centuries, for reasons that included an increasing need for insurance and other precautions against capture as prize.[15] In the 19th century, they decline dramatically. No one knows what it would have cost to ship a bushel of grain from New York to Liverpool in 1800, since it would not have occurred to anyone to try it. In 1874, however, it cost 20 cents on a piston-engine steamer. In 1881, thanks to the introduction of the Parsons turbine, it cost 2 cents.[16]

The market efficiencies embodied in new technologies were realized in large part because of the advance of political liberalism, which shifted state attitudes in the direction of free enterprise, and because of the prevalence of peace among the Great Powers following the defeat of Napoleon in 1815.[17] Although it would be wrong to suggest that Europeans had lost their taste for "prize and booty" as a consequence of the wars engendered by the French Revolution, there is no question that the Concert of Europe was less prone to adopt war as an all-purpose instrument of policy than the Old Regime had been. As one recent study of the period has noted, no European state threatened with war in the decades before 1789 ever succeeded in avoiding it, even if it tried hard to do so.[18] This was certainly not the case after 1815.

The defeat of France allowed high wartime tariffs to be dispensed with, an adjustment that marked the beginning of a secular trend toward trade liberalization. Internal customs duties disappeared in Germany and much of the Habsburg Empire; the paramilitary royal companies that had dominated global trade under the Old Regime were disbanded; and Britain, now uncontested master of the high seas, shifted its weight decisively in favor of free trade by abolishing its tariffs on imported grain. In the second half of the 19th century, global terms of trade shifted permanently in favor of finished goods and against primary commodities, whose prices fall regardless of where they are produced. The rate of trade expansion between 1820 and 1914 more than tripled compared to that of the previous 3 centuries, to 3.5 per cent per annum, a rate that has persisted to this day.[19] Labor and capital followed the flow of goods. The plummeting cost of transoceanic transportation allowed tens of millions of Europeans to migrate to the Americas. In 1910, 17 percent of the population of the United States and 24 percent of its work force consisted of immigrants. By 1913, overseas investment (as a percentage of total investment) had reached a level comparable to that of today, and possibly exceeded it.[20]

Free Trade and Belligerent Rights

The rise of free trade demanded a new approach to the international law of the sea, in which the theoretical structure developed during the Enlightenment would be adapted to an environment in which private interests and the rights of neutrals counted for far more than they had in the past. And here one could do worse than to recall Clausewitz's "paradoxical Trinity," by which war was imagined to be a phenomenon suspended among three magnets: violence, chance, and reason.[21] In considering the evolution of the law of the sea, one might think of the magnets as three sets of interests, each in need of legal protection. The first are the interests of warfare; the second, those of trade, which requires unfettered use of the high seas and uninterrupted access to the ports of trading partners; the third, those of direct economic exploitation, which seeks to harvest resources for use and to bar competitors from doing the same.

The customary prize law of the Old Regime was transformed into the modern, treaty-based law of the sea because of the increasing strength of the second magnet during the 19th century. The elemental tug of commerce was strengthened by the emergence, for the first time, of a major trading state indifferent to the rivalries of the European powers and without a strong navy of its own. This was, of course, the United

States, whose economic might was arrayed behind a policy that sought to extend the protection of international law to all private property on the high seas.

Like most strongly held principles, this one was capable of forcing some unattractive tradeoffs. Thus the United States, having outlawed the slave trade in 1808 (a year after the British did so), nevertheless refused to cooperate in its suppression on the high seas, on the grounds that the only thing worse than slavery, in the words of Secretary of State John Quincy Adams, would be "admitting the right of search . . . for that would be making slaves of ourselves."[22] America's adamant stance weighed heavily with its biggest trading partner, Great Britain. Britain had gotten itself into war with its former colonies in 1812 because of the Royal Navy's too-forcible assertion of belligerent rights. When the Crimean War began in 1854, it sought to avoid any repetition by announcing that it would forego its right to search neutral vessels engaged in trade with the enemy. This concession, initially conceived as a wartime expedient, became impossible to withdraw once granted and was incorporated in a declaration accompanying the Treaty of Paris in 1856. Under its terms, the Old Rule was supplanted by the New, whose provisions were that privateering—the licensing of private ships as commerce raiders—was abolished; that enemy goods (save contraband) could move freely on neutral ships; that neutral goods (again save contraband) could move freely on enemy ships; and that a blockade had to be "effective" to convey belligerent rights—meaning it had to be maintained by large naval forces and not simply proclaimed as a pro forma means to legalize prize-taking.[23]

Only seven countries signed the Declaration of Paris, but all the major maritime powers adhered to it, including the United States, which declined to sign because the declaration's provisions fell short of complete immunity for all private vessels, including those of belligerents. The declaration codified a fundamental change in the balance of interests between warfare and trade on the high seas, in effect shifting the benefit of the doubt from the one to the other. It did so, however, at a time when the globalization of world commerce was altering the strategic landscape in ways whose implications were decidedly puzzling, at least for those who favored the advance of liberty in politics.

It was not simply that the cause of freedom on the oceans might confound the same cause elsewhere, as Adams's painful remark about slavery makes plain enough. It was that it was not easy to agree on what kind of legal regime would be most conducive to the cause of peace, upon which the progress of global trade depended. The triumph of the New Rule reflected the rise of commercial interests and a specific interpretation of how those interests would play out militarily. Advocates of immunity believed they were creating "a partial commercial peace in the midst of . . . political war."[24] If war persisted, then at least it would be reduced to "a duel between Governments and their professional fighters."[25] Precisely for that reason, however, others were convinced that the restraining effects of globalization on the bellicosity of governments would be lost if commercial interests were not at risk. In their eyes, the true hope of peace, and the only true security for commerce in wartime, lay in the continued assertion of belligerent rights by peaceloving commercial democracies.[26]

Diplomatically, immunity was a legal position endorsed by states without strong navies, a fact that advocates sought to finesse by arguing that, like other advances of free trade, its benefits would accrue to maritime nations—quoting Adams again—"in proportion to their interests . . . upon the Ocean." Strong maritime states need not fear the loss of belligerent rights, since they were gaining "entire security" for their own commerce, the true source of national strength in modern times.[27] As the naval strength of the United States grew, however, its experts came to doubt the wisdom of its traditional policy. Thus Alfred Thayer Mahan wrote to President Theodore Roosevelt in 1904, warning that America's insistence upon "free ships, free goods" had "lost the fitness it possibly once had to national conditions." Roosevelt saw the point, while noting that the advance of civilization had brought with it "a strong tendency to protect private property and private life on sea and land."[28] In the event, it proved difficult to abandon an ideological commitment of such long standing. The United States voted with Germany and a host of small neutrals at The Hague in 1907, in an unsuccessful attempt to abolish the right of search and capture on the high seas. It was still hectoring Great Britain about freedom of the seas until a few weeks before it entered the war against Germany in 1917.

Globalization in Retreat

By then, however, the real strategic significance of globalization was becoming apparent, particularly for the inhabitants of continental states cut off by the competing blockades mounted by Germany and Great Britain. Not only had the expanding web of commercial relationships created during the 19th century failed to avert war among trading partners, it also had created new forms of strategic vulnerability. One reason the British had gone as far as they had in accepting the New Rule was that they had come to regard war against commerce as an unprofitable diversion of naval forces—a point of view shared by American navalists like Mahan. The revolution in the terms of trade that globalization had brought about falsified this tactical assumption no less thoroughly that it had dashed liberal hopes for perpetual peace.

All major belligerents in World War I (except the United States) were dependent upon primary commodities imported from overseas—most critically food, for which demand is constant and substitution difficult. In 1917, Germans were consuming 40 percent fewer calories per day than they had been 3 years before, thanks to the British blockade. The unlimited submarine campaign they unleashed by way of reprisal brought Britain to the brink of defeat in its turn, an outcome narrowly avoided only when major naval assets were grudgingly diverted from fleet operations to commerce protection.

Such effects were unknown to maritime warfare in the past. Under the Old Regime, the major impact of a naval blockade was financial. In a globally interdependent world, it struck directly at society as a whole. Prolonged deprivation of a kind never before experienced by an industrial population eroded German civilian and military morale and confronted the government in Berlin with almost insoluble problems of manpower allocation, as the army and war industries relentlessly absorbed the labor needed to increase domestic food production. Nor were the effects purely psychological. Upward of 700,000 German civilians died in World War I, a toll directly attributable to their being cut off from the vast, unseen network of overseas farmers and grain merchants on which they had become dependent. In searching for the roots of Germany's defeat in 1918, the advent of free trade in grain 80 years before is not a bad place to start.[29]

World War I brought an end the world's first great era of globalization. The subsequent retreat into autarky, which persisted until after 1945, was due partly to the economic dislocation the war caused and partly to new apprehensions about excessive dependence on overseas trade.[30] Although the creation of the League of Nations in 1919 promised to inject new vitality into international law, the impact of collective security on the law of the sea was limited. The general drift of legal development before 1914, as reflected in the Declaration of Paris, The Hague and Geneva conventions, and countless other agreements, had been to protect the rights of private persons and property, soldiers (as individuals), and neutrals from the consequences of military action. In the era of collective security, the aim was raised to incorporate a ban upon international violence per se, a goal for which legal remedies would prove inadequate in the face of determined aggression by strong states.

Economic globalization resumed in the 1950s, stimulated by a combination of proactive measures to hasten postwar reconstruction—the Marshall Plan and the founding of the World Bank and the International Monetary Fund most prominently—and the final breakdown of European empires, which left successor states more exposed to the risks and rewards of international markets than ever before. At the same time, certain basic premises of international life had been permanently altered by protracted global conflict and the advent of collective security. Even at the turn of the 20th century, the right of developed states to use force to manage their relations with the less developed world was scarcely questioned. In the aftermath of the world wars, this would no longer be true.

The United Nations and Law of the Sea

These developments coincided with a renewed concern with the law of the sea, pulled along now by economic exploitation, the third of the magnets described earlier. In Grotius' day, or for that matter in Mahan's, the direct appropriation of ocean resources was chiefly the business of fishermen and whalers, whose disputes, while perennially contentious, are ultimately parochial. As the industrialized world shifted from coal to oil as its principal source of energy, however, the attractions of the seabed for the world's oil industry became intense, and the stakes involved in regulating economic use of the ocean grew large. American companies began drilling a few thousand yards offshore in the Gulf of Mexico in the 1930s, and as technology improved, the question of how to manage expansion into deeper, international waters arose. In September 1945, the United States formally asserted its "jurisdiction and control" over its continental shelf out to a depth of 200 meters, a zone extending far beyond its 3-mile territorial sea. Because the claim was specifically to seabed resources, however, the waters above remained "high seas," through which free passage was guaranteed.[31]

Over the next few years, dozens of states followed the American example, albeit with significant variation in legal form, and in some cases with express reservations about the international status of the superjacent sea. In 1958, the first United Nations Conference on the Law of the Sea (UNCLOS) sought to get the cat back in the bag by, in effect, codifying what must have seemed to the Truman administration a simple enough distinction: national sovereignty (roughly) for the seabed, but not for the water above it.[32] By then, however, the process of subdividing and refining jurisdictional claims beyond the territorial sea, for purposes of regulating mining, drilling, fishing, environmental pollution, and so on, had acquired a highly contentious life of its own. In the process, the longstanding but uncodified convention limiting the territorial sea to 3 miles collapsed, under pressure from post-colonial regimes with scant means of exploiting or defending maritime rights, and fearful of encroachment by more capable outsiders. Among the 101 states that joined the UN between 1946 and 1980, only 8 settled for a 3-mile territorial sea—most claimed 12 miles, a few as many as 200—a tide the UN was unable to stem at a second conference (UNCLOS II) in 1960.

For the developed world, the expansion of the territorial sea posed a threat to navigation and overflight, above all as applied to international straits. Special rules of access to a few critical straits have been a feature of black-letter international law since 1841, when the British forced the abrogation of an earlier treaty between the Russians and the Ottoman Empire, restricting the right to transit the Dardanelles (which are less than a mile wide at their narrowest point). For most such vital waterways, however, the 3-mile limit provided de facto assurance of a middle channel through international water. If 3 miles were stretched to 12, however, over 100 international straits would become subject to the sovereign claims of the nations that bordered them. To this concrete concern must be added nebulous unease about the fact of disorder as such. As Adams pointed out to the British in the 1820s, powerful maritime states will profit from an orderly oceans regime in proportion to their interests on the water, even if achieving order means giving up familiar advantages. The United States would now find itself on the receiving end of this very argument.

The political leverage by which the major maritime powers would arrest the creep of sovereignty onto the high seas arose because the prospect of anarchy began to trouble the developing world as well. In particular, it was feared that new technologies would allow the mining of polymetallic nodules on and beneath the ocean floor, an activity in which Third World nations could not compete for lack of technology and expertise, and which if successful might ruin land-based producers of the same metals, many of which are found in poor countries. Extravagant territorial claims projecting outward from the shoreline could not protect against this threat. In the late 1960s, something between a gold rush and an arms race seemed to impend, as envisioned most candidly by Malta's ambassador to the UN, Arvid Pardo. In an August 1967 speech delivered before the UN Ad Hoc Committee to Study the Peaceful Uses of the Seabed and the Ocean Floor beyond the Limits of National Jurisdiction, Pardo prophesized that as the seabed became "progressively and competitively subject to national appropriation and use," rapid militarization and resource depletion would follow, through which "the common heritage of mankind" would be siphoned off "for the national advantage of technologically developed countries."[33]

Pardo's phrase, "the common heritage of mankind," would become the watchword of contemporary ocean law 15 years later, with the promulgation of UNCLOS. The convention, the fruit of 9 years of negotiation involving 149 countries and nongovernmental organizations, is in textual terms the longest international agreement ever recorded. Much of its contents are devoted to technical questions—the precise methods for drawing the baselines from which territorial and archipelagic seas are measured, for instance—whose resolutions are mainly of administrative and juridical significance.[34] At the treaty's heart, however, lay a pathbreaking political compromise, by which the developed world's concern with commercial access and navigation was assuaged in return for concessions designed to assure poor countries a share in any future development of ocean resources. And here the treaty's framers failed to allay the qualms of key constituents, notably the United States, which balked at the convention's provisions regarding seabed mining. Ratification was delayed an additional 12 years while a separate agreement amending the relevant articles was hammered out. The resulting treaty, plus the associated agreement, finally entered into force on November 16, 1994, and is now regarded by most nations, including the United States, as "an authoritative expression of existing international law"[35] (though it still awaits ratification by the U.S. Senate).

From the point of view of the continued expansion and integration of the world economy, the most important achievement of UNCLOS III is undoubtedly its statutory definition of the territorial sea, which is now limited to 12 miles and linked to two other legally defined zones, across which a coastal state's authority gradually diminishes. Thus an additional 12 miles may be claimed as a contiguous zone, where a state may enforce its own regulations respecting customs, immigration, fiscal, and sanitary matters; and beyond that an additional exclusive economic zone (EEZ), extending out to 200 miles, over which it may claim exclusive rights with respect to all living and nonliving resources of the water, seabed, and subsoil. Travel through international straits and archipelagic sea lanes falling within territorial seas are governed by special rules of transit passage, which must remained unobstructed at all times for civilian and military vessels alike, including submerged submarines.

All these provisions have attracted comment and concern. It is by no means unreasonable to worry, for instance, about states adopting onerous conditions respecting the treaty's provision for innocent passage for all ships (including warships) through territorial seas (as has already happened in a number of instances[36]—though it must be admitted that a propensity for onerous behavior does not depend on the depth of the water in which it occurs). The enormous size of the EEZ is sufficient in itself to give pause. Together with the territorial sea and contiguous zone, it comprises about one-third of the world's oceans, and 99 percent of the world catch of fish is taken there.[37] Its extent ensures that the zones of neighboring states often overlap, and drawing the lines necessary to separate them is by no means a purely mechanical process.[38] At the same time, because the EEZ is defined from a baseline drawn along the shore, it does not always encompass the resource-rich continental shelf, for which many additional rules and exceptions are provided—rules that have no bearing on the status of the superjacent waters. From such intricacies, friction will surely come, as well as from numerous points at which UNCLOS III provisions transgress expectations based upon earlier treaty law.[39]

The central issue, however, is whether the hierarchy of zones established by UNCLOS III checks the drift toward extended sovereignty that began with the Truman Declaration in 1945 or simply applies an additional layer of grease to an already slippery slope. History, it has been proposed, shows that "claims to jurisdiction have always tended to harden into claims to sovereignty,"[40] a proposition that should not be taken at face value. If history shows anything in the matter, it is that, in international law, practice trumps theory. The question, for instance, whether the EEZ is high seas, over which coastal states exercise a few special rights, or alternatively an extension of the territorial sea, in which outsiders are accorded a few special privileges, is left unsettled by

UNCLOS III, and remains fair game for contestation. Yet it is equally reasonable to view UNCLOS III as having injected an element of elasticity into a process in which rigidity is usually a portent of rupture. As long as the major maritime states persist in treating the EEZ as high seas for purposes of war and trade, that is what it will be. In this regard, the fact that the largest zones are claimed by states with a profound interest in freedom of navigation—the largest EEZ of all is that of the United States—is an additional source of reassurance.

UNCLOS III initially failed ratification not because of doubts about its regime of zones, but because of the way it handled what was left over once all the lines were drawn—specifically the international seabed beneath the high seas, known in the treaty as "the Area." It is in the Area that the "common heritage of mankind" is found, and it was to get a share of it that the developing world was prepared to curtail its exfoliating claims to sovereignty. UNCLOS III placed the Area under the jurisdiction of a new agency, the International Seabed Authority (ISA), which was responsible for regulating exploration and exploitation and for equitable sharing of benefits. To achieve the latter, it was envisioned that commercial development would proceed along parallel tracks. Applicants who wished to mine the seabed would be required to submit plans identifying two sites of equal estimated value, one of which would be reserved for development by the ISA commercial organ, called the "Enterprise," which would distribute proceeds to the treaty's poor signatories. Private-sector and national companies that wished to mine in the Area would be required to sell their technology to the Enterprise and to pay annual fees for working their designated sites. They would also be subject to ISA-administered environmental rules and to production limits intended to protect land-based producers of the same minerals.

These provisions proved troubling to a number of developed countries and wholly unacceptable to the United States, which became one of only four conference participants to refuse signature of the treaty in 1982. Much has been written about the nature of America's objections and about the cynicism with which they were advanced, for it was clear to all that the provisions about which the United States cared most—the new rules defining the territorial sea, the contiguous zone, and the EEZ— were certain to become customary law, regardless of whether the United States signed or not. Subsequent negotiations amended the deep seabed regime in fundamental ways by eliminating access fees, mandatory technology transfers, and production limits; and by changing the ISA composition to ensure that the interests of developed states were represented in proportion to their economic weight, rather than their numbers among the UN membership. It was with these emendations that the treaty finally entered into force.

Beyond UNCLOS

It is difficult today to recapture the intensity of feeling that once attached to UN-CLOS III seabed mining provisions. The celebrated polymetallic nodules have proven to be among nature's more elusive creations, whose successful recovery is now conceded to be many years away.[41] In the meantime, the industrialized world's anxiety about "strategic metals" has faded with the ending of the Cold War, while many of the Third World states that hoped to gain from a centralized scheme for redistributing wealth now prefer market solutions instead. It was, indeed, precisely because of these exogenous changes in the political and economic environment that a seabed treaty acceptable to all was finally achieved.

Which, in the present context, is very much the point. During the years in which UNCLOS III was aborning—roughly the late 1960s to the early 1990s—the world economy more than doubled in size and developed wholly unanticipated new forms of dynamism, integration, and growth—forms in which activities like mining, however esoteric, play a far less prominent role than anyone imagined a generation ago. When UNCLOS III was first negotiated, its proponents imagined that it was a harbinger of the future, "a new platform from which to launch a new international order."

> The concept [is] of a public international institution that is operational, capable of generating revenue, imposing international taxation, bringing multinational companies into a structured relationship; responsible for resource planning on a global scale, as well as for the protection and conservation of the marine environment and scientific research. An institution linking politics, economics and science in new ways—a model, potentially, for international organizations in the twenty-first century.[42]

That the past should have been wrong about what the future would hold is unsurprising. We are undoubtedly equally mistaken in our expectations. The question UNCLOS III raises is not about failed prophecy but about responsiveness to the modern pace of social and economic change. And here we must recall a point made at the start: that international law is made by and for states, which are not the lead actors in the drama of globalization and may be among the less quick of the supporting players. UNCLOS III was and is distinguished by a desire to elevate global interests above those of state governments; quite apart from its creation of a wholly new international regime for the ocean floor, its signatories are bound to settle treaty-related disputes either in international courts or through binding arbitration. Yet the convention's effort to visualize how those interests should be embodied in institutions already looked outdated on the day it came into force.

Law of the Sea versus Global Terrorism: Wrong Place to Look

The terrorist attacks directed against the United States in September 2001 seem certain to challenge the law's capacity to adapt to strategic change as well. The modern law of war aims to discriminate between the civil and the military, between belligerents and bystanders, between the use of lethal force and the larger interests of humanity. Its capacity to interpret events and render justice will be sorely tested by new forms of massive social violence designed precisely to blur all such distinctions. How far the global war on terrorism will impact the distinctive interests of the law of the sea is difficult to judge, though it is easy to imagine scenarios by which that impact could be profound. Had the attacks of September 11 been delivered not by hijacked airliners but by liquefied natural gas tankers detonated in New York Harbor and the Delaware Bay, the subsequent actions of the U.S. Navy probably would not have been much constrained by concern for a 12-mile territorial sea. Yet it is generally true that international legal structures fall short when confronted with worst-case scenarios, and in their absence it is perhaps equally likely that the habits of compromise and conciliation that UNCLOS III embodied will prove their worth in strategic terms as well.

Still, the international law of the sea has evolved to support global trade and enterprise. Its value in the eradication of a global scourge is as yet untested. The best historical precedent, the suppression of the slave trade, is not reassuring. Rather like terrorism, slavery in the 19th century was a practice that found few open defenders beyond the narrow ranks of those directly involved in it. It was declared anathema by the Treaty of Paris in 1815 and outlawed everywhere in Europe, even by states that tacitly supported the overseas trade between Africa and the Americas. Yet the British, who were determined to end the trade, were unable to construct an international legal consensus, because action against slavery was thought to jeopardize other important interests—free trade in the case of the United States, and national pride and autonomy in the case of small countries such as Portugal and Belgium, which profited surreptitiously from the trade. In the end, the British proceeded instead on the basis of bilateral treaties and by asserting what was in fact a belligerent right—the right of search—in peacetime, a borderline illegal practice that heightened Britain's reputation for arrogant unilateralism.[43] Slavery and the trade in slaves were proscribed by international law only in 1926, long after the issue had been substantially settled by more forcible means.

It therefore bears repeating: in matters of international law, practice trumps theory. Or, more precisely, it precedes it, both logically and for the most part historically, as the developments surveyed in this essay illustrate clearly enough. This deference of theory to practice is not a defect of international law. On the contrary, it is testimony to its underlying realism and utility. Yet it does suggest that international law is probably not the place to look for leadership in solving the problems of the emergent global economy or in addressing the strategic challenges that have followed in its wake.

Notes

[1] Adam Smith, *The Wealth of Nations*, vol. 2 (London, 1776; reprinted 1791), 139. Among scholars who accept the Columbian era as a watershed dividing a globalizing modernity from a parochial past, see Andre Gunder Frank, *ReOrient: Global Economy in the Asian Age* (Berkeley: University of California Press, 1998), 52; Jerry H. Bentley, "Cross-Cultural Interaction and Periodization in World History," *American Historical Review* 101, no. 3 (June 1996), 749–770; Immanuel Wallerstein, *The Modern World System, vol. 1: Capitalist Agriculture and the Origins of the European World-Economy in the Sixteenth Century* (New York: Academic Press, 1974), 67; William H. McNeill, *A World History*, 4th ed., rev. (New York: Oxford University Press, 1999).

[2] Pacific islanders did transit the open ocean to spread out across the Pacific, but not in the numbers of the prehistoric Asian or post-Columbian migrations.

[3] Robert O. Keohane and Joseph S. Nye, Jr., "Introduction," in *Governance in a Globalizing World*, ed. Joseph S. Nye and John D. Donahue (Washington, DC: The Brookings Institution Press, 2000), 1–6; see also Alan W. Heston and Neil A. Weiner, eds., "Dimensions of Globalization," in *The Annals of the American Academy of Political and Social Science* 570 (London: Sage Publications, 2000), which adopts a similar scheme with different results. For Keohane and Nye, globalization dates from the campaigns of Alexander the Great (4); for Heston and Weiner, it is a phenomenon of the last 20 years (8–17).

[4] Kevin H. O'Rourke and Jeffrey G. Williamson, *Globalization and History* (Cambridge, MA: MIT Press, 1999); Jeffrey G. Williamson, "Globalization, Convergence, and History," *Journal of Economic History* 56, no. 2 (June 1996), 1–30.

[5] Richard Langhorne, *The Coming of Globalization* (New York: Palgrave, 2001); see also Pippa Norris, "Global Governance and Cosmopolitan Citizens," in Nye and Donahue, 155–177.

[6] Whether international law is an expression of international society—that is, the society created by states among themselves—is another question, on which see Kai Alderson and Andrew Hurrell, *Hedley Bull on International Society* (New York: Palgrave, 2000).

[7] Cornelius van Bynkershoek, *De dominio maris* (Leyden, 1702), chap. 2. The principle of a maritime belt began to command general acceptance after it was taken up by Emer de Vattel in his influential *Le Droit des Gens* (1758). It was subsequently incorporated into the customs and fishery regulations of a number of states. See Ian Brownlie, *Principles of Public International Law*, 5th ed., rev. (New York: Oxford, 1998), 179. The formalization of the "cannon-shot rule" into the now-defunct 3-mile limit for territorial waters was the work of British and American prize courts during the Napoleonic wars.

[8] Grotius, *Mare Liberum*, chap. 5. Grotius' work does not include the idea of a maritime belt as sovereign territory. For him, the high seas extended from shore to shore.

[9] The most serious objections to Grotius' arguments involved his assumption that the resources of the sea were unlimited, a claim that even 17th-century fisherman knew to be false. See William Welwood, *An Abridgment of All Sea Lawes* (London, 1613), and John Selden, *Mare Clausum* (London, 1635), book 1.

[10] The outcome of the struggle for precedence in early modern Europe testifies to the limited weight of preindustrial globalization. Except for Spain in the 16th century, none of the countries that rise to the top during this period do so on the strength of gains from overseas trade and empire. See David Eltis and Stanley L. Engerman, "The Importance of Slavery and the Slave Trade to Industrializing Britain," *Journal of Economic History* 60, no. 1 (March 2000), 123–144.

[11] Carl von Clausewitz, *On War* (1832), ed. and trans. by Michael Howard and Peter Paret (Princeton: Princeton University Press, 1976), 75.

[12] The Duke of Newcastle's *Letter by His Majesty's Order*, to Monsieur Michell, the King of Prussia's Secretary of the Embassy (London, 1753), 10. Newcastle, citing Grotius as his authority, wrote to defend Britain's wartime seizure of French goods on a neutral Prussian merchantman. The original text is not in the form of a bullet list; it appears here in that form for clarification.

[13] Kevin H. O'Rourke and Jeffrey G. Williamson, *After Columbus: Explaining the Global Trade Boom, 1500–1800*, National Bureau of Economic Research Working Paper 8186 (Cambridge, MA: MIT Press, 2001), 3. During the century and a half studied by Mahan in his *Influence of Seapower* series (1660–1815), there were no more than a score of years in which at least one of the major maritime states (France, Britain, Spain, and the Netherlands) was not at war.

[14] *Mare Liberum*, chap. 1.

[15] Ralph Davis, *The Rise of the English Shipping Industry in the Seventeenth and Eighteenth Centuries* (London: David and Charles, 1962), 262–264; Russell Menard, "Transport Costs and Long-Range Trade, 1300–1800: Was There a European 'Transport Revolution' in the Early Modern Era?" in *The Political Economy of Merchant Empires*, ed. James D. Tracy (Cambridge, Cambridge University Press, 1991), 228–275.

[16] Norman Stone, *Europe Transformed, 1878–1919* (Cambridge, MA: Harvard University Press, 1983), 25.

[17] Kevin H. O'Rourke and Jeffrey G. Williamson, *When Did Globalization Begin?* National Bureau of Economic Research Working Paper 7632 (Cambridge, MA: MIT Press, 2001), argues that about 75 percent of price convergence in the 19th century is due to declining transportation costs, with the remainder attributable to the liberal policy shift.

[18] Paul Schroeder, *The Transformation of European Politics, 1763–1848* (New York: Oxford University Press, 1994), 52.

[19] O'Rourke and Williamson, *After Columbus*, 3.

[20] Peter H. Lindert and Jeffrey G. Williamson, *Does Globalization Make the World More Unequal?* National Bureau of Economic Research Working Paper 8228 (Cambridge, MA: MIT Press, 2001), 13–14 and table 2.

[21] Clausewitz, 89.

[22] Adams was of course an ardent abolitionist himself. The quoted statement, made to the British Ambassador, is in H.G. Soulsby, *The Right of Search and the Slave Trade in Anglo-American Relations, 1814–1862* (Baltimore: Johns Hopkins University Press, 1933), 18. On Anglo-American maritime relations generally, see Bernard Semmel, *Liberalism and Naval Strategy: Ideology, Interest, and Sea Power during the Pax Britannica* (Boston: Allen and Unwin, 1986), especially 31–67, 152–171.

[23] "Paris Declaration Respecting Maritime Law," April 16, 1856, in *Documents on the Laws of War*, ed. Robert Adams and Richard Guelff, 3rd ed., rev. (New York: Oxford University Press, 2000), 47–49.

[24] [Henry Reeve], "The Orders in Council on Trade During War," *Edinburgh Review*, July 1854, 221–222.

[25] Richard Cobden to W. S. Lindsay, August 29, 1856, in Semmel, 71.

[26] John Stuart Mill, speech of August 5, 1867, in *Parliamentary Debates: House of Commons*, 3d series (London: HMS Stationary Office, 1869), 880.

[27] Adams to [British] Minister Rush, July 28, 1823, in *Policy of the United States Toward Maritime Commerce in War* vol. 1, ed. Carlton Savage (Washington, DC: Government Printing Office,1934), 306–307.

[28] For this exchange of letters see Semmel, 155.

[29] On the consequence of food shortage for the German war effort, see Avner Offer, *The First World War: An Agrarian Interpretation* (New York: Oxford University Press, 1989). The severe German death toll was the result not of starvation but of declining resistance to disease, increased infant mortality, and so on. For the original statistics, see the League of Nations study compiled by Frank W. Notestein et al., *The Future Population of Europe and the Soviet Union: Population Projections, 1940–1970* (Geneva: League of Nations, 1944).

[30] A third cause, less immediately germane to our theme, was the increasing economic inequality that accompanied globalization in Europe. Socialist, national-socialist, fascist, and communist parties all sought to limit the impact of international capitalism on the mass of the population, and liberal regimes that feared radical opposition forces were disposed to do likewise by way of self-defense. Scholars are uncertain whether a similar link between globalization and inequality exits today. See Adrian Wood, *North-South Trade, Employment, and Inequality: Changing Fortunes in a Skill-Driven World* (New York: Oxford, 1994); and Kevin H. O'Rourke, *Globalization and Inequality: Historical Trends*, National Bureau of Economic Research Working Paper 8339 (Cambridge, MA: MIT Press, 2001).

[31] The text of the U.S. declaration is in Marjorie M. Whiteman, *Digest of International Law* 4 (Washington, DC: U.S. Department of State, 1963–1973), 756.

[32] UN Convention on the Continental Shelf, excerpted in Brownlie, 213.

[33] Excerpted in George V. Galdorisi and Kevin R. Vienna, *Beyond the Law of the Sea: New Directions of U.S. Oceans Policy* (Westport, CT: Praeger, 1997), 25.

[34] For an authoritative analysis of the convention's legal meaning, see *United Nations Convention on the Law of the Sea: A Commentary*, 5 vols., ed. Myron H. Nordquist (Boston: Martinus Nijhoff, 1985). The first volume includes the text of the treaty itself (206–403). The best non-technical account, with emphasis upon American policy, is Galdorisi and Vienna. The older work by Ken Booth, *Law, Force, and Diplomacy at Sea* (Boston: Allen and Unwin, 1985), now somewhat overtaken by events, remains useful for its insights into the convention's political and strategic context.

[35] Lung-Chu Chen, *An Introduction to Contemporary International Law: A Policy-Oriented Perspective*, 2d ed. (New Haven, Yale University Press, 2000), 133

[36] Galdorisi and Vienna, 145–147.

[37] Chen, 137.

[38] There is a useful map illustrating the zone's extent and the complexity of its definition where neighboring zones collide in Booth, following page 220.

[39] See H. Caminos and M.R. Molitor, "Progressive Development of International Law and the Package Deal," *American Journal of International Law* 79, no. 4 (October 1985); and Malcolm N. Shaw, *International Law*, 4th ed. (Cambridge: Cambridge University Press, 1997), 443.

[40] Brownlie, 180.

[41] Chen, 141.

[42] Elisabeth Mann Borgese, "Law of the Sea: The Next Phase," *Third World Quarterly* (October 1982), 708; see also discussion in Booth, 28.

[43] See Chaim D. Kaufmann and Robert A. Pape, "Explaining Costly International Moral Action: Britain's Sixty-Year Campaign Against the Atlantic Slave Trade," *International Organization* (Autumn 1999), 631–668.

Chapter 13

Beyond Integration: Globalization and Maritime Power from a European Perspective

James H. Bergeron

I t is common in discussions of U.S.–European Union (EU) relations to point out a supposed difference in strategic viewpoint between the two. The United States is often depicted (especially in Europe) as being overly committed to a neorealist vision of international relations—a world of friends and foes, deterrence, power, and conflict. In turn, European political culture is often described (especially in the United States) as immature, insular, naïve in its reliance on supposed international norms, and overly focused on diplomacy, development aid, and crisis management solutions to international problems. At the heart of these differences (and there *are* differences, although they often are distorted out of proportion) lies competing visions of globalization, based on different (but intertwined) historical experiences. This chapter explores the European concepts of globalization and examines how they have changed over time, particularly since September 11, 2001. It will then consider the implication of the European global perspectives for EU maritime doctrine and the future of its force structure.

Europe is at a crossroads in its global vision, a situation that has been developing since the end of the Cold War but has become an imperative issue since September 11 and the potential changes in U.S.–EU relations that may come in its wake. European states do not view the world similarly, but it has been the case the most European states have, since 1945, focused their vision on the European integration project to the exclusion of wider geostrategic concerns. This was partly and understandably due to the roles played by the United States and the North Atlantic Treaty Organization (NATO) during those years as the guarantors of Western defense. In contrast, the 1990s witnessed a slow

James H. Bergeron is a law professor at University College, Dublin (on leave). He currently serves as NATO–EU Policy Officer on the staff of the Commander, United States Naval Forces Europe, in London. The author thanks Sean Colman, Simon Duke, and Terry Terriff for their comments on an earlier draft of this chapter.

development of European strategic consciousness at the level of EU institutions, culminating in the European Security and Defense Policy (ESDP) and the development (at least on paper) of a European Rapid Reaction Force. All of this has been accelerated since September 11. The post-September 11 world creates both challenges and opportunities for Europe different from anything they have had to address for over 30 years, and for many EU member states, the revival of an old conundrum: the need for Europe to act as a global, rather than a regional, power.

European Integration as a Surrogate for Globalization

A linkage has always existed between the parallel European projects of integration and defense. Thus it was at the beginning. It is now mostly forgotten (especially in Washington) that the United States was among the main promoters of the failed European Defense Community initiative in the early 1950s. Instead of a separate European defense alliance, what developed was a selective European Economic Community (EEC)—guided by France and West Germany—with security provided by NATO, whose membership extended beyond the EEC.[1] By the 1960s, Europe was an economic, political, and security part of a grander transatlantic whole, of variable geometry, and with high tensions. It was the era of the Berlin airlift, the Cuban missile crisis, and the John F. Kennedy assassination. The Cold War was truly cold and threatened to become hot.

The period between the failure of the first EEC applications of the United Kingdom and Ireland in 1962, and the final accession of the United Kingdom, Ireland, and Denmark to the community in 1973 witnessed a substantial transformation in the global context of European integration. U.S.-Soviet relations stabilized. President Richard Nixon initiated a policy of détente with the Soviet Union and opened a diplomatic door to China. U.S. defense spending fell, the Navy shrank. The threat, such as it was, existed more in Southeast Asia than in Europe. Although at the epicenter of nuclear confrontation, the very enormity of such a confrontation reduced the likelihood, in the eyes of many Europeans, of a nuclear war ever occurring in Europe. Détente and the advent of arms control agreements reduced the nuclear specter still further. In Europe, the world of détente had become a more peaceable one, and it made possible the emergence of a different kind of EEC.

For just at that time, in the late 1960s, began the construction of a more autonomous, civilianized European Community (EC) that represented an inward shift in the global paradigm for many European states. Although the De Gaulle plan for a European Political and Defense Union had come to naught, his historic *rapproachment* with Konrad Adenauer in 1962 had created Franco-Germany as the center of gravity of a European project that would have a more commercial and social focus. The expansion of EEC economic and social law, including especially the free movement of persons, and the expanding constitutional law of the EEC Treaty emerging from the European Court of Justice in Luxembourg provided a foundation for a view of Europe as a quasi-federal entity, a constitutional legal order based on treaty.

This new Europe was one of trade and travel, of increasing labor and capital mobility, competition law and economic regulation, a bright Europe whose new optimism (at least within the EC institutions) was unblemished by the defense and security concerns that were the responsibility of the United States or the member states acting through NATO. Or perhaps, from an institutional perspective, the new Europe was a project of national foreign ministries, trade ministries, other ministries such as labor, environment, and finance, judges, lawyers, corporations, business and interest groups. Ministries of defense and the military had almost no role within the scope of the community and so naturally took their lead, and their focus, from NATO.

In effect, the common market had created a space for positive European cooperation, outside of the sphere of superpower confrontation (although supported by the United States for political and economic reasons). It also played an important psychological function, in making the EC member states masters of their own destiny, albeit within a narrow confine of interests, in an era of decolonization, the economic domination of the United States and growing economic rivalry of Japan, and the arrival from the late 1950s of new immigrant populations from the former colonies.[2] European integration itself thus represented a form of globalization, based on the rule of international law, supranational institutions, harmonization of laws and policies, and the free flow of goods, persons, capital, culture and ideas. It was a *rational* or planned globalization, brought about as an act of the sovereign wills of EC member states pooling their sovereignty. It was a very "European" globalization based on the assumption of managing technological forces through cooperation and legal regulation.[3]

The presence of the United States, in Europe and globally, was of course an essential precondition for this Brussels worldview. Defense could be ignored within the corridors of the European institutions precisely because it had been the first European market to have been integrated, through NATO.[4] With defense sovereignty pooled in NATO under the leadership of the United States—and thus depoliticized from an internal European perspective—the EEC could develop a remarkable power-sharing model that gave influence to smaller states and the European Commission. In particular, the "big four" powers—France, West Germany, Italy, and the United Kingdom—did not exercise the kind four-power *directoire* over Europe that might have been the case were political and security policy issues in play in the Council.

Ironically, the more stable world of détente allowed for the creation of a greater space for European foreign policy, at least in the sense of formal political declarations. The early 1970s witnessed the emergence of an informal European Political Cooperation in the Council of Ministers, European support for the Conference on Security and

Cooperation in Europe (against U.S. policy wishes), and the rebuff of Secretary of State Henry Kissinger's "Year of Europe" attempt to reexert a more robust U.S. foreign policy hegemony. The new emphasis from the 1970s to the 1990s was on the internal market, employment policy, competition, regulation, state aids, cohesion and development funds, free movement, economic and monetary union, subsidiarity, European citizenship. External relations were primarily concerned with economic relations, in particular the General Agreement on Trade and Tariffs, but also trade association agreements, and preferential agreements for former colonies and developing countries.

Yet it was in these years of European development, the heyday of the EC in the view of many, that Europe as a set of institutions withdrew further from security and defense concerns. It is noteworthy that during the Second Cold War following the Soviet invasion of Afghanistan in 1979 and through the Intermediate-Range Nuclear Forces crisis, the Community developed no significant autonomous security policy or institutions. NATO, led by the United States, remained firmly at the helm of European defense policy. This was also the era of declining European defense expenditures and of a growing gap between European and U.S. military capabilities, as the United States turned to computer and information technologies to reinvent the art of post-Vietnam warfare.

The Cold War Ends: First Crack in the Assumed Security Paradigm of Europe

In 1986, the great European initiative was the completion of the internal market—the creation of a Europe without frontiers. Three hundred directives were to be implemented by the member states in areas such as banking and financial services harmonization, mutual recognition of professional qualifications, technical standards, and labor mobility. The process was to be completed by January 1, 1993. In fact, by that date, history had moved forward so quickly that the ambitious schemes of 1986 appeared as safe, technocratic, almost nostalgic in their orientation. In the interim period, the Berlin Wall had fallen, the Soviet Union had dissolved, a war had been fought in the Persian Gulf, Yugoslavia collapsed, and the Balkan wars had begun. The member states of the EC, seeing the changes of the late 1980s and fearing in particular the prospect of a reunited Germany not solidly integrated into larger European structures, rapidly negotiated and signed at Maastricht the Treaty on European Union. The new treaty included plans for economic and monetary union, introduced the concepts of subsidiarity and European citizenship, and established two intergovernmental pillars for European cooperation in the areas of foreign and security policy, and in the area of justice and internal affairs. After 30 years of slow functionalist groping toward a political end, the process of European integration shifted into high gear.

This was so because the fall of the Berlin Wall and the end of the Soviet Union had partly undermined the foundations on which the détente model EEC had been built. The decline of Russia recreated the possibility of achieving the long-stated NATO goal of a "Europe whole and free," but it also meant a reintegration project for Western Europe of gigantic proportions. American leadership in NATO, although not challenged, was less of an imperative of survival than it had been, and indeed substantial U.S. forces were withdrawn from Europe as part of the peace dividend. NATO was casting about for a role in the world. After 30 years of successful European integration, it was no longer clear that—as a sardonic adage maintains—NATO was needed to keep "the Americans in, the Russians out, and the Germans down."

In response to the new situation, all major international security actors— NATO, the EU, the Organization for Security and Cooperation in Europe (OSCE), the United States, and the European member states—attempted a reinvention of their missions. With the threat of invasion and war receding, policy emphasis shifted to instability and engagement as the practical justifications for NATO, ESDP, U.S. forward presence in Europe, and the defense budgets of the major European powers. General George Joulwan, the Supreme Allied Commander, Europe (SACEUR), summed it up in 1995: "Instability is the Enemy." Across the transatlantic world, policy staffs set about building partnership programs, military to military contact programs with Eastern European states, a NATO Mediterranean dialogue and EU Barcelona Process with the southern Mediterranean states, a South East European Initiative for the greater Balkans, innumerable engagement plans attempting to prioritize engagement in favor of states representing both vital interests and high instability. By 1998, it was hard to justify military forces on the basis of defense alone.

Although the détente EEC has been undermined by the demise of the Soviet Union, a surrogate was provided during the 1990s by the prospect of security—but not defense—cooperation. The 1991 Maastricht Treaty on European Union created a European Common Foreign and Security Policy (CFSP) for the pursuit of the Petersberg Tasks of peacekeeping and crisis management, including peacemaking. Although the CFSP chapter envisaged a future common defense policy, and perhaps in time, a common defense, all accepted this to be a distant and contentious aspiration. For the foreseeable future, security cooperation would be about solving other people's problems, would not alter of central role of NATO in the defense of Europe, and would not put too great a burden on national defense budgets. The use of the term European Security and Defense Identity (ESDI) was apposite—what was at stake in the first phase of the CFSP was the project of European state building and identity formation, to which a foreign and security policy was intended to contribute. CFSP/ESDI reflected a new awareness of global forces, and their potential impact on Europe, but these forces were viewed through the Balkan paradigm, as rooted in ethnic and religious strife, and having as consequences mostly human rights abuses, immigration flows, and perhaps the export of criminal activities.

ESDP and the Regionalization of European Global Vision

The end of the Cold War offered the EU the opportunity to create itself as a powerful entity and strategic partner of the United States in dealing with the challenges posed by peacekeeping, crisis management, and humanitarian intervention. But that opportunity was fumbled for almost a decade. In 1994, NATO agreed to a compromise in the form of the European Security and Defense Identity, a plan for separable but not separate European forces acting as a combined Joint Task Force, under the command of the Western European Union (WEU) but still within the overall NATO structure. Despite extensive doctrinal development, the WEU-led combined joint task force (CJTF) concept went nowhere. Divisions over recognition of the new Balkan states exacerbated—some would say caused—the onset of the first Balkan conflicts. In 1994, the EU was not able to take common action in Bosnia, leaving the initiative first to the United Kingdom and France, and then the United States. European states were once again startled, as they had been in the Gulf War, by the scale of American military superiority. They were also aware of the antagonisms that the dual-key UN–NATO arrangements had created, and of the evident desire of the United States for NATO to henceforth act outside UN control, perhaps without UN authorization. The hard bargain forced by Richard Holbrook at Dayton reminded the Europeans that, once engaged, the United States would insist upon the right to lead and set the terms of both conflict and closure.

The crunch came in Kosovo. Under U.S. leadership, NATO conducted an air campaign to force the secession of ethnic cleansing. Whether the air strategy was a success is debatable. But what was beyond debate in the capitals of Europe was the immense superiority of American air power, their command and control (C^2) systems, satellite intelligence, strategic lift, and logistics, proven once again in the skies over former Yugoslavia. With almost 4 million men under arms, the collective member states of the EU were unable to rapidly deploy even 40,000 troops to Kosovo. Command and control relations were strained in the conflict, with several states demanding target list approval, and rumors of senior U.S. officers waiting until the allies were absent from the targeting table to "get down to business." Even the United Kingdom felt a sense of exclusion from decisionmaking.

The NATO command structure was problematic in Kosovo, raising in clear relief a tension always latent in it: the role of the NATO SACEUR, the U.S. four-star general who was also combatant commander of the U.S. European Command. When NATO went to war, was SACEUR to act as an ally or as an American? Was he at liberty to consult with the members of the North Atlantic Council or heads of member states, or did he take direction from the Pentagon? As Wesley Clark notes in his recent book *Waging Modern War*, Washington was solidly of the latter view.[5] General Clark's difficulties with Washington and his early transfer from the SACEUR position convinced many in Europe that the NATO command structure was moribund, never to be used again. And not only because of a U.S. unwillingness to share decisionmaking with allies, but also because of an internal unwillingness in Washington to split decisionmaking between two top U.S. officers—the Chairman of the Joint Chiefs of Staff and SACEUR.

Kosovo represented a moment of truth for the EU, and especially for France and the United Kingdom, the two remaining great powers in Europe. A sense of relative weakness in security capabilities coincided with a new Suez feeling that the United States could not always be expected to act in accordance with European wishes. For the United Kingdom, the experience of Kosovo coincided with the felt need of the new Labor government in Britain to exert more influence of European Union affairs, a prospect daunted by their nonparticipation in the Economic and Monetary Union. The result was the December 1998 communiqué of Tony Blair and French President Jacques Chirac at St. Malo, calling for the rapid development of a European Security and Defense Policy and the establishment of a credible, rapidly deployable European force for peacekeeping and crisis management operations. The European Summit in Helsinki confirmed the new Anglo-French initiative as a European project and established a Headline Goal process that would allow the EU to field 50,000 to 60,000 troops, plus required naval and air assets and to sustain them in the field for one year. The EU held a Capabilities Commitment Conference in November 2000, and a follow-on in November 2001, to develop its catalogue of force contributions. At Nice in December 2000, the European Council set out its proposal for cooperation with NATO, and the establishment of EU security institutions in the form of a Political and Security Committee of the Council, an EU Military Committee, and an EU Military Staff.

The emergence of ESDP is a foreign policy challenge for Washington, which has long called for greater burdensharing on the part of its European allies, while reluctant to accept a diminution of America's leadership role in NATO that a more powerful Europe would demand. NATO–EU cooperation is a fraught issue and has not yet been resolved. In the aftermath of the St. Malo declaration, the United States took a hard line on ESDP, insisting that the EU not duplicate the planning role of Supreme Headquarters Allied Powers Europe, and that EU force planning and generation be integrated with NATO in the person of Deputy Supreme Allied Commander Europe, the senior European officer in the NATO command structure. The United States also sought regular meetings between NATO and EU committees, a form of diplomatic escalation dominance. In return, the United States agreed to grant the EU "assured access" to common NATO planning and command and control assets, and on a case-by-case basis, U.S. capabilities such as intelligence, reconnaissance, and strategic lift. NATO and the

EU agreed a verbal formula that ESDP would be undertaken "where the Alliance as a whole was not engaged." Whether that meant that the United States has a right of first refusal, or only whether the decision to take action must first be presented to NATO for agreement by consensus, has been left constructively ambiguous.

These so-called Berlin Plus negotiations between NATO and the EU continue and are in stalemate due to the Cyprus dispute between Greece and Turkey. An associate member of the Western European Union, Turkey considers the ESDP to undermine its strategic leverage in the eastern Mediterranean. It is concerned that the EU could take action in that area, and especially in Cyprus, without a Turkish veto as would be the case in NATO. The efforts of Greece to achieve accession of the island of Cyprus in the next round of EU enlargement, to the extent of threatening to veto any enlargement that does not include Cyprus, has added to Turkish concerns. Although promising negotiation between the two Cypriot governments are ongoing, no break in the Berlin Plus negotiations appeared to be on the cards at the time of writing.

Notwithstanding the lack of a formal cooperation agreement, NATO and EU political cooperation has been effective because of the excellent working relations between Secretary General Lord Robertson and Javier Solana, the EU High Representative for CFSP. There has also been very efficient coordination on the ground in Kosovo. As a French diplomat recently said, apparently with great concern, "NATO–EU cooperation works well in practice, but not in theory."

Split in European Global Vision: The Neutrals

The European neutrals—Austria, Finland, Sweden, and Ireland—have watched these developments with interest and caution. The trend in European security relations after 1991 presents substantial challenges and opportunities for nonaligned foreign and security policy. The NATO Partnership for Peace and the establishment of the Euro-Atlantic Partnership Council shifted the defense debate away from questions of neutrality toward those of capabilities. Whether formal mutual defense agreements existed ceased to matter. With the threat of a unifying Soviet land invasion gone, not all NATO members would provide forces for every operation, and many of those contributing would be not members but partners. A new NATO convention was developing in which influence and even command responsibility would depend on the level of contribution, not the fact of NATO membership. Coalitions of the willing, based on individual and common interests, would go forth when necessary—a model followed in the Persian Gulf, Bosnia, Kosovo, and Afghanistan. This change meant that the neutrals could play a greater role in international security affairs on a case-by-case basis without joining NATO or abandoning their formal neutrality. Of course, for those who associated neutrality with nonintervention except for UN peacekeeping missions, this was also a portent of deeper involvement in a detested realpolitik of international relations, in cooperation with a "nuclear alliance."

For traditional peacekeeping, the experiences of the UN Protection Force in Bosnia and then NATO in Kosovo marked the end of an era. Bosnia was not ripe for a peacekeeping mission, and the UN forces were tragically incapable of carrying out their mandate. Peacekeeping had become peacemaking, not only in that case, but in paradigmatic terms. The UN, although still central to the global peacekeeping mission, increasingly mandates command and control to regional organizations such as NATO and perhaps the EU or to lead nations. Especially in the Balkans, support for peacekeeping would have to be done under UN authorization but NATO command. Having a voice in NATO operations meant having a voice in NATO, via the 1994 Partnership for Peace initiative.

The Irish example is illustrative of the difficult path between EU membership and security alliance. In the aftermath of Kosovo, the St. Malo declaration and Helsinki Summit propelled the EU into the security realm, making the decision by Ireland to earmark a light infantry battalion and Ranger platoon—850 soldiers—to the EU Rapid Reaction Force (RRF) a politically volatile one. In his November 18, 2000, announcement, Irish Foreign Minister Brian Cowen laid out the concept and framework for Ireland's participation in ESDP.[6] In the view of the Irish government, the RRF provides the EU with the opportunity to engage in humanitarian and crisis management operations, including both military and nonmilitary aspects, while fully respecting the principles of the UN Charter. The RRF will not affect Ireland's policy of neutrality, as Irish Defense Forces would participate only when UN authorization is in place, when the requirements of Irish legislation have been met, and on the basis of a specific government decision. Irish involvement with EU/NATO operations would occur only where Irish peacekeepers act under the UN flag. Of interest in the foreign minister's speech was the lack of any linkage between collective capability and de facto alliance, based on political solidarity and economic interdependence. ESDP exists to provide peace and stability elsewhere; it is reactive but not defensive. In short, it is seen as optional—a morally nice thing to do.

This pacific view of EU security and defense functions was not shared by a growing section of the Irish public, which recognized—whether in favor of defense cooperation or isolation—that a de facto alliance was emerging in the EU toward which Ireland and the other nonaligned EU member states would be expected to show loyalty. It also sits ill with the EU vision of itself. EU Commission President Romano Prodi told Eastern European states in September 2001 that the security that EU states enjoy by membership of the Union "is of the same level" as NATO membership. An EU state "cannot be damaged or attacked without reaction from the EU. Otherwise there is no Union."[7] Although the reference is to de facto solidarity, the message is nonetheless

clear that EU member states—including the neutrals—were pooling their essential interests to such an extent that mutual support was a high expectation, notwithstanding
the lack of a formal mutual defense treaty commitment.

The New European Maritime Posture: Doctrine and Forces

Europe's maritime posture is a good indicator of its global vision, and during the
waning years of the Cold War, that posture was strongly defensive. NATO non-U.S.
maritime forces were focused mostly on antisubmarine warfare (ASW), mine countermeasures, sea control, and interdiction. The guided missile or ASW frigate, supplemented by the conventional submarine, was the paradigm European naval unit. Although most large European states maintained carrier strike and amphibious
capabilities, these forces were modest.

Although European defense budgets have not improved in recent years, there
have been interesting shifts in procurement and force planning. Of greatest significance in the maritime area has been the development of amphibious capabilities. A
number of European navies are investing in amphibious lift and C² capabilities as part
of the European Amphibious Initiative (EAI).

EAI brings together amphibious forces from the United Kingdom, Netherlands,
France, Spain, and Italy, including the United Kingdom/Netherlands Amphibious
Force built around three commando Royal Marines, the Spanish-Italian Amphibious
Force, and the French amphibious force, possibly augmented to brigade strength by a
German troop contribution.[8] Currently, the core of this force could be organized
around the amphibious assault ship HMS *Fearless* and amphibious assault (helicopter)
ships HMS *Ocean*, Netherlands amphibious assault transport dock (LPD) HrMs *Rotterdam*, and Spanish LPD *Galicia*. To remedy national and combined weaknesses in
amphibious lift and C², Spain plans to add a second *Rotterdam*-class vessel. Likewise,
the United Kingdom has agreed to purchase four Royal Schelde *Enforcer* design *Bay*-
class LPDs to enter service in 2004, replacing its old *Sir*-class landing ship logistic vessels, which will serve alongside its new landing personnel dock replacement
(LPD[R])ships HMS *Albion* and HMS *Bulwark*. The Netherlands has ordered a modified *Rotterdam*-class LPD to be named *Johan de Witt*, scheduled to enter service in
2007. Of note, the new craft (referred to as LPD–2) will be capable of hosting a 400-
person headquarters staff for a CJTF of up to division strength. It will also have a sophisticated command, control, communications, computers, and intelligence (C⁴I) infrastructure, with the American command ship USS *Mount Whitney* as its model.[9] The
EAI navies have long had the manpower to deploy an amphibious division. With these
improvements in amphibious lift and C⁴I, a European capability to project and sustain
an embarked amphibious force, roughly equivalent to a U.S. marine expeditionary
unit/amphibious ready group, should be in place by 2008.[10]

European carrier strike capabilities have also gradually developed, including the deployment of French aircraft carrier *Charles De Gaulle*, the recent return to service of HMS *Ark Royal*, and the combat experience of ITS *Garibaldi* in support of coalition operations in the war against terrorism. However, given the relative scarcity of carrier strike assets, ESDP planning probably will need to emphasize nonopposed landings, or, if opposed, operations in areas where substantial land-based air force strike capabilities could be brought to bear in a supporting role.

The maritime concept of ESDP may take on a stronger institutional form as a result of an initiative at the Chiefs of European Navies (CHENs) Conference of May 2002 to consider a NATO Channel Committee proposal for a European Maritime Initiative (EMI).[11] The EMI paper sets out a vision of the enabling role that naval forces will play in ESDP joint operations. Substantial emphasis is placed on amphibious operations and, to a lesser extent, carrier strike capabilities. EMI was motivated by a sense of overemphasis on land forces in the European Headline Goal establishing the Rapid Reaction Force, and the intent of the European naval chiefs is to convince their military and political masters of the key enabling role that naval forces play in joint operations. It is interesting to note that the CHENs initiative is replaying many of the arguments raised during the development of joint operations within the Department of Defense, leading to the reorientation of U.S. naval forces under the naval strategic vision . . . *From the Sea*.

EMI identifies European naval weaknesses in command, control, communications, computers, intelligence, surveillance, and reconnaissance; theater ballistic missile defense; interoperable CJTF headquarters facilities; and logistics. A joint procurement program for the Airbus A400M heavy lift transport plane is at an advanced stage, and the development of autonomous satellite positioning and intelligence system (Galileo) was approved by the European Council at the March 2002 EU Summit in Barcelona. By 2008—if current plans are implemented—Europeans will collectively possess a credible force capable of carrying out the range of Petersburg Tasks, albeit at a higher level of risk than the United States (with its more robust capabilities) would need to accept.

The period from the high point of the Kosovo operations to the September 11 terrorist attacks saw a shift in European strategic thinking, including their concept of globalization as applied to military and naval forces. A new European appreciation for dangers of instability in the greater European region emerged, as did—even more important—a conviction that Europe needed the capability to address these challenges on its own. However, the focus remained regional, and the threat remained *instability*. European defense budgets are at best stagnant, and some are in decline. The demographics of an aging population do not bode well for further defense expenditures, and domestic regional and employment priorities in many states constrain governments from moving away from the static land force structure of the Cold War toward a lighter, more mobile force. Most of all, there is no certainty that EU foreign policy during 21st-century crises will be any more coherent than existed during crisis moments in Bosnia, Kosovo, or indeed Afghanistan.

That being said, however, it should be noted that within the maritime realm, there are some contraindications of a "merely ancilliary" status for European forces. During Operation *Enduring Freedom*, many European nations (along with Japan and others) found it easier to provide support for U.S. efforts in the form of warships and naval units than land forces—for very practical reasons. For one thing, many European land forces are not globally deployable or are primarily deployable in very small numbers or through American logistical support. Seagoing warships are generally designed to deploy independently and are easier to sustain via overall NATO maritime capabilities. Also—perhaps somewhat cynically—sailors were less likely to suffer casualties than soldiers in a war where there were no opposing naval forces, thereby lessening the prospects that European voters might call their countries' participation in the counterterrorism war (particularly the phase against the Taliban and al Qaeda) into question. On the other hand, the forces provided at sea were combat-capable: British and French naval aircraft conducted combat sorties. The French contribution of the newly operational aircraft carrier *Charles de Gaulle* was a strong symbolic show of support—and, while not as large as U.S. carriers, she was a potential substitute for U.S. carrier airpower. As noted, Italy also sent its primary naval assets, the aircraft carrier *Giuseppe Garibaldi* and her escorts.[12]

More importantly, command of the interdiction patrol tasked with preventing al Qaeda forces from escaping by sea (focusing on the coast of Somalia as a primary terrorist destination) was eventual turned over by the United States to a German admiral—another very symbolic act of multilateral solidarity, this time in the U.S.-to-Europe direction.[13] The obvious suggestion is that even with the disparity in capabilities identified by the European naval chiefs of staff, maritime operations are primary areas where European forces could make more than a "very junior partner" contribution.

World Turned Upside Down: September 11 and Revival of a European Global Paradigm?

To the observer on September 10, ESDP was bound for rapid institutional, but slow military, growth; its mandate would be limited to Europe or its very near abroad. Some form of NATO–EU cooperation would be agreed eventually, and defense issues would remain largely external affairs, focused around peacekeeping, crisis management, and constructive engagement. U.S. commitment to the Alliance was assumed to be strong, notwithstanding the gradual drawdown of U.S. forces in Europe. U.S. strategic presence in Europe would maintain the strategic status quo. And instability and insecurity was consensually seen as an externality, part of the state of anarchy that exists outside the realm of peace and stability that is the nation-state.

September 11 changed all that. The United States has been seriously attacked on its soil for the first time in living memory. Both NATO and the UN define this situation as, if not war, then at least war's closest surrogate in the world of modern international law—an "armed attack" triggering the right of individual and collective self-defense under Article 51 of the UN Charter, as well as the NATO Article 5 collective defense guarantee. Alliances shifted: Pakistan, who could have been condemned as a promoter of the Taliban regime, became a partner in Operation *Enduring Freedom*. Russia threw its weight solidly behind the United States, and even China acquiesced in the need for action in Afghanistan. The members of NATO stood as one in declaring an attack on the United States as an attack on them all; as a *Le Monde* headline put it, "We are all Americans." The European response demonstrated that, whatever the future of NATO as a formal structure, Atlanticism—in the sense of shared basic interests and values—was alive and well. But the expressed conviction that September 11 "could have happened anywhere" was not only rhetoric; there was (and is) a very real appreciation in European capitals that international terrorism, the sharp end of instability, now has a prodigious capability to inflict domestic harm. Globalization could no longer be viewed as something that happened to other people, and military intervention as a moral option. The European paradigm of globalization is likely to expand yet again.

September 11 has pushed the trans-Atlantic relationship into new territory. Post-September 11 America is seen as pulled simultaneously toward unilateralism and multilateralism—as a country coming to grips with the simultaneous realization that its power and its vulnerability are much greater then previously perceived. The wave of national unity following the attacks took many European commentators by surprise. Nor was it lost on the Europeans that the United States, while welcoming allies, intended to fight its war on terrorism by itself if necessary. NATO served only an ancillary, although important, role. The NATO command structure was not utilized (although, particularly at sea, NATO procedures were utilized in organizing task force operations). Operation *Enduring Freedom* demonstrated once again the substantial and growing capabilities gap between Europe and the United States at the sharp end of war fighting. Several commentators, Paul Kennedy most recently, have argued that the United States has pulled so far ahead of all allies and rivals that the NATO alliance cannot expect to exercise a decisive influence over U.S. decisionmaking.[14] The hand of those who argue for a strategic reorientation toward an arc of instability ranging from the Mahgreb to the Central Asian republics, toward the Pacific, or indeed in favor of "fortress America," have been strengthened. Europeans are aware that they soon may need to look to their own devices and to take on a greater security role in their own backyard. They are also increasingly aware that their capability of influencing U.S. policy globally—a policy in which their fortunes are very much implicated—will rest on their own global capabilities.

As did détente and the fall of the Berlin Wall, September 11 has upset the underpinnings of the emerging European security order. As Dominique David wrote, the September attacks "place the United States permanently in the position of a target, which corresponds to the extent of its power."[15] For the first time in the post-war period, the military capability and central global role of a state were seen as a direct form of vulnerability. It was not war in the normal sense of a conflict between territorially based groups, nor a war capable of being waged or countered by conventional means. Most fundamentally, as David notes, the attacks challenged the prime assumption of U.S. security policy: the primacy of technologically advanced societies. At stake was the proposition whether "the overall vulnerability of sophisticated societies increases more rapidly than the technical means to remedy it."[16] Technology became recognized as part of the strategic problem, as much as the strategic solution.

Faced with a challenge of such magnitude, the U.S. Government appears to be rethinking its global defense strategy. It is too early to see the direction of future policy, but some trends do stand out. Emphasis is shifting to homeland defense, from the low-tech level of a greater guard presence at airports to high-tech plans for missile defense. It is likely that U.S. forces will draw down in the Balkans, in tandem with other contributing states but motivated by U.S. needs elsewhere. The Bush administration's continuing emphasis on the need for further military action against al Qaeda and other terrorist groups, and perhaps states, indicates that this war is not over. It is surely not over from the point of view of the terrorists. Deputy Secretary of Defense Paul Wolfowitz was very clear at the 2002 Munich Conference on Security Policy that NATO support was welcome, but ancillary to, the U.S. effort.[17] Even in Mediterranean operations, the United States may choose to go it alone and not employ the NATO command structure in operations (let alone allow a NATO political veto) in its own backyard. Increasingly, there have been calls for the recognition that the United States—the 800-pound gorilla—can no longer be constrained within the Alliance, even as the EU has moved naturally toward an economic and foreign policy caucus different from, although close to, that of the United States. Given threats in other parts of the world, the undeniable linkage between Middle East presence and policy (particularly in Saudi Arabia, Israel, and Iraq) and anti-American violence, and the need to redistribute resources, it is possible (although by no means certain or desirable) that the United States will gradually disengage from European security structures, ceasing to be effectively "a European power" and becoming an "American power, occasionally in Europe."

September 11, the war on terrorism, and the prospect of U.S. disengagement from European security structures raise crucial questions for ESDP and come at a decisive time in the history of European integration. The euro went into full effect in January 2002. In December 2002, the EU will decide on the next round of enlargement, probably bringing 10 states within the EU by 2008, with ultimate plans for a European Union of 27 states. EU expansion to that level cannot be achieved on the current institutional model, and an intergovernmental conference has been planned for 2004 to create a constitutional charter for the EU. Europe is faced, for the first time since the collapse of the Soviet Union, with the possibility of aggression against itself by the forces of international terrorism using weapons of mass destruction. The impact of the war on terrorism may unsettle vital European interests in the Middle East. And U.S. engagement elsewhere may require the European Union to take on defense, as well as a security, roles.

Given the continuing coincidence of U.S. and EU vital interests and the financial reluctance of the EU states to invest in defense, it is likely that the scope for an autonomous ESDP will be directly linked to U.S. decisions about its European presence. Should the status quo be generally maintained, ESDP will remain somewhat minimalist: a UN Security Council resolution would be required for EU action, few states would contribute more than token forces, and there would need to be a broad European consensus to undertake action under the EU flag. Given the current political split in Europe between the new center-right governments of Jose Maria Anzar in Spain and Silvio Berlusconi in Italy, and the traditional Euro-elites, that consensus would need to be wide, indeed. Greater political opportunities may lie in First and Third Pillar initiatives to intensify internal police cooperation, increase intelligence surveillance, and promote financial transparency in the antiterrorist campaign.

Greater challenges would confront Europe in what seems the most likely outcome: a gradual and moderate American disengagement from Europe. The U.S. war on terrorism may lead to a substantial drawdown in Balkans forces. With aircraft carrier or amphibious ready group presence only intermittent in the Mediterranean, U.S. naval presence would be considerably curtailed, an effect not offset by the presence of air force jets in northern Italy or soldiers in Germany. Reduced U.S. presence in Europe might increase pressure to surrender one or more top NATO commands. The United States might keep SACEUR, but of course this would be a somewhat Pyrrhic victory as NATO would have become a defense services organization—a kind of OSCE with weapons. The EU would need to assume responsibility for Balkans peacekeeping (which they currently resist), and probably for any future crisis in Eastern Europe or the Maghreb. Europe might even obtain a larger role in mediating the Middle East crisis.

For Europe, this is the option that is officially espoused but quietly feared. The financial cost of creating viable forces for regional power projection will be substantial, and defense budgets would have to rise significantly in the face of an aging population and increased social spending. European political solidarity would be put to the test in the foreign policy area. And in a deeper sense, the European project would need to find its equilibrium sans the role of the United States in Europe. For smaller states such as Ireland, there is a danger of the emergence of a four-power *directoire* of the greater European powers, a possibility already foreshadowed by British, French, and German meetings on defense policy prior to the Laeken summit last December, Tony Blair's famous foreign policy dinner, and recent ideas that have been mooted for a UN Security Council-like arrangement in the European Council, with the larger states having veto power. For national foreign policy, dangers may exist not so much in the theory of participation but the greater risk of losses at the sharp edge of Petersberg Tasks.

A final possible outcome, although very remote, must be considered. Should unilateralist tendencies in the United States predominate, or should a second and larger terrorist attack shake American confidence, a partial drawdown of U.S. forces from the Middle East and the Persian Gulf is not impossible. As the United States draws most of its energy supplies from non-Middle East sources, its primary strategic interest in the Gulf is based on the commercial vulnerability of Europe and Japan to a loss of energy supplies. In a more vulnerable international environment, the U.S. Government could decide to demand a greater European role in the policing of these regions. The EU would have to take on a super-regional hegemonic and deterrent role, requiring substantial power-projection forces. In a smaller version of the U.S.–EU capabilities gap, the United Kingdom, France, Germany, and Italy would clearly dominate such European efforts. For the neutral states, and indeed Germany, this option is the least appealing. Lacking U.S. responsibility for defense of the larger global infrastructure of energy, trade, and finance, the EU would be forced to take on a more aggressive foreign policy stance; to speak in terms of *vital interests, escalation dominance,* and warfighting, not peacekeeping; to plan military options should the EU need to participate in (if not lead) the repulse of an Iraqi invasion or a Saudi revolution, or broker a forced peace in Gaza or the West Bank.

Regardless of the exact endstate in U.S.–EU relations, Europe must now address the possibility of an Atlanticism that may no longer be based on traditional NATO alliance structures and political assumptions. A U.S.–EU grand coalition, the weakening of NATO, and an increased defense role for the EU are all serious options at present. The new international environment will put the European Union on the world stage as a security actor and place Council solidarity under intense pressure. It is probable that, under these conditions, the EU will rather rapidly coalesce into a stronger state model, possibly to the detriment of smaller countries. But is it also possible that the EU may crack under the strain. It is a turning point in the project of European integration. Robert Schuman, the famed post-World War II French finance minister and premier, once said that Europe would not be built all at once but by small steps. The next step is large indeed.

Notes

[1] In July 1961, when the Irish government applied to join the European Economic Community (EEC), a number of capitals were concerned that Ireland, given her non-membership of NATO and stated policy of neutrality, would be unable to play a full role in the development of European integration, including French initiatives to bring about a European political and defense community. The Irish government of the day was under no illusion—and indeed was reminded several times—that EEC membership in 1961 was part of a much larger geopolitical package including the role of Western Europe in the confrontation with the Soviet Union, the primacy of NATO in European defense, and the leadership role of the United States. See Dermot Keogh, "The Diplomacy of 'Dignified Calm': An Analysis of Ireland's Application for Membership in the EEC, 1961–1963," *Chronicon* 1, no. 4 (1997), 1–68.

[2] See James Henry Bergeron, "An Ever Whiter Myth: The Colonization of Modernity in European Community Law," in *Europe's Other: European Law between Modernity and Postmodernity*, ed. Peter Fitzpatrick and James Henry Bergeron (Aldershot, UK: Ashgate, 1998), 3–26.

[3] See James Henry Bergeron, "Europe's Emprise: Symbolic Economy and the Postmodern Condition," in Fitzpatrick and Bergeron, 67–92.

[4] See Paul Kapteyn, *The Stateless Market* (London: Routledge, 1996), 51–59.

[5] Wesley K. Clark, *Waging Modern War: Bosnia, Kosovo and the Future of Combat* (New York: Public Affairs Press, 2001), 77–106.

[6] Brian Coward, "Ireland's New Duties in a Changing Europe," *Irish Times*, November 18, 2000; Jim Cusack, "Infantry Battalion will be Irish RRF Contribution," *Irish Times*, November 21, 2000.

[7] Briffni O'Rourke, "EU: Prodi Seeks to Reassure Candidates on Security," Radio Free Europe/Radio Liberty, September 6, 2001, accessed at <http://www.rferl.org/nca/features/2001/09/06092001114157.asp>.

[8] Joris Janssen Lok and Richard Scott, "Amphibious Lift Bound by a Common Thread," *Jane's Navy International* (January/February 2002), 16–21.

[9] Ibid.

[10] It should be noted that this improvement is based on *planned capabilities*. It remains to be seen whether—like other recent European procurement plans—the improvements will be developed as envisioned or will be scaled back in the face of increasing cost estimates.

[11] Joris Janssen Lok, "Promoting a European Maritime Initiative," *Jane's Navy International* (Web version), December 12, 2001, accessed at <http://jni.janes.com/docs/jni/search/shtml>.

[12] Paolo Valpolini, "Italian Combat Forces to Join Coalition," *Jane's Defence Weekly*, November 14, 2001, 4.

[13] See Michael Nitz, "Germany to Take Command of Task Force," *Jane's Defence Weekly*, May 22, 2002, accessed at <http://jdw.janes.com/jdw01452.htm>.

[14] Paul Kennedy, "The Eagle Has Landed," *The Financial Times*, February 1, 2002, accessed at <http://globalarchive.ft.com/globalarchieve/article.htm?id=020201011552&query=NATO+>.

[15] Dominique David, "The First Strategic Lessons to be Drawn from September 11," *Paris Politique Etrangere* (October-December 2001), 766–775.

[16] Ibid.

[17] See "U.S. Ready to Go It Alone, " BBC News, February 2, 2002, accessed at <http://news.bbc.co.uk/hi/english/world/europe/newsid_1798000/1798132.stm>; Gerold Buchner, "What is Security," *Berliner Zeitung*, February 4, 2002, accessed at <http://www.berlinonline.de/suche.bin/>.

Chapter 14

Implications for Multinational Naval Doctrine

James J. Tritten

G lobalization has shattered the reliable predictability of the Cold War, engendering greater interdependence, opportunity, and perhaps insecurity as we move into the global 21st century. It will be a century that has continued conflicts over territory and new conflicts with nonstate actors—much the same as previous global wars against piracy. There are natural breeding grounds for conflict born out of deep-rooted historical animosities, regional instability, vulnerabilities, and the proliferation of the means of war.

Despite efforts to bring global outliers being left behind into the growing prosperity and stability offered by the new global 21st century, governments have an obligation to be prepared to use military forces and force to achieve political objectives. The future use of military power will continue to include operations in areas that do not have prepared support infrastructure, thus making operations from the sea a national core competency that must be maintained. The U.S. Armed Forces will need to be able to wage major theater warfare (MTW) and major regional contingencies (MRCs) as well as execute small-scale contingency operations (SSCOs) and lesser regional contingencies (LRCs) and a whole series of military operations other than war (MOOTW).

The implication for navies in such an environment is to shift to a capabilities-based fleet that maximizes its flexibility to respond to a wider range of wars than the

James J. Tritten is a career civil servant who has worked for a variety of organizations and currently serves as chief of the Training and Inspection Division of the Defense Threat Reduction Agency. He was previously chief of transformation in the Joint Doctrine Division of U.S. Joint Forces Command Joint Warfighting Center, special adviser to the Commander of the Naval Doctrine Command, and, prior to that, chairman of the national security affairs department at the Naval Postgraduate School (NPS). Dr. Tritten's publications have won a number of awards, including the Alfred Thayer Mahan Award for Literary Achievement from the Navy League of the United States. Dr. Tritten retired from active duty with the Navy in 1989 after serving as chairman of the national security department at NPS, as Assistant Director of Net Assessment in the Office of the Secretary of Defense, as a joint strategic planner in the Office of the Chief of Naval Operations, and previously in the fleet as a carrier-based naval aviator.

heretofore canonical MTW scenarios. The U.S. Navy and all of the U.S. Armed Forces are now in an international security environment that mandates the participation of other nations if we are to succeed in any actions taken at the MTW/MRC level—if for no other reason than the need for host nation support. SSCOs/LRCs might be undertaken unilaterally but would naturally benefit from the contributions and legitimacy afforded by the participation of other nations.

What Is Multinational Navy Doctrine, and Why Is It Needed?

One way to increase the combat potential of U.S. forces is to improve their ability to act with allied or coalition forces that join together for specific military actions. The U.S. National Military Strategy in the 1990s specifically highlighted recent efforts to strengthen allied doctrine as a means to improve readiness.[1] *Doctrine* is a term that is not often or fully recognized by fleet sailors and is used often by other nations and academics in a way that does not parallel its use by the U.S. military. Just what is this doctrine, and how might it help achieve readiness?

The primary definition of *doctrine* is "something taught" or "a piece of instruction . . . that which is taught . . . in the most general sense."[2] Doctrine is also defined as "a principle or body of principles presented by a specific field, system, or organization for acceptance or belief" or "a body or system of principles or tenets; a doctrinal or theoretical system; a theory; a science, or department of knowledge." From an organizational perspective, doctrine is those shared beliefs and principles that define the work of a profession. Doctrine also determines the *behavior* of the profession. Doctrine is not meant to be just what is taught or the ink in booklets that line bookshelves.

Doctrine is a form of policy. Less perishable than current policy, it is policy nonetheless. General policy is not designed to standardize decisionmaking—military doctrine *is*.[3] Doctrine is the basis of the "contract" under which forces provided by nations are expected to operate. Because they are expected to operate under doctrine, these forces can and do fit quickly into multinational ad hoc joint organizations.

Like other professions, militaries have always had doctrine that defines how they do their job. Unlike some professions, however, military doctrine does not have one standard approach or common thread that can be found in all nations and in all military services. In some cases, doctrine in the armed forces has been written and centralized. In other cases, doctrine has been unwritten and decentralized. In many cases, especially in U.S. Navy and other navies, doctrine was not published under that term and instead doctrinal publications had other titles, such as *War Instructions* or *Fighting Instructions*.[4]

The term is used in some countries in a fundamentally different manner. Doctrine under Soviet, and now Russian, military terminology refers to a determination of who will be fought in war, the character and objectives of the armed conflict portion of a war, the type of armed forces needed for war and their organization, the resources required for war and the overall preparation of the armed forces for war, and the strategic-level methods for waging war.[5] This use of the term is often also found in other nations that were influenced by Soviet military thought and also in the writings of many Western academics who use the term to refer to national military policy or grand strategy—for example, the doctrine of containment or flexible response. This political-military use of the term is *not* the focus of this present chapter.

The official starting point in the U.S. Armed Forces for a definition of doctrine is the *Department of Defense Dictionary of Military and Associated Terms*, Joint Publication 1–02.[6] According to this authoritative publication, doctrine is the "fundamental principles by which the military forces or elements thereof guide their actions in support of national objectives. It is authoritative but requires judgment in application."

Generally in the United States, the word also applies, conceptually, to subordinate tactics, techniques, and procedures (TTP). The joint doctrine development process includes management of both doctrine and joint TTP.

Joint Publication 1, *Joint Warfare of the Armed Forces of the United States*, mentions the term *military doctrine*. Military doctrine:

> shapes the way the Armed Forces think about the use of the military instrument of national power... presents fundamental principles that guide the employment of forces... establishes principles that provide direction for the employment of those capabilities.[7]

A subset of military doctrine would be that doctrine that applies to the navy. Another subset would be multiservice doctrine that applied to navies and their associated naval infantry or Marine Corps-type organizations. A final category would be maritime doctrine or that applying to the navies, naval infantry, coast guard and similar border patrol and revenue services, nonmilitary shipping managed by governments, the civilian merchant marine, and the like.

There are two essential elements in all forms of military doctrine: how the military profession thinks about warfare and how it acts when in combat. Without each element, doctrine would be incomplete. If it were merely how we thought about war, such a doctrine would be just the unfulfilled wishes of the leadership. If it only codified how we acted, without having created a theory, it might represent the documentation of mob violence.

Doctrine also has a multinational dimension. The term *multinational* refers to anything international—that is, bilateral, regional, global, ad hoc, standing alliances, etc. Multinational doctrine could be defined as the fundamental principles that guide the employment of forces of two or more nations in coordinated action toward a common objective. It is ratified by participating nations.

The *NATO Glossary of Terms and Definition* defines doctrine much like the United States does with the exception of removing the word *national* in front of objectives: "Fundamental principles by which the military forces guide their actions in support of objectives. It is authoritative but requires judgment in application."[8] The importance that the North Atlantic Treaty Organization (NATO) places on doctrine is demonstrated by how that organization defines *commonality*: "The state achieved when the same *doctrine*, procedures, or equipment are used."

For clarification, since the terms are often used interchangeably, doctrine and *concepts* are not the same thing. The United States and NATO define a *tactical concept* as "a statement, in broad outline, which provides a common basis for future development of tactical doctrine." Thus concepts are future doctrine—ideas that might become doctrine if validated and supported.

If we are going to operate more with other nations, it would appear that we are going to have to agree upon those principles or professional practices that will allow successful interaction. Fortunately, modern navies have operated for years from a very large base of shared professional knowledge. That knowledge was the basis for successful multinational operations that have been conducted at sea for hundreds of years. In today's new political environment, including the fundamental change in threat, resources, and goals for military forces, and the intrusion of ground, air, and joint force doctrine into the maritime realm, navies must get together to once again agree on this shared basis. That basis has now been changed since the end of the Cold War, resulting in fundamental changes to national navy doctrines that mean that if navies are to operate again successfully in the future in a multinational manner, they must agree upon the doctrinal basis for such actions.

One possible solution to the need for multinational navy doctrine would be to release existing NATO doctrine to non-NATO nations. This could be a quick solution, assuming that all NATO nations agreed. This problem is exacerbated when it comes to the release of classified NATO doctrine. Efforts to prepare generic tactical-level signaling books[9] based upon existing NATO doctrine is insufficient—released NATO doctrine cannot provide all the multinational doctrine that is needed.

Governments can and will spend their national treasure on new hardware for their militaries. Unlike expensive hardware, doctrine development is relatively inexpensive. Not all advances in combat potential, and therefore readiness, need come about by the purchase of new equipment. Relatively small amounts of money spent on training the force with existing hardware in accordance with current doctrine could yield a visible improvement in readiness. Additional small amounts of money spent on concept development to improve doctrine again based on existing hardware could also yield visible improvements.

As an example, by the mid-1930s, the Imperial Japanese Navy recognized that, despite all of the technological and industrial efforts being made to upgrade the fleet, its projected capabilities would not result in a force capable of meeting the rapidly improving U.S. Navy in a decisive battle at sea—the preferred doctrine on both sides. The Japanese, therefore, gave impetus to the development of night tactics and eventually formed specialized night combat groupings (*yasengun*) that would weaken the U.S. Pacific Fleet to such a degree that, subsequent to night battle between main fleets, daylight battle would be a foregone conclusion.[10] Thus a major improvement in combat potential was made as a result of doctrinal innovation.

One final aspect of the importance of doctrine in the new international security environment is that of shaping the behavior of other nations. When NATO initiated its Partnership for Peace program to train and exercise with nations that were formerly in the Warsaw Pact, it needed doctrine as the basis for the training and exercises. If our intent is now to expand that effort to other nations to bring them into the fold of supporters of democracy and the free enterprise system, we will need doctrine as the basis for this expanded training/exercise program. Navies will have to play their part and will have to deliver doctrine to these new partners.

In short, military doctrine affects how we fight, train, exercise, organize, and plan, and what we buy. It is about setting the standards for professional behavior. Figure 14–1 illustrates what doctrine can influence and the high payoff possible by actions taken to ensure that our doctrine is sound.

Figure 14–1. **What Is Affected by Doctrine**

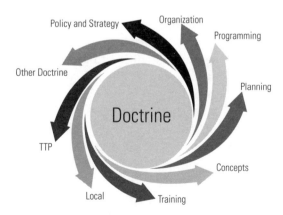

Preparation of Multinational Naval Doctrine

There are many ways to approach the preparation of multinational navy doctrine. At one extreme, the United States could assume that the United Nations (UN) would take over the supervision of navies, a recommendation that periodically appears in journals.[11] Despite the initial views of some in the Clinton administration to embrace UN control over peacekeeping operations, it is clear that the U.S. Congress is not ready to support a transfer of command or significant amounts of control to the UN, and this option is not currently realistic, nor supported by the administration of George W. Bush.

Existing regional organizations could be used to prepare multinational navy doctrine—there are many existing NATO tactical-level doctrinal publications on which to draw. Although many of these doctrinal publications are classified, unclassified versions are being prepared. These publications, however, do not address all of the tasks that navies currently need to face, and they also were primarily designed for a European-centered war within a standing alliance with decades of experience operating together. The use of existing NATO doctrine would really only be a temporary substitute for more robust multinational navy doctrine designed for all forms of multinational navy interactions.

The U.S. Navy routinely prepares national tactical-level navy doctrine and TTP used by its battlegroup commanders and below and limited amounts of operational-level naval doctrine that serve the Navy-Marine Corps team.[12] It also contributes to the preparation of U.S. joint TTP and operational-level joint doctrine. The Navy has a long history of contributing to and operating routinely under NATO tactical-level doctrine, and it is currently developing NATO joint doctrine for the operational level. All of these efforts are necessary but are not enough.

What seems to be needed is more generic navy doctrine that can be used by all nations and navies—including nations that have not previously been included in U.S. Navy exercise programs. An overarching framework of operational-level doctrine in a non-NATO environment is needed in addition to the tactical-level signal books and TTP that will be easier to prepare. A start would be to rekindle the efforts made by the former Naval Doctrine Command in producing generic navy doctrine. An entire series of publications was envisaged, but only one has been produced.[13]

Dealing with the issue of multinational navy doctrine outside of NATO will be somewhat new for the U.S. Navy. It is not new at all, however, for nations who field medium-power navies. Rear Admiral J.R. Hill of the Royal Navy prepared an excellent study on the role of medium-power Western navies during the mid-1980s, when such navies were struggling to understand their role vis-à-vis the U.S. Navy when national missions had to be performed that would not automatically involve the United States. Hill described medium powers as those that lie between the totally self-sufficient and the insufficient. *Medium powers* "try to create and keep under national control enough means of power to initiate and sustain coercive actions whose outcomes will be the preservation of its vital interests."[14] The keyword defining a medium-power's aspirations is autonomy.

A medium-power navy, therefore, is a navy of a nation-state that can use the sea to manipulate power to its own advantage—primarily to preserve national autonomy. The most important issue facing a medium-power navy is its relationship to a super-power navy. There was no way that a medium-power navy could successfully challenge the navy of a superpower in combat during the Cold War era; hence, alliance with a superpower was axiomatic. Obviously even smaller navies have successfully challenged medium-power navies in operations other than war (OOTW)—the 1976 Icelandic/British "Cod" War being an excellent example.

The self-identity of a medium-power navy was determined during the Cold War not only by its ethnocentric view, but also by its relationship to the superpower with which it was allied. For this reason, it was the medium-power navies of the Cold War era that championed the use of allied doctrine. Such doctrine would establish the behavior of the superpower vis-à-vis the medium-power navy and the roles that each would play in operations.

During the Cold War, the self-identity of the U.S. or Soviet Navy, however, was *not* expressed in terms of its relationship to allied and friendly medium-power navies. Rather, the self-identify of the U.S. Navy was determined by its relationship with its major competitor. Hence, the Navy approached the preparation of NATO maritime doctrine with recognition that it was necessary but without the need to use doctrine to establish its relationship with its allies. NATO allies knew that the U.S. Navy was supreme. Under today's international security environment, the Navy is in a class by itself, and it is likely to assume an international position of leadership more than anyone else.

After World War II, the U.S. Navy issued a doctrinal publication entitled *Principles and Applications of Naval Warfare: United States Fleets, 1947*, USF–1. Signed out by then-Chief of Naval Operations Admiral of the Fleet Chester W. Nimitz, USN, this publication set forth the "general instructions to the naval service in the preparation for and conduct of future wars." USF–1 addressed a number of issues that can cause difficulties when operating with multinational partners. There were the obvious problems of:

> different supply specifications, difference communications, lack of common language, national pride, different standards of living, different personal relationships. . . . There were also more substantive issues, including different tactics and

techniques, extra time required for the establishment of integrated commands and staffs, and lack of knowledge of capabilities.[15]

International liaison officers populate many U.S. military commands charged with the development and review of military doctrine. Such officers were in residence at the U.S. Naval Doctrine Command during its existence. Similar arrangements exist for U.S. officers assigned to multinational staffs. All of these foreign officers have been requested by the U.S. Armed Forces, and they bring a wealth of experience and talent that contributes to the development of U.S. military and multinational doctrine. The influence of these foreign and combined staff liaison officers, however, does not extend to having formal review authority.

The United States has published *Joint Doctrine for Multinational Operations*, Joint Publication 3–16. This publication, like all joint doctrinal publications, was not officially staffed by any foreign governments, although it is likely that foreign liaison officers attached to U.S. commands did review the draft. Joint Publication 3–16 addresses substantive issues during the planning and execution of multinational operations, saying "U.S. commanders should expect to conduct operations as part of a multinational force (MNF)."[16] The assumption must be that this U.S. doctrinal document will govern U.S. behavior and should also be understood by multinational partners who intend acting with us.

One possible way to develop multinational navy doctrine is to build upon this joint model by use of existing U.S. Navy or multiservice naval doctrine. It would be offered to foreign nations or international organizations, such as Joint Publication 3–16 apparently would be. Although this would appear to be an easy plan, it might not be once nations more carefully consider the sources of any U.S. doctrine.

Military doctrine is derived from various national considerations: government policy, available resources, strategy and campaign concepts, existing doctrine, the threat, history and lessons learned, strategic and service culture, fielded and/or emerging technology, geography and demographics, types of government, and existing doctrine and TTP. It is extremely hard to see how many foreign governments would allow U.S. military doctrine, at the strategic or operational levels, to govern the behavior of their own national military forces. Figure 14–2 illustrates the various inputs that influence the creation of doctrine.

More likely, foreign governments would prefer to participate in the creation of any operational-level doctrine that would dictate how their forces would behave in a multinational scenario. Foreign navies can, and should, assist in the preparation of doctrine in many specific areas where they have demonstrated expertise. On the other hand, for some nations, such as Japan, there may be constitutional limitations on the type of combat or other actions that they are allowed to explore.

Figure 14–2. **What Affects Doctrine**

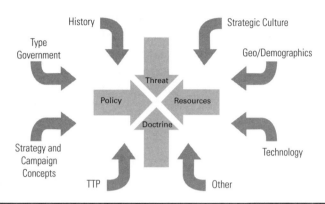

The creation of TTP would likely be reviewed as a professional military matter not requiring political oversight—hence it might be possible to simply transfer some existing U.S. joint (or other) TTP at this level directly to a medium-power navy. The one stumbling block here might be that U.S. joint doctrine and TTP have taken on more of a prescriptive tone. Since 1994, U.S. joint doctrine and joint TTP have a standard phrase in the front of each publication: "This doctrine will be followed except when, in the judgment of the commander, exceptional circumstances dictate otherwise." Such direction might cause U.S. military doctrine to be rejected out of hand by foreign navies that have no requirement or desire to have a doctrine that *must* be followed except in "exceptional" circumstances.

Another very real problem is associated with the foreign perception of various terms that are taken for granted in the United States. For example, the term *power projection* may be viewed as threatening to some nations whose governments might not allow their navies to cooperate with any doctrinal development that uses such words. Although *expeditionary* is a term the U.S. Armed Forces have used frequently and for many years, European navies might be reluctant to embrace such concepts for fears of being associated with colonialism.

Similarly, *ballistic missile defense*, whether it is against tactical, operational, naval, or strategic missiles, is a loaded term that has association with the Strategic Defense Initiative, still commonly referred to as "Star Wars" by foreign nations. Despite successful U.S. efforts to distinguish theater ballistic missile defense efforts from "Star Wars," this subtlety is lost on some foreign governments that will reject any participation in such doctrinal development. As U.S. joint military doctrine and emerging naval doctrine embrace such terms, they will be more difficult to "sell" to foreign governments.

The Tricky Problems of Interoperability

When the *Principles and Applications of Naval Warfare: United States Fleets, 1947*, was issued, it addressed the need for standardized communications capabilities: "allies of this nation should standardize with us."[17] Unwritten is the assumption today that U.S. Navy doctrine is the standard to which medium-power navies will have to adapt if they desire to be fully integrated with a U.S. Navy that continues to evolve with costly new technology. If they are unable to integrate fully, such as with some navies within NATO, then a separate command structure and area of operations provides them an opportunity to perform tasks under national military doctrine.

It is possible to have a medium-power navy operate successfully in support of the U.S. Navy *without* fully integrated doctrine. It is entirely possible that U.S. Armed Forces might have one doctrine when operating in a national environment and another when working a combined force. It is also possible for a medium-power navy to be the lead agency on doctrine for which the U.S. military services operate in a supporting role. Many foreign navies have specialized expertise in other areas, such as diesel-electric submarines and mine warfare. In these cases, the U.S. Navy would operate as a supporting agency or service. Could there be parallels for multinational naval doctrine specialization?

The reality of multinational military operations is that although it is entirely appropriate to have full interoperability by military forces, more often, only navies will have the ability to cooperate in the attainment of multinational military objectives with coordinated but separate military activities. For example, although some NATO navies have diesel-electric submarines, their operations are not always fully integrated with NATO nuclear submarines. Usually submarine operations are separated into different sectors, but all submarines contribute to the attainment of appropriate naval tasks and missions.

Another paradigm would be the full interoperability of a medium-power navy with the U.S. Coast Guard (essentially a medium-power navy), probably in a discrete sector. From the perspective of a small- or medium-power navy, interoperability with the U.S. Coast Guard might be preferred since it would occur without the political "baggage" associated with the U.S. Navy.[18] An example is that a Royal New Zealand Navy relationship with the U.S. Coast Guard might be a stepping-stone to resumption of normal relations between the "Kiwis" and the U.S. Navy.

It is also possible that a medium-power navy will have to be assigned a separate sector where it pursues independent maritime tasks—being interoperable with neither the U.S. Navy nor other national armed forces. This does not mean that such navies are less capable, only that they must be dealt with differently. Smaller navies would most likely need to be handled in this manner—capable of working toward a common political goal despite not being interoperable with the U.S. Navy or Coast Guard.

It is also possible for a medium-power navy to operate successfully in a multinational context totally integrated with U.S. Navy. The U.S. Coast Guard attempts to do this. A nation that desires to influence U.S. political decisionmaking may strive for such a degree of interoperability in order to ensure that they are represented "at the table."[19]

Many medium-power navies, however, can be interoperable with the U.S. Navy but might not be fully interoperable with their national air forces. Given the choice of being joint with their own national military services or interoperable with the U.S. Navy, many medium-power navies might opt for the latter since it probably would be less expensive and provide a higher payoff to that navy.

In addition to a range of possibilities with medium-power navies within NATO, there exists the need to consider operations with other medium-power and smaller navies outside of the NATO environment or North Atlantic Treaty-approved areas of operations. Although the smaller navy will have more difficulty in integrating with the U.S. Navy, it will have fewer problems with the Coast Guard and navy forces operated by the U.S. Special Operations Command (USSOCOM), since their missions are not dissimilar to those of the Coast Guard or USSOCOM.

The smaller navy and some medium-power navies may prefer to operate with the U.S. Coast Guard rather than the Navy. Indeed, many medium-power and smaller navies make no artificial distinctions between the navy, constabulary, and special operations forces. Since the Navy maintains such distinctions, it is necessary for medium-power and smaller navies to have a relationship with the Coast Guard and USSOCOM in addition to one with the Navy. This suggests that multinational navy doctrine also must have an interagency component.

At a minimum, this relationship with the U.S. Coast Guard should be studied and form the basis of how we might approach the role of the U.S. Navy vis-à-vis other medium-power navies. That is not to say that the Navy and Coast Guard relationship ought to define the Navy's relationship with medium-power foreign navies. Creative parallels may need to be drawn between such issues as the difficulties in creating multinational rules of engagement (ROEs) and the difficulties in training the U.S. Coast Guard in both civilian law enforcement standards (such as the "use of force continuum" dealing with a suspect who has not exhibited manifest intent to harm) and military combat ROEs designed to deal with "hostile intent" prior to actual hostile action. This issue becomes readily apparent during the efforts of allied and coalition navies (with potentially conflicting ROEs) in conducting maritime interception operations.

Complicating the integration and interoperability of navies will be the impact of the various transformational efforts that attempt to harness the ongoing revolution in military affairs (RMA). Most of those associated with the concepts being investigated with an RMA tend to assume that once the new technology arrives, it will be fielded and used by the fleet. Internalizing the RMA is much more complicated and includes a major role to be played by doctrine and challenges for multinational interoperability.

New concepts of warfare associated with the RMA must first be made part of official national service, multiservice, joint, and multinational doctrine, and also our military culture. They must be taught at a myriad of national and multinational war and command and staff colleges and various training institutions and become an integral part of a vast empire of national and multinational exercise programs.

Doctrine has a major role in the RMA and the transformation of the armed forces to operate in the new international security environment. This role is primarily that of being an engine or a voice of change.[20] Once all parties agree to new concepts for warfare, they need to be codified in doctrine that all agree to teach and use in military exercises and actual operations. Without the training and education to support change, doctrine is merely the unfulfilled wishes of how one would like to operate.

Many of the specific concepts being studied in U.S. national transformation efforts include similar activities such as smart and rapid targeting of key vulnerabilities and weaknesses. Doctrine writers will need a list of such weaknesses in order to formulate how to gain the advantage. From a navy perspective, this list might include such things as: geography, training, readiness, organizational and doctrinal rigidity, intelligence and warning, reconnaissance, damage assessment, combat beyond visual range, combined-arms/joint/multinational warfighting, command and control, battle management, targeting, air support for naval operations, air control, air defense, all-weather and night combat, munitions lethality, maneuver and mobility, sustainability and logistics, and countermeasures.[21]

Concepts associated with the RMA also tend to address taking advantage of windows of opportunity as they occur. Naval forces would be shifted from secondary to main areas of combat actions in order to mass them for the main effort during a window of opportunity. It is not easy to know when windows of opportunity are going to be available, let alone to create them, in a multinational maritime environment. New concepts also stress the need to maximize opportunity and also achieve synchronization or strength—both inherently good at sea but in need of balance by the navy commander. Multinational combat leaders will need to decide when to take advantage of opportunities with forces at hand or to await the advantages of greater strength as the result of massing.

Political Issues and the Sector Approach

The *Principles and Applications of Naval Warfare: United States Fleets, 1947,* is instructive in other areas, because when it was written, the United States had just fought a coalition war on two fronts and had ample experience with multinational partners. Admiral Nimitz highlighted difficulties associated with "differences of national aims and involvement."[22]

Joint Doctrine for Multinational Operations states, "The degree of involvement of each participant is likely to be a purely political decision, and the commander must be cognizant of national mandates placed on individual units. It may be necessary to employ the force according to national and political considerations." [23] The text of this 2000 joint doctrine publication was influenced by the results of Operation *Allied Force,* undertaken by NATO in 1999, against the Federal Republic of Yugoslavia. One of the most important lessons from that operation was the degree that political decisions influenced military actions. A 2001 U.S. General Accounting Office study observed:

> military commanders of multinational operations should not expect to always apply decisive military force with a strict adherence to military doctrine. As a result, to balance the variety of interests and concerns that arise during multinational operations, these operations may not be conducted as effectively or efficiently as operations that more closely follow U.S. military doctrine, which may lead to higher costs.[24]

Whereas a current U.S. task force or task group commander might have as his objective the attainment of a U.S. military objective, it is clearly the political objective of some governments of medium-power navies today to use their fleets to influence U.S. behavior. This is generally accomplished by having their fleets integrated into American forces and by attempting to stake out staff and subordinate command positions.

An extremely good example of this is the continuation of submarine forces by many navies of the world who might otherwise not find them cost-effective. Although there might not be a viable combat mission for submarines by many medium-power navies, the mere possession of such forces gives that government entrée into world of underwater traffic management. This is an extremely important method of learning about what is going on not only in distant international waters but also in one's own exclusive economic zones, archipelagic waters, straits, and transit lanes. With no need to declare submerged transit through these waters, an effective way to learn about submerged transit and perhaps to influence planned transits is to be a player at the table of subsurface operations.

The fact that navies of the world routinely train together today is not a commitment to actually fight together in any MRC/MTW that their government chooses to oppose. If the U.S. Government allows medium-power navies to become so integrated with the U.S. Navy that the American force will not be able to operate on its own, we may find ourselves unable to provide a unilateral LRC/SSCO combat capability. Although the size of the U.S. Navy will probably not shrink to that level, it must have a balance between the ability to operate under joint and multinational navy doctrine so that national tasks are not precluded.

The governments of medium-power navies determine whether their navies are sent to MRC/MTWs or LRC/SSCOs merely to provide the impression of participating or to actually participate in combat. Some forces will be sent merely to be seen as having participated—casualties are neither expected nor desired. Yet it may be necessary from a purely U.S. perspective to have foreign forces participate in a crisis response. Hence, multinational navy doctrine is needed to account not only for how to fight together, but also for how to ensure that the forces of some navies are perceived as participating without being placed in harm's way—without it looking like that.[25]

Multinational naval doctrine should both provide navies with honorable options to operate in a multinational environment as a fully integrated member of a U.S.-led task group and as a foreign-led separate task group operating in separate waters. Although the current group of medium-power navies probably views full integration as the only honorable alternative, this will become increasingly difficult as the U.S. Navy adds even more costly technologies to the fleet, thus precluding full integration even by the U.S. Coast Guard.

During World War II, the British Pacific Fleet (BPF) operated in a separate sector and not as an integral part of the U.S. Pacific Fleet even though fully integrated forces were in the Atlantic. The BPF had even adopted U.S. Navy doctrine and aircraft. Yet its aircraft carrier design and lack of an integrated logistical train precluded the BPF from fully integrated operations. In the Atlantic, convoy escort duty presented fewer difficulties in integrating forces from a variety of nations. There was no issue of diminished honor or respect due the Royal Navy because the BPF operated on its own. Perhaps it is time to remember that in history, navies from different nations have rarely operated in a fully integrated manner.

During the Persian Gulf War, coalition navy forces were divided into three main task groups that were organized around their political instructions.[26] One group was committed to perform the original UN-sanctioned tasking of maritime interception operations. Another group under more expanded political authority was permitted to engage in support tasks and protection of the sea lines of communication. Finally, the third group was permitted to participate in the wider range of offensive tasks associated with the U.S. Navy. Within each group, national subgroups were organized related to levels of risk allowed and proximity to the battle area.

During coalition naval operations off Haiti from 1993 to 1994, national forces were divided into three distinct missions. A range of multinational participants enforced UN sanctions. U.S. naval forces conducted a noncombatant evacuation operation. Finally, the U.S. Coast Guard handled refugee control.[27]

Unfortunately, by acknowledging the sector option as an honorable alternative, the U.S. Navy would undermine the argument made by medium-power navies to their governments that they need additional technology or more capable forces. In turn, this might affect the sale of technologies or hardware to these countries. The unintended consequences of multinational doctrine development might not be apparent to officers whose primary expertise is with the various combat arms.

Foreign navies operating under some multinational context will eventually come up against multinational tasking that conflicts with their own national policy. An example might be the deliberate testing of the right of innocent passage or the sailing of ships into waters considered closed to non-littoral nations. If a foreign warship is operating with a U.S. task group that has been asked to perform such a mission and that ship's government opposes such a move, procedures will need to be established to provide a face-saving way out. This issue does not appear to be insurmountable but should be addressed before the situation occurs so that standing doctrine can guide behavior in the fleet. More complicated will be the handling of national missions that are intended to be carried out while operating as a part of a multinational force—for example, the gathering of intelligence.

Rules of engagement are another problem area for multinational naval operations. During the Persian Gulf War, coalition navy forces had different ROEs for different nations. The usual issues with terms such as *hostile intent* came up for interpretation and debate, as it does when the U.S. Navy addresses this issue with other U.S. Armed Forces. In 1993–1994, UN-sanctioned operations in the Adriatic against the Federal Republic of Yugoslavia saw German ships restricted by national ROEs from firing of weapons except in self-defense and lacking a charter to conduct boardings.[28]

Because ROEs do not drive doctrine, the inability to reach prior agreement on them does not preclude the development of multinational navy doctrine.[29] The problems associated with ROEs themselves are not insurmountable, and navies have demonstrated the ability to operate in highly complex environments in which ROEs might actually change during the flight of naval aircraft launched from an aircraft carrier but operating under the tactical control of some other organization. Different national ROEs may themselves force the use of a sector approach and force a multinational commander to accept less than direct command over coalition forces.

As a precedent, the *Principles and Applications of Naval Warfare: United States Fleets, 1947*, stated:

It has been the practice of this government to recognize and to require the right of communications, and if necessary of appeal, through national channels in order to allow:

(1) Notification to a government by its national commander if he considers that his force is in danger of reduction that would imperil its further effectiveness for the purposes of its own government.

(2) Protest to a government by its national commander if he considers that his force is being subjected to unusual or discriminatory action.[30]

Joint Doctrine for Multinational Operations addresses the need for individual nations to have appropriate lines of communication to their parent nation.[31]

Levels of Preparation for Warfighting

Most medium-power navies cannot afford to be provided with capabilities for both the high end of warfighting and for constabulary national missions. Over time, the U.S. Navy has evolved and been expected to provide certain capabilities to the medium-power navy, thus eliminating the need for the governments of such navies to provide them for themselves. For example, the U.S. Navy provides to most medium-power navies: modern aircraft carriers with fixed-wing aircraft capable of a full range of missions; nuclear-powered ballistic missile submarines and nuclear-powered attack submarines; a power projection across the beach capability; various intelligence sources and capabilities; and certain training facilities.

From a doctrinal standpoint, the U.S. Navy provides the bulk of the expertise at the higher ends of warfighting—power projection. On the other hand, medium-power navies have provided things that the U.S. Navy does not normally concern itself with, including escorts, diesel-electric submarines, patrol craft, mine warfare capabilities,[32] and expertise in nonmilitary operations other than war. Again, the U.S. Coast Guard is an excellent parallel. The U.S. Coast Guard is maximized for performance at the lower spectrum of conflict and has divested itself of certain open-ocean antisubmarine warfare capabilities and offensive surface warfare missile systems.

A number of substantive questions stem from this current division of labor. Is doctrine one of those things that the superpower navy should provide to other navies of the world? Where other nations have demonstrated expertise in various individual aspects of combat or OOTW, should the U.S. Navy ask them to take the lead on the development of multinational navy doctrine? If not, is there an alternative way to gain their expertise so that the U.S. Navy need not "reinvent the wheel"? Since destroyers and frigates are capital ships in many medium-power navies, we might find that some doctrine for the employment of these forces has been more fully developed in foreign navies than it has in the U.S. Navy. Not all navies are capable of all missions that can be performed by the American one. On the other hand, medium-power and smaller navies routinely perform tasks that are not performed by the U.S. Navy.

Can navies train equally well for both the high end of warfighting and OOTW? An Indian observer noted the failure of American forces in Somalia to master the doctrine of low-intensity conflict and counterinsurgency operations and contrasted it to the extensive experience of Indian forces in these same areas and their relative success in Somalia.[33] Although the theoretical answer is "Yes, navies can do both," the behavior of the U.S. Navy has demonstrated that it prefers to dominate the high end and to "subcontract" OOTW functions to the U.S. Coast Guard. The Coast Guard routinely provides detachments aboard Navy warships to handle OOTW functions for which U.S. Navy officers have not been trained. Similarly, the Coast Guard has moved away from being able to be fully interoperable with the Navy in offensive and undersea warfare at sea. Such an approach does not appear to be a problem; both the Navy and Coast Guard appear to be comfortable in their roles and self-identities.[34]

Such a division of labor is liable to have unintended consequences for medium-power navies with histories that include significant combat at sea. The self-identity of most navies is still that of a combat force. The more that navies are forced to move into the area of OOTW, the less likely that they are going to seek and be successful at combat at the higher end of the warfighting spectrum. Naturally, most medium-power navies will have the opportunity to retain warfighting skills at commensurate levels of capability. Navy officers may resent being considered only "good enough" to handle medium or lower end tasks and OOTW. Yet the reality of future hardware procurement by many governments that field medium-power navies is that they will be increasingly specialized out of the higher ends of combat.

As younger navy officers in some medium-power navies having more self-identity with constabulary and other OOTW tasks advance into leadership positions, they will probably embrace these roles for their own navy, thus changing their service culture. Today, the identity of the U.S. Coast Guard is more akin to the policeman rather than the combat warrior. The Coast Guard protects its noncombat roles from "mission creep" by the U.S. Navy.

Perhaps medium-power navies could provide detachments, like the U.S. Coast Guard, in multinational scenarios for OOTW areas of expertise that are not developed by the U.S. Navy. Currently this is done by the Coast Guard, but neither the Navy nor Coast Guard have a sufficiently trained cadre of foreign area officers—an area of expertise that might be better provided by multinational navy partners rather than turning to the U.S. Army for that support. Navy detachments offer a foreign government the ability to advertise its presence and participation in a multinational crisis response at far less cost than sending even one small ship. They also offer these governments an opportunity to influence U.S. behavior and extremely low visibility when they do not desire to advertise participation.

Visibility is another area that can be highlighted or reduced, depending upon the political object of governments. When a nation does not desire to advertise its support for a multinational effort, it can do so with assistance in the areas of communications, intelligence, transportation, logistics, and other inconspicuous assets. The United States could use "stealthy" support when it is not in the best interests of the attainment of the political objective to send in a U.S. warship. In such cases, multinational navy partners can provide the visible presence while the United States operates behind the scenes, essentially invisible to the world press. There are ways to interact multinationally other than sending a ship.

Some will suggest that the U.S. Navy not take the lead in the preparation of multinational navy doctrine and that such efforts should be better left to organizations such as the United Nations. If the Navy is left to take the lead, it will undoubtedly work out the issues described herein and in doing so will satisfy the need for medium-power navies to establish their working relations with the superpower navy. It will also satisfy the need for the United States to determine how it will operate in an MTW/MRC and LRC/SSCO environments with partners. The writing of lower-end doctrine for MOOTW and OOTW tasks could be a collective effort of medium-power navies or one that could be championed by one of these navies, to include the U.S. Coast Guard.

Conclusions

In the 21st century, the U.S. Navy stands at the crossroads of national doctrinal development and multinational leadership. The Navy is fully cooperating with the development of U.S. joint doctrine and is a partner with the Marine Corps in the development of multiservice naval doctrine focused upon warfare in the littorals. The Navy also has the ability to act as the inspirational leader of the navies of the world with the development of multinational navy doctrine that may be equally as important as the development of joint and naval doctrine.

Some medium-power navies might be more willing to embrace multinational navy doctrine than to become joint-capable within their own nation. The U.S. Navy and many medium-power navies have no choice but to be both joint and multinational. If the U.S. Government and Armed Forces count on multinational navies for the attainment of U.S. national security and military objectives, then the development of multinational navy doctrine for navies that are not also joint-capable is also a priority. Doctrine is needed for both navies that can fully integrate with the U.S. Navy and those that must cooperate without full integration.

Regardless of the degree of cooperation between navies in the development of doctrine, in routine operations at sea in time of peace, in conducting multinational naval exercises, in various exchange programs, and so forth, the fleets remain instruments of national power wielded by government. As has happened in the past, we may see nations, including the United States, plan to operate together, train to do so, and then fail to act in a collective manner.[35] This reality must be accounted for in our doctrine; otherwise, we will have no viable options.

If the U.S. Navy desires to get into the business of providing multinational navy doctrine to other countries, a series of extremely sophisticated political and diplomatic issues of substance will need to be addressed. This strongly suggests that expertise in areas other than actual combat arms is required for such doctrinal development and, if not made available to the U.S. Navy, might result in unintended international repercussions.

Many nations that field medium-power navies do not have stand-alone doctrine commands or centers. They do, however, have some dozen or so academics that are interested in navies and may even have a group of political retired navy officers. These individuals have an extraordinary ability to influence force development and policy in these nations. The U.S. Navy would probably be well served by a continuing dialogue with such academics and retired officers so that the major issues that have been raised in this essay can be fully discussed with such influential individuals. Discussions only with navies are not a satisfactory manner to deal with the operational level of multinational navy doctrine.

Dealing with the sector approach is the single most important challenge facing naval doctrine in the near future. The solution to this challenge is to write doctrine that has a more reasonable basis than the unrealistic but politically correct assumption that navies will be fully integrated and interoperable. That basis should start with the assumptions that naval forces will have different political objectives and restrictions and they will *not* be fully interoperable. The doctrinal challenge is then how to operate as a multinational force given those assumptions. Differences do not mean that multinational operations are not possible, only that in performing them, the participants need to acknowledge those differences and find solutions. It is in the best interests of the United States to ensure that mechanisms are in place, to include doctrine that will allow a diverse array of forces to join in unexpected and unplanned ad hoc coalitions and will permit U.S. forces to operate in a less than favorable environment.

Notes

[1] General John M. Shalikashvili, U.S. Army, Chairman of the Joint Chiefs of Staff, *National Military Strategy of the United States of America* (Washington, DC: Government Printing Office, February 1995), 18.

[2] *Webster's II New Riverside University Dictionary* (Boston, MA: The Riverside Publishing Co., 1984, 1988); *The Oxford English Dictionary*, 2d ed. (Oxford, England: Clarendon Press, 1991 [reprint with corrections]).

[3] See especially on this issue, Wayne P. Hughes, Jr., "The Power in Doctrine," *Naval War College Review* 48, no. 3 (Summer 1995), 9–31; a response by Irving Brinton Holley, "Doctrine on the Wrong Foot," *Naval War College Review* 49, no. 1 (Winter 1996), 117–118; and two responses by Hughes and Mike Bowman, "Doctrine on the Wrong Foot," *Naval War College Review* 49, no. 2 (Spring 1996), 108–112.

[4] For an example of the finest U.S. Navy doctrine written, see Admiral Ernest J. King, USN, Commander-in-Chief, United States Fleet and Chief of Naval Operations, *War Instructions: United States Navy, 1944*, F.T.P. 143(A) (Washington, DC: Government Printing Office, November 1944).

[5] Genrikh Trofimenko, *The U.S. Military Doctrine* (Moscow: Progress Publishers, 1986).

[6] Director of the Joint Staff, *Department of Defense Dictionary of Military and Associated Terms*, Joint Publication 1–02 (Washington, DC: Government Printing Office, April 12, 2001), 132. This document was used for all definitions hereafter unless otherwise noted.

[7] Chairman of the Joint Chiefs of Staff, *Joint Warfare of the Armed Forces of the United States*, Joint Publication 1 (Washington, DC: Government Printing Office, November 14, 2000), vi, I–1, I–8.

[8] North Atlantic Treaty Organization, *NATO Glossary of Terms and Definitions (English and French)*, AAP–6(V) Modified Version 2 (August 7, 2000), 2–D–6. This document is the source for NATO terms used in this chapter.

[9] Barry Coombs and Les Sim, "The Russians Are Here," U.S. Naval Institute *Proceedings* (March 1995), 69, discusses the creation of an unclassified NATO publication, *Maritime Maneuvering and Tactical Procedures* (Experimental Tactic [EXTAC] 768) and a bilateral set of terms based upon the *Department of Defense Dictionary of Military and Associated Terms*, Joint Publication 1–02, shared with the Russians.

[10] David C. Evans and Mark R. Peattie, *Kaigun [Navy]: Strategy, Tactics, and Technology in the Imperial Japanese Navy, 1887–1941* (Annapolis, MD: Naval Institute Press, 1997), 273–280.

[11] A skeptical but balanced discussion of various proposals prior to 1990 is Sam J. Tangredi, *A United Nations Navy: Solution, Illusion or Delusion?* Working Paper in International Studies I–91–1 (Stanford, CA: Hoover Institution on War, Revolution and Peace, Stanford University, March 1991). More recent proposals are advocated in Robert Stephens Stanley, *The Wave of the Future: The United Nations and Naval Peacekeeping* (Boulder, CO: Lynne Rienner Publications, 1992), and Michael C. Pugh, ed., *Maritime Security and Peacekeeping: A Framework for United Nations Operations* (New York: St. Martin's Press, 1994).

[12] A good example of multiservice naval doctrine is Naval Doctrine Command, *Naval Warfare*, NDP–1 (Washington, DC: Government Printing Office, March 28, 1994).

[13] Naval Doctrine Command, *Multinational Maritime Operations* (Washington, DC: Government Printing Office, September 1996).

[14] John Richard Hill, *Maritime Strategy for Medium Powers* (Annapolis, MD: Naval Institute Press, 1986), 31.

[15] Admiral of the Fleet Chester W. Nimitz, USN, *Principles and Applications of Naval Warfare: United States Fleets, 1947*, USF–1 (Washington, DC: Office of the Chief of Naval Operations, May 1, 1947), 9–4, 9–5.

[16] Chairman of the Joint Chiefs of Staff, *Joint Doctrine for Multinational Operations*, Joint Publication 3–16 (Washington, DC: Department of Defense, April 5, 2000), I–3.

[17] Nimitz, 9–6.

[18] Bruce B. Stubbs, "The U.S. Coast Guard: A Unique Instrument of U.S. National Security," *Marine Policy* 18, no. 6 (1994), 513, documents a number of instances of use of the U.S. Coast Guard to show U.S. resolve but with a force that has a humanitarian and law enforcement image.

[19] See, for example, the rather frank admission by Fred W. Crickard and Richard H. Cimblett, "The Navy as an Instrument of Middle Power Foreign Policy: Canada in Korea 1950 and the Persian Gulf 1990," in *Maritime Forces in Global Security*, ed. Ann L. Griffiths and Peter T. Haydon (Halifax, Nova Scotia: Centre for Foreign Policy Studies, Dalhousie University, 1995), 335: "In terms of Canada's national interest, leverage with coalition partners and in particular the United States was as important as defeating the enemy."

[20] *Joint Warfare of the Armed Forces of the United States*, Joint Publication 1 (Washington, DC: Department of Defense, November 14, 2000), I–8–I–9.

[21] List is suggested by Anthony H. Cordesman, "Compensating for Smaller Forces: Adjusting Ways and Means Through Technology," in *Strategy and Technology* (Carlisle Barracks, PA: Strategic Studies Institute, Army War College,

April 1, 1992), 16–19, and *Australian Maritime Doctrine*, Royal Australian Navy Doctrine 1 (Canberra: Defence Publishing Service, 2000), 112.

[22] Nimitz, 9–5.

[23] *Joint Doctrine for Multinational Operations*, III–2. Of interest is more cautionary wording found in a March 1995 draft of the previous edition: "that the national objectives of participating forces may interfere with or limit how their military contingents participate [and] . . . National mandates may differ when forces are committed to a multinational operation, even if the nations are in agreement with respect to the ultimate objective." Joint Chiefs of Staff, *Joint Doctrine for Multinational Operations*, draft Joint Publication 3–16, March 1995, I–14, IV–1 and IV–2.

[24] U.S. General Accounting Office, *Kosovo Air Operations: Need to Maintain Alliance Cohesion Resulted in Doctrinal Departures*, GAO–01–784 (Washington, DC: General Accounting Office, July 2001), 15.

[25] An early draft of the previous version of *Joint Doctrine for Multinational Operations* stated that: "It may be necessary to divide the force according to national and/or political considerations. For example, in an environment in which hostilities become likely, a portion of the multinational force (those nations authorized the full range of forces) may be assigned to offensive operations, a second group (with more political constraint) may be assigned to support and to protect lines of communication in the theater, while a third (with greater constraint) may be assigned to interdiction operations on the periphery of the theater." *Joint Doctrine for Multinational Operations*, draft Joint Publication 3–16, IV–2.

[26] Juan Carlos Neves, "Interoperability in Multinational Coalitions: Lessons from the Persian Gulf War," *Naval War College Review* 48, no. 1 (Winter 1995), 56–57.

[27] Peter Jones, "Multi-National Operations: Their Demands and Impact on Medium Power Navies," *Maritime Security Working Papers* No. 3 (Halifax, Nova Scotia: Centre for Foreign Policy Studies, Dalhousie University, May 1996), 54.

[28] G.R. Maddison, "Operations in the Adriatic," in Griffiths and Haydon, 198–199.

[29] *Joint Doctrine for Multinational Operations*, III–19, states: "Complete consensus or standardization of R[ules] O[f] E[ngagement] should be sought, but may not be achievable."

[30] Nimitz, 9–3.

[31] *Joint Doctrine for Multinational Operations*, II–7 and II–8 (figure II–3 clearly shows these national lines of command).

[32] Indeed, the lack of maturity in U.S. Navy mine warfare was the apparent cause for a Royal Navy commodore to refuse to risk his ships under an American-designed plan. See Edward J. Marolda and Robert J. Schneller, Jr., *Shield and Sword: The United States Navy and the Persian Gulf War* (Annapolis, MD: Naval Institute Press, 2001), 254.

[33] Vinod Anand, "Evolution of a Joint Doctrine for Indian Armed Forces," *Strategic Analysis* (July 2000), 733–750.

[34] Colin S. Gray has recommended that the U.S. Coast Guard be transferred to the U.S. Department of Defense (DOD). In making this recommendation, Gray cautions, "Above all, a Coast Guard within DOD would need to preserve its distinctive warrior-policeman culture." See "The Coast Guard and Navy: It's Time for a 'National Fleet'," *Naval War College Review* 54, no. 3 (Summer 2001), 133.

[35] Joe J. Sokolsky, "NATO's New Maritime Role: The Sea Power Solution or Allies Adrift?" in Griffiths and Haydon, 150.

Chapter 15

Naval Overseas Presence in the New U.S. Defense Strategy

Richard L. Kugler

The 2001 *Quadrennial Defense Review Report* (*QDR Report*) announced a new U.S. defense strategy that will bring important changes to the U.S. overseas presence in all key theaters.[1] In addition to waging the war against terrorism, this new strategy shifts away from the previous preoccupation with preparing for two major theater wars (MTWs) in Northeast Asia and the Persian Gulf.[2] Instead, it calls upon the armed services to provide flexible capabilities for a wide spectrum of purposes and contingencies, especially along the unstable southern strategic arc that stretches from the Middle East to the Asian littoral.[3] In addition, it calls for U.S. forces not only to be modernized, but also to pursue transformation in order to adopt new technologies, structures, and doctrines for the long haul.

What implications does this important development pose for the future of naval overseas presence, including the structure of both naval services—the U.S. Navy and U.S. Marine Corps? This important question is the focus of this chapter. The aim is not to advocate any single response as a fixed blueprint but instead to illuminate the key issues, analyze them systematically, and suggest a strategic framework for thinking about the options ahead.

This chapter's main thesis is that the Navy faces not only challenges in this arena, but also opportunities. The most difficult challenge lies in coping with a fluid global situation—characterized by the effects of globalization detailed throughout this volume—that promises to uproot old ways of thinking and alter the traditional rationale for stationing naval forces abroad in peacetime. But at the same time, there is an opportunity to use emerging, innovative thinking to craft a newly energetic,

Richard L. Kugler is a distinguished research professor in the Institute for National Strategic Studies at National Defense University. Formerly, he was a research leader at RAND and a senior executive in the Department of Defense. He is co-editor of *The Global Century: Globalization and National Security* (Washington, DC: National Defense University Press, 2001) and author of numerous books and studies, including *Commitment to Purpose: How Alliance Partnership Won the Cold War* (Santa Monica, CA: RAND, 1993).

effective role for naval forces—one that is affordable and feasible, yet contributing uniquely and importantly to future U.S. defense strategy in peace, crisis, and war. To some, the challenges loom large (see, in particular, chapters 25 and 27), but when emerging strategic dynamics are considered, the opportunities are substantial if the Pentagon and the Navy can take advantage of them. If future naval overseas presence is well designed, it may come to play an equal or even greater role in U.S. defense strategy than is the case today.[4]

Analyzing the Shift from Europe to Asia

The *QDR Report* suggests that naval forces will participate in a shift of some overseas presence forces from Europe to Asia. Obviously, the shifting of highly maneuverable, self-contained naval units such as warships is different than the shifting of land-based forces. The details of the shift are to be determined, but regardless of how they unfold, an underlying point is quite important. The key to crafting a successful response to the task is not to think in terms of such traditional metrics as numbers of carriers, combatants, and marines stationed abroad, apportioned among theaters according to some fixed mathematical formula. Such metrics and formulas are merely surface manifestations of the Navy's role in overseas presence; they can change, and should change, when new trends are encountered. Rather, the future overseas presence should first be analyzed in terms of the new strategic missions that naval forces will be called upon to perform and the fresh requirements that will flow from these missions. Only then will it be possible to decide upon force levels and apportionments abroad.

As described in chapter 2, today's global climate of accelerating globalization and chaotic security affairs seems destined to create a future of fast-paced changes and surprising developments rather than static, predictable continuity. Overseas deployed naval forces—more commonly known in naval parlance as *forward presence* forces—will be called upon to contribute to the new U.S. defense strategy in political and military ways that will be different from today and will change contours as the future unfolds. Most likely, no single model of overseas naval/forward presence will endure throughout the coming decade or two. Indeed, one model may give way to another with unaccustomed frequency. What can be definitely said, however, is that the new U.S. defense strategy will need strong naval forces abroad for as far into the future as the eye can see, and it will need to employ these forces flexibly and assertively on behalf of multiple strategic purposes. This enduring strategic reality provides a starting point for considering how a future of considerable dynamism should be charted.

Legacy of the Past

The practice of stationing large naval forces abroad in peacetime has been a hardy perennial of U.S. defense strategy since World War II. For varying reasons, all U.S. presidential administrations have valued a sizable overseas/forward naval presence and have resisted arguments in favor of reducing it in big ways. Indeed, U.S. defense strategy has changed often during the past five decades, but the overseas/forward naval presence—in its core assets and main missions—has been marked by considerable continuity, not regular change, even though the Navy as a whole has mutated a great deal.[5]

At the end of World War II, the Navy presided over a huge force of 40 aircraft carriers, 24 battleships, several hundred smaller surface combatants and submarines, 24,000 aircraft, and 3 million sailors supported by an additional 480,000 marines. Because defeat of Germany and Japan had eliminated these two threats to U.S. control of the seas, a smaller Navy was seen as appropriate in the postwar world. However, mounting tensions with the Soviet Union dictated that the United States could not withdraw into its old pattern of isolationism and military unpreparedness. Fortunately, the network of bases and facilities inherited from World War II in both Europe and Asia made it relatively easy for the United States to turn to a permanent overseas naval presence as a key part of its emerging strategy.[6] The act of deploying naval forces overseas, in turn, required a sizable Navy, a portion of which could constantly be stationed abroad even as the remainder guarded the U.S. coastline and provided a pool for rotationally deployed forces in peacetime and sending reinforcements overseas in wartime.

To perform its new missions in the postwar years, Navy leaders recommended a total peacetime force of 15 carriers, 400 combatants, 550,000 sailors, and 100,000 marines. By 1948, however, pell-mell disarmament had reduced the Navy to 11 aging carriers, 289 combatants, 429,000 sailors and 86,000 marines. The other services were in similarly bad shape; indeed, General Omar Bradley said that the Army could not fight its way out of a wet paper bag. In this situation, naval forces played a big role in U.S. defense plans, which anticipated that a Soviet attack in Europe and elsewhere would result in major initial reversals, compelling a mostly naval and air effort to cling to strategic footholds in England, North Africa, and Japan, pending a World War II-style buildup and counterattack. But the problem was that the Navy would have been hard-pressed at that time to carry out this global strategic mission.

The outbreak of the Korean War led to major rearmament, including a larger Navy. When U.S. defense strategy for waging the Cold War was first formed in the early 1950s, and the North Atlantic Treaty Organization (NATO) integrated military command was created, naval forces were assigned the key mission of patrolling the North Atlantic, the Mediterranean, and Asian waters on behalf of containment, deterrence, and forward defense. During the mid-1950s, a new U.S. strategy focused on nuclear weapons and massive retaliation, bringing about big changes in U.S. and NATO forces, but sizable naval forces remained overseas, continuing to perform their traditional missions even as they prepared for nuclear war.[7] A decade later, U.S. strategy was again switching directions, this time away from massive nuclear retaliation toward flexible response and stronger conventional forces. This development reinforced the rationale for stationing carrier battlegroups and marines aboard, for they provided valuable assets for showing the American flag in peacetime and for providing initial crisis response options in the lengthy period before reinforcements from the United States could converge on the scene.

The Vietnam War of the late 1960s resulted in several carriers being regularly stationed off the Vietnamese coast, where they played a key role in conducting bombing missions and supporting forces ashore. Withdrawal from Vietnam in the early 1970s led to another shift in overall U.S. defense strategy, with less emphasis on Southeast Asia and greater attention to the growing NATO-Warsaw Pact rivalry in Central Europe and the North Atlantic. Post-Vietnam drawdowns led to a smaller military posture, but as the Soviet Union began challenging for control of the seas, this threat underscored the need to modernize the Navy with new nuclear carriers, other ships, and warplanes. During the Carter administration, big debates erupted over the Navy's future, with some proponents advocating smaller and fewer carriers plus greater reliance on land-based aircraft for maritime missions. When the dust settled, the Navy emerged intact, with a force of 13 carriers, 204 surface combatants, 94 attack submarines, 66 amphibious warfare ships, and 150 support ships. Its overseas presence settled into a comfortable groove of two carrier battlegroups (CVBGs) in the Atlantic and Mediterranean, one to two CVBGs in the Western Pacific, deployed amphibious ready groups (ARGs) in both regions, and a marine expeditionary force (MEF) stationed on Okinawa.

During the 1980s, the Reagan administration charted a big naval buildup to 15–16 carriers and 580–600 ships. The Navy's overseas presence remained mostly stable during this period. But larger changes swept over the U.S. military posture in ways affecting force operations, including those of naval forces. One of the biggest changes was that the U.S. military acquired significantly better strategic mobility forces in the form of airlift, sealift, and prepositioned assets. This step enhanced the Department of Defense (DOD) capacity to swiftly project power overseas, thus lessening dependence upon overseas presence to conduct a lengthy initial defense until reinforcements could arrive. Faster reinforcement, in turn, helped broaden U.S. military options in wartime in ways that were magnified by the major modernization effort carried out then. The U.S. Air Force (USAF) acquired better aircraft, munitions, and support systems that allowed it not only to win the air battle quickly, but also to influence the ground battle. The Army acquired better tanks, infantry fighting vehicles, and other weapons that permitted it to switch away from stationary linear defense to mobile operations and strong counterattacks. The combined effect was to enable both services to work together in increasingly using offensive operations, rather than passive defense, to attain their battlefield goals.

A similar trend swept over the Navy, which acquired the modern weapons and systems that permitted defensive and offensive doctrines aimed at taking the fight to the enemy in event of a global war. For example, modernization brought the Aegis air defense system, the F–14 and F–18 fighters, and cruise missiles. More than ever before, the Navy emerged as the world's dominant sea power, and overall, the U.S. military emerged as the world's best fighting force, capable of projecting power across the globe and of pursuing offensive strategies against enemies who lacked the power to resist them. In this setting, overseas presence, including naval forces, changed from being a stopgap measure for initial defense against aggression to become the vanguard of a U.S. superpower in pursuit of a proactive global strategic agenda. This proactive naval role was highlighted by the public release of *The Maritime Strategy* in 1986.[8]

Throughout the Cold War's last decades, the Navy maintained a sizable overseas presence in support of a national defense strategy that was mostly continental in its outlook—that is, focused on defending Europe and Northeast Asia against big enemy land and air threats. Even so, the Navy role was quite important because it provided assured access to key strategic regions while helping safeguard against surprise attacks against Central Europe and the North Atlantic, and against South Korea and Japan. Key Navy missions were to maintain control of the seas, swiftly defeat enemy maritime threats, protect the passage of large ground and air reinforcements to crisis zones, and project power ashore where appropriate. As naval technology improved Navy strike capabilities, the power projection role for a potential global confrontation with the Soviet Union increased. In the late 1980s, defense of the Persian Gulf also grew in importance, thereby providing naval forces a significant mission there as well. Initial U.S. strategy in the Persian Gulf focused on defending oil fields against a possible Soviet attack, but the eruption of the bitter Iran-Iraq war signaled that dealing with these two menacing powers would become a dominating theme of the coming years. The Navy soon found itself patrolling Gulf waters to secure safe passage of commercial ships and to signal U.S. determination to protect its strategic interests there.[9] Emergence of the Persian Gulf as a key factor in U.S. defense plans helped complete the Navy's transition into a truly global force, with sizable overseas presence assets continuously present in all three key theaters.

The end of the Cold War in 1990 and the victorious Persian Gulf War of 1991 triggered another searching review of U.S. defense strategy and forces. The Bush administration initiated the process of adjusting to the new era by crafting a regional defense strategy that abandoned the earlier premise of global war.[10] With Central Europe's security no longer directly threatened, the Clinton administration focused its new U.S. defense strategy on being prepared for two concurrent MTW conflicts in the Persian Gulf and Korea, while performing peacekeeping, enforcing no-fly zones over Iraq, and carrying out periodic crisis interventions that erupted with surprising frequency. Overall U.S. forces were reduced to about 30 percent lower than their Cold War levels, and the Navy began its steady drawdown to today's posture while focusing increasingly on littoral operations. The total U.S. overseas presence declined from about 450,000 troops during the Cold War to today's posture of about 235,000 troops. But these withdrawals were mostly carried out by ground and air forces, and especially in Europe, where the U.S. presence shrank from 330,000 troops to 109,000. The Navy's overseas presence remained largely intact, for two reasons: it was seen as a valuable instrument for pursuing the political and military goals of the post-Cold War era in Europe, Asia, and the Persian Gulf; and forward presence was carried out through rotational forces (ships and deployed aircraft squadrons), rather than permanently stationed personnel. The political and military goals included not only being prepared to fight regional wars on short notice but also using overseas presence to help shape the new international security system. By the end of the 1990s, overseas-stationed/forward deployed naval forces found themselves carrying out a plethora of new missions: guarding against MTW conflicts, participating in smaller-scale contingencies (SSCs), and performing defense diplomacy for environment shaping.

Today's Overseas Naval Presence

This historical legacy has bequeathed the naval overseas presence of today. The exact number of naval personnel deployed abroad—sailors and marines—is not a constant. Instead, it is a variable that depends upon not only permanently stationed forces but also the ebb and flow of ship deployments, including rotational duty by almost all continental U.S. (CONUS)-based ships. As a general rule, about 60,000 sailors and 25,000 marines are normally deployed abroad, counting command staffs, ships, bases, and other support facilities. This total includes about 20,000 sailors and 2,500 marines in Europe and the Mediterranean, 20,000 sailors and 20,000 marines in Asia-Pacific (not counting Hawaii), and 15,000 sailors and 3,000 marines in Southwest Asia. In peacetime, naval forces thus account for fully one-third of U.S. military personnel deployed overseas.

What matters more than manpower levels is the nature of the combat forces stationed abroad, for they are large and powerful. In terms of the entire U.S. fleet, roughly one-third is forward deployed on any given day. In the Mediterranean, the Navy's 6th fleet typically consists of a CVBG and an ARG, including a carrier, attack submarines, surface combatants, amphibious ships, prepositioned marine equipment, and various support ships. In Asia and the Western Pacific, the 7th Fleet typically includes a CVBG and an ARG; in addition, the Marine MEF on Okinawa includes about two-thirds of a division and fighter wing. Unique to the 7th Fleet is the fact that a number of ships, including an aircraft carrier and entire ARG, are continuously homeported in the region (in Japan). In Southwest Asia, the 5th Fleet normally commands a CVBG and an ARG and can draw upon marine prepositioned equipment on Diego Garcia. These forces in all three theaters, of course, can be reinforced by the large Atlantic/2d Fleet stationed on the east coast of the United States, the Pacific/3rd Fleet stationed on the west coast and Hawaii, and the two Marine divisions based in the United States.[11] Recent years have seen reinforcements regularly deploy to deal with crises in the Balkans, the Persian Gulf, Afghanistan, and Taiwan. During such crises, the amount of naval power deployed abroad has surged well above the peacetime norm, but the norm itself is widely seen as reflecting a weighty contribution to U.S. global defense strategy.

These naval forces, of course, are embedded in a larger joint overseas presence that includes sizable ground and air forces. Worldwide, about 84,000 Army personnel and 65,000 Air Force personnel are also deployed. The result is today's pattern of about 109,000 military personnel from all services in Europe, 100,000 in Northeast Asia, 25,000 in the Persian Gulf, and a few thousand elsewhere. In Europe, the joint combat posture of 2 Army divisions (4 brigades), $2\frac{1}{3}$ USAF wings, a CVBG, and an ARG is intended to fulfill U.S. military commitments to NATO. In Northeast Asia, the posture of an Army division, a MEF, $2\frac{1}{3}$ USAF wings, a CVBG, and an ARG helps defend Korea, reassure Japan, and perform region-wide security missions. In the Persian Gulf, the normal presence of a USAF fighter wing, a CVBG, an ARG, and small Army units provides initial defense against threats posed by Iraq and others.

Since naval forces account for about one-third of the U.S. military manpower deployed abroad, they presumably provide about one-third of the posture's strategic performance. Such a simple metric, however, conceals many complexities in gauging the contribution of naval forces, as well as those from ground and air forces. The United States deploys a balanced joint posture abroad because each service component performs uniquely important missions, all of which are critical to an effective overseas presence. Moreover, U.S. strategy calls for the missions and activities of the service components to be blended in ways that not only produce joint teamwork but also have synergistic effects. In essence, the whole is intended to exceed the sum of its parts.

Whereas ground and air forces mostly perform missions on land, naval forces perform maritime missions while also possessing a significant capacity to contribute to joint land operations. Naval forces maintain control of the seas, operate along the littorals, and train with a large number of navies from allies and partners. Their contribution to multilateral activities is especially important in Europe and Asia, where maritime collaboration has long been a key aspect of U.S. collective defense and coalition-building endeavors. Naval forces are also invaluable because of their mobility on the seas, which provides U.S. defense strategy with significant strategic reach through power projection. Their normal peacetime missions allow them to operate along vast stretches of the world's oceans and the Eurasian littoral, influencing strategic affairs in many places. In crises, they can converge quickly on littoral hotspots—provided, of course, that they are deployed overseas in a manner that maintains them within swift sailing range of places where U.S. interests might be threatened.

Today's overseas naval presence not only makes many contributions to national security strategy but also plays a key role in maintaining the rationale for a sizable navy force posture.[12] The Army, Air Force, and Marines are readily able to find a requirement for their combat forces in the framework for waging two concurrent MTWs that DOD used for force-sizing from 1993 until recently. But owing to the two contingencies that are usually identified as constituting MTWs—wars against Iraq and North Korea—the requirement for 12 carriers and the rest of the navy posture of about 300 ships becomes less clear (from an MTW warfighting perspective). Sensible defense planners know that other contingencies could require larger naval forces than these two MTWs: for example, a sustained confrontation with China over control of the Asian littoral. But even so, a stressful debate over the Navy posture has been avoided because a force of this size is needed to sustain the current overseas/forward presence. In essence, rotational dynamics necessitate today's posture in order to sustain deployment of three CVBGs, three ARGs, and other ships overseas. In a major crisis, of course, far larger navy forces could be surged by extracting CONUS-based ships from their normal cycles of preparation and recovery, replenishing them quickly, and sending them overseas.

In recent years, some observers have claimed that because the United States has become so proficient at power projection, it no longer needs to station large forces overseas on a permanent basis. Their argument is that a small overseas presence, composed of command staffs and command, control, communications, computers, intelligence, surveillance, and reconnaissance (C4ISR) units, will suffice if it is supported by CONUS-stationed combat forces that can swiftly deploy overseas in event of an emergency. This argument, however, overlooks a compelling political reality. The constant presence of large combat forces not only is a visual manifestation of U.S. strategic power but also is needed to convince allies and adversaries that the United States can be relied upon to protect its interests and meet its security commitments in a still-dangerous world. The need to perform daily training and exercises with allies is another reason for keeping sizable forces overseas. Moreover, some forces must be present to deal with surprise attacks that could result in defeat for the United States and its allies in the days before U.S. reinforcements can arrive; Korea is an example.

Beyond this, the idea that large U.S. combat forces can deploy overseas at a moment's notice from CONUS is an illusion. The reality of constraints is certainly the case for naval forces, which would have to sail long distances to reach remote crisis zones. Likewise, ground forces are so heavy that they mostly must deploy by sealift: a single heavy division, with its support assets, weighs 300,000 tons. While tactical combat aircraft can quickly fly overseas, each fighter wing must be accompanied by 10,000 to 20,000 tons of supplies. A force of 10 fighter wings (now organized as air expeditionary forces) can itself take 2 weeks or more to deploy even if all strategic airlift is allocated to it. DOD has endlessly studied the dynamics of rushing reinforcements overseas over the past two decades. The conclusion always has been that while relatively small forces can be sped to a distant location in a week or two, deployment of the large forces needed to win a big regional war takes far longer, often 2 to 3 months or more. In the interim, a sizable overseas presence of combat forces, including naval forces, is needed in order to provide initial defense in ways that make power projection from CONUS a viable strategy. This conclusion seems unlikely to change in fundamental ways, even though the exact mix of overseas presence and power projection will be a variable in the coming years.

Other critics argue that because USAF forces have acquired growing capabilities for a wide variety of operations, they potentially can substitute for naval forces in overseas presence missions. When strategic and military realities are examined closely, however, they rebut any wholesale acceptance of this claim. To a degree, USAF and Naval air forces can substitute for one another in limited ways and for limited periods. This complementary nature helps enhance the flexibility of overseas forces, gaining greater mileage from them. But for practical reasons, the act of employing this practice in big, permanent ways is another matter. In Europe, for example, the 2 ⅓ USAF fighter wings are widely scattered among Britain, Germany, Italy, and Turkey. If they were assigned the added duty of patrolling the Mediterranean, they would be less able to perform their normal missions of providing high-tech fighters for NATO integrated continental air defense system, participating in NATO reaction forces for expeditionary missions, and training with allied air forces. In Northeast Asia, the 2 ⅓ USAF fighter wings help defend South Korea and Japan, missions that totally engage their time and efforts. If they were assigned the mission of substituting for Navy carrier battlegroups, they would be required regularly to deploy elsewhere across the Asia-Pacific region and thereby would be less able to help guard against a surprise attack against South Korea or violations of Japan's airspace. The key point is that the regular presence of Navy CVBGs in all three theaters not only provides assets for demanding maritime operations but also enables scarce USAF forces to focus intently on their normal continental missions.

Other practical realities enter the equation in constraining ways. While USAF forces can perform some maritime missions, they cannot perform the full set of such missions, and they lack the equipment and training to perform key missions for which they might otherwise be suitable. For example, they cannot conduct antisubmarine warfare, fire long-range intercept missiles, provide layered defense against air attack, fully support amphibious assault operations, clear minefields, provide constant protection of convoys, or help train allied navies. Although they can fly quickly to distant locations, they require bases and facilities in order to operate there continuously for long periods. The counterterrorist war in Afghanistan shows the value of naval forces that do not depend on immediate access to bases that might not be available owing to political constraints or the absence of prepared infrastructure.

Beyond this, a sense of perspective is needed in gauging the relative importance of USAF and Navy forces to overseas presence and in assessing options for change. Whereas today, the Air Force deploys about 4 fighter wings and 260 combat aircraft abroad, the Navy and Marines deploy an equal number of wings, with 260 combat aircraft and many other forms of air-delivered firepower, including cruise missiles. If the goal is to maintain an equal amount of overseas combat power, any reduction of naval forces presumably must be accompanied by deployment of enough additional USAF forces to make up the difference. Would one USAF fighter wing (organized into an air expeditionary unit) be an adequate substitute for one CVBG, or would two or three wings be needed? Regardless of the answer, the practical impediments must be considered. The Air Force already deploys nearly one-half of its active fighter wings overseas and nearly one-third of its total active and reserve forces. Especially with homeland defense missions gaining importance, the Air Force would be hard pressed to support additional overseas deployments and easily could be stretched to the breaking point—as indeed was the case in Kosovo operations.[13]

In theory, additional USAF wings could be fielded by retiring CVBGs and using the savings for this purpose. On the surface, such a tradeoff may look attractive because a USAF fighter wing costs less than a CVBG. But each USAF fighter wing must be accompanied by a large number of expensive support aircraft to perform such roles as command and control, search and rescue, reconnaissance, suppression of enemy defenses, and refueling. Such aircraft are an inherent part of CVBGs. If new USAF fighter wings are to perform a full set of maritime missions, they also would have to be given special equipment and training that would be costly. Moreover, additional bases and facilities would have to be developed in many places in order to provide USAF forces with the geographic reach of CVBGs. These added expenses narrow the cost advantage of substituting USAF forces for naval forces. The idea of pursuing such a substitution was examined in earlier years, and when the full set of strategic considerations and cost-effectiveness tradeoffs was considered, it always was rejected for valid reasons. Whether this calculus will change in the future remains to be seen, but until it does, CVBGs and naval forces seem likely to retain their current attractiveness as part of the joint team for overseas presence.

Costs of Naval Presence

Although today's naval overseas presence offers many strategic advantages, it is not without downsides and impediments. The Navy and Marine Corps are required to sustain today's overseas presence with military manpower that is about 30 percent smaller than during the Cold War. The effect is to put added strains on manpower policies for both services, strains that are magnified when crises and peacekeeping missions require commitment of more ships and personnel than is normal. Since the Navy has only 12 carriers, moreover, it is unable to keep 3 carriers deployed abroad full-time. Owing to rotational dynamics—that is, preparing for extended deployments and recovering from them—a larger force of 15–16 carriers would be needed to sustain 3 carriers abroad.[14] Not surprisingly, carrier deployments in recent years have slipped below the goal of three CVBGs, averaging instead about 2.5 carriers on a month-to-month basis. The effect has been to deprive one or more regional commands of a CVBG for lengthy periods. If the overall navy posture declines from 310 ships to about 285 ships, as is widely expected, strains on overseas presence likely will grow further, perhaps resulting in fewer deployments.

If the Navy did not have to maintain any overseas presence, it would be freed to focus on keeping its forces ready for crises. As a result, it likely would be able to surge more forces in crises than currently is the case; for example, a significant portion of its forces would not be undergoing the shakedown and recovery period that normally accompanies a long overseas deployment. This is one price to be paid for having today's overseas presence. Also, the naval overseas presence elevates spending on operations and maintenance (O&M), thus further inflating the DOD budget for O&M, which has surged upward to $125 billion annually today—50 percent higher than historical levels for per capita spending. Another expense is the cost of extensive bases and facilities overseas, especially in Europe and Asia. As a result, the Navy has fewer funds for spending on readiness, training, and modernization, accounts that have experienced shortfalls in recent years. These direct and indirect expenses do not mean that the money could be better spent elsewhere, but they do underscore the judgment that today's overseas naval presence is not a free lunch. It consumes significant resources, and it requires careful planning to ensure that it provides maximum benefits for the manpower and money invested.

The same, of course, can be said about the total U.S. overseas military presence. Today, DOD stations nearly 20 percent of its active military manpower overseas. In addition to the troops and formations abroad, overseas presence includes many activities that are easily overlooked but are quite important: command staffs, support bases and facilities, prepositioned equipment and war reserve stockpiles, training and exercises with many countries, and security assistance to a variety of nations. For all these reasons, overseas presence is quite an important instrument of U.S. national security policy; indeed, it often is the main way that the United States manifests its power and interests in key regions. While the budget costs of overseas presence are hazy, a reasonable estimate is that they total about $10–$15 billion per year: this is the incremental cost of keeping already-funded forces overseas, operating them in current ways, and pursuing associated activities. A defense effort this important and costly arguably should be treated as a separate program in the DOD planning, programming, and budgeting system process.

Even short of this step, strong management oversight is needed to ensure that vital requirements are met and resources are spent wisely. A few years ago, DOD created the Theater Engagement Plan (TEP) system to help accomplish this purpose. While the TEP system has helped identify key strategic objectives in each region, it has fallen short of providing serious analysis of the critical relationship between resource inputs and performance outputs. Something better is needed. The Secretary of Defense and the Joint Staff need good analytical tools for gauging requirements and policies for overseas presence both globally and in each key region. The services need tools for gauging how overseas presence measures should be fitted into their budgets and programs. The commanders of the regional unified commands need tools for articulating the case for improvements critical to their missions. Crafting a management process that performs these functions and provides participants the necessary analytical tools should be a key goal for the coming years.[15]

Future Strategic and Political Purposes of Overseas Presence

Only a few years ago, U.S. national security policy portrayed world affairs as headed toward ever-growing stability and peace as a result of the onward march of democracy and economic markets. By contrast, the *QDR Report* portrays a world of mounting turmoil and dangers owing to terrorism and other threats. In response, it puts forth a new U.S. defense strategy that emphasizes enhanced homeland defense and assertive security policies abroad. In this new strategy, overseas military presence is to play an increasingly important role on behalf of new strategic and political purposes, as well as to help carry out new operational concepts for warfighting.

As a consequence, two important strategic changes will be occurring. First, overseas presence will be seen as an integrated global asset in DOD force planning, not as a set of disconnected regional postures with wholly separate rationales of their own. This global perspective likely will leave DOD willing to regularly shift overseas presence back and forth among the regions as the security situations dictate, rather than rely on an immutable apportionment plan. Second, overseas presence will be seen not as an instrument of local forward defense in fixed locations but as a tool of power projection that interacts with reinforcements from CONUS to provide a capacity to swiftly apply U.S. military power across a wide range of locations in all key regions.

Overseas-stationed/forward naval forces, of course, have always possessed the inherent mobility to perform this mission. The change is that they will now be regularly employing this mobility more often, and in more sweeping ways, than in the past.

Beyond this, the *QDR Report* calls for design of regionally tailored forces in key theaters as well as transformation efforts aimed at strengthening their capabilities to deter aggression and to permit reallocation of CONUS-based forces now dedicated to reinforcement missions. In order to pursue these goals, the *QDR Report* makes clear that the current overseas presence will be changing in specific ways. It instructs that the U.S. global military posture will be reoriented to:

- develop a basing system that provides greater flexibility for U.S. forces in the world, placing emphasis on additional bases and stations beyond Western Europe and northeast Asia. Current bases in Europe and northeast Asia will be retained, but they will also be used as regional hubs for power projection elsewhere.
- provide temporary access to facilities in foreign countries that enable U.S. forces to conduct training and exercises in the absence of permanent ranges and bases.
- redistribute forces and equipment based on regional deterrence requirements.
- provide sufficient mobility, bases, debarkation points, and new logistical concepts to conduct expeditionary operations in distant theaters against adversaries armed with weapons of mass destruction (WMD) and other means to deny access to U.S. forces.[16]

To help achieve these goals, the *QDR Report* announced the following specific changes to overseas presence forces:

- The Navy will increase CVBG presence in the western Pacific and will explore options for homeporting three or four more surface combatants and guided missile cruise submarines there.[17]
- The Navy also will develop new concepts for maritime prepositioning, high-speed sealift, and new amphibious capabilities for the Marines. In addition, the Navy will develop options to shift some Marine prepositioned equipment from the Mediterranean toward the Indian Ocean and Arabian Gulf in order to become more responsive to Middle East contingencies and will explore prospects for the Marine Corps to conduct training for littoral warfare in the Western Pacific.[18]
- The Army will accelerate the forward stationing of interim brigade combat teams in Europe and will explore options to enhance ground force capabilities in the Arabian Gulf.[19]
- The Air Force will develop plans to increase contingency basing in the Pacific and Indian Oceans as well as the Arabian Gulf.[20]
- DOD will develop a new joint presence policy that establishes steady-state levels of ground, air, and naval presence in critical regions and that synchronizes force

deployments and cross-service trades in order to increase the flexibility of forward-stationed forces while coordinating the readiness and operational tempo of all U.S. forces.[21]

Beyond question, these are major changes to the U.S. overseas presence, and they may be forerunners of bigger changes to come. They are being heavily driven by the DOD judgment that globalization, new-era geopolitics, and other trends are interacting to create a vast southern arc of instability stretching from the Middle East to the Asian littoral (part of which constitutes President George W. Bush's "axis of evil") that menaces world peace in the 21st century.[22] In this strategic calculus, the democratic community is becoming healthier and prosperous as the globalizing world economy gains momentum, and the old troubled zones of Europe and Northeast Asia are becoming more stable as well. But in worrisome ways, the southern arc is moving in the opposite direction. Animated by slow economic progress, troubled countries, WMD proliferation, and red-hot security affairs, it is creating a zone of chaos: a boiling primordial stew lacking orderly relationships and capable of erupting into conflict and violence at multiple places. Across this vast zone, the United States does not confront a new peer rival akin to the Soviet Union during the Cold War. But it does face multiple dangerous threats: terrorists and other nonstate actors, failing states and ethnic conflict, regional rogues armed with asymmetric strategies and WMD systems, and big powers with newly assertive geopolitical agendas of their own. If these threats are left unchecked, the risk is that they will fester, grow, and interact to endanger not only U.S. interests and values overseas, but the physical safety of the United States and its people as well.

In dealing with this situation, the *QDR Report* articulates three core U.S. interests for guiding national security policy:

- ensuring U.S. security and freedom of action, including U.S. sovereignty, the safety of its citizens at home and abroad, and protection of critical infrastructure.
- honoring international commitments, including the security of allies and friends, precluding hostile domination of critical regions on the Eurasian landmass, and peaceful stability in the Western Hemisphere.
- contributing to economic well-being, including a productive global economy, the security of international sea, air and space, and information lines of communication, and access to key markets and strategic resources.[23]

To help safeguard these interests, the *QDR Report* identifies four key goals to guide the new U.S. defense strategy: assuring allies and friends; dissuading future military competition; deterring threats and coercion against U.S. interests; if deterrence fails, decisively defeating any adversary.[24] It articulates all four goals with language underscoring the need to pursue them through assertive security policies abroad and high levels of U.S. military preparedness. Although three of these goals are written about with a sharper edge than in earlier years, they are familiar features of U.S. policy. By contrast, the goal of "dissuading future military competition" is a fresh strategic concept that reflects stressful, unfamiliar aspects of new-era geopolitical dynamics.[25] This goal calls for U.S. defense strategy and forces to be shaped in an explicit manner that powerfully influences potential adversaries not to compete with the United States and its allies in the military domain by making clear that they will lose any such competition. Essentially, this goal addresses the murky geopolitical arena between peaceful relations and outright military confrontation, focusing on countries that might otherwise be tempted to build military forces aimed at challenging the United States and its allies. By maintaining unquestioned U.S. military superiority, this goal aspires to end competitive efforts by adversaries before they begin.

To pursue these four goals, the *QDR Report* puts forth a "paradigm shift" in force planning that is aimed at sizing and shaping future U.S. forces to defend the U.S. homeland, deter coercion forward in critical regions, swiftly defeat aggression in overlapping major conflicts, and conduct a limited number of SSC operations.[26] The new defense strategy broadens the earlier focus on fixed threats and contingencies with an emphasis on building capabilities for multiple purposes. It does not wholly dismantle the previous two-MTW framework. Indeed, it says that DOD should retain a strong capability to wage two such concurrent conflicts if necessary. But it articulates a new approach to force allocations for them. The *QDR Report* instructs that DOD should allocate sufficient forces to win one MTW in overwhelming ways (to include occupation of enemy territory), assign sufficient forces to conduct a stalwart defense in the other MTW, and make available significant forces for SSC commitments.[27] It thus asserts that the act of staying ready for two MTWs should not be carried to the point of so consuming the entire defense posture that forces cannot be freed for dealing with the SSC contingencies that erupt frequently.

Beyond this, the *QDR Report* makes clear that the central thrust of defense planning will be to create capabilities for handling a wide spectrum of military conflicts: not only MTWs against regional rogues, but conflicts at the lower end of the spectrum—including peacekeeping and small crisis interventions—and those at the higher end, including wars against WMD-armed opponents and big powers. The clarion call of the new strategy is for highly capable forces that are flexible, versatile, agile, and adaptable. Indeed, the *QDR Report* states that DOD will not be able to predict where and when wars will erupt and often will be caught by surprise. Accordingly, it calls for a flexible portfolio of military assets that can quickly be combined and recombined to deal with the conflicts at hand in each case and with an ever-shifting set of military challenges as the future unfolds.[28] Compared to the earlier DOD focus on highly predictable MTWs in northeast Asia and the Persian Gulf, this new approach, with its emphasis on generic capabilities and flexible response options, is decidedly new and different. If taken seriously, it promises to move U.S. defense planning into a new realm in which being capable of multiple warfighting efforts will be more important than being optimized for a small number of them.

The *QDR Report* identifies a set of strategic tenets to accompany this new emphasis on flexible capabilities. Of them, three are especially important for the future overseas presence. One tenet states that while defending the U.S. homeland must receive considerable emphasis, possessing the capability swiftly to project strong forces abroad will be key to disrupting and destroying threats at long distances.[29] The second tenet states that U.S forces must train and operate with the forces of allies and friends in order to build strengthened alliances and partnerships capable of performing new-era security operations.[30] The third tenet states that U.S. forces must play a central role in maintaining favorable regional force balances, so that allies are protected, adversaries are dissuaded and deterred, and a foundation of peaceful stability is established.[31] As the *QDR Report* acknowledges, these tenets underscore the strategic need for the future U.S. overseas presence to be strong, energetic, and highly capable—indeed, more capable than now.

What implications does this new strategic framework pose for the future strategic and political purposes of overseas naval presence? It creates not only challenges for the Navy, but for several reasons, important opportunities as well. The emergence of the southern arc of instability as a key worry means that U.S. defense strategy will be switching away from its old focus on continental Europe. Instead, it will be addressing a vast zone whose turbulent security dynamics will be greatly influenced by littoral and maritime affairs, by control of nearby seas, and by the projection of naval power ashore. This new geography alone elevates the importance of overseas naval presence in the strategic calculus. Equally important, the strategic goals and tenets articulated by the new U.S. defense strategy clearly mandate the systematic application of overseas naval power as part of the joint team. Along the southern arc from the Middle East to the Asian littoral, a strong overseas naval presence will be needed to pursue the four goals of assurance, dissuasion, deterrence, and defeat of aggression—in the face of difficult security conditions that make attainment of these goals difficult. Likewise, strong naval forces will be needed to provide readily available and flexible military capabilities, to build strengthened multilateral alliances and partnerships, and to maintain favorable force balances. Perhaps it is an exaggeration to say that the southern arc is tailor-made for naval forces; air and ground forces will have important roles to play as well. But naval forces do seem destined often to play a front-and-center role in U.S. strategy and joint operations there because their inherent characteristics are well suited to the new-era requirements facing the armed services.

Regional Effects of Overseas Naval Presence

While these general principles apply across the southern arc and elsewhere, the specific opportunities for overseas naval presence to contribute to the new U.S. defense strategy differ greatly from one region to the next. In Europe, the prevailing sentiment is to shift some U.S. forces from there to other endangered regions where they will be more needed. Even so, U.S. naval forces still will be expected to contribute importantly to stabilizing the Mediterranean region, which is the northern flank of the southern arc. If events in the Middle East make the Mediterranean a growing hot spot, U.S. naval forces—whose assets are stronger than those of NATO allies there—will need to help defend the sea lanes, to help protect such NATO members as Italy, Greece, and Turkey, and to provide forces for crisis interventions along the littorals, including the Balkans and North Africa. Equally important, U.S. naval forces can be used to help energize sluggish NATO efforts to develop better European expeditionary forces for power projection operations along Europe's periphery and beyond. Apart from Britain, the European allies currently lack the mobility and logistics support assets needed to swiftly deploy large ground and air forces outside their borders. But many of their naval forces are better suited to expeditionary and power-projection missions while being interoperable with U.S. forces and providing valuable niche capabilities in such areas as mine-clearing, sea lane protection, and patrol of littoral areas. Potentially, U.S. naval forces could work closely with allied forces to create enhanced multilateral cooperation in ways that provide a foundation for progress on ground and air forces as well. If NATO becomes a reformed alliance whose power projection assets are led by U.S. and European naval forces and supplemented by appropriate land and air forces, it will be able to play a stronger role in global security affairs than it does today.

Surface appearances suggest that the big landmass stretching from the Middle East to South Asia is mostly the province of U.S. air and ground forces. The problem with this formulation, however, is that the prevailing political climate in these regions seems likely to prevent the permanent stationing of such forces there. Indeed, the small U.S. air and ground forces now temporarily based in Saudi Arabia and neighboring Gulf sheikdoms have increasingly become lightning rods for Islamic protests against alleged U.S. hegemony and cultural domination. Whether the United States will succeed in clinging to its current foothold in the Persian Gulf is to be seen. But it is hard to envisage larger U.S. forces being welcomed there, or major U.S. air and ground forces being stationed in India, Pakistan, and other South Asian countries.[32] Naval forces deployed offshore, however, are less politically contentious and are capable of reaching most littoral regions through their air and missile assets, as well as performing daily patrolling and periodic base visits. As a result, naval forces, coupled with maritime prepositioning of equipment sets and greater temporary access to bases and infrastructure of friendly nations, likely will remain the main military instrument by which the United States asserts its interests in these regions. Indeed, turbulent security affairs there could compel the United States to deploy larger naval forces than currently is the case. This especially will be the case for as long as the war against terrorists and their sponsors is being fought—a conflict that could take years.

The Asian littoral indisputably is a fluid geostrategic zone well suited to maritime strategic concepts and force operations. There, the principal danger is that China's growing power will result in it posing a maritime threat to several countries there and to U.S. access to the vital sea lines of communication stretching from the Malacca Straits along the great Asian crescent to Taiwan and Japan. The emerging strategic situation calls for U.S. defense strategy to broaden its focus beyond northeast Asia, to work with Japan and South Korea in projecting stability along the Asian littoral, and to pursue enhanced collaboration with such countries as Australia, the Philippines, Indonesia, Malaysia, Thailand, and others. Clearly, U.S. air forces can help pursue this geopolitical and military agenda, but their numbers will be limited in relation to the requirements ahead. Especially because most countries of East Asia and the Western Pacific think in terms of naval power and maritime security relationships, the future role to be played by the Navy in this murky region will be critical to achieving U.S. security goals. The decision by the *QDR Report* to call for larger U.S. naval deployments along the Asian littoral, and for better access to bases and facilities there, may be a forerunner of things to come.

The future U.S. overseas presence in Asia will depend heavily upon geopolitical trends. For as long as North Korea poses a serious military threat, large U.S. forces will remain in South Korea, supported by reinforcements in Japan, to enforce deterrence and defense on the Korean Peninsula. In the event this threat fades and Korea unifies, a partial drawdown of U.S. ground and air forces may be possible, perhaps including the marines on Okinawa. Yet sizable forces likely will remain as part of U.S. strategy to maintain a stable balance of power in Asia and to perform power-projection missions across East Asia and along the Asian littoral. China's growing power seems likely to reinforce the DOD call for large Navy ship deployments in Asia and a widening geographic scope of peacetime operations. The Navy currently has adequate bases in Northeast Asia, but it likely will be seeking better bases and facilities in the Philippines, Singapore, and elsewhere in Southeast Asia—not necessarily to deploy ships and marines there in a permanent arrangement, but instead to gain access for temporary deployments and surge missions.

The bottom line is that the new U.S. defense strategy faces powerful incentives to retain a strong overseas naval presence and even to increase it in critical regions where threats and requirements are growing. Yet the Navy's resources for this mission—measured in terms of carriers, other ships, and marines—are already limited and may shrink somewhat in the coming years. For this reason, the proper response is not to continue deploying naval forces, as well as ground and air forces, according to the same mechanical logic of force apportionments that has applied in the past. Instead, a tailored response should be designed for each region. The need to employ scarce assets with maximum effectiveness mandates careful analyses aimed at determining, as precisely as possible, the exact relationship between overseas presence and the attainment of U.S. security objectives—which is the genesis of studies such as that described in chapter 6. Such analyses will need to assess not only technical military issues, but also the political influence of naval forces and other overseas presence assets on the proclivities and policies of many nations, including friends and adversaries.

Both globally and for each key region, the strategic goal should be to design the kind of overseas presence in size and force mix that does the best job of achieving U.S. political-military goals. Some regions may demand more naval overseas presence than others, with the optimal mix among them fluctuating as strategic conditions evolve. In some cases, overseas naval presence may be more effective, or more necessary, than is commonly believed. In other cases, it may be less effective, or less critical, than imagined. In some situations, the proper response may be naval forces; in other situations, it may be air or ground forces, or such other measures as C⁴ISR assets, bases and infrastructure, prepositioned equipment, or security assistance. If such differences in requirements and performance arise, they need to be discovered and acted upon wisely, for they may be critical to determining whether the future U.S. overseas presence actually achieves the strategic and political purposes for which it is designed.

Warfighting and Operational Requirements for Naval Presence

Future directions in the U.S. overseas naval presence also will be influenced by requirements for waging wars and carrying out new operational concepts that U.S. forces will adopt as transformation gains momentum. Here, too, the Navy faces challenges as well as opportunities. For example, U.S. naval forces likely will acquire key assets for the new network of theater missile defenses that will be erected to help protect U.S. forces and allied countries against WMD proliferation in the coming years. Equally important, overseas naval forces will help provide the vanguard of initial defenses that will be needed to gain early control of conflicts in ways that permit reinforcements from CONUS to deploy swiftly and effectively. During the past decade, naval forces have primarily been focused on providing initial defense for the two MTWs in the Persian Gulf and Korea. In the coming years, they will be facing a widening spectrum of conflict, including different types of wars in new and unfamiliar places. If the conflicts in Kosovo and Afghanistan are prologue, future operations may be neither big nor small, but instead will require medium-sized strike packages: for example, one to three CVBGs, four to six USAF expeditionary air units (fighter wings), and one to three Army and Marine divisions. If this proves the case, overseas forces may provide a lion's share of the total forces committed and thus will be more than a mere vanguard for a much larger buildup.

Nobody can pretend to know what the future holds, but if current trends are an indicator, U.S. forces may be called upon to wage war frequently in the years ahead— not necessarily big and calamitous conflicts, but instead a lengthy sequence of small- to medium-sized conflicts in shifting places, in unique ways tailored to the occasion, and against a varying cast of enemies. Operations in Afghanistan may be a forerunner—but this example is on the lower end of this scale in terms of forces committed. The new U.S. defense strategy's call for flexible military capabilities is not only a wise response to this prospect, but it also means that the future naval posture probably will not have to find its sizing rationale in overseas presence. The need for flexible capabilities for a spectrum of wars will provide ample rationale for a large and diverse naval posture. Equally important, the overseas naval presence will need to be adjusted and equipped so that it fits effectively into this new doctrine for warfighting.

Emerging operational concepts will play a large role in determining how the overseas naval presence should be prepared for this purpose. A number of such concepts already are provided by *Joint Vision 2020,* which calls for full-spectrum dominance, and by such associated concepts as network centric warfare, rapid decisive operations, and effects-based operations.[33] In addition, the *QDR Report* identifies the following operational goals as critical to guiding force transformation:

- protecting critical bases of operations at home and abroad and defeating WMD systems and their means of delivery
- protecting information systems in the face of attack and using them to conduct effective operations
- projecting and sustaining U.S. forces in distant antiaccess or area-denial environments and defeating associated threats
- denying sanctuary to enemies by carrying out accurate long-distance strike operations against industrial and military targets as well as critical mobile and fixed targets in forward areas near the battlefield
- enhancing the capability and survivability of space systems and supporting infrastructure
- leveraging information systems and innovative concepts to develop an interoperable, joint C[4]ISR architecture and joint operational capability.[34]

To develop an improved capacity to carry out new operational doctrines for using naval overseas presence in warfighting, there will be a premium on understanding future military threats and the best ways to counter them. The past decade has seen an unusually high degree of U.S. military superiority in virtually all areas, such that today U.S. ground, air, and naval forces operate virtually free from serious worry about having large casualties inflicted upon them. While U.S. forces will remain superior over future opponents, this degree of total dominance likely will erode as enemies acquire asymmetric strategies, information-age weapons and systems, long-range strike assets, WMD systems, and other enhanced capabilities of their own. As a result, U.S. forces, including naval forces, likely will again confront competitive environments in which they will need to operate with new technologies, weapons, information systems, and doctrines in order to minimize heavy casualties and to achieve their warfighting goals. Reacting wisely to this challenge will be a key imperative ahead.

As the naval overseas presence is adjusted to deal with growing military threats across a widening spectrum of conflicts and geographic zones, it will be essential for DOD and the Navy to get the strategic basics right. This especially is the case in dealing with future antiaccess/area denial threats. As will be discussed in chapter 25, some analysts are so apprehensive of such threats that they judge U.S. forces should switch away from their traditional emphasis on forward defense of endangered friends and allies, and instead should resort to a new military strategy of standoff operations from distant rearward areas that lie over the horizon. This strategy mainly would be characterized by long-distance bombardment of enemy targets in a war. Two reasons account for this stance. The first reason is concern that in many places, allied and friendly governments will be too cowed by nearby adversaries to allow U.S. forces access to their bases and facilities. The second reason is fear that adversaries will develop the missiles and other offensive assets needed to sink U.S. naval warships and to destroy ground and air forces if they draw within striking range of crisis zones. The implication is that U.S. military strategy should resort to strategic bombers, long-range cruise missiles, and space assets in order to wage war outside the envelope of such threats.

As U.S. forces become better at long-range strikes, clearly they should include standoff operations as part of their armory; there may be situations in which such operations are either the only recourse or can help complement forward operations by suppressing enemy defenses before large forces arrive on the scene. But wholly embracing standoff operations to the point of abandoning heavy reliance on forward operations is another matter. Today, U.S. strategic bombers, cruise missiles, and other standoff strike assets provide only about 25 percent of the U.S. military's capacity for air-delivered firepower. Even if they are upgraded significantly, they likely will not possess the firepower, maneuverability, and agility needed to win future wars on their own. For most conflicts, a hefty infusion of shorter-range airpower and ground maneuver forces will also be needed. This is a practical reason for not relying too exclusively on standoff assets: they normally will not be able to get the job done alone, and especially so if more than one contingency occurs at a time.

Moreover, U.S. defense strategy has long portrayed forward deployments, with forces based on the soil or in nearby waters of allies and friends, as a key element in signaling its political resolve and credibility. Any wholesale resort to standoff operations inevitably would be seen as a serious weakening of the U.S. commitment to their security. How would such long-standing friends and allies as Turkey, Kuwait, Saudi Arabia, the Philippines, Taiwan, South Korea, and Japan react if U.S. forces are no longer on the soil or closely offshore, available to help directly defend their borders and airspace? The reaction likely would be negative in ways that could have serious, ripple-effect damages on larger U.S. policies and interests in these regions. The idea that such countries will be so cowed by new-era adversaries to insist that U.S. forces keep distant seems a stretch. During the Cold War, most of these countries eagerly sought U.S. forward commitments even though the consequence was to risk Soviet nuclear weapons being targeted on them. Having withstood such a threat then, they are unlikely to be cowed by the new-era threats facing them now. Indeed, their reaction to these threats likely will be one of seeking stronger U.S. forward commitments, not weaker relationships.

In addition, future antiaccess/area-denial threats should be kept in perspective. As argued in chapter 26, U.S. forces will be less vulnerable to them than surface appearances suggest. Throughout the Cold War, the U.S. Navy faced, and surmounted, a major antiaccess/area-denial threat posed by the Soviet Union. The Soviets built a huge naval force of long-range bombers, cruise missiles, nuclear warheads, and attack submarines aimed not only at denying the U.S. Navy access to northern waters but also at interdicting NATO reinforcing convoys sailing to Central Europe. In order to ward off these threats and suppress them, the Navy greatly increased its defensive capabilities with such systems as F–14 fighters with Phoenix missiles, Aegis, and point-defense assets for air defense, and with P–3 aircraft, lethal attack submarines, and modern destroyers and frigates for antisubmarine warfare. By the end of the Cold War, the Navy had become relatively immune to these threats, to the point of judging that it could sail close to northern Soviet ports and strike them without suffering major losses in return.

A similar trend occurred on the European continent. Here too, the Soviet Union assembled a huge threat of several hundred bombers, 4,000 tactical combat aircraft, and hundreds of nuclear-tipped ballistic missiles for suppressing NATO airbases, ports, supply dumps, and road and rail networks, all aimed at preventing NATO from mounting a forward defense of Germany's borders. The United States and NATO counteracted by erecting a formidable defense screen of airborne warning and control systems, modern fighters, the Patriot air defense system, point defenses, and hardened facilities. By the end of the Cold War, the Soviet air threat was fading, and the NATO capacity to reinforce and mount a formidable forward defense was not in doubt. The central lesson is that on sea, land, and air, the U.S. military confronted a serious antiaccess/area denial threat, chose to confront it rather than retreat from forward defense, and won the contest going away—against a rival with big military forces and modern technology.

In this arena, the past seems likely to be prologue if U.S. forces merely take the necessary precautionary steps, for the new threats are likely to be smaller and less well-armed than those posed by the Soviet Union in the Cold War. Owing to its existing formidable defensive systems, a U.S. CVBG is enormously hard to damage significantly, much less sink entirely. Because it moves constantly on the high seas, the act of locating it with enough precision to target it effectively is itself quite difficult, even for countries that may gradually gain access to space-based assets and other modern reconnaissance systems. To be sure, enemy cruise missiles, ballistic missiles, diesel submarines, and mines pose new-era threats to the Navy's survivability. But these threats can be countered by acquiring the modernized information systems, defense assets, and offensive strike capabilities needed to ensure that naval forces remain survivable even when they approach littoral hot spots. The same applies to the act of sending ground and air forces ashore in the face of enemy efforts to destroy them. Measures to modernize their defense systems, disperse them, and harden ports, facilities, and bases—while upgrading allied forces for initial defense—can accomplish a great deal to ensure that as these U.S. forces converge on a crisis, they will be able to enter the fray safely and operate effectively. The bottom line is that while new-era antiaccess/area-denial threats should be taken seriously, the proper response is to counteract them, not to be driven into weak defense strategy that might be unable to win future wars.

If strategic retreat in the face of antiaccess/area-denial threats is not necessary, what new operational concepts should be employed to help guide the wartime use of overseas naval presence? A good candidate may be the concept of "joint response forces for early and forcible entry" that surfaced, with considerable fanfare, during the recent DOD defense strategy review and is highlighted as a wave of the future by the *QDR Report*.[35] This concept calls for creation of standing joint task forces in key commands that would be equipped to carry out the swift deployment of small or medium-sized spearhead forces to a crisis zone. These joint response forces would be composed of naval, air, and ground units. Heavily transformed with new-era technologies, they would be ultra-sophisticated, equipped with modern C4ISR systems, information networks, modern munitions, and weapons capable of lethal strike operations, especially from the air. They would be given the high readiness and strong mobility assets needed for them to deploy within a week or two of a decision to send them. Their mission would not be to win the war on their own, but instead to gain sufficient control of the battle to pave the way for the prompt arrival of larger reinforcements, which mostly would be modernized legacy forces. In essence, they would be high-tech "tip of the spear" forces, capable of being fitted atop multiple different shafts of bigger forces for fighting a wide spectrum of wars to successful completion.

The concept of joint response forces for early entry is not the only new operational concept under consideration, nor is it a cure-all for all future wars. But it seems likely to take hold in ways that will influence not only future U.S. defense strategy but transformation as well. It provides a conceptual tool for focusing transformation in limited ways that have high leverage and battlefield potency, without prematurely calling for the overhaul of the entire U.S. defense posture. As a new approach to warfighting, this concept provides an attractive, natural mission for naval overseas presence. Owing to their deployment patterns, emphasis on network centric operations, and high-technology strike assets, overseas naval forces should be well endowed for participation in joint response forces and missions. Indeed, for missions that have a strong littoral and maritime dimension, overseas naval forces may often serve not only as a cutting edge for early and forcible entry, but also as a central organizer and choreographer of the entire operation. That is, naval forces would provide a firm foundation upon which swift interventions by other service components would be built.

The future in this arena will depend upon many considerations. Most likely, other requirements will dictate that overseas presence naval forces should not be optimized solely for the "joint response force" concept. But if future overseas naval forces can acquire significant capabilities for contributing to this key concept and become a leading-edge participant in the Navy's transformation efforts, they will gain a role of enduring importance in the new U.S. defense strategy—not only because of their political influence abroad and overall versatility, but also because of their ability to fight the high-tech wars of the future.

Conclusion: Toward a Future of Flexibility

The days are gone in which the Navy could rely on continuously deploying a CVBG and an ARG in each key region: Europe and the Mediterranean, the Persian Gulf, and Asia. Significant shifts away from this longstanding pattern are already under way and may lie ahead. Irrespective of how redeployments are carried out in the near term, no single new model of regional apportionments is likely to rule throughout the coming decade or two. In the coming period during which the war on terrorism will be carried out, larger-than-normal forces may be concentrated in the Persian Gulf and the Arabian Sea. Afterward, forces may be concentrated in Asia. Yet it also is possible that major deployments might again be needed in the Mediterranean, at least temporarily, if events there heat up, perhaps as a byproduct of WMD proliferation, tensions with Islam, or ethnic wars in the Balkans and Caucasus. The key judgment is that flexibility and adaptability likely will need to be the watchwords for the future. The Navy likely will need to be able regularly to shift Navy and Marine forces among the key regions in order to deal with the long period of great fluidity and surprising changes that apparently lies ahead.

The exact numbers of naval forces deployed abroad—manpower, combat units, and support assets for the Navy and Marines—should be determined by future missions and requirements, not the other way around. However, there is a distinct relationship between the amount of forces that can be forward deployed and the overall size of the Navy and Marine Corps. If we are to maintain approximately the same amount of forces on overseas/forward deployment—even if they are sent to changing locations—cuts in naval force structure cannot be justified. Another important influence will be the course of transformation. The *QDR Report 2001* implies that transformation will not be pursued at a breakneck pace, but it will be carried out in meaningful ways that are purposeful and measured. Most likely the Navy and Marines will retain many of their legacy platforms and forces, while modernizing and recapitalizing them. But depending upon the outcome of joint experiments and ongoing research and development activities, new systems and platforms likely will begin appearing in the coming years and gradually will become more significant as the distant future unfolds. To what extent will the future Navy be marked by smaller carriers, surface combatants with far smaller crews than now, submarines that fire many cruise missiles, unmanned combat aircraft, smaller craft and patrol boats, mobile offshore bases, light ground combat vehicles, bigger and faster cargo ships, and other new platforms beloved by some proponents of transformation? The answer remains to be seen, but it will play a significant role in shaping the naval overseas presence of the future.

Notes

[1] Department of Defense, *Quadrennial Defense Review Report* (Washington, DC: Department of Defense, September 2001), 20, 25–28.

[2] Ibid., 17.

[3] In the 2001 State of the Union Address, President George W. Bush referred to three dictatorial regimes within this strategic arc—Iraq, Iran, and North Korea—as part of an "axis of evil" dedicated to destabilizing their neighbors and the world order.

[4] This is the prime thesis of Sam J. Tangredi, "The Fall and Rise of Naval Forward Presence," U.S. Naval Institute *Proceedings* 126, no. 5 (May 2000), 28–32, which also illuminates many of the challenges. A reply to this article by Philip A. Dur appears in *Proceedings* 126, no. 7 (July 2000), 22–23.

[5] A recent conference, "U.S. Navy Forward Presence Bicentennial Symposium—Forward . . . From the Start," sponsored by the CNA Corporations, the Naval Historical Foundation, and the Naval Historical Center on June 21,2001, lauded the fact that the conceptual roots of naval overseas/forward presence can be traced back—relatively unchanged—to July 1, 1801.

[6] By providing the overseas base infrastructure that allowed for permanent stationing (as opposed to only rotational deployment)of ships in foreign ports, closer to the Soviet Union. This infrastructure also allowed for longer stationing times and better supply for those ships on rotational deployment from U.S. ports. The actual degree of dependency of the rotational forces on overseas bases is a matter of considerable, often parochial, debate.

[7] A fascinating recent study of naval preparations for nuclear war during that era can be found in Jerry Miller, *Nuclear Weapons and Aircraft Carriers* (Washington, DC: Smithsonian Institution Press, 2001). Vice Admiral Miller was a direct participant in many of these preparations.

[8] Public version released as "The Maritime Strategy," U.S. Naval Institute *Proceedings* (January 1986 supplement). An excellent analysis is Norman Friedman, *The U.S. Maritime Strategy* (New York: Jane's Publishing Company, 1988).

[9] An excellent source on the naval role in the pre-*Desert Storm* Arabian Gulf is Michael A. Palmer, *On Course to Desert Storm: The U.S. Navy and the Persian Gulf*, Contributions to Naval History Series no. 5 (Washington, DC: Naval Historical Center, 1992).

[10] A comprehensive analysis of the Bush administration's "reconstitution strategy" that was unfortunately released only shortly before the election of President Clinton is *Reconstituting America's Defense: The New U.S. National Security Strategy*, ed. James J. Tritten and Paul N. Stockton (New York: Praeger Publishers, 1992). See also James J. Tritten, *Our New National Security Strategy: America Promises to Come Back* (New York: Praeger Publishers, 1992).

[11] The Atlantic and Pacific Fleets are the administrative organizations (for training, maintenance, repair, etc.) of ships; the 2nd and 3rd Fleets are the operational organizations.

[12] See discussion in Tangredi, "The Fall and Rise of Naval Forward Presence," 28–29.

[13] See, for example, statements of Air Force leaders in "Can't Get There From Here," *Armed Forces Journal International* (September 2000), 4–5.

[14] A good discussion of rotational dynamics is Gregory V. Cox, *Keeping Carriers Forward Deployed: Harder Than It Seems* (Alexandria, VA: Center for Naval Analyses, 2000).

[15] A key issue raised in Roger Cliff, Sam J. Tangredi, and Christine E. Wormuth, "The Future of U.S. Overseas Presence," in *QDR 2001: Strategy-Driven Choices for America's Security*, ed. Michéle Flournoy (Washington, DC: National Defense University Press, 2001), 235–262.

[16] *QDR Report*, 26.

[17] Ibid., 27.

[18] Ibid.

[19] Ibid.

[20] Ibid.

[21] Ibid., 35.

[22] On "arc of strategic instability," see Stephen J. Flanagan, Ellen L. Frost, and Richard L. Kugler, *Challenges of the Global Century: Report of the Project on Globalization and National Security* (Washington, DC: National Defense University Press, 2001), 16–17.

[23] *QDR Report*, 2.

[24] Ibid., 11.

[25] Ibid., 12.

[26] Ibid., 17.

[27] Ibid., 21.

[28] Ibid., 13–14.

[29] Ibid., 14.

[30] Ibid., 14–15.

[31] Ibid., 15.

[32] Albeit, the United States has made considerable progress in getting permission to selectively base small numbers of troops and aircraft in the former Soviet republics in Asia for the purposes of antiterrorism operations.

[33] Chairman, Joint Chiefs of Staff, *Joint Vision 2020* (Washington, DC: Government Printing Office, 2000).

[34] These are the "transformation initiatives" described in *QDR Report*, 42–47.

[35] Characteristics of the "joint response forces" can be found in *QDR Report*, 32–34.

Part IV

Globalization and Naval Operations

Chapter 16

From Effects-Based Operations to Effects-Based Deterrence: Military Planning and Concept Development

Edward A. Smith, Jr.

T he concept of globalization and its potential for changing the world rest on an
enormous and routinely ignored assumption: that conflict between nations
and within nations will not impede globalization from taking place.[1] Conflicts,
whether economic, political, cultural, or military, are the antithesis of globalization
and can be its undoing. Conflict can halt or reverse progress in crucial areas and can
be used by those who oppose globalization to do just that. Also, and perhaps of greater
concern to the United States and the West, free trade and travel, a vital element of globalization, both make countries and regions beyond the conflict area vulnerable in ways
that they have never been before.

In this new emerging global environment, deterrence becomes ever more important. It is no longer sufficient for military forces to be able to "fight and win" the wars.
The potential impacts and fallout from conflicts in such a tightly linked world could well
be so great that fighting and winning could be too little, too late. Rather, globalization
will shift the focus of military efforts to preventing wars from occurring, containing
those conflicts that do occur, and discouraging the emergence of a hostile peer competitor.

Edward A. Smith, Jr., is a senior defense analyst in the Boeing Company's Washington Studies
and Analysis Office. Before retiring as a captain in the U.S. Navy, he served in combat and on numerous planning staffs. He was one of the principal authors of the U.S. Navy's seminal ... *From
the Sea* (1992) and wrote the Navy's *Anytime, Anywhere* vision (1997). He recently completed a
book on effects-based operations, entitled *Effects-Based Operations: Applying Network Centric
Warfare in Peace, Crisis, and War,* to be published by the Department of Defense Cooperative
C4ISR Research Project.

Forward Engagement

For the United States, deterrence in the new global environment has two dimensions: homeland defense and forward engagement. The question of U.S. homeland defense is under closer scrutiny today than ever before because of the potential for terrorist use of weapons of mass effect and because globalization has made threats easier to conceal and our ocean buffers less effective. Accordingly, forward engagement and its component military missions of presence and crisis response have emerged from its Cold War "containment" mentality to become a primary and increasing focus of military efforts.[2] The two are closely related. For decades, our national security strategy has maintained that a forward defense is the best way to defend the homeland. Simply put, challenges and unrest are best met and dealt with far from our shores. However, in the turmoil of the post-Cold War and of an expanding globalization, this strategy of forward engagement has taken on new meaning.

Our national strategy of forward engagement has rested on three interlocking pillars: economic, political/cultural, and military. Over the decades of the Cold War, our national security strategy often described these pillars in terms of U.S. efforts to promote free enterprise, democracy, and regional stability. But, amid accelerating globalization, especially in the period since the end of the Cold War, it has become particularly apparent that the reality is somewhat different.

The expansion of free market economies in the post-Cold War period was not so much a function of U.S. efforts to promote any ideology of free enterprise as it was of the attraction that such an economic model held. The reason is simple. The free market economy is essentially a complex adaptive economic system that has proven to be a much more efficient producer of goods and services than command economies or more traditional economies. Moreover, the continuing introduction of new information technologies stands to enhance further the flexibility and efficiency of the system. Since economic efficiency manifests itself in the form of expanded quantities of goods and services, the free market system visibly translates into not so much "mass consumption" as into "consumption by the masses," the idea that everyone can aspire to material goods and some semblance of "the American dream." It was this prospect that drew Eastern Europe from its Soviet tutelage, and it is this prospect that is laying the foundation for fundamental changes in China and elsewhere. It is worth noting that the driving force for this change is not any American effort to proselytize an ideology of free enterprise. It is rather a self-sustaining movement driven by the hope of a better life.

Similarly, democracy, the equivalent complex adaptive political system, has proven attractive to a changing and more knowledgeable world. Democratic forms of government have demonstrated the flexibility both to cope with the accelerating pace of change that accompanies the free market and information-driven globalization and, at the same time, to ameliorate the potential abuses of the free market system. The idea of a continuing "revolution at the ballot box," thus, is no longer the luxury of the affluent countries. It has become a political necessity in a world whose pace and awareness of change have been accelerated by information technology. Yet it is not just democracy that has proven attractive. A globalization of the free, mass culture of the West has been fostered by pervasive media whose reach has also been rapidly expanded by the revolution in information technology. This media revolution not only has heightened demands for more open government but also has reinforced the demand for the goods that a more efficient free market economy can bring. Once again, it is not an American effort to create democratic bastions and a free press that drives the change, but rather the spread of information and an increased awareness of how life might be different and how governments might be better.

These changes are accepted as a matter of course in the United States and the West where they have long since taken place. However, the farther away from the North American and Western European epicenter we proceed, the more likely the "revolutions" are to produce changes in cultures and institutions that can be destabilizing. Eastern Europe's transition to a free market economy, for example, caused major economic difficulties spanning a full decade, while the states of the former Soviet Union continue to grapple with an economic aftermath that is still far from resolved. Similarly, the progressive Westernization and secularization of Arab culture has evoked a violent reaction by many in the Arab world who see it as a threat to their very identity, a reaction that lies at the root of the anti-Western terrorism of an Osama bin Laden. Finally, in areas such as China, there is an uneasy combination of an economic revolution-in-progress and a political stagnation that has yet to be resolved and that may prove destabilizing in the decades to come. In general, the further we move toward the periphery, the greater the change in other societies is likely to be, the greater the degree of instability likely, and the further they will probably be from completing the transition that we have begun.

Put in this light, our forward-engagement strategy takes on a somewhat different character. It presents a paradox. It seeks both change and stability. Free market economies and democracy require some modicum of both internal and external stability to succeed. Yet those same changes tend to produce instability both inside the countries experiencing the transition and in the region in general. In fact, we might hypothesize that the greater the instability a country must confront during the transition, the longer it is likely to take to complete and the more unrest it is likely to propagate both to the countries surrounding it and to the world as a whole. This latter threat, most apparent in the attacks of terrorists such as Osama bin Laden, underlines what is perhaps the most basic rationale for our espousal of forward engagement. The United States is clearly the prime target for any antiglobalization backlash, a problem that directly menaces not only the American diaspora overseas but the homeland as well. Thus, by adopting regionally focused strategies aimed at aiding the needed transition to a successful and speedy conclusion, we lessen the danger that we ourselves face at home and abroad.

. . . And the Military Role?

How do military forces contribute to this strategy? Obviously, the long-term solutions to the unrest must derive from the economic and political transformations that are now taking place. In other words, the economic and political/cultural pillars of our forward engagement—not the military pillar—are the source of any ultimate solution. Only they can deal with the root cause of the instability. They aid the transformation to the degree that American and Western businesspersons, teachers, diplomats, and journalists are free to play an active role. But this role, like the transformation itself, demands stability to succeed and is retarded by instability such as the threat of anti-Western terrorism, particularly that directed at overseas Americans.

This is where the military role in forward engagement really comes into play. We have been looking at the military role in forward engagement in terms of reactive operations, such as the evacuation of American nationals threatened by local terrorism or crisis responses to block local aggression, whether internal or external. However, these are at best operations to deal with the symptoms of the instability that we have been discussing, and they do not reflect the most fundamental and essential role of our forward and forward-deployable military power. That role is to act as the guarantor of stability. It is to buy time for peaceful change to succeed, and—to the degree that military power can do—to ensure that peaceful change remains *peaceful*. In this equation, military power is not itself the solution; the solutions lie instead in the economic and sociopolitical domain. The military pillar enables those solutions to be effective by promoting stability and keeping the peace. Stated in more formal terms, the role of military forces in forward engagement is to establish a local regime of conventional deterrence within which the needed economic and political changes can take place.[3]

How do these economic, political, and military roles combine to carry out forward engagement? Based on the above discussion, we can conceive of forward engagement in terms of three overlapping economic, political, and military circles, as depicted in figure 16–1. The overlaps are instructive. For example, by opening new markets, businesspersons also engage in people-to-people contacts that help to expand cultural and political frontiers. Yet, despite the overlap, the role of the businessperson clearly remains economic. Similarly, a diplomat might aid the business in opening new markets while remaining still a diplomat advancing U.S. policy. The same is true of military power. One role of a military force in forward engagement, for example, may be to take up a position permitting it to evacuate American nationals. Or that force may keep the

Figure 16–1. **Forward Engagement**

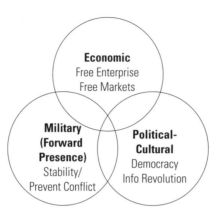

seas safe for commerce or engage people-to-people contacts such as exercises with local militaries. However, we need to be clear that each of these examples do not describe the entire military role but only the areas in which military operations overlap the economic and political spheres (that is, where military forces are used to support directly the actions of sociopolitical or the economic pillars). In this sense, they are missions that are peripheral to the actual and most critical military role: creating and maintaining local stability. It is this conventional deterrence role with its forward presence and crisis response components that is the true focus of the military pillar of forward engagement. It is also the hinge upon which a peaceful globalization process turns.

Deterrence

After 40 years of the Cold War, when issues of strategic nuclear deterrence loomed large, there is a natural tendency to think of the word *deterrence* with an implicit *strategic nuclear* in front of it. It is, therefore, useful to understand how that strategic nuclear aspect has shaped our thinking in order to distinguish how *conventional* or *non*strategic nuclear deterrence differs.[4]

Strategic Nuclear Deterrence

The strategic nuclear deterrence with which we have become so familiar rested on the threat of retaliation. It worked because each nuclear-armed power could threaten its opponent(s) with consequences that were so catastrophic that the opponent was deterred from taking action, a so-called balance of terror. As secure second-strike capabilities emerged, this threat of retaliation even became the security of mutually assured destruction, in which the ability to retaliate with horrendous consequences was guaranteed, even if one side managed to deliver the first blow. Despite numerous crises and a number of tense military confrontations between the great powers during the Cold War, the consequences of a nuclear exchange combined with the acknowledged difficulty of controlling the escalation of even a tactical nuclear exchange made a strategic nuclear conflict unlikely.

Deterrence worked—or so it seemed at the time. In reality, the scale of the consequences involved had another dimension embodied in the failure of the Dulles Doctrine.[5] In effect, the horrendous scale and scope of the consequences involved in nuclear warfare set a credibility threshold. A nuclear war that would result in the annihilation of a large portion of the populations on both sides could only be credibly threatened to the degree that the issue at hand threatened the very existence of the nuclear powers qua nations.[6] The greater the risks incurred by the threat, the more important the interest threatened had to be if the threat were to be plausible.

Beneath this sliding and uncertain threshold, conflicts occurred in which the vital interests of the superpowers were not directly threatened, and, thus, strategic nuclear capabilities appeared irrelevant. The list of such Cold War substrategic nonnuclear conflicts included everything from conflicts in Vietnam and Afghanistan, to the Czech and Hungarian revolutions, to the Grenada operation. To some extent, the United States attempted to deal with this threshold by evolving variants on the strategic nuclear deterrence concept, such as graduated response or flexible response. However, in actuality, the United States resorted to a second, parallel level of *conventional* deterrence centered on forward presence and rapid response to crises through global power projection.

Conventional Deterrence

For purposes of this chapter, the term *conventional deterrence* is used to encompass everything but strategic deterrence (that is, nuclear, weapons of mass destruction or mass effect). Perhaps in a reflex left over from Cold War strategic nuclear deterrence thinking, we tend to think of conventional deterrence as a miniature version of strategic deterrence, that is, in terms of destroying predetermined lists of targets, but simply using conventional rather than nuclear weapons. However, there are really two aspects to this conventional deterrence: the threat of retaliation and prevention.

Threat of Retaliation

Like its strategic nuclear counterpart, conventional deterrence uses threats of retaliation.[7] Even though this retaliation may be executed with conventional weapons, the deterrent value of the threat follows much the same logic as strategic nuclear deterrence. It threatens by holding at risk something an enemy holds dear. However, where strategic nuclear arms may hold whole societies at risk, the conventional threat is limited to finite targets or actions that only in some vast aggregate might purport to hold a society as a whole at risk.

Nevertheless, over the years, the potential impact of that conventional threat has been multiplied by a succession of developments. First, the development of precision weapons made it possible to destroy very specific targets reliably without a large-scale effort. Then, nodal targeting bolstered the impact of precise weapons further by enabling warfighters to focus destruction where it would create the greatest impact. Finally, the introduction of cruise missiles into the equation meant that these precisely targeted strikes could be accomplished without risking personnel—a change that made the political credibility of military action far greater.

However, retaliation-based conventional deterrence runs into some of the same problems encountered in retaliation-based strategic nuclear deterrence. In accordance with international law, the general principle of *repelling* attack is well accepted, but the legality of retaliation after attack is not. The threat of retaliation, too, has a credibility threshold. The same sort of logic applies to conventional threats as to those at the strategic nuclear level. The less direct a challenge is to the interests of the state retaliating, the less credible a threat of a large-scale retaliation is likely to be—just as in the case of the doctrine of massive response.[8] But there is a second, almost catch-22 aspect to this. The less the magnitude of the damage threatened, the lower the consequences and risks attached to the conduct that is to be deterred. The lower the risks, the more likely the deterrence is to be tested—time and again—just as long as, from the adversary's perspective, the risks remain manageable and do not outweigh potential gains.

To make matters worse, this risks-versus-gains calculation is likely to be heavily colored by what the adversary wants to see and by a consequent tendency to rationalize away the possibility of retaliation entirely or to minimize its impact. The more intellectually isolated adversary decisionmakers are, the more such rationalization is likely to occur.[9] In short, conventional-level threats of retaliation cannot be counted upon to be very effective deterrents.

Prevention

The more successful approach to conventional deterrence appears to revolve instead around prevention (that is, the foreclosure of a reasonable prospect of success for a potential adversary). Logically and quite apart from any risks-versus-gains calculation, if protagonists perceive that they simply cannot succeed in the action being contemplated, then the action becomes pointless, and they probably will not proceed.[10] The idea of prevention and specifically its military corollary, foreclosure, creates a very different arena for the use of military power as a deterrent.[11]

What type of conduct are we trying to deter, and how might an adversary use the capabilities at his disposal to that end? The central thesis in these questions is that if we know what a challenger is attempting to do and how he intends to do it, we can array the capabilities to prevent him from succeeding and thus deter him. This thesis is open-ended on several levels. It does not necessarily imply a military-on-military confrontation or a formal campaign of any sort, though both may be part of an effort to foreclose. It does not necessarily imply a violent use of military force, though the actions of military forces are very likely to be part of any response. And it may be either an active foreclosure in which specific moves are countered or a passive foreclosure in which a continuing local security calculus discourages the development of challenges.[12]

In essence, prevention focuses on one specific kind of effect: the idea of foreclosure. We bring an observer to conclude that a challenge to stability simply cannot succeed. As the above discussion of foreclosure indicated, there are two types of foreclosure to be considered, passive and active.

Passive Foreclosure

Passive foreclosure is embodied in Mahan's concept of a "fleet in being," that is, a force or capability that cannot be ignored by observers and whose very existence shapes what the observers do. In the context of forward engagement, this would mean becoming a key and unavoidable part of a local security calculus as the player whose intervention would change the entire risks-gains assessment in any given situation. This kind of deterrence would likely be played out at two levels. At its most basic level, it would be represented by all of the challenges to local stability that would not be made even though potential local challengers might otherwise have had the capability and will to do so. At a more advanced level, it might be reflected in decisions not to develop the military or other capabilities to threaten stability in the first place.[13] Stated simply, because the fleet in being was there and able to intervene, neither the capabilities nor the strategy that they were to support could have failed. Forward-presence forces and alert crisis-response forces such as an airborne division or an air expeditionary force are examples of forces whose very existence becomes part of a local security calculus and thus who contribute to passive foreclosure.

Active Foreclosure

Active foreclosure centers on the actions taken by forces to block or negate an emerging challenge to stability or one already in progress. It is, thus, the form of deterrence that occurs when passive foreclosure fails. Active foreclosure is evident in the active positioning of forces either to ensure that a challenge cannot succeed or to raise the level of risks to the point that continuing the challenge no longer makes sense. Such foreclosure can involve combat operations as well as maneuver.

Active foreclosure is embodied in crisis-response operations, whether by forces already forward deployed at the onset of a challenge or by those readily deployed from distant bases outside the region. Indeed, the history of crisis responses by U.S. military forces—more than 500 over the past 50 years—is an illustration of active foreclosure at work. In many of these responses, especially those in the Mediterranean in the late 1960s and early 1970s, there was in fact a conscious effort by participants to follow a strategy of *interposition*.[14]

We can define *conventional deterrence* in terms of threat of retaliation and prevention, but how do we describe what is going on, and how might we better use our military forces to build a stable local regime of conventional deterrence? This is the core challenge for the emerging concepts of network-centric and effects-based operations.

Effects-based Operations

In studies of both network-centric operations and effects-based operations, the emphasis has been on combat operations. This is certainly understandable; after all, the only military force worth having is one that can fight and win. Yet in the context of globalization and the requirement to deter conflict, to focus solely or almost exclusively on combat operations would be a mistake. If the mark of a truly successful 21st-century military force is the ability to win without fighting or to prevent the combat in the first place, then clearly network-centric and effects-based operations must be examined in that light. A concept of effects-based operations that is focused on *actions* rather than weapons or targets enables us to do just this and to take a theoretical and conceptual look at the use of military forces and network-centric operations not only in combat but in peace and crisis as well. If we conceive of effects-based operations in terms of operations in the cognitive domain, we can take a step in this direction and provide the basis for looking at how military operations might best be orchestrated to shape behavior so as to keep the peace and prevent war. Finally, by understanding the role of network-centric operations in this same context, we can assess the applicability of network-centric warfare to the core military problem of deterrence.

In the context of globalization, the ideas of effects-based deterrence, effects-based forward engagement, and effects-based presence all seem eminently reasonable. After all, deterrence is inherently a question of human behavior, and behavior is the ultimate focus of effects-based operations. Any concept of effects-based deterrence, then, must address the question of how the actions we take, military or otherwise, influence behavior in peace and crisis with or without the violent use of military or other force. Not only is deterrence a logical focus of any study of either network-centric or effects-based operations, but it is also a reflection of the operational realities of our current world. Deterrence has been a core mission of our military forces, and it is the mission toward which most of their day-to-day activity is directed. Moreover, if we consider that deterrence is far from being a peacetime-only mission that disappears when combat begins but is instead a fundamental facet of military operations in combat as well, then understanding the role of effects-based operations in deterrence becomes even more essential.

What are effects-based operations? The concept itself is not new. It is certainly reflected in the focus both of Sun Tzu and of Carl von Clausewitz on decisions and outcomes. It is also reflected in *nodal targeting* that seeks to create second- and third-order effects from the destruction of targets. However, the previous discussion suggests that effects-based operations need to be considered in a context that is much wider than targeting and that points to the utility of a broad definition along the following lines: *Effects-based operations* are coordinated sets of actions directed at shaping the behavior of friends, neutrals, and foes in peace, crisis, and war.[15]

The actions that may be undertaken by military forces certainly include combat and specifically strike operations, but military forces clearly do a great deal more. They shape the behavior of observers by their actions or by their very presence in a particular area. These actions and presence often are deliberately planned to create a particular effect that usually is not limited to overwhelming and confounding enemies, but extends equally to supporting friends and reassuring neutrals. The basic building block for creating effects is what might be termed an *action-reaction* cycle (see figure 16–2), that is, a two-sided interaction in which each side tries to persuade its opponent to adopt a particular course of action while dissuading it from alternate, unacceptable courses of action.[16]

These action-reaction building blocks can be seen at each level of interaction—tactical, operational, military-strategic, and geostrategic—and appear to be operative in a long chain of military operations in peace, crisis, and war, but especially in the crisis responses of U.S. military forces over the last 50 years. In fact, a closer examination of the history of those operations points to six basic rules of thumb that define an effects-based operation. The first three of these basic rules are analogous to those of a game of chess, while the last three point to a degree of complexity that is well beyond that of a chess game—specifically because they center on the human dimension of the interaction. This human dimension is where the nonlinear payoff for effects-based operations occurs and is the same focal point that we must address in trying to create a regime of conventional deterrence.

Rule One: **All actions create effects; some create more than others.**

In a chess game, it is not necessary to take a piece to have an effect on the game (for example, putting an opponent into check). Many or indeed most of the moves undertaken during a game probably do not involve taking an opponent's pieces, but instead are directed at foreclosing a future move threatening a future move, or positioning a

Figure 16–2. **Basic Building Block: Action-Reaction Cycle**

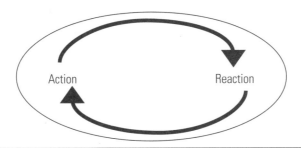

piece for a future move that we might like to take. Similarly, in an effects-based operation, it is not necessary to destroy an opponent's capabilities to have an impact or to create an effect. Action-reaction cycles need not involve combat, and even those effects-based operations that do include combat can consist primarily of the noncombat operations. This does not exclude destruction of capabilities and targets. It says rather that there is much more to creating an effect than striking a target and that effects-based targeting is but one way to accomplish our ends.

During many of the crisis responses of the last 50 years, particularly those involving some form of military confrontation, opposing sides maneuvered for tactical advantage while avoiding actual combat. During responses by naval forces in particular, the coordination of participating ships, aircraft, and submarines bore all of the marks of maneuver warfare because of the agility, flexibility, and responsiveness of action required. In many respects, they resembled nothing so much as a modern version of 18th-century positional warfare in which the object was not necessarily to destroy the opposing army but to outmaneuver it so much as to foreclose any possibility of success and, thus, force its cession.[17] The encounters were, in essence, *maneuver warfare— without the warfare.*

Rule Two: Interactions are likely to be multiple and produce a cumulative effect.

A chess game is comprised of a series of moves by two players that continue to capitulation, checkmate, or a draw. Moves do not occur in isolation. Pieces may be lost, formations dispersed, and gambits foreclosed in each move with the effect of that move setting the cumulative parameters for succeeding moves. This effect may be felt either immediately by forcing a reaction in the next move, such as putting a king into check, or it may not be felt until later in the game, such as in the impact of the loss of a powerful piece. As the latter implies, the ultimate effect of a move cannot be entirely known. Thus, a move undertaken at one point in the game may well produce serendipitous or unintended consequences in subsequent moves.

The action-reaction cycles of crisis reactions follow a similar pattern. The effect of an action may be immediate, an impact that either independently or when added to what has gone before causes a change in the current mode of operation. Or it may be long term, a part of a continuing effect that will ultimately produce an aggregate impact. This indicates that, just as in a chess game, the action-reaction cycles in an effects-based operation cannot be isolated. The effects created are likely to be multiple and to multiply over time with the effects created by each cycle carrying over into the next cycles to create a cumulative overall effect.

Rule Three: Any action-reaction cycle will have both active and passive participants.

The idea of cumulative effect can be taken a step further. Consider that, in tournament chess, the impact of a move is not confined to an individual game but may influence the play in succeeding games. Each move or series of moves may be studied for the novel way in which they deal with a given situation on the board or for what they say about an individual player's thinking. These lessons can then be carried over to other encounters. But this learning process is not confined to the two active agents; rather, it applies to all those who can observe the game or who can study it in some fashion. In this manner, the impact of a move may extend not only to rematches of the same two players but also to all who can put the knowledge to use for their own ends, whether in future competition with one of the two players or with a different player.

The same principle applies to effects-based operations. The actions undertaken stand to have an impact upon the active participants in a given action-reaction cycle and over the course of their interaction and upon any other party who can see them. Again, this impact may be immediate, as in the case of the next challenger in line, or over the longer term by influencing the way in which military or political strategists assess an encounter and adjust their own thinking for future interactions. Thus, the effect of an action may assume many different dimensions that stretch far beyond the initial battlespace and the original players, and over the longer term may have an impact, in fact, that greatly exceeds the original effect on either of the active players.

Whereas the above rules have clear analogies to a chess game, they also hint at a more complex interaction that transcends the kind of competition reflected therein. This dimension is reflected in the remaining three rules that focus on the human dimension of the interactions, that is, the way in which each action-reaction cycle is seen and understood by both active and passive observers.

Rule Four: **Action-reaction cycles occur simultaneously in multiple dimensions.**

Crisis interactions by military forces typically demonstrate three degrees of complication that are not reflected in the chess game used to illustrate the first three rule sets.

First, the action-reaction cycles in crises occur at four different levels: tactical, operational, military strategic, and geostrategic. At the tactical level, for example, there may be air-to-air intercepts or maneuvers and countermaneuvers by ships. At the operational level, there may be a face-off between an entire fleet and an opponent's air and sea forces in the area. At the military strategic level, there may be some form of confrontation between the two opposing militaries as a whole with each alerting and/or drawing assets from outside the immediate geographic area of the interaction. And at the geostrategic level, the military interactions will likely be paralleled by a standoff between the two governments that stretches into the domestic and international political arena and, perhaps, the economic arena as well.

Second, as this latter point suggests, action-reaction cycles are not limited to the military arena but will extend at a minimum to the political dimension. At the diplomatic-strategic level of the international arena, for example, the Department of State will need to formulate a plan for explaining operations and U.S. policy to area allies and neutrals. At the State Department's operational level, the foreign policy apparatus would coordinate the execution of this plan in international forums, such as the United Nations (UN) and individual embassies. At the tactical diplomatic level, different action officers in each venue would be called upon to act. On the domestic political front, similarly, the White House would be obliged to present the situation to Congress, the press, and the American public. Where either the tools of the interaction or its results might be economic in nature, that too must be coordinated.

Finally, as the above implies, this military, political, diplomatic, and economic chess game must be played simultaneously on all levels.

Thus, in place of a single chess game, we have multiple, complex interactions on four levels and in three or more arenas. This only stands to reason, since the objects of the effects we seek to create—the actors and the behavior to be shaped—also reside on four different levels of a military arena and at multiple levels of the political and economic arenas.

Rule Five: **All actions and effects at each level and in each arena are interrelated.**

If we consider, further, that actions and effects cannot be isolated but, as noted in rule two, produce cumulative effects, then all of the above interactions—at each level, from one level to the next, and from one arena to the next—must also be treated as interrelated and cumulative. In crisis operations, for example, the impact of an aircraft being shot down and its pilots captured is instantaneously felt from the tactical through the geostrategic level in the military arena and spreads just as quickly into the political and diplomatic arenas. Moreover, in this already complex interrelationship, we must consider that, again as indicated in rule two, effects are cumulative over time. By extension, all these interrelated effects at each level and in each arena are cumulative over time. Thus, it is not only what we do now that might create an effect on another level or in another arena, but also how that action (or actions) appears in the context of what we have done in the past—again at each level and in each arena. The effect of any individual action stands to be enhanced or diminished by the cumulative context within which they were undertaken.

If we combine these last two rule sets, what emerges is something akin to a nesting of actions and effects as shown in figure 16–3. An air intercept, for example, would appear as an interaction between two active players, but that interaction takes place in the context of an air picture that might include other, for the moment, passive aviation players in the area. Moreover, these passive air players might be paralleled by other passive ground, surface, and subsurface players who constitute the land and sea maneuver forces for the operations, or they might be paralleled by the reconnaissance and communications assets that present a space context. When all of these elements are taken together, they comprise the operational picture of the joint commander. That operational picture in its turn is but one theater picture that, when combined with the situations presented by supporting commanders and other theaters of operation, comprises the military strategic dimension of the U.S. response.[18] Finally, this entire military picture is but one facet of the overall national problem that must be considered at the level of the President and his senior advisers.

The decisionmaking problem is further complicated by the fact that effects overlap from one arena to the next, as illustrated in figure 16–4. In the example given, not only would the Department of State have been left to explain the nature of a tactical action in the event of a shoot-down, but its actions in other areas might well have affected the access to allied ports and airfields that Joint Task Force units enjoyed during the interaction. Thus, actions by an Embassy action officer in one country might well have an impact on tactical actions undertaken by military forces off the coast of another country entirely.

The challenge is to coordinate the interrelated actions of all of a nation's actors at each level and in each arena so as to create the desired overall effect. Since no level of the nest can be isolated or ignored so long as its actions can be observed, this coordination is at best complex. The decisionmaking challenge is especially great as it involves coordinating diverse and often seemingly unconnected actions in three arenas so as to create a coordinated effect. As if this were not complicated enough, the

Figure 16–3. **Effects Nesting**

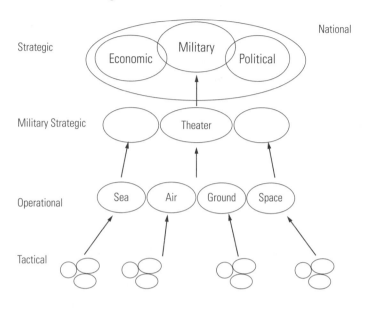

Figure 16–4. **Effects Nesting: Multiple Overlapping Nests**

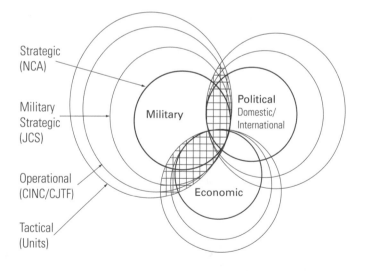

actions that can be undertaken by the military, political, and economic instruments of national power have vastly different time lines associated with their exercise. If political, economic, and military actions must be timed to occur either simultaneously or in some specific sequence, then no matter how fast the military operations may be in theory, they will still be held hostage to the slower pace at which governing action, usually political, can take place. For example, a military response may be held pending the presentation of the U.S. case at a meeting of the UN Security Council or, even longer, pending international enforcement of a quarantine. But the reverse can also be true. Political actions such as the announcement of a quarantine may be held up pending the arrival of the military forces needed to enforce it.

Rule Six: Effects have both physical and psychological dimensions.

It should be readily evident that the effects discussed above are both physical and psychological in nature. In the context of attrition-based warfare, the word *effects* implies *physical* effects that are usually measured in terms of capabilities destroyed, such as the degree of target destruction or, more narrowly still, in the sense of weapons effects. However, this physical destruction clearly can have another dimension beyond straightforward attrition. The destruction of a particular set of capabilities can cause a cascade of impacts as, for example, the destruction of a rail junction might translate into a blockage of rail lines of communications and, in turn, into a decrease in the production of war matériel. Even more, that physical destruction might cascade into an impact on how the enemy thinks and acts, for example, by disrupting his plans and forcing him to look for alternatives. That is, the physical action might produce a *psychological* effect—one of the central ideas in nodal targeting efforts. In this cascade from the physical to the psychological, the destruction of the rail junction might become a stimulus that the foe must take into account in his decisionmaking process.[19] The physical effect thus takes on a human dimension. If the destruction and subsequent disruption are particularly sudden or severe, or if there are no good alternatives, then the physical destruction may shock the opponent. Or it may induce an incapacitating despair either immediately or over a period of time. The physical destruction creates a psychological effect that can stretch far beyond the immediate tactical impact of the targets destroyed.

The earlier rule sets provide additional dimensions in this cascade of effects from the physical to the psychological.

First, they suggest that physical actions at the tactical level can create a chain of physical and psychological effects that will echo at the operational, military strategic, and geostrategic levels of the military arena and that may extend to the domestic and international political arena as well as into the economic world.

Second, they indicate that effects are not restricted to the active participants in the physical action but extend to anyone who can observe it.

Lastly, they indicate that the actions that create this rippling effect do not have to involve destruction of physical capabilities; they merely need to be observable.

The effect, then, derives not only from what physical destruction is meted out but also how an audience perceives the action, which stretches far beyond the immediate battlefield.

From Observations to Perceptions to Effects

Our starting definition of effects-based operations proposed that they were directed at shaping behavior. Destroying forces and capabilities obviously can shape behavior by foreclosing options that an actor might have otherwise exercised. But both the definition and the rule sets just discussed indicate that this is a rather narrow view of effects somewhat colored by attrition-based thinking. Moreover, such shaping presupposes the existence of a state of conflict that would countenance the destruction. If we are to understand how effects-based operations might apply to peacetime operations and deterrence, much less to realize their full potential, we must instead think in terms of actions or stimuli to which an opponent might react. Such actions encompass the destruction of forces and capabilities and extend as well to all observable military force moves and thus serve as a stimulus. In this context, the question of how actions are perceived is critical. But how does this process of perception and reaction occur?

The transition from the physical to the psychological effect is the result of observations made, of the perceptions that those observations in turn create, and the decisions made—consciously or unconsciously—as a result of those perceptions. In this chain, the physical action is only the first step. If the behavior of the observer is to be affected, obviously, he must "see" what has been done and this process of "seeing" will itself be shaped by the sensors or other means available to discern what is going on. Given that neither sensors nor displays of sensor data are ever perfect, the observer is unlikely to see *exactly* what the action was. Rather, he will be reacting to some variation of that action as presented through the filters of his sensors, his displays, and his doctrine and organization for conducting surveillance and relaying data and information.[20] The better his sensors and surveillance system, the closer to reality the observations are likely to be. Then, the observer will need to correlate what he has observed with other observations so as to create a bigger picture of the situation. This picture may fuse inputs from other levels of conflict and other arenas, each of which will have its own variation on reality. Then, the observer will attempt to contextualize the observation, comparing it with other actions and any known history of previous actions. Finally, he will attempt to make sense of the observation in light of a personal experience base shaped by culture, education, and position in an organization. This process of making sense of the external stimulus and assessing the options open, in turn, will lead to a decision as to a course of action.[21] In this entire process, there are only two inputs over which we may exert any control—the initial action or stimulus and the history of our own previous actions in the same geographic or operational area. Our challenge in creating a stable deterrence regime is to orchestrate both sets of actions to produce the deterrent state we desire, recognizing that each action we take will be filtered both by what our target decisionmaker can and cannot observe and by his individual predilections. The observations, perceptions, and decisions we seek, thus, are a function not only of *what* destruction might have been meted out or what action taken, but also of what was observed, that is, *how* it was done. This implies that, from the standpoint of an observer, our physical actions have at least six different attributes, each of which may contribute to shaping perceptions.

Focus. There is of course the question of the physical nature of the action itself. For the observer, this *what* is the aspect of the stimulus that should provoke a specific line of questions. What was done? What capability was destroyed? How does it affect my options? In short, this *what* encompasses most of the reactions on which nodal targeting or a carefully crafted target list might focus.

Force Applied. However, not only what is done, but also how it is done—that is, what kind of force was used—will affect an observer's reactions. Was the stimulus primarily political, economic, or military? Did it demonstrate a willingness to take risks and undertake a commitment (for example, "boots on the ground")? Or was it a relatively risk-free surgical missile strike? The *what* also extends to the kinds of questions toward which maneuver warfare might be directed. Where did the force interpose itself? What action did it take, and how might that action inhibit my operations? As these latter questions imply, the *what* need not involve destruction but must be something that the observer would have to take into account in his decisionmaking.

Scale. The scale of the action has two dimensions: the scale of the effort involved in the action and the scale of the impact. Together, they set the quantitative size of the problem that the adversary must deal with. Obviously, a single missile might destroy a target and create an effect, but it seems evident that the use of 100 missiles on the same target will—for good or bad—create a different impression upon the observer. Similarly, using 100 missiles against one target has a different significance from the use against 100 different targets. Moreover, the effect created by the same scale action will vary from one observer to the next and from one situation to the next. Was a 100-missile strike a disproportionate response? Was it sufficient to induce shock and to deter future actions, or were a greater scale of effort and impact required? Would a strike by a single missile against a single target convey an impression of weakness or of confidence in an ability to detect and strike exactly the right target at exactly the right time? While these questions underline how separate the question of scale is from that of focus, they also point to the need to tailor the scale to a particular set of observers and a particular situation.

Scope. Scope encompasses two dimensions, one geographic and the other operational. The geographic scope of the action defines the physical area within which the foe may be obliged to act or within which he may be vulnerable. The broader the area, the greater his problem is likely to be. For example, a barrage of 100 missiles aimed at a single target will be observed to present a different challenge in many respects than a similar scale strike directed at 100 separate targets spread across the breadth of a country.

The operational scope defines the battlespace—air, sea, undersea, ground, space—and warfare environments in which the foe might be challenged. However, it also defines those warfare areas in which the foe is not likely to be challenged and in which opportunities might be provided to counter or balance a challenge, such as mine warfare. In general, the greater the number of warfare environments, the more stressing a threat is likely to be seen to be. A complex, multiple threat simply will tax an adversary's assets and command and control to a greater degree and is more likely to leave him guessing where the full weight of an attack or maneuver will be placed.

Timing. Timing encompasses three different dimensions: speed, duration, and what might be called synchronicity.

Speed is the ability to execute an action or reaction rapidly enough to create a desired effect. This may mean creating an operations tempo so overwhelmingly fast as to allow no coherent response and, perhaps, to induce shock or chaos. Or it may mean being able to react quickly enough to changes in either the warfare environment or the political arena to foreclose courses of action that the foe might wish to take.

Duration (or the period of time over which an operation can be sustained) is how long a foe might have to endure an action. An action that can only be initiated once or cannot be repeated very often invites the foe to ride it out and then return to previous behavior, whereas an operation that has no such limitation means that the pressure is not going to end before the unacceptable behavior ceases.

Synchronicity (or the ability to cause actions to occur at exactly the right time or in exactly the right sequence) is the level of difficulty of the military problem that the potential foe faces. The wider the diversity of closely timed operations the foe might face, the more difficult it will be for him to counter them and the more likely it is that they will result in a cascade of problems that he will be unable to control.

Visibility. Any action that is observed, whether intended or part of our effects-based plan, will create some effect. Conversely, any actions that are not observed, no matter how carefully orchestrated, will create no psychological effect.[22] The visibility of our actions is key. If the foe cannot see the scale, scope, and timing of our actions—including virtual actions—or cannot get a report of the actions in a manner that is timely enough to enter his decisionmaking process, then these actions will have no effect beyond their attrition value, if any. But that is not all. If the dimensions of our actions are misreported and misperceived, the observer may overreact—a particularly dangerous prospect when confronting a foe armed with weapons of mass destruction. Knowing what the foe or observer is likely to see, therefore, is a critical factor in effects-based planning.

While there is clearly a need to appreciate what observers are likely to see and react to, there is also an opportunity in having an ability to do so because it provides one more variable that can be manipulated and controlled to create the desired effect. If our knowledge of the observer's sensor system and how it operates is sufficient, for example, we may be able to orchestrate our actions so as to control what is observed and when.

Keeping the *Peace* in Peaceful Global Change

How do the effects-based operations that we have been describing translate into an effects-based deterrence that can simultaneously thwart would-be aggressors and reassure friends and neutrals? It should be clear from the preceding discussions that deterrence itself is inherently effects-based. After all, it is in great measure about shaping human behavior and the use of physical actions to create psychological effects, a process that takes place in the minds of regional decisionmakers and local publics. The decisions made and courses of action pursued arise from an aggregation of economic, political, cultural, and military perceptions (both rational and emotional components) that may take place over a period of years or even generations. In part, the perceptions reflect assessments of physical capabilities such as the economic and military power of local and extraregional contenders and of patterns of past behavior by these actors that might indicate how the physical capabilities may or may not translate into action. In part, they reflect human elements such as national pride, trust, and friendship. It is within this context that we must consider conventional deterrence and its twin components of presence and crisis response.

How do military forces build a deterrence regime? We need to recognize from the start that all conventional deterrence is local; it is about the balance of power and threats in a given area, that is, about a *local* security calculus. Our challenge is to create a local constellation of military capabilities that would force a would-be aggressor to ask a series of hard questions about his intended course of action and then bring him to conclude that aggression could not succeed. The effects-based discussions above provide some key insights as to the nature of this local security calculus.

First, any deterrence regime will rest on local perceptions of our action, actions observed in the past, actions undertaken on a day-to-day basis, and actions that might potentially be taken in the future. The key words in shaping a local security calculus are *actions* and *perceptions*. Having a capability to thwart or reassure is not sufficient to deter. We must also demonstrate both the capability and a willingness to use it in such a way as to be readily observed by all concerned. Also, we must do so on a regular basis if we are to translate a past history of action into a current and continuing expectation of future action whenever and wherever needed.

Second, as this implies, building local deterrence is a continuous process. Effects are cumulative over time. There is no sharp dividing line between peace and war but rather a continuous chain of observed interactions that stretches from routine peacetime presence to combat operations. Effects-based operations do not begin with combat or even target planning. Peacetime actions are critical to wartime success—as well as to avoiding conflict in the first place. It is the peacetime actions that condition observers as to what to expect in the face of a threat. The history of those actions constitutes the experience base upon which crisis and wartime perceptions and, thus, effects are built. If we wait for a crisis or war before beginning to shape perceptions, we are likely to discover either that it is too late or that we must first overcome a local perception of *in*action before our crisis actions will be taken seriously.

Third, the military components of deterrence do not exist in isolation. All actions—tactical, operational, military strategic, and geostrategic, as well as political, military, and economic—are interrelated and will be seen by others as a whole.

Fourth, choosing the right actions to undertake and creating the right effects depends on knowing the observer sufficiently to have some idea of how those actions will be perceived by the intended audience and a larger world audience.

To shape the security calculus of a would-be foe, therefore, we must first understand how our capabilities and actions constrain or fail to constrain would-be local aggressors. Then we must force home the perception by demonstrating repeatedly both the capability and willingness to act. It is this combination of capability and willingness that constitutes the credibility of any form of deterrence. In short, forward-engagement forces must by their makeup and actions define the military problem that a would-be foe must overcome in order to achieve a successful outcome. The five attributes of an action examined earlier provide the framework for setting the dimensions of the local military problem. For example, the focus on what we and our allies can do collectively or separately forces the would-be aggressor to address the kinds of risks entailed by aggression. The scale of military power we collectively can bring to bear forces him to question whether he has sufficient numbers either to reach his objectives or to defend his homeland. The scope of what we can do forces him to assess just how far he is likely to have to spread his efforts. The speed of what we can do, especially how fast additional forces can be brought to bear, sets his time line and thus increases or decreases the challenge involved. The duration of the effort we can sustain forces him to assess the "what-ifs" of an operation that is not swiftly concluded and his own ability to withstand a long war.

Designing Forces that Deter Aggression

If these are the general dimensions of the perceptions that we are trying to create, then what do they say about the forces we might need? That is, based on the above discussion, what kinds of military power and in what combinations could prevent successful aggression?

Logically, the military power making up our deterrent relies on a balance of both the forces and capabilities of local allies[23] and those of the nonregional players that demonstrably would be applicable to a local crisis. The half-century history of real-world crisis responses by U.S. military forces indicates that these latter forces are really of two kinds. The first is the visible forward military presence by which the physical capabilities become an insistent part of local perceptions and thus the local security calculus. The second is the crisis response by which these capabilities and the still greater extraregional capabilities of major powers are brought into the balance. All three of these forces play roles in shaping the local security calculus and must be thought of in terms of interlocking capabilities. For example, the greater the capabilities of the local allies and the greater their will, the less reinforcement will be required from nonregional players to maintain the same level of deterrence. The greater the capabilities of the forward-deployed forces, the less dependent the deterrence will be either on local capabilities or those deployed from distant bases. Finally, the greater the forces that can be rapidly deployed, the less reliant the deterrence will be on either local or forward-deployed forces. In this equation, the local forces component is the independent variable. That is, the amount of outside intervention required to maintain deterrence and stability in the area will depend on the level of local capabilities rather than the reverse. The United States, for example, might encourage local allies to take a greater part in their own defense, but in the last analysis it cannot control what they actually do or the proficiency and will that they bring to the task.

However, as the discussion of shaping the would-be aggressor's challenge points out, there are several additional dimensions that must be added to the equation.

First, as previously identified, there is the question of speed, that is, of shaping a would-be aggressor's time line for military or other operations. How immediate must a response to aggression be in order to collapse the aggressor's time line to the point that his objectives can no longer be realized? For the aggressor, there will probably be a trade-off between the scale of the objectives and consequent scale of operations on the one hand and the time required to achieve those objectives on the other. The bigger the required operation, the longer the operation will take to mount, thus the more warning opposing forces are likely to have and the more likely it is that heavy forces stationed outside the region will enter into the balance. The smaller operations and more limited objectives will require less time, thus the less warning opposing forces will have and the more likely that any response will depend on forces already in the region and those lighter forces that can be readily deployed. This is where the balance in the local deterrent comes into play. If smaller operations by a would-be aggressor (for example, cross-border or guerrilla operations) could be met immediately and decisively with some combination of local forces and forward-deployed forces,[24] then the aggressor is likely to conclude that aggression cannot succeed. If he were to increase the size of the operations so as to overwhelm the forces in the region but, in so doing, were to increase the warning time to the point that a decisive intervention by forces from outside the region became possible, then he would lose again. By contrast, if our deterrent were to rely heavily upon a very large force from outside the region, but the endeavor took 6 months to accomplish, then there would be a high probability that the aggressor could achieve his objectives before we could act effectively and the deterrent effect would be minimal.

Second, the key to the deterrence equation is not forces, but capabilities that are applicable to particular warfare challenges. Capabilities that cannot or will not[25] be brought to bear do not figure in the local security calculus. Capabilities that cannot be used against the threats at hand (for example, long-range cruise missiles in an urban conflict) will likewise be discounted in any local security calculus. This aspect of the equation is made all the more important by the likelihood that the would-be foe probably will have based his calculations on an identified capabilities and political niche within which he believes he can compete with local and nonregional forces. This means he will have tried to identify warfare areas in which our collective capabilities are lacking or weak. Mine warfare and urban warfare are obvious examples. To this end, the regional deterrent must include diverse capabilities from low end to high end that permit local, forward-deployed or forward-deployable elements to deal with such threats. Then, these diverse capabilities must be constantly adapted and demonstrated as the opponent continues to seek new niches for competition.

Third, the question of applicability extends likewise to simply getting forces to where they can be effective. If the potential adversary can impede or deny access to needed facilities or to the local battlespace, then the capabilities that are subject to denial are also likely to be discounted. The potential impact on deterrence here is threefold. If the foe calculates that his denial efforts can impede either the arrival of forces from outside the region or the movement of forces within the region for some amount of time, then that time will be added to his operational time line, giving him extra latitude and a greater probability of success. If he calculates that he can restrict access to local bases and, thus, force nonregional forces to operate from distant areas, he will likely discount the scale, speed, and, perhaps, duration of those capabilities in his balancing of risks. Finally, if he can either deny access entirely or inflict sufficient damage to force the nonregional powers to withdraw or reconsider their involvement, then capabilities that can be so denied are not likely to deter. The converse of this calculation is that, to the degree that we can demonstrate an ability to deal with area denial threats, our deterrent is made more credible.

As the above should make clear, there is no *one size fits all* or *cookie-cutter* combination of military capabilities and actions that adds up to a stable local conventional deterrence regime. Asymmetry in the stakes of the contending parties must be evaluated and included in the calculus. The requirements will also vary from one region to the next, and they will vary over time to reflect the changing constellation of potential adversaries and allies in each region. Perhaps the two most critical factors in the creation and maintenance of deterrence are the knowledge of friends, foes, and neutrals who let us adapt the deterrent to the changing challenge, and the visibility of our responses to that changing challenge. Friends, foes, and neutrals must see what local allies and we can and will do if the capabilities are to enter into their security calculus and become part of the deterrence regime. Moreover, they must see those capabilities demonstrated repeatedly enough to become a norm in their perceptions and thinking.

Conclusions

The scale and scope of the changes now going on in the world are so vast that we cannot really hope to control them. These changes have been destabilizing to the point that one of the greatest challenges of forward engagement will be to keep the peace in a peaceful change. Thus, although we tend to think of globalization in economic or perhaps political and cultural terms, it in fact rests on a critical military mission: to maintain local and regional stability by deterring those who would either disrupt a peaceful change or turn instability to their own advantage.

The military task of creating and sustaining a broad regime of conventional deterrence to support globalization is essentially about shaping and reinforcing behavior. That is, it is inherently effects-based. The long history of presence and crisis response operations by U.S. forces points to a series of effects-based rules of thumb to guide us in this task:

- Actions, rather than weapons, do most shaping. The effects wrought by destroying a foe's forces and capabilities, however good these might be, are confined to combat operations, whereas the effects created by actions both span the spectrum from peace to crisis to war and determine in large part how wartime weapons effects will be seen and understood.

- The effect of actions is continuous and cumulative. There is no sharp break between effects-based operations in peacetime and those in war. Rather, each move contributes to or detracts from the overall effect we seek to create: a stable local conventional deterrence.
- Our actions will have an effect on all who can see them, not only upon a would-be foe but also upon friends and neutrals.
- Actions to add to or detract from deterrence can take place on four levels of military operations—tactical, operational, military strategic, and geostrategic—and with actions in the international and domestic political arenas and the economic arena as well.
- Actions at any level or in any arena cannot be isolated from those in other levels or arenas. Observers will tend to look at all of the actions in all of the arenas and on all levels, whether intended or unintended, supporting or contradictory, as a whole. To create a coherent overall effect, coordination is imperative.
- Our challenge is to translate physical actions from simply being there to conducting combat operations into the psychological effect of deterrence and an expectation of stability. The psychological effect is the fruit not of our actions themselves but of what observers see and perceive those actions to be and to mean. To shape behavior rather than react to it, therefore, we must orchestrate not only what we do but also how we do it.

All these considerations apply to shaping a local security calculus that will prevent aggression. However, prevention hinges on confronting adversaries with a military problem that they cannot solve. The United States and its local allies must present a capability to pose so many risks as to outweigh any possible gain; a speed of reaction that affords no opportunity to attain military objectives; a balance of diverse capabilities that leaves no warfare niche to be exploited; and a certainty that all capabilities will be brought to bear regardless of any effort to deny access.

In practice, this is an interlocking threefold task. Local partners provide the basic capabilities to defend themselves and deal with internal instability. Balanced forward-deployed forces provide the ability to deal with smaller, swiftly moving threats, a capacity to multiply the capability of local forces (for example, with information and sensors), a means of ensuring or obtaining access for heavier forces, and a day-to-day presence to reinforce deterrence continually. Forward-deployable forces, in turn, provide both a wider array of capabilities and the scale and endurance to overwhelm an adversary's efforts. The key to this whole endeavor is visibility. What an adversary cannot see or has not seen recently will probably not enter his calculus. Thus, it is not sufficient only to *have* capabilities; they must be *demonstrated* time and again if they are to be a continuing part of the calculus we wish to shape.

The tasks outlined above are not new; nor is the concept of effects-based operations. What is new, rather, is a change in the emphasis in how we approach the tasks that underline the interrelationship of the political, economic, and military elements of forward engagement, and, perhaps, a new urgency generated by both the promises and perils of globalization. Both demand a new attention to an old problem: how to prevent wars and shape a more stable peace.

Notes

[1] The relative stability of the last decade has become the foundation for incipient globalization, much as the *Pax Britannica* became the foundation for the globalization of commerce that occurred in the 19th century.

[2] This does not detract from the need to deal with eventual peer or near-peer opponents. Rather, it indicates that, over the next few decades, the day-to-day operation of the forward-engagement strategy is likely to focus on a succession of local and regional crises. Furthermore, the history of the Cold War underlines that, even in the midst of peer competition, a substantial proportion of military efforts remains focused on dealing with local crises—a task that may be worsened by a peer opponent's efforts to foment further unrest to its own ends.

[3] A frequent criticism of military crisis responses is that 6 months or so later, there is no discernible change in the local situation as a result of the intervention. However, if we consider the military role not as one of solving the underlying problem but of buying time for an economic or sociopolitical solution, the intervention and its outcome take on a new perspective. It may not be the intervention that failed at all, but the inability of the political and economic tools to provide a lasting solution in the period allotted.

[4] See Edward Rhodes, "Conventional Deterrence," *Comparative Strategy* 19, no. 3 (July-September 2000), 221–254.

[5] The 1953 proposal by the Eisenhower administration Secretary of State, John Foster Dulles, was that the United States would meet conventional attacks with a massive—read *nuclear*—response.

[6] This was the essence of the French argument for an independent *force de frappe*, which was deemed a credible response to any threat to France where a U.S. response that endangered American cities might not be.

[7] Given the United Nations charter injunction against retaliatory warfare, such retaliation is usually couched in terms of self-defense, but the logic remains the same.

[8] In the case of conventional deterrence, most probably the unacceptable result will not be the annihilation of society, but rather a political fallout that can be counterproductive and that would negate the effect that the using power had sought. Obviously, this sets up a sliding scale. The more important the interest to be defended, the more likely any negative fallout is to be acceptable. The less important the interest, the more likely it is that possible negative repercussions will outweigh any gains to be made from successful deterrence.

[9] Although it can be postulated that such a rational process of calculation would have little to do with the reaction of an irrational decisionmaker, it is probably more precise to say that any senior-level decisionmaker is, by virtue of having attained that position, rational. This does not mean that the rationality would match Western notions of a rational decisionmaker, but simply that some form of rational calculation will almost inevitably be involved in perceiving and reacting to the threat of retaliation. It is upon that calculation, in whatever form it takes, that deterrence relies.

[10] Rhodes, 222–223.

[11] The concept of foreclosure bears resemblance to the new preemptive approach to national security outlined by President George W. Bush in his speech at West Point on June 1, 2002. In encountering the emerging enemies of the 21st century, the President maintained, "If we wait for threats to fully materialize, we will have waited too long." However, U.S. defense policy has yet to develop and describe this approach fully. It may be assumed that significant differences may exist between the concept of foreclosure discussed in this chapter and the new U.S. defense concept. On President Bush's speech, see Elisabeth Bumiller, "U.S. Must Act First to Battle Terror, Bush Tells Cadets," *The New York Times*, June 2, 2002, 1,6; and Mike Allen and Karen DeYoung, "Bush: U.S. Will Strike First at Enemies," *The Washington Post*, June 2, 2002, A1, A8.

[12] While prevention is likely to rest on the political as well as the military components of that local calculus, the focus here is on the military dimension and specifically how effects-based operational concepts might help us better use military forces to deter.

[13] These are both negative events, that is, actions that did not take place because they were deterred. Since one cannot logically prove a negative, the perennial difficulty with passive foreclosure is proving that deterrence did in fact take place.

[14] This occurred most notably in the Soviet-American confrontations during the 1967, 1970, and 1973 Middle East wars.

[15] This is a definition of effects-based *operations*. Effects-based *warfare* would be a subset of these operations applying to wartime operations, while effects-based *targeting* would be in turn a subset of effects-based warfare.

[16] In the draft book from which this essay is drawn, the author uses a detailed example drawn from the January-April 1986 operations off Libya, omitted here for brevity.

[17] According to the Barry M. Blechman and Stephen S. Kaplan study, this figure stood at 331 as of 1978. As later updated by Siegel and the Center for Naval Analyses using the same methodology, the figure had reached more than 400 crisis responses by U.S. military forces by the end of 1996. See Blechman and Kaplan, *Force Without War: U.S. Armed Forces as a Political Instrument* (Washington, DC: The Brookings Institution Press, 1978).

[18] In response to the Libyan crisis, for example, the *Saratoga* carrier battlegroup was dispatched from the Pacific theater and later, the *America* battlegroup reinforced the operation from the Atlantic theater.

[19] See Edward A. Smith, Jr., "Network Centric Warfare: What's the Point?" *Naval War College Review* 54, no. 1 (Winter 2001), 64.

[20] The latter determine how sensors are deployed and used, what is collected, and how it is handled.

[21] As this implies, the course of action decided then becomes a reaction or set of events that we in turn will have to consider as a stimulus proceeding through our own sensors and cognitive process to another decision and reaction in what can be seen as a spiral of actions and reactions.

[22] This was expressed in one wargame in the comment, "What if the other guy doesn't know he has lost?"

[23] These local capabilities include both those applicable to conflicts with would-be external aggressors and those to deal with internal unrest.

[24] This combined capability might rest, for example, principally on local forces but with U.S. forward-deployed forces providing more sophisticated support such as sensors and communications to enhance those capabilities.

[25] For example, forces that require access to ports and airfields to operate or that require overflight permission to reach an area are only a factor to the degree that the necessary permissions can be assured. Similarly, a vast strategic nuclear arsenal matters little in a local security calculus if the perception by would-be aggressors is that it will not be used short of a WMD attack on the nuclear power's homeland.

Chapter 17

Globalization under the Sea

William J. Holland, Jr.

The new realms of space and under the sea are the hallmarks of the globalization of the U.S. Navy that began after the end of World War II. These elements differentiate today's maritime reality from that experienced by the Royal Navy in the previous 2 centuries. Submarines, nuclear power, and mines make today's world much more problematical than the one the Royal Navy ruled. When coupled with Earth-orbiting satellites, nuclear submarines make the current and future global maritime environment substantially different than even that which existed in the first part of the 20th century.

While distance has yielded to technology, the ocean's complexity remains challenging. Scientists who deal with the ocean attest:

> The ocean is not transparent. This bold, flat statement, eminently testable and tirelessly tested, carries a truth that has far-reaching, even global implications. Both a blessing and a curse to undersea warfare, it may, indeed, be the preeminent catch-22 of geopolitical strategy today.[1]

The opaqueness of the ocean to light and electromagnetic energy make it a singular environment. Operations in this medium have a character unlike any other. Invisible from all but the most sophisticated sensors, which have to be based in the same medium, ships operating inside the ocean generally disclose their presence only by leaving their adversary "a flaming datum," a sinking or severely damaged opponent. No technology is even forecast that will change this situation.

Thus visibility in the ocean is asymmetric in two ways. The ocean is more visible to advanced powers than to others. The combination of space-based sensors, sea-bottom sensors, wide area mobile sensor arrays, and long-range acoustic detections by

William J. "Jerry" Holland, Jr., is an adviser and consultant on command, control, communications, computers, intelligence, surveillance, and reconnaissance (C⁴ISR) matters, submarine warfare, and nuclear weapons policy for a number of individual clients, government agencies, and policy organizations. He retired as a rear admiral after 32 years of naval service, including 13 years in command of nuclear submarines, submarine squadrons and group, and the Submarine School. He is currently vice president of the Naval Historical Foundation and recently edited *The United States Navy* (Washington, DC: Naval Historical Foundation, 2000).

submarine sonars make the oceans vastly more visible to the United States than to any other country. This visibility extends even into the littorals of other countries.[2] Submarines, the other facet of this asymmetry of visibility, like space-based sensors, are expensive and require skilled work forces to operate. This is not a description of systems likely to be available to Second and Third World nations. While the interior of the sea will remain a challenging environment for all, the asymmetry in this global environment will likely continue to favor the United States for years to come. The proliferation of antiaccess sensors and weapons systems that may be a characteristic of military globalization has not penetrated the open ocean.

The Nuclear Powered Submarine: Queen of the Seas

The foremost change in maritime warfare since World War II has been the appearance of a new capital ship. Operating as a true submersible with an endurance of months at high speed, submarines propelled by nuclear power have the ability to go to every part of the ocean. No place is too far. Forces need not be dispatched far in advance of a perceived need, nor is a global infrastructure of logistic ports necessary. The nuclear powered submarines dominate the maritime scene to an extent never before seen. This situation has few precedents and thus far only one war, the Falkland Islands campaign, to demonstrate this change to maritime affairs. This war demonstrated that other forces can operate in the vicinity of nuclear powered submarines only with the submarines' acquiescence.[3]

Properly operated, a nuclear submarine wishing to remain undetected is undetectable by any surface- or space-based platform except for chance encounters.[4] Submarines are not now and for the foreseeable future will not be subject to attack by cruise or ballistic missiles, chemical or biological weapons, or electromagnetic pulse. This characteristic makes these submerged platforms ideal bases for strategic weapons and allows them to conduct operations in areas otherwise denied or sensitive.

In 1988, the editor of *Jane's Fighting Ships*, a world authority on the subject, declared that the mark of a first-class navy was possession of nuclear submarines.[5] So pervasive is the ability of the nuclear submarine to dominate the sea that the first and most dramatic effect has been disappearance of surface warships in other than the dominant Navy and those of America's allies. Just the existence of the American fleet of nuclear submarines makes surface warships of all other nations poor investments. American nuclear submarines deter naval arms races more effectively than any line of battleships has in the past. The size of this modern fleet and its continuing improvement set a standard that no one else can reach or sustain and so few try—the so-called dissuasion effect.[6] Even in the United States, surface warships are not designed to fight other surface warships and have abdicated most antisubmarine warfare (ASW) capabilities, making little pretense that they can operate in the vicinity of submarines.

This inherently stealthy platform, unlike a surface ship or aircraft, can operate with impunity in a high threat area without the need for self-defense. Invulnerability is inherent in the medium. This remarkable feature, available in any submarine and demonstrated in every maritime theater since 1914, becomes truly formidable when coupled with advantages of high speed and unlimited endurance. Nuclear submarines have long been used for sensitive operations in littorals because of their ability to operate undetected and to remain unsupported for long periods of time. These kinds of operations, cloaked in much secrecy and double talk, is sufficiently important that, according to public pronouncements and documents, the time devoted to them has increased since the end of the Cold War.[7]

Nuclear power enables submarines to deploy to the ends of the Earth without dependence on any infrastructure for months. This precludes the need to preposition stocks in theater, provides the flexibility to go to whatever area is deemed advisable, and allows the ship to stay as long as necessary. Submarine deployments can be conducted in relative obscurity if desired, and forces can be in place in any littoral of the Atlantic, Mediterranean, or Pacific within a week.[8] Coupling routine operations in areas of interest with this ability for rapid deployment of reinforcements of forces gives the United States great flexibility in shaping the battlespace. Undersea assets are particularly effective in sensing enemy intentions, observing ports and lines of communications, laying the basis for the sensor grid, and negating the effect of antiaccess preparations—including sinking minelayers. While submarines are unlikely to field antiaircraft weapons, the ability of their weapons to interdict airfields is excellent. Versions of the Tomahawk missiles that are designed for just such efforts are particularly effective against unbunkered aircraft. With their short time of flight to target and the launch from unsuspected locations and azimuths, missiles from submarines can be crucial weapons in the first days of operations against an enemy land-based air force, missile launchers, and air defenses.

High speed, unlimited endurance, and logistic independence allow massing of weapons in a theater before an engagement, at the first outbreak, or later as desired. Because submarines can so swiftly close the area of operations, they can bring large numbers of weapons to bear—not in a single platform—but in a number of platforms. During the Cold War, the Navy demonstrated the ability to sortie virtually the entire submarine force not in the shipyard in 2 or 3 days. As a result, this whole force is an available reserve that can mass weapons on scene very quickly and totally independently of political considerations or overseas infrastructure. In a world punctuated by unexpected and unanticipated crises, speed of response and the ability to manage risk become highly sought commodities. These are the forté of nuclear submarines that possess the stealth and agility to deploy without fanfare, adding nothing to media pressures to heighten tensions or shorten time lines.[9]

Future submarines will be expected to carry "countermine capabilities, unmanned undersea vehicles, [and] strike weapons," as well as all the necessary weapons and sensors to conduct antisubmarine warfare.[10] Such hulls will not be smaller or less costly until some technical breakthrough such as direct conversion of fission to electricity comes to fruition, reducing equipment size.

Diesel Boats Forever . . . but Not for Us

As Paul Scully-Powers states, ocean opaqueness is a double-edged sword. While not every country with a navy can build or operate nuclear powered submarines, conventionally powered submarines are a realistic mechanism for many nations without an otherwise functioning navy to challenge, locally and for some finite time, the dominance of the United States. While the piston engine and the biplane are anachronisms in the air, conventionally powered submarines represent a weapon system that can be thwarted only after substantial investment of resources and time by even the most advanced navy. Though lacking the mobility, endurance, and sensor suite of modern nuclear powered submarines, conventionally powered submarines operate in the same opaque medium and, at least for a time, can be as stealthy, difficult to detect, and lethal a threat to surface ship operation in their vicinity. The obvious disadvantages of slow speed, time limitations to their stealth, and restricted endurance severely inhibit the utility of the conventional submarine. But where the area of conflict can be predicted or is geographically constrained, these submarines are a substantial challenge to even the most dominant maritime power.[11]

However dangerous in their areas of operations, conventional submarines are essentially "mobile minefields" lacking both the endurance and the speed to be useful in maintaining forward presence or power projection. With a speed of advance of 10 or 12 knots when stealthy (and that is very wearing on the crew) or even 18 to 20 knots surfaced, conventional submarines are slow to reach station. Once on station, they cannot be easily moved or quickly reinforced. For the United States, a country that expects to fight in distant oceans or deep seas, conventionally powered submarines are expensive anachronisms. The fate of the Royal Navy's *Upholders* (fine conventional submarines constructed under the rubric of "more conventional is better than fewer nukes") is a lesson in economics. These submarines served for a very short time before being laid up and offered for sale, cheap, to any buyer. Those who advocate that the United States should buy or build conventional submarines are heirs to the traditions of Thomas Jefferson's gunboats or the coast defense battleships that served no purpose. Though less costly to build than nuclear powered submarines, with no utility these ships are very expensive.[12]

ASW Is Still Job One

The only serious threat to America's sea lines of communications/commerce (SLOCs) comes from submarines. With the Navy's emphasis shift to strike warfare, antisubmarine warfare has died as a matter of priority in every warfare community. Only the maritime patrol air and the submarine forces pay more than lip service to ASW. Maritime air faces a problematical future as its aircraft, the venerable P–3C, begins to reach the end of service life in 2005 with no evidence of a program to replace the aircraft.[13] This leaves submarines as the primary Navy ASW vehicle and the only carrier of a reliable and proven ASW weapon.

This deficiency in naval capability bothers few in the Navy and even fewer leaders in the Government. American dominance at sea has been unchallenged for so long that most are dazzled by the illusion of instantaneous and total American naval hegemony. However, no navy can cope in a short period with even a few diesel submarines, particularly if they are positioned along a SLOC before a crisis. With no ability to confront the U.S. fleet directly, the only recourse that nations have in trying to oppose this country at sea is either to attempt to interdict the SLOCs or to make it difficult to establish a blockade or strike the homeland from close ashore.

Antisubmarine warfare is as much a matter of time and endurance as of technology and operational procedure. The conventionally powered submarine can be thwarted, but only through patient endurance and careful use of resources on the side of the dominant navy.[14] One observer comments that "Even if the U.S. Navy can detect and destroy enemy submarines it is unlikely that it could do so before they inflict unacceptable damage on both the U. S. fleet and allied shipping."[15]

Should a forehanded enemy choose, deployment of conventional submarines to chokepoints or harbor exits distant from the area of conflict can be devastating, as the Germans proved in 1942 and 1943. Properly operated and adequately armed, two not unsubstantial or easily satisfied requirements, conventional submarines could be major deterrents in flow of forces out of the United States and into theater. Karl Doenitz did not defend his littorals by holding his U-boats in the North Sea; he did it by sending them to the east coast of the United States and the middle Atlantic. Sooner or later an opponent with submarines, probably conventional ones much like those used by the Germans 60 years ago, will challenge U.S. maritime dominance off Savannah, Sandy Hook, the Strait of Gibraltar, the channels into the Strait of Malacca, or any one of a dozen other sites where trade routes pass. When that occurs, the calls for ASW forces will be frantic, and no one will respond but the submarine force and its auxiliaries, the Integrated Undersea Surveillance System's towed array ships. The ability to counter submarines depends on training, equipment, and weapons. Such investments are being made only in the submarine force of the U.S. Navy.

The Fleet Ballistic Missile Submarine: Invulnerable Base for Strategic Arms

Nuclear submarines are the ideal bases for strategic weapons and will remain so as long as nuclear weapons exist and the oceans remain opaque. Undetectable and invulnerable, they offer no incentive for an enemy to try to strike first because the ocean provides complete concealment. Equally important, by basing missiles in an invulnerable mode, any enemy is assured that the owners of such forces will be able to strike back after an attack of any kind. Now that the characteristics of the missiles carried on submarines (for example, range, accuracy, readiness, and communication connectivity) are as good or better than those based on land, there is little reason to support other weapons systems. Able to attack any point on Earth from their operating areas, fleet ballistic missile submarines (SSBNs) will continue to provide the most effective disincentive to the use of nuclear weapons.[16]

The British have led the way toward rationalization of national nuclear weapons forces by moving all of their deterrent weapons to sea, closing the land-based missile sites, and retiring bombers as strategic weapons systems. Land-based missiles are natural targets both for missiles and terrorists while no longer having any attribute superior to their sea-based brethren. Every country having nuclear weapons that can build and operate nuclear powered submarines will probably imitate this French initiative except perhaps Russia. Because of its continental mentality and vast space allowing land-based missiles to be mobile, Russia may remain an exception.[17] There, the ratio of land- to sea-based weapons will be as much a matter of cultural heritage as any military or political analysis. China has been trying to make a sea-based missile system work for a number of years and will, eventually, deploy an operative missile on a submarine. Both India and Pakistan have nuclear weapons and missiles, operate conventional submarines, and have hopes of someday being able to operate nuclear submarines. It is not unreasonable to assume that they will eventually achieve the goal of putting their strategic nuclear weapons on a submarine platform.

The extent to which one country is seen as being able to hold at risk another's seaborne strategic weapons is a major issue in this equation. While this is a matter of perception as well as expertise, there is no question that the United States believed that it could threaten the sea-based strategic forces of the former Soviet Union. At the same time, the United States also believed that its SSBNs were absolutely secure and invulnerable to interdiction by any foreign power. Exercises at sea under real conditions indicated both of these beliefs were well founded.[18]

Unless there is an abolition of nuclear weapons, a most doubtful scenario, the next fleet ballistic missile submarine will be designed in the coming decade. As the total number of weapons deployed decreases, questions about the number of needed ships will be in the forefront of this design. Part of the equation that makes up the invulnerability of these weapons is the number of platforms at sea at any time and the difficulty inherent in trying to threaten all of those simultaneously to create a convincing first-strike scenario. Ten submarines is generally accepted as the very minimum to deploy an untargetable mass while allowing some maintenance.[19]

Scouting: Watching without Being Seen

Submarine ability to conduct surveillance and reconnaissance has long been veiled in mystery—as any good intelligence operation should be. But the present emphasis on design of hull number 5 of the *Virginia*-class as a platform dedicated to intelligence gathering and reconnaissance gives some indication of past successes and future expectations. While the exact nature of the modern submarine's intelligence gathering, scouting, and reconnaissance functions remains closely held, a current statement of the capability by Commander, Submarine Force, U.S. Atlantic Fleet gives some indication of the capability: "We now have the ability to collect information in ways that no one else can . . . stay on station a long time . . . [and] integrate what they collect at a level of sophistications that you just can't do with a machine."[20]

Submarine sensors complement space-based sensors and in some cases can detect activities that space-based or air-based sensors cannot. The synergism between space sensors and the sensors carried on and deployed by submarines grows as their complementary abilities are exploited and respective limitations recognized. While some space-based systems will become more capable in detecting emissions of interest on Earth, detections will continue to depend upon a cooperative target, that is, one big enough, loud enough, in the frequency being watched, and so forth. The presence of a space-based system sensor can be predicted well in advance of its arrival. The submarine on the other hand operates without notice and even when suspected to be in the vicinity is often ignored by those targeted. In addition to finding information on manners and mechanisms that would be concealed if their operators were conscious of the presence of an observer, the submarine can detect and act upon data found in real time. Low power communications, for example, are more likely to be intercepted by small antennae close aboard than by a large antenna hundreds or thousands of miles away.

Some submarines, the USS *Jimmy Carter* for example, will have a flexible ocean interface that will allow submerged launches of a number of various kinds of payloads. Special forces unmanned and manned underwater vehicles are part of these. Other capabilities that hold great promise in the globalized world include sensor devices on the ocean bottom, communications links using fiber cable laid on the seabed, and ocean engineering machinery for retrieving and planting equipment.

Submarine Reconnaissance: Forward Node of the Expeditionary Sensor Grid

Submarine intelligence gathering and scouting, normally started long before the battlespace has begun to blossom, are not the same as serving as a node of a sensor network providing near-real-time data. Submarines can bring a synergistic combination of on-board sensors, manned and unmanned deployable vehicles, off-hull land, sea, and air sensors, and special forces that can become the forward elements of the theater's expeditionary sensor grid. Unlike space-based sensors and long-range airborne assets, submarine sensors have agility and staying power. Submarine sensors form a segment of this sensor network that can be moved wherever needed with little regard to threat or logistics considerations. In the Falklands campaign, for example, a submarine operating close inshore off the Argentine airbase served as the air early warning sensor.[21]

In addition to on-board sensors and analytical personnel, the submarine promises to bring a number of sensors to the preparation of the battlespace by deploying families of unmanned devices. Exploitation of the undersea environment and coupling to space-based assets promise to make any part of the globe as visible as home waters. Among the future prospects are unattended ground sensors to detect radio frequency transmissions, particularly low-level personal communications, acoustic and seismic sensors to indicate movement, and thermal sensors to indicate presence of people or machinery. Increasingly sophisticated small unmanned undersea vehicles for mine detection and oceanographic survey are projected. Unattended sensors on the sea bottom and afloat will become key sensors in observing enemy maritime operations in areas of potential conflicts, important to cue ASW actions and countermining. With lives of hours or days and refurbishment without risk to the delivery platform, these devices can be covertly laid to allow preparation of the battlespace in near real time without alerting the enemy.

Improvements in signal recognition, data stowage, knowledge-based comparison, data compression computer processing, and communications will allow sensors to be deployed in small packages yet be able to describe where they are and much of what they detect without transmitting data for analysis. Such capabilities will open a new realm of tactics. Combining data from both space and submarines in near real time is a technique perfected years ago when the targets were the Soviet surface fleet and the weapon was the Tomahawk Attack (Sea) Missile. The same techniques can provide inputs to the expeditionary sensor grid. Since the platform doing the sensing is also capable of launching weapons and supporting special forces operations, the reaction time to developments sensed is reduced to a minimum.

Special Forces: Getting In and Out without Being Seen

No more avid proponent of exploitation under the sea exists than the special forces that use the submarine as a delivery system for surreptitious entry ashore. The submarine provides adequate space, sufficient communications for planning and execution, and assured access to the area of employment. This capability will be more important in areas where land bases within aircraft operational range of targets are unavailable or denied by political considerations. The ability to place special forces near targets, without exhausting the physical condition of the forces and without alerting the enemy, is likely to grow in importance. Where operatives provide intelligence from ashore, low probability of intercept (low power spread spectrum) communications directly to the submarine and then to the special forces is realistic and particularly attractive.

With the advent of advanced swimmer delivery vehicles, small battery-powered submarines, accomplishing these tasks is easier because the submarine can remain further from shore while putting the special forces close to the beach before having to swim. The limitations of past miniature submarines are addressed by the mother ship—a stealthy source of electrical charging, air, and equipment space.

Beyond the well-recognized special forces operations against land targets, submarines can also bring ocean engineering techniques to exploit the ocean bottom. Particularly intriguing for these diver operations are schemes to exploit enemy sensors or to move enemy mines.

Thwarting Antiaccess Strategies: Penetrating the Defended Littoral

Much of the current promotion of short wars through rapid attack assumes the United States will control the air and sea before the conflict begins. But access to a defended littoral—like most battles—will be sequential, not simultaneous. The United States and its allies will have to fight their way in, sometimes against heavy odds. Countries intending to defend themselves against attack will create perimeters fortified by submarines, mines, land-based over-the-horizon sensors, antiship cruise missiles, theater ballistic missiles, antiair defenses, tactical aircraft, and command and control systems secure from distant interception. Eventually technologies already identified will allow defense to seaward of 100 miles or more by any moderately adept country. In this environment, the survivability of surface ships becomes problematic at best.[22]

Submarines and their associated underwater vehicles offer the necessary mechanisms to overcome an antiaccess strategy. The advantages of the stealthy nature of the submarine in this situation cannot be overstated. Development of a capability to detect submarines, let alone classify and attack them, is immensely expensive and difficult. Few countries have mastered it and then only for limited periods of time and after great expense. It does not exist today.

Stealth permits submarines to act as the key that unlocks the door when opponents adopt antiaccess strategies. With no ability even to detect a submarine, an opponent is helpless to defend itself against the threats that such a vehicle can present. "Pushing back entry points and interdicting forces"[23] have no meaning for submarines. The stealthy aspect of the submarine allows it to operate with impunity in areas that are too hazardous for other forces. The strike weapons that the submarine can bring to bear raise the assured cost of opposition limiting the effectiveness of an antiaccess strategy. Further, open literature demonstrates that the presence of U.S. submarines can be inferred in any country that has a littoral, and the threat from submarine launched strike weapons will be limited only by the time to deploy a number of submarines into the threatened area and to reload them after their initial salvos are expended.

Strike from Inside the Defended Perimeter and the Real Arsenal Ships

The current Navy vision document, . . . *From the Sea*, recognizing there is no competition on the high seas, emphasizes strikes against shore targets. The combination of the strategies advocating early strikes of great precision and concerns for surface ship operations in defended littorals gives weight to providing such strikes from secure vehicles (that is, submarines).

Unlike surface ships, the submarine needs no antiair/antimissile protection and, against likely maritime opponents, few torpedoes. Almost every ammunition stowage, certainly every missile space, can contain a strike weapon. The advantages of nuclear power, enumerated earlier, allow these ships to be deployed, redeployed, or held in readiness, able to transit to any theater quickly. No matter where these ships may be located at the beginning of a crisis or how well defended a littoral may be, any potential enemy will have to consider the weapons that these ships carry will be delivered on their territory and from locations well inside the horizon line of their shores.

The greatest benefits arise when the submarine platform operates for some period of time in a littoral area during crisis buildup and before conflict begins. Conducting clandestine surveillance of the enemy coast and littoral, coupling information from on-board sensors to data from space and air sensors directly with intelligence from databases on board and information supplied from theater headquarters, the submarine and, if embarked, special forces can plan optimum missions well before shooting begins. Should a crisis develop into a conflict, the submarine can approach close to shore ready on D-day to deliver the initial salvos to shock enemy command systems, to overwhelm and suppress the enemy air defenses enhancing the effectiveness of air strikes, and to destroy surface sensors and antiship weapons enabling entry of surface ships into the defended littoral.

Submarines can enhance the effectiveness of other forces in several ways. Attacking air defenses (for example, suppressing them) makes air strikes more effective because fewer planes need be devoted to force protection. Destruction of the enemy theater cruise and ballistic missile weapons, launchers, arsenals, and planes reduces the sizes of subsequent salvos with which the antiair/antimissile forces must contend and reduces the demands on the theater inventory of antiair/antimissile weapons.

Missile inventory is one of a theater commander's major concerns, particularly in the early stages of conflict. Today, attack submarines bring a significant contribution to the land attack capabilities because 80 percent of the magazines of missile-armed surface ships contain antiair/antimissile weapons. In any crisis in which a potential enemy can field ballistic or cruise missiles, this ratio is likely to tip toward more antiair/antimissile weapons. Magazine spaces in surface ships will be most important in defending the ports of entry and in-theater forces logistics bases. Land- and air-based missile defenses are likely to be limited or absent in the opening days of a campaign and during the flow of air and ground forces to the theater. In such cases, missile and air defense will have to be exercised almost completely by the Navy. The most important mission of the Aegis and its follow-on systems will be defending the movement of follow-on forces: there will be few missile spaces available for strike in air defense capable ships.[24]

With submarines furnishing much of the land attack missile capacity needed, surface ship design can be optimized for antimissile defense or other purposes. Furthermore, with submarines clearing the littoral for follow-on forces; suppressing first any enemy warship operations and then air defenses; and attacking land-based sensors, command and control facilities, and missile launchers, the design requirements for surface ships operating in the littoral are greatly eased. Stealth is advantageous, but the expense of design and construction of stealthy vehicles is exponential; cost increases by several orders of magnitude for each incremental gain in target cross-section reduction. For a submarine, stealth is provided by the medium, and while reduction in noise levels to improve stealth is expensive, the order of expense for vehicles operating on or above the surface of the ocean is much greater. No surface ship can ever be as stealthy as a submarine no matter the expenditure, but using submarines to crack open a defended littoral, no surface ship needs to be.

Among the advantages that submarine launched strike weapons bring is their short time of flight. Able to attack from relatively close inshore, these weapons can respond to urgent targets—those that may move or disperse—or highly valuable, strongly defended ones. Weapons launched from submarines inside the perimeter of a defended littoral have the shortest distance to travel, can come from a wide azimuth, and so provide little warning to the defender.

The ultimate shore strike vehicle is, of course, the fleet ballistic missile submarine. With the end of the Cold War, 4 of the 18 Trident hulls were declared excess to American's strategic needs. These redundant hulls, each with about 20 years of ship life left, offer the opportunity to convert them to tactical land attack platforms. The advantages offered by this kind of platform now and even more in the future suggest that these Tridents will be the model for future submarines designed specifically, although not exclusively, for this task. With a crew half the size of *Arleigh Burke*-class destroyers and no requirement for fueling or other logistic support until the magazine is exhausted, the submarine embodies all the attributes desired for the arsenal ship plus invulnerability and sustainability not possible in a surface ship.[25]

Finally, the very existence of the submarines capable of entering any littoral and attacking targets afloat and ashore with powerful weapons should serve as a deterrent to construction of littoral defenses. Like the dominance of the nuclear submarine on the high seas, little can be done to prevent these submarines from accomplishing their mission: discouraging endeavors to fortify the littorals.[26]

Command and Control of Stealthy Forces: Works in Progress

Today's passion for jointness contains a danger in employing stealth vehicles. Submarines, the prototype stealth vehicle, are best employed independently, not tied tightly to the movements of other forces. Submarines can enhance the effectiveness of joint operations (for example, improving the efficiency of tactical air by suppressing enemy air defenses or by countermine operations enabling access by follow-on amphibious forces), but even in doing so need not, indeed *should not*, be maneuvered as units to remain fixed on station or in constant communication. Invariably, attempts to employ submarines by officers not familiar with their attributes are limited by unnecessary requirements placed on operation so that they look like surface ships or communicate like combat air patrol units.

Direct downlink from space-based sensors will inevitably link the sensitive on-scene sensors deployed on and by the submarine with the big picture from overhead. Together, these inputs can confirm or contradict, allow immediate on-scene analysis of data, and provide a basis for immediate action. Rules of engagement for vehicles with these kinds of capabilities will eventually need to incorporate directions to fire on indications at predetermined types of targets and to maneuver without further orders to improve the probability of successful accomplishment of their mission. Development of the tactical concepts for use of these kind of vehicles, whether under the sea or airborne, are still being developed. This development, though, is hindered by the traditional concepts of hierarchical command and control in spite of the doctrinal advocates of decentralized execution.

Space was not the only place where wide area sensors were developed during the Cold War. The threat from the Soviet submarine fleet led the United States to discover and exploit the phenomenon of low frequency sound propagation in the sea, wiring the North Atlantic and North Pacific for sound. Then came movable arrays for use in areas that the fixed detectors could not reach because of geographic shielding or that were outside of the coverage of the fixed arrays. The combination of space-based and in-the-sea sensors created a new information habitat that permitted near-real-time direction of the fleet to avoid or engage likely opponents both on and under the sea. Maritime patrol aircraft and submarines enabled by nuclear power to move rapidly to any area and remain there for long periods unattended became a potent combination that could over time classify and attack, sanitizing an area to allow surface forces to operate there. The Integrated Undersea Surveillance System was the Navy's first sensor grid. This command showed the way to develop remotely sensed data into tactical procedures for others to exploit.

The difficulties of optimizing naval fires with tactical air and coordination with the Air Tasking Order have been identified even in leisurely campaigns.[27] In a major campaign, where weight of explosive, inventory, and target mobility become important issues, the difficulty in trying to optimize utility of individual platforms and weapons will have to be addressed. Not all cruise missiles are equal. In a defended littoral, for example, submarine weapons will have a shorter time of flight than those from surface ships or aircraft that launch outside the defensive perimeter. For small salvo sizes, weapons in a submarine torpedo room should be preferred over those in other ships because they can be reloaded. Presently no mechanism or process takes these considerations into account. As the numbers and types of weapons proliferate, and as total missile inventories decline because of resource constraints, these considerations will complicate weapons allocations and strike command and control.

One of the challenges for operating a fleet that includes dispersed and stealthy forces such as submarines and special forces will be development of command and control processes that optimize the use of each component and coordinates individual capabilities to maximize the total effort. Even within a single service, understanding the contributions and limitations of individual arms is sufficiently parochial that coordination of employment is a skill set hard to develop. As yet, the mechanics of developing the broad understanding for application of force among components while maintaining the necessary skills in the specific warfare specialties have not been achieved. The difficulties are not only related to submarines (though especially acute there) but also to other stealthy vehicles, independent operators such as special forces, and network information systems. Procedures to optimize fires from a variety of platforms on a variety of targets and to employ stealthy vehicles in a centralized decision/decentralized execution mode remain to be created.

Mines and Countermining

Thwarting of amphibious attacks by mines at Wonsan in Korea and off Kuwait in Operation *Desert Storm* demonstrated the effectiveness of mines in the hands of even primitive powers. As discussed in chapter 20 of the present volume, proliferation of mines into the hands of many is a well-identified problem for the dominant navy. Mining is not a trivial undertaking, regardless of mine availability. Far less complex or costly than other antiaccess strategies, unless the field is very thick or defended by other forces, mine utility is limited, and it will eventually be breached. The essence of the problem is *time*.

The most successful and efficient countermining operation is to sink the minelayers. As Admiral Stanley Arthur stated, "First of all, you should never let the guys lay mines if you can prevent them."[28] Laying mines in international waters is an act of war. While obtaining political permission to execute such action may be difficult, submarines have a particular value in their ability to linger, observe, and act. By lying inshore, alert to moves of a potential enemy, linked to space-based or air-deployed platforms that are able to conduct wide area surveillance and thereby able to direct the submarine to the appropriate area, and then to act with short time of flight weapons to sink or totally disable a minelayer, the submarine forms the first line of offense against minelaying.

To make this tactic effective, however, the mindset of the Navy and Department of Defense (DOD) political leadership needs to recognize that laying mines in international waters is an act of war. Attempts to get permission to sink the minelayers during *Desert Storm* failed at high levels of government.[29] Establishing the conditions necessary for offensive action against minelayers before a hostile environment exists is vital. The rules of engagement to be implemented when minelayers are detected must be widely advertised in order to lay the groundwork for a timely decision that may have to be made in the heat of battle—something upper-level leaderships do particularly poorly. The United States should seize the very first occasion in the future when someone lays mines in international waters as an opportunity to demonstrate that such actions are acts of war and will be responded to immediately as such.

Next to sinking the minelayers, the next most effective countermining tactic is sanitization (that is, the process of finding where the mines have or have not been laid). Not entering mined waters is the best defense against an existing minefield. Combinations of space assets, airborne observers, and submarine surveillance can observe the laying of mines with some precision so that major fields can be avoided. Finding and avoiding covertly laid mines that are sparsely separated or drift mines is more challenging. In the presence of minefields with known characteristics but un-known dimensions, approaching from seaward takes time to locate, disable, or move the defenders' mines. Submarines can start covertly before D-day or even in the absence of a conflict or crisis. Among their advantages, submarines are built to withstand great pressures. Also, operating in the sea rather than at water interface (half in, half out), submarines are not as vulnerable to pressure mines as surface ships.[30]

Mine reconnaissance by covert vehicles keeps the enemy in the dark or at least confused as to the location of an intended landing or penetration. Scouting by un-manned vehicles will be vital, and their entry into suspect waters will be an early priority task in any operation against a defended littoral. If the fields can be mapped, at-tackers can maneuver rather than having to attrite the mines. Using the sea as a maneuver space requires early detection so avoidance paths can be established, gaps can be exploited, and countermining plans can be developed. Finding poorly mined areas may require a multitude of sensors—here small, unmanned underwater vehicles will be at their best, keys to preparation of the battlespace. This reconnaissance is best conducted in a clandestine manner so as not to alert the enemy of the proposed pen-etrations. Unmanned vehicles, covertly launched from submarines, are now being pro-posed to examine the near shore, surf zone, and beaches. The procedures and processes to permit follow-ships to penetrate enemy minefields have still to be ex-plored when submarines scout waters.

Mines present a number of interesting tactical opportunities when covert re-sources are used to exploit them. Ideas are in a fledgling state as to how countermin-ing conducted by stealthy activities can contribute to U.S. control of a defended lit-toral. Moving an enemy mine from where it was planted into an area that the enemy plans to use, for example, complicates not only enemy use of the area but also con-founds the command and control system that laid the mine in the first place.[31] Per-mutations for this sort of mental warfare are large and can be effected using covert and overt methods.

The submarine offers great potential as a minelayer in its own right. To mine into port an enemy's seagoing assets is a stroke of great worth when the enemy needs harbor egress or littoral access for military or economic reasons. Covert mining re-quires only a few mines to be effective, and the ability to resow the field after minesweeping operations have begun can demoralize a countermine force. The capa-bility for covert mining by submarines is present today and does not require unique skills or expensive technology.

The Potential Enemy under the Sea

No submarine force has ever gone to war with a torpedo that worked. This sorry history is particularly embedded in the ethos of the American submarine force. Armed today with the best torpedo in the world, the MK 48 ADCAP, the submarine force continues the practice of expending real torpedoes on real targets at regular intervals expressly to provide confidence that if this torpedo is to be used in war, it will explode when it is supposed to. Expensive underwater ranges and regular exercise by every submarine guarantee that capability in each unit of the American submarine force. Few nations have the resources or are willing to afford the expense involved with this kind of program. That expense marks the difference between owning a submarine and having a submarine force.

Similar practices with other weapons are necessary to achieve the assurance that weapons, when employed, will accomplish the tasks necessary. This historic track record must be considered when deciding what sort of threat is represented by a nation possessing submarines. Simple possession of a hull is no more than the first step in acquiring the ability to use submarines and other undersea resources.

In addition to having an adequate platform and useful technology, the ability to employ submarine platforms relies on the competence of the operators, intelligent command and control processes that have been practiced, and familiarity with the sea, particularly its internal environment and the geography of the area in which they are operating. These are not casual skills gained by schooling or sitting in port. A submarine that does not go to sea regularly and for reasonable periods of time is a monument, not a military asset. This description applies to most of the submarine forces of the world.

The performance of the Argentine navy's submarines in the Falkland campaigns indicates the truth of these descriptions. The Argentine navy was well regarded before the war, and in some other respects, particularly strike aircraft, it performed well against the Royal Navy. But of the submarines that got under way, only one reached a position where it could take action, and of the many torpedoes fired, none ran true. To find that the fire control system is wired improperly only after going into action is indicative of the obstacles in the way of creating effective undersea forces.[32]

Interactions with Other Navies: Unifying under the Global Seas

Similar to other parts of the U.S. Navy, submarines have contributed to the globalizing functions outlined throughout this volume. A unique application arises in operations under the sea: the prevention of collisions by submerged submarines. Over the past 5 decades, the Navy has developed careful and elegant procedures to prevent such accidents. Cooperation with other navies operating submarines to share these processes has expanded steadily.

In the Cold War battle of the North Atlantic, the Royal Navy's submarine force became a total partner with the U.S. Atlantic Fleet Submarine Force. In the Mediterranean, Italian, Greek, and Spanish submarines operations managed their operations in close cooperation with the U.S. Sixth Fleet submarine commander. Similarly in Japan, the Japanese Maritime Self-Defense Force submarines operations outside their local immediate operation areas were conducted in close association with the Seventh Fleet submarine headquarters in Yokosuka. For almost 20 years, a major fleet exercise in the Pacific annually has brought together ships from the Pacific Rim, including submarines from Japan, Australia, Canada, and Chile, under the operational direction of the Pacific Fleet submarine force. The annual UNITAS cruise around South America has included submarines of most of the littoral countries for more than 30 years. The resulting interoperability of the submarine forces and recognition of strengths and abilities of each country's navy is enhanced in these relationships.

Hammers and Mosquitoes: Submarines in Operations Other Than War

The submarine's roles in counterterrorism and operations other than war are fairly minimal. Scouting and reconnaissance are performed in many circumstances and have been declared very effective. The perceived need has grown as more operations take place in the immediate vicinity of other naval forces. "Now that lots of people know what submarines do, everybody wants one!" declared then-Vice Chief of Naval Operations Admiral Arthur. But as the number of submarines has declined, these less central operations have been suspended, indicating their value is less important than other ongoing missions. In general, submarines, like bombers and armored divisions, have only marginal relevancy to operations other than war, but, like a tuxedo, when you need one, hardly anything else will do.

Summary

Control of the sea has been American for so long that it is taken for granted. Few officers on active duty have actual wartime experience and then only against enemies with very limited capabilities. One could wish for this condition to last forever, but history suggests it will not. Someday this control will not be given but will have to be earned or taken. In that fight, warfare under sea surface will play a major role. British historian John Keegan characterizes such a war and the ability of nuclear submarines to so dominate the sea and throttle surface forces as "An Empty Ocean."[33] While conventionally powered submarines do not pose the same threat, the concentration of movement into the superports described in chapter 7 offers tempting targets for any nation bent on interdicting a general trade route. Submarines are not restricted to the dominant navy, the defended littorals, or supporting antiaccess strategies. They may be most effective by operating as offensive systems deployed off the coats of their opponent, read *the United States*, or along the sea lines between ports of embarkation and debarkation. Control of the sea in the future will involve dominating the depths before being able to exploit the surface as the broad commons described by Mahan. Submarines will be the primary vehicles in this endeavor, the first requirement upon which all else follows.

Notes

[1] Paul Scully-Power and Richard J. Stevenson, "Swallowing the Transparency Pill?" U.S. Naval Institute *Proceedings* 113, no. 12 (December 1987), 149–152.

[2] Owen Cote, Jr., *Precision Strike from the Sea: New Missions for a New Navy* (Cambridge, MA: MIT Press, 1998), 10–13.

[3] Department of the Navy, *Lessons of the Falklands, Summary Report* (Washington, DC: Department of the Navy, 1983).

[4] George P. Steele, "Killing Nuclear Submarines," U.S. Naval Institute *Proceedings* 86, no. 11 (November 1960), 45–51, is the seminal public description of this superiority.

[5] Richard G. Sharp, "Forward," *Jane's Fighting Ships 1989–1990*, reprinted in SEAPOWER, Arlington, VA, July 1989, 37–47.

[6] Paul Wolfowitz, *Remarks to the Submarine Technical Symposium*, Johns Hopkins University Applied Physics Laboratory, May 12, 1999, and Vernon Clark, Chief of Naval Operations, *Remarks to Naval Submarine League Convention*, Arlington, VA, June 14, 2001.

[7] Testimony of VADM Edmund P. Giambastiani, USN, Commander, Submarine Force, U.S. Atlantic Fleet; RADM Malcolm I. Fages, USN, Director of Submarine Warfare; and RADM Lowell E. Jacoby, Director of Naval Intelligence, to the Seapower Subcommittee of the Senate Armed Services Committee on "Submarine Warfare in the 21st Century," accessed at <http://www.senate.gov/~armed_services/hearings/1999/s990413.htm>.

[8] James H. Patton developed the concept of virtual presence. His concept demonstrates that even with a small number of deployed submarines, no place on Earth is ever more than 48 hours sailing time from a nuclear powered submarine. See Patton, "Impact of Weapons Proliferation on Naval Forces," in *Naval Forward Presence and the National Military Strategy*, ed. Robert L. Pfaltzgraf, Jr., and Robert H. Schultz, Jr. (Annapolis, MD: U.S. Naval Institute Press, 1993), 133–142.

[9] For example, one characterization of the kind of forces needed in the future was, "Historically, more threatening forces are characterized by high mobility (able to rapidly move to effective engagement range), high lethal range (able to outreach opponents and strike them quickly with lethal force), and a low signature (difficult to detect for various reasons). Such forces seem to have consistent values and drive preferences for specific kinds and levels of knowledge." The speaker did not recognize that he was accurately describing modern nuclear powered submarines. See C. Frank Strickland, "It's Not About Mousetraps—Measuring the Value of Knowledge for Operators," *Joint Force Quarterly* no. 13 (Autumn 1998), 90–96.

[10] Thomas Keating, "Naval Power Is Vital," U. S. Naval Institute *Proceedings* 127, no. 7 (July 2001), 46–49.

[11] William J. Holland, Jr., "ASW Is Still Job One," U.S. Naval Institute *Proceedings* 118, no. 8 (August 1992), 30–34.

[12] Kenneth M. Cox and Thomas P. Maloney, "Applied Submarine Technology for the 1990s," *Proceedings of the Submarine Technical Symposium*, Johns Hopkins University Applied Physics Laboratory, May 1993, discusses the technical issues; Nils R. Thunman, "Diesel Submarines for the U. S. Navy?" U.S. Naval Institute *Proceedings* 111, no. 8 (August 1985), 136–137, describes the strategic considerations; and Vago Muradian, "Canada to Buy British Upholder Subs in $525 Million Deal," *Defense Daily*, April 7, 1998, 1, describes the end of the *Upholders'* saga.

[13] Keith W. May, "Building on a Proven Record," U.S. Naval Institute *Proceedings* 127, no. 7 (July 2001), 64–65, argues for replacement aircraft program.

[14] For a more detailed discussion of the tactical considerations, see William J. Holland, Jr., "Battling Battery Boats," U.S. Naval Institute *Proceedings* 123, no. 6 (June 1997), 30–33.

[15] David Adams, "We Are Not Invincible," U.S. Naval Institute *Proceedings* 123, no. 5 (May 1997), 35–39, describes the potential problems with a submarine-armed opponent.

[16] Jeffrey A. Zink, "The End of the Triad: Morality, Reality, and the Ideal Deterrent," *Naval War College Review* 47, no. 3 (Summer 1994), 51–66.

[17] Richard W. Mies, "CINCSTRAT Interview," *Undersea Warfare* (Fall 1999).

[18] Robert L.J. Long, "Foreword," *The Role of Seapower in U.S. National Security in the 21st Century* (Washington, DC: Center for Strategic and International Studies, 1998), viii; and Thomas B. Allen, "Run Silent, Run Deep," *Smithsonian Magazine*, March 2001, 50–61.

[19] For the considerations in making these judgments, see William J. Holland, Jr., "How Many SSBNs Are Enough?" *The Submarine Review*, July 1989.

[20] John Grossenbacher, *Seapower*, July 2001, 13.

[21] Department of the Navy, *Lessons*.

[22] Yeddia Ya'ari, "A Case for Maneuverability," *Naval War College Review* 50, no. 4 (Autumn 1997), 125–132; and "The Littoral Arena, A Word of Caution," *Naval War College Review* 48, no. 2 (Spring 1995), 7–21.

[23] Thomas G. Mahnken, "Deny U.S. Access?" U.S. Naval Institute *Proceedings* 124, no. 9 (September 1998), 36–39.

[24] George Galdorisi, "Navy Theater Missile Defense," *Shipmate*, July-August 2000, 43.

[25] Cote, *Precision*, 25: "In theory, with 288 VLS cell equivalents, an SSGN (TRIDENT Conversion) is equal to roughly 2.5 Aegis cruisers . . . a single SSGN will provide about as much long range, standoff precision weapon capability as resides today in all the escorts in a typical battle group."

[26] William J. Holland, Jr., "A Fleet to Fight in the Littorals," *Naval Submarine Review*, April 2001, 33–44.

[27] In the Global 2001 War Game at the Naval War College, the Joint Force Air Commander (USAF) refused to use submarine-launched weapons for suppression of enemy air defenses, preferring to conduct all such missions using only air-based weapons. Difficulties in incorporating sea-based weapons in Air Tasking Orders have been reported routinely since the Gulf War. This cultural impasse continues to defy solution.

[28] Stanley R. Arthur, Interview, *Desert Shield/Desert Storm: The 10th Anniversary of the Gulf War* (Tampa: Faircloth, 2001), 113.

[29] Ibid.

[30] James H. Patton, "Submarines versus Mines," *Submarine Review*, April 1995, 23–26.

[31] James H. Patton, "Coping With ASW Minefields," *Defense Science*, March 1988, 25–30.

[32] Department of the Navy, *Lessons*.

[33] John Keegan, *The Price of Admiralty: The Evolution of Naval Warfare* (New York: Penguin Books, 1988), 319–327.

Chapter 18

Globalization and Naval Aviation

J. Kevin Mattonen

T he trends identified in this volume as affecting maritime roles in a globalized world have a demonstrated impact on naval aviation. As of the time of writing, carrier-based naval aircraft are operating with great effect against terrorist and Taliban forces in Afghanistan. But the roles of naval aviation are multiple and complex, and this complexity increases as the result of globalization. Depending on one's perspective, aviation in the U.S. Navy may be viewed as approaching a crossroads or a precipice. The crossroads signal questions for naval aviation: Will naval aviation be able to compete with technologically advanced threats and doctrines designed to confound conventional application of force while avoiding needless destruction? Can naval aviation continue along planned growth rates with iterative improvements through the established budgeting and acquisition process, or must it break with that plan?

The precipice represents the question of whether naval aviation will decay to a point of no longer being capable of fulfilling its envisioned role because of the cumulative effects of increasing tactical threats and decreased operational readiness due to aging, training, retention, and other conditions of its own making. The dilemma for naval leaders is that to take a wrong turn at this juncture may seal its fate. The outlook for naval aviation is further complicated by a myriad of internal factors that—unlike the overall force of globalization—are within the span of control of both military and legislative leaders.

Globalization Trends and Naval Aviation

The earlier chapters introduced readers to an emerging panorama of global challenges to maritime forces. This chapter attempts to address the specific impact of some of these challenges on naval aviation.

J. Kevin Mattonen is currently a consultant to several national security organizations, including Joint Forces Command. He served for over 20 years as a naval flight officer and naval strategic planner and earned the master of arts in law and diplomacy from the Fletcher School at Tufts University. In addition to service in numerous maritime patrol (P–3) squadrons, the U.S. Naval Academy, and as a staff member of the Chief of Naval Operations Executive Panel, he commanded the Undersea Surveillance Station in Keflavik, Iceland.

Antiaccess Weapons Proliferation

Denial of access to U.S. and friendly forces is by far the least expensive and most effective strategy that a potential adversary can adopt. This trend of denying access appears to be the single greatest military threat to maritime forces operating in the new globalized environment. Several already existing antiaccess capabilities directly affect the ability of naval aviation to complete its missions.

Integrated Air Defense Systems (IADS). Over the next decade, advances in air defenses, such as terminal guidance in long-range surface-to-air missiles and improvements in man-portable air defense systems, will continue. These air defense systems and their anticipated variants will continue to present a tangible threat to our attack and reconnaissance aircraft. Specifically, advances in and exports of the Russian S–300 (SA–10) series of missiles and associated acquisition and guidance systems currently present strike packages with a formidable counter that can engage aircraft at ranges of more than 120 nautical miles. Their supporting radars are capable of functioning from hardened sites, providing them with an additional defensive layer against radar seeking missiles.[1]

Global Positioning System (GPS) Jammers. These systems present a threat to current and future standoff weapon systems, including cruise missiles and unmanned aerial vehicles.[2] The experience of allied forces in the air campaign over Kosovo revealed that sortie rates could be reduced by as much as one-half with a concomitant increase in the dependence on GPS-guided munitions to overcome weather obstructing target sites.[3] In February of 2001, naval aviation forces struck against predetermined target points in Iraq with GPS-aided munitions and achieved disappointing results. While there is considerable debate in the public domain as to whether this was a failure of targeting or the result of GPS jamming, the military establishment has already identified and acknowledged the susceptibility of their newest generation GPS-assisted weapons to jamming.[4] Without the availability of precision munitions and the conditions necessary for their successful employment, the requirement for numbers of sorties and the risk associated with every strike increases exponentially.

Camouflage, Concealment, and Deception (CCD). These comprise measures that an opponent can employ to deny or mislead our intelligence, surveillance, and reconnaissance systems. CCD may result in incorrectly deploying U.S. combat assets or wasting limited collection assets chasing false targets. Disrupting and delaying the search-locate-identify-attack loop buys time for adversaries to mask intentions, redeploy forces, and strengthen defenses.

None of these particular measures should be viewed as directed solely against carrier-borne aircraft. Land-based patrol and reconnaissance forces add a vital element to developing the operational intelligence picture, identifying targets and launching weapons against those targets. Hence, they too would be affected by such antiaccess measures. Conditions that preclude patrol and reconnaissance forces' entry into viable operating areas or that disrupt their ability to reconnoiter and attack further degrade the overall safety and efficiency of naval aviation.

Other elements of the antiaccess suite further hinder naval aviation in planning and executing its role in a combat or near-combat environment. These elements are those directed against forces at sea or their support establishments ashore. Because the fates of aircraft and the place from which they must launch or recover are intertwined, these threats are potentially as lethal to mission accomplishment as those discussed above.

Sea Mines and Submarines. Antiship mines can close sea lanes and ports. Potential adversaries already possess submarines in their inventories with new technologies making them difficult to detect and neutralize. Experts anticipate advances to reduce further detection vulnerability and increase the killing power of submarine weapons systems. Antiship cruise missiles are far less expensive for an adversary to acquire than surface ships designed to slug it out with the modern carrier battlegroup. All of these antiaccess measures serve to restrict the *sea room* that has been a great advantage of naval forces since battle was first joined on the seas. Restricting the mobility of naval forces can, in turn, restrict the options available to the entire joint force with which they will operate.

As discussed in chapter 20, the experience of the U.S. Navy in Operations *Desert Shield* and *Desert Storm* is illustrative of the effects that mining can have on ships at sea. Because of political restrictions, continuous in-situ surveillance of the approaches to Iraq and Kuwait was not allowed during the 5 months preceding *Desert Storm*. During this time, the Iraqis laid more than 1,100 mines of a design dating back nearly 75 years. Upon commencement of *Desert Storm*, the Iraqis had effectively neutralized the option for large-scale amphibious assault by eliminating havens for maneuver within the potential amphibious operating area within the Kuwaiti littoral. The fates of two ships, USS *Princeton* and USS *Tripoli*, were cast in doubt after both struck mines.[5] Intelligence indicating large numbers of floating mines in restricted waters may only confound operational planning for carrier operations. The potential impact of a hit on an aircraft carrier operating in space already restricted because of coordination requirements and airspace or draft limitations might well be devastating.

The lessons of the British in the Falklands conflict are also instructive when considering what havoc the mere reported presence of a hostile submarine can wreak upon maneuver forces afloat. During the period of hostilities, a single Argentine submarine could not be located. Hundreds of sightings were passed over the reporting networks, and more than 50 antisubmarine warfare torpedoes were launched without a single weapon ever endangering the *San Luis*, a relatively modern quiet diesel powered submarine. Had the captain of the *San Luis* not suffered the same miserable weapons performance that beleaguered his air force counterparts, the outcome of the conflict could have been considerably different.[6]

Theater Ballistic Missiles. Theater ballistic missiles, while difficult to impossible to deliver against mobile maritime forces, can negate access to in-theater ports, airfields, and staging areas that may be required for logistical support to forward deployed naval forces. Terrorist attacks against logistical and command and control centers should be anticipated, especially when operating from a lodgement on foreign soil. Low-technology yet highly destructive measures have already been employed to disrupt the tempo of battle for naval aviation and its supporting assets as witnessed in the environmental warfare tactics employed by the Iraqis, who ignited oil wells throughout Kuwait to mask their movements.[7] Using "human shields," collocating of military operations and sensitive cultural features, and choosing urban terrain for combat are options that must be considered further when trying to anticipate obstacles to naval aviation in a combat role.

To echo the point made in chapter 1, the absence of a globalized maritime adversary does not mean U.S. naval aviation will not have to contend with threats. In fact, because the investment in antiaccess capability is minuscule compared to the economic burden of building and maintaining a globally capable and competent navy, leaders and planners must anticipate encountering any or all of these capabilities and operate with a healthy respect for the new enemy.

Proliferation of Information Systems and Sensors

Proliferation of high-speed information systems and remote sensing capability does not appear to present the direct threat to forces of naval aviation that the antiaccess suite entails. Even if one were to argue successfully that combination of these two elements places maneuver forces at sea at risk, there has been little discussion to argue that they present a danger to operations of elements of naval aviation. What may be argued is that any combination of high-speed information processing and survivable high-data-rate communications, especially if combined with near-real-time imagery or other sources of detection, increases the efficiency of both offensive targeting and defensive reaction measures.

Increases in Maritime Trade and Traffic

Modern navies clearly have a role in protecting sea lines of communication against threats that would disrupt the free movement of trade between nations. This authority derives, in part, international legitimacy from Article 87 of the United Nations Convention on the Law of the Sea. Article 87 specifically identifies the freedom of nations to operate aircraft over international waters.[8] The role of the U.S. Navy with regard to protection of seaborne trade is vaguely articulated in their only current strategic "operational concept" entitled *Forward . . . from the Sea*.[9] While the forces of global navies and their aviation components have only rarely been called upon to defend directly the free movement of maritime commerce between nations in contemporary times, their role in that regard is nonetheless vital.

This was borne out to some extent by the rapid decision to deploy U.S. Navy forces for the specific role of homeland defense including the protection of ports and harbors on the day that terrorists hijacked commercial aircraft and struck the World Trade Center and the Pentagon.[10] While this volume was in draft form, protection of homeland seaports for the United States was considered a potential role for Navy forces. The deployment of the USS *George Washington* and its embarked air wing to an operating area in Long Island Sound brought that potential scenario to reality.

The escort of reflagged Kuwaiti tankers in 1987 during Operation *Earnest Will* was the most conspicuous armed escort of U.S. shipping to and from ports of call since World War II. Although conducted on a relatively small scale (only 11 Kuwaiti tankers were reflagged), the effort nearly cost the Navy the loss of two ships and ultimately resulted in lives lost. While the conditions that generated the reflagging and escort initiatives were arguably the fault of both Iran and Iraq, military action by U.S. forces was directed only against Iranian interests, most notably in the strikes conducted during Operation *Praying Mantis*.[11] *Earnest Will* was to be a campaign with limited military goals, yet the U.S. Navy suffered loss of prestige and credibility when the USS *Vincennes* mistakenly downed an Iranian commercial aircraft subsequent to an engagement with Iranian Republican Guard forces operating from armed patrol craft in the approaches to the Strait of Hormuz.

As noted in chapters 4 and 8, the increasing prevalence of piracy and armed robbery at sea has gained the attention of ship owners for bulk carriers and passenger liners, insurance brokers, professional maritime organizations, and military planners.[12] What role the U.S. Navy may play in suppressing criminals who strike on the seas has not been publicly discussed in any depth in recent times. It may be worthwhile to remember that naval forces have a long tradition of fighting piracy in earlier times, and, therefore, a look at the history books might be due in short order.

Because discussion of the Navy role in protection of increased maritime trade and traffic is not well developed, the same follows for the role of naval aviation (for example, antipiracy has received only passing mention in Pacific Fleet and Pacific Command public briefing materials and speeches). As these explorations mature, determining the contribution that naval aviation can play should follow quickly because the extant and near-term capabilities of naval aviation are well known.

The recent attacks on American territory and the accompanying threats of follow-on terrorist actions should focus the thinking of military and government leaders. Global shipping clearly carries the weight of world commerce on its shoulders.

Increasing attacks upon maritime shipping can serve to disrupt the free flow of goods between nations. More frightening are the implications of providing terrorists with platforms from which to stage or launch further attacks on maritime ports.

Peace Operations, Small-Scale Contingencies, and Regional Warfighting

The trinity of peace operations—peacemaking, peacekeeping, and peace enforcement—are usually murky distinctions in the mind of the naval aviator. All three can entail risk beyond the inherent dangers of aviation. Attaching the *peace* connotation to their label does nothing to reduce the negative consequences that can occur. The same can be said for the diminution that is implied in *small*-scale contingencies and *regional* war fighting. One would have to doubt that individual aircrews consider these differences in mission planning.

The same should not hold true for those who are faced with the task of analyzing needs and requirements for training, readiness, and force structure. Operations *Southern Watch*, *Vigilant Sentinel*, *Desert Thunder*, *Desert Fox*, Somalia, the Taiwan Straits, North Korea, Bosnia, Kosovo, counterterrorism, and counternarcotics patrols are but part of the list of exhausting contingencies that naval aviation has faced through the past decade. Developing a budget plan for a two-major-theater-war force structure was a frustrating exercise in trying to make the real world fit into the constraints of domestic political considerations. The multitude of contingency operations involving potential and actual hostile fire through the past 10 years is fairly clear testament that these operations will continue and, in all likelihood, increase in frequency in the near term. The reality is that the intensity and frequency of these operations is placing a heavy burden on maintaining a ready force.[13]

Emerging Concerns about Economic Security

The attacks of September 11, 2001, brought home the reality of war waged on American soil and their direct ties to globalized economic security. Despite a suspension of trading on many exchanges, the reverberations were tumultuous throughout world financial markets. Previously only discussed as a scenario,[14] these strikes brought relevance to the role and mission of naval forces in homeland defense.

The impact of the attacks and the accompanying shift to defense of the homeland outlined in the most recent Quadrennial Defense Review will undoubtedly be significant in the totality of the Nation's defense budget.[15] What is less clear at this point is what that budgetary and operational impact will have on naval aviation.

Naval Aviation: "Inside the Lifelines"

Naval aviation as an entity bears examination before undertaking further discussion of potential changes for naval aviation driven by increased globalization. Major factors are negatively affecting the future of naval aviation. These issues include recapitalization, retention, and ranges. The label *inside the lifelines* is attached to these issues because changes in these areas are within the span of control and business practices of the uniformed, political, and legislative leadership of the government. One must attempt to foresee the totality of change that may be necessary throughout the naval aviation community, both to support the benefits of increased globalization and to protect the Nation and its partners from emerging threats.

Recapitalization and Readiness. For the first time in its history, the average age of naval aviation aircraft is older than the average of ships in the fleet: nearly 18 years old.[16] Even if the Navy and Marine Corps were to achieve their most optimistic goals of procurement and delivery, the situation with respect to the average age of aircraft in the inventory is not predicted to improve but rather worsen, especially with regard to tactical aircraft.[17] To place this aging into perspective, consider the decline of patrol aviation and the P–3C with an average age per airframe exceeding 22 years. Had these conditions prevailed during the Cold War, the Navy would have fielded airships and PBY Catalina flying boats in Vietnam.

Aging has been exacerbated over the past 4 years by the unplanned migration of more than $6 billion in funding that was targeted to procure new aircraft to readiness funding to meet the commitments of everyday operations.[18] Even at planned procurement rates, the Government Accounting Office has determined that for tactical aircraft, aging will not be reversed until 2011. The situation is even bleaker for the Air Force tactical inventory, as its average age is expected to climb to 21 years by 2011.[19] As Admiral Vernon Clark offered in his prepared testimony before the House Armed Services Committee, "For too long, we have deferred modernization and recapitalization of our force and paid for mission accomplishment by postponing maintenance and the repair of our infrastructure. That trend now poses, in my view, in my opinion, a serious risk to our Navy's future."[20]

There is a wide range of effects that accompany the aging of aircraft. They include decreased reliability, increased maintenance requirements, decreased readiness, lower availability for training, and increased operating and support costs. In 2000, the inspector general (IG) of the Navy delivered a detailed analysis of these and other factors continuing to plague naval aviation.

Achieving and maintaining combat readiness for naval aviation has become increasingly problematic. Availability of spare parts has been near the forefront of the problem, but this alone does not encompass the entirety of the issue of how aging inventory has affected readiness. Furthermore, however convenient it might be to try and place the blame on the support of the systems commander, this would not be fair.

The lack of adequate spares has cascaded throughout the entire community. This is not a chain of events with a discrete end and beginning, but, as the IG noted, it is a loop of interrelated activities, causes and effects. These complex interrelationships and their potential effects have only recently become visible:

> Naval Aviation and its myriad supporting organizations suffer from a lack of total system visibility, connectivity and single-point managerial oversight. During times of more robust funding and ample asset inventory, these disconnects in linkage tended to be masked and compensated for by the (sic) shear vitality and numbers, and at times, excesses, of the system's various component parts.[21]

The term *bathtub effect* has become pervasive in discussions about readiness dilemmas. From a broad view, this phenomenon is marked from the point where a squadron departs its homeport nominally manned, trained, and equipped to fulfill its deployed assignments. As the deployment ends, the squadron is assigned a lower priority for spares, manning, and training. It is forced to transfer aircraft and parts to those following them. This begins the downward slide (as measured in readiness terms) of *entering the bathtub*.

As the interdeployment training cycle (IDTC) progresses, the squadron must begin the workup cycle anew. In more prosperous times, this might have meant the transfer of one or two aircraft to extensive depot-level rework and increased time in training flights, but there would be a relatively steady state maintenance workload. In the current environment, squadrons are routinely subjected to multiple aircraft transfers to other squadrons (which entails additional paperwork and maintenance man-hours). Because spares are not readily available, the aircraft that are assigned to the individual units experience significant periods of unavailability for training. Squadrons are then forced to "cannabalize" parts from other aircraft in an effort to patch together sufficient numbers of flyable aircraft to achieve a minimum of training proficiency. This describes the bottoming-out phase of the IDTC where readiness simply cannot get any lower.

The climb back to full readiness (*out of the bathtub*) for deployment begins as aircraft and parts are made available. These aircraft must be inducted, inspected, and flown before they can be accepted as part of the squadron inventory. Training intensifies along with the accompanying workload to prepare people and aircraft for deployment. As the squadron deploys, it has ideally reached the pinnacle of its readiness to fulfill its wartime assignments.

The IG pointed out that systemic faults in the naval aviation support system were worsened by the decades-long practice, which was only corrected in fiscal year 1998 by action of the Chief of Naval Operations, of using the type commander's (Naval Air Forces Pacific and Atlantic) operating funds as a source of funding unforeseen expenditures. In recent years, these have included computer buys, temporary additional duty funding, range support, and contingency operations. As these funds disappeared off the balance sheets of the type commanders, something had to give. In many cases, it was funding for aviation spares (usually deferred until the following fiscal year) and depot-level maintenance. This deferral created a bow wave because the supply systems could not obligate funds to support their customers until the next fiscal year. In depot-level maintenance, this meant that work was stopped for often months at a time until funding was available to support that work. At one point in 1998, the Pacific Naval Air Force had more than 200 bare firewalls (that is, aircraft engine compartments without engines) as a result of the lack of funding.[22]

These costs of doing business were made all the more inimical to readiness by the aging of aircraft beyond what any of the forecast models could foresee. The reality appears to be that as aging increases, support increases in proportions that are almost logarithmic. As a result, despite well-intentioned forecasts of requirements, support systems have been ill prepared to predict the support and spares requirements for the inventory.

Seemingly innocuous budget designations, such as program-related engineering and program-related logistics, have long been buried under various subtitles within the myriad of budget documents. As yet another target for underfunding, the effect of doing so did not appear until the situation achieved glaring visibility. In 1999 and continuing into 2000, the SH–60 community was unable to fund the printing of sufficient numbers of the Naval Aviation Training and Operating Procedures Standardization (NATOPS) flight manuals to provide one to each pilot and aircrewman undergoing training in the Fleet Replacement Squadron (FRS). One of the workarounds was to use squadron funds for operation to contract private printing of the manuals. Unfortunately, the manuals did not include enclosures such as wiring and systems diagrams. The potential impact on safety of flight for aircrew not operating with current and readable flight manuals quite plausibly crosses the line of "acceptable levels of risk" for naval aviation.

The Chief of Naval Operations has testified rather bluntly that "the cost of operating Naval Air, because it is so old, is spiraling out of control. And there is no magic way out of this except [to] buy new airplanes."[23]

Retention. As mentioned earlier, the aging of aircraft results in decreased reliability and increased maintenance requirements. The increase in workload on sailors in particular, and to some extent marines as well, has created a host of morale problems that range across the entire rank structure. In what must have been a startling revelation, Navy leadership found that more than 70 percent of those queried responded that the conditions under which they were working negatively influenced their decision to stay in the Navy.

Across the board in aviation-related ratings for sailors, the Navy was found to be undermanned. Even today, the desired retention rate of 42 percent for pilots and naval flight officers has not been achieved for several years.[24] The result is a loss of combat-experienced aircrew and an increased workload for the training and recruiting commands.

Long an institutional bugaboo for those who have served in the operational forces of the Navy has been the inability of the personnel system to stabilize manning for deploying forces. The stories of training the ship or squadron to "get up to speed for deployment" only to have a host of newly reported bootcamp and FRS graduates show up in the 2 weeks prior to getting under way are a common theme. The burden of training and qualifying new people in what should be an arena manned by experts is usually made all the more difficult by the departure of senior and experienced people throughout the course of the deployment. In the report of the IG investigation, the frustration of the fleet with this situation is clearly evident. What may surprise sailors is the revelation that the Marine Corps has simply refused this situation as an acceptable mode of operations. Marine manning is stabilized 6 months prior to deployment, and no gains or losses (except for exceptional circumstances) are allowed during that time.

Another highlighted frustration to optimal manning has been the long accepted practice of reassigning people to temporary additional duty from their ordered billets. For many years, this was looked upon as an almost necessary rite of passage wherein sailors, including those who had completed advanced courses of instruction in aviation systems, were welcomed aboard and promptly assigned duties such as "compartment cleaning" and food service attendant (FSA, commonly referred to as mess cooking). This loss of a sailor could constitute anywhere from 8 to 12 percent of his availability during his tour. The IG report pinpointed especially egregious instances wherein aviation technicians assigned to depot-level facilities ashore were reassigned to duties as FSAs aboard flagships, duties for public relations oriented event support, "honors support teams," and auxiliary security forces. Coupled with the financial bow wave phenomenon discussed previously that complicates workload management and productivity for depot-level maintenance, this is yet another bothersome factor, well within the span of control of the Navy, that can be ameliorated.

Ranges. Rather than attempt to document the numerous sources that have testified to the necessity of live fire ranges for maritime forces and naval aviation, we must realize that no one within Navy leadership is presently on record as supporting the elimination of that capability.

Much attention has been garnered by the controversy surrounding Navy use of impact ranges on the island of Vieques, a part of the Commonwealth of Puerto Rico. The Puerto Rico Operating Area has been an integral part of naval task force training evolutions since World War II. Debate concerning continued Navy use of the Vieques range became divisive and contentious throughout the Clinton and Bush administrations. The death of a government employee on the range during a bombing exercise in April of 1999 seemed to ignite a conflagration of lobby and legal proceedings, including the filing of more than 2,000 tort suits. This public pressure ultimately resulted in the Bush administration decision to leave the island by 2003 and search for alternatives.[25]

One of the profound effects of not being able to collocate live fire target ranges with the other ranges used for deployment preparation has been the expense involved in finding suitable alternatives. In recent congressional testimony, the Deputy Chief of Naval Operations for Fleet Readiness and Logistics estimated these costs at more than $1.5 billion for the most recent fiscal year.[26] These expenses have the potential to become extraordinary unfunded requirements over the coming years. As discussed above, unfunded requirements have decimated the recapitalization efforts of naval aviation. Further pressures on the budget will increase the likelihood of further degradation of readiness.

A further point of consideration is in what ways the factors outlined above, which can be summarized as reduced training opportunities, affect the ability of naval aviation to deliver ordnance accurately and effectively.

Carrier air wings, and more recently maritime patrol aircraft and strike capable helicopters, deploy to the Naval Strike and Warfare Center (NSAWC) in Fallon, Nevada, for 4 to 5 weeks of intensive strike oriented training prior to their deployments. At the Fallon ranges, where access is essentially unencumbered (as opposed to Vieques), ordnance delivery accuracy has displayed alarming and declining trends. Over a 2-year period, the percentage of aircraft able to hit their targets successfully in the first week of training declined from an historic average of 60 percent to 40 percent. In the words of the IG, "air wings are receiving people, parts, critical combat systems and advanced ordnance training later in the [interdeployment training cycle] . . . air wings are arriving at NSAWC less prepared for graduate level training effort because they have not received the support required to train in the basics."

The readiness bathtub discussed above appears to be a problem more vexing than the lack of suitable target ranges. What the IG report appears to reflect is that even if naval aviation is provided all the range capacity that it desires for delivery of ordnance, it will be essentially unprepared to do so. The leadership of NSAWC apparently shares this belief as reflected in the following from the report:

> NSAWC believes that the lack of training opportunities with FMC (Full Mission Capable) aircraft, FLIR (Forward Looking Infrared) Pods, and PGMs (Precision-Guided Munitions) has resulted in strike success rates in Iraq and the former Yugoslavia far below those that should be achievable.

Quo Vadis, Aircraft Carrier?

Any number of perspectives enters into this debate, most of which center around programmatic decisions about *how many of what* does the Navy need *to get the job done* for naval aviation operating in a globalized environment.

One fundamental question deals with the very nature of the aircraft carrier. Three specific issues are generally debated with regard to the carrier. The first is whether we should have carriers. The second is how many of them are needed to do the job. The third is what size should they be. The debate tends to be joined on all fronts by active duty and retired military, individual services, the Office of the Secretary of Defense, any number of lobbying agencies and think tanks, shipbuilders, weapons and system design companies, scholars, and observers. The realities of carrier construction are ultimately in the hands of the elected officials in Congress. Their individual and collective votes in committee or meeting as a body of the whole are the quintessential arbiter in these debates. Thus, it is Congress—not the lobbyists or think tanks—that has to remain convinced as to the value of large aircraft carriers. But to maintain this conviction requires that the Navy understand the opposing arguments and participate in the public debate, not merely dismiss the critics.

A recent journal article by two respected former carrier-qualified aviators likened aircraft carriers to "today's battleships—national treasures that may become too valuable to risk when some Osama bin Laden figures out (soon) how to do them in. . . . [T]he danger here is that carriers and their aircraft constitute a senile weapon system, rapidly approaching obsolescence." The authors go on to advocate adoption and innovation in development and use of unmanned airborne vehicles and unmanned combat airborne vehicles.[27] While these arguments are certainly debatable, they are illustrative of contending points of view to the conventional wisdom of press statements and advertising brochures.

Numbers of aircraft carriers have been operational and legislative conundrums for years. During the Gulf War, the Navy had six carriers forward deployed to support combat operations. This was possible because the Navy inventory of carriers was 15 (although this total included the soon to be decommissioned USS *Coral Sea* and the recently commissioned USS *Abraham Lincoln*, neither of which were available for combat operations.) The Navy has attempted to maintain a carrier presence in the Mediterranean since shortly after the end of World War II and in the Persian Gulf/Indian Ocean since the early 1970s, along with a forward presence in the Western Pacific. Under the anecdotal calculus applied in the Cold War, this required three forward-deployed aircraft carriers at all times; three in post-deployment standdown and training; three in deployment preparations; three undergoing extended overhaul; a combination of three more nearing decommissioning or commissioning; and perhaps up to three more in transit or on alert for surge operations for a total of 18.[28] One of the more pragmatic and operative equations was that envisioned under the maritime strategy of the Reagan years. This equation required 16 carrier battlegroups forward in event of hostilities with the Soviet Union.[29] However these equations were calculated or debated, their numbers were determined by Congress, and the end result is that there are 12 aircraft carriers on active duty today.

The final debate centers around so-called large deck (*Nimitz*-class and beyond) carriers and alternative designs. Commonly discussed alternatives have included smaller-deck carriers, mobile offshore bases, and significant changes to the carrier force structure. The near-term reality is that a large-deck *Nimitz*-class derivative design (CVNX) will be the newest generation of aircraft carriers for the U.S. Navy.

The *Nimitz*-class design was introduced in the late 1960s. Incremental upgrades to ship systems have been developed and installed over the years that reflect changes and advances in communications, navigation, sensors, and information warfare systems (a term that did not exist in Navy doctrine at the time of the ship's original design). As currently approved, an evolutionary approach to ship systems upgrades will be incorporated over the build of the next three carriers, CVN–77, CVNX–1, and CVNX–2.[30] Envisioned changes include an integrated combat systems package, advanced propulsion plant (with reduced operator support requirements), eventual incorporation of electric-drive systems, and potentially an electromagnetic launch system that would eliminate steam powered catapult systems.[31]

The decision to adhere to an evolutionary incorporation of emerging technologies was supported by a years-long research effort that focused on a myriad of potential carrier designs. This study, led by the Center for Naval Analyses, concluded that continuation with the large-deck configuration yielded economies of scale that could not be replicated through other alternatives. The commonly quoted analysis is that a large-deck carrier with 75 aircraft assigned can deliver 100 percent more sorties than a ship with 55 aircraft with only an 8 percent increase in overall operating expense.[32]

Even as debate was appearing to diminish about the long-term plans for aircraft carriers, the Secretary of Defense directed the Defense Science Board to conduct yet another study to assess the future naval environment, the role of the Navy over the next half-century, and what transformations might be necessary for carriers to incorporate to adapt to the changing world.[33]

What Does It Take to Win?

Congressman Ike Skelton (D–MO), at the end of a long day of testimony by the Secretary of the Navy, Chief of Naval Operations, and Commandant of the Marine Corps, decided to impart a history lesson to the leadership of the Navy:

Admiral Clark, a few moments ago, [I] asked the question, what does it take to win? And that question, of course, is usually asked at the time a conflict begins. But I refer to 1934 when this Congress passed the Vincent Trammel Act that authorized eventual construction of 92 war ships, which was the birth of the two-ocean Navy.

Those members of the Congress asked themselves, what does it take to win? They had no idea of the threat that was hanging over us from the empire of Japan. But thanks to the question, the ships were built. None of the ships that won the battle of Midway were built after the war started. They were built as a result of what the Congress did in anticipating worst-case scenario.[34]

This author does not presume to have the answers to all or any of the questions previously discussed. What can be offered, however, is the reasoned argument that should the Navy and its aviation community desire to play a continued and survivable role in a globalized environment, significant changes must take place.

The Navy must identify doctrinal and technological counters to the emerging antiaccess regimes of future adversaries. These are *right now* threats. A scenario of denied forward basing, denied access to the littoral, denied overflight, and unacceptable risks in the vicinity of targets will not allow naval aviation to fight and win.

Increasing requirements for military responses to global contingencies will continue to increase the demands on naval aviation. Should national leadership continue to choose to respond at the rates of the past decade, the effects of attrition on aircraft, ships, and people must be reversed through increased procurement, increased end-strength, and increased training opportunities to hone combat skills and maintain the required edge of readiness.

Most troubling to Navy leadership should be the potential for a continued downward spiral in readiness of naval aviation due to the conditions and trends identified by the inspector general in his report. This environment is not survivable if allowed to continue. Aggressive and continuous response and monitoring are required to reverse these trends.

These answers are within the span of control of elected and appointed leaders of the military forces. All of the above will require significant financial investment. Naval aviation cannot continue along its present path and remain a viable force in a globalized maritime environment.

Notes

[1] Various sources. Data available at <http://www.fas.org/nuke/guide/russia/airdef/s-300pmu.htm>.

[2] Norman Polmar, "A Problem with Precision?" U.S. Naval Institute *Proceedings* 127, no. 4 (April 2001), 4–6.

[3] See discussions by Anthony H. Cordesman, "The Lessons and Non-Lessons of the Air and Missile War in Kosovo," Center for Strategic and International Studies, September 29, 1999, accessed at <http://www.csis.org/kosovo/Lessons.html>.

[4] David A. Fulghum, Robert Wall, and John D. Morrocco, "Strikes Hit Old Targets, Reveal New Problems," *Aviation Week*, February 23, 2001, accessed at <www.aviationnow.com/avnow/new/channel_military.jsp>.

[5] Department of Defense, *Final Report to Congress: Conduct of the Persian Gulf War* (Washington, DC: Department of Defense, April 1992), 200–208.

[6] John Lehman, *Command of the Seas* (New York: Scribners, 1988), 285–286.

[7] *Final Report to Congress: Conduct of the Persian Gulf War*, 147.

[8] United Nations Convention on the Law of the Sea, Office of Legal Affairs, United Nations, accessed at <http://www.un.org/Depts/los/convention_agreements/texts/unclos/closindx.htm>.

[9] Department of the Navy, *Forward…from the Sea*, 1994, accessed at <http://www.chinfo.navy.mil/navpalib/policy/fromsea/forward.txt>, 3.

[10] Robert Burns, "Warships on Guard Amid High Alert," *Hampton-Newport News Daily Press*, September 13, 2001, A4.

[11] Accessed at <www.history.navy.mil/wars/dstorm/ds1.htm>.

[12] The United Nations International Maritime Organization provides sources of information on international agreements and forums relating to maritime piracy through their Web site at <www.imo.org>. Current worldwide incident reports are available through <www.maritimesecurity.com>.

[13] Scott C. Truver, "The U.S. Navy in Review," U.S. Naval Institute *Proceedings* 126, no. 5 (May 2000), 76, 78.

[14] Alarik Fritz, et al., *Navy Role in Homeland Defense Against Asymmetric Threats*, Volume One: Summary Report (Alexandria, VA: Center for Naval Analyses, September 2001), 13–14.

[15] Department of Defense, *Quadrennial Defense Review Report* (Washington, DC: Department of Defense, September 30, 2001), 14, 17, 27.

[16] John Nathman, "'In Harm's Way'—Naval Aviation at the Dawn of the 21st Century," articles and interviews with *Hook, Association of Naval Aviation*, and *Seapower* (Navy League of the United States) accessed at <http://www.anahq.org/In%20Harm's%20Way%20–%20%20Naval%20Aviation%20at%20the%20Dawn%20of%20the%2021st%20Century.htm>.

[17] Government Accounting Office, "TACTICAL AIRCRAFT: Modernization Plans Will Not Reduce Average Age of Aircraft," GAO–01–163BR, February 16, 2001, accessed at <http://commdocs.house.gov/committees/security/has193000.000/has193000_0f.htm>.

[18] Hearings on the National Defense Authorization Act for Fiscal Year 2002: H.R. 2586 and Oversight Previously Authorized Programs before the Committee on Armed Services House of Representatives, 107th Congress, First Session, July 12, 2001, accessed at <http://www.house.gov/hasc/openingstatementsandpressreleases/107thcongress/01-07-12clark.html>.

[19] Government Accounting Office, February 16, 2001.

[20] Ibid.

[21] U.S. Navy, Navy Inspector General, *Final Report of Naval Aviation Spares and Readiness*, April 28, 2000, 2.

[22] John Nathman, Interview, "A Balanced and Lethal Force," *Seapower*, June 2001, accessed at <www.navyleague.org/seapower_mag/june2001/balanced_and_lethal.htm>.

[23] HASC, July 12, 2001.

[24] "Running the Fleet Ragged—Duct Tape Aviation," *Navy Times*, September 10, 2001.

[25] Remarks of the Secretary of the Navy Gordon England at Vieques, Puerto Rico, June 15, 2001, accessed at <www.chinfo.navy.mil/navpalib/people/secnav/england/speeches/eng-vieques.txt>.

[26] U.S. House of Representatives, House Armed Service Committee, Hearings on the National Defense Authorization Act for Fiscal Year 2002: H.R. 2586 and Oversight Previously Authorized Programs before the Committee on Armed Services House of Representatives, 107th Congress, First Session, Military Readiness Subcommittee Hearings on Title III—Operation and Maintenance, May 22, 2001, accessed at <http://commdocs.house.gov/committees/security/has142030.000/has142030_0f.htm>. This hearing was marked by an almost surreal discussion of environmental issues, including the fate of the snowy plover that overtook most of the discussion of the impact of "'encroachment" on military ranges on readiness and training.

[27] Joseph A. Gattuso, Jr., and Lori J. Tanner, "Naval Force in the New Century," *Naval War College Review* 54, no. 1 (Winter 2001).

[28] A more recent version of this ratio—based on operations research analysis techniques—appears in Gregory V. Cox, *Keeping Carriers Forward Deployed: Harder Than It Seems* (Alexandria, VA: Center for Naval Analyses, 2000).

[29] Lehman, 115–143.

[30] Scott C. Truver, "Tomorrow's U.S. Fleet," U.S. Naval Institute *Proceedings* 126, no. 3 (March 2000), 107–109.

[31] J. Talbot Manvel, "The Next-Generation Aircraft Carrier," U.S. Naval Institute *Proceedings* 126, no. 6 (June 2000), 70–72.

[32] David Perin, "Are Big Decks Still the Answer?" U.S. Naval Institute *Proceedings* 127, no. 6 (June 2001), 30–33.

[33] Robert Holzer, "Rumsfeld Directs DSB To Assess Future Role of U.S. Aircraft Carriers," DefenseNews.com, August 29, 2001, accessed at <www.paxriver.org/news/010829.htm>.

[34] U.S. House of Representatives, House Armed Services Committee, Hearings on the National Defense Authorization Act for Fiscal Year 2002, June 12, 2001.

Chapter 19

Globalization and Surface Warfare

Norman Friedman, James S. O'Brasky, and Sam J. Tangredi

Surface warfare is the soul of the Navy. Yet within all souls, there are sometimes issues of faith and periods of doubt and reassessment. For the surface warfare community, the end of the Cold War brought a period of reassessment that is still ongoing. It will not be complete until the community grapples with the implications of the era of globalization and resolves a series of issues that appear to place long-term faith in collision with current requirements.

We say that surface warfare is the soul of the Navy because all operational concepts for naval forces—and to a great extent, land-based tactical air forces—have their historical origins in the individual ship-to-ship, fleet-versus-fleet, and fleet-versus-shore combat that constitutes traditional war at sea.[1] The aircraft carrier and submarine have indeed replaced the surface vessel as the capital ship and primary sea control ship, respectively. But the development of fundamental tactical concepts, crew structure, and naval culture lie within the historical evolution of the surface ship. Arguably, if one understands the organizational structure of the prototypical surface warfare ship—the destroyer—one can understand the internal functioning and departmental structure of almost every U.S. Navy organization.

What Is Surface Warfare?

Surface warfare can be narrowly defined as warfare conducted from maritime surface platforms against surface targets. This is a preferred definition for those looking solely at the technologies or individual tactics optimized for a particular type of engagement—hence, surface warfare (against surface targets) differs from antisubmarine warfare (against subsurface targets), antiair warfare (against aircraft or missiles), or strike warfare (strikes against targets ashore). But the individual surface ship operates

Norman Friedman has been a consultant to the Department of the Navy on numerous issues, including surface ship design. James S. O'Brasky formerly served with the Naval Surface Warfare Center, Dahlgren Division. Captain Sam J. Tangredi commanded USS *Harpers Ferry* (LSD–49).

at the very nexus of the air, surface, undersea, and littoral (coastal) environments and is generally designed to conduct all the above types of engagements. In that sense, the surface ship is the most multidimensional of naval platforms. To capture this multidimensionality, surface warfare can be more broadly defined as any activity carried out by multipurpose surface ships.[2]

Utilizing such a broad definition is, in fact, one of the issues where faith (or perhaps culture) collides with requirements. If one looks at the organizational chart of the Office of the Chief of Naval Operations (OPNAV), one would note that the Director for Surface Warfare has no direct responsibility for amphibious warships. This is of considerable irony since the current Department of the Navy vision, . . . *From the Sea* (with slight modifications by *Forward . . . from the Sea*), implies that littoral warfare— of which expeditionary and amphibious operations would appear to be the dominant component—is now the primary focus of the surface fleet, carrier battlegroups as well as amphibious ready groups. This vision makes considerable sense, since the collapse of the Soviet Navy at the end of the Cold War resulted in a historically rare situation in which there is but one global navy (the U.S. Navy with maritime allies) against which there is no effective maritime opposition. In other words, fleet-versus-fleet surface warfare has become the *least likely* form of combat in which the U.S. Navy will engage for the foreseeable future.[3]

And yet the amphibious fleet appears to remain relegated to second-class status in the culture of surface warfare (represented in OPNAV by a Marine general), and surface platforms look and function much like they did in the later stages of the Cold War—technological advances in ordnance aside. In creating a new land attack platform suitable for littoral operations in a fleet combat-absent and globalized world, the initial preference (DD 21) of senior surface warfare leaders was a modified fleet destroyer.[4] DD 21 was subsequently cancelled by the Secretary of Defense under the impression that the program was not suitably "transformational."[5]

Along with the declining possibility of a major fleet-on-fleet engagement, the combat experience of modern *combined arms* naval forces indicates that asymmetrical attacks tend to produce more efficient results at longer ranges than symmetrical means. Thus, aircraft and submarine attacks against surface ships have become the preferred means of surface engagement, rather than surface ship versus surface ship combat (which explains the dominance of aircraft carriers and submarines).[6]

Our conclusion from the above observation is that one of the first steps facing the surface community in any attempt to adapt to the implications of globalization would be to redefine surface warfare to be more inclusive of the activities that it is most likely to perform: landing and supporting ground forces ashore. Until it does so, the surface platforms required for these activities will neither keep up with the potential technological advances nor be optimized to perform these missions in an antiaccess environment.

In fairness, it must be admitted that the surface community has adapted to two of the other significant roles that it performs and/or will perform in the future security environment: long-range land attack with Tomahawk cruise missiles and ballistic missile defense. Then again, both missions are adaptable to destroyers. However, recent development of the littoral combat ship (LCS) concept does indicate recognition that nontraditional platforms might be future requirements.[7]

Impact of and on Globalization

Like the other aspects of maritime power, U.S. naval surface forces are directly affected by, and in turn, directly involved in, globalization. For the purpose of this chapter, we focus on six of the seven effects identified in the introduction but in a different order: interventions in locations not previously considered of vital interest (effect 4), increasing nonstate and transnational threats (effect 1), increasing maritime traffic and trade (effect 2), proliferation of antiaccess or area-denial weapons and strategies (effect 7), new effects on alliances and coalitions (effect 5), and proliferation of information technology and sensors (effect 6).

Increasing Interventions and the Revolution in Surface Warfare. Naval forces in general are uniquely well equipped for global operations, because, unlike land-based forces, they can remain in place for a protracted period without the support of, or permission from, local governments. Moreover, ships can carry heavy enough weights of weaponry to make their presence off a foreign coast a meaningful gesture either of support or of coercion.[8] But to handle increasing intervention requires either a more efficient manner of employment or a bigger fleet.

The great question for any navy is how many areas it must affect simultaneously. During the Cold War, when the U.S. Navy was built around carrier battlegroups (CVBGs) composed of an aircraft carrier, one or two replenishment ships, and six or seven surface combatants, the answer was generally no more than two or three areas: one locale in the Mediterranean or the Middle East and one or two in the Far East; later the Arabian Sea was added. Surface ships did in fact visit many more places at any one time, but there was little expectation that they would actually have to fight in these various places. Toward the end of the Cold War, the Navy acknowledged that the CVBGs could not cover enough contingencies. It therefore formed surface action groups (SAGs) around the four battleships. The battleship SAGs presaged an important likely future role of surface combatants in a more globalized world.[9]

Complementing the realization that the U.S. Navy could not afford the number of CVBGs required for true global coverage, a revolution in surface warfare occurred through the development of the land-attack cruise missile. The development of the

Tomahawk land-attack cruise missile in the 1980s effectively increased the striking range of an individual surface ship from approximately 24 nautical miles (the range of the largest battleship gun) to over 1,500 nautical miles. Effectively demonstrated in Operation *Desert Storm*, by 1998 the sea-launched Tomahawk had become a contingency weapon of choice, being used for strikes in even a completely landlocked country (Afghanistan). Brushing aside the question of whether this was the wisest use for such a weapon,[10] the success of the Tomahawk effectively *globalized* naval surface warfare—at least for the surface forces of the U.S. Navy and her closest allies. This allows SAGs—even without the now-decommissioned battleships—to have an independent strike capability that they had not had since the beginning of naval aviation, at a range unfathomable to the classical naval strategists.

SAGs were now strike groups; they derived their value from the Tomahawk land attack missiles they deployed—but also from the defensive capability of the *Aegis* antiair combat systems aboard some of the ships. The combination of these capabilities meant that SAGs now had a capacity to defend themselves from sophisticated air attack as well as strike targets deep inland.

Thus, our second conclusion is that with the advent of the long-range land-attack cruise missile, the U.S. Navy had already answered one of the major effects of globalization: the ability to affect contingencies in areas not previously considered of vital interest. And it is now able to do so with platforms (surface ships) that were not previously viewed as having a strategic impact. This brings up another question of faith: why can't SAGs deploy as forward presence formations to critical locations in lieu of our overtaxed CVBGs? Globalization implies the need for great agility on our own part. Whatever forces the United States brings to bear must appear quickly. They must be self-contained, in the sense that they enjoy independent endurance, can defend themselves against a realistic scale of attack, and, perhaps most importantly, can execute significant offensive operations. Carrier battlegroups are self-contained and have enormous offensive and defensive firepower, but they are also massive and expensive, and it seems unlikely that the United States can ever afford a large number of them. The next level down has to be SAGs, with individual high-capacity surface combatants another level down.

Our second recommendation is that the Navy fully use this capability by breaking the traditional cycle of providing a CVBG as the standard deployment formation in every situation. Surface SAGs would seem to have the appropriate capabilities for many deployment locations and could increase the number of places where the United States could maintain combat-credible forces. The Office of the Chief of Naval Operations has recently initiated development of a concept of an expeditionary assault group consisting of *Aegis* guided missile destroyers, nuclear attack submarines, and combat logistics ships attached to (and trained with) current amphibious ready groups. If put in place, these adjustments may prove beneficial in satisfying the recommendations of chapter 15 concerning shifts in overseas presence requirements.

The continuing reduction in forward land-based forces and the emergence of antiaccess threats place a variety of increased demands on sea-based forces, including the emerging need to operate sea-based forces in littoral regions in the continual presence of threat. New combinations of naval assets in tailored task forces would appear the solution to maximize our capabilities. For example, the global war on terror may require strike and small-scale amphibious operations on short notice and in the absence of accessible infrastructure. Relying on a limited number of standard-configuration CVBGs/ARGs no longer makes sense. Discussion of alternative task force combinations (naval operational architecture) is the focus of chapter 28.

Increasing Transnational Threats and Increasing Maritime Traffic. Experience since the Cold War has shown that surface combatants also play very important roles in embargoes and sanctions enforcement, in which numbers of units may be more important than unit strike capability. The most prominent cases in point are the sanctions against Iraq, interdiction operations against Serbia in the Adriatic, and now the effort to prevent members of the al Qaeda terrorist network from fleeing Pakistan by sea. Newspaper reports suggest that there may be an essential U.S. security role as well, since the sponsors of al Qaeda apparently control merchant ships that may be used to transport weapons or other terrorist materiel to the United States.[11]

Chapter 4 discusses the potential roles of surface combatants in interdicting transnational threats, so we will not describe them here. Similarly, chapter 8 describes the increase in maritime traffic and potential need for greater sea lane security, a mission that presumably will be assigned to surface ships (of which most are helicopter equipped) and maritime patrol aircraft. Ocean, coastal, and riverine surface transportation will increase in volume and value with the rise of littoral economic activity. We may expect that the demand for transportation in the newly and rapidly expanding urbanized and industrialized areas will overwhelm land and air transportation infrastructures, creating even greater dependence on maritime transportation features. This plethora of high-value ocean and coastal commerce and the concentration of economic and political activity in the littoral regions create a large and valuable array of potential surface targets to defend or attack.

Our observation on these points is in consonance with our first recommendation: there are more aspects to the surface fleet than cruiser/destroyer-type combatants. If the need for interdiction/sea lane security is increasing, it would seem logical to also assign amphibious warships, the remaining fleet of patrol combatants, and the future LCSs to these tasks. As noted in chapter 4, this has been done to some extent in the Persian Gulf, but could also be done elsewhere (such as the Malacca straits). Interdiction does not require Tomahawk-capable ships; our third recommendation would be to balance this globalized role throughout the surface community. This might require increased cross-training between platforms and greater professionalism regarding these missions. These missions also call for the development of coalition fleets, a function in which the U.S. Navy has previously proved quite adept.

Proliferation of Antiaccess Weapons: Battle Space and Ballistic Missile Defense. Extensive discussion of antiaccess weapons proliferation appears in chapters 25 and 26 in this volume. There is a significant debate on the level of threat that antiaccess or area denial weapons entail and whether potential opponents are actually acquiring robust and integrated antiaccess defense systems. Chapters 25 and 26 reflect this debate and reach different conclusions—both of which hold differing implications for the surface fleet. A robust antiaccess network would suggest a greater opportunity for opponents to target large surface platforms, suggesting the need for smaller, potentially expendable ships—networked in line with the network-centric warfare principles of retired Vice Admiral Arthur Cebrowski's Streetfighter concept. We will discuss the issue of smaller surface combatants later; however, two elements related to the globalization of antiaccess weapons are indisputable under any interpretation: that the littoral battle space is collapsing (that is, becoming more difficult and dangerous to operate within), and that development of ballistic missile defense capabilities for surface ships would be a very significant means of ensuring both expeditionary force and allied state survivability in an antiaccess environment.

The challenge of the contested littoral battlespace is much greater than that faced by the surface fleet in the open ocean. In the complex cluttered littoral, survival depends upon an even higher standard of situational awareness, requiring low signature platforms operating in quiet modes and quick reaction weapons of a most discriminate and effective nature. This high standard of situational awareness demanded by sustained littoral operations can be achieved only if a well-instrumented battlespace can be created and sustained in the face of a determined and adaptive enemy with relatively large local resources (no matter their level of sophistication). As noted in Admiral Cebrowski's proposals, a comprehensive sensing grid could develop sufficient information to allow a conditioning of the littoral battlespace so as to reduce the effectiveness of antiaccess threats before the entrance of U.S. and allied forces. But layered defenses are still problematic. The possibility of attack from a hidden position at relatively close range cannot be ignored. The only viable countermeasure is a well-integrated hard-kill and soft-kill defense of a low signature platform—which might be, of necessity, vastly different in configuration than today's surface combatants.

In such a collapsed battlespace, mutual support distances rarely exceed 30 nautical miles. This is both an advantage and disadvantage for U.S. naval forces. A network-centric sensing grid may enable the documentation and reconstruction of the engagement to characterize the enemy attack mode and platform. This would facilitate the orchestration of a force-level response to a platform-level attack. (This assumes, of course, that the opponent has fewer naval platforms available than U.S. and allied naval forces.) But conversely, the short operating distance means that U.S. naval forces themselves could be subject to greater detection and repeated attacks from land-based missiles and aircraft.

This is a particular danger for *unalerted* surface platforms performing a forward presence mission. To be an effective deterrent, forward-deployed forces must maintain access to the theater and provide essential services to the joint and combined force commanders. These functions require the ability to rapidly assert maritime battlespace dominance in the open ocean approaches to the theater and in the littoral regions of the theater. But they also expose a forward-deployed force to a "battle for the first salvo" in a no-warning engagement.[12] We conclude, therefore, that combat in a contested littoral will involve platform losses. We may also conclude that the modes of combat that are suitable for operations in the "relatively expansive desert" of the open ocean will prove quite ineffective if not counterproductive in the " urban sprawl" of the littoral. Regardless of the size and characteristics of U.S. warships or the sophistication and robustness of enemy antiaccess systems, littoral operations will require tactics much different than those in open-ocean fleet combat. This tactical development has begun only recently.[13] Our fourth recommendation is for the surface community—in addition to internal tactical development—to strenuously encourage discussion of littoral tactics in the open professional literature as an intellectual "force multiplier."[14]

The ballistic missile defense mission could bring back a naval role that has not been a major mission of the surface navy since 1918: defense of coastal cities. Access to ballistic missile technology is widespread, despite diplomatic efforts to restrict it. The current effort to develop a sea-based theater ballistic missile defense (TBMD) integrates nicely with our current forward presence posture since TBMD is generally predicated on the need to protect allies against enemies, and at the least to protect necessary points of access, such as container ports, against attack. Prime threats would be such rogue states as North Korea and Iraq, both of which have developed medium-range ballistic missile capabilities. It should be noted, however, that many of our current allies or friends oppose other allies or friends. It may well be in our interest to be able to negate strategic attacks one tries to mount against the other. As this is written, India and Pakistan, both armed with nuclear-tipped missiles, seem to be on the point of war. They may well not fight, or their fight may be on a much smaller scale. However, American policymakers would probably prize the ability to cool off such a fight by intercepting opposing missiles from a neutral position—from the sea.

The related but more difficult mission of integrating sea-based missile defense with a national missile defense (NMD) to protect the U.S. homeland is discussed in detail in chapter 24. Until recently, surface navy leaders have been reluctant to countenance NMD as a major surface fleet mission due to the perception that such an assignment would force ships to remain close to the continental United States, thereby taking them away from their *real* missions of providing forward presence and crisis response overseas. This view has since begun to change, particular in light of the Bush administration's unwavering commitment to NMD. Our fifth recommendation is that the surface navy begin to develop the concepts and tactics for this inevitable mission.[15] As the 2001 *Quadrennial Defense Review Report* states, "To be effective abroad, America must be safe at home."[16]

Effects on Alliances and Coalitions: Toward a Global Coalition Navy? Globalization has a complementary economic face: very wide-scale access to markets, not only for peacetime commodities, but for military products. That face affects the projected capabilities of possible enemies and also those of allies and potential partners. As noted in chapter 11, it may also affect the fortunes of producers of military systems and thereby the course of weapon system development globally. Earlier we asked how the United States could gain the numbers of ships it needs for some operations, such as maritime interdiction.[17] The answer may be coalitions with navies that individually are weak but that together operate large numbers of frigates and smaller oceangoing craft.

Paradoxically, in recent crises it has been the U.S. ability to operate independently at sea that has drawn other governments into coalitions with us. In the political vernacular, the ability to act unilaterally is the catalyst to attract multilateral participation. Indeed, other governments see coalition operation as quite important, to the point that, for example, the Danes are buying substantial frigate-sized ships (a size larger than those in their current fleet) specifically to participate in allied/coalition operations—a trend not seen since the Cold War.[18] Such is the allure that a global-capable navy, such as the U.S. Navy, has for the professional naval services of like-minded nations. Unlike their army counterparts, which frequently rely on conscripts, most world navies are highly professional and have enjoyed the benefits of personnel trained at staff colleges (including attendance at the U.S. Naval War College and National Defense University) for several generations. The very best have and maintain very high professional standards. These navies can be both formidable opponents and valued partners.

Our observation is that the current level of maritime dominance of the United States is the best way to dissuade potential enemies from building large oceangoing navies *and* the best way to attract a maritime coalition of friends and allies. Other navies see interoperability with U.S. naval forces as substantial support to their own defense policies. Since international law of the sea allows global naval operations without infringement on sovereignty or the need for permanent foreign bases, it is easier to draw skeptical potential allies/former antagonists into combined naval exercises than it is to persuade them to allow combined land exercises—Russia being an example in this regard. Naval dominance (used thoughtfully) holds positive diplomatic benefits in a globalized world. Our sixth recommendation is for the United States to make every effort to retain the overall naval dominance (in an operational and technological sense) developed during the Cold War and use it as a prime method of political-military engagement—even with Russia, China, and, in the future, reformed/modified rogue states.[19]

Proliferation of Information Systems and Sensors. We have left the discussion of the proliferation of information systems and sensors (effect 6) for last, because we are uncertain of the *real* effect that this has had on naval surface fleets other than those of the United States and its closest allies. Obviously, naval surface combatants appear to have become more capable in almost every navy. For example, China has recently taken delivery of two more *Sovremenny*-class destroyers from Russia (for a total of four). The *Sovremenny*-class is a legacy system of the late Cold War, armed with SS–N–22 Sunburn cruise missiles, still reputedly the most fearsome ship killer.[20] Increases in weapons capability are dependent on increased capabilities in detection and battle management. Individual warships have indeed been transformed through increased access to tactical and navigational information and communications via satellite. However, since the collapse of the Soviet Navy at the end of the Cold War, no non-NATO nation has developed a comprehensive, sophisticated maritime surveillance system that could significantly improve its surface warfare capabilities (that is, for long-range maritime defense). From this perspective, there has thus far been a definite limit on the effect that information technology (IT) proliferation has had on surface warfare globally.

This is a fact (as discussed in chapter 26) that places the more alarmist views of the need for radical military transformation into question. Nations that operate sophisticated integrated air defense systems (such as the Russian-built SA–10) simply have not developed the comparable maritime information systems that would make their surface (as well as undersea and air) forces substantially more effective. This may be due to the perception that sea mines, diesel submarines, and land-based antiship missiles—currently the primary weapons of maritime antiaccess—do not need extensive cueing and battle management in the short distances of the collapsed littoral battlespace.[21] (See discussion of sea mines in chapter 20.) Or it may be due to the fact that these expensive systems are not high in most militaries' budget priorities. Operating such systems requires a level of training and maintenance outside the current capabilities of most nations (no matter their level of naval professionalism). This is particularly true of the rogue states.[22]

Our conclusion in this regard is that global advances in IT have made surface warships individually more lethal, but outside the U.S. Navy and NATO partners, these advances have not been applied to increasing overall maritime power. One result is that in a coalition context, the United States must contribute the essential intelligence to support sanctions/embargo operations. Both in the Gulf and in the Adriatic, it seems that U.S. systems built to track the Soviet fleet during the Cold War played an essential role in tracking and then intercepting merchant ships. A decade after the Gulf War, the United States still enjoys a near-monopoly on such capability, although our allies certainly contribute vital information in support of the effort. The U.S. contribution is very much in the emerging spirit of network-centric warfare: the tactical picture (which is much of our part of the operation) makes up much of the cost and value of the operation.

More generally, surface combatants gain their offensive firepower largely from their ability to fire weapons, particularly cruise missiles, beyond their horizons. Thus, they must rely on remote targeting, which will come from some sort of netted large-area picture of a remote area. The picture must be available wherever surface combatants have to operate. Our experience even during the Cold War, and certainly since, has been an almost total inability to predict venues of conflict, and at the least an inability to guess national priorities (imagine writing the same analysis before and after September 11, 2001). Thus integral with future surface warfare ought to be a globally agile sensor system—which means space-based sensors. The United States already enjoys unparalleled space-based sensor systems; few other nations have any such capability. Our recommendation is for the U.S. Navy to maintain and improve these capabilities, even to the extent of considering a ship's satellite antenna its primary sensor.[23]

Streetfighter, the Littoral Combat Ship, and the Case for Smaller Warships

Do littoral operations in the antiaccess environment globalized world ipso facto require the U.S. Navy to rely on smaller ships? This is a primary question in the debate over military transformation. Many of the proponents of transformation—arguing that opposing forces will be replete with high-technology information systems and sensors—view surface ships as increasingly easy targets, especially in the littoral but at sea as well. (See chapter 25.) To some extent, this view is a legacy of the "carriers as sitting ducks" debate that first emerged during the Carter administration and that periodically resurfaces—a debate based on budget concerns but on little, if any, tactical analysis. However, even supporters of a robust surface fleet have become convinced that a Streetfighter-type vessel—netted together by an extensive tactical network and sensor grid—is needed to conduct high-intensity combat in the collapsing littoral battlespace. Having fought strenuously against the Streetfighter concept since its articulation by Admiral Cebrowski, the surface warfare leadership now appears to have (of necessity) endorsed it in the form of the LCS program.[24] But is this a valid conclusion?

Our answer appears a vacillating one: it depends on the missions that the surface force is expected to carry out. If the primary mission of U.S. surface vessels will be to strike targets ashore in support of a joint and combined campaign against a regional opponent (that is, a major regional war), their primary weapon would be long- and medium-range cruise missiles. Substantial missile firepower is expensive in ship size. The bigger the ship, the larger the magazine, the more firepower that can be placed on target. If this is the dominant mission, smaller ships would not seem to present any advantage.

Probably the appropriate measure of a globalized U.S. surface combatant force is the number of separate self-sufficient units that can be maintained abroad at any one time. That leaves open a choice between larger, effectively self-sufficient ships and smaller ones that must operate in groups. Hull steel is relatively inexpensive, and in terms of personnel, the smaller number of larger ships would probably be far less expensive to operate. The argument in favor of smaller ships—say, the size of existing frigates—would be that some important operations, such as maritime interception, require a more dispersed force. It may also be argued that the more numerous smaller ships are more difficult to destroy. However, a larger ship can probably survive several hits, whereas a smaller one may succumb to only one. Moreover, the cost to support units of smaller ships may be prohibitive.

A key point is probably that a smaller ship would buy very little in terms of armed presence, because it would have so little inherent capability of its own; it would be effective only as part of a larger group, if then. That is, a large ship can accommodate both substantial defensive and offensive armament; it takes a major effort to sink. A smaller one would be armed with either offensive or area-defensive weapons, and quite possibly with very few in either case. Numbers of smaller ships could combine to provide serious capabilities; but one or two such ships would have neither. It must be admitted that at present, foreign navies seem quite content to use ships with very limited capabilities for naval presence missions, presumably on the theory that the locals are not sophisticated enough to realize just how empty their threat may be.[25] Alternatively, they may feel that a weak ship suffices, on the theory that the locals realize that attacking it will bring down a much more massive attack from really powerful forces beyond the horizon. But, most recently, that has been bluff. When the Iraqis nearly sank the USS *Stark*, there were no real consequences for them.

However, if a primary mission of the surface fleet is to maintain littoral sea control throughout a sustained joint military campaign in which the United States seeks to place land forces ashore—while the enemy retains the capability to repeatedly strike naval forces from shore—then Streetfighter/LCS-type warships in sufficiently large numbers would be key assets in any balanced fleet portfolio. This was a lesson the U.S. Navy learned during combat in the Pacific archipelagoes in World War II. Streetfighter/LCS can only be a successful innovation with a network-centric approach. But network-centric does not mean being unconcerned about numbers—smaller ships are effective as a coordinated fleet, not as individual units. The case for smaller ships is only convincing if they are bought in sufficient numbers, provide stealth advantages in a confused littoral battlespace, and can maintain their network capabilities even in the face of inevitable losses. Streetfighter/LCS development cannot be about cost savings because, as the discussion above indicates, they will not provide the economies of scale that a smaller number of bigger ships might provide.

Global Warship Trends

What, then, of that other side of globalization—the diffusion of the defense and shipbuilding industry? In contrast to the Streetfighter approach, foreign navies are now building larger ships because they expect to operate further from home, which means that they can join in the sort of out-of-area operations that were previously almost the exclusive domain of the U.S. Navy. In the past, that would have been very good news for specialist warship-builders in the United States, Britain, and France. However, as in the world of merchant shipbuilding, assembly of hulls and machinery is increasingly the province of other countries with lower labor costs. For example, just as the Republic of Korea gained prominence in merchant ship construction, it is now building frigates and has just exported one to Bangladesh (which presumably could never have afforded a European-built ship). China has sold frigates to Egypt and Thailand. This trend has not gone very far yet, but it is not too difficult to imagine a future in which very few countries feel compelled to go to classical builders for their hulls. (See discussion in chapter 11.)

Combat systems, as indicated above, are still a very different proposition. The Bangladeshi frigate is Western-equipped. The latest Thai frigates, built in China, have a mixture of Western and Chinese (reverse-engineered Russian) weapons and sensors, and U.S. experts had to modify the Chinese combat direction system to suit Thai requirements.

Since combat systems make up as much as half the cost of a ship, Western makers of naval systems probably will not suffer too badly in future global competition. However, U.S. shipbuilders may well be driven to the wall. Even now they are in substantial trouble. The trend for decades has been toward smaller numbers of larger ships with more elaborate systems on board. The smaller number of hulls requires less shipyard effort; more and more of the total naval ship procurement budget goes to systems. The net effect is likely to be to focus innovation on systems rather than on hull and machinery combinations. The U.S. choice of all-electric machinery does go against this trend, but then again it was justified on the ground that it made for better combatant performance, including better resistance to damage. In the past, few navies have been willing to analyze their requirements to a comparable depth.

The preeminence of U.S. combat system design may be our greatest military advantage in creating a global coalition navy under U.S. leadership. Right now, a NATO battlegroup is held together by formatted data links, particularly by Link 11. The data links work because ships all have computer combat direction systems amenable to processing the linked picture. At one time, most non-NATO ships of Western origin, even if they had computer-based combat direction, used a much less capable Link Y. Because computers are now so much more capable, and because money was available for combat direction development, a Link Y Mark 2, comparable in capacity to Link 11, was developed and is now installed on board many non-NATO ships. Such a link makes possible coordination with NATO ships, given the appropriate translation devices.[26]

Of course, not everyone operates combat direction systems similar enough to ours to be compatible. It may be that the great technological challenge of the next few years will be not some implementing of stealth but rather gaining the ability to cooperate with dissimilar systems such as those of Russian warships. After all, before September 11, who would have thought of the Russians as likely partners in the war against al Qaeda?

At the least, globalization will mean that potential partners have the technical wherewithal actually to be coalition partners, but only if we can provide them with the necessary data inputs. That in turn may allow us to concentrate our own limited resources on the sort of surface combatants we cannot expect our potential partners to provide for joint operations.[27]

Conclusions

Our conclusions on the future of the surface navy in a globalized world take the form of recommendations.

First, the surface warfare community must define itself more broadly, working to eliminate the status distinctions among platform types and to distribute firepower across all warships. To launch land-attack missiles in a relatively benign environment does not require cruiser/destroyer-type ships. Assets should not be confined to their traditional roles.

Second—and in order to implement the first recommendation—the U.S. Navy should experiment with new deployment configurations and operational architectures for surface groups. Suggested configurations are discussed in chapter 28.

Third, transnational threats will require the surface navy to utilize its assets in a more creative fashion for interdiction. This will require distribution of the mission across assets as well as greater interoperability with coalition forces. The key to achieving such interoperability remains tactical information (an in some cases the necessary information systems) provided by United States forces.

Fourth, the network-centric approach to future fleet capabilities remains sound logic and should be continued. If the Streetfighter/LCS concept is adopted, network-centricity becomes even more important in achieving effective contributions from smaller ships.

Our fifth recommendation is that the surface navy needs to embrace the national missile defense mission as well as the countertransnational threat role. Or, if a deliberate decision is made to utilize U.S. Navy assets *only* for forward-deployed overseas operations, then substantial deep-water resources need to flow to the U.S. Coast Guard to be effective in the NMD and countertransnational threat roles.

Sixth, there are clear political-diplomatic reasons for the United States to actively maintain its naval dominance in a post-Cold War world. These reasons make maritime coalitions more likely and maritime rivals less likely. No apparent action/reaction arms race dynamics are currently in place to make maritime supremacy a hazard.

Seventh, the surface navy needs to improve its tactical development for littoral operations and seek to provide open forums for creative and unorthodox tactical thinking. Professional associations such as the U.S. Naval Institute and Surface Navy Association could help best in that regard. But the keys are *open* forums and professional rewards.

Eighth, the surface navy must retain its strong interest in connectivity with space-based assets—which are probably the best way to maintain U.S. naval global capabilities, even with a shrinking fleet. (This is not meant to advocate a shrinking fleet, only to advocate preparations to maximize assets no matter the number of platforms.) Space is and will be a part of the multidimensional medium of naval combat—especially for surface forces.

Ninth, the decision to adopt Streetfighter/LCS concepts hinges on a clear understanding of the missions that the surface navy is expected to undertake in a future antiaccess environment. Also, the difficulty of this antiaccess environment must be patiently analyzed, not taken for granted. Our sense is that the surface navy has not yet accepted the difficulty of the future challenge (currently we are unchallenged), but that the *transformation school* is also overstating the enormity of the antiaccess threat. In any regard, a balanced fleet that combines high-end/low-end, large/small assets in a broad portfolio is the best naval insurance policy toward the future security environment. We hesitate to use former Chief of Naval Operations Admiral Elmo Zumwalt's term of *high/low mix* because of the historical baggage that term brings, but the concept still makes considerable sense if prudently applied. Surface ships are not obsolete—but one size (type) does not fit all.

Finally, the health of U.S. warship construction capacity hinges not on shipbuilding but on combat systems. (Chapter 11 also comes to this conclusion.) Primary effort to maintain U.S. leadership in naval technology must focus on combat systems development. This is also the most important aspect the United States brings in encouraging the development of an effective and interoperable global coalition navy.

The effects of globalization may require some collective self-searching, but surface warfare seems destined to remain the soul of the Navy.

Notes

[1] One school of thought argues that amphibious warfare and strike against shore actually predate the history of war at sea. See representative discussion in Sam J. Tangredi, "Sea Power: Theory and Practice," in *Strategy in the Contemporary World*, ed. John Baylis, James Wirtz, Eliot Cohen, and Colin S. Gray (New York: Oxford University Press, 2002), 118–119.

[2] Although aircraft carriers, amphibious warships, mine-countermeasure ships, and combat logistics ships all operate on the surface of the ocean, they can all be specialized, not multipurpose. However, new technologies are gradually eliminating such distinctions.

[3] See argument in Sam J. Tangredi, *All Possible Wars? Toward a Consensus View of the Future Security Environment*, McNair Paper 63 (Washington, DC: National Defense University Press, November 2000), 73–78.

[4] See, for example, Timothy LaFleur, "Taking Defense Littorally," *Washington Times*, August 5, 2001, B5.

[5] One of the new program "transformational concepts" is *spiral development*. See Nathan Hodge, "Admiral Sees Stiff Competition For New Surface Combatant," *Defense Week*, February 4, 2002, 2.

[6] Similarly, air-to-ground and surface-to-air engagements tend to achieve air superiority more efficiently than air-to-air engagements.

[7] Dale Eisman, "Navy Moves to Develop a Novel Type of Warship," *The Virginian-Pilot*, February 4, 2002.

[8] It is sometimes argued that small surface ships are excellent as means of observing a developing situation, pending arrival of more substantial forces. For example, a surface ship might define a baseline situation, so that significant changes would be detectable. No transient detector, such as a satellite, would offer the same coverage. However, the surface ship would also advertise U.S. interest and thus might well aggravate a situation. The observation role, then, would more likely be appropriate to a submarine operating sensors such as unmanned underwater vehicles and small unmanned aerial vehicles.

[9] During the Cold War, the Joint Chiefs of Staff called for as many as 22 carrier battlegroups for wartime. The Navy's judgment was that no more than 15 were affordable, even at the height of the Reagan budget. The number of battleship surface action groups (SAGs) was based entirely on the number of battleships available; suggestions to activate a pair of heavy cruiser SAGs (to exploit the two available hulls) were dropped, presumably because of affordability. All of this was for a significantly less distributed set of potential crises than are anticipated today.

[10] See discussion in Sam J. Tangredi, "Are We Firing Tomahawks Too Easily?" U. S. Naval Institute *Proceedings* 122, no. 12 (December 1996), 8, 10.

[11] In December 2001, British authorities detained and searched a bulk carrier headed for London, on the official ground that they had received a tip that it was carrying "terrorist materials." It was released after a fruitless 3-day search, as "other information" (presumably that the first tip was false) had been received. However, British newspapers carried claims that Norwegian intelligence had identified a fleet of 20 "terror ships"—ships controlled by al Qaeda interests—but that identifying them was proving difficult because the financial network involved was so complex.

[12] "Battle for the first salvo" was a phrase used in the writings of Admiral of the Fleet of the Soviet Union S.G. Gorshkov to indicate the Soviet Navy's doctrinal requirement to detect and strike the enemy first in any naval engagement. In Gorshkov's view, history indicated that ships that launched the first well-aimed salvo would inevitably be victorious. Soviet pre-engagement tactics were continually focused on maneuvering to ensure victory in the initial positional struggle to launch the first salvo (for example, fixed missile launchers pointed directly at the enemy's high value target). See Milan N. Vego, *Soviet Naval Tactics* (Annapolis, MD: Naval Institute Press, 1992), 44.

[13] A representative change occurred in the highly regarded book on tactics by Wayne P. Hughes, Jr., *Fleet Tactics* (Annapolis, MD: Naval Institute Press, 1986), whose second edition (2000) is now titled *Fleet Tactics and Coastal Combat*. The best overall publication on littoral operations is currently Milan N. Vego, *Naval Strategy and Operations in Narrow Seas* (Portland, OR: Frank Cass, 1999).

[14] The U.S. Naval Institute *Proceedings* is an excellent forum, but for more specialized discussions of surface tactics, we would recommend the establishment of a set of open-forum professional journals with prizes for good writing and ideas. In these journals, an eminent leader of the community would open topics for discussion for a period of 2 years. At the end of this period, the community leadership would make a decision, announce it, and close the discussion except for implementation progress reports. Journal prizes and credit for successful implementations would be significant factors in a person's record. A partial near-term solution would be for the Surface Navy Association to establish a general community professional journal along the lines of the Naval Submarine League's *The Submarine Review*.

[15] As an alternative, the sea-based national missile defense mission off the coast of the United States—along with the necessary assets—could be transferred to the U.S. Coast Guard.

[16] Department of Defense, *Quadrennial Defense Review Report* (Washington, DC: Department of Defense, September 2001), III.

[17] Indeed, it could be argued that for us to concentrate unduly on providing all the necessary ships would be a reversion to platform-centric thinking.

[18] The Danish case is particularly interesting because the 300-ton Stanflex corvette is often used as a case in point of the value and capability of a small well-designed ship. The Danes decided that "small was not beautiful" after operating a small frigate (much larger than a Stanflex) in support of the coalition force in the Gulf in 1990–1991. The new Danish frigates will displace about 5,000 tons.

[19] As a rough estimate, an overall defense budget of about 4 percent of gross domestic product is necessary to fully fund the recapitalization of the existing joint force structure and to fund the defense transformation.

[20] According to reports, the United States attempted in the mid-1990s to buy the entire former Soviet inventory of 841 Sunburn missiles from Russia before they could reach the global market. See Norman Friedman, *World Naval Weapons Systems 1997–1998* (Annapolis, MD: Naval Institute Press, 1997), 243–244. With speed in excess of Mach 2, SS–N–22 is extremely difficult to shoot down once locked on target. However, in April 2000, the U.S. point defense system rolling airframe missile (RAM) reportedly had successfully engaged a simulated SS–N–22 conducting a high-speed weave. Report in "RAM Passes OpEval," U.S. Naval Institute *Proceedings* 126, no. 4 (April 2000), 6.

[21] Surface ships in a littoral denial role may serve as adjuncts to a land-force-dominated coastal defense based on land-based antiship cruise missile systems; remote controlled minefields; a small tactical airforce with very limited maritime strike potential; and/or a naval militia capable of operating an inshore guerrilla force.

[22] A national maritime approaches and littoral surveillance system with national and regional command elements and with a coordinated sea space denial capability may be difficult for an enemy to achieve, but it is certainly conceivable, which is why it is a staple of the literature pushing military transformation.

[23] See Norman Friedman, *Seapower and Space: From the Dawn of the Missile Age to Net-Centric Warfare* (Annapolis: Naval Institute Press, 2000), for details of existing systems. One irony of the current situation is that support for space systems is declining even as they are becoming more vital. Unmanned aerial vehicles are often proposed as alternatives to space-based sensors, but they generally require local support, at least in the form of airfields.

[24] See Andrew Koch, "USN Pushes Littoral Combat Ship," *Jane's Defence Weekly*, January 23, 2002, 6.

[25] The British Type 23 frigate, which has no land-attack capability beyond its 4.5-inch gun, would seem to be a case in point.

[26] The key point was that, due to multipath problems, high-frequency radio (the medium for Link 11) could support only 75 pulses per second. Using a very ingenious technique of parallel transmission, Link 11 operates at 2,250 bits/second. Without the computer-intensive technique, Link Y (a variant of NATO Link 10) operates at only 75 bits/second. For example, Link 11 transmitted vectors with identifiers; Link Y transmits only positional information. Link Y Mk 2 uses a computer sampling technique, which is now quite common, to sort out multipath and increase its data rate to Link 11 standard (about 2,400 bits/second) without using the elaborate radio system associated with Link 11.

[27] For a very limited number of operations, moreover, the U.S. Coast Guard can provide the sort of numerous embargo-enforcing ships we may need. We may then want to invest in the sort of mobile support that would be needed to maintain a force of Coast Guard cutters in an overseas embargo operation.

Chapter 20

Mine Warfare and Globalization: Low-Tech Warfare in a High-Tech World

Thomas R. Bernitt and Sam J. Tangredi

In a conventional military sense, globalization has been with us for many decades. The era of an abundant and seemingly unlimited supply of military weapons—fanned by the subsidies of the Cold War—has made it possible for just about every military and paramilitary force to have access to everything short of nuclear ballistic weapons (and that gap may soon be closing as well). The irony is that while many would argue that the economic effects of globalization have bifurcated the world more precisely into haves and have-nots, just the opposite is true in regard to the globalization of conventional weapons. From the grenade launcher to the shoulder-fired surface-to-air missile, the process of globalization has, in some ways, facilitated a democratization of conventional forces. Now every military has some degree of access to technology that can support a slice of the modern technological forms of warfare. But despite such a spectrum of death available to the highest bidder, the most democratic of these weapons is also the least technologically advanced: the mine.

Whether on land or at sea, the mine now constitutes the true *everyman* weapon whose very universality serves as a reminder of the *progress* of modern life. If globalization means the ability for consumers and producers to create a world where everyone has access to all the world's products (if not necessarily the ability to purchase

---

Thomas R. Bernitt is president of Bernitt Services, a management consulting firm working primarily in the field of demining and environmental remediation. Retiring from the U.S. Navy in 2000, Captain Bernitt's previous commands included Explosive Ordnance Mobile Unit 5, Explosive Ordnance Group 1, and Naval Weapons Station, Seal Beach. During Operation *Desert Storm*, then-Commander Bernitt served as primary mine warfare adviser to the naval forces commander, Admiral Stanley Arthur, Commander, 7th Fleet. Early in his naval career, he directed American and Egyptian divers in demining operation in the Suez Canal. He earned masters degrees in history, national security affairs, and business administration, and is an adjunct professor at several universities. As a surface warfare officer, Captain Sam J. Tangredi has spent his operational career avoiding mines.

them), then the very proliferation of mines to arsenals throughout the world—including those of nonstate actors—means that we are all more or less equal. At least, we are all more or less vulnerable on a scale not witnessed before.

This means that most average citizens in the Third World are threatened to some degree (some much more than others, such as in Afghanistan or Cambodia or parts of Africa) every day by landmines. It also means that every navy, along with commercial shipping, is threatened to some degree by the sea mine, even when operating in neutral waters or offshore the most technologically *unadvanced* of nations. The annual report issued by the International Campaign to Ban Landmines, founded by Nobel laureate Jody Williams, lists 76 countries where mine clearance is occurring, excluding the countries that might have them in their territories but are unable to exorcise them.[1]

Although landmines can be (relatively) technologically advanced either with plastic casings that make locating and thus neutralizing them almost impossible or with computer chip sensors that can discriminate between the most similar of targets (or both), the sad truth is that landmines do not have to be that sophisticated to be effective. Rather, the sheer number of mines, the impenetrability of the medium (soil), and the lack of technologically advanced methods for clearance make them just as effective when employing World War I technology as when they contain 21st-century technologies. In fact, the United States still clears landmines basically the same way that the Armed Forces did during World War II: through either brute force or one at a time by single soldiers armed with magnetometers. The new technologies of ground-penetrating radar, chemical analysis, and sonar mapping all have been confounded by the imperviousness of the soil to give up what it considers its own secrets willingly. Thus, the mine-clearer, whether Afghani, Egyptian, Cambodian, or American, usually moves inch by inch in a painstaking advance of modern blind man's bluff.

Yet to this point, we have been addressing the effects that the availability of landmines has on the civilian populations of the world. Although problematic in a very serious way to these people—if only because of the humanitarian element of the argument—landmines nevertheless do not necessarily pose insurmountable problems to most modern armies of the world because of the air mobility that these armies possess, especially the armies of the United States and Western Europe. Landmines instead tend to restrict the movements of ground-based forces that one tends to find almost exclusively in the Third World. Afghanistan provides the perfect current example of the efficacy of the landmine when opposing unsophisticated armies, hence the universal appeal of landmines as defensive weapons to these kinds of land forces.

But it is the sea mine that still presents the greatest impediment to modern military forces. To understand this modern threat, a cursory overview of the development of the sea mine as a viable weapon is necessary.

Anatomy of a Weapon

Although the modern sea mine bears little resemblance to its 19th-century antecedent in terms of technical sophistication, the original definition given to what then were called torpedoes still holds true: an unattended underwater explosive. Antiship devices of one sort or another have been used since Grecian times with a fairly consistent failure rate. The primary problem that plagued the early proponents of mine warfare was the design of a firing system that would fire at the most opportune moment—preferably when an enemy ship was within striking distance and not when the mine was being planted.

It was not until the 19th century that the first practical firing mechanism for an underwater explosive device was developed.[2] Essentially, the device consisted of a glass tube that contained sulfuric acid in a mixture of sugar and potassium chlorate powder. It, in turn, was protected in a sheath of lead. When something large, such as a ship, ran into the explosive container, the glass tube broke and the chemicals reacted exothermically with one another, causing the explosive to detonate. In addition, the mines were anchored in a stationary location in order to wait passively for targets to move toward them. This concept of passive operational deployment was to remain the norm until the development of active target-seeking mines in the 1960s. However, many of the mines still stockpiled by Third World nations remain based on this principle.

Many of the early mines were extremely unreliable because of their primitive firing systems and unpredictable explosives (gun cotton and black powder). Furthermore, when deployed in saltwater, they corroded easily and quickly became totally ineffective. It was not until the beginning of the 20th century that such engineering problems would be sufficiently solved so that mines could be used extensively and contribute strategically to the outcome of a war.

The Hague Conference was convened in 1907 as the first attempt to negotiate viable restrictions upon the employment of mine warfare by belligerent nations. Essentially, four basic points were agreed upon: it was forbidden to lay drifting mines unless "they are so constructed as to become harmless one hour at most after those who have laid them have lost control over them"; it was forbidden to lay "automatic contact mines which do not become harmless as soon as they have broken loose from their moorings"; it was forbidden to lay automatic contact mines off the coasts and ports of the enemy with the sole purpose of intercepting commercial navigation; and every possible precaution must be used to ensure safe navigation to nonbelligerents when moored minefields are employed. That these agreements were largely unenforceable and (from a military standpoint) essentially impractical if mining was to offer any tactical or strategic advantage is borne out by the actions of the belligerents during World War I when they were largely ignored. The Hague agreements were scheduled for renewal in 1914, but the war prevented it, and consequently the stipulations of the original 1907 Hague Convention were never updated or amended. It remains, for all practical purposes, the basic international agreement on mine warfare in force today.

World War I witnessed the first extensive use of sea mines as a major weapon in a total war as the allies and central powers used mines in tactical situations up through 1918. The most significant employment of mines was the result of the inability of the United States and Britain to counter the German U-boat threat with conventional surface actions. Consequently, the two allies embarked on what has come to be termed the North Sea Barrage in which over 72,000 mines were laid between the Orkney Islands off the coast of Scotland to the northern coast of Norway. According to several sources, the effects of the barrage ranged from negligible to questionable, due to the extent of the area coverage (over 250 nautical miles), the depth of the water, and the unreliability of the mines.[3] However, despite its minimal success, it was becoming increasingly apparent to military planners throughout the world that "the mine would make the difference if [it was] properly designed, properly reliable, and properly supplemented by other forces."[4]

World War II ushered in the modern age of mines through the development of the bottom influence mine. The significance was twofold. First, the underwater mine no longer required a heavy anchor in order to be moored within the path of a ship. Instead, the new influence mines could detect ship presence as they lay on the sea bottom, detonating at the precise opportune moment of the ship's passage. With this development, the mine could now be delivered by airplane against an enemy's protected harbors, giving the mine an offensive potential for the first time. Secondly, the coverage of a minefield was dramatically increased since a ship no longer was required to run into an influence mine. In other words, fewer mines could threaten a much larger area.

This combination was not lost on U.S. Navy planners who formulated a massive offensive mining campaign, code-named Operation *Starvation*, against the Japanese homeland from March 27, 1945, until the first of August of the same year. Over 12,000 mines were laid, primarily by airplane but supplemented by submarine. By the war's end, the operation was successful in cutting the total imports of the Japanese by 97 percent. It has been debated whether the dropping of the atomic bombs on Hiroshima and Nagasaki would have been necessary if Operation *Starvation* had begun 6 months earlier.[5]

Just as World War II demonstrated the offensive potential of mine warfare, the Korean War reaffirmed the mine's defensive possibilities, especially when used by a qualitatively inferior force to stop a technically superior one. Specifically, North Korea effectively prevented the U.S. Army from landing at Wonson Harbor in October 1950 primarily through the use of Russian MKB mines, one of the world's most unsophisticated moored mines.[6] Approximately 3,000 of these mines were laid by sampan and junk in combination with a few bottom influence mines. Despite the relative crudeness of the operation, the North Koreans were able to sink four U.S. minesweepers, damage several destroyers, and—more importantly from a strategic aspect—delay the landing of U.S. troops by a full week at a critical juncture of the war.[7]

The modern underwater mine has evolved from the crude and (by today's standards) largely ineffective influence mine employed near the end of World War II to a highly sophisticated, computerized weapon that in some cases can seek and destroy targets autonomously. The electronic arming and fuzing devices that have been incorporated into today's mines allow them to be extremely sensitive in the target acquisition phase yet impervious to incidental background influences. They are also highly selective and accurate in target discrimination capabilities and rugged enough to withstand tremendous depth pressures for extended periods of time. In addition, simultaneous improvements in explosive blast/weight ratios, as well as the recent advances in the miniaturization of electronic circuitries, have made mines smaller and hence easier to deploy. As a result, a few mines can be used with strategic effect when employed in low-intensity conflicts in which the objectives are primarily disruption of seaborne supply channels in and out of principal ports. Additionally, the ease of concealment and deployment has facilitated their attractiveness as a preemptive weapon prior to the beginning of conventional hostilities.

The actual assessment of mine effectiveness is a fairly arcane process that attempts to quantify a statistical probability of kill against certain types of shipping based on such factors as minefield density, damage criteria, and parameters of ship traffic. Strictly counting the number of ships sunk by mines has never been considered an accurate method of determining a particular minefield's utility. For example, during World War II, the United States aerially planted mines in the mouth of Palau atoll in the Pacific. Due to their disinclination to move through the minefield, the Japanese elected to keep their fleet of 32 ships in the harbor where they became sitting ducks for American torpedo planes and bombers, which were able to sink every ship the very next day.[8] Consequently, minefield planners frequently argue what a minefield could have accomplished rather than what the actual results were. It is necessary to keep in mind, therefore, the ability of a minefield to deny access to or out of a particular geographic area (a capability admittedly not easily measured but rather inferred) as opposed to a numerical accounting of mine to ships sunk ratio.

Modern Use of Sea Mines

Mines today can be roughly classified into four major categories: moored contact mines (World War I technology); bottom influence mines (with significant improvements on what was introduced during World War II); moored influence mines (post-World War II antisubmarine weapons); and moored influence target-seeking mines.

This last category is considered to be the most significant development in mine technology since the advent of influence mines at the beginning of World War II.

Moored contact mines still in service today have not radically altered in design since World War I. They consist basically of two types: the chemical-horn design previously described and the galvanic antenna mine, a device suspending a copper wire several feet above a chemical-horn mine by means of a float. The contact of a ship's steel hull with the copper wire in saltwater produces an electrical current that subsequently fires the mine. Using this procedure, the target range of the contact mine was increased threefold. Most moored mines are difficult to deploy because of size (a large air cavity must be contained in the mine body) and because of their weight (a heavy anchor and steel cable are necessary for mooring). Consequently, only surface ships and a few specially configured submarines operating on the surface are suitable for planting these mines. A minefield containing only moored contact mines, for all intents and purposes, has to be planted overtly in one's own waters as a defensive barrier against enemy combatants rather than in enemy-controlled harbors and chokepoints.[9]

The bottom influence mine, by eliminating the requirement for an air cavity in the mine as well as an anchor, significantly reduces mine size and weight. As a result, influence mines are now configured for aircraft and submarine deployment into hostile environments. The early influence mines were strictly magnetically actuated, firing only when the magnetic field of a ship was detected by a sensor inside the mine. These mines were unreliable and frequently fired either before or after the ship was overhead, thus causing minimal or no damage to the intended target. Today, however, bottom influence mines are not only much more reliable but also use two other kinds of influence signals to fire: an acoustic signal and pressure signal. Mines can now be set to detect a variety of ship signals before firing, which increases both the mine's reliability and discrimination capabilities. In the more sophisticated bottom influence mines, microcircuit computer technology has been incorporated into sensing and firing systems with the result that they can be set to fire against a much more specific range of targets. In fact, it is now theoretically possible to adjust the sensitivity setting of a programmable mine to the point where the mine will fire only on certain classes of ships.[10] However, such exclusive targeting is usually not considered to be an effective use of mine capabilities since this *fine-tuning* overly restricts the range of available targets that the minefield can attack.

Mine technology has also developed various counter-countermeasure devices that have made bottom influence mines more resistant to sweeping and other countermeasure techniques. These include delay-arming devices that allow the minefield to remain dormant until such time as it is required to become active; ship counters that allow the mines to fire only after a prescribed number of ships has transited the area; probability actuator circuits that randomly turn mine circuitry on and off; and nonferrous mine casings and anechoic mine coatings that reduce the sonar reflection of the mine and, consequently, increase the difficulty of minehunting.

During and immediately following World War II, the nominal target range of bottom influence mines was sufficient to be effective against surface ships as well as submarines operating in shallow water. The physics of underwater explosions basically restricts the effectiveness of bottom mines against surface targets to a maximum depth of 200 feet because the air bubble that the explosive creates—the primary destructive element of the mine against ships—dissipates to such a degree after 200 feet that it no longer contains sufficient force to effect consistent damage beyond that range. This does not usually pose insurmountable problems when the intended target areas include harbors, channels, and amphibious landing beaches—normally areas close enough to shore that the depths would not be greater than 200 feet.

Improvements in the design of modern submarines, however, significantly altered the necessary depth capabilities of the mine. Initially, the moored influence mine was designed specifically to counter the deep-water submarine threat. These mines, however, proved to be ineffective at depths near the continental shelf (600 feet) and practically useless when used in deeper waters—the prime operating area of the modern submarine—because of the relatively small target width provided by their stationary explosive charge.[11] Nevertheless, they are still in the inventory of the U.S. Navy, despite efforts since 1960 to develop a replacement. The Russian Navy also has retained a shallow water moored influence mine in their inventory whose principal utility seems to be for export rather than for Russian operational use.

Consequently, the problem was to develop a mine that, while planted in the operating depths of the submarine, would be effective against an area large enough to require relatively few mines. Thus the requirement for the prohibitive number of mines that would have to be planted to pose a serious threat to the submarine in forward operating areas would be eliminated. Ironically, the answer was arrived at more or less simultaneously by both Soviet and American mine engineers in the late 1960s: marry the concept of the mine and the torpedo into an independently deployable package that, once the mine has detected an appropriate target, would automatically launch and destroy it. The result was the moored influence, target-seeking mine.

These mines (presently in both U.S. and Russian inventories) have basically taken the advanced arming and firing technology of the most sophisticated influence mines and incorporated it into available torpedo and rocket hardware so that, in essence, the new mines are unmanned torpedo platforms that deploy in the deep operating depths of the modern submarine. When the mine senses an enemy submarine within a target detection range of several hundred yards, it will fire its single torpedo or rocket toward the target.

Mines have been used extensively since the Korean War by a growing number of nations. Known mining incidents have occurred in:

- Long Tau Channel in 1965 (North Vietnam)
- Suez Canal and the Straits of Aqaba in 1967 (Egypt)
- Straits of Gubal and Chittagona, Bangladesh, in 1971 (India)
- Haiphong Harbor in 1972 (United States)
- Tripoli, Benghazi, and Bomba in 1973 (Egypt and Libya)
- Khowr-E-Musa, Iraq, in 1982 (Iran)
- Corinta, Nicaragua, in 1983–1984 (Nicaraguan contras with U.S. support)[12]
- Approaches to the Suez Canal in the Red Sea in 1984 (suspected to have been Libya).

Today, there is obviously no longer a monopoly by the wealthy industrialized nations on mine warfare since mines have become increasingly available to the Third World. The technology of today's mines makes them ideally suited to low-intensity conflicts when the strategic objective becomes a cut-off of sea transported supplies rather than naval confrontation. Until the Persian Gulf War, however, deploying mines remained only within the purview of the major nations. That all changed in 1990.

A simple World War I design (patterned after the Imperial Russian MKB moored mine), the LUGM 140, an indigenous mine manufactured by Iraq, was deployed in late 1990 as a floating mine throughout the Arabian Gulf. Although specifically in violation of the 1907 Hague Treaty, which prohibited such "floaters," the mines complicated the maneuver capabilities of the naval armada positioned in the Gulf prior to and during the outbreak of hostilities. Additionally, and probably more importantly, the mines helped to stall the world's greatest Navy in its tracks in February 1991 off the shore of Kuwait because of the inability of the U.S. Navy, and anyone else for that matter, to sweep the sea lanes effectively prior to an amphibious invasion. The LUGM presence, as well as the presence of the more sophisticated Swedish manufactured Mantas (a magnetically activated mine that caused the damage to USS *Tripoli* and USS *Princeton* during the Gulf War), was a prime consideration of war planners designing options for landing marines ashore near Kuwait City. During that war, with no credible countermine capability, the U.S. Navy actually experimented, midwar, with individual swimmers armed with snorkels and facemasks merely to try to create an ad hoc minimalist capability that might ascertain the presence or nonpresence of mines in the assault lanes. Most of this effort was expended for a mine essentially based on a pre-World War I design.

For purposes of our argument on the globalization and subsequent proliferation of the mining capability, not only are the sea mines a threat from a traditional government organization, such as the Iraqi military, but, similar to their land mine brethren, they also can be employed effectively by paramilitary forces as well. Our own Central Intelligence Agency proved the point during the mid-1980s when it mined some ports off the coast of Nicaragua during the contra conflicts. Using a 55-gallon drum filled with explosives and fuzing devices, these homemade mines were intended to disrupt military supplies and commercial activities supplying the Sandinista government of Daniel Ortega.

The capabilities of a modern armed force to countermine these sea mines in a timely manner has not significantly improved. Still without verified methodologies within the shallow water zone, the principle stumbling block to Gulf War access from the sea, the U.S. Navy and by extension the remainder of the world, is still vulnerable to the strategically laid sea mine. The question then could be whether globalization has been the culprit. One could easily say that economies of scale and simplicity of design came long before the weapons supermarket became a fact of life. Certainly, the global nature today of weapons availability made them all the easier to obtain but not necessarily easier to clear. Therein lies the Faustian bargain. Something that is cheap, easy to deploy, and thwarts the most powerful adversary through sheer numbers and simplicity becomes the hardest to counteract.

Problems of Countermeasures

As indicated earlier, there are technical countermeasures to mines, and the U.S. Navy continues to pursue both organic and mission-dedicated solutions. No problem is insolvable as long as one is willing to pay the cost to solve it. As chapter 17 notes, submarines may be the optimal platform to hunt mines at the outer edges of the littoral regions and possible in chokepoints and sea lines of communication. But the author of that chapter does not go so far as to advocate building specialized minehunting submarines; other missions appear to be a greater priority.

The U.S. Navy and many allied and friendly navies do have dedicated surface minehunters and minesweepers, but it is obvious to anyone who has studied American naval force structure that mine countermeasures still are not a priority to our fleet. Otherwise, countermine forces would not be as starved for resources as they have traditionally been. The programs that are funded, such as the Galveston-based countermine squadron, helicopter squadrons, and explosive ordnance disposal programs (such as marine mammals) are a miniscule part of the overall Navy budget, well below 5 percent—even with generous amounts of service overhead added in.

This situation is understandable. During the Cold War, minehunting and minesweeping were the primary responsibilities of the smaller North Atlantic Treaty Organization (NATO) navies. The expected threat was a Soviet minelaying campaign directed against Western European ports in order to prevent military reinforcements from being transported across the Atlantic from the United States and Canada. It was natural enough to expect the nations to whom the ports belonged, such as the Dutch, Belgians, Germans, Norwegians, and Danes, to be responsible for neutralizing the mine threats to their own ports. More importantly, these nations could not afford to build their own large oceangoing warships in great numbers. Under the logic of scarce resources and comparative advantage, it made sense for many of the smaller NATO navies to put much or the majority of their resources into mine countermeasures, while the United States put most or almost all of its resources into globally deployable combatants. Since it is impossible to mine deep water effectively, the sea mine threat would not affect U.S. and Canadian forces until they were in the littoral regions where the smaller NATO navies could sweep channels and escort them.

However, with the end of the Cold War, this supposedly easy solution lost its rationale. If a war with Russia was so unlikely, protecting the European ports was no longer a focus of mine countermeasures. A part of the NATO capability atrophied; there were now more important priorities than naval spending. But even more critical, the local mine countermeasure capabilities could not be swiftly deployed to regions in which conflict was now expected. At a transit speed of 10 knots or less (less than half of that of a globally capable surface combatant or aircraft carrier), NATO mine countermeasures ships coming from Western European ports and their U.S. equivalents coming from across the Atlantic for Operation *Desert Shield/Desert Storm* were not timely enough or in sufficient numbers to have much of an impact on the mine threat until the Gulf War was over. The United States has kept two mine countermeasures ships homeported (or, technically, permanently forward deployed) to the Arabian Gulf region, rotating their crews from the United States by air. But two ships, supplemented by the faster arriving helicopter squadrons, could hardly make a dent against a prepared (albeit poorly coordinated) Iraqi mine campaign. As noted in chapter 19, the mines were already in place before coalition navies arrived in numbers, and, more importantly, before they were allowed to fire at the Iraqi minelayers—hence, the damage to USS *Tripoli* and USS *Princeton*.

As indicated, an even more difficult threat than the mines lurking on the littoral edge (after all, oceangoing warships could avoid them by staying clear and using long-range weapons to attack Iraqi forces) were the mines planted in the near-shore littoral and surf zone against which there was little the coalition could do at minimal risk. Certainly countermine swimmers could have been sacrificed in large numbers (assuming large numbers could be quickly trained); countermine vessels could have been exposed to greater, almost-certain chance of destruction; even the old, sardonic suggestion of filling empty merchant vessels with ping-pong balls and driving them through the minefields to set off the mines could have been tried (although with little success against the more sophisticated bottom mines). But none of these would have been particularly effective, even if the losses were acceptable. In the American style of war, few potential opponents are worth a damn-the-torpedoes amphibious assault when long-range air strikes could provide gradual attrition.

All of this would seem a wakeup call for a global Navy focused on littoral operations. Indeed, there has been a renewed interest in countermine programs. But a technological silver bullet has not arrived. As chapter 17 discusses, even relatively shallow water has remained remarkably opaque. So, if a degree of certainty against the littoral mine threat is desired, the issue becomes one of how many resources (for instance, in terms of aircraft or countermeasure ships) should be devoted to the problem. Currently the U.S. Navy has elected to focus on *organic* minehunting capabilities from existing oceangoing platforms. While this can afford more protection to a deep-water fleet, it can provide little to solve the antiamphibious assault mines in the surf zone.

Unilateral Solutions

If the sea mine threat is as difficult a threat as presented above—and continues to be proliferated during this era of globalization—it seems logical that the United States should devote considerable thought and resources to solving the mine problem. This is not simply a naval issue; it is a joint military issue, since most ground force combat vehicles and Army and Air Force sustainment logistics must travel by sea in any power projection scenario. There are at least three potential unilateral methods toward a near-term solution to the mine threat: a declaratory policy of preemption; a substantial increase in minehunting/clearing research and development; and a substantial increase in mine countermeasure forces and capabilities.

Preemption. In terms of operational effectiveness, the best way to prevent the use of sea mines in an antiaccess/area denial strategy against U.S. maritime forces would be to prevent the mines from ever being laid. Of course, since sea mines must be laid largely before the commencement of hostilities in order to be effective, destroying minelayers would require a preemptive or *prehostilities* strike. This is a policy that has been advocated by individual senior naval officers (as evident from chapter 17), but not one with which political leaders have been comfortable. Unless U.S. and/or allied decisionmakers were convinced that war with a state (or nonstate actor) was inevitable, it is unlikely that they would order a preemptive strike on ships or aircraft involved in minelaying. But they might be more inclined to do so if there was an existing declaratory policy that the United States would automatically take such action. Arguably, this is in consonance with the Bush administration's recently released National Security Strategy.

There are certainly precedents in international law that could be used to justify a preemptive attack on any vessel or aircraft laying mines in international water. As noted in chapter 18, the existing International Law of the Sea would appear to mandate action in these circumstances. Since almost any type of watercraft can lay mines, it may be difficult to gather intelligence in a timely enough fashion to prevent actual emplacement. However, a declaratory policy that includes a defined, assured response against the state or nonstate organization perpetrating the mining may have a deterrent effect. Mine laying in international waters could be perceived in the same manner as piracy—that any state aware of such action is empowered to act against the perpetrator. This would appear in consonance with the Hague Conference of 1907.

Such a policy would have little effect on mine laying as part of emplacing antiaccess defense within a state's own territorial waters, making it ineffectual against the rationale of globalized mine proliferation. It would require a multilateral agreement banning sea mines to justify the violation of sovereignty needed to stop coastal mine seeding.

Increase in Research and Development. As noted in chapter 17, detection of any object under the sea is a difficult art. But there is a significant difference between submarines and sea mines: mines do not (or are not supposed to) move. Thus, there is always the potential that substantial increase in minehunting/clearing research and development—particularly research and development involving space-based means of detection—might have considerable effect in blunting the mine threat. There have been experiments using space-based systems, but the amount spent on such research is miniscule in comparison to more favored defense programs. Part of the reason is that counter-sea mine efforts are seen as exclusively a naval problem, to be funded solely within the resources allocated to the Department of the Navy. But as pointed out earlier, sea mines are in effect a joint problem. Arguably, sea mines are actually less of a problem for the Navy in its sea control and land attack roles than they are for the power projection of the Army (and, ultimately, expeditionary air forces). They could be a substantial problem for amphibious forces and the U.S. Marine Corps; however, vertical assault by air from amphibious ships just outside of coastal waters may neutralize the mine threat for the light, self-sustaining Marine forces. All of this points to the need for a *joint* program, funded in a manner such as ballistic missile defense to ensure the level of resourcing that could spur significant technical advances. Advanced mine countermeasures might be a fruitful area for Department of Defense experimentation and transformation.

Increase in Countermeasure Forces. If sea mines are indeed the number one global antiaccess threat, then a substantial increase in mine countermeasure forces and capabilities would seem to be the logical counter. Currently, the U.S. Navy has avoided that route, opting for *organic* minehunting capabilities that improve protection for the oceangoing fleet but do relatively little to improve the coastal clearance necessary for amphibious landings or port debarkation.

The relative neglect of mine forces has become something of a tradition for all the reasons discussed earlier—as a *lesson learned* that has to be continuously *re-*

learned. As soon as it is relearned, it seems forgotten. The primary official study of the naval aspects of the Korean War optimistically noted, "There was one residual result of the mine war in Korea. It was to make mine warfare a more dependable career specialty in the United States Navy."[13] That statement was probably true for a few years in the 1950s, but it is not a true statement today.

In organizational politics, mine warfare is considered but a subset of expeditionary warfare, which is but a subset (if that) of surface warfare. Rarely does it have a strong advocate within the surface community (whose personnel crew the mine countermeasures ships). In aviation, it is a subset of the helicopter community, which is itself somewhat of a second-class (possibly third-class) branch of the fighter/strike-focused world of naval air. The community on which the mine clearing responsibility inevitably (and perhaps naturally) devolves is the explosive ordnance disposal specialty—a warfare community that has no flag officer billets. All of this adds to a lack of a powerful advocate for mine warfare in the competition for limited defense resources. This neglect makes little sense if sea mines are to be a significant antiaccess threat in the future and argues for more dedicated resources (in both personnel and platforms) for the mission.

Multilateral/Global Solutions

Globalization is about the interconnectedness of human society, with reduced hazard to freedom of trade or movement. Mine warfare is all about disconnecting and hazarding. In the same spirit of the international campaign to ban landmines, it would seem logical that multilateral or global steps could be taken to eliminate the proliferation of sea mines. Three potential global solutions would be an arms control regime to stop the proliferation of sea mines; an outright ban on the production and use of sea mines; and a commitment by the United Nations to take immediate sanctions or police action toward any state or nonstate actor emplacing sea mines in any part of the ocean or littoral.[14]

The second option—a ban on the production, trafficking, and use of sea mines—would most closely resemble the efforts of the International Campaign to Ban Landmines. However, gaining public interest for such a campaign against sea mines would likely be much more difficult. Although civilian deaths on land as well as sea may have resulted from sea mines—consider Operation *Starvation* of World War II—there are simply not enough graphic public images such as paraplegic men and women or injured children to stir a strong sense of outrage. Sea mines are not the same sort of media exploitable threat to everyday activity as landmines—particularly in the most unfortunate, war-wracked Third World countries. It is difficult to portray the destructive effects of sea mines on the global economy.

Critics would claim that banning sea mines would be of disproportionate advantage to the U.S. Navy as the world's last global navy. But that argument could easily be applicable to landmines, which are not needed to defend American territory and whose removal would be of advantage to U.S. power projection forces on land. If the security of the positive benefits of globalization is enhanced by today's de facto *global* Navy, then there seems to be no good reason for a global proliferation of sea mines.

The other global solutions do not currently possess much support from proponents of arms control or international organization, but they are not any more difficult to achieve than the host of arms control, disarmament, or confidence building measures currently on the intellectual agenda. (The first option would be an attempt to complete the existing Hague Conference.) Inclusion of a complete ban on sea mines in the existing law of the sea might gain international support, particularly if encouraged by those states most capable of producing advanced mines, such as the United States, Russia, China, France, United Kingdom, and Italy. Sea mines have been particularly destructive in civil wars in coastal states, such as Sri Lanka, so it is quite possible that lesser developed states might be encouraged to join such an agreement. The issues of adherence, verification, and enforcement of controls on sea mines would be no more challenging than those of any other arms control regime.

Conclusion

The sea mine—perhaps the *lowest tech* of antiaccess weaponry—has become one of the world's most proliferated weapons (small arms being the most proliferated). Sea mines are also a threat that has not received the attention or resources that is their due. The globalization process would benefit if a stabilizing power, such as the United States, maintained the resources to deal with this threat on a global basis. Doing so is also of obvious tactical benefit to the U.S. Navy and America's joint armed forces. But increased resources alone would not result in a significant improvement unless there is a corresponding change in the cultural attitude of the joint forces that currently relegates the countermine mission to a relatively low priority. Part of this attitude is left over from the Cold War days in which mine countermeasures was a mission assigned to the smaller NATO allies. But the Cold War is over.

Moving beyond unilateral solutions toward a global regime to eliminate sea mines would be of even greater benefit in the long run. Whether a nongovernmental campaign such as that against landmines can be sparked seems to hinge on the degree to which individuals will come to recognize how much the beneficial activities of globalization are directly or indirectly dependent on the sea.

Notes

[1] The 76 countries and regions in which mine clearance operations were carried out during 2000 and early 2001 are Abkhazia, Afghanistan, Albania, Angola, Armenia, Azerbaijan, Bangladesh, Bosnia and Herzegovina, Belarus, Burma Myanmar, Cambodia, Chad, Chechnya, Costa Rica, Croatia, Cyprus, Czech Republic, Djibouti, Democratic Republic of Congo, Ecuador, Egypt, Eritrea, Ethiopia, Estonia, Georgia, Greece, Guatemala, Guinea-Bissau, Honduras, India, northern Iraq, Iran, Israel, Jordan, Kenya, Kosovo, Kyrgyzstan, Latvia, Lebanon, Laos, Liberia, Libya, Lithuania, Federal Yugoslav Republic of Macedonia, Mauritania, Moldova, Mongolia, Mozambique, Nagorno-Karabakh, Namibia, Nepal, Nicaragua, Oman, Pakistan, Peru, Philippines, Poland, Russia, Rwanda, Senegal, Somaliland, Sri Lanka, Sudan, Syria, Taiwan, Tajikistan, Thailand, Tunisia, Uganda, Ukraine, Vietnam, Western Sahara, Yemen, Federal Republic of Yugoslavia, Zambia, and Zimbabwe. See International Campaign to Ban Landmines, *Landmine Monitor Report: Toward a Mine Free World*, Executive Summary, Mine Clearance section, September 12, 2001, accessed at <www.icbl.org/lm2001/exec/hma.html#Heading680>.

[2] Moritz von Jacobi, a Prussian émigré who worked at the Russian Committee on Underwater Experiments, is credited with designing the first practical mine, although many others, including American David Bushnell, the "father" of the submarine, have been given recognition. An interesting depiction of torpedo (mine) warfare in the War of 1812 can be found in James Tertius De Kay, *The Battle of Stonington: Torpedoes, Submarines and Rockets in the War of 1812* (Annapolis, MD: U.S. Naval Institute Press, 1990).

[3] See E.B. Potter, *Sea Power: A Naval History* (Annapolis: U.S. Naval Institute Press, 1981), 235. Interview conducted by Thomas R. Bernitt with Charles Hayden, U.S. Navy participant in the North Sea Barrage, December 1975.

[4] Gregory K. Hartmann, *Weapons That Wait* (Annapolis, MD: U.S. Naval Institute Press, 1979), 55.

[5] Ibid., 78.

[6] The basic design had not changed since 1904.

[7] Hartmann, 81.

[8] Ibid., 231.

[9] Surface sea mines covertly deployed by Libya in the Red Sea from commercial ships in the 1980s were not moored but allowed to float, which eliminated the weight of the mooring device and the effort required for mooring.

[10] Based on such specifics as the ship's size, design characteristics, composition of materials, and, at times, even the location of its construction.

[11] The requirement for an air cavity, necessary for buoyancy, reduces the available space within the mine for explosives.

[12] Walter LaFeber, *Inevitable Revolutions: The United States in Central America* (New York: Norton, 1984), 305.

[13] Malcolm W. Cagle and Frank A. Manson, *The Sea War in Korea* (Annapolis, MD: U.S. Naval Institute Press, 1957), 220.

[14] In proposing "global solutions" via an arms control process, we are proceeding in a similar spirit as the International Campaign to Ban Landmines. This opens the chapter to criticism from both sides of the arms control argument. On the one hand, it can be argued that arms control regimes have never actually worked during times of war (the Hague agreements on mines did not in World War I or subsequent wars), and to develop a sea mine ban is but a deceptive fiction. This criticism can also be leveled at the recent treaty to ban landmines—an effort supported most vocally by European nations and Canada (who presumably have a sophisticated understanding of the effectiveness of treaty law) and considered of sufficient merit to earn a Nobel Peace Prize. On the other hand, it could be argued that a ban on sea/littoral mines would prove a "military advantage" to naval powers as the United States—as if such an advantage somehow lessens the moral principles on which the case for arms control is publicly argued by most proponents. The same military advantage case can also be made against bans on landmines. In garnering publicity, any movement for a ban on sea/littoral mines would suffer from a lack of widely publicized photographs of children being blown up by mines washed ashore on beaches (or planted in the surf zone) or drowned merchant sailors.

Chapter 21

Expeditionary and Amphibious Warfare

George V. Galdorisi

The war the nation fights today is not a war of America's choosing. It is a war that was brought violently and brutally to America's shores by the evil forces of terror. It is a war against America and America's way of life. It is a war against all that America holds dear. It is a war against freedom itself.[1]

—*Quadrennial Defense Review Report*, September 30, 2001

A military, naval, littoral war, when wisely prepared and discreetly conducted, is a terrible sort of war. Happy for that people who are sovereigns enough of the sea to put it into execution! For it comes like thunder and lightning to some unprepared part of the world.[2]

—Thomas More Molyneux, *Conjunct Expeditions*, 1759

In his Foreword to the *Quadrennial Defense Review Report* (*QDR Report*), Secretary of Defense Donald Rumsfeld puts an exclamation point on the impact that the terrorist attacks of September 11, 2001, had on the United States. A variety of forces were already causing the United States to place an enhanced emphasis on defeating terrorism and on ensuring the security of America by elevating homeland security as a new mission area. The attacks accelerated those efforts.

Some commentators have suggested that the forces of globalization make America more vulnerable. Others have suggested that these same forces contribute to America's position as the world's sole superpower and provide the wherewithal for the

George V. Galdorisi serves as senior adviser in the Space and Naval Warfare Systems Center, San Diego, California, where he helps direct center efforts in strategic planning and corporate communications. Prior to joining the center, he completed a 30-year career as a naval aviator, culminating in 14 years of consecutive experience as executive officer, commanding officer, commodore, and chief of staff. He served several tours in the expeditionary warfare forces, including command of USS *Cleveland* (LPD–7) and Amphibious Squadron Seven. He is the author of over 100 articles in professional journals, as well as two books on the law of the sea and two novels, *The Coronado Conspiracy* and *For Duty and Honor*.

United States to defend itself against a wide range of threats.[3] Regardless of the school of thought to which one subscribes, one thing is clear: the U.S. security paradigm has dramatically changed at the dawn of a millennium marked by globalization.

The *QDR Report* and the Secretary of Defense's 2002 *Annual Report to the President and Congress* provide a roadmap to this new security paradigm. Significantly, these reports do not envision a strategy that causes America to hunker down and devolve into a "Fortress America" solution for dealing with terrorism and homeland security. Rather, it articulates four overarching defense policy goals that keep America engaged in a globalizing world.

These goals—assuring allies and friends; dissuading future military competition; deterring threats and coercion against U.S. interests; and if deterrence fails, decisively defeating any adversary—underscore America's commitment to remain engaged globally, thus continuing to make forward defense an essential part of the homeland security equation.[4] A substantial part of that forward defense is provided by naval expeditionary forces writ large—and by amphibious warfare forces specifically.

While globalization is a relatively new term, expeditionary and amphibious warfare have existed for several millennia, and this way of war has been part of the U.S. lexicon for well over 2 centuries, dating back as far as 1775.[5] (For much of this chapter, amphibious warfare will be subsumed under the term *expeditionary warfare*, which is current Navy and Marine Corps usage.) In light of the profound impact of globalization and the historical importance that naval expeditionary warfare has played in the U.S. security paradigm, it is important to understand the trade space where these two intersect. How do U.S. expeditionary warfare forces impact globalization? Conversely, how does globalization impact the mission of current and future U.S. expeditionary warfare forces?

Understanding this intersection between globalization and expeditionary warfare can help ensure that expeditionary warfare forces fielded by the United States will be as relevant as possible throughout this century. The available evidence strongly suggests that the changes wrought by globalization are profound—and they profoundly affect the ways in which expeditionary warfare forces will be shaped. As nations, and especially the United States, have interests overseas that are critical to national political and economic survival, the ability to react quickly to crises across the globe is more essential now than it ever was before. A robust expeditionary warfare capability is a critical element of the ability to provide this response.

Globalization: Accelerating in the 21st Century

U.S. security goals are framed within the context of dramatic changes to the international security environment. *Globalization*—which is defined as the international interaction of information, financial capital, commerce, technology, and labor at exponentially greater speeds than previously thought possible—is perhaps the seminal factor impacting this environment.[6] For the Nation to remain strong, its security policy must respond to globalization by shaping the emerging world order in a way that protects vital interests, including the American homeland, as well as those of our allies and friends.[7]

A previous study, *The Global Century: Globalization and National Security*, frames the environment in which naval expeditionary forces will operate and emphasizes the enduring value that these forces have in shaping the global security environment. The broad consensus of many commentators contributing to this study is that the global era calls for a military strategy that combines peacetime regional engagement, crisis management, and maintenance of warfighting capabilities to mitigate and contain likely conflicts and that this overarching strategy argues strongly for a reorientation of military operations toward expeditionary warfare.

The ongoing migration of world population to cities on or near coasts, combined with the growing reach of modern weapons, makes the objective area for decisive military operations more accessible to naval expeditionary forces, which promises to place even greater demands on the use of carrier battlegroups (CVBGs) and amphibious ready groups (ARGs).[8] Furthermore, the inability of airpower alone to defeat an enemy decisively—as evidenced by recent operations in Iraq, Kosovo, and Afghanistan—argues strongly that forces such as the Marine air-ground task forces (MAGTFs) embarked in ARGs will be essential to bring future crises to a successful resolution.[9]

Changes wrought by globalization, especially the dramatic expansion of international trade between and among emerging economies, increase the likelihood that America's naval expeditionary forces will operate most frequently in areas of growing strategic instability. These areas include the southern belt of strategic instability that stretches from the Balkans, through the Middle East and the Persian Gulf, across South Asia, and through the Asian Crescent from Southeast Asia northward to Taiwan and Japan.[10] Importantly, these are areas where ARGs and MAGTFs operate most effectively.

Naval expeditionary forces are ideally suited to operate in these forward areas and take on the mission of peacetime environment shaping for the strategic purpose of promoting favorable changes while dampening chaos and preventing damaging trends. This strategic shaping is crucial to bring about stable conditions and constructive changes that likely would not evolve on their own.

The strategy employed by these naval expeditionary forces will not be positional or continental but instead will focus on applying flexible, adaptive, and decisive military power projection at ever-shifting locations. The new strategic landscape suggests that naval expeditionary forces will perform a more critical role than they did in the past, that they will not act alone but in concert with joint and coalition forces to enable these forces to enter the fight and perform their missions, and that they will be used more frequently as the searing forces of globalization create worldwide crises requiring their use.

Thus, while globalization impacts many aspects of the U.S. security paradigm, it impacts naval expeditionary forces in general and amphibious warfare forces in particular perhaps more significantly than other components of America's arsenal. At issue is whether the Department of Defense has the flexibility and agility to respond to the impacts of globalization in a way that enhances the ability of these forces to maximize their contribution to the national defense.

Expeditionary Warfare: Focused on Amphibious Warfare Forces

It is possible to become adrift in a sea of similar definitions: expeditionary warfare, naval expeditionary warfare, amphibious warfare, amphibious operations, and others. These terms often mean different things to different people; therefore, a moment spent on definitional accuracy is a moment well spent.

At one end of the definitional spectrum, *expeditionary warfare* can be understood to mean any combination of joint or coalition forces operating outside of the continental United States to accomplish some military mission. In this context, we include virtually all naval forces, CVBGs, ARGs, independent formations of surface combatants, and strategic submarines, as well as Army and Air Force expeditionary forces and the like. At the other end of the spectrum, the term *amphibious operations* is typically used in the context of assaults against an enemy beachhead in much the same way that these operations were conducted over a half-century ago during World War II.

A more nuanced definition, focused on naval expeditionary warfare and amphibious warfare in the changed security environment of the 21st century, requires that we sharpen our terms and agree upon precisely what these terms mean. For the purpose of this analysis, *naval expeditionary warfare* refers to operations carried out by forward-deployed CVBGs and ARGs, sometimes working independently but more often operating in mutual support.

With respect to the ARG, this should be understood to mean a group of three Navy ships designed specifically for amphibious warfare—typically a general purpose amphibious assault ship (LHA)/multipurpose amphibious assault ship (LHD), an amphibious transport dock (LPD), a landing ship dock (LSD), and an embarked Marine expeditionary unit (special operations capable) (MEU[SOC]). This is the smallest unit of a MAGTF. Larger MAGTFs are comprised of at least one ARG/MEU(SOC) and additional assets.

Finally, amphibious warfare must be defined in more universal terms than World War II-type assaults on enemy beaches. For the purposes of this analysis, we define *amphibious warfare* as the broad scope of those operations conducted by a MAGTF embarked in one or more ARGs (along with other associated forces comprising the MAGTF). A CVBG or other forces in theater may support these forces, but the ARG/MAGTF team provides the essential elements of the forces for the operation.[11]

Maintaining expeditionary forces that can conduct amphibious warfare (and prevail over any type of enemy) will be one of the central challenges for U.S. force planners in the years ahead. The U.S. Commission on National Security/21st Century brought this into sharp focus in their report *Roadmap for National Security: Imperative for Change*, which noted that:

> Ultimately, the transformation process will blur the distinction between expeditionary and conventional forces, as both types of capabilities will eventually possess the technological superiority, deployability, survivability, and lethality now called for in the expeditionary forces. For the near term, however, those we call expeditionary capabilities require the most emphasis. Consequently, we recommend that the Defense Department devote its highest priority to improving and further developing its expeditionary capabilities.[12]

At the intersection of globalization and amphibious warfare, the issue remains whether the United States ascertains clearly the impact of globalization on amphibious warfare and makes needed changes to amphibious warfare force structure and doctrine to maximize the utility and viability of these forces. To address this issue, we need to examine where expeditionary warfare in general and amphibious warfare in particular have been and where this complex warfighting discipline appears to be going.

A Century of Change

The expeditionary warfare tradition of the U.S. Navy and Marine Corps is as old as the Nation itself. It is a tradition and capability unmatched or even approached by any military force in the world. Expeditionary warfighting is a mindset derived from a naval character that has allowed the Navy-Marine Corps team to provide the Nation the enduring means to shape and influence global events with military operations mounted from the sea. Modern naval expeditionary warfare had its origins in exercises conducted during the decades preceding World War II, which has led to the development of today's unique operational capabilities, tailored support equipment, and the finely honed skills that continue to ensure success.

During half a century of hot and cold wars since the end of World War II, the Navy and Marine Corps together have maintained a strong maritime forward presence, influencing the perceptions of friends and potential foes simply by being on-scene when events develop. Centered on multimission CVBGs and ARGs, forward-deployed naval forces have been formidable instruments for peacetime engagement and crisis response, as well as conflict deterrence and conflict resolution. Their inherent flexibility has allowed them to operate effectively in a wide range of scenarios and across different levels of conflict—an unparalleled capability.

Sea-based forward presence enables the United States to maintain regional stability in the least intrusive way by avoiding the stationing of ground forces on foreign soil. Experience has shown that many countries prefer the less provocative, low-profile presence of a naval expeditionary force that remains continuously on-scene with a sustainable, combat-credible punch that is both understood and respected. These forces can deploy from the sea and withdraw again very quickly, or they can remain on station—over the horizon and out of sight—monitoring an emerging crisis while preparing to intervene. Their appearance does not necessarily signal a long-term presence, but it still affords sustained reassurance of commitment to friend and foe alike.

Commandant of the Marine Corps, General James Jones, recently underscored this capability in remarks that highlighted the enduring value of forward-deployed naval expeditionary forces:

> What we want here is balance, and the balance has to be, for a superpower, to be able to do a little bit of everything very well. It seems to me there's tremendous value in having an expeditionary service that is forward-deployed, that on a moment's notice can bring to bear all of the elements of combined arms to make a point—whether it is to deter, to influence, to shape, or to respond to an actual crisis. . . . The Marine Corps is the only branch of the military that can deploy rapidly around the world from Navy ships, sustain itself for weeks and bring "combined arms"—ground troops, air support and naval firepower—to bear against an adversary.[13]

Expeditionary Warfare Forces: First Responders and Force Enablers

Joint Vision 2020 (the Chairman of the Joint Chiefs of Staff strategic vision) "operationalizes" the way in which the United States intends to employ its military forces to accomplish the missions assigned by the President and Secretary of Defense. This emerging vision of military operations has U.S. forces maintaining a strong forward-presence posture and fighting in and through the littorals. Naval expeditionary forces are the bedrock of this capability.[14]

These forward-deployed naval expeditionary forces provide the first responders when crisis erupts and also become the joint and coalition force enablers if a conflict persists after these forces first respond. The multimission capability of amphibious warfare forces causes these forces—and particularly the MAGTF—to be the expeditionary warfare forces used most frequently in response to a wide spectrum of crises, especially in the last decade of the last century. There are profound reasons for this.

Naval expeditionary forces provide credible combat power forward deployed to achieve regional stability, deter aggression, provide timely crisis response, and defeat an enemy that seeks to pursue actions inimical to our interests. They provide the President and Secretary of Defense with a flexible and effective instrument to promote stability and project power in regions of importance. Combat-credible formations such as the MAGTF contribute substantially to this effort by providing ready, robust, credible, and scalable forward presence to assure access for and enable other joint forces to make their unique contributions.

The ability to reassure friends and allies, deter potential adversaries, and, when necessary, engage in combat at all levels of intensity makes these naval expeditionary forces especially valuable as the indispensable force that enables the United States to put its entire military into play. Rotational CVBGs and ARGs help shape and stabilize the regional security environment by being continuously on-scene with a combat-credible and sustainable presence. Serving as sovereign and maneuverable U.S. bases, unencumbered by any footprint ashore, they are well positioned to project influence and reassure allies and friends.

This combat-credible presence can deter regional foes from initiating a crisis. Presence is provided by rotational and surged CVBGs and ARGs and suggests to a potential adversary that response to aggression will be swift and massive. These forces are task organized, sized, and configured to deter aggression by their presence. Should a regional aggressor not respond to deterrence, these naval expeditionary forces deployed forward to provide deterrence are also the forces most likely to respond rapidly to an emerging crisis.

The deployment patterns of CVBGs and ARGs are carefully constructed by theater combatant commanders to ensure that at least one of these battle formations is within striking distance—or a short steaming distance away—of likely areas of concern. Importantly, in addition to serving as first responders to a crisis, they provide the wherewithal for the application of joint combat power as the crisis continues.

Should a crisis or conflict require U.S. response beyond that provided by on-scene CVBGs and ARGs, a more robust joint or coalition response will be required. The unique contribution of these naval expeditionary forces comes through their value as an enabling force during the transition from crisis to conflict since they are also shaped specifically to be the backbone for the rapid and scalable application of joint forces.

The ability of naval expeditionary forces to form this backbone for the application of joint combat power by all branches of the U.S. military makes them the indispensable element in the application of joint and coalition combat power. The Marines embarked with the ARG typically provide the initial combat power ashore and assure access for follow-on joint forces as they arrive on-scene. By denying the enemy sanctuary and seizing beachheads, ports, and airfields early on in a conflict, these MAGTFs foreclose enemy options and enable joint forces to focus on delivering combat power deep inland.

Without forward-deployed, combat-credible naval forces on station in littoral areas and without a force such as a MAGTF able to provide boots on the ground immediately, it is difficult to imagine a scenario in which joint forces could be effectively employed. Being there before the start of a crisis or conflict is the cardinal prerequisite for the application of our joint military power, and the recurring cost of our entry—the cost of fighting our way in—is considerably less if the forces that help enable power projection are present beforehand in peacetime.

Thus in crises across the broad spectrum of conflict, it is amphibious warfare forces delivering the capabilities of a MAGTF that are called upon most frequently to deal with events ranging from humanitarian assistance, to peacemaking, to noncombatant evacuation, to peacekeeping, to a wide range of other missions. How do these amphibious warfare forces impact the pace of globalization, and has globalization fundamentally changed the nature of the amphibious warfare mission?

Globalization and Expeditionary Warfare: A Symbiotic Relationship?

The forces impelling globalization suggest the need for a military strategy that combines peacetime regional engagement, crisis management, and maintenance of warfighting capabilities to mitigate and contain likely conflicts. As concerns about the impact of globalization on U.S. security have gained traction during the past decade, U.S. forces have often been called upon to operate in multiple, simultaneous, lesser regional contingencies.[15] The number of contingencies is striking. During the 1990s, the United States engaged in more than 500 lesser regional contingencies.[16] The ability to respond to these contingencies—occurring at the rate of one per week—depends upon the ability of naval expeditionary forces to remain forward deployed, mobile, flexible, and combat-credible.

Expeditionary warfare forces in general and amphibious warfare forces in particular have provided first responders to these crises that occur more frequently. Less well understood is the impact that these forces have on the globalization process. What effect does the ability of the United States to field a robust amphibious warfare capability have on the ongoing process of globalization? Are these forces a facilitating element, or are they merely crisis response forces operating on the margins?

The economy that essentially defines globalization is built on the worldwide transport of goods and services as well as the accelerating connectivity wrought by modern telecommunications and information technology. Although some time-critical material travels by air, the overwhelming bulk of this worldwide transport occurs by sea and is facilitated by international law such as the 1982 United Nations Convention on the Law of the Sea and other accords.[17] However, regional aggressors, international pirates, rogue states, international terrorists, and the like have little respect for international law. Ultimately, it is incumbent on maritime powers such as the United States to guarantee this worldwide transport of goods and services by protecting the ocean commons—both the high seas and the ports of embarkation and debarkation.

In concert with the navies of allied nations, the Navy and Marine Corps are the guarantors of international trade, allowing it to flourish and expand without the fear of long-term disruption. While localized crises such as the Iraq-Iran tanker war during the 1980s can temporarily disrupt international trade, ultimately the maritime powers in general, and the United States in particular, restore order on the global commons with their naval forces. Clearly, without this worldwide naval presence—and the threat of retaliation against those who would disrupt world trade—it is unlikely that globalization as we know it today would be a reality, and thus, the continued expansion of a globalizing economy could well be an uncertain thing.

Increasingly, expeditionary warfare forces are becoming more visible in their role in undergirding the political stability necessary for globalization. Other naval assets—such as CVBGs, submarines, independently operating surface combatants, and long-range tactical aviation—play key roles in enforcing order on the high seas portion of the global commons. But it is the nature of amphibious forces—that is, the ability to project power from the sea onto the land in a measured, tailored fashion—that makes them the most likely asset to be called upon to perform stability operations. Landing marines ashore has an obviously longer-term impact (and more flexible outcome) than aerial bombing or a missile strike. In this sense, amphibious forces are the most visible sign of reassurance for friendly nations and deterrence for potential hostile actors.

Should an aggressor threaten commerce on the global commons—either on the high seas or in the littorals—expeditionary warfare forces are structured to extract swift retribution: from destroying ships, aircraft, ports, or airfields that disrupt or even threaten to disrupt global commerce, to protecting the ports and airfields of friendly nations to ensure the continued free flow of trade, to directly attacking pirates or other rogue entities that seize or otherwise hazard international merchant shipping, to escorting this same shipping during selected portions of their transits.

The ability of expeditionary warfare forces to serve as key guarantors of international commerce from terminus to terminus makes them indispensable assets in facilitating and accelerating globalization. While these forces dramatically impact globalization, so too does globalization impact the rule set for the conduct of amphibious warfare. This suggests that the paradigm for expeditionary warfare may be changing as rapidly as globalization is changing the world.[18]

Changing the Rules of Expeditionary Warfare

The U.S. paradigm for expeditionary warfare may be undergoing fundamental change as Navy and Marine forces dedicated to this mission seek to remain relevant throughout the ensuing decades. This paradigm shift may move us away not only from what we were accustomed to in the post-Cold War world of the last decade or so but also from what we were accustomed to at the turn of the century. This new rule set for expeditionary warfare may change the way that expeditionary warfare forces will be employed across the spectrum of conflict.

While there is no way to predict accurately the precise scope of the increasing demands on the use of expeditionary warfare forces, the available evidence suggests that these forces will be used, at a minimum episodically and at a maximum continuously, as regional and international tensions ebb and flow in response to the searing forces of globalization. While there will be demands for these forces for a host of reasons, they will be most frequently called upon to deter or defeat direct threats to the United States or its allies.

Threats to the United States now come from a widely dispersed group of nations as well as from transnational groups. Given the vast distances involved, it is unlikely America can respond to these threats by surging forces from the continental United States. Naval expeditionary warfare forces, especially amphibious warfare forces, will need to be on-scene simultaneously in multiple theaters and will have to be prepared to take decisive action without immediate reinforcement. This argues for a larger footprint than that to be provided by the 36 amphibious warfare ships currently in the Future Years Defense Plan.[19]

Economic macro-trends and demographic shifts unleashed by globalization will likely increase the need for expeditionary warfare forces to protect what globalization has wrought. As more goods move by sea, protection of ships and ports will place increasing demands on amphibious warfare forces, particularly when an armed force on the ground may be required on short notice to protect port facilities. Globalization has accelerated dramatic demographic shifts as populations have moved toward the coastline, drawn by the economic vitality of coastal cites that are the terminus points for the tremendously enhanced worldwide trade. The mega-cities of this century will be clustered along the coast. Thus, the objective area for the overwhelming number of world crises will be within the operational and tactical reach of amphibious warfare forces.

Other forces of globalization exacerbate this need for expeditionary warfare forces. As the Cold War camps continue to dissolve, economic independence makes the world community less dependent on superpower (even the lone superpower) protection, and nations become more conscious of their own individual sovereignty, U.S.

access to overseas bases continues to decline. This makes the need for amphibious warfare forces that can operate independent of these bases even greater.

The potent combination of modern Navy amphibious assault ships and a modern and modernizing Marine Corps tactical mobility triad built around the MV–22 Osprey tilt-rotor aircraft, the landing craft air cushion (LCAC) and the advanced amphibious assault vehicle (AAAV) will provide the ARG and MAGTF with a power projection capability—not replicated anywhere else—and with the operational agility, strategic mobility, potent lethality, and embedded sustainment to influence events ashore decisively. This makes these amphibious warfare forces best suited to respond to ongoing crises in the littorals.

Once ashore, MAGTFs are task organized, armed, equipped, and trained to deal with the spectrum of crises unleashed by the forces of globalization. This is articulated perhaps most vividly in the Marine Corps view of future warfighting in urban areas—the so-called three-block war in which the MAGTF will operate in highly populated areas, often conducting humanitarian assistance, peacekeeping, and warfighting simultaneously in a three-block area. An almost hypothetical notion when the Marines first proposed it, this taxonomy has gained traction as the realities of intervention in the littorals have made this the new paradigm for our expeditionary warfare forces.

As noted throughout this volume (particularly in chapter 25), the international trade in increasingly lethal weapons systems is increasing as globalization continues to break down trade barriers. The access to these weapons on the part of potentially hostile nations or groups will continue to shape both the offensive and defensive makeup of expeditionary warfare forces. The ability to cope with a wide array of antiaccess threats ranging from ballistic missiles, to naval mines, to cruise missiles, to adversary aircraft, ships, submarines and craft, to suicide attackers across a wide spectrum will drive the systems, sensors, platforms, and weapons for expeditionary warfare forces being built for the future.

While the exact nature of these threats continues to evolve, some of the capabilities that future expeditionary warfare forces must leverage are becoming evident. A first-order requirement is for these forces to leverage the tremendous American advantage in command, control, communications, computers, intelligence, surveillance, and reconnaissance (C^{4}ISR) in order to fight in a network-centric versus a platform-centric manner and thus to maximize the warfighting capabilities of the entire force. Another first-order requirement is to harness similarly the full range and depth of U.S. intelligence capabilities—those traditionally used by expeditionary warfare forces as well as those not as leveraged as frequently.

Changing the rule set to take on the additional missions, as well as to increase the scope of some specialized missions that will likely fall to these forces, could impossibly strain current and future amphibious warfare forces if they also continue to take on the full spectrum of missions that they currently perform. While there is an understandable unwillingness on the part of any military organization to give up missions due to the fear that this may lead to the loss of force structure, this is a case in which—given the broad scope of the missions that the ARG and MAGTF team must be prepared to conduct—decreasing the emphasis on some missions should not cause Navy planners and budgeters undue concern.

Given the dramatic shifts in the global security paradigm, it is unlikely that naval expeditionary forces will fight a pitched battle with a peer-competitor navy on the high seas. Thus, systems, sensors, platforms, and weapons focused on that mission can probably receive a decreased emphasis. More directly relevant to expeditionary warfare forces, it is increasingly unlikely that the entire expeditionary warfare force will be required to make simultaneously a full-blown amphibious assault against a hostile beach. Clearly, we should not divest ourselves of all our amphibious assault capability built up so carefully over the past decades. However, a portion of those platforms and systems optimized for such assaults might be reconstituted to go around, go over, or otherwise avoid such direct assaults.

Conversely, based on their actions in recent contingencies, as well as an extrapolation of plausible scenarios, expeditionary warfare forces will likely be called upon to intensify their focus on a number of mission areas as they continue to operate in areas of growing strategic instability, especially along the southern belt of Asia.

Missions that put a premium on the inherent mobility and ability of amphibious warfare forces are missions that these forces will likely be called upon to conduct with more regularity. Thus, missions such as in extremis hostage rescue, clandestine operations, noncombatant evacuation, intelligence gathering, tactical recovery of downed aviators, force protection, and other small unit operations are the kinds of missions that amphibious warfare forces will continue to undertake with increasing frequency.

Significantly, all of these missions require small numbers of highly trained, elite marines to be transported quickly to an objective area. There, they must be supported by robust C4ISR systems and be backed up by on-call combat-credible power should adversary forces gain the upper hand. These small units will be required to operate autonomously and covertly or in mutual support of other small units. Upon completion of an operation, these forces must be quickly extracted, and sufficient backup extraction capability must exist in order to ensure that no marines are left behind in hostile territory.

These are the mission areas that can be seen on the horizon based on an informed extrapolation of the changes that globalization has already made to our security paradigm. But what about the changes that cannot be seen yet? Capabilities cannot be built into our amphibious warfare forces based on what is not yet known.

However, a process can be put in place that can be responsive to the ongoing changes wrought by globalization.

To hedge against ongoing changes in the security paradigm impelled by globalization, Navy and Marine Corps amphibious warfare forces need to maintain a robust science and technology and research and development base that keeps pace with technologies being developed in response to emerging threats. Given the lengthy Department of Defense procurement process, a responsive capability must include the ability to prototype rapidly systems, sensors, platforms, and weapons and get them into the hands of the warfighters without undue delay.

Ultimately, the ability of amphibious warfare forces to deal with a dramatically changing security paradigm wrought by globalization will be dependent on the men and women of the force, the platforms that they serve on, and the sensors and weapons that they bring to the fight. In light of the crucial role that these forces play in the Nation's defense, a thorough review of these important parts of the equation is imperative.

Keeping Expeditionary Warfare Relevant in a Globalizing Century

Expeditionary warfare forces are crucial contributors to national security today, but they will only remain so in the future if they continuously change to meet emerging threats impelled by a globalizing world. While the precise outlines of these changes are difficult to discern, there are reasonable vectors that can be taken to ensure that expeditionary warfare forces continue to remain relevant throughout this century of dramatic changes. The 10 policy choices or *vectors* presented here (categorized by component or capability) are not final solutions, but rather proposals that should be vetted throughout Navy and Marine Corps leadership to determine if they have the potential to enhance the effectiveness of our expeditionary warfare forces today—and well into the future.

Personnel. The missions that MAGTFs are likely to be involved in over the next several decades will most frequently involve small unit tactics with perhaps a squad or platoon of marines operating in rapid-action, high-stress environments. These operations will likely mirror missions conducted by special operations forces, such as Navy SEALS, Army Rangers, and Air Force Special Forces, much more closely than they mirror the more generalized amphibious assault operations that MAGTFs are currently task-organized and trained to conduct. The Corps will need to determine whether some of the resources spent on maintaining a large force of capable—but generally skilled—marines would be better spent on a smaller force of elite special forces marines and on the equipment that they need to conduct specialized missions.

C^4ISR. While upgrades to equipment across the board are required for MAGTFs to conduct the special missions that they will need to conduct in a globalizing world, there are some upgrades that are more critical than others. Small Marine Corps units operating independently in hostile territory where they will need to have extensive reach-back and fire support clearly need top-of-the-line integrated and interoperable C⁴ISR capability to have a high probability of achieving success in their missions. This C⁴ISR capability must seamlessly connect Marine units with each other and with Navy support units. Perhaps as importantly, this capability must connect these small units with the broad spectrum of joint force capabilities that may be brought to bear in a crisis—from satellites, to unmanned aerial vehicles, to other autonomous sensing and weapons platforms.

Surface Assault Platforms. In a globalizing security paradigm in which emphasis is placed on small unit tactics delivered rapidly and often covertly by elite marines, the Navy and Marine Corps should reevaluate the emerging tactical mobility triad (MV–22, LCAC, and AAAV) and determine if the tremendous and ongoing investment in surface assault platforms is prudent and affordable. This is not to say that the Marine Corps should divest itself of all surface assault capability; clearly the service must hedge its bets and retain significant capability in this area. However, with the decreasing likelihood of major, opposed amphibious assault on hostile beaches, perhaps a scaled-down platform commitment is worth considering. This change would also impact the makeup of the Navy hulls that transport the MAGTF, especially given the large footprint of craft such as the LCAC and the AAAV.

Air Assault Platforms. In an environment in which small MAGTF units must be transported by air quickly and often covertly, the composition of the Marine Corps air combat element (ACE) should be closely scrutinized. The current ACE, built around the venerable CH–46, CH–53–E, AH–1W, and UH–1 helicopters, as well as the AV–8B Harrier, is aging rapidly and is stressed to conduct current missions effectively. The Marine Corps is counting on the MV–22 Osprey to replace its aging CH–46 helicopters and perhaps eventually the CH–53E helicopter. The Osprey is a technologically advanced and highly capable platform, but it has been plagued by technical challenges and its long-term survival is not assured. Initially, the Marine Corps might be well served to develop a Plan-B for another air vehicle to replace its aging ACE transport aircraft should the Osprey not reach fruition. If the Osprey does survive and if the MAGTF moves toward an Osprey-dominant force, the capabilities of the entire ACE must be further evaluated in this context. The Osprey can outfly and outrange ACE components such as the AH–1W Cobra gunship that historically have provided the preponderance of escort support for Marine transport helicopters. If the Osprey is to transport Marines inland on special missions, than a companion support platform must be added to the mix to ensure that these helicopters are properly escorted.

Maritime Prepositioning Ships. The Navy has made a substantial investment in hulls, and the Marine Corps has made an equally large investment in equipment that is prepositioned aboard these ships. Three squadrons of maritime prepositioning ships (MPS) are strategically deployed worldwide close to areas where expeditionary warfare forces are likely to be engaged. The purpose of these ships is both to sustain a MEU(SOC) embarked in an ARG and to provide the equipment and supplies to enable an airlifted MAGTF to be configured for combat operations as an adjunct to amphibious warfare forces already in theater. Among other items, these ships carry an expeditionary airfield, a naval construction battalion, and a fleet hospital. While they deliver a robust capability, the enormous cost to both the Navy and Marine Corps should be reevaluated in light of the new role that expeditionary warfare forces are playing in the 21st century.[20] The Marine Corps may no longer need all of the heavy equipment resident in the ships of a maritime prepositioning squadron to be on-call and readily available simultaneously in three theaters of operation. Clearly, given the Title 10 requirement that the Marine Corps have three divisions and three air wings, this is not a decision that the Department of the Navy can make unilaterally. However, the issue should be dealt with forthrightly, not ignored. Additionally, as emerging technology makes high speed vessels more affordable, the Navy and Marine Corps should examine the viability of transitioning to a fleet of fewer—but faster—MPS in order to reduce both the number of hulls needed as well as the amount of Marine equipment tied up in these ships.

Seabasing and High Speed Vessels. Closely related to the issue of maritime prepositioning ships is the issue of seabasing and the viability of high speed vessels—both as MPS hulls and as high speed lift between and among ships. Seabasing is one of the primary tenets of the Navy Capstone Concept of naval operations. It is a concept that enhances the rapid, sustainable enabling force capabilities provided by forward-deployed expeditionary warfare forces.[21] Expeditionary warfare forces operating in an objective area for a sustained period require ongoing and substantial resupply. The seabasing concept provides this via sea-based as opposed to land-based sites. Among its primary attributes, seabasing provides the ability to resupply forces rapidly in an objective area while dramatically decreasing the risk to these forces. However, this concept of seabasing is critically dependent on the movement of enormous quantities of material between the sea base (notionally 100–200 miles off an adversary's coast) to the amphibious warfare forces operating in the objective area (notionally 25–50 miles off that same coast). This concept has been evaluated in simulations and in wargames. The Corps has begun experimenting with catamarans to move marines and material between bases in the Western Pacific. However, unless or until the Navy and Marine Corps make a substantial commitment to some form of high speed vessel as an adjunct to complement ARGs and maritime prepositioning squadrons, the concept of seabasing will remain just that—a concept.[22]

Unmanned Aerial Vehicles. The Navy and Marine Corps have been at the fore-front of unmanned aerial vehicle (UAV) development and have fielded the Pioneer UAV system that has been successfully employed in Operation *Desert Storm*, Kosovo, and numerous contingency operations, including Somalia and counterdrug missions. The capabilities delivered by UAV systems are critical to expeditionary warfare opera-tions in a globalizing world as these operations increasingly depend on extensive in-telligence preparation of the battlefield, C[4]ISR connectivity, battle damage assessment, and other capabilities that are delivered by UAVs in increasingly frequent situations where the risk of conducting such missions with a manned aircraft is deemed too high. The U.S. experience in Afghanistan validated the utility of UAVs and showcased the ca-pabilities of emerging UAV technology. To ensure the continued viability of amphibi-ous warfare forces, the Navy and Marine Corps must acquire this new technology as a matter of priority, since the extant Navy-Marine Corps UAV system, Pioneer, is based on late 1970s technology and has limitations that proscribe its tactical utility.[23] As the Navy and Marine Corps embrace the technology of emerging UAV technology, espe-cially systems such as Global Hawk, the capability built into these systems must enable them to link directly with ARG and MAGTF forces on the ground in order to exploit fully their tactical utility.

Tactical Fixed-Wing Aviation. Prior to the changes wrought by a globalizing world—and when the United States and Soviet Union were still locked in a Cold War paradigm—U.S. war plans envisioned scenarios in which an entire Marine division might be locked in a land battle in sites as remote as Norway. This spawned the need for large expeditionary airfields and for a substantial investment in Marine Corps tac-tical aviation so that sustained division-level operations could be conducted without the dependence on Navy or Air Force tactical aviation. While the Cold War paradigm has been eliminated, the enormous investment in Marine tactical aviation has been sustained. In light of the increasing downward pressure on Navy and Marine force structure, a thorough analysis of this mission area appears to be in order to determine if these funds might be more effectively used for other expeditionary warfare needs. In light of the integration, interoperability, and transformation of the Armed Forces envisioned in *Joint Vision 2020*, a thorough review of Marine tactical aviation—and the ability to meet these needs with other joint forces—would seem prudent.

Expeditionary/Amphibious Warfare Combatants. The pace of expeditionary war-fare wrought by globalization requires that Navy contribution to mission success in-volve more than the old paradigm of providing amphibious shipping to move a MEU-sized force from point to point. When the Navy shifted its strategic paradigm from the early-1980s maritime strategy to a littoral-focused *Forward . . . from the Sea* strategy, it placed greater emphasis on modernized amphibious warfare ships and new operating concepts for the amphibious fleet.[24] Through the end of the last decade, this change in emphasis was increasingly evident and resulted in the construction and fleet introduction of new classes of amphibious warships such as the LHD multipurpose amphibious assault ship and the LSD–41 and LSD–49 dock landing ships.[25] However, as naval budgets have come under increasing pressure, naval shipbuilding programs have been trimmed—often significantly—and absent a substantial infusion of new procurement funds. In fact, by the end of the decade, a navy of less than 300 ships is a reality. This downward pressure has negative impacts on expeditionary warfare, specifically in the delay of the LPD–17 *San Antonio*-class amphibious transport dock, sorely needed to replace the aging LPD–4 *Austin*-class, and the virtual elimination of the DD 21 (DD[X]) program, a ship that was counted upon to provide the Marines with significant fire support.[26] As the forces of globalization continue to require interventions in the world's littoral regions, a reevaluation of naval shipbuilding priorities with a view toward providing a more robust littoral warfare capability would seem advisable.

Development of Doctrine, Tactics, Techniques, and Procedures. More so than any two services of any nations, the U.S. Navy and Marine Corps must operate together effectively in order to have any chance of success. The establishment of the Director of Expeditionary Warfare (a Marine Corps major general with a Navy rear admiral as his deputy) within the Navy staff was one important step in coordinating Navy and Marine Corps procurement efforts in support of amphibious warfare. However, it is not clear that the same coordination exists in the area of development of Navy and Marine Corps doctrine, as well as associated tactics, techniques, and procedures. While some progress is being made in the field in forward-thinking organizations such as the expeditionary warfare training groups in the Atlantic and Pacific fleets, it is important that this coordination be matched in the area of the crucial doctrinal development that undergirds the way in which the Navy and Marine Corps operate together. Navy doctrine is developed and written by the Navy Warfare Development Command in Newport, Rhode Island, while Marine Corps doctrine is developed and written by the Marine Corps Combat Development Command in Quantico, Virginia. Coordination and cooperation in doctrinal development between these two commands is an area that would benefit from increased focus and emphasis.[27] In view of the absolute requirement for Navy and Marine Corps forces to work in close coordination with one another, ongoing efforts must be focused on avoiding a doctrinal divide between the two military services that must operate together most effectively.

These 10 vectors are not all-inclusive but represent primary issues that the Navy and Marine Corps must come to grips with to ensure that amphibious warfare forces are manned and equipped in a manner that guarantees that they remain relevant in the decades to come. Manned and equipped in this manner, these forces will continue to be major contributors to the accelerating pace of globalization.

Coming Full Circle: Expeditionary Warfare and the Pace of Globalization

At the intersection of globalization and expeditionary warfare, the question is not whether these two paradigms intersect—the available evidence strongly suggests that they do. Nor is the issue whether expeditionary warfare impacts globalization and whether globalization impacts expeditionary warfare. Clearly the impact on one upon the other is profound. The real issue is to what extent is the United States willing to invest in expeditionary warfare forces in order to ensure that international trade on the global commons—as well as other trends that undergird globalization—accelerate in ways that ensure the political and economic success of United States, its allies, and its friends.

In a summer 2001 radio interview, Deputy Secretary of Defense Paul Wolfowitz made the point that "The defense of our country isn't cheap, but it's proven to be a terrifically valuable investment."[28] The deputy secretary's comments are especially germane as they apply to amphibious warfare forces. The substantial investment in Navy and Marine Corps personnel, systems, sensors, platforms, and weapons is not cheap, and it must be evaluated against other needed capabilities among all of the military services. However, based on what these forces add to the political and economic security of the Nation, continued investment in naval expeditionary forces is the best way to ensure the Nation's continued prosperity in a globalizing world.

The core issue then becomes, as defense budgets rise and fall, what portion of those budgets are dedicated to assuring the viability of the Nation's expeditionary warfare forces? The answers belie simple statistical comparisons and go straight to the issue of national commitment and national will. The dialogue seems positive—but rhetoric is not reality. Where procurement dollars are spent will ultimately determine whether we have funded expeditionary warfare forces in a way that makes these forces viable assets in a globalizing world. As Presidents react to emerging international crises in this new millennium by asking, "Where are the expeditionary warfare forces?" the answer to this question will become self-evident.

Toward an Essential Expeditionary/Amphibious Warfare Force

When invading an enemy's country, men should always be confident in spirit, but they should fear, too, and take measures of precaution: and thus they will be at once most valorous in attack and impregnable in defense.[29]

> —Archidamus of Sparta, Speech to the Lacadaemonian expeditionary forces departing against Athens, 431 BCE

Amphibious flexibility is the greatest strategic asset that a sea power possesses.[30]

> —B.H. Liddell Hart
> *Deterrent or Defense*, 1960

These two quotations, proffered almost two and one-half millennia apart, suggest that much has changed—and that much remains the same. While technological advances have changed the face of warfare, what has not changed is that putting forces on the ground is often the only certain way to impose one's will on an adversary. These forces travel most efficiently by sea and operate most effectively in the near shore area where they can strike any littoral area almost without warning.

Expeditionary/amphibious warfare forces—especially the tailored force package comprising the ARG–MAGTF team—were accomplishing the expeditionary mission well before the 21st-century version of this mission emerged. Building on a long tradition of excellence, today's expeditionary warfare forces are engaged worldwide at a rate unprecedented in history. As macro-trends such as globalization make the need for naval expeditionary forces more imperative, the Navy-Marine Corps team is adapting to a changing world by leading military transformation with revolutionary new warfighting concepts, systems, sensors, platforms, and weapons designed to ensure this force's viability well into this century.

Notes

[1] U.S. Department of Defense, *Quadrennial Defense Review Report* (Washington, DC: Department of Defense, September 30, 2001), iii. Henceforth referred to as *QDR Report*.

[2] This quotation is from Thomas More Molyneux, *Conjunct Expeditions*, 1759, and is reproduced in U.S. Navy, *The Naval Amphibious Warfare Plan* (Washington, DC: Government Printing Office, October 1999), 11.

[3] There is an extensive body of literature articulating the manifest ways in which globalization benefits the United States. Some of this work asserts that globalization's benefits are uneven and benefit the industrialized nations more than those that are emerging. Other works focus on the antiglobalization movement in general. Nonetheless, the preponderance of the literature comes down squarely on the side of globalization as a force that benefits the United States. See, for example, Joseph S. Nye, Jr., "Globalization's Democratic Deficit," *Foreign Affairs* (July/August 2001), 2–6; John Micklethwait and Adrian Wooldridge, "The Globalization Backlash," *Foreign Policy* (September 2001), 16–27; Mary Kaldor, "Wanted: Global Politics," *The Nation* (November 5, 2001), 15–17; Robert Reich, "A Proper Global Agenda," *The American Prospect* (September 24, 2001), accessed at <www.prospect.org/print/v12/17reich-r.html>; and Kurt Campbell, "Globalization at War," *The Washington Post*, October 22, 2001, A19, for a sampling of recent literature on the subject.

[4] *QDR Report*, 11.

[5] For an excellent Web site offering links to Navy and Marine Corps history, see the Chief of Naval Operations Expeditionary Warfare (N75) Web site at <www.exwar.org>. The Marine Corps history Web site notes that the Continental Congress established the Marine Corps in November 1775 and that the first amphibious raid was conducted at New Providence, Bahamas, on March 3, 1776—four months before the signing of the Declaration of Independence.

[6] Richard L. Kugler and Ellen L. Frost, eds. *The Global Century: Globalization and National Security* (Washington, DC: National Defense University Press, 2001). Many contributors to these two volumes provide several somewhat similar definitions of *globalization*. The definition provided in the Foreword of this publication is perhaps the most useful in this context. Alternative definitions of globalization abound. See also Martin Wolf, "Will the Nation-State Survive Globalization," *Foreign Affairs* (January/February 2001), 178–190. Wolf states, "A 'globalized' economy could be defined as one in which neither distance nor national borders impede economic transactions." Joseph S. Nye, Jr., dean of Harvard University's Kennedy School of Government offers, "Globalization—networks of interdependence at worldwide distances," See Nye, "Globalization's Democratic Deficit."

[7] Craig Elwell, *CRS Report for Congress: Global Markets: Evaluating Some Risks the U.S. May Face* (Washington, DC: Congressional Research Service, February 11, 2001), 1–15. This document discusses some of the ways in which globalization benefits the United States and makes a strong case for U.S. backing of trends supporting globalization.

[8] *Naval Amphibious Warfare Plan*, 13. This document emphasizes the fact that by 2010, the littoral areas of the world will be home to over 70 percent of the world's population and over 80 percent of the world's capitals. Furthermore, these littoral areas represent the centers of economic activity and provide the land-sea-air juncture that enables trade and international interactions.

[9] The definition of a MAGTF can be found in the Marine Corps capstone doctrinal publication *MCDP–1: Warfighting* (Washington, DC: Government Printing Office, 1997). *MCDP–1* defines a *MAGTF* as "task organizations consisting of ground, aviation, combat service support, and command elements. They have no standard structure, but rather are constituted as appropriate for the specific situation," 55.

[10] Stephen J. Flanagan, Ellen L. Frost, and Richard L. Kugler, *Challenges of the Global Century: Report of the Project on Globalization and National Security* (Washington, DC: National Defense University Press, 2001), 16–17.

[11] As noted in chapter 19 of the current volume, the Office of the Chief of Naval Operations has recently initiated the development of a concept of an expeditionary assault group consisting of Aegis DDGs, SSNs, and combat logistics ships attached to (and trained with) current amphibious ready groups. This proposal is a significant step but can be assessed skeptically. Similar proposals have been studied in the past without resulting in changes to current ARGs. Likewise, it is unclear whether large surface combatants and submarines as currently configured can effectively defend amphibious forces within the littoral combat zone. Current surface capabilities can certainly defend amphibious warships while in deep water; however, significant deep-water threats to amphibious transit are currently few.

[12] The three publications of the U.S. Commission on National Security/21st Century (the Hart-Rudman Commission) include *New World Coming: American Security in the 21st Century* (Washington, DC: September 1999); *Seeking a National Strategy: A Concert for Preserving Security and Promoting Freedom* (Washington, DC: April 2000); and *Road Map for National Security: Imperative for Change* (Washington, DC: March 2001).

[13] Vernon Loeb, "For Jones, Marines, Time for a Change," *The Washington Post*, September 4, 2001, 17.

[14] *Joint Vision 2020: America's Military—Preparing for Tomorrow* (Washington, DC: Government Printing Office, June 2000). *Joint Vision 2020* is the DOD and joint staff capstone document that operationalizes the strategic direction for the Armed Forces and speaks to the ways in which joint forces will operate together to achieve full-spectrum dominance over an adversary.

[15] Barry Blechman, "Alternative Force Sizing Mechanism for the Department of Defense," unpublished briefing for DOD, September 2000.

[16] *Global Century*, 24.

[17] *1982 United Nations Convention on the Law of the Sea*, United Nations publication 1261 (1982), reproduced from UN Document/CONF.62/122 of October 7, 1982.

[18] According to chapter 13 of the current volume, European navies have come to recognize the increased importance of modern amphibious capabilities.

[19] Navy Program Objective Memorandum (POM) submission for fiscal years 2003–2007. The Navy POM and Future Years Defense Plan submissions are reported in multiple sources. For this analysis, the weekly newsletter compilation *Inside the Navy* was used as a primary source. For a concise analysis of the issues surrounding the size of the Navy, particularly the number of Navy ships, see Ronald O'Rourke, *CRS Report to Congress: Navy Ship Procurement Rate and the Planned Size of the Navy: Background and Issues for Congress* (Washington, DC: Congressional Research Service, August 28, 2001), 1–6. Additionally, for a recent analysis of the costs associated with maintaining the kind of forward naval presence practiced by our forward-deployed amphibious warfare forces, see Daniel Gouré, "The Tyranny of Forward Presence," *Naval War College Review* 54, no. 3 (Summer 2001), 11–24.

[20] *Naval Amphibious Warfare Plan*, 70. The current maritime prepositioned force consists of 13 ships deployed in 3 forward-deployed squadrons. These ships are privately owned and operated by three companies and leased by DOD. The Navy and Marine Corps are seeking funding for 2 additional hulls to bring the total force up to 15 ships.

[21] Navy Warfare Development Command, *Network Centric Operations: A Capstone Concept for Naval Operations in the Information Age*, draft report, 2001. The Capstone Concept envisions a Navy and Marine Corps team conducting network-centric operations in which U.S. and allied forces will derive power from the robust rapid networking of well-informed, geographically dispersed forces. The four principal tenets of network-centric operations include

information and knowledge advantage, assured access, effects-based operations, and forward sea-based forces. These forward sea-based forces rely on seabasing (that is, the rapid resupply of forces from mobile bases at sea) as an alternative to a dependence on land-based resupply sites. Emerging threats, particularly cruise missiles, make these land-based sites especially attractive and vulnerable targets. In the Navy-Marine Corps context, seabasing eliminates the standard practice of moving supplies delivered by maritime prepositioning ships ashore and marrying them to marines flown in to the same site, dramatically decreasing the risk to these forces.

[22] A point made with great frequency by Arthur Cebrowski, current director of the Office of Force Transformation. Cebrowski has been the most vocal proponent for the testing of high speed transport craft, such as H.M.A.S. *Jervis Bay.* On such testing, see, for example, William Polson, "Navy goes Down Under, explores future of amphib warfare: Australian catamaran gives possible glimpse of next generation gator," accessed at <www.c7f.navy.mil/news/200/09/16.html>.

[23] *Naval Amphibious Warfare Plan*, 64. The Pioneer UAV is the current naval tactical UAV system. Its missions are reconnaissance, surveillance, target acquisition, and battle damage assessment. The air vehicle has a range of 100 nautical miles, cruise speed of 65 knots, endurance of up to 5 hours, and an operational ceiling of 10,000 feet.

[24] *Global Century*, 485.

[25] *Naval Amphibious Warfare Plan*, 49–56.

[26] Navy Program Objective Memorandum and Future Years Defense Plan submissions and for fiscal years 2003–2007. For this analysis, the weekly newsletter compilation *Inside the Navy* was used as a primary source. The specific citation in this case is from *Inside the Navy*, November 5, 2001.

[27] One example of the degree of autonomy between Navy Warfare Development Command (NWDC) and Marine Corps Combat Development Command is the lack of coordination and cooperation in the development of the capstone documents for both Services, *MCDP–1 Warfighting* (Marine Corps) and *NDP–1 Naval Warfare* (Navy). The similarities in naming conventions belie completely separate paths to publication. The Marine Corps published *MCDP–1 Warfighting* in 1997 without significant Navy involvement. *Naval Warfare*, first published in 1994, recently went through extensive revision at NWDC but has been delayed indefinitely, largely due to a lack of consensus by the Marine Corps.

[28] Paul Wolfowitz, radio interview with Luis Torres, KNX News Radio, August 2, 2001.

[29] *Naval Amphibious Warfare Plan*, 77.

[30] Ibid., 5.

Chapter 22

A Marine Corps for a Global Century: Expeditionary Maneuver Brigades

Frank G. Hoffman

A globalizing world will place new demands on the U.S. Marine Corps. In such a world, the requirement for rapidly deployable expeditionary forces that are adept at complex contingencies will be much greater and certainly more frequent than the need to engage in simultaneous major theater wars. Developing preventative strategies and shifting locations of potential instability highlight an increased need for rapid strategic deployability and politically viable presence. It also demands greater readiness over a broader mission spectrum, but much of this mission spectrum is in the middle of the scale, in the "small wars" where Marine culture, experience, and history have evidenced a very nuanced and successful performance.

Operational Concepts

The Marines are well aware of the strategic context facing them and have been developing a strategy for matching their contribution to a changed national security emphasis. A new strategic vision and a number of innovative operational concepts have been developed to meet emerging demands. *Marine Corps Strategy 21* was recently issued to address how the Marines intend to respond to the complexities of the global century, and two concepts have particular utility in the coming decades.[1]

Expeditionary maneuver warfare (EMW) is the latest Corps capstone operational concept.[2] It is an umbrella concept that incorporates previously published operational concepts including *Operational Maneuver from the Sea* (OMFTS) and its supporting

Frank G. Hoffman is a civilian strategic planner at the Marine Corps Warfighting Laboratory in Quantico, Virginia. He is also a lieutenant colonel in the U.S. Marine Corps Reserve. In addition to his service on the staff of the Commission on Roles and Missions of the Armed Forces and the Hart-Rudman Commission, he has held policy planning positions in the Department of Defense. He is also the author of *Decisive Force: The New American Way of War* (Westport, CT: Praeger, 1996).

concept, *Ship to Objective Maneuver* (STOM). Expeditionary maneuver warfare frames these concepts and their application across the entire spectrum of conflict and combines the Marine warfighting philosophy of maneuver warfare with the Marine expeditionary mindset and culture. Expeditionary maneuver warfare focuses on:

- *Joint enabling*: the ability to use Marine forces to serve as a lead element of a joint task force, act as joint enablers, or serve as a maneuver element to exploit success.
- *Strategic agility*: the ability to transition rapidly from precrisis readiness to full combat capability while deployed in a distant theater.
- *Operational reach*: the ability to project and sustain relevant and effective power across the depth of a battlespace.
- *Tactical flexibility*: the capability to conduct a range of dissimilar missions, *concurrently*, in support of a joint team across the entire spectrum of conflict.

The Marine Corps developed the operational concept OMFTS beginning in the late 1980s, and the Commandant signed it in 1996. It applies maneuver warfare to expeditionary power projection and relies extensively upon the tightly integrated capabilities of the Navy-Marine Corps team. The major underlying tenet of OMFTS is the use of sea-based naval forces. Seabasing facilitates maneuver warfare by eliminating the requirement for an operational pause as the landing force builds combat power ashore, thereby freeing the Marine air-ground task force (MAGTF) from the slow build-up and protection of a traditional beachhead. This allows the force to exploit the sea as maneuver space while applying combat power ashore to achieve the operational objectives. Such a concept affords surprise, the ability to generate mass at a point of choosing, and much greater force protection. The latter is especially valuable in a weapons of mass destruction (WMD) environment or when enemy forces retain a ballistic missile capability.

OMFTS is applicable across the range of military operations, from major theater war to smaller-scale contingencies. It reflects the Corps expeditionary maneuver warfare concept in the context of amphibious operations from a sea base, as it enables the force to maximize effects, exploit opportunity, maintain tempo and initiative, while striking unexpectedly against enemy critical vulnerabilities. OMFTS provides increased operational flexibility through enhanced capabilities for sea-based logistics, fires, and command and control. If this increased operational flexibility is going to be achieved, the deliberate design and integration of naval capabilities is a must.

Operational Forces

Given the complexities of military operations in this millennium, and the revolutionary concepts being offered to drive combat development efforts, it should come as no surprise that the size and shape of military forces must adapt. While new concepts and technologies are clearly called for, equally innovative force designs are needed to maximize the overall impact of these concepts and systems. The Marines understand this, and several experiments have explored various tactical organizational designs from the basic Marine rifle squad to regimental structures designed to conduct widely dispersed operations. Some of these have been controversial.[3]

However, the full benefit of the technological revolution will never be incorporated if industrial age forces try to laminate new systems on old tactics or outdated structures. A sharply new strategic context mandates new capabilities that are the composite of concepts, technologies, and organizations. Changing only one component of the elements of innovation will retard progress and limit the contributions that the Corps makes to the Nation's security. Expeditionary maneuver warfare builds on existing concepts of organization, deployment, and employment, *and adapts them to the future strategic landscape.* Ultimately, adapting the Marines for the dynamic security environment that we find ourselves in will require serious evaluation of new organizational concepts. A fundamental principle in such an evaluation will be the need to view operations *as a continuous event from the port of embarkation to the operational objective ashore.*

The remainder of this chapter focuses on a proposal for adapting Marine forces to the future strategic landscape and designing forces that are fully ready and capable of executing operations seamlessly from deployment to decisive operations aimed at the operational objective. This proposal details a strategy-driven force structure that is optimized for the latest Corps operational concepts.

Proposal: Expeditionary Maneuver Brigades

The essence of this proposal is a transition from the Marine Corps basic structure of Marine expeditionary forces (MEFs) built around division and wings to MEFs comprised of two expeditionary maneuver brigades (EMBs) each. The active Corps would total 3 MEF headquarters and 6 EMBs of roughly 15,000 marines each. These organizations would not resemble a current Marine expeditionary brigade, as detailed later, nor would they be a mirror image.

In the past, there have been numerous proposals to organize into brigade-based systems.[4] Earlier proposals were rejected in the 1980s because of the Cold War threat environment and the need for robust combat forces for high-intensity conflict. Proposals made immediately after the demise of the Soviet Union were delayed due to the uncertainty of the emerging security environment and since then to assess new technology and innovative tactics. Proposals also face significant political obstacles since the Marine Corps is shielded by statutory provisions set out by Congress nearly half a century ago.[5] This legislation prescribes a specific force structure of three divisions and three aircraft wings and associated support. The Marine Corps has been officially reticent to discuss force structure changes but has been willing to debate internally and examine wide-ranging proposals in its experimentation program. In particular, the Marine Corps Warfighting Laboratory has postulated significantly different force designs in response to threat and technological developments.[6]

Sufficient granularity has been achieved now with respect to U.S. strategic interests and available technologies to evolve toward new organizational alternatives that are more modular and adaptive. Such modular force designs are being used by the Army and should have even greater utility for the Corps given its assigned missions.[7] In fact, given the tremendous costs postulated for the Army transformation initiative and the growing interest in joint response forces as part of the 2001 Quadrennial Defense Review, there seems to be a growing market for capabilities that the Marine Corps could and should provide the Nation, at a substantially lower cost.[8]

The expeditionary maneuver brigade would still contain the four basic elements of the MAGTF concept.[9] Each element would be altered, however, as outlined below.

Command Element. Each EMB would be commanded by a major general. The headquarters staff must be robust enough for *continuous* operations, be capable of independent operations, or serve as a joint task force headquarters. The staff would be kept to a minimum and redesigned to support a joint task force headquarters capability and support rapid and continuous staff planning and oversight processes.

Ground Combat Element (GCE). The GCE would be built around four infantry battalions and a tactical mobility battalion. The infantry battalions would be modified to be lighter and smaller with 11-man rifle squads and the elimination of 81-millimeter (mm) mortars in the battalion. The regiment would contain unmanned tactical vehicles including ground robotic systems and tactical unmanned aerial vehicles (UAVs). The size of the infantry battalion would be 700 to 750 marines versus today's 882 officers and enlisted personnel. Four infantry battalions per EMB are necessary to support rotating forward deployments and also reflect the manpower requirements for stability operations, humanitarian crises, and urban combat.

One EMB in each MEF would be oriented toward amphibious assault and would have an amphibious assault battalion with the new advanced amphibious assault vehicle (AAAV). The other EMB would be configured for rapid movement by strategic air assets and would contain a light armored battalion as its principal tactical mobility asset. These brigades would be responsible for planning and executing missions employing maritime prepositioned assets. There would be no tanks in either formation.

The organic fire support for the EMB would be provided by a fire support battalion comprised of 2 batteries of 155 mm howitzers, a 120 mm battery of 8 systems, and a high mobility mobile rocket battery for deep and area denial fires.

Combat Service Support (CSS). A brigade service support group would provide the requisite combat service support to its parent EMB. The CSS element would be shaped by reduced deliberate engineering, maintenance, and supply functions. It would focus instead on providing tailored expeditionary support with greater precision and velocity. It would have to be carefully tailored to be able to operate from a sea base. Extensive engineering and maintenance capabilities would be transferred to supporting establishments, outsourced, or shifted to the Marine Corps reserve.

Aviation Element. The aviation component of the EMB would contain three composite Marine aviation groups (MAGs). One MAG would be an assault support MAG, comprised of 3 MV–22 Osprey squadrons, a squadron of light attack helicopters, and a heavy support squadron with the CH–53. The fixed wing MAG would contain three squadrons of the short take-off, vertical landing (STOVL) version of the Joint Strike Fighter (JSF). The final group would contain air control and air defense assets, as well as operational UAVs. Consideration should be given to naval support elements that combine common Navy and Marine aircraft to a greater degree, perhaps in UAVs, utility and electronic warfare aircraft, and aerial refueling assets.

Budget and Programmatic Impacts. The principal purpose of an EMB proposal is to align the contributions of the Marine Corps better with the emerging strategic environment. Secondarily, the proposal has significant budget and program impacts. These will narrow the capability/resource gap that has plagued the Marines for the last decade. However, the emphasis must be on creating a better Marine Corps, not a smaller or cheaper force. Of particular note, the end-strength of the active Corps could be reduced by approximately 15,000 marines to roughly 159,000. However, this study recommends that manning of the fleet Marine force be increased from its resource-constrained level (roughly 90 percent) to 100 percent. This manning level is consistent with the Corps role as a force in readiness. An end-strength of 165,000 is projected, with the savings of this reduction focused on training and education enhancements.

The Marine Corps has been operating for a decade at about 80 to 85 percent of its necessary funding. Near-term readiness was achieved for a decade by deferring investments and eating seed corn. The barn and field are both now barren. Resource realignments will ensure that limited resources are allocated to the greatest operational priorities. The annual $1.5 billion budget shortfall that the Commandant of the Marine Corps has identified will not be eliminated, but it certainly will be narrowed appreciably. No longer should the Corps struggle with inadequate manning of its operating forces, and the fielding of trucks and helicopters that are older than the marines driving and repairing them. In an age of resource constraints, this focus on operational priorities will become more valuable every year. For the first time in many years, the *Force in Readiness* will be ready in more than name.

Reductions in major ground programs reduce the coming modernization "train wreck" and speed the introduction of improved capabilities into the force.[10] The elimination of tanks and a reduced purchase of AAAVs will lighten up the Corps and reduce its operating and support costs.[11] Resources could then be used to introduce enhanced light armored and fast attack vehicles sooner. Capabilities lost through conventional artillery reductions are more than offset by enhanced Marine aviation and naval surface fire support, as well as the 120 mm mortar and rocket systems.

Aviation requirements will have to be carefully considered. Marine aviation is an expensive but valuable commodity, and its relevance in a naval or joint context must be evaluated as such. Some analysts have recently challenged the need for Marine fixed-wing support.[12] However, such analyses overlook the synergy of combined arms and its suitability to the types of expeditionary operations that are anticipated in the coming decades. Currently programmed assets such as the V–22 and the JSF are ideally suited to meet the emerging strategic environment, and while acquisition objectives have been reduced somewhat, these systems remain crucial to both expeditionary maneuver warfare and OMFTS concepts. Options to integrate Marine air assets into carrier air groups are viable, but not at the expense of losing the capacity to conduct expeditionary operations.

While the force design of the EMB is lighter and somewhat leaner than its MEF predecessor, there appears to be no major impact on amphibious lift requirements. Troop berthing spaces may be saved, and some vehicle lift is reduced by the tank cuts. These are offsets by necessary additions, and naval support requirements for ship-to-objective mobility. Thus, current amphibious fleet requirements seem sound. Space savings can be employed to enhance habitability, command spaces for embarked staffs, and training. Furthermore, the combat service support community will need additional flexibility in accessing supplies and consumables to support OMFTS and STOM operations and for mobility assets to increase the velocity of CSS.

Rationale

This proposal is consistent with the strategic context generated by globalization and U.S. security interests. In an age stressing speed, flexibility, adaptability, and versatility, expeditionary maneuver brigades offer a responsive solution. Additionally, it is more consistent with the Marine strategic organizational concept and major warfighting doctrine. Maneuver warfare is an approach that stresses speed of thought and action over mass and attrition. For these reasons, the proposal has merit for further refinement and implementation.

Strategic Consistency. Realigning the Corps standing forces toward the middle end of the conflict spectrum will optimize the Marine Corps for the most probable conflicts of the global century. Instead of structuring for high-end, sustained land combat, as it did during the Cold War, the Marine Corps will be positioned and fully prepared for more likely scenarios. Instead of absorbing risks by trying to be all things, the Corps will be tailored to a more specific role, within a strategic and joint context. This proposal aligns the most enduring and unique core Marine competencies to the strategic context facing the Nation. This will ensure its strategic relevance, as well as ensuring the country has an agile instrument of national power focused on preserving stability or suppressing conflicts.

Part of the strategic consistency is supported by ensuring rapid deployability of Marine forces through configuring them for amphibious shipping and by airlift. It does *not* size the overall active duty Marine Corps to available lift, but it does size and shape the Marine force structure to its principal deployment modes. This will simplify planning and logically tie the Corps structure to strategic mobility means, while increasing Corps utility to commanders. More than "first to fight," commanders will increasingly be able to depend on the Corps as the "first to respond."

Conceptual Consistency. In response to Congressional direction, the Marine Corps has consistently framed its purpose and raison d'etre as the Nation's Force in Readiness.[13] While not codified in Title 10, there is clear historical precedent and legislative intent for this strategic concept. However, this rationale was laid out in the early 1950s, and the strategic context has been altered by time and legislation. The original concept made sense given the strategic culture and strategy, but both have changed. Containment was originally designed to address Soviet vulnerabilities along its periphery at a time and point of our choosing. Amphibious striking power was tailored to operationalize the strategy of containment. Furthermore, the underlying strategic culture of the United States precluded creating a large standing Army. The solution was to frame a single service force in readiness of combined arms that was posed for rapid deployment. Framing it so was a way around the mobilization dilemma. Yet ultimately, the extent of the ideological struggle with the Soviet Union produced a strategic synthesis that avoided creation of a garrison state, while still developing a national security system of substantial size and complexity.[14]

In the midst of the Cold War, such an institutional rationale for the Marines made sense. However, it was a concept borne of the Cold War over half a century ago. Today's national security planners need not think that all our Cold War constructs are outdated or carved in stone. We live within a new context today, and a fresh evaluation of the role of the Marine Corps and naval expeditionary forces is warranted. Furthermore, with the passage of Goldwater-Nichols legislation in 1986, previous Congressional direction about service roles and functions should be reconstituted in light of the need for a greater rationalization and integration of the armed services.[15]

However, the emerging security environment—what is known and that which is enshrouded by wild cards—still clearly calls for highly ready, rapidly deployable expeditionary forces that can stand poised near an incipient crisis to deter or contain the problem or that can forcibly enter and respond to a contingency, whether it is a humanitarian disaster, a civil disorder, or a violent armed conflict. Rather than containing communism and Russian hegemony, we are now containing chaos and instability. In a globalized world, specific Corps competencies retain great utility. However, greater strategic focus on its principal role will narrow the gap between its concept and its force structure and facilitate rapid deployment and higher readiness levels. In short, the EMB design retains those core competencies associated with historic Marine roles and enhances them for a new century.

Doctrinal Consistency. The force design articulated as part of this study is also consistent with fundamental Marine Corps philosophy and doctrine of maneuver warfare. Maneuver warfare stresses decentralized decisionmaking based on the commander's intent and understanding of the mission. Underlying this approach is an appreciation of the chaos, uncertainty, and friction of combat, and the concomitant desire to offset these factors with organizational cohesion, a common understanding of the commander's intent and initiative at the lowest organizational level. Command and control (C^2) doctrine inherent to maneuver warfare mandates that subordinate commanders make their own decisions at the lowest level possible. The ability for senior commanders and their subordinate elements to communicate through a mutual understanding and to anticipate reactions is fundamental to this approach.[16]

Mutual understanding and implicit communications cannot be gained just through shared doctrine or occasional exercise. They can only be generated through extensive interaction in peacetime and through the familiarity and trust that are produced through established and regular interaction. The ad hoc nature of the current brigade task-organizing approach fails to support this regular interaction since brigade commanders do not have designated forces and subordinate commanders, and their staffs and even some of the commanding generals are dual-tasked in other positions. Thus, the long-term daily working relationships necessary to underwrite the fundamental warfighting doctrine of the Corps are undermined by the current approach of task-organizing the subordinate elements of the MAGTF in the midst of a crisis. Permanent MAGTF structures as proposed herein will correct this readiness gap and facilitate the further institutionalization of maneuver warfare.

The apparent rigidity of Marine warfighting units warrants examination in light of the dramatic doctrinal changes that the Marines have undergone. Looking back over the basic force structure of the Marine Corps since World War II, there is remarkably little change. The fundamental structures of the squad, rifle platoon, company, battalion, regiment, and division have remained remarkably stable. A division commander or a rifle platoon commander from the World War II battle of Tarawa would instantly recognize and be entirely comfortable with the current organizational design.

However, the Corps does not fight the same way, nor does it have the same doctrine it employed at Tarawa. The basic squad and platoon designs of that generation were constructed with the high attrition inherent to high-intensity amphibious assaults in mind. In the 1980s, the Corps formally adopted maneuver warfare as its basic doctrine, an approach that was formulated in many ways as an antidote to the reliance on mass and attrition inherent to Vietnam and the American way of war. Yet the basic organizational structure remains. It is difficult to square the sharp changes in basic doctrine and warfighting approaches with the stability of Marine ground force structure from 1945 to the present. This gives credence to critics who define maneuver warfare as an aborted innovation in the Marine Corps.[17]

The Case for Strategic Adjustment

This volume began with an overview of numerous challenges and changes in the evolving strategic environment.[18] We face an age of nonlinearity, vulnerability, and intense competition. There is little reason to believe that America will be immune to the resentments of this age. Nor is there any reason to suspect that America will be able to disconnect itself from leadership responsibilities or critical interests around the globe. Our own interests are too globally distributed, and we cannot easily separate them for judicious or selective involvement.[19] Instead, the United States will become increasingly involved in preserving or reestablishing stability in many forms.

"A persistent and repeated error through the ages," Don Kagan reminds us, "has been the failure to understand that the preservation of peace requires active effort, planning, the expenditure of resources and sacrifice, just as war does."[20] This is even truer of the future than the past. We cannot afford to shrink from the active effort, planning, and sacrifice that it will take to preserve U.S. interests.

The conflicts of this era will shock us with their violence, unconstrained by Western norms. Globalization has a leveling effect for our adversaries, and we should take little comfort in the litany of past Western success.[21] Nor should we accept the notion that we live in an age of virtual warfare in which success can be guaranteed by warfare from afar.[22] Technological advances in conventional warfare are impressive but offer few advantages to the most probable intervention cases. American forces excel at their preferred operational paradigm; however, our more likely and most dangerous intervention requirement will place Americans on the ground in an incipient crisis. Most likely this will occur in an urban setting, probably along the world's littorals, with an ambiguous admixture of protagonists to contend with. This is not something that we typically excel at, but as Michael Howard recently warned:

> Peoples who are not prepared to put their forces in harm's way fight at some disadvantage against those who are. Tomahawk cruise missiles may command the air,

but it is Kalashnikov sub-machine guns that still rule the ground. It is an imbalance that makes the enforcement of world order a rather problematic affair.[23]

If peace is actually an invention, as Howard suggests, then the evolving era will challenge that invention in many ways. Given the sharp differences between the age that the current national security system was created to address and our new environment, a strategic adjustment is needed if we are to enhance our chances of preserving peace in a world order of such problematic circumstances.[24] A strategic adjustment is:

> The business of refining security objectives when established ends no longer bear a compelling relation to evolving circumstances, and of altering the relation between ends and means, resources and security needs, when changing conditions make these relations obsolete.[25]

Much of our present military remains relevant to the Nation's security interests. It would be a sweeping exaggeration to assert that the U.S. military is obsolete. However, it would be an equally sweeping claim to argue that evolving circumstances have not changed conditions and weakened the fit between political ends and military means.

The Challenge of Change

A period of national strategic adjustment mandates that civilian and military leaders face up to the challenge of change. Such periods produce tensions and risks for bureaucratic and professional institutions such as the military. The most acute tension is between continuity and change, "between preserving that which has met the needs of the past and adapting to the challenge of change in a confusing and uncertain future."[26]

This confusing and uncertain future can be used to justify strategic and operational stasis. Uncertainty about future requirements and constrained resources can combine to produce a protracted paralysis in planning and organizational change. Yet military history is replete with successful innovations, even revolutionary and discontinuous leaps in capability under similar circumstances. The strategies for dealing with uncertainty and abetting progressive change are fairly clear. Neither perfect intelligence about enemy intentions or capabilities nor massive resources are required.[27]

Leadership, vision, and an organizational proclivity to debate fundamental assumptions are the principal ingredients to successful change. Credible military leadership is the most important element. Additionally, the ability and willingness to cope with ambiguity is a distinctive attribute. Finally, the most adaptive military organizations cultivate a culture that combines intellectual curiosity and relentless improvement. They tolerate diversity and the rigorous evaluation of both old assumptions and new proposals.[28]

Scholarship on military innovation frequently points to the Marines as an example of institutional adaptation in the face of dynamic environmental change.[29] Much of this reputation was established 50 years ago when the Marines created the doctrinal foundation and capabilities for amphibious warfare. Pressed by the Navy in 1920 to take on the mission of seizing and defending forward bases, the Corps ultimately created the fleet Marine force in 1933.[30] By 1941, out of an effort of two decades, the requisite components for meeting U.S. strategic needs in the Pacific campaigns were in place.

Today, a similar effort is required. This time, however, we do not have the luxuries of our predecessors. We do not have the time or the certainty of a predetermined opponent and War Plan Orange. The challenge of change in the global century requires embracing greater uncertainty. Historically, this is not an anomaly. As one highly regarded historian put it, the one aspect of military science that should be studied above all others is "the capacity to adapt oneself to the utterly unpredictable, the entirely unknown."[31]

Greater Institutional Adaptation

Given the emerging security environment, the Nation's interests strongly suggest that greater institutional adaptation and organizational change are necessary. The Corps does not have to adapt itself to "the utterly unpredictable or the entirely unknown." Both chaos in the littorals and small wars are something that the Marine Corps has experience with, and the EMB concept is not a radical departure from its combined arms and MAGTF philosophy. But if Corps commitment to being ready whenever the Nation calls is immutable, it must adapt to new demands for complex contingencies, greater strategic deployability, higher readiness levels, and far greater operational agility. If the Corps is to provide combat-ready MAGTFs as an adaptive instrument of national power, it must evolve in response to the strategic, political, and technological revolution that swirls around it.

This chapter has explored the parameters of the new security environment and the corresponding need for new capabilities and adaptive institutions to meet the country's interests. Alterations are needed in our current national security architecture to match the pressures created by globalization.[32] The Marine Corps is neither immune to these pressures nor vaccinated against the need for change by its past contributions. Tomorrow's complexities portend a heightened need for ready expeditionary forces that are organized, trained, and equipped to advance America's interests in a nonlinear and unpredictable world.

As in the past, a ready, relevant, and capable Marine Corps fulfills a vital role in the Nation's security. However, this role is never a constant one. To better prepare for a global century, the Marines should evaluate the expeditionary maneuver brigade to ensure that it remains as ready, relevant, and capable tomorrow as it has been in the past.

Notes

[1] James L. Jones, *Marine Corps Strategy 21* (Washington, DC: Department of the Navy, November 3, 2000).

[2] James L. Jones, *Expeditionary Maneuver Warfare* (Washington, DC: Headquarters, U.S. Marine Corps, November 10, 2001).

[3] John F. Schmidt, "A Critique of the Hunter Warrior Concept," *Marine Corps Gazette*, June 1998, 13–19. For an overview of the experiment, see James A. Lasswell, "Assessing Hunter Warrior," *Armed Forces Journal International*, May 1997, 14–15.

[4] See Joseph H. Schmid, "Reorganizing the Fleet Marine Force: From Division-Wing Teams to Marine Expeditionary Brigades," (M.S. thesis, Marine Corps University, 1989). The current author has also proposed similar arguments in Frank G. Hoffman, "Strategic Concepts and Marine Corps Force Structure in the 21st Century," *Marine Corps Gazette*, December 1993, 70–75.

[5] The best history for this period remains Allan R. Millett, *Semper Fidelis: The History of the United States Marine Corps* (New York: Free Press, 1991), 445–474.

[6] The original "Green Dragon" concept paper that was the progenitor for the hunter-warrior experiments postulated a division-based structure comprised of one heavy Marine regiment and two light regiments. The heavy regiment contained five battalions, including two infantry battalions plus all mechanized division assets (tanks, light armored vehicles, and amphibious assault vehicles). The lighter regiments were composed of battalions almost half the size of today's force, with each battalion designed to function as a highly maneuverable reconnaissance assault battalion whose mission was to seek out enemy forces and targets and to engage them with long-range supporting arms.

[7] Douglas A. Macgregor has proposed a widely cited modular design for the U.S. Army. See *Breaking the Phalanx: A New Design for Landpower in the 21st Century* (Westport, CT: Praeger, 1997). For another brigade-oriented approach for Marine units, see James T. Quinliven, "Flexible Ground Forces," in *Holding the Line: U.S. Defense Alternatives for the Early 21st Century*, ed. Cindy Williams (Cambridge, MA: Massachusetts Institute of Technology Press, 2001), 181–204.

[8] Department of Defense, *Report of the Quadrennial Defense Review* (Washington, DC: Department of Defense, September 30, 2001).

[9] The Marine Corps organizes its operating forces into Marine air-ground task forces (MAGTFs), which are task-organized entities that can be tailored to specific contingencies. Each MAGTF has similar organization, containing a command element, a ground combat element, an aviation combat element, and a combat service support element. The largest MAGTF is the Marine expeditionary force that is normally composed of a Marine expeditionary force command element, a division, a Marine aircraft wing, and a force service support group. These elements are the standing forces. Other smaller MAGTFs are formed by detaching battalions and subordinate units from the major MEF components.

[10] Daniel Goure and Jeffrey M. Ranney, *Averting the Defense Train Wreck in the New Millennium* (Washington, DC: Center for Strategic and International Studies, 1999).

[11] The AAAV would not be prepositioned aboard maritime prepositioning force shipping, thus reducing the Marine acquisition objective of 1,013 vehicles to roughly 600 units and saving more than $3.6 billion in acquisition and life cycle costs.

[12] Michael E. O'Hanlon, *Defense Policy Choices for the Bush Administration 2001–2005* (Washington, DC: The Brookings Institution Press, 2001), 103; Thomas Donnelly, *Rebuilding America's Defenses: Strategy, Forces and Resources For a New Century* (Washington, DC: Project for the New American Century, 2000), 63–71.

[13] Samuel P. Huntington, "National Policy and Transoceanic Navy," U.S. Naval Institute *Proceedings* (May 1954), 483. Huntington has spoken in the past on the importance of a strategic concept for each of the military services. He noted, "If a service does not possess a well-defined strategic concept, the public and political leaders will be confused as to the role of the service, uncertain as to the necessity of its existence, and apathetic or hostile to the claims made by the service upon the resources of society."

[14] For superb scholarship on this issue, see Aaron L. Friedberg, *In the Shadow of the Garrison State, America's Anti-Statism and Its Cold War Grand Strategy* (Princeton, NJ: Princeton University Press, 2000).

[15] William Owens with Edward Offley, *Lifting the Fog of War* (New York: Farrar, Straus and Giroux, 2000).

[16] Marine Corps Doctrinal Publication 1, *Warfighting* (Washington, DC: U.S. Marine Corps, 1997).

[17] Terry Pierce, *Disguised Innovation* (Ph.D. diss., Harvard University, 2001).

[18] See in particular chapter 2.

[19] Jonathan T. Howe, "A Global Agenda for Foreign and Defense Policy," in *The Global Century: Globalization and National Security*, ed. Richard L. Kugler and Ellen L. Frost (Washington, DC: National Defense University Press, 2001), 179; and Hugh De Santis, "Mutualism: An American Strategy for the Next Century," Strategic Forum 162 (Washington, DC: National Defense University Press, May 1999).

[20] Donald Kagan, *On the Origins of War and the Preservation of Peace* (New York: Doubleday, 1995), 567.

[21] For an alternative view, see Victor Davis Hanson, *Culture and Carnage: Landmark Battles in the Rise of Western Power* (New York: Doubleday, 2001). In a brilliant overview of the development of Western military power, Hanson argues that Western military supremacy is predicated on more than superior technology. Culture, rather than chance or geography, plays the dominant role in his explanation. Traditional institutions, consensual government, individual freedom and initiative, free inquiry, and rationalism have produced the individual initiative, discipline, social cohesiveness, and tactical adaptation that is the hallmark of Western military history.

[22] Michael Ignatieff, *Virtual War: Kosovo and Beyond* (New York: Metropolitan Books, 2000).

[23] Michael Howard, *The Invention of Peace: Reflections on War and International Order* (New Haven: Yale University Press, 2001), 102.

[24] Peter Turbowitz, Emily O. Goldman, and Edward Rhodes, eds., *The Politics of Strategic Adjustment: Ideas, Institutions, and Interests* (New York: Columbia University Press, 1999).

[25] Miroslav Nincic, Roger Rose, and Gerard Gorski, "The Social Foundations of Strategic Adjustment," in *The Politics of Strategic Adjustment*, ed. Turbowitz, Goldman, and Rhodes, 176.

[26] Harold R. Winton, "Introduction on Military Change," in *The Challenge of Change: Military Institutions and New Realities, 1918–1941*, ed. Harold R. Winton and David R. Mets (Lincoln: University of Nebraska Press, 2000), xi.

[27] Stephen Peter Rosen, *Winning the Next War: Innovation and the Modern Military* (Ithaca: Cornell University Press, 1991).

[28] Williamson Murray and Allan R. Millett, *Military Innovation in the Interwar Period* (Cambridge, MA: Cambridge University Press, 1996). Additionally, see James Corum, "A Comprehensive Approach to Change: Reform in the German Army in the Interwar Period," in *The Challenge of Change*, ed. Winton and Mets, 35–73.

[29] Emily O. Goldman, "Mission Possible: Organizational Learning in Peacetime," in *The Politics of Strategic Adjustment*, ed. Turbowitz, Goldman, and Rhodes, 243–247.

[30] For a concise overview of Navy and Marine innovation in the development of amphibious warfare, see Allan R. Millett, "Assault from the Sea: The Development of Amphibious Warfare between the Wars," in *Military Innovation in the Interwar Period*, ed. Murray and Millett, 70–95; Rosen, 59.

[31] Michael Howard, Chesney Memorial Gold Medal Lecture, October 3, 1973.

[32] For one perspective on needed changes to the U.S. national security architecture, see U.S. Commission on National Security/21st Century, *Road Map for National Security: Imperative For Change* (Washington, DC: Government Printing Office, March 2001).

Chapter 23

Homeland Security: Implications for the Coast Guard

Edward Feege and Scott C. Truver

What if January [2000] had started with 1,000 Americans dead in six or seven locations around the world? We came very close to having that happen.[1]

—Richard A. Clarke
National Coordinator for Infrastructure Protection and
Counterterrorism, December 2000

On September 11, 2001, America received a horrific, first-hand demonstration of asymmetric warfare: the unconventional strategies that self-proclaimed enemies of the United States, unable to stand up to U.S. conventional military power, have increasingly adopted to achieve their aims. The use of hijacked airliners to attack the World Trade Center and the Pentagon underscored the fact that the United States is at war with a global network of terrorist forces as well as the groups and states that support them.

In retrospect, the Nation had been at war for some time, even if U.S. leaders and citizens did not wish to acknowledge this unsettling fact. During the past 5 years, terrorist groups bombed the Khobar Tower barracks in Saudi Arabia, U.S. embassies in Nairobi, Kenya, and Dar as Salaam, Tanzania, and the Navy destroyer USS *Cole* during a brief stop for fuel in Aden, Yemen. Moreover, the September 2001 attacks were not the first attempts to strike the United States. Indeed, the Islamic militants had already bombed the World Trade Center in 1993. And as then-counterterrorism national coordinator Richard Clarke noted, attempts were planned for the millennium celebration.

Edward Feege is a senior maritime security analyst with the Center for Security Strategies and Operations at the Anteon Corporation. Scott C. Truver is vice president of national security studies at the Anteon Corporation. Research for this chapter was completed prior to January 2002.

In December 1999, U.S. Customs Service agents in Washington state apprehended a would-be Algerian terrorist on the U.S.-Canadian border as he departed from a ferry, his vehicle loaded with the ingredients to make a powerful bomb. Ahmed Ressam's potential targets reportedly were in the Los Angeles area. Subsequent reports identified Ressam as a member of terrorist leader Osama bin Laden's al Qaeda network—the leading suspect for the September airliner attacks. Only a fortuitous hunch by a Customs Service agent resulted in Ressam's arrest. The terrorist might have had better luck if his vehicle had blended better into cross-border traffic or if Ressam had tried entering the United States another way. Little wonder, then, that the first report of the Hart-Rudman Commission in 1999 concluded:

> States, terrorists, and other disaffected groups will acquire weapons of mass destruction and mass disruption, and some will use them. Americans will likely die on American soil, possibly in large numbers.[2]

The September 2001 terrorist attacks on New York and Washington occurred despite efforts to improve the security at U.S. airports. They also proved that innovative terrorists can and will use a broad array of methods and techniques to infiltrate the United States and attack its citizens. As U.S. law enforcement agencies now concentrate on closing one gap in U.S. defenses—significantly beefing up airport security and conducting reconnaissance sweeps of the country's airspace with armed fighter aircraft—terrorists will most assuredly be seeking other ways of entering the country and launching additional terror operations, including maritime means.

Ironically, shortly after Customs agents apprehended Ressam, 600 Haitians in a ramshackle boat almost accomplished what he had not: penetrating U.S. maritime borders and escaping inland. If their boat had not run aground in Biscayne Bay, only a mile from the Florida coast, there is a good chance that at least some of the illegal migrants would have made it to shore. These Haitians were unlucky; scores of other illegal migrants from Cuba, China, and some 20 other countries in recent years have entered the United States successfully, some with help from savvy smugglers in fast pleasure craft or hidden on board commercial vessels. Drug smugglers have also used such tactics to penetrate U.S. maritime frontiers, usually successfully, for decades.

While posing a danger to America's social fabric, drug traffickers and illegal migrants do not represent the same type of threat as a lone terrorist or well-heeled terrorist group, particularly one that may be attempting to bring chemical, biological, radiological, or nuclear weapons of mass destruction and disruption onto U.S. soil. But smuggler ability to infiltrate U.S. borders *is* cause for serious concern. The routes and procedures they use offer similar opportunities for the more dangerous foes of the United States. Hence, it is becoming increasingly important that the United States be able to identify and stop anyone attempting to breach America's maritime sovereignty.

This is easier said than done. Extremely high volumes of maritime traffic—commercial freighters and tankers, fishing vessels, tugs and barges, cruise ships, ferries, and recreational boats—cross our maritime borders every day. Anyone wishing to attack the United States by sea could choose to do so by blending in with peaceful, legal traffic approaching our coasts and ports from all points of the compass. Once inside U.S. waters, for example, naval mines could be clandestinely planted (as was done by Libya using a commercial ferry in the Red Sea and Gulf of Suez during summer 1984) or worse.

Traditional naval forces, while offering important surveillance and tracking capabilities, are inadequate for stopping this kind of maritime infiltration. The problem ultimately requires the apprehension of individuals, both foreign nationals and U.S. citizens, who offer assistance. This activity, at its core, is a law enforcement function and thus falls under the responsibility of the U.S. Coast Guard, although in its roles, missions, and tasks the Coast Guard links to numerous departments, services, and agencies in the United States and abroad.

Law Enforcement in Deep Water

As the only U.S. armed service with law enforcement authority, the Coast Guard is charged with guarding America's maritime frontiers, along with a host of other duties. It is already heavily involved in interdicting drug and illegal migrant traffic, two missions that entail protecting American citizens and territories from transnational foreign threats that are not military in the traditional sense. In carrying them out, the Coast Guard is already contributing to U.S. homeland defense.[3] Immediately following the September 11 attacks, the Coast Guard strengthened patrols of critical ports, harbors, and roadsteads. Surveillance of offshore areas increased, and the service activated its special interest vessel (SIV) program. This program closed U.S. inland and territorial waters and offshore zones to vessels that were flying the flags of certain suspect states, that were owned by citizens or groups of these countries, or that had recently visited a port in these states.

As currently equipped, however, the Coast Guard is only partially able to meet the demands of these critical missions. Plagued by obsolescent equipment, perennial budgetary constraints, and severe readiness problems, while at the same time tasked with a growing array of missions and tasks, particularly in its deepwater operating regions, the service has struggled to hold its own in recent years. It is in these deepwater areas—more than 50 miles off U.S. shores—where the Coast Guard maintains America's first line of defense, against drug smugglers, migrants, and any other individuals or groups that may wish to breach U.S. sovereignty from the sea. These offshore operations allow the Coast Guard to conduct a layered defense that give the service, and its law enforcement and military partners, time to react to emerging maritime threats.

Nevertheless, there is light at the end of the Coast Guard tunnel. In 1997, the service established the Integrated Deepwater System Capabilities Replacement Project (the "Deepwater Program" for short) designed to replace the aging cutters, aircraft, and support systems that routinely operate in waters. More than just replacing a collection of aging ships and aircraft, the Deepwater Program promises to transform the Coast Guard into a modern force able to leverage advanced technology to perform its security missions more effectively. The program is a central element in the ongoing Coast Guard attempt to develop a comprehensive means of tracking, analyzing, and interpreting maritime activities that can impact the security and well-being of the United States and its citizens and, when necessary, responding with an active defense.

Deepwater cutters and aircraft will be participants in—and beneficiaries of—the emerging integrated maritime intelligence and surveillance system that the Coast Guard is also pursuing. As planned, the new Deepwater national security cutters also will be more effective than their current counterparts in acting as forward sensor and operations platforms. Their embarked aircraft and boats will be able to deliver boarding teams to the decks of a wide variety of threat vessels, thus consummating the critical interdiction endgame and apprehending those who would endanger the safety and security of the United States and its citizens. Overall, with new and strengthened existing capabilities that derive from the Deepwater Program, the Coast Guard and the Nation will have taken an immense step forward in securing its maritime borders against any and all unconventional threats.

The Coast Guard, Homeland Security, and Homeland Defense

The Coast Guard has five major roles, each associated with specific mission areas. These roles include maritime security, maritime safety, marine environmental protection, protection of natural resources, and national defense.

Conceptually, the Coast Guard places its roles and missions on a continuum of activities that contribute to U.S. national security. In particular, the service plays a key role in the area of homeland *security.* Besides encompassing the Coast Guard's homeland defense activities, homeland security also includes sovereignty missions associated with maritime safety, marine environmental protection, and protection of natural resources.[4] (*Homeland defense* per se and *border protection* both fall under a more expansive definition of homeland security.)

But no matter how one divides the Coast Guard's roles and missions, the expertise and capabilities that it has developed to perform them—along with the legal authorities it has been given under U.S. law—are central to effective U.S. homeland defense and security in the maritime realm. The Coast Guard is the only member of the U.S. Armed Forces with domestic and international law enforcement authority. Additionally, its missions require extensive interagency coordination at the Federal, state, and local levels, and the Coast Guard routinely coordinates its operations with other U.S. and foreign military services, as well as with civil law enforcement agencies at home and abroad.

Coast Guard activities and forces that contribute to U.S. homeland security, and homeland defense, occur over a wide geographic area, encompassing U.S. inland waterways, ports, and coastal waters, as well as the deepwater region well beyond U.S. coasts. Together, they comprise a layered system of defense that extends outward from U.S. territory and territorial waters—and in some cases thousands of miles into international ocean space.

An important example of the Coast Guard's inshore effort is the service's port safety and security program. Coast Guard captains of the port (COTPs)—and the marine safety offices that they command—enforce laws dealing with the protection and security of vessels, harbors, waterfront facilities, and deepwater ports. COTPs have the authority to establish security and safety zones, regulate navigation areas, and control the anchorage and movement of any vessel within their assigned areas. The COTPs also serve as officers in charge of marine inspection and as predesignated Federal on-scene coordinators for pollution emergencies.

Routine Coast Guard activities and programs under the cognizance of COTPs not only safeguard ports, vessels, and waterfront facilities from accidents and negligence but also from terrorism and sabotage.[5] COTPs can direct vessels or waterfront facilities to take specific actions to prevent sabotage. They can enlist the aid and cooperation of other governmental and private agencies to ensure the protection and security of these vessels or facilities. Also, they implement the service SIV program that identifies and targets vessels and crews from foreign countries that may pose a threat to U.S. security. COTPs can either deny these ships or people entry into U.S. ports, or, if they are permitted into U.S. waters, they can be placed under additional controls. As such, COTPs are critical elements of any first-response to a terrorist attack from the sea, and, in the wake of the 2001 attacks, COTPs on all U.S. coasts were ordered to highest alert.

The Coast Guard also is responsible for maritime defense zone (MDZ) activities that protect the strategic U.S. ports from which U.S. military forces deploy. Coast Guard port security and Navy coastal warfare units routinely work together to secure critical seaports and shipping operations, both in the United States and overseas, under the command of the Coast Guard MDZ commanders, who in turn report to Navy fleet commanders.[6] COTPs also chair port readiness committees in 13 strategic seaports from which U.S. forces would deploy during a crisis or war, ensuring multiagency coordination and resolution of local defense readiness issues.

In the event of an emergency, other Coast Guard commands back up COTPs with key consequence management capabilities. For instance, three Coast Guard national strike teams are poised to respond to oil or hazardous material spills in any U.S. waterway or port. The teams also provide expertise, equipment, and command and control support to the Environmental Protection Agency for inland spills. To increase usefulness in homeland defense, the Coast Guard is working with the Federal Bureau of Investigation, the Federal Emergency Management Agency, and the Department of Defense (DOD) to give the strike teams the capability to respond to nuclear, biological, or chemical attacks as well.

Coast Guard inshore homeland defense activities represent only one part of broader service capabilities. In effect, however, they are the last line of a layered defense-in-depth against threats that may already be on the high seas, headed to the United States, already in U.S. territorial waters and proceeding to a U.S. port or even anchored in a roadstead or tied to a pier. Moreover, these capabilities are specifically structured to detect and prevent security (as well as safety and environmental) threats within the massive stream of commercial traffic that passes through U.S. ports and surrounding coastal waters on a daily basis. But ports are just one gateway through which dangerous materials and people can cross U.S. maritime borders.

The Coast Guard is also called upon to protect the entire 95,000-mile expanse of U.S. coastline and 3.5-million-square-mile expanse of territorial seas and economic zones against smugglers carrying illicit drugs and illegal migrants. Countering these traffickers and their operations is important for reducing the drug scourge on American streets and upholding immigration laws.

From a broader perspective, however, these illegal networks and contraband routes also offer any nation or group a means of short-circuiting U.S. sovereignty and bypassing the U.S. border controls that keep dangerous individuals and materials out of the country. Closing them down is a vital security issue for the United States, one with which the Coast Guard has been grappling for decades, if not since its birth as the Revenue Cutter Service in 1790. The importance—and difficulty—of this task only highlights further the importance of the Coast Guard in the Nation's future and the need for its Deepwater Program.

Deepwater Challenges

Deepwater forces are crucial to Coast Guard ability to fulfill its maritime security role. Maritime security encompasses multiple missions, in particular drug interdiction, alien migrant interdiction, and the protection of fisheries and other organic marine resources. While critically important to the livelihood of a $30 billion industry, the fisheries protection mission does not have a direct impact on U.S. homeland defense. As discussed above, however, the first two are closely intertwined with overall U.S. efforts to defend its borders. Additionally, the Coast Guard's national defense role and its capabilities in this area also have a direct impact on the service's ability to defend the United States from asymmetric and unconventional attacks as well as to contribute to conventional, general-purpose naval missions and tasks.

Drug Interdiction

In mid-2001, the U.S. Government estimated that 242 tons of cocaine had already entered the United States since the first of the year, setting a pace that exceeded that of the year before. Likewise, the importation of marijuana, heroin, and other illegal narcotics appeared to be holding steady or increasing as well, demonstrating that the drug trade is thriving despite a banner year for drug seizures, including a record number carried out by the Coast Guard.[7]

Most of the supply of illicit drugs sold in the United States either originates in or passes through Central and South America. Ninety percent of the cocaine peddled on U.S. streets is produced in Colombia, as is a significant amount of heroin. Jamaica and, to a lesser extent, Mexico supply American drug users with marijuana. Meanwhile, Haiti, the poorest country in the Western Hemisphere, lacking a stable government and suffering from endemic corruption, serves as a major drug transshipment point for the Western Hemisphere.[8]

Illegal narcotics are transported by a variety of means, but most shipments travel at least part of the way to the United States along Caribbean and Eastern Pacific routes. The primary method for smuggling large quantities of cocaine through the Caribbean to the United States is by vessel, including "go-fast" boats (typically 30- to 50-foot, multiengine boats that can carry 500 to 1,500 kilograms of cocaine in each trip), fishing vessels, bulk cargo freighters, and even containerized cargo vessels. Private aircraft also make airdrops to vessels—mainly go-fasts—which then smuggle the drugs into Caribbean nations for staging and subsequent delivery to the United States.[9]

Getting drugs into Haiti or the Dominican Republic, its neighbor on the island of Hispaniola, is often the immediate goal of the smuggler. From there, others can attempt to move the drugs into Puerto Rico, which is easily accessible from Hispaniola by plane or boat. Since Puerto Rico has U.S. commonwealth status, a shipment of cocaine from there to the United States will usually not be inspected by U.S. Customs Service agents upon arrival on the U.S. mainland. A similar procedure occurs in the Pacific, where large cocaine shipments from Colombia are often offloaded to smaller go-fasts or *pangas* for further transport into Central America and Mexico, from which much of the cocaine is then transported primarily via land routes—or sometimes near-shore routes in an illegal version of cabotage—into southern California.[10]

Staunching these flows of illegal drugs is a daunting problem, which is compounded by the sheer size—six million square miles—of the Caribbean and Pacific areas that encompass the drug transit zones, trafficker ingenuity, and the volume and variety of commercial cargo flowing through these areas. Nevertheless, this is what the

Coast Guard and its Federal partners are called upon to do. The Coast Guard has been designated the lead agency for maritime drug interdiction under the National Drug Control Strategy.[11] It has established an international presence in drug enforcement and cooperates with other Federal agencies within the framework established by the U.S. Interdiction Coordinator.

For more than 2 decades, Coast Guard cutters, aircraft, and legal detachments operating from Navy warships have been deployed in Pacific and Caribbean drug transit corridors. The service supports both the Joint Interagency Task Force (JIATF)-West and JIATF-East, commands that coordinate Federal counterdrug efforts—including both military and civilian agencies—in their respective areas. The Coast Guard contribution, including high- and medium-endurance cutters, patrol boats, and long-range aircraft, has resulted in significant cocaine seizures and smuggling activity disruptions. In fiscal year 2000, for example, the Coast Guard seized a record 62 tons of cocaine, much of it traveling Eastern Pacific routes. Those drugs, along with another 25 tons of marijuana seized during the year, had a street value of approximately $4.1 billion—equal to the Coast Guard's entire budget.

An overarching, multiyear strategic plan, dubbed Steel Web, guides Coast Guard drug-interdiction efforts. Within this framework, the service has employed a variety of innovative interdiction tactics. For instance, during Operation *New Frontier*, which began in August 1999, armed Coast Guard helicopters used nonlethal, disabling force to stop go-fasts.[12] The helicopters work in tandem with Zodiac rigid-hull inflatable boats, whose crews handle the final boarding and apprehension of suspects.

Even with its past successes, however, the Coast Guard estimates that it is interdicting at most only 10 percent of the drugs that enter the transit zone. Moreover, the traffickers are not standing still. They are increasingly employing leading-edge equipment and technology such as hard-to-detect low-profile boats and aircraft, higher endurance go-fast boats, global positioning system equipment, satellite communications, cellular telephones, worldwide paging, e-mail, and sophisticated counterinformation technologies. All of this enables the drug traffickers to challenge law enforcement organizations with greater daring and boldness and highlights the critical need for more effective U.S. intelligence, surveillance, and interdiction capabilities.

Alien Migrant Interdiction

Stemming the tide of illegal migrants seeking entry into the United States is likewise a major Coast Guard maritime security mission. With continuing economic and political upheaval in the Caribbean and Asia, turning back the resulting flow of illegal migrants will remain a difficult challenge. In the recent past, the numbers have been extraordinary: 125,000 illegal migrants interdicted in 1980 during an attempted mass migration from Cuba to south Florida and 37,600 from Haiti in 1990 and 1991. Then, in 1994, Coast Guard cutters and aircraft responded to two nearly simultaneous mass migrations from Cuba and Haiti, working closely with Navy and other DOD assets. An afloat Coast Guard task force commander directed operations for the largest fleet of cutters since World War II, interdicting more than 25,300 Haitian migrants in Operation *Able Manner* and nearly 38,600 Cuban migrants in Operation *Able Vigil*.

During fiscal years 1999 and 2000, the Coast Guard interdicted 9,036 illegal immigrants, for an average of 4,400 per year. The origin of these migrant flows varies from year to year. In 1999, for instance, Chinese immigrants accounted for almost one-third of the total apprehended by the Coast Guard. In 2000, the service interdicted more than 1,300 Haitians, while the number of Chinese immigrants dropped precipitously. Moreover, these numbers do not represent the entire illegal migration picture. Some illegal migrants avoid Coast Guard defenses, while others change their routes or mode of entry in response to Coast Guard and other Federal activities.

Illegal migration into the United States by maritime means involves many different types of vessels. Cuban and Haitian migrants have relied upon craft ranging in size from small freighters and fishing boats to small boats and rafts. There also have been several well-publicized incidents in which superannuated and unseaworthy merchant ships have run aground on U.S. beaches in attempts to land other illegal migrants from South Asia. In late August 1998, for example, the Coast Guard intercepted the converted Chinese fishing vessel *Chih Yung*, crammed full of illegal migrants, many of whom were in very poor health and in desperate need of food and water.

Recently, many would-be migrants have been turning to professional smugglers to get them into the United States. Maritime immigrant smuggling is a potentially lucrative undertaking: one large boatload of Chinese aliens is worth some $6 million to the smugglers, with some migrants paying $45,000 or more for the hazardous voyage that might last as long as 4 months. Likewise, smugglers of Cuban immigrants are demanding anywhere from $2,000 to $8,000 per person to transport them to the United States.

Professional migrant smuggling has brought more sophisticated tactics, similar to those used by drug traffickers. Some smugglers pick up their human cargo from vessels at sea. Significantly, migrant smugglers also have begun to rely heavily on high-speed boats, similar to the go-fasts used by drug traffickers, to elude the Coast Guard. As is the case in drug interdiction, current Coast Guard forces are not always sufficient to stem the immigrant flow. As one Coast Guard officer based in Key West, Florida, noted in early 2001, "We may be missing more than we're getting."[13]

Alien migrant interdiction operations (AMIO) do not end when the Coast Guard intercepts a vessel. There are extensive follow-on requirements for removing (sometimes large numbers of) individuals from unsafe vessels at sea: providing medical care, sustenance, and security, as well as transporting them safely to the custody of the Immigration and Naturalization Service. AMIO is a complex mission, yet it is critical if the United States is to control the number and ascertain the identities of people crossing into its territory.

Interdiction for National Defense

As the Nation's fifth and smallest armed service, the Coast Guard acts as part of the Navy in times of war or whenever the President directs. The Coast Guard participates routinely in naval operations, both within the Western Hemisphere and overseas. Specific Coast Guard responsibilities for supporting DOD military operations and contingencies in key areas are spelled out in a memorandum of agreement that was signed in 1995 between the Department of Transportation and DOD.[14]

Existing command relationships, along with a continuing quest for better interservice interoperability, allow the Coast Guard and Navy, and the other services, to work together and integrate their efforts. This is critical both for the Coast Guard's support to the Navy's overseas operations and also to Navy (and other service) support for Coast Guard law enforcement efforts. As noted, the Coast Guard, Navy, other U.S. armed services, and law enforcement agencies all work together in Joint Inter-Agency Task Forces. Coast Guard high-endurance cutters deploy overseas to participate in maritime interdiction operations aimed at nations such as Iraq or to operate as part of Navy battlegroups. Likewise, the service's cutters, boats, and aircraft play an important role in U.S. overseas warfighting and crisis-response plans. Conversely, Navy forces can operate under Coast Guard operational command, as occurred during past Caribbean mass migrations.

Together, the Coast Guard and Navy comprise a broad national fleet, which can handle a range of maritime threats to the United States and its interests, from conventional to asymmetric.[15] The Navy is best suited to ensuring access to overseas regions, responding to crises, and fighting conventional wars, while the Coast Guard is more expert in performing law enforcement missions and tasks at the lower end of the defense-military operational spectrum. The capabilities and requirements of both overlap, sometimes to great extent, so that the Coast Guard can conduct specialized naval missions and the Navy can support Coast Guard operations by providing highly capable sensors, command and control links, and platforms from which Coast Guard law enforcement detachments can operate. This mutual support will likely be critical when facing unconventional threats—both overseas and in the Western Hemisphere—in the years ahead.

A Deepwater Solution

A common factor in all Coast Guard missions that impact homeland defense is the need for a robust capability for *interdiction* at sea.[16] In simplest terms, this means the ability to detect, track, arrest, and board suspect vessels at will, both off our coasts and in deepwater regions farther offshore. Interdiction at sea is a sequential process that includes *surveillance* of often broad ocean areas, *detection* of targets that might be potential threats to U.S. security or sovereignty, *sorting* of these targets (mostly surface platforms, but occasionally aircraft), *identification* of targets of interest, and finally *interception* and boarding if necessary.

Current Coast Guard capabilities are marginal in many of these areas, shortfalls that the Deepwater Program is designed to rectify. One of the more glaring inadequacies is service inability to gather, process, and disseminate tactical information reliably—activities that are critical in interdiction operations.

The execution of these activities occurs at both the tactical and the operational level. Events at the tactical level involve deployed Coast Guard cutters or maritime patrol aircraft, which use onboard sensors or off-board systems such as helicopters or unmanned aerial vehicles to locate and react to threats in their vicinity. Tactical maritime domain awareness is a prerequisite for the final stage of the operational sequence (interception) and the subsequent boarding of a suspect vessel and, if necessary, the apprehension of its crew, passengers, or cargo.

Before tactical domain awareness even becomes an issue, Coast Guard commanders functioning at the operational level must direct their cutters and aircraft to optimal patrol stations. They must also provide these forces with the outside *cueing* that allows them to react expeditiously to events occurring beyond the range of their own sensors. Without this outside support, deployed Coast Guard forces would be forced to cover large ocean areas with their own range-limited sensors while attempting to sort through a wide variety of maritime traffic. Most of this traffic will seem to be—and in reality *will* be—peaceful and legitimate. However, the flow of legal commercial and recreational vessels also provides camouflage for the activities of dangerous or illegal operators, many of whom will be trying to appear innocuous as well. Thus, outside intelligence that provides deployed forces with cues as to what and whom to look for, and where to look, is indispensable in establishing broader or operational-level maritime domain awareness and is a key to effective operations in the deepwater zone.[17]

The Coast Guard has an existing infrastructure for building maritime domain awareness at the operational level, but it needs to be modernized and better integrated to be more effective, and significant investment is needed to enhance tactical capabilities, which are meager. The Coast Guard requires improved fusion of its intelligence and increased integration between its deployed deepwater forces, the network of Coast Guard command and control nodes, and the service's coastal, near-shore forces. It also requires greater interoperability with intelligence and information nodes and the operational units of other military and civil law enforcement units.

At the tactical level, the Coast Guard needs new platforms and sensors that can deal with existing and projected threats—those in its inventory now are no longer sufficient. As noted by one naval analyst in 1998:

> The cutters now in the Coast Guard inventory have no air-search radars, no modern synthetic-aperture radars, no sonar systems, no infrared sensors, and no night-vision equipment. They also lack the equipment needed to allow the analysis and sharing of tactical information between Coast Guard units. With the best equipment the Coast Guard now has, a cutter may be able to identify a 60-foot vessel at 2,000 yards—but that means that the 25-foot "cigarette boats" favored by drug runners have little to fear.[18]

The Coast Guard is working to achieve greater maritime domain awareness at all levels. Its ongoing effort to modernize the National Distress and Response System is designed to provide an integrated command, control, and sensor system in the coastal and port zones. This effort, along with modernization and integration of other key maritime information systems such as the Marine Information for Safety and Law Enforcement, the Law Enforcement Information System, and the Joint Maritime Information Element, may eventually allow the Coast Guard to provide its forces with a common maritime operational picture throughout U.S. territorial waters and beyond.

At the platform level, the cutters and aircraft that emerge from the Deepwater Program will be designed to take advantage of—and be key participants in—this integrated Coast Guard maritime information network. Unlike the assets they will replace, the new Deepwater forces should have a more comprehensive understanding of ongoing maritime events in homeland waters. Deployed Coast Guard crews and coastal command centers will be able to exchange information readily using both voice and data. Also, because Deepwater command, control, communications, computers, and intelligence (C^4I) systems will be interoperable with those of DOD and those of other Federal agencies, joint and multiagency operations will be significantly more efficient and effective.

Additionally, the nature of Coast Guard missions requires that the final phase of any interdiction operation—boardings, inspections, and possibly arrests—require the close-quarters and physical presence of Coast Guard personnel on the scene, whether the target is a drug-runner, pirate, or terrorist. A key difference between the Coast Guard and other naval forces, this requirement means that the new Deepwater cutters will be equipped to embark, deploy rapidly and safely, support logistically, and provide control for helicopters, rigid-hull inflatable boats, and possibly other craft such as deployable pursuit boats. As such, they will become more effective bases for the employment of integrated teams of armed helicopters and fast boats, a tactic that proved highly successful in Operation *New Frontier*.

Preparing for the Coming Challenge

Since it was established as a consolidated force in 1915, the Coast Guard has been performing missions that today fall under the rubric of homeland defense. However, the stakes in the homeland defense battle will likely rise sharply in the coming years, as hostile states and groups increasingly incorporate asymmetrical or unconventional tactics into their military repertoires. The Coast Guard—a pivotal part of America's seaward defenses—must prepare itself to meet this emerging threat.

Improving Coast Guard interdiction capabilities is a key part of this preparation. Drug and alien migrant smugglers have already shown how porous America's maritime borders can be. For either financial or ideological reasons, these criminal entrepreneurs could one day agree to smuggle weapons or terrorists or both, using the same methods and routes that they do to deliver narcotics or illegal aliens to U.S. territory. When that day comes, it will be in the Nation's best interest to have a modern, effective Coast Guard that is able to stop these smugglers and their deadly cargoes before they reach American shores. Without the new capabilities that will originate with the Deepwater Program, that kind of Coast Guard will not exist.

Notes

[1] Vernon Loeb, "Planned Jan. 2000 Attacks Failed or Were Thwarted," *The Washington Post*, December 24, 2000, A2.

[2] U.S. Commission on National Security/21st Century, *New World Coming: American Security in the 21st Century, Major Themes and Implications* (Washington, DC: Government Printing Office, 1999), 141.

[3] As noted in chapter 4 of the current volume, critics have suggested that less-than-abundant funding will force the Coast Guard to *reduce* the amount of assets devoted to the counterdrug mission to carry out counterterrorism missions. Others maintain that the two missions essentially go hand in hand.

[4] This definition of homeland defense is from a traditional Coast Guard viewpoint and does not exactly coincide with current DOD definitions for homeland defense or homeland security, which are not specifically concerned with the listed sovereignty missions.

[5] The port safety component of the Port Safety and Security (PSS) program is concerned primarily with prevention of accidental damage to vessels and port facilities. This is generally accomplished through various activities, including inspections, hazardous materials-loading supervision, and cargo-transfer monitoring. The port security component is concerned with the prevention of intentional destruction, loss, or damage to port assets. During peacetime, port security is a law enforcement function. During time of armed conflict, port security can quickly change from being primarily a law enforcement function to a military mission carried out in ports within the United States as well as overseas.

[6] *Naval Coastal Warfare Doctrine* (NWP 39) delineates Navy and Coast Guard responsibilities for port security, harbor defense, and coastal sea control. It describes the maritime defense zone concept and states the command relationships and roles of the Coast Guard captain of the port, the MDZ sector commander, Naval forces, and other involved agencies. This doctrine was developed to support coastal warfare efforts in both domestic ports and in ports overseas where United States forces are deployed.

[7] Office of the National Drug Control Policy Coordinator, *The National Drug Control Strategy 2001 Annual Report* (Washington, DC: Government Printing Office, 2001), 15–16.

[8] Approximately 15 percent of the cocaine heading to the United States passes through Haiti or the Dominican Republic. Statement of Michael S. Vigil, Special Agent-in-Charge, Caribbean Field Division, Drug Enforcement Administration, before the Subcommittee on Criminal Justice, Drug Policy, and Human Resources, April 12, 2000.

[9] Statement of John C. Varrone, Acting Deputy Assistant Commissioner, Office of Investigations, U.S. Customs Service, before the Senate Judiciary Committee Subcommittee on Criminal Justice Oversight on Drug Smuggling in the Caribbean, May 9, 2000

[10] Statement of Robert D. Allen, Commander, Coast Guard Activities San Diego, before the Subcommittee on Criminal Justice, Drug Policy, and Human Resources, Committee on Government Reform, U.S. House of Representatives, March 7, 2000.

[11] Presidential Decision Directive 14, "Western Hemisphere Counter-Drug Strategy," established the Coast Guard as the lead agency for maritime interdiction. The Coast Guard shares lead agency responsibility for air interdiction with the U.S. Customs Service.

[12] Previously, service helicopters could only monitor the progress of go-fasts and were powerless to stop them. In addition to deadly force, the Coast Guard is investigating a variety of nonlethal/disabling technologies for drug enforcement and other interdiction tasks. See Mike Emerson, "Coast Guard Helos: A Call to Arms," *U.S. Naval Institute Proceedings* 125, no. 10 (October 1999), 30–33.

[13] Thomas Walker, "Coast Guard Expects Smuggling to Increase," *Daily Citizen* (Key West, FL), March 24, 2001, 1.

[14] "Memorandum of Agreement between the Department of Defense and the Department of Transportation on the Use of U.S. Coast Guard Capabilities in Support of the National Military Strategy," October 3, 1995. This document identifies 1) maritime intercept operations; 2) military environmental response operations; and 3) deployed port operations, security, and defense as Coast Guard capabilities that DOD planners may rely on as being available during military operations and other contingencies. This agreement was amended in 2001 to add "coastal sea control" operations as an area of mutual support.

[15] This is the term used by Chief of Naval Operations and the Commandant of the Coast Guard to refer to complementary forces. See Jay Johnson and James Loy, National Fleet Policy Statement, September 28, 1998. In March 2001, Vernon Clark and Loy reissued the National Fleet Policy Statement and expanded it beyond cutters and surface warships to include aircraft and C⁴ISR systems. In the fall 2001, a joint Navy-Coast Guard Review Team was established to review the National Fleet Policy Statement and the 1995 memorandum of agreement (as amended) to "identify enhancements to our partnership to ensure interoperability and complementary operations between the Navy and the Coast Guard, especially in the area of homeland security."

[16] Several recent studies have argued that at-sea interdiction is not effective for the monitoring of large container vessels. Instead, a mixture of inspection and sophisticated monitoring technologies needs to be adopted. This requires considerable cooperation between the Coast Guard, the Customs Service, and local port authorities, with post authorities taking the lead on developing and maintaining the computer-based systems for tracking individual containers. See, for example, Charles Pope and Chris McGann, "Ports Getting Top-Notch Security: Seattle, Tacoma are First on Nation's List for New, Tougher System," *Seattle Post Intelligencer*, July 11, 2002, 1.

[17] For instance, noting the vast area and the countries that must be monitored to interdict drug shipments in the Caribbean basin, DEA agent Vigil insisted in 2000 congressional testimony that "any meaningful, effective interdiction program must almost exclusively depend on quality, time sensitive intelligence. See Vigil.

[18] James B. Thach, "USCG's Urgent Need for Deepwater Replacements," *Sea Power*, April 1998.

Chapter 24

Naval Contributions to National Missile Defense

Hans Binnendijk and George Stewart

S everal previous chapters have identified ballistic missile defense as a potential mission for naval forces in a globalized world—a world characterized by continuing proliferation of weapons of mass destruction and their means of delivery. Events of the past 18 months have created new possibilities for the U.S. Navy to contribute to defenses against intercontinental ballistic missiles (ICBMs). Some potential contributions by naval forces to this national effort would enhance the prospects for defeating a missile attack on the United States and its allies by rogue states, while others could undermine strategic stability with Russia and China. The purpose of this chapter is to review the state of the naval missile defense program and to evaluate its prospects, both as an enhancement and as a potential destabilizer. Our conclusion is that the most efficacious architecture for a national missile defense (NMD) system—from both a technical and strategic perspective—would include a Navy boost-phase intercept program and selective sea-based radars.

Recent History of the NMD Program

The Clinton administration developed its NMD strategy in an effort to defend all 50 states as soon as possible against a limited ICBM threat from rogue states. Emphasis was placed on amending but retaining the 1972 Anti-Ballistic Missile (ABM) Treaty to secure strategic stability with Russia. The resulting architecture relied on land-based midcourse interceptors guided by both land- and space-based sensors. But by September 2000, the technologies needed for this architecture were not yet mature and President William Clinton decided not to deploy the system in 2001. Although significant progress was made to develop naval-based theater missile defenses during

Hans Binnendijk is Roosevelt Professor of National Security Policy at the National Defense University and director of the Center for Technology and National Security Policy. He previously served at the National Security Council as Senior Director for Defense Policy and Arms Control. George Stewart is a research analyst at the Center for Naval Analyses.

the Clinton administration, there was no naval component to the basic NMD architecture because that administration sought deployments that could be in place by 2005–2006.[1]

The Bush administration entered office determined to accelerate progress on missile defenses, expand research and development efforts, accept a greater degree of technological risk, and redesign the NMD architecture. The clear line established in 1997 that delineated theater missile defenses from national missile defenses was blurred. This opened the door to a greater seaborne contribution to defense against ICBMs, and the Navy began to analyze this new potential.[2] A broad array of options was developed to exploit the progress that had been made in the Navy's theater ballistic missile defense programs. Then three events occurred in December 2001 and January 2002 that further shaped the Navy's program—in both positive and negative directions.

On December 13, 2001, the Bush administration announced that the United States would withdraw from the ABM Treaty in 6 months time.[3] Despite its diplomatic drawbacks, this step allows the United States the legal standing to experiment with ship-based and other mobile ICBM defense systems and to build the land-based test site in Alaska.[4] With the treaty expiring in June 2002, the Pentagon is scheduled to test the ability of the Navy Aegis radar to track both the interceptor and target missiles. The decision to withdraw from the ABM Treaty also removes constraints from the development of Navy systems designed to be effective against shorter-range ballistic missiles. The effect is to begin moving tests of future sea-based systems from the virtual world of high-speed computers to the test range.

But the day after the administration announced its intention to withdraw from the ABM Treaty, it terminated Navy Area—the Navy's program for terminal defense against short-range ballistic missiles—for failure to meet the goals set by the Nunn-McCurdy Act.[5] Up to that point, some in the administration had envisioned using Navy Area as an emergency boost-phase interceptor against North Korea. Since termination, work has ceased on all aspects of Navy Area, while the Navy and the new Missile Defense Agency study how best to fulfill the requirement for a ship-based short-range missile defense system. This work included efforts such as the integration of missile defense functions with the rest of the Aegis weapon system that would have helped support the development of other Navy systems effective against long-range ballistic missiles. Navy Area had been scheduled to begin testing in 2002 with an operational deployment by 2004.[6] One likely consequence of the termination decision will be to delay any operational (as opposed to an experimental or test-bed) sea-based missile defense system by some 2 to 5 years.

Then on January 25, 2002, the Navy successfully flight-tested the first fully functional SM–3 (standard missile) and scored a direct hit, using hit-to-kill technology against a Scud-type test missile.[7] The SM–3 is the missile associated with the Aegis

Light Exo-Atmospheric Projectile Intercept (ALI) Program, which is the core of the Navy Mid-Course (formerly Navy Theater Wide) system. Navy Mid-Course is the only Navy missile defense program to enjoy any significant funding, with seven SM–3 test firings now scheduled. But there is currently no funding for procurement or any official plan for transitioning what is currently a risk reduction/proof of principle effort toward a procurement program. The date is not at all certain when the technologies being tested as part of Navy Mid-Course could meld into an operational system. Optimistic guesses start at around 5 years, more pessimistic guesses at 10 years.

The net effect of these three events was to encourage additional testing of naval missile defenses while actually delaying much of the foundation upon which the systems being tested was built. As a result, the Navy program is being reengineered, and much of the steam has been taken out of efforts to focus it on ICBM defenses.

An Overall Approach to National Defense against ICBMs

U.S. Navy contribution to missile defenses needs to be placed in the context of emerging rogue state threats and the need to maintain strategic stability with former adversaries. During the past several years, national intelligence estimates have indicated a growing missile threat from North Korea, Iran, and Iraq that will continue to develop throughout this decade. At the same time, relations with former adversaries have improved, and the recent Nuclear Posture Review suggests that the United States is no longer sizing its offensive nuclear forces based primarily upon the need to strike specific Russian targets. In this context, a reasonable architecture to defend against ICBMs would:

- be oriented primarily against missiles launched from rogue states
- emphasize the systems that attack the missile during its boost phase
- contain a thin layer of systems designed to attack the missile during its midcourse should they leak through the first line of defenses.[8]

The emphasis on boost-phase missile defense systems is consistent with emphasizing defense of the United States against attacks launched from rogue states. Unless the missile defense system is space-based, its operating area will necessarily be within about 1,000 kilometers of the launchsite. This greatly limits the impact that a terrestrial boost-phase missile defense system could have on the strategic deterrents of Russia or China. We would not recommend deploying boost-phased interceptors in space because such deployments would be able to intercept Russian and Chinese missiles and would prove destabilizing. Similarly, deploying ground-based boost-phased interceptors would require stationing them in Russia to deal with the North Korean threat.

Boost-phase missile defense systems also have the advantage of attacking an ICBM during the most vulnerable portion of its trajectory. During boost phase, an

ICBM is a large object with a bright booster plume. The large stresses of launch mean that even the slightest amount of damage to the ICBM can result in total destruction of the entire system. Boost-phase missile defense systems also attack the ICBM before the offense can disperse countermeasures or multiple warheads. Another strong advantage to focusing on boost-phase defenses is that the United States would be able to defend its allies as it defends itself.

The technical and operational challenges of the boost phase involve the requirement to consummate the engagement in a very short time, less than 3 to 5 minutes.[9] Since the decision to engage must be made in a fraction of that time, command, control, and surveillance systems must be tailored to flow information very quickly to the command center where the decision to engage will be made. Although in the information age such data can be piped anywhere instantaneously, the person most likely to have his hand on the trigger will be the local commanding officer of an individual unit, not the geographic commander or civilian authorities in Washington, DC. Also, while that commander will have some information available as to the type of missile and the direction of the missile, he will not have an unambiguous estimate of its aim point (and therefore clear proof of its hostile intent) at the time when the decision must be made to engage or forgo the opportunity. Therefore, operational usage of boost-phase systems will require that special procedures be established in advance. These procedures could range from no-fly zones similar to those being enforced over Iraq to prelaunch notifications for commercial launches.

Since most missile defense development to date has concentrated on midcourse or terminal defense, the technical challenges of building a system capable of detecting, identifying, tracking, and engaging a ballistic missile during its boost phase have not yet been fully developed. In addition, even a limited barrage attack could result in a few missiles leaking through boost-phase defenses. It is therefore prudent to augment the boost-phase missile defense systems with a thin layer of perhaps 100 midcourse interceptors that could engage leakers from the boost-phase layer. Providing that the problem of midcourse countermeasures can be managed, midcourse defense systems also have the advantage of allowing a single missile interceptor base to defend large areas. For example, under the Clinton administration NMD program, a single site in Alaska would have been capable of defending the United States against an ICBM launched from much of the Northern Hemisphere. Such a midcourse insurance policy should not affect Russian deterrent posture.

While the United States need not have many sites from which missile interceptors are fired for a midcourse defense, it will require a large network of sensors (for example, radars, infrared, and visible) to detect, identify, and track all ICBM components. After the last booster of an ICBM burns out, the payload deploys. What deploys and how long this process takes depends on the complexity of the weapon system. Simple

ICBMs may merely separate the warhead from the booster with the concurrent deployment of simple countermeasures such as balloons. More complex weapon systems may include a bus that performs additional maneuvers to distribute countermeasures and warheads over a wide swath of space. Sorting out this picture of launch debris, spent boosters, deliberate countermeasures, and warheads will require both sensors and a sophisticated battle management system to direct successful engagements.[10]

This proposed architecture would be both highly effective against a rogue state and relatively cost effective. Rogue states are unlikely to possess more than about 20 ICBMs during the next few decades.[11] Assuming all are launched at the same time, a robust boost-phased system should be able to engage successfully well over 60 percent of those missiles. In this stressful scenario, the remaining 8 missiles would disperse a total of 8 warheads and additional decoys to face 100 U.S. midcourse interceptors. The United States could afford to launch four midcourse interceptors against each real warhead and up to 17 of the decoys as a further insurance policy. The cost of this system would be no more than the 2 phases of the system proposed by President Clinton, which included a total of up to 250 midcourse interceptors.

Our suggested missile defense architecture would not include terminal defenses for the continental United States or for those who attack the missile after it begins to reenter the atmosphere. The advantage of terminal defense is that the atmosphere strips off the lighter countermeasures used by the offense to fool the defense. The disadvantage is that very little time is left to consummate the engagement. Also, if the device is nuclear, the effects of salvage fusing can still deliver a very damaging electromagnetic pulse to the intended target. The physics involved limit the footprint (that is, the area defended by a single missile interceptor site) of terminal defense systems to less than 10,000 square nautical miles or so. This is an area large enough to be useful for defending a port, airfield, coastal city, or troop concentrations, but it is a minute fraction of the land area of the United States. There may be value in using terminal phase deployments to defend some of our European allies or Japan against theater-range missiles. But as far as the *overall* defense of the United States is concerned, there seems little rationale for building a terminal defense system capable of engaging high-speed, long-range ICBMs.[12]

Pros and Cons of Sea-based Defense against ICBMs

The systems being considered by the new Missile Defense Agency (MDA) and the Navy for sea-based ICBM defense are not unique to ships; in fact, given an appropriate site, they could all be employed equally well on land. Thus, it is reasonable to ask: "Why deploy the ICBM defense systems at sea?" The primary advantages offered by seabasing are:

■ *Flexibility offered by making part of the ICBM defense architecture mobile.* The radars and missile interceptors required for defense against ICBMs are large and heavy. Placing them onboard a ship is a very cost effective way to make them mobile. Mobility offers two advantages. First, it makes the defensive missile system less vulnerable to a preemptive strike. Second, it allows the United States to change the architecture quickly in response to changes in the world situation. Ships could be withdrawn if no longer needed or moved if new threats appear.

■ *Unambiguous control over ICBM defense sites in international waters.* Over two-thirds of the world's surface is covered by oceans. With the notable exception of the ice-covered Artic, U.S. Navy ships can operate year-round in any of them without the approval of foreign governments. Thus seabasing may allow the appropriate placement of ICBM defense elements outside of the United States without requiring the permission of a host-nation that could be revoked if our interests and theirs diverge.

While the advantages of seabasing are significant, they must be balanced with potential disadvantages.

■ *Multiple ships are required to operate continuously in a single ICBM defense site.* No matter how efficiently the Navy operates, ICBM defense-capable ships will eventually need to return to port for maintenance and/or crew rest. As a consequence, the United States will need to purchase multiple copies of each ICBM defense system if continuous on-station presence is desired. In addition to cost and efficiency, the surge capacity inherent in the extra ships may create political concerns.

■ *Missile defenses deployed on Navy ships must be integrated with other combat systems.* Current Navy ships are complex platforms capable of performing multiple missions. Each new combat system added to the ship must solve technical problems of shipboard integration as well as the technical issues inherent in the system itself. This requires significant resources, particularly when the system is as complex as the Aegis weapon system that has figured prominently in many proposals to host missile defense capabilities on Navy ships. Integration issues are not insoluble, but they are ones that must be factored into the costs and time required to put a missile defense system to sea.

■ *Missile defenses deployed on Navy ships create the potential for conflicts between ICBM defense and other Navy missions.* In practice, several considerations may rule out *simultaneous* usage of ships for traditional missions and ICBM defense. While some ICBM defense areas overlap nicely with expected Navy crisis operating areas, others do not. For example, the original Clinton administration architecture relied on radars in the United Kingdom and Greenland. If due to host-nation concerns we decided to put these radars on Navy ships instead, they would not be of much use for other missions during a crisis in the Middle East. In addition, executing many traditional Navy missions requires putting a ship in harm's way. If a ship is participating in defense of the United States against ICBMs, we might prefer to limit that ship's exposure to risks not associated with ICBM defense.

Before leaving the subject of generic advantages and disadvantages to sea-based missile defense systems, we should point out that in hosting missile defense systems at sea there is an important policy decision to make: should the missile defense systems be hosted on existing Navy ships or on noncombatants? For example, interceptor missiles could be deployed on special ships akin to the cancelled arsenal ship, and radars could be deployed on special radar ships such as the Cobra Judy radar in USNS *Observation Island*.

Hosting the systems on combatants such as an Aegis cruiser has the advantage that the ship can participate in its own defense. There are also good solid policy reasons for keeping major weapon systems such as missile interceptors on military platforms. However, as pointed out above, adding missile defense to the list of existing missions incurs overhead in both the form of integration of the missile defense system with other combat systems and a potential opportunity cost of diverting the ship from the missions that we originally built it to perform. Hosting sea-based systems on noncombatants avoids the integration and potential opportunity costs. It is not a free solution, however. One has to procure the additional platforms and then provide for their defense. It still might be the preferable solution for some applications.

Potential Sea-based Contributions to Boost-Phase Defense

While the radar presently in place on Aegis combatants has enough power and resolution to detect and track ICBMs during the boost phase, its performance and displays have been optimized for defense against air-breathing targets (for example, cruise missiles and airplanes). While the required modifications for missile defense are nontrivial, they are still judged as achievable. What is totally missing at present is a suitable boost-phase missile interceptor.

While some Navy officials proposed using missiles being built for the now-terminated Navy Area program (the SM–2 Block IV) to engage boosting ICBMs in the upper atmosphere, that proposal was fraught with a great deal of technical risk and required the ship to be within 50 kilometers of the launchsite, making the ship itself vulnerable. A more practical approach seems to be the development of a missile interceptor intended to engage the boosting ICBM above the atmosphere.

Suitable missiles could be developed using the SM–3 test missiles being produced for the Navy Mid-Course risk reduction effort as a starting point. Successful boost-phase intercept missiles would have to be faster than the SM–3 test missiles. Fortunately, the vertical launching system on Navy combatants has enough growth potential to support a variety of solutions, such as modifying the second stage of the SM–3 to increase the diameter of the rocket engine to 21 inches, hosting a faster, more maneuverable kill vehicle with a liquid fueled divert and attitude control system, or even increasing the overall diameter of the missile interceptor to 27 inches.

We can only speculate as to how long development of a suitable missile and its integration with the Aegis weapon system would require. Prior to the cancellation of the Navy Area program, optimistic estimates by some Navy officials were as low as 6 years to produce boost-phase missile interceptors for ship tests. Since all work on shipboard integration of missile defense systems is currently in suspense, this timeline has probably increased.

Using the modified SM–3 or wide diameter missiles, the ship could be positioned as far as 1,000 kilometers from the launch point. Using international waters, Navy ships so equipped could engage missiles launched from all of North Korea or Iraq. The effectiveness of sea-based boost-phase missile interceptors against ICBMs launched from Iran would depend on the part of the country from which the ICBMs were launched, and ground-based or airborne supplements would be needed in some cases.

There are clear political advantages and some disadvantages to a sea-based boost-phase capability. The main advantage is that it would provide the potential to defend against ICBMs launched from North Korea and most parts of the Middle East. At the same time, it would present no threat to the land-based ICBM deterrent of Russia and China because their launch points are far inland.

There are some disadvantages. First, a sea-based boost-phase system would present a potential threat to the submarine-launched deterrent of Russia, assuming a capability to estimate the general location of the submarine. Second, this concept would require the establishment of a "no-launch zone" or other special procedures over the rogue state and a willingness in extremis to delegate the engagement decision to the ship commander. Both requirements may be difficult to sustain politically. Finally, the concept would require the interceptors to be launched in the direction of the country launching the ICBMs and third parties. For example, defending against North Korea with boost-phase missile interceptors will entail their launch on azimuths toward both North Korea and China. When defending against Iraq and Iran, the boost-phase missile interceptors would fly over several countries on an azimuth toward Russia. Debris from the engagement (such as damaged warheads or spent interceptor boosters) could impact third countries.

If the United States is willing to accept these political disadvantages, the operational advantages of a sea-based boost-phase interceptor are significant. With the potential exception of Iran, they are most effective against the countries that we wish to dissuade and deter, and they are less effective against former adversaries that we wish to reassure. If we require continuous protection, several Aegis ships would needed to be deployed for the mission, but that investment is relatively small compared to the potential cost of a missile strike against the United States. However, with the short time lines involved in such an attack, it seems prudent to develop an additional layer to meet the goal of designing a robust defense against rogue state ICBMs.

Potential Sea-based Contributions to Mid-Course Defense

Given the critical dependence of any midcourse ICBM defense system on sensor support, we first discuss the possibility of seabasing high power, fine resolution radars to provide sensor support and then discuss the possibility of seabasing midcourse missile interceptors. While we discuss these separately, it would be quite possible to put both on the same ship.

Sea-based Radars

While the ABM Treaty has prohibited formal testing, the current S-band radar (SPY–1) used by the Aegis weapon system has the capability to track large objects such as boosters at ranges well above the atmosphere. While testing is required to determine just how much the current SPY–1 radar can contribute to a midcourse defense system, it seems likely that any solution to the countermeasure problem will require the development of radars with even higher power and finer resolution.

Navy officials have stated that the near-term possibility would be to use the existing SPY–1 radar coupled with software modifications to tailor the waveform for the tracking of objects in space. Depending upon the cross section of the target, its maximum detection and tracking ranges would be somewhere between 500 to 1,000 kilometers. This capability would support midcourse engagements of early generation ICBM systems developed by rogue states with few or no countermeasures. The same Navy officials estimate that increasing the power and resolution of the systems to detect, to provide discrimination clues, and to track all individual elements of a cluster at range out to 3,000 kilometers will require approximately 9 years to produce and will involve the development of new technology X-band and S-band radars.

Another possibility is taking the current X-band technology developed for the national missile defense program, marinizing it, and placing it onboard a ship. These radars have maximum detection and tracking ranges between 2,000 and 4,000 kilometers. While these radars could be backfit onto existing Navy combatants, their weight, power, and cooling needs would require the removal of many combat systems currently in place. As a result, some proponents of this idea suggest that the ship should be a noncombatant and utilize a commercial hull. The minimum time required for the integration, design, and conversion of an existing hull is likely in the vicinity of 5 years.

Sea-based radars can make a unique contribution to midcourse intercepts. Earth curvature limits the detection and tracking ranges of any radar. Presumably appropriate land-based sites will be found for radars to track incoming missiles as they approach the United States. Seabasing can locate a radar totally under U.S. control much closer to the launchsite than is possible from sovereign U.S. territory. Indeed, if host-nation support is not forthcoming, it might be the only way to put high power radars closer to the launchsite. Two factors make this radar placement desirable:

- It would help develop sufficient information to engage the ICBM in the early midcourse. This is an important consideration in a battle that will be over for better or worse in 15 to 30 minutes.
- Observing deployment of the payload would provide additional information that might be of great value in picking out the warhead(s) amid the cluster of debris and deliberate countermeasures.

There are two other reasons why naval deployment of radars to detect ICBMs might be useful. First, there has been reluctance in both Britain and Denmark to the deployment suggested by the Clinton administration of X-band radars at Fylingdales and Thule. While ground-based radars might be more reliable, naval deployments do provide an alternative. Second, if the space-based infrared systems (SBIRS, High and Low) now in development continue to face technological and funding problems, naval radar deployments could be in greater demand.

Sea-based radars should not undermine strategic stability. They would not enable similar early detection/tracking of ICBMs launched from the interior of Russia and China. One potential complication, however, relates to verification for future arms control regimes. If the United States makes provisions to link existing Aegis radars (or any other radar used widely throughout the Navy) into an ICBM missile defense network, then all the ships with that radar become potential strategic assets.

Using radars onboard naval combatants for a midcourse defense system against ICBMs appears to be feasible and to have definite advantages. The disadvantage again would include the potential opportunity cost of diverting those ships from the missions that they were originally constructed for. This disadvantage is offset somewhat when the ships are employed in forward locations where they might be able to participate simultaneously in other missions that did not put their strategic mission at risk.

Sea-based Missile Interceptors

The SM–3 test missiles with the Aegis Light Exo-Atmospheric Projectile Intercept Program currently being purchased for risk reduction testing have a maximum speed of about 3.1 kilometers per second. This is adequate for defending against intermediate-range ballistic missiles. But to have a robust capability against ICBMs, the speed of the interceptor missile will need to be increased. Engineers estimate that the current launch systems used on Navy combatants could be modified to accept larger diameter missiles with speeds of 6.5 kilometers per second or greater. An interceptor missile with a speed of 6.5 kilometers per second would be capable of defending a huge area, the size of a continent or larger, and it could address advanced capability ICBMs. Developing these new missiles will take time. Estimates for development of faster missile interceptors with improved kill vehicles generally range between 6 and 15 years.

Unlike other weapon systems, the technology does not impose natural boundaries between midcourse missile defense systems developed to defend against long-range theater missiles (with ranges up to 3,500 kilometers) and ICBMs. The Navy and geographic commanders have, as a priority, the development of missile defense systems effective against longer-range theater missiles now being developed by some of the rogue states. Given appropriate sensor support, such missiles would have at least a rudimentary capability against ICBMs. In fact, at times they could perform both missions simultaneously. For example, given proper sensor support, a ship with fast mid-course missile interceptors in the North Sea could defend large parts of Europe and the east coast of the United States against missiles launched from the Middle East. This is good in that it enhances the utility of these weapon systems. But it is bad in that it blurs the boundary between the strategic and nonstrategic for arms control purposes.

Notwithstanding the large areas that can be defended by a single missile interceptor facility, there are advantages to having missile interceptors for midcourse systems launched from multiple sites:

- System suppression becomes more difficult.
- Target engagement becomes more flexible, which is important in dealing with salvage-fused nuclear warheads.
- Shoot-look-shoot firing doctrine can be used.

A shoot-look-shoot doctrine is one in which the defense fires one interceptor missile, evaluates the results, and fires a second (or more) interceptor missile only if the first interceptor misses. Shoot-look-shoot preserves missile inventory and greatly simplifies battle management by minimizing the number of interceptor missiles in flight at any given time. This becomes important when one envisions defending against small raids of more than one ICBM. Shoot-look-shoot is only feasible if the durations of individual engagements are a small fraction of the overall flight time of the ICBM.

Since multiple land-based sites can be built within the territory of the United States to permit multiple engagements in the latter part of the midcourse, this suggests operating areas for ships with midcourse ICBM interceptors be based on either engaging the ICBM early in the midcourse or extending the defended area to cover portions of the world far from the United States in defense of allies or U.S. forces deployed forward. Even with these general guidelines it is difficult to define fixed operating areas for Navy ships in support of midcourse missile defense against ICBMs.

What political impacts might the seabasing of midcourse missile interceptors have? These ships could be positioned to engage ICBMs originating from anywhere on the globe. This gives them great flexibility, but also makes them of intense interest to Russia and China. Also, the numbers of missiles and platforms that we might desire to build for *theater* defense purposes could become entangled in strategic issues.

For the sake of efficiency, the Navy would like to limit the numbers of special purpose combatants and weapon systems. If we build midcourse missile interceptors capable of engaging ICBMs that are compatible with the Navy's standard missile launching system (the vertical launch system), then most of the fleet will be viewed as strategic assets and as the potential basis for a huge surge in defensive capabilities. (An Aegis cruiser has 122 missile launch tubes. With 20+ cruisers in the fleet, the Navy could theoretically surge over 2,000 missile tubes with midcourse interceptors in them to sea in an operational posture.)

Maintaining Strategic Stability

While the ABM Treaty terminates in summer 2002, there remains a need to maintain strategic stability with Russia and China. If a new strategic framework with Russia is to be successfully concluded, some constraints on missile defenses will have to be accepted by the United States. The question is whether those constraints would allow for the eventual deployment of a limited number of naval ships with radars and interceptors capable of defeating an ICBM.

Such a new framework could be negotiated without abandoning sea-based missile defenses. If the sea-based interceptors are limited to boost phase, they would not have adequate range to intercept ICBMs launched from Russia. Line-of-sight radars based on ships deployed near North Korea and the Persian Gulf would also have very limited capabilities against Russian ICBMs. Russia might seek to limit the number of ships deployed with ICBM defense capabilities or to limit their stationing area. They might also seek assurances that sea-based systems will not be used against their submarine-launched missiles.

The most difficult arms control problem to solve is that if some naval systems with theater missile defense capabilities are netted into the national missile defense system, Russia might assume that all Aegis radars and all interceptors have at least some NMD capabilities. The arms control task will be to convince the Russians that this capability is limited and does not undermine Russian deterrence. One possibility would be to create a boost-phase interceptor that requires a modified launch system whose presence can be verified by visual inspection of the outside of the ship and then to limit the number of those systems deployed on Aegis ships.

The Chinese problem is more difficult because they have only a few dozen land-based single warhead missiles capable of striking the United States. Sea-based boost-phased interceptors should not present a threat to Chinese ICBMs launched from the Chinese interior. On the other hand, sea-based radars linked to even a limited number of midcourse interceptors could be seen by the Chinese as affecting their current deterrence force. But the Chinese are modernizing their ICBM force anyway, and the number of warheads capable of striking the United States could multiply several times during the coming decade even without U.S. missile defenses.[13] The best that can be hoped for is that China does not pursue options to create multiple warheads on their missiles. The missile defense architecture suggested above provides the best prospect of preventing the Chinese from MIRVing their ICBMs while still providing credible protection against rogue states.

Conclusions

There are several general advantages to using seabasing for defense of the United States against ICBMs. The most important are flexibility and control. But there are costs as well, including operational limitations for other missions and competition for resources to build new ships.

From the perspective of cost effectiveness, the most attractive option for a potential seaborne deployment is using upgraded Aegis radars and modified SM–3 missiles for boost-phase intercepts onboard existing combat ships stationed near Korea and the Eastern Mediterranean. In addition to providing a layer of boost-phase defense, ships at these locations would provide radar coverage early in the ICBM's flight that would be valuable to the midcourse defense layer. These locations overlap with current Navy forward-operating areas. The overlap would help mitigate the opportunity cost entailed by the new mission.

It is difficult to estimate when this capability will be available. The end of the decade is a reasonable estimate providing the United States decides to pursue this approach in the near future. It is possible that systems for the midcourse defense layer would mature earlier. In that case, the ships could deploy initially to provide radar support with the boost-phase capability being added as it becomes available.

There are several costs to this option, which would need management. The first is maintaining strategic stability with the Russians. They would need to be convinced that such deployments would not undermine their deterrent. That would be a difficult but not impossible task. Second, the Navy would need to accept that Aegis ships deployed with this capability would have missile defense as their principal mission and that all other missions would be secondary. Third, the President would have to delegate the authority to shoot down a missile in boost phase to the commander of the ship or some other regional commander. This might cause potential diplomatic problems, but in practice other missile defense concepts would probably also have to delegate a similar authority to the operational level.

An alternative, which might have some arms control and operational benefits, would be to pursue the construction of separate ships designed solely for the intercept and radar missions. That way the missile defense ships would be separate from the Aegis fleet and could be more easily verified. But new construction might slow down the existing Navy shipbuilding program due to cost considerations.

Seabasing of midcourse missile interceptors or terminal defense systems against ICBMs is a much less attractive alternative. There are better land-based alternatives for midcourse intercepts that would be less destabilizing and would not mix theater and national missile defenses. The terminal defense systems for the continental United States simply cannot defend a large enough area to be attractive for anything other than the last-ditch defense of very important strategic facilities. Since those defense facilities generally do not move, there seems to be no reason to pay a premium for making the defense system mobile.

In summary, deployment of a small number of sea-based radars and boost-phase interceptors would make sense in dealing with a limited rogue state threat. There are costs to be managed, not the least of which is persuading Russia and China that such deployments do not undermine strategic stability. But if the architecture is properly designed, this should not be an impossible task.

Notes

[1] A critical assessment of the decision not to include a naval component can be found in Jack Spencer and Joseph Dougherty, "The Quickest Way to Global Missile Defense: First From the Sea," *The Heritage Foundation Back-grounder*, No. 1384, July 13, 2000, accessed at <www.heritage.org/library/backgrounder/bg1384.html>.

[2] On July 5, 2000, Chief of Naval Operations Jay Johnson announced the establishment of a new office on his immediate staff, the Assistant Chief of Naval Operations (ACNO) for Missile Defense. See remarks in Kauai Economic Development Board, "Navy Establishes Missile Defense Office," *Kauai Now*, July 5, 2000, accessed at <www.kedb.com/news/navy-missile-office.html>. Kauai is the location of the instrumentation center for the Navy's Pacific missile test range.

[3] Merle D. Kellerhals, "U.S. Will Withdraw From 1972 Anti-Ballistic Missile Treaty," U.S. Department of State, International Information Programs, December 13, 2001, accessed at <http://usinfo.state.gov/topical/pol/arms/stories/01121301.htm>; The White House, Office of the Press Secretary, "Remarks by the President on National Missile Defense," December 13, 2001, accessed at <http://usinfo.state.gov/topical/pol/arms/stories/01121302.htm>.

[4] For brief discussion of diplomatic drawbacks, see U.S. Department of State, International Information Programs, "Powell says U.S. Withdrawal from ABM not creating crisis or arms race," December 16, 2001, accessed at <http://usinfo.state.gov/topical/pol/arms/stories/01121610.htm>.

[5] U.S. Department of Defense, "Navy Area Missile Defense Program Cancelled," News Release 637–01, December 2001, accessed at <www.defenselink.mil/news/Dec2001>; Bradley Graham, "Rise and Fall of a Navy Missile," *The Washington Post*, March 28, 2002, A3.

[6] Robert Wall and David A. Fulgham, "What's Next For Navy Missile Defense," *Aviation Week & Space Technology*, December 24, 2001, accessed at <www.aviationnow.com/content/publication/awst/20011224/aw43b.htm>.

[7] U.S. Navy, "Navy intercepts ballistic missile; accelerates TBMD program," January 24, 2002, accessed at <www.chinfo.navy.mil/navpalib/weapons/missiles/standard/standard.html>. See commentary in Henry F. Cooper, "New Life for Sea-Based Defense," *National Review* Online, January 30, 2002, accessed at <www.nationalreview.com/comment/ comment-cooper013002.shtml>.

[8] See Hans Binnendijk, "How to Build an International Consensus for Missile Defense," *International Herald Tribune*, March 7, 2001.

[9] While some advanced ICBM concepts such as fast burn and depressed trajectories can reduce this time still further, rogue states will not have this capability in their first-generation ICBMs.

[10] Many critics of missile defense programs argue that the countermeasure problem is fundamentally insoluble. While that is not the position of the scientists and engineers engaged in system design, it is fair to say that the final solution to the countermeasure problem has not yet been identified. The debate is complicated by a lack of agreement (between the critics and proponents) on what types of countermeasures an ICBM defense system can expect to encounter in various time frames.

[11] This is the current estimate for a potential North Korean ICBM missile arsenal as noted in interview of Deputy Secretary of State Richard Armitage by the Australian Broadcasting Corporation. See Four Corners, "Rogue State," August 6, 2001, accessed at <www.abc.net.au/4corners/stories/s341915.htm>.

[12] The currently operational Patriot missile system has no capability against ICBMs. The ICBMs are simply too fast for the system to engage.

[13] Trends generally accepted as valid by all sources. See, for example, "NRDC Nuclear Notebook," *Bulletin of the Atomic Scientists*, November/December 2000, 78–79.

Part V

Globalization and Force Structure

Chapter 25

The Navy in an Antiaccess World

Clark A. Murdock

Early in this volume, the proliferation of antiaccess (or area-denial) systems and strategies was identified as a key military feature of globalization. The *Quadrennial Defense Review Report* (*QDR Report*) identifies the antiaccess challenge—"Projecting and sustaining U.S. forces in distant anti-access or area-denial environments, and defeat anti-access threats"—as one of the six critical "emerging strategic and operational challenges" that will focus and drive the transformation of the U.S. military:[1]

> Future adversaries could have the means to render ineffective much of our current ability to project military power overseas. Saturation attacks with ballistic and cruise missiles could deny or delay U.S. military access to overseas bases, airfields and ports. Advanced air defense systems could deny access to hostile airspace to all but extremely low-observable aircraft. Military and commercial space capabilities, over-the-horizon radars, and low-observable unmanned aerial vehicles could give potential adversaries the means to conduct wide-area surveillance and track and target American forces and assets. Anti-ship cruise missiles, advanced diesel submarines, and advanced mines could threaten the ability of U.S. naval and amphibious forces to operate in littoral waters. *New approaches for projecting power must be developed to meet these threats.*[2]

In the past, the Department of Defense (DOD) has been somewhat in denial about the antiaccess challenge. Many of these capabilities are, in fact, already part of the current threat environment. But the *QDR Report*'s full embrace of the imperative to change is a significant step forward.

Clark A. Murdock is president of Murdock Associates and a senior fellow at the Center for Strategic and International Studies in Washington, DC. Among other policy planning positions, he served as counselor to U.S. Representative and later Secretary of Defense Les Aspin, Deputy Director of Strategic Planning for the U.S. Air Force, and distinguished professor at the National War College.

After first analyzing the general nature of the U.S. power projection versus antiaccess competition, this chapter addresses how the U.S. Navy should meet the antiaccess challenge.

Projecting Power and Presence into Antiaccess Environments[3]

How the United States projects power and presence into an antiaccess environment will be central to the global security dynamic for at least 2 decades. All grand strategies—such as balance of power, containment, and deterrence—depend both on capability and will. That the United States has the capability to project power into any regional theater is beyond question. What is at issue is America's willingness to do so. The question of *what* constitutes unacceptable losses to Americans in the pursuit of *what kinds* of interests has been tested by regional aggressors and would-be hegemons.

Americans clearly will support high-intensity, military operations (such as Operations *Desert Storm* and *Allied Force*) of important regional interests as long as casualties are minimal and the campaign is successful. In the immediate wake of the September 11, 2001, terrorist attack on the World Trade Center and the Pentagon, 83 percent of those polled by *The Washington Post* backed military action against the perpetrators, even if it led to war, and two-thirds of the respondents favored going to war even if it should prove a long one with large numbers of U.S. military casualties—including 45 percent who "strongly supported" it.[4] However, just as clearly (consider Somalia), Americans will not support an inconclusive or ineffective military operation involving casualties "disproportionate" to minor U.S. interests.

In both *Desert Storm* and *Allied Force,* U.S. opponents tried to inflict casualties on American forces but failed, largely because the United States refused to engage in a manner that exposed U.S. and allied forces to significant losses. In the Gulf War, ground forces were not committed until Iraqi forces were decimated by the air campaign. In *Allied Force,* the air campaign was conducted beyond the effective range of Serbian air defenses. The results were minimal or no allied military casualties, even at the cost of longer campaigns (no one envisioned a 78-day air campaign against Serbia) or at the expense of more ambitious political objectives (such as the removal of Saddam Husayn from power).

In light of American (and coalition) successes, the offense-defense competition between the United States and its potential regional opponents has turned asymmetric. The United States can now project power and employ force at politically acceptable costs to the President. Unable to directly defend against superior U.S. conventional forces, potential opponents are acquiring antiaccess capabilities (in the case of China, advanced conventional capabilities; in other cases, biological and chemical weapons and their means of delivery) to increase their ability to inflict higher casualties on U.S. power projection forces. The United States, in turn, must increase the survivability of its forces in the face of increasing antiaccess threats. Reducing the vulnerability of U.S. power projection forces is not only intrinsically worthy—after all, the lives of young American men and women are at stake—but is also critical to America's global role. Although many (including myself) believe the American aversion to casualties has been overstated, why test it? Once an adversary discovers what the actual American tolerance is (that is, what kinds of costs Americans will accept for what kinds of interests), the limits of U.S. power will have been defined. From a strategic perspective, it is sensible to maintain *strategic ambiguity* about the real limits to U.S. power.

The U.S. ability to ensure that U.S. power projection forces remain highly survivable even as antiaccess capabilities grow and proliferate will ultimately dissuade potential opponents from further efforts. The vulnerability of U.S. forces to antiaccess attacks increases as they come in closer to engage the enemy. The U.S. capability to defeat large-scale aggression should reside largely in forces capable of operating initially from beyond adversary killing zones. If U.S. power projection forces have to come deep into the theater to engage, the United States, in effect, is putting its center of gravity (American casualties) into the adversary's wheelhouse. For the next couple of decades, *highly survivable* means standoff and (good) stealth.

Future large-scale military campaigns will be phased campaigns; the United States will fight at a distance until it is safe to close. Improving standoff, force protection, and forcible entry capabilities will shorten the time required before land forces can close, but large forces deployed deep in the theater during peacetime will remain too vulnerable to surprise attacks. U.S. power projection forces must work patiently from the outside in, as they first punish aggression and take down adversary antiaccess capability before closing with the enemy.

Deploying *some* forces forward in critical areas, however, is essential as an expression of U.S. commitment and willingness to protect its regional interests. "Tripwires" helped contain the Soviet Union during the Cold War and will constrain would-be hegemons in the 21st century. Forward-deployed forces also can serve as a casus belli; Americans will support fighting anyone who kills many Americans, regardless of how important U.S. interests in the region are. *Deter forward* is not the same thing as *defend forward*.

The presence of U.S. forces in a region (unless they are just passing through) sends a message to everyone in the region that U.S. interests are of such importance that it may military force to defend or advance them. The act of deploying forces forward during peacetime also signals an awareness (on the part of the United States) that its interests in the region are being threatened. If there is no threat, why send military forces? This message, if credible, should reassure friends and allies and deter potential threats to those interests. U.S. forward presence makes the United States a global power. It reassures allies and friends; it sends a message to potential aggressors;

and it positions the United States for rapid response to smaller-scale contingencies and humanitarian relief missions. U.S. presence forces are there to be *seen* and deal with lesser contingencies. They address the *will* side of the U.S. deterrent against large-scale aggression.

U.S. presence forces should not be shaped for defending forward against large-scale aggression. Requiring forward stationed and deployed forces to defeat large-scale aggression with minimum reinforcement ensures that a regional aggressor will have many lucrative "antiaccess" targets to hit at the outset of the conflict. The potential payoff (to the aggressor) would be twofold. First, it would send a message to the American people: "Are U.S. interests here worth these kinds of costs?" Second, it could disable U.S. forces to defeat the aggressor's subsequent attack. Much in the same way that Saddam Husayn was criticized (in rogue state circles) for giving the United States 5 months to build up its forces in Southwest Asia, Slobodan Milosevic was criticized for not attacking the 20-plus bases from which the coalition mounted *Allied Force*. The next regional aggressor is likely to attack U.S. assets in theater early in the conflict in order to test the will of the United States to intervene. Since large forward-deployed forces in peacetime will always be vulnerable to surprise attacks, the United States should not have its ability to defeat large-scale aggression within range of the enemy. U.S. presence forces should raise the bar for large-scale aggression but not tempt potential aggressors into believing that it could disable through preemption the main portion of America's capability for defeating large-scale aggression.

U.S. power projection forces, on the other hand, must be highly lethal and highly survivable, capable of frustrating an aggressor's plans and inflicting great pain. These forces address the *capability* side of the deterrent against large-scale aggression. Conducting *rapid global strike* strictly from the continental United States (CONUS), however, makes it too difficult to mass the fires needed to halt aggression. U.S. power projection capabilities would be greatly enhanced if the United States could operate from robust, heavily defended, assured access bases on the periphery of a regional theater. The United States would initially wage standoff war from these *periphery bases* and then use them as staging areas for follow-on forces. For example, bombers operating from Guam, western Australia, and Diego Garcia could cover the vast Asian theater. Defending these periphery bases from missile attacks would be critical but much easier than defending closer-in bases from heavier antiaccess attacks.

Neither presence nor power projection in an antiaccess world should be viewed as lesser-included cases of each other. Moving more Air Force firepower into standoff systems could begin a division of labor among the military services across the spectrum of conflict. Although naval standoff systems (missile-carrying ships and submarines) are an important global strike asset, the Navy-Marine team is critical to global presence and more than capable of handling challenging smaller-scale contingencies. Air Force standoff forces and strategically mobile, CONUS-based Army maneuver forces should be optimized for the high end of the spectrum, although lighter Army-Air Force forces provide an important land-based element of global presence. In the midterm, space provides the global surveillance that enables all U.S. forces, but in the long term will provide silver bullet global strike assets. Greater role specialization from the services will be necessary to ensure that the U.S. military as a whole can project power and presence effectively and affordably in the 21st century.

The Emerging QDR Construct

At first blush, the QDR construct for forward presence seems inconsistent with the argument made here that U.S. presence forces should be shaped for handling lesser contingencies, not for defending forward against large-scale aggression. In describing how the U.S. military global posture would be reoriented to meet new challenges (including the antiaccess one), the QDR said that one of its goals is "to render forward forces capable of defeating an adversary's military and political objectives with only modest reinforcement."[5] The *QDR Report*, however, envisions new forms of forward presence that would include "immediately employable supplement[s]" to forward deployed and stationed forces:[6]

> A reorientation of the [military global] posture must take account of new challenges, *such as antiaccess and area denial threats.* New combinations of immediately employable forward stationed and deployed forces; globally available reconnaissance, strike, command and control assets; information operations capabilities; and rapidly deployable, highly lethal forces that may have to come from outside a theater of operations have the potential to be a significant force multiplier for forward stationed forces, including forcible entry forces.[7]

An earlier draft version of the *QDR Report* expressed the need for new forms of forward presence in even stronger terms. Although the stronger verbiage was excised from the final report and does not necessarily reflect official DOD policy, it does indicate that significant segments of DOD are sympathetic toward the argument that new forms of forward presence are indeed needed. According to the earlier draft, "in an information age that enables rapid, networked operations," forward forces can be augmented by immediately employable supplemental forces (that are either globally distributed or CONUS-based) and are capable of creating strategic and operational effects "almost instantly both from within as well as from beyond a theater."[8] The draft continued by implying that no longer would DOD measure "forward presence in terms of the troops, naval tonnage, and the number of aircraft visible to the eye in any given theater" but that new measures of effectiveness were needed for these "new forms of forward presence."[9]

The final *QDR Report* clearly recognizes that the ability of the U.S. military to project firepower rapidly, massively, and precisely into a theater is growing. In its effort to increase the deterrent impact of its forward forces, it has effectively broadened the definition of forward presence (what I call presence forces) to include rapidly deployable forces. Broadening the definition of *presence forces* is exactly right; potential aggressors must understand that the United States has an immediately employable force to frustrate their aggression. U.S. forward forces should be capable of handling conflicts short of major aggression—a carrier battlegroup or amphibious ready group represents a substantial capability—but the capability to defeat large-scale aggression is increasingly resident in U.S. rapidly deployable power projection forces, of which naval forward presence forces are but one part.

The U.S. Navy in an Antiaccess World

In its April 2000 Strategic Planning Guidance, the Navy identified "combat-credible forward presence" as its "enduring contribution" to the Nation.[10] According to this document, "sea-based, self-contained and self-sustaining" naval expeditionary forces project power and influence through the means of "Knowledge Superiority and Forward Presence," defined as follows:

> Knowledge Superiority is the ability to achieve a real-time, shared understanding of the battlespace at all levels through a network which provides the rapid accumulation of all information that is needed—and the dissemination of that information to the commander as the knowledge needed—to make a timely and informed decision inside any potential adversary's sensor and engagement timeline.

> Forward Presence is being physically present with combat credible forces to Deter Aggression, Enhance Regional Stability, Protect and Promote U.S. interests, Improve Interoperability, and provide Timely Initial Crisis Response where our national interests dictate.[11]

The issue, as I have often debated with Navy officers, is "combat credible" to do what? Even though the Navy often says that it is the Army and the Air Force that win the Nation's war, the Navy clearly wants a part of the action:

> At the other end [that is, high end] of the spectrum, on-station naval expeditionary forces can provide timely and powerful sea-based response through the full range of amphibious and precision strike operations.... Ultimately, naval expeditionary forces, capable of direct and decisive influence through maritime power projection, are the nation's essential first responders and shape the early phases of hostilities to set the conditions for victory.[12]

The Navy enables its war-winning sister services by providing them "assured access" to the forward bases and ports they require. This is a commitment that even the Navy recognizes as flying into the face of the antiaccess threat:

> In order to assure U.S. access forward, naval forces will be required to counter a host of threats: sea and land mines, cruise missiles, submarines, chemical and biological weapons, space-based sensors, and information warfare. Maintaining our ability to assure access and project power in light of these threats will be increasingly vital and remains one of our most important priorities.[13]

"Knocking down the antiaccess door" (as one Navy briefing expressed it) in order to give the Air Force and Navy access to close-in bases and ports early in the conflict makes little strategic sense. After noting the widespread proliferation of antiaccess capabilities, driven by the need of lesser powers to focus military investments, Owen Cote states flatly, "Fixed targets on the surface will be indefensible if within range of an opponent's likely arsenal of precision TBMs [tactical ballistic missiles] and cruise missiles, for as long as the supply of those weapons last."[14] Gaining access to indefensible bases is not how to fight large-scale aggression.

This is bad news for the Army and Air Force. The news for the Navy is not much better. Cote continues, "Even mobile targets will be at much greater risk of prompt destruction if the opponent retains access to wide-area battlefield surveillance assets."[15] As Steven Kosiak, Andrew Krepinevich, and Michael Vickers observed, today's antiaccess threat to naval forces—"a mix of diesel submarines, sophisticated anti-ship mines, land- and sea-based high-speed anti-ship cruise missiles, and land-based aircraft and ballistic missiles"—is tough, but the future threat is even worse:

> It is also possible to envision new forms of extended-range blockade in which an adversary employs maritime forces (e.g., submarines and mines) in combination with land- (e.g., aircraft, cruise and ballistic missiles, UAVs [unmanned aerial vehicles] and UCAVs [unmanned combat aerial vehicles]) and space-based systems. Such an adversary would employ extended-range scouting systems to identify slow-moving maritime craft movement, while extended-range strike forces engage the target. One suspects that this form of blockade is likely to emerge initially at choke points . . . or be focused on a few ports . . . [but] It does not require a huge leap in imagination to envision how an enemy's blockade capabilities might be brought to bear against critical targets in more open waters, as the means for conducting extended-range reconnaissance proliferate and mature, along with the means to conduct attacks at ever greater ranges.[16]

This is far from a benign threat environment.

The Navy excelled at defending itself when it was a blue-water navy, but it must now fight in the littorals, where it is not only easier for adversaries to acquire surface ships as targets but they are within range of greater array of land- and sea-based capabilities as well. The proliferating threats to naval surface vessels—from SS–N–22 Sunburn antiship cruise missiles to sophisticated naval mines—is rapidly reducing the survivability delta between bases that move at zero knots per hour to those that move at 25 knots per hour. Everything forward is becoming a biological and chemical weapons magnet. Although the Navy is investing in active and passive defenses, increasing global transparency and the proliferation of antiaccess capabilities is outpacing the force protection capabilities of U.S. power projection forces, including naval surface vessels. The Navy needs a new paradigm for projecting presence and power in an antiaccess world.

Projecting Naval Presence

The growing vulnerability of naval presence does not mean that virtual presence is the answer. One cannot do gunboat diplomacy without a gunboat. From a purely military perspective, the United States can see who is doing what to whom and hurt them badly without being there. But drawing a line in the sand and threatening to wreak havoc from the skies if a regional rogue crosses that line invites failure; it passes the initiative to the aggressor and stresses our will or resolve to carry out threats. Being there does not always solve the will problem—consider U.S. "air occupations" of Bosnia-Herzegovina in 1992 and of northern Iraq in 1996—but it can help. The United States has global interests, but it is hard to advance these interests without a global presence.

The primary purpose for deploying U.S. forces in a region during peacetime is political: their very presence signals that the United States is a power in that region and intends to remain so. The more continuous the presence in a particular region is, the stronger the message. For example, U.S. forces stationed permanently in Japan and Korea leave no room for ambiguity: the United States will defend Japan and Korea if attacked. Less permanent forms of presence, rotational deployments, and temporary deployments for exercises and training leave more room for miscalculation, which can be offset by the continuity of the deployments.

The *QDR Report* notes that Asia, which "contains a volatile mix of both rising and declining regional powers," is "gradually emerging as a region susceptible to large-scale military competition."[17] The vast distances of the Asian theater put a premium on naval forward presence, in part because the U.S. Navy budget includes funds for its presence operations. The Air Force and Army, on the other hand, not only must fund the extra resources required for rotational or temporary deployments but also must suffer the vagaries of the military airlift system. But even the Navy finds it difficult to "show the flag" anywhere (except in Japan) in the huge Asian theater on a continuous basis. Naval forward presence forces spend far too much time crossing oceans that no one covets. The carrier is widely viewed as the flagship of U.S. forward presence, and its presence in Asia should be increased.

Homeporting a second carrier in Asia, perhaps in northern or western Australia, would greatly enhance the U.S. presence in Asia.[18] Not only would homeporting a second carrier significantly enhance carrier time forward,[19] establishing a new permanent installation in Asia, but it also would signal clearly and loudly that the United States was in Asia to stay. As an alternative, the United States should consider ending the requirement for a continuous presence of a carrier in the Mediterranean. Europe is both a small theater and hosts several U.S. Army and Air Force units. The U.S. commitment to European security is not in doubt; the U.S. commitment to Asian security is. The *QDR Report* calls for the Navy to "increase its aircraft carrier battlegroup presence in the Western Pacific and . . . explore options for homeporting an additional three to four surface combatants, and guided cruise missile submarines (SSGNs), near that area."[20] That is a good start. As Asia's importance rises, U.S interests will grow, as should the U.S. naval presence.

As argued previously, U.S. naval presence forces should be shaped largely for smaller-scale contingencies and humanitarian relief missions, not for defeating large-scale aggressions. This does not mean that the Navy will need less force protection. As symbols of American military might, U.S. Navy assets will always be a favorite target for terrorist attacks, as seen most recently in the 2000 attack on the USS *Cole*. U.S. involvement in smaller-scale contingencies will always carry the risk of reprisal attacks. The Navy's improving force protection capabilities should be increasingly capable of defense against small-scale attacks.

Although the *QDR Report* eschews *shaping* and *engagement*, terms favored by the previous administration, there is no downgrading of the importance of U.S. forward presence that plays a key role in three of the four Defense Policy Goals—assuring allies and friends, deterring threats to U.S. interests, and defeating aggression if deterrence fails (dissuading future military competition is the fourth goal).[21] The *QDR Report*, however, maintains that

> the U.S. military will promote security cooperation with allies and friendly nations. A primary objective of U.S. security cooperation will be to help allies and friends create favorable balances of military power in critical areas of the world to deter aggression and coercion. Security cooperation will serve as an important means for linking [DOD] strategic direction with those of its allies and friends.[22]

DOD will focus its peacetime overseas activities on security cooperation to help create favorable balances of military power in critical areas of the world and to deter aggression and coercion. A particular aim of DOD security cooperation efforts will be to ensure access, interoperability, and intelligence cooperation, while expanding the range of preconflict options available to counter coercive threats, deter aggression, or favorably prosecute war on U.S. terms.[23]

Being there still matters immensely, but Secretary of Defense Donald Rumsfeld prefers a focus on "security cooperation," not engagement for engagement's sake.

In addition to being prepared for a wide variety of potential missions short of large-scale aggression, U.S. naval forces deployed forward will contribute significantly in several important areas.

Prewar Situational Awareness. In line with its embrace of "Knowledge Superiority" as one of its two "means" (the other is forward presence), the Navy is investing heavily in the command, control, communications, computers, and intelligence (C⁴I) capabilities that enable network-centric warfare. While the Navy focuses on how the knowledge gained from its forward presence will help it conduct its missions, the Navy recognizes, as it stated in the 2000 Strategic Planning Guidance, that the "U.S. Armed Forces . . . will benefit from a regional knowledge base that is built and enhanced by day-to-day naval presence, familiarity with forward operating environments, and foreign-area expertise."[24] Previously acquired "close-in" knowledge is, in fact, more valuable when the fight against large-scale aggression begins at standoff ranges.

Sea-Based Theater Missile Defense. U.S. power projection forces should operate initially from robust, heavily defended bases on the periphery of contested theaters. Defending these periphery bases will be much easier than defending close-in bases and ports from much thicker antiaccess attacks. But in some instances, the United States will want to defend an ally or friend against missile attack, even if the scale of attack threatens to overwhelm U.S. defenses. Sea-based TMD will play a critical role in these scenarios.

Antiterrorist Operations. In the wake of the horrific attacks of September 11, 2001, the United States has committed itself to a war against global terrorism that will probably have no end. New concepts of operations for attacking terrorists will require new mixes of capabilities—special operations forces, UAVs, distributed sensor networks, and so on—that can be hosted on forward-deployed naval assets that can operate autonomously from international waters. The U.S. Marine Corps announced within 2 weeks of the attack that it would reactivate the 4th Marine Expeditionary Brigade as a specialized counterterrorism unit of 4,800 personnel, which would include the existing Chemical/Biological Incident Response Force Marines.[25] The urgency of the campaign against terrorism will undoubtedly fuel a major growth in sea-based antiterrorist capabilities.

In short, there is no lack of critical missions for U.S. naval presence forces. In fact, what the United States needs is more naval forward presence in more places. This is what a global power needs to stay a global power.

Naval Power Projection

In confronting large-scale aggression, U.S. power projection forces must initially fight from a distance, as they first punish aggression and take down an adversary's antiaccess capability before closing with the enemy. The Navy, of course, already has substantial standoff capability in its conventional missile-carrying submarines and surface ships. The Navy's Tomahawk cruise missile has been prominently featured in several campaigns and retaliatory raids. The Navy is also planning to convert four Trident ballistic missiles submarines to conventional missile carriers, which will greatly augment the Navy's standoff capabilities (particularly if the nuclear-powered cruise missile attack submarines retain the same crew rotation policy they did as nuclear-powered ballistic missile submarines). Naval standoff capabilities have proven particularly useful early in a conflict in attacks on the enemy's integrated air defenses. The Navy, however, should accelerate its acquisition of a land-attack missile to give it a prompt target kill capability.

Navy carriers and amphibious ready groups also project power, but they have to deploy deep into the theater in order to apply force against land targets. Modernizing with the planned Joint Strike Fighter helps somewhat, but its range (at 900 miles, 200 more than the Air Force) is too short for severe antiaccess environments, and it is not stealthy enough for advanced surface-to-air missile environments. In future large-scale campaigns, naval surface vessels are simply too valuable and too vulnerable to risk forward early in the conflict. That is probably true even for the notion of a Streetfighter warship, which would be a smaller, faster, presumably more expendable ship. For a casualty-adverse America, however, there is no such thing as an expendable ship, and in the event of an actual large-scale war, the United States, in the same manner it rejected an amphibious attack in the Persian Gulf War, will be reluctant to bring naval surface ships forward into the teeth of an adversary's still functioning antiaccess capability.

Navy carriers and amphibious vehicles, however, will be in the force for decades. The introduction of new technologies—intelligence, surveillance, and reconnaissance UAVs, particularly a stealthy variant; combat UAVs; unmanned underwater vehicles; and smaller and cheaper land-attack missiles—could significantly increase their standoff capability, although it would come at the expense of shorter-range capabilities. The Navy's introduction of its Cooperative Engagement Capability will greatly increase the ability of its fleet to fight as a distributed network, making it much easier to integrate new longer-range assets.

Final Thought

The U.S. Navy will have to change to meet the challenges of an antiaccess environment, but less profoundly than its sister services. It does not need forward bases and ports from which to operate. The Navy, which embraced the presence role in the

1993 Bottom-Up Review (BUR), will remain the Nation's premier presence force. Its role in high-intensity conflict has been declining, but most of the demand for the Nation's military forces has been in areas where the Navy and Marines excel—peacetime overseas activities (now focused on security cooperation), smaller-scale contingencies, and humanitarian relief missions. In 1993, the BUR used presence as a force structure justifier for the first time. But in 2001, the *QDR Report* said that DOD will now use smaller-scale contingencies as a force-planning tool, not as lesser-included cases of its warfighting capabilities.

The antiaccess world provides serious challenges to the Navy at the high end of the spectrum of conflict, even as the demand for its capabilities on the lower end seems to be growing.[26] Conducting the forward presence mission as if it were our primary response to high-intensity conflict is a recipe for disaster, both for the naval forces involved and our Nation.

Notes

[1] U.S. Department of Defense, *Quadrennial Defense Review Report* (Washington, DC: Department of Defense, September 30, 2001) (hereafter referred to as *QDR Report*), 30. The other critical challenges include protecting the U.S. homeland, forces abroad, allies, and friends from nuclear, biological, and chemical weapons and their means of delivery; assuring information security and conducting effective information operations; providing persistent surveillance and rapid engagement with high-volume precision strike against all targets under all conditions; enhancing the capability and survivability of space assets; and developing an interoperable, joint C⁴ISR architecture.

[2] Ibid., 31. Emphasis added.

[3] Many of the ideas in this section were first explored in Clark A. Murdock, *Projecting Power and Presence into 21st Century Asia* (Washington, DC: DFI-International Paper, 2001). Office of the Secretary of Defense, Office of Net Assessment, supported the project for which that paper was written.

[4] *The Washington Post,* September 29, 2001, A14.

[5] *QDR Report*, 25. In a much earlier draft, the force planning paradigm for "deterring forward" used the phrase "with minimum reinforcement" instead of "only modest reinforcement," a requirement sufficiently stringent that one Office of the Secretary of Defense office maintained that the U.S. Navy would need 36 carriers to meet it.

[6] Ibid., 26.

[7] Unreleased earlier draft of *QDR Report* (early September 2001), 38. Emphasis added.

[8] Ibid., 39.

[9] Ibid.

[10] U.S. Navy Chief of Naval Operations, *Navy Strategic Planning Guidance with Long Range Planning Objectives*, April 2000, 36.

[11] Ibid., 19–21.

[12] Ibid., 20.

[13] Ibid., 27.

[14] Owen R. Cote, Jr., "Buying '. . . From the Sea': A Defense Budget for a Maritime Strategy," in *Holding the Line: U.S. Defense Alternatives for the Early 21st Century*, ed. Cindy Williams (Cambridge, MA: Massachusetts Institute of Technology Press, 2001), 156.

[15] Ibid.

[16] Steven Kosiak, Andrew Krepinevich, and Michael Vickers, *A Strategy for a Long Peace* (Washington, DC: Center for Strategic and Budgetary Assessments, January 2001), 36.

[17] *QDR Report*, 4.

[18] Homeporting a second carrier in Guam would also increase naval presence in Asia, but not quite as much as a port in Australia (Guam is still over 1,000 miles from theater). Moreover, the political statement made by basing a carrier in Australia would be much stronger for both the United States and Australia.

[19] Cote observes that today's 12-carrier force with 1 homeport abroad provides 2.5 carrier battlegroups (CVBGs) forward at any one time, while an 11-carrier force with 2 homeports abroad would provide between 3.5 and 4 CVBGs forward at any one time. See Cote, 177.

[20] *QDR Report*, 27. The U.S. Marine Corps was also told to "develop plans to shift some of its afloat prepositioned equipment from the Mediterranean toward the Indian Ocean and Persian Gulf" and to "explore the feasibility of conducting training for littoral warfare in the Western Pacific."

[21] Ibid., iii–iv.

[22] Ibid., 11.

[23] Ibid., 20.

[24] U.S. Navy Chief of Naval Operations, 22.

[25] Joshua S. Higgins, "Anti-Terrorism Unit Set For Activation," October 17, 2001, accessed at <www.usmc.mil/marinelink/mcn2000.nsf/>. Article reference number 200110221060.

[26] For a discussion and redefinition of the concept of the *spectrum of conflict*, see Sam J. Tangredi, "Assessing New Missions" in *Transforming America's Military*, ed. Hans Binnendijk (Washington, DC: National Defense University Press, 2002).

Chapter 26

Globalization of Antiaccess Strategies?

Norman Friedman

G reat powers such as the United States buy navies in order to assure global access, despite whatever countermeasures other countries may take. In the aftermath of the Cold War, globalization seems to have made sophisticated weaponry much more available to many potential opponents than in the past. Does this mean we are losing our ability to enforce access? What trends can we discern in the world arms market? There is certainly a great amount of new technology that, if implemented, might cause us considerable problems. However, in projecting ahead, we have a choice. We can look at the most likely future, or we can concentrate on potential enemy access to technology. If we choose the former, the future is at least mildly encouraging, if not more so. If we choose to respond to the latter, we may be unable to afford anything resembling our current capabilities. Which should it be?

Moreover, if we overemphasize the wrong categories of antiaccess weapons—perhaps by underestimating the problems of our prospective enemies—then we risk overspending on the wrong kinds of countermeasures and neglecting those weapons that we are more likely to face. There is also a dangerous potential to ignore system aspects of enemy capabilities. We naturally concentrate on the terminal engagement, in which the missile pops up over a ship's horizon and runs in, or in which a submarine fires a torpedo, or in which a ship triggers a mine. In several such cases, it can be argued that terminal countermeasures are lacking.

Norman Friedman is a widely published defense analyst and historian who spent over a decade as consultant to the Department of the Navy. He writes the *Naval Institute Guide to World Naval Weapons Systems* and the Raytheon handbook of world missiles and rockets (now in its second edition). His most recent books include *The Fifty-Year War: Conflict and Strategy in the Cold War* (Annapolis, MD: Naval Institute Press, 2000) which examines the political, military, and economic factors in the Cold War, and *Seapower as Strategy: Navies and National Interests* (Annapolis, MD: Naval Institute Press, 2001).

Yet the battle is not between a missile and a ship, or a submarine and a ship, or a mine and a ship. It is between our fleet and an enemy. The missile or mine or submarine has to come into proximity with the ship, and to do that effectively the attacker has to detect the ship and arrange an engagement. In some very important cases, prospective enemies seem not to have appreciated the extent to which other capabilities are needed to make their missiles or mines or torpedoes effective against us. Conversely, our own countermeasures may be most effective against elements of enemy force other than the actual weapons.

Much of the current debate on military transformation is animated by the argument that U.S. forces are not sufficiently network centric. In fact, all warfare can be described in network terms, the real issue being to what extent investment is concentrated at different points in the network. That is, some sort of network connects the long-range sensors that detect, for example, a carrier and the launcher that fires a missile at her. Just as investment may be concentrated in the long-range sensors, the command and control system that makes sense of their product (that is, decides what has been seen really is a carrier and also where it is going and what it is doing), the communications network, or the antiship missiles, our countermeasures to the enemy's capability can strike at various points in his network. Evaluation of antiaccess capability, then, must take into account both how well the enemy can negate the existing sanctuary enjoyed by ships well out beyond the enemy's horizon and how well those ships can engage enemy land targets without losing the protection of that sanctuary.

These are not trivial issues. It seems that our potential enemies have spent very little to negate the sea sanctuary; they seem to imagine that we have to come inshore to deal with them. They may not be alone. Discussions of a new littoral warfare combatant ship carry similar assumptions. Reality, however, is that remote sensing makes standoff attack both possible and attractive. It is difficult to avoid a comparison with the Taliban in Afghanistan. Commenting on the bombing—much of it directed against critical Taliban capabilities—Mullah Omar, the Taliban leader, said that he could not stop such attacks but that the Americans would suffer "when the real ground war" began—that is, when the Americans were forced to move in masses of troops in a "real man's" war. But by that time the coalition partners—the Northern Alliance and rebels in the Pushtun south—had already begun to move, exploiting the standoff attacks carried out by the Americans. The ground war was almost over. It seems most unlikely that massed American troops will ever be involved in Afghanistan. Perhaps the Mullah's overall defense system lacked something. (Incidentally, much of the standoff attack had been mounted from the sea, bypassing important political defenses erected by the Taliban in nearby places like Pakistan.)

There is a strong temptation to ensure against surprise by assuming the most of enemy capabilities. Certainly past underestimates have sometimes been extremely embarrassing, as in the case of Japan in 1941. However, overestimates may well deter us from actions that are clearly in our interests. For example, overestimates of Iraqi capability probably explain why the United States took so long to act in 1990 and 1991. Although our action was ultimately successful, the image of vast U.S. forces not quite crushing Iraq gave Saddam Husayn considerable political capital within the Third World. In retrospect, scratch forces assembled in the fall of 1990 probably would have sufficed, and ending the war as early as possible might have been well worth our while. In a truly post–Cold War situation, the mass forces used in 1990 and 1991 are no longer available. Meanwhile, crises are likely to be both more frequent and more widely distributed. For example, U.S. strategy and tactics in Afghanistan have almost certainly been dictated by the absence of nearby bases and distance from the sea. In this particular case, a realistic view of the adversary made it possible for the U.S. Government to take the political decision to attack. Admittedly, given the scale of the September 11 attack, the Government could not have waited much longer, but it could have chosen a lengthy build-up with more limited attacks.

Realism matters because we cannot possibly match resources to every perceived scale of threat. It is easy to assemble threats that make current and projected forces useless, but unless those threats are plausible, they merely serve to discourage us and to distort our force structure. That applies particularly to future threats that seem, in retrospect, to have been designed to affect only particular kinds of forces.

Globalization and Defense Economics

Indeed, one key question is just how much technology, in quantitative and qualitative terms, our prospective opponents will have. In the past, the Soviets were the primary source of weapons directed against us. Presumably, globalization means both that our opponents have access to more varied sources of weaponry and that Russian- and Chinese-made equipment may incorporate Western technology, to our cost.

During the Cold War, we faced a highly militarized Soviet Union whose economy was drastically different from ours. The Soviets could and did afford to develop a very wide range of exotic military technologies, at least some of which entered production. In some important cases, we failed to understand what the Soviets were building, at considerable potential danger to us.[1] The character of the Soviet economy favored massive production runs, creating considerable surpluses of weapons and their associated platforms. These surpluses were often made available gratis to Soviet client states. Since it was the client states to which we needed naval access on a year-to-year basis, the sheer size of the Soviet military production machine was a problem for us.

On the other hand, the Soviets were apparently unable to produce computers or microchips in great quantities, to the point that it was widely claimed that one of their intercontinental ballistic missiles used chips from Western hand-held calculators, bought in quantity for just that application. Indeed, it seems in retrospect that Mikhail Gorbachev was driven into a suicidal loosening of the Soviet system largely to grow his economy enough to produce military computers on a Western scale.[2] Clearly, our opponents now enjoy fairly free access to computer technology, at least at the level of personal computers. There are still technology embargoes, but they cannot stop the diffusion of quite powerful chips embedded in devices such as the Sony PlayStation. Of course, whether these devices can be exploited for military purposes is another question.

So one side of globalization is access to raw technology. If there is some way in which a particular chip radically improves the performance of a given Soviet-era missile, then that improvement seems likely. The Russians themselves have been advertising upgraded versions of their missiles, using new (presumably Western) electronics. The chips involved may be quite inexpensive, but that does not make the overall upgrade inexpensive—as the cost is mainly in the software and integration (including adaptation of existing hardware). In the case of an antiship missile, there seems to be a considerable difference between first-generation hardwired weapons, which must be rebuilt completely to accommodate any major modification, and second-generation weapons incorporating internal data buses, which buffer components from each other. The Russian Styx (P–15/NATO SS–N–2) is a first-generation weapon, hence probably almost impossible to modify cheaply. So is the Exocet MM 38. However, Harpoon and Exocet MM 40 are quite clearly second-generation weapons. Both have enjoyed substantial upgrades, which are available as modifications to existing missiles (Exocet Block II, with its evasive terminal maneuvers, is a case in point). Presumably, the new Russian missiles currently on sale also incorporate data buses and, hence, can be modified.[3]

This aspect of globalization can cause us considerable problems because we will probably face hybrid weapons incorporating Western electronics and emitting signals that we have not previously encountered. To the extent that countermeasures are tailored to particular missile seekers, we may find that emissions may often be unrecognizable and that soft countermeasures often fail. In a larger sense, identification of friend or foe will become more and more difficult—simply because friends may turn out to be using ex-Soviet weaponry, whereas enemies may often be armed with Western equipment. In fact, these issues are part of a larger trend in which software-controlled electronic emissions are more difficult to recognize automatically.[4]

At least as important is the economic aspect of globalization. A great deal of flashy technology is on offer, but how much actually sells? It is striking how, from year to year, attractive projects for new weapons slide from the sketch stage to the no-longer-marketed stage. Much depends on the balance between internal and external investment on the part of the prospective producer. Currently, the United States represents the single largest defense market in the world. Although U.S. investment is far below the Cold War level, it is high enough to support the development and production of many weapons without any kind of reference to the foreign market (although many of these same weapons do eventually find foreign buyers). The other major suppliers are a different story. Some European countries still try to develop weapons entirely for the home (or European) market, but the number of such weapons, particularly major ones, is declining. Of course, this situation may reverse if the Europeans truly develop a pan-European Union (EU) defense market and if the current consolidation of defense producers continues. At present, although the European missile builders have largely merged into the Matra-BAe-Dynamics-SAS (MBDS) conglomerate, the resulting entity still finds itself supporting numerous legacy systems bought in limited numbers by different European users. Moreover, many navies have already invested in these legacy weapons and are unlikely to dispose of them in favor of some single future weapon.

At the very least, any observer of the European defense scene must be struck by the drastic decline in funding, which in turn has curtailed major new developments. Those systems that seem not to promise major exports appear to be the principal victims, exemplified by the French supersonic Anti-Navire Nouvelle Generation (ANNG) antiship missile. European politicians still seem to subscribe to the view that a national (or EU-wide) combat aircraft industry is vital, so airplane projects such as the Eurofighter have survived.[5]

Then there are the two major Third World mass suppliers, Russia and China. During the Cold War, the Soviet Union accounted for mass sales of weapons such as antiship missiles; Western missiles and aircraft tended to be exported in much smaller numbers. At least in the case of aircraft, the argument was that the West supplied maintenance support and spares to keep the number supplied flying whereas the Soviet system supplied numbers because there were few spares, and only a fraction of the total number supplied was expected to be usable at any one time. This distinction matters because if economics change, the sheer number of weapons involved will fall drastically, as buyers are forced to confront the high unit costs of weapons produced in limited quantities. From the point of view of the defender, there is a world of difference between the flood of missiles with which the Soviets were credited and the small numbers that a Third World navy may be able to field, particularly after Cold War supplies run out.

As the Soviet Union dissolved, a cash economy gradually arose. That took time. For some years, Soviet-era enterprises could still assemble weapons from parts accumulated under the Soviet regime. In effect their only costs were payrolls and associated expenses; they could then sell almost-new weapons fairly cheaply. Some of those weapons were still within reach of impoverished ex-client states. However, the supply of spares was always finite. There had to come a day when something approaching Western defense economics began to apply. At that point buyers were pulled up embarrassingly short. Indeed, the situation was even worse than for Western suppliers because the Russian state lacked the cash resources to subsidize arms sales.[6] As a consequence, whatever the magnitude of Cold War transfers, post-Cold War sales of Russian weaponry seem to involve small numbers of weapons, comparable in magnitude to Western sales.[7]

Economics has a stronger effect on new development. In the past, new developments were financed internally, and Soviet developers produced some very exotic weapons, sometimes with details unsuspected by the West.[8] Now internal financing has largely evaporated, along with the Russian budget. There is considerable talk of new-generation weapons, but what is offered for sale now is largely what might have been offered a decade ago, had security restrictions not applied. Thus, Russia seems not to be a major source of new designs or design concepts. Moreover, the more sophisticated Russian weapons seem not to have sold very well.

Somewhat similar questions apply to China. At one time, China maintained a command economy, which could be ordered, at least in theory, to produce floods of missiles, aircraft, and ships. The production side is still government-owned. However, China has a mixed economy, which must at least sometimes pay attention to questions of cash. For example, urban workers are fed by the products of a peasantry who expect to be paid in real cash. If the government cannot take in enough cash because its own enterprises are effectively bankrupt and because it cannot efficiently collect taxes, then it will soon find maintenance of the big enterprises impossible. Similar to other communist bureaucracies, the Chinese government presumably does not produce realistic statistics. However, there is anecdotal evidence that tax collection is ineffective because the ruling Communist Party in effect skims most of what would otherwise go for taxes. Repeated demands that the Chinese armed forces withdraw from the civil economy indicate that the central government has failed to control the economy and that it has failed to pay the military enough to turn it from what is seen as corruption. This is a very serious issue because, given its economic desires, the military can fix overall policy in ways inimical to continued communist rule.[9]

These considerations are crucial because the antiaccess threat is, in part, a combination of numbers of antiaccess weapons and the technologies that they incorporate. If weapons are made in large numbers and are easy to obtain, we face a serious saturation threat, as we certainly did from the Soviet armed services. If not, then the threat is much less severe. Similarly, if some weapons producer is encouraged to insert ever more advanced technology in its weapons, then we may well find our own countersystems obsolescing rapidly. Conversely, if potential enemies (or their suppliers) find such investment difficult or unimportant, then access itself is likely not to be a serious problem.

Antiship Missiles: Case in Point

A survey of current defense development suggests that, apart from a very few producers such as the United States and perhaps the United Kingdom, development is financed mainly by exports. That is, the global defense market literally defines what is and is not developed. Russia is a case in point. The first major release of defense information came at the 1991 Moscow Air Show. Weapons for sale were those already in Russian service. Then there was a second category: weapons available for cooperative development (that is, for development financed by the prospective buyer). Some of them were quite impressive, many in antiaccess roles. For example, the Russians already had a short-range air-launched ballistic missile, Kh-15, comparable to the old U.S. SRAM (AGM–69). What they offered at the show—for cooperative development—was a version guided by an active millimeter-wave radar to attack ships. Arriving at Mach 5, such a missile would have been nearly impossible to shoot down. If it was characteristic of future threats, then the future of large surface ships such as carriers was decidedly bleak. However, the antiship Kh-15S would have been quite expensive to develop. After some years, it apparently became clear that no prospective buyer had anything like sufficient resources, and no more was heard of it.

This experience might have been set down to Russian poverty, but it is hardly unique. During the 1960s, the French government discovered that it could not continue to develop the full range of weapon systems it associated with French national independence and grandeur. The solution was largely to tailor future French weapons to the Third World export market. Examples were the Mirage fighter, the AMX 30 tank, and the Exocet antiship missile.[10] One consequence was that, through at least the early 1980s, French forces were considered ill suited for a future European war. In the 1980s, as the North Atlantic Treaty Organization (NATO) revived, French development strategy turned to more sophisticated weapons suited for high-end NATO adoption. Ironically, these weapons matured as the Soviet threat collapsed, and, based on the motivation, the French investment strategy failed. One delayed victim of this failure was probably the supersonic ANNG antiship missile (which was not, however, canceled until 2000).

More generally, the Western antiship missile market is largely an export market, as Western navies have not recently invested heavily in such weapons. Since these missiles are major elements of any antiaccess threat, failures in marketing suggest that the likely customers, who are also likely victims of Western naval access, have little interest in antiaccess investment. Major recent failures have been the French supersonic ANNG, initially a Franco-German project for next-generation frigates; and Teseo Mk

3, a stealthy Otomat follow-on.[11] The German Daimler-Benz Aerospace (DASA) conglomerate was unable to convince the German government to finance a ship-launched version of its Taurus missile; the new German K130 corvettes are to be armed instead with an existing weapon, either the Swedish RBS 15 Mk 3 or the new Norwegian Naval Strike Missile (NSM)—assuming the latter ever enters service.

It may be argued that any such comments are disingenuous, since the most likely victims of U.S. naval access are rogue states dependent on Russian and Chinese arms suppliers. But that makes the failure of many Russian missile programs particularly striking. There are four current Russian antiaccess programs: Kh-35 (SS–N–25, similar in outline to the U.S. Harpoon), Moskit (3M80), Alfa (3M54), and Yakhont. Of these, Kh-35 seems to sell mainly as a direct replacement for the Cold War-era Styx (P–15), a very dangerous (to its operators) missile that at least one navy, the Finnish, was happy to discard. But Kh-35 offers much the same performance as Harpoon, so it can hardly be considered a major change in the antiaccess threat. The other three missiles all offer supersonic performance, which can be considered a major advance in the threat. Yet they have sold quite poorly. Thus far, the only customer for Moskit has been China, and the Chinese bought the missile because they bought its platform, the *Sovremenny*-class destroyer. They seem to have bought no more than two missiles per launch tube, which suggests a pessimistic view of ship survivability. The only customer for Alfa has been India. Yakhont enjoyed no sales at all but has been the subject of a cooperative development effort with India. Indian press reports suggest that the main projected role of the missile is as a nuclear delivery vehicle aimed at Pakistan. More generally, it is difficult to see why India is buying Yakhont when the Indian Navy already has a broadly equivalent missile in hand in the form of Alfa.[12] Reports of sales of Moskit or other advanced Russian antiship missiles to Iran seem to have been erroneous.

The other potential supplier of missiles to roguish states is China; the usual export weapons are the subsonic rocket-powered C–801 (apparently a somewhat larger illicit cousin to Exocet) and a turbojet derivative, C–802. Like the Russians, the Chinese have developed supersonic antiship missiles, C–101 and C–301. They were announced in 1985 and 1988, but they seem not to have entered service—even though the Chinese Navy announced that it wanted to equip all its fast missile attack boats with C–101 during the Ninth Five-Year Plan, which ended in 2000 (a single boat armed with a test canister for C–101 has been seen). The implication seems to be that fully indigenous missile programs have generally failed. The sole new weapon displayed in recent years is C–701, a small missile designed to attack missile boats rather than substantial warships (it is broadly comparable with such Western weapons as Sea Skua). It might indeed be difficult to shoot down, but its 29-kilogram (64-pound) warhead is unlikely to do enormous damage. The only Chinese antiship missiles currently in production are two apparently unlicensed Exocet derivatives, C–801 and C–802; a C–803 may also exist.[13] In 2001, the Chinese announced that they were buying the Russian Kh-59MEK, a turbojet antiship missile (in this case, air-launched, though there may be a ship-launched version) roughly equivalent to C–802. This purchase suggests that C–802 may be inadequate.[14]

The other major non-Western state trying to develop indigenous tactical missiles is India. It began a very ambitious program in the 1980s, but the only successful products have been strategic weapons. Even the short-range Prithvi surface-to-surface missile, using an engine copied from the Soviet SA–2 surface-to-air missile, has not been particularly successful (the naval version, Dhanush, failed spectacularly in its first test). The Indian press has complained about the ocean of money wasted on failed programs, and India has repeatedly had to buy foreign weapons, such as the Israeli Barak defensive missile. The Indian experience does not make for confidence that other lesser-developed countries can or will develop their own tactical weapons. For that matter, widespread reports that countries such as Iran and Pakistan are totally dependent on China and North Korea for ballistic missile design and components lead to much the same conclusion: there are very few independent missile developers, and cash is thus a key issue in any national missile program.

None of this is to deny that many countries have antiship missiles, though usually in rather smaller numbers than might be imagined. Limited purchases are borne out by reported sales figures for the three leading Western antiship missiles; about 6,000 Harpoons, about 3,800 Exocets, and about 1,000 Otomats have been sold. If one subtracts the major buyers, such as the United States and Britain, one ends up with one or two missiles per existing launcher. That is, the typical surface ship fit is 8 tubes, so 3,800 Exocets, less 600 (worldwide!) for aircraft, submarines, and coastal batteries, comes to a total of all of 400 ship-loads, which on average is about 20 ship-loads per country using the missile. However, the British and the Germans bought heavily, about 600 missiles each, which would leave only about 2,000 for everyone else—about 250 ship-loads, or roughly 10 per using country on average—and countries often have more than 10 Exocet-shooting ships (not to mention submarines and aircraft). These are crude figures, but they do suggest that anything that decoys small numbers of antiship missiles will typically exhaust a national war reserve.

Elements of Antiaccess Power

Ultimately, access to a foreign country involves either landing troops or landing weapons, or both. Just how effective antiaccess measures can be depends on our own technology and tactics. For example, for years the Marine Corps concept for deploying troops required that heavy matériel, such as organic artillery, be landed over a beach, regardless of how the troops themselves arrived (possibly by long-range air transports).

Thus, minefields were an effective barrier to Marine operations ashore. However, current Marine Corps ship-to-objective maneuver tactics emphasize the infiltration of relatively small units, whose heavy firepower would be primarily provided by ships and aircraft based well offshore. These small units may well be air-landed. Coastal minefields have only a limited effect on this type of operation. The main anti-infiltration weapon would probably be antiaircraft fire designed to deal with the troop carriers, and even it might not be capable of handling dispersed assaults. The infiltration concept was a tactical riposte to the mine (and, incidentally, the coast defense) threat, and it required the new technology making real-time deep fire support possible.

The Marines may still want to land heavy equipment over selected beaches, and it can still be argued that small missile-armed attack boats can be a serious threat to Corps landing craft. That raises the question of effective counters. For example, during the Gulf War, British helicopters quite successfully destroyed a large force of Iraqi missile-armed attack boats. Antiaircraft missiles on board such boats could potentially deal with helicopters, but in that case the cost per boat would rise dramatically, and the numbers of affordable boats would fall drastically. The resulting small force would find it difficult to deal with dispersed landings and would have to rely more and more on some external source of cueing—in other words, on a substantial investment in expensive over-the-horizon sensing.

Then there are submarines, which certainly can attack ships well offshore. Moreover, Russian-supplied submarines, including some fairly old ones, are armed with wake-following weapons, which are particularly difficult to counter. It can certainly be argued that the U.S. Navy has failed to devise sufficient countermeasures. However, virtually all the submarines involved are diesel powered. They cannot easily transit covertly at high speed submerged. The usual tactical countermeasure against diesel submarines is sustained high speed and random maneuver on the part of potential targets. Moreover, the further offshore the submarine target, the less likely that the submarine can be coached into attack position. Much depends on just how far offshore access forces can lie, which, in turn, depends not on the quality of torpedo countermeasures but on the ranges of guns, aircraft, and missiles of the access forces themselves.[15]

As in any other form of warfare, antiaccess warfare requires the defender first to detect the attacker far enough away to react, then to make sense of what the detection implies, and then to react with weaponry. Any evaluation of future antiaccess warfare would have to take all three of these elements into account. For example, current U.S. thinking entails attacks mounted by ships well beyond a defender's physical horizon. A defender possessing the appropriate missiles but no sensors with sufficient range might well find engagement impossible. Conversely, given the right sensors but only short-range missiles, success would depend on whether the platforms carrying those missiles could get to the ships. Another aspect of antiaccess warfare would simply be to defend against the offshore force at the point of contact ashore. Antiaircraft defenses fall into this latter category.

The use of decoys makes the defender's job much more difficult. The main antidote to decoying is good surveillance feeding good command and control. Sophisticated navies tasked with defensive antiaccess operations certainly understand as much. It is clear that the Nordic countries invested heavily in coastal radars and in computer command centers that they feed. Even so, these are short-range sensors. They would do no good against an enemy standing more than about 20 miles offshore, except under ducting conditions (which are by no means always present).[16] As it happens, three alternative surveillance schemes, independent of the seasonal conditions that permit ducting, have been advertised. One is high frequency (HF) surface-wave radar, offered by several companies and by the Russians. A second is passive underwater acoustics, offered by U.S., German, and Russian developers. A third is intense surveillance by maritime patrol aircraft. It seems striking that few, if any, commercial successes have been reported. Only Canada seems to have bought HF radar to detect poachers in fishing grounds. Advertising for underwater surveillance systems has virtually ceased, suggesting a total lack of interest. As for aircraft, no one seems to be buying them in sufficient numbers to achieve solid coverage. Readers may recall that the large U.S. fleet of P–3s depended heavily on fixed (in effect, staring) surveillance assets, mainly the sound surveillance system (SOSUS), for Cold War coverage of the North Atlantic and North Pacific.

Many navies probably do have HF/Direction Finder (DF) networks, but with the rise of satellite communications these surveillance systems are less and less valuable. The Soviets did enjoy some important early successes in exploiting U.S. satellite communications, but once those were known, countermeasures were deployed. As for other Cold War naval surveillance techniques, it seems most unlikely that any potential target country will field an equivalent to the very specialized satellite systems deployed by the two Cold War superpowers. Without either such systems or specialized fixed surveillance systems, the sea would seem to be an effective sanctuary. Striking from well offshore would seem an effective counter to antiaccess weaponry.

It will be pointed out that mobile platforms could offer effective resistance to the U.S. fleet even well offshore, particularly aircraft armed with antiship missiles, missile-bearing boats and corvettes, and submarines. All Third World littoral states invest in some or all of these platforms. Certainly, too, globalization offers both better platforms and improvements to existing ones. For example, France reportedly sold modern sonars to China for installation on Chinese submarines. Israel is currently offering a modernization package for the MiG–21 fighter, and it has enjoyed some success in this venture. What is less clear is how effective such upgraded weapons are likely to be, particularly in the absence of modernized command and control.

Again, however, prospective Third World enemies seem to show little interest in the less glamorous sea surveillance required to make an antiaccess force truly effective. That may be entirely logical. Most countries are concerned more with local politics than with the larger threat of U.S. intervention. Given limited resources, they buy forces that will impress their neighbors. If their neighbors are unsophisticated, expensive sea surveillance is an apparent waste of money.

Incidentally, somewhat similar considerations apply to mines. It is certainly true that an inexpensive mine can destroy a costly ship, but bringing that mine into proximity with the ship is not a trivial matter. Mine warfare is a statistical proposition, which means that a large field must be laid in order to gain a few successes. One modern mine may cost $50,000, but it is ineffective unless it is part of a field of (for example) a thousand mines. Then, suddenly, the cost per victim rises to $50 million. That may seem little to pay to deal with a ship costing ten times as much, but then again the defender's economy will likely be far less than a tenth the size of the attacker's. The cost of the minefield may seem anything but trivial to most states. Moreover, a minefield is a single-use weapon. Once the mines are laid, they are essentially impossible to recover for reuse, at least at present.[17]

The need to lay large numbers of mines to get useful results suggests the countermeasure that the U.S. Navy is adopting, mine reconnaissance, will be effective. If the planting of the field can be observed, our forces can avoid it. Much obviously depends on just how flexible our amphibious over-the-beach craft are, but it was specifically to gain flexibility that the Navy adopted air cushion landing craft. Of course, reconnaissance can fail. The two minings in the Persian Gulf in 1991 were due to just such a failure, which in turn was due to a failure to realize that the Iraqis were laying mines from extemporized platforms. The planned future reconnaissance technique involves unmanned underwater vehicles and is likely to be more effective. Again, the wider the variety of areas off which ships can operate, the better the chance that they can find clear water.

There are, of course, technologies that present special threats. One is the destructor, a mechanism that converts a standard bomb into a mine. It is not new; the U.S. Navy used destructors in Vietnam and turned over aspects of the mechanism to the North Vietnamese as part of the end-of-war settlement. Later, Argentina advertised a destructor family of mines that it was manufacturing. Presumably others have done the same. The real threat of the destructor is that it is inexpensive to stockpile. Using destructors, a minefield can be extemporized, without earmarking major facilities for mine maintenance in peacetime.

Another technology of interest is the rising mine, pioneered by the Russians and now widely advertised. China manufactures a simple rising mine, based on an early Russian type. From time to time, the United States has considered buying rising mines.

These weapons are dangerous because, at least in their later versions, they can cover wide areas and thus make it almost impossible to designate a safe channel. However, they are costly, and the arguments against Third World mine purchases certainly apply to them. They may also be vulnerable to simple deceptive countermeasures.

The overriding point is that the economics of globalization can cripple an enemy's mine effort. Reports of mine sales generally indicate that buyers purchase sophisticated mines in very small numbers—usually fewer than a hundred. In the past, the Soviets produced vast numbers of mines, which they gave to their client states. Of these, only a limited percentage were modern sensor mines. Such mines demand a considerable investment in storage and maintenance. Contrary to popular conceptions, they can and do go bad.[18]

On the other hand, many countries have bought, or have tried to buy, ballistic missiles (which are best used against fixed targets). Some of the same countries have invested in chemical and biological weapons as a kind of nuclear surrogate. At the same time, it can be argued that commercial imaging satellites offer countries much better information concerning any sustained buildup nearby. The main conclusion one might draw is that fixed bases and massive buildups ashore are becoming more vulnerable—although current and future missile defense weapons may well solve that problem. At the least, any fixed buildup, such as that in the desert prior to the Gulf War, will become more difficult to conceal. Conversely, mobile forces are very difficult to spot using imaging satellites because satellite revisit times and swath widths are quite limited. This limitation is unlikely to vanish. One might, therefore, conclude that the balance between ground-based and sea-based intervention forces is changing radically in favor of the sea.

Conclusion

None of this is to suggest that the U.S. Navy can or should cease investment in systems designed to counter antiaccess weaponry. It is, however, to suggest that the threats we face are not nearly so severe as those of the Cold War and, moreover, that the military effects of globalization may be more disastrous to our prospective enemies than to ourselves. That will probably be true as long as the export market rules, and as long as the countries involved do not have wealthy patrons to solve their military problems.

Can things change? Certainly, but that will take time. For example, the Chinese may solve their financial problems and come to resemble the Cold War Soviets—but that will demand not only an internal political renaissance but also gross militarization of Chinese society. Given that the economic vitality of China comes entirely from a nonmilitary sector of its economy, that particular combination is difficult to imagine. A revitalized Soviet Union is easier to imagine, but as time passes nationalist passions in the former republics will make reconstitution much more difficult. The two areas with the economic power to arm against us, Europe and Japan, seem disinclined to do so—although radical shifts are of course possible.[19]

Our own foreign policy demands access. If we raise the conceptual bar for force protection unrealistically high, we will deter ourselves, derail a successful foreign policy, and probably lay ourselves more—rather than less—open to foreign attacks like the ones carried out on September 11. We are the engine of globalization, and militarily it is helping, not hurting, us.

Notes

[1] As a case in point, at the end of the Cold War, the U.S. Navy feared a future Soviet capability to lock air-launched antiship missiles onto U.S. ships after launch, but we considered that only a potential problem. In reality, the Soviets fielded just such a missile, Kh-22M (a version of AS–4) in parallel with the "Backfire" (Tu-22M) bomber. This particular reality seems to have emerged only as Russian writers began to discuss Cold War weapons systems in detail.

[2] The author made this case in his *The Fifty-Year War: Conflict and Strategy in the Cold War* (Annapolis, MD: U.S. Naval Institute Press, 2000). Anyone who read Soviet articles about military technology will remember the emphasis on "reconnaissance-strike complexes" in the late 1970s and early 1980s. Presumably the key Western prototype was Assault Breaker. Given what we now know was an enormous Soviet effort to derail the development of the neutron bomb (which would have given NATO a potent antiarmor weapon to stop a mass attack against Europe), it seems reasonable to see in Assault Breaker and its ilk something even worse, a counter to mass armored attacks that could not be stopped politically. Given the military orientation of the Soviet state, its leader would have been uncomfortably aware of what, in the West, might have been dismissed as a military technicality.

[3] The Chinese did radically modify Styx (as the series of weapons that NATO nicknamed Silkworm) to create their current antiship missiles, but it is not clear just how much industrial effort was involved. Nor is it clear how easily weapons such as C–801 can be modernized. Official Chinese accounts of missile production suggest vast effort expended for slow progress, but that may have been due to the stress of the Cultural Revolution, which killed off many skilled engineers and technicians, rather than to purely technical problems. It is certainly true that the Soviets produced modified versions of the original Styx (P–15), but it seems notable that development has now stopped in favor of a different missile, Kh-35 (NATO SS–N–25). Aside from any other deficiencies, Styx may have been dropped because it was so unsafe because of its use of hypergolic propellants: dropping one would literally cause a catastrophic explosion. That was why, for example, the Finnish Navy discarded the missile. The Russians seem to be promoting Kh-35 as a preferable replacement, on a four-for-one basis.

[4] At present the most prominent case is fighter multirole radars, which switch among radically varied radar waveforms by computer (the waveform is generated by software and amplified by a tube, typically a traveling-wave tube). The first such radar was probably the AWG–9 of the U.S. F–14 Tomcat fighter (the multirole character of the APG–65 radar on board the F/A–18 was more widely publicized). As an example of the effect of such variability, when the USS *Stark* was illuminated by the multirole radar of an Iraqi fighter (a French-built Mirage), the ship's electronic countermeasures operator, who had been coached to fear an *Iranian* attack, assumed he was picking up the multirole radar of an Iranian F–14. Since both radars had been adapted to the same antiship mission, there was really no gross difference between their emissions. In the past, when radar signals were produced by specialized tubes (magnetrons or klystrons), signal characteristics reflected physical characteristics of the tubes. That is less and less the case. Individual radars still can be identified, but only by much more subtle features, which presumably reflect the physical character of waveguide and antenna.

[5] The British Nimrod replacement is an odd and perhaps telling case. The choice lay between a British airframe equipped with a U.S. combat system (by Boeing) and a U.S. airframe with a British system. The choice was the British-looking airplane with the U.S. combat system. The implication may be that those in charge of the selection were blissfully unaware that combat systems are the major element of the price of this type of airplane (MPA). Their choice was particularly bizarre, since it entailed remanufacture of an existing airframe that probably cannot be duplicated for ex-

port—whereas the combat system choice could easily be adapted to other aircraft. In other words, they chose *against* British suppliers of the only exportable element of the system. The implication seems to be that even sophisticated buyers such as the U.K. Ministry of Defence can become fixated on the airframe element of a larger system.

6 Some Western European sellers (of submarines, for example) reportedly benefit from very low interest sales loans, which amount to grants to buyers. The rationale is that the governments involved want to preserve key military industries. This subsidy practice is, in theory, illegal within the European Union, so presumably it will gradually decline.

7 Because the arms market is so central to the survival of the Russian military industry, the Russians have made an unusually public effort to analyze the world arms market and, incidentally, to convince themselves that their industry can survive without many Russian orders. One result was a rather comprehensive account of recent arms sales. See B. Kuzik, N. Novichkov, V. Shvarev, M. Kenshetaev, and A. Simakov, *Rossiia na mirovom rynke oruzhiia: Analiz i perspektivy* [*Russia on the Global Arms Market: Encyclopedia of the Russian Arms Trade and Military-Technical Cooperation*] (Moscow: Voennyi parad, 2001). Despite its title, it includes accounts of Western sales. Table 7.2–8 (166178) lists post-Soviet exports. The scale of supply seems to be two missiles (Styx or Kh-35) per missile tube. In some cases, such as the large Indian order for Kh-35, the Russians seem not to have been able to fill the order on time. Other tables in the same volume suggest that at most the Chinese received two missiles per tube of their new *Sovremenny*-class destroyers. Overall, the implication is that any countermeasure that causes missile craft to waste their weapons would quickly disarm the antiaccess force. Moreover, the number of modern missile-firing craft is quite limited.

8 A major case in point is Granit (SS–N–19), which employs a scheme of missile-to-missile communication among the weapons in a salvo, to ensure that fire-and-forget operation can be combined with efficient distribution of weapons among targets. Even the configuration of the Granit missile seems not to have been known outside the Cold War Soviet Union. The fire control scheme was revealed at Euronaval 1996, and the configuration only in 2001 (with some earlier hints). Yakhont, now for sale, apparently incorporates the Granit guidance scheme, at least in the version currently on offer.

9 As a case in point, some years ago the Chinese central government decided to prohibit satellite dishes so as to deny Chinese citizens access to subversive foreign broadcasts. The general staff of the People's Liberation Army rejected the order because one of its commercial subsidiaries was doing so well producing and selling the dishes.

10 Exocet was conceived as a fast attack boat weapon. At about the same time this weapon began development, the French went into partnership with the Italians in a longer-range weapon, Otomat, which seems in retrospect to have been intended mainly for larger ships (it was also mounted on board some fast attack boats, and, like Exocet, it was sold for coast defense).

11 Teseo is advertised as the weapon to arm the Italian version of the European Horizon frigate, but private conversations with MBDA representatives at the 2001 Paris Air Show indicate that it is little more than a component development effort, badly underfunded.

12 One possibility might be interservice rivalries among the Indian armed forces.

13 In October 2001, a Chinese officer claimed to the author that his missile frigate was armed with C–803 or YJ–3, no details being supplied. The missile-launching boxes were apparently the same as those used for C–801 and C–802.

14 Similar to many Western jet-powered antiship missiles, C–802 is powered by a Microturbo engine—export of which to China is banned. Reportedly, the Chinese managed to obtain a lot of 50 such engines, which powered the first 50 C–802s. Efforts to obtain more missile-suitable engines failed. Reports vary as to whether the Chinese tried a domestic engine (which was too heavy) or a less suitable version of the Microturbo engine. In either case, it would seem that further C–802 production was difficult at best. Exports have been limited.

15 In World War II, both sides depended heavily on external cueing to direct submarines into position to deal with fast combatant ships, and fairly small errors in cueing could negate such attacks. Cueing depends on offshore sensing (in World War II, often on code breaking, which was in effect a kind of sensing). Without cueing, the submarine commander has to guess where the carrier will be. In the Falklands, for example, the Argentine commander knew that the British Sea Harrier had a very short range and that the H.M.S. *Hermes* would try to stay as far east of the air operating area (Falkland Sound) as possible in order to limit exposure to Argentine air attack. That easily defined her likely location, and he found the carrier—and almost sank her. Presumably, a carrier equipped with longer-range aircraft would have been almost invulnerable. Reports of carriers sunk by diesel submarines during Cold War wargames often

or always referred to a practice in which carriers were deliberately confined to small areas in order to allow NATO diesel submarines to practice the attacks. The famous 1968 episode in which a Soviet November-class nuclear attack submarine intercepted the carrier USS *Enterprise* en route to the Far East required considerable cueing from what the U.S. Navy called the Soviet Ocean Surveillance System. That system has largely died due to the decline of Russian funding. It is also open to question whether the Russians would be inclined to distribute operational intelligence to a third party in some future minor war.

[16] Indeed, ducting is frequent in some important parts of the world, such as the Eastern Baltic, the Eastern Mediterranean, the Indian Ocean, the Persian Gulf, and the South China Sea. However, the attacker would certainly be aware of ducting conditions and might well be able to avoid them. The Italian Navy actually uses ducting in an experimental frigate radar, and the Indian Navy modified its "Square Tie" (Rangout) missile fire control radars to exploit ducting. Note, however, that the claimed range was no more than 50 nautical miles, which would not be enough to detect a formation launching aircraft against coastal installations. Presumably, the boats equipped with ducting radars still had to be cued to attack their targets.

[17] Periodically, interest is shown in remote control technologies, which can turn a field on and off. Presumably it might be safe to recover mines disabled in this way, though it seems doubtful that anyone would trust a control mechanism immersed in water for months at a time.

[18] After the end of the Cold War, the Royal Navy seems to have abandoned offensive mining altogether because all of the explosive in its remaining mines required replacement (explosives can go bad over time).

[19] Any historian/analyst must be uncomfortably aware that, if he or she were writing about Germany in 1925, rearmament and revived militarism would have seemed impossible.

Chapter 27

The Future of American Naval Power: Propositions and Recommendations

Donald C.F. Daniel

This chapter sets down eight propositions about American naval power over the next 25 years, a period many would characterize as an era of increased globalization.[1] Several propositions are hypotheses subject to being judged true or false. Others are more properly postulates, statements not so much provably true or false as subject to validation (that is, to being judged as to whether they provide sensible bases for follow-on analysis and policymaking). Nine recommendations that flow naturally from these propositions are also listed for consideration by U.S. decisionmakers. The purpose for both propositions and recommendations is to help contribute to the ongoing policy debates on the role of naval power in the future international security environment.

U.S. Naval Superiority

The United States will possess the world's premier navy for at least 2 to 3 decades. No one disputes the Navy's present superiority, only the degree, and it is probably increasing as evidenced in the lament of allies who fear a loss of interoperability if they fall too far behind.[2] American efforts to develop network-centric naval operational capabilities have only compounded these fears. Network-centric operations involve interconnecting dispersed command elements, sensors, and weapons platforms so

Donald C.F. Daniel is a professor in the Security Studies Program, School of Foreign Service, at Georgetown University. He was formerly Milton E. Miles Professor of International Relations and director of the Strategic Research Department at the Center for Naval Warfare Studies at the U.S. Naval War College. Among other government assignments, he recently served as a special assistant to the National Intelligence Council. He has written and coedited numerous books, including *Beyond the 600 Ship Navy*, *Anti-Submarine Warfare and Superpower Strategic Stability*, *Strategic Military Deception*, and *Beyond Traditional Peacekeeping*. An earlier version of this chapter appeared in the Canadian journal *Maritime Affairs*.

Figure 27–1. **Eight Propositions on the Future of American Naval Power**

1. The United States will possess the world's premier navy for at least 2 to 3 decades.
2. Unless there is a radical transformation in the type of naval platforms that the Navy will build, the force will continue to dwindle in number.
3. Nevertheless, the quality of the platforms and their supporting infrastructure means no other navy will match it.
4. The best option available for most state-based adversaries would be to build an anti-navy, not a comparable navy.
5. The naval element of the U.S. strategic nuclear deterrence arsenal has been and will likely remain for another 25 years or so the foundation for strategic nuclear stability.
6. The critical quality of a naval task force is that it inherently offers political leaders flexibility.
7. Outside the context of a specific crisis, constant day-to-day naval presence does not do much to deter unwanted behavior.
8. The statement "balanced forward naval presence will be increasingly vital in shaping the peace" seems true only vis-à-vis friends but not potential adversaries or third parties. What is vital instead is that U.S. naval forces show up when needed (during the run-up to and the onset of a contingency) and because of prior operations with regional friends, that it immediately act effectively in concert with them.

---

that informed combat decisions can be made at a speed that overwhelms enemy ability to keep up. That vision today is as much promise as it is reality, but over the next 2 decades, the Navy should move significantly down the road toward achievement.[3]

Unless there is a radical transformation in the type of naval platforms that the Navy will build, the force will continue to dwindle in number. With a near 50 percent decrease in the last decade alone, the Navy today has 315 mostly large, capital-intensive ships. This number could well drop to about 285 over the next 2 to 3 decades at present building trends.[4]

Nevertheless, the quality of the platforms and their supporting infrastructure means no other navy will match it. As the Soviet Union experienced during the Cold War, growing a world-class naval capability is expensive and involves more than just building platforms and supporting elements; it requires sorting out how to use them, and that process takes considerable time.

Indeed, the best option available for most state-based adversaries would be to build an anti-navy, *not a* comparable *navy.* This anti-navy is a relatively inexpensive sea denial force of afloat expendable surface elements, small quiet submarines, mines, shore-based aircraft, antiship missiles, and associated sensors and jammers. Its aim would be to deny U.S. naval forces access to littoral areas,[5] and, depending upon circumstances, its threat could be significant in coastal waters and the high seas approaches.[6]

During the Falklands/Malvinas War, for example, the British Royal Navy, with 2 antisubmarine aircraft carriers, 7 destroyers, 15 frigates, and 6 submarines, had to engage in extensive efforts to deal with only 2 Argentine submarines, one of which was caught on the surface early in the conflict. The campaign showed that antisubmarine warfare aimed at protecting surface ships operating in predictable areas familiar to an enemy is an inherently unfair game biased in favor of enemy submarines (see chapter 17).[7] Similarly, during Operation *Desert Storm*, both the amphibious ship *Tripoli* and the guided missile cruiser *Princeton* struck Iraqi mines, developments that probably contributed to the allied decision not to undertake an amphibious landing (see chapter 20).

Unique Tasks and Roles?

What difference will it make that the United States will have the premier navy for the next quarter century? What does the U.S. Navy have to offer that is special or unique? Its assigned tasks include several overlapping activities, many of which come under the general rubric of contingency response and some of which have only recently come into prominence: maintaining a presence in various distant regions; providing humanitarian assistance; enforcing international sanctions (such as embargoes and no-fly zones); participating in or supporting peace operations, as well as supporting civil authorities including law enforcement agencies; evacuating Americans from danger areas; controlling sea areas so as to allow follow-on military operations or the secure transport of goods; deterring nuclear weapons strategically; engaging in retaliatory or compellence strikes; defending the American homeland and that of friends and allies; and conducting sustained offensive combat operations including interdiction of an enemy's sea lines and the opposed seizure of coastal regions.

Of these activities, the only ones specific to the Navy involve sea control, the interdiction of sea lines, and the seizure of hostile coasts.[8] Yet being able to perform these tasks in the past constituted a necessary feature of the infrastructure[9] for success in land-sea wars (that is, wars that "include a significant maritime aspect"[10]). With these capabilities, the winning coalition could adjust to setbacks on land,[11] compel its enemy to disperse his forces to deal with the threat of amphibious assault, and limit its enemy's ability to draw on and consolidate resources from his friends and suppliers across water boundaries. Conversely, such capabilities could allow coalition members to bring to the fight—often at times and places of their own choosing—assets drawn from within and without their nations.[12] This is not to say that naval capabilities were the principal contributors to victory, but without them victory in land-sea wars might not have been achieved.

All of the other listed tasks and subtasks could or are regularly performed by the other services, and the issue thus becomes whether the Navy can make a special contribution to carrying them out.

Certainly *the naval element of the U.S. strategic nuclear deterrence arsenal has been and will likely remain for another 25 years or so the foundation for strategic nuclear stability.*[13] Deployed U.S. ballistic missile submarines, unlike their fixed land-based counterparts, are and almost certainly will remain immune from attack since there is no evidence of any potential adversary nation being close to the technological breakthrough required to challenge underwater stealth. In fact, submarines now carry a significantly higher percentage of the Nation's attributed missile warheads—63 percent in 2000, scheduled to rise to 77 percent in 2007, according to Strategic Arms Reduction Treaty (START) II provisions (that is, if the United States goes to allowable limits.)[14]

Some hold, however, that the special Navy role could eventually be eliminated. Their logic is that ballistic missile submarines are so expensive to develop and maintain that, when time comes to build a new fleet or if the United States significantly reduces its arsenal of strategic weapons, U.S. decisionmakers may conclude that the cost per warhead is too prohibitive. In either case, this argument goes, it would make more sense overall—notwithstanding the invulnerability of submarine basing—to revert to a nuclear dyad of land-based missiles and bombers.[15]

Until that happens, the special nuclear role of the Navy will remain, and it may complement a no less significant new responsibility: ballistic missile defense.[16] Specifically, if the United States deploys a missile defense shield for itself or allies, basing parts at sea may be sensible should its combatant-based Aegis air defense system also prove effective as a missile interceptor.[17] Seabasing is attractive because it can provide the capability to strike at missiles in boost or cruise phase while still relatively distant from the U.S. homeland or that of an ally (see chapter 24).

This role, however, would tie down valuable ships in an essentially static mission. Also, since they would be restricted to operating in predictable areas, extensive resources would have to be applied to protect them. But seabasing would still be attractive if alternative systems, most notably the Air Force experimental airborne laser, do not become operational.

Many of the Navy's remaining tasks fall under the rubric of contingency response, and here the Navy does indeed have much to offer—but not as much as some naval proponents would argue. A baseline for discussion is the fact that U.S. naval surface ships responded to 325 political crises or an average of 6 times per year during the Cold War.[18] They did so in 81 cases or 8 times yearly in the 1990s with 50 percent of the latter consisting of sequential operations involving Iraq, Somalia, Haiti, and Yugoslavia (Bosnia/Kosovo).[19] Considering the longevity of the trend of six responses a year and the fact that there was no lessening with the end of the Cold War, it seems reasonable to extrapolate that level of utilization forward. In addition, naval use should further become more attractive as the United States reduces its reliance on foreign bases[20] and traditional allies and as Asia "moves to the forefront" of America's geopolitical planning in Washington.[21]

Globalization, Flexibility, and Contingency Response

Reinforcing these trends are the characteristics of U.S. naval forces that have made their use almost second nature to American policymakers[22] and that seem in tune with changing conceptions of strategy and scenarios. Jean-Marie Guehenno has argued that, because of globalization, determining long-term goals and political strategies to attain them "may become increasingly unrealistic: too many factors are beyond our control, and there are too many unknowns." Hence, he concludes:

> A successful [political] strategy may be no more than a series of successful tactics. Under these circumstances, strategy's goal becomes, not identifying the best outcome and finding the means to attain it, but keeping as many options open for as long as possible to provide maximum tactical flexibility. The intrinsic value of having the option to make or not to make a decision, long recognized in the financial world, may increasingly become part of politics.[23]

In line with Guehenno's call for flexibility is the rising significance of what Thomas Barnett and Henry Gaffney call "horizontal scenarios," such as those that have characterized our dealing with the Iraqi and Yugoslav leaderships. These entail a recurring pattern of unfriendly interactions that may go on for years and in which specific issues and contexts for each crisis or encounter may well differ. Barnett and Gaffney stated, "In horizontal scenarios, everything and everyone is free to evolve over time, meaning positions change, allies come and go, and definitions of 'what the real issue is' abound."[24]

The critical quality of a naval task force is that it inherently offers political leaders flexibility. Such flexibility enables leaders to deal with the strategic uncertainties of a globalizing world and the inconstancies of horizontal scenarios.[25] Without legal constraint, the Navy can readily transit to and operate off foreign littorals. Its smaller footprint makes "maritime presence . . . most welcome" to local friends for whom "there is absolutely no enthusiasm whatsoever for increasing the levels of land-based forces in the Eastern Mediterranean, or the Arabian Peninsula, or East Asia."[26] It can modulate the visibility, level, and makeup of its presence to match the political situation. It can loiter indefinitely in international waters off a coast, ready to go into action on short notice.[27] While loitering, its underway replenishment capability makes it relatively less dependent on nearby land bases,[28] and, notwithstanding the USS *Cole* tragedy, its afloat mobility minimizes the prospect of its personnel being captured or subjected to sabotage.[29]

Naval task forces are generally more assured of arriving fully prepared for combat operations compared with ground-based forces that may need weeks to set up if their support infrastructure is not already in place.[30] With today's aircraft carriers, cruise missile shooters, and marines, a naval task force can provide the full spectrum of conventional power projection for small to mid-level contingencies in coastal and adjacent areas, as well as enable the entry of ground-based army and air forces for larger events.[31] Finally, should the Navy transform into a network-centric force, it would significantly increase the scope of what it could accomplish on its own against shore as well as sea targets.

The Effect of Presence?

In sum, there would seem to be a special role for the U.S. Navy in contingency response along littorals, but, *outside the context of a specific crisis, constant day-to-day presence does not do much to deter unwanted behavior.*[32]

Thus, it would seem a raising of false expectations to argue, for example, that the "gapping of aircraft carriers in areas of potential crisis is an invitation to disaster—and therefore represents culpable negligence on the part of America's defense decision-makers."[33] In the early 1960s, the United States maintained three aircraft carrier battlegroups in the Mediterranean Sea but later gradually found that it needed to scale back. Currently, a single battlegroup operates there for less than 9 months of the year on average. This is a significant reduction, but no one can prove that the Mediterranean region became less stable. Conversely, the Navy began to maintain a regular presence in the Arabian Gulf in 1979, but this did not prevent Iran or Iraq from attacking ships during their war. In the 1980s, attacks generally increased in number over the 8 years of the war.[34]

As for deterring the initiation of a crisis in the first place, it is essentially impossible for an outsider to prove that such deterrence was successful except in the rare case in which a deterred party admits that he was deterred and states the reasons.[35] Adam Siegel, John Arquilla, Paul Huth, Paul Davis, and a Rutgers Center for Global Security and Democracy team led by Edward Rhodes have each attempted to study the effects of forward presence and general deterrence. The deficiency of such study is always in making the definitive link between them. The majority of these studies suggest that "[h]istorically seapower has not done well as a deterrent" in preventing the outbreak of conflicts,[36] principally because land-based powers not dependent on overseas trade are relatively "insensitive" to the operations of naval forces.[37]

One instance when continuous noncrisis naval presence may have contributed to general deterrence may have been in the Cold War when the U.S. and Soviet navies regularly rubbed shoulders in the Mediterranean Sea and Indian Ocean. Each navy maintained forward-deployed forces that could be counted upon to react to one another in a crisis. Hence it seems reasonable to assume that this reality became incorporated in each side's calculations and may have had some deterrent effect, but, again, evidence is the problem.[38]

If the evidence is slim concerning deterring the onset of a crisis, it is only slightly better when it comes to the issue of shaping events (that is, to positively changing the political landscape of an area in a manner favoring American interests). Systematic analytic attempts are few and definitive results are sparse. The Rutgers team did conclude in their study on shaping that it works best when it is limited to deterring external actions and is not based on a sweeping set of goals.[39]

As against that conclusion, several studies that involved interviews of U.S. country teams and foreign political leaders suggest that military presence can be seen by friendly nations as a commitment to a security environment in which stability provides for greater economic development. This environment of stability leads to both greater local investment and trade by U.S. companies and greater local support for U.S. policies. Some foreign interviewees specifically linked their willingness to support the U.S. politically to the reassurance they received from a U.S. presence.[40]

In short, then, to say that *"balanced forward naval presence will be increasingly vital in shaping the peace"*[41]*seems true only vis-à-vis friends* but *not potential adversaries or third parties.* It would not seem to have much direct impact on the shape of a friend's domestic politics but could affect its economy (and thus indirectly the domestic political scene) and its willingness to support U.S. foreign policy. There is no evidence, however, that presence need be continuous to achieve these effects. The Mediterranean analysis suggests that, at the end of the day, *what is vital instead is that U.S. naval forces show up when needed—that is, during the run-up to and the onset of a contingency—and because of prior operations with regional friends, that it immediately act effectively in concert with them.*

Recommendations

If the above propositions do in fact accurately represent the prospective and potential roles of naval forces in the future security environment characterized by globalization, then nine recommendations are worthy of consideration for future defense policy:

1. The United States must maintain a force that can exercise sea control throughout the oceans and in chokepoints and littoral regions. Considering its geographic location, if *the United States* is to fight wars in the next quarter-century, they *will* almost surely be "land-sea" affairs—if only to use the seas to move military cargoes—at far removed areas from its homeland. As a consequence, it *should maintain in its military*

arsenal those capabilities—to control the seas, interdict sea lines, and seize hostile coasts—that form part of the infrastructure of success in land-sea campaigns.

2. This sea-control force should be part of a transformed fleet that can fight through enemy anti-access systems, maximizing its knowledge of the enemy while, at the same time, being able to absorb his initial strike.[42] Transformation could involve significantly spreading out the sensors and firepower of the fleet so that they are not concentrated in a decreasing number of large and expensive hulls. Consistent with the network-centric concept, it would certainly mean developing or blending with existing intelligence, communications, and command infrastructures to produce a rapid reaction, synergistic fighting force whose overall capability exceeds the sum of its parts.

3. Due to their relative invulnerability, ballistic missile submarines should be retained as prime guarantors of strategic nuclear stability, even if the cost per warhead continues to increase. *At some point the cost per warhead of relying on submarines may indeed become too high, but significant price tolerance should be accepted.*

4. If land- or air-based national missile defense forces are deployed and prove capable, they should retain primary responsibility for the task rather than Aegis ships. Assuming that they can do the job, the opportunity costs of employing Aegis-capable surface ships in ballistic missile defense are high because the mission toes down versatile platforms to one role and to specific areas of operation dictated by the geometry of missile flight.

5. The inherent flexibility of naval forces optimizes them for small- and medium-level contingencies along the littorals and reassures friends and allies of U.S. support. *The United States ought to capitalize on the* inherent *flexibility of naval forces to respond to small- and medium-level contingencies along littorals,* and when appropriate, *enable the entry of army and air forces for medium- to high-level contingencies along* littorals, *and reassure friends,* thereby helping to shape their economic development and willingness to support U.S. policies.

6. Naval advocates should take care not to oversell the impact that day-to-day naval presence might have on deterring the onset of crises. It is unclear whether day-to-day naval presence actually deters regional crises.

7. A new formula is needed for determining routine (noncrisis) naval presence. If the United States possessed the 600-ship navy that it aimed for in the 1980s, meeting its presence requirements would not be a problem, but it is roughly half that size and getting smaller. As such, it needs to rethink how it will do presence. *What should drive U.S. decisions on noncrisis forward deployments is not a relatively inflexible set of standards* (such as one carrier group full time in region A and another present three-quarters time in region B with a tether of so many days transit to region C), *but rather a more flexible rule set based on the requirements for being prepared for quick action.*

Preparing would necessitate periodically deploying to areas where contingencies might arise. The U.S. Coast Guard should be included in this formula.

8. Routine naval presence should be tailored to meet a very specific set of objectives rather as a general effort to "deter" crises. The military objectives should include acclimating U.S. naval forces to those physical and meteorological idiosyncrasies of the area that affect how well sailors and systems would perform; and exercising with indigenous militaries so as to enhance interoperability should they combine with the United States to respond to a contingency. Political objectives should include reassuring friends that America will help defend them, while also helping condition them and others to support U.S. efforts if and when a crisis does occur.[43]

9. Top quality strategic intelligence should be as much a U.S. naval priority as buying the next capital ship. The efficient and timely *deployment* of American naval forces depends on the quality of the strategic intelligence available to those authorities that direct movement. The right mix of ships needs to be deployed to the right spot with the right missions or tactics, rather than deploying a standard package to a standard location. Quality information maximizes the time available for U.S. naval forces to assemble the right mix at the right spots with the right mission capabilities, or, as with the USS *Cole*, to avoid certain spots altogether.

Conclusion

While the United States will possess the world's premier Navy for the foreseeable future, it will nevertheless face crucial decisions about how to transform and employ it. The force should be employed to ensure that its comparative advantages are maximized with full recognition of where limits exist. The point of the above recommendations is to emphasis that naval forces possess unique flexibility as politico-military instruments, but there are also limitations to what they can achieve as elements of conventional deterrence to regional crises. Naval forces can be effective instruments in training toward interoperability with friends, allies, and potential coalition members and do appear to have a reassuring effect on treaty allies. But this does not necessarily require the current rigorous force deployment schedule.

In the globalizing world, naval forces will be critical elements in *responding* to crises and will have a modest role in *shaping* the environment, but it is not certain that they can have considerable direct effect in *deterring* the inevitable politico-military crises that will occur in less stable regions buffeted by the effects of globalization. U.S. Navy force structure should be optimized for what it can do, not for tasks that cannot be proven effective.

Notes

¹ The author wishes to acknowledge the assistance of William Murray, Bradd Hayes, Frank Uhlig, Edward Rhodes, Henry Kamradt, Robert Rubel, George Kasten, Roger Barnett, Peter Swartz, Harlan Ullman, Thomas Barnett, Henry Gaffney, Timothy Somes, Ronald O'Rourke, Robert Reilly, and 35 participants at a Naval War College workshop called to debate the propositions offered in this article.

² On the prospect of continued superiority in the future, see Congressional Budget Office, *Budgeting for Naval Forces: Structuring Tomorrow's Navy at Today's Funding Level* (October 2000), 13–15, accessed at <http://www.cbo.gov/showdoc.cfm?index-2603&sequcncc=0&from-7>.

³ The promise of a network-centric navy is well summarized in a recent report of the Naval Studies Board: "Within the physical limits of time required for movement and weapon range and speed, the force commanders operating in a network-centric mode *will* be able to concentrate widely dispersed forces' fire and maneuvers at decisive *locations* and times. The forces *will* be able to achieve the precision needed to identify and engage opposing forces and specific targets with minimal casualties and least civilian damage. And they will be able to do so at a pace that overwhelms the opposition's ability to prevent the actions or to respond in time to avoid defeat." See National Research Council, Naval Studies Board, *Network-Centric Naval Forces: A Transition Strategy for Enhancing Operational Capabilities* (Washington, DC: National Academy Press, 2000), 2. William Owens provides some sense of the spatial dimension within which a network-centric naval force might operate when he writes that the technology available today "can give us the ability to see a 'battlefield' as large as Iraq or Korea—an area 200 miles on a side . . . all the time." Owens with Edward Offley, *Lifting the Fog of War* (New York: Farrar, Straus and Giroux, 2000), 14.

⁴ To have a fleet of 305 ships in the year 2030, it would be necessary to build 8.7 ships a year, but the projected building rate through 2005 is only 7.5 a year with little expectation that it will rise much beyond that as long as the Navy continues to opt for high-end ships such as are presently programmed. See "Cohen Sends Navy Shipbuilding Report To Congress," *Inside the Navy*, July 3, 2000, 6–7; Statement of Ronald O'Rourke, Specialist in National Defense, Congressional Research Service, before the Senate Armed Services Committee, Subcommittee on Seapower, Hearing on Ship Procurement and Research and Development Programs, March 2, 2000, photocopy, 6; Ronald O'Rourke, *Navy Ship Procurement Rate and the Planned Size of the Navy: Background and Issues for Congress* (Washington, DC: Congressional Research Service, April 4, 2000); and Congressional Budget Office, chapter 2.

⁵ It may be worth noting that "population diminishes rapidly with elevation and with distance from coastlines and major rivers." In particular, "there are far more people per available land area within 100 km of the coastlines and within 200 meters of sea level than further inland or at higher elevations." Christopher Small and Joel Cohen, "Continental Physiography, Climate and the Global Distribution of Human Population," *Proceedings of the International Symposium on Digital Earth*, 1999, accessed at <http://www.ldeo.columbia.edu/-small/pdf/isde_mallcohen.pdf>.

⁶ It would also put Americans off balance if the sea-denial force included capability to attack transport ships on the open ocean. With the increased size of such ships, the value of each attack could be quite significant. Such *guerre de course* would be the oceanic equivalent of guerrilla warfare, forcing Americans to expend time and considerable resources to contend with it (especially if the attacks were against military transports), but it would require the attackers to have access to sources of resupply if the threat is to be maintained. Americans presumably would be blockading whatever ports such attackers would operate from. They might also have prior intelligence of such a threat and seek to deal with it early on before it becomes an extensive open-ocean menace.

⁷ Donald C. Daniel, "Antisubmarine Warfare in the Nuclear Age," *Orbis* (Fall 1984), 549–551.

⁸ In its effort to become expeditionary, the U.S. Army is investigating the purchase of its own tactical support vessels to bring its troops ashore. The troops would move in after an air assault had secured a point of entry.

⁹ George Modelski and William R. Thompson, *Seapower in Global Politics, 1494–1993* (Seattle: University of Washington Press, 1988), 22.

¹⁰ John Arquilla, *Dubious Battles* (Washington, DC: Crane Russak, 1992), 132.

¹¹ S.W. Roskill points out that it is often because of setbacks on land that states with seapower potential capitalize on it. He states, "To turn to the manner in which *our* strategy developed during [World War II], it is something of a paradox that it was our total expulsion from the European continent in 1940 that forced us to change from a predominantly continental to a predominantly maritime strategy: and the reason for the change was that no other means of achieving victory then remained to us. Thus the reversion to a strategy which strongly resembled that of the elder

Pitt in the Seven Years War, and also that adopted during the greater part of the Napoleonic War, took place not under any voluntary act on our part, but under the Axis victories on land." See Roskill, *The Strategy of Sea Power* (London: Collin's, 1962), 240.

[12] Modelski and Thompson, 11–12; Colin Gray, *The Leverage of Sea Power: The Strategic Advantage of Navies in War* (New York: Free Press, 1992), 283; Colin Gray, *The Navy in the Post-Cold War Period: The Uses and Value of Strategic Sea Power* (University Park, PA: Pennsylvania State University Press, 1992), 162–163, 193; Colin Gray, "Seapower and Landpower;" in *Seapower and Strategy*, ed. Colin Gray and Roger Barnett (Annapolis, MD: U.S. Naval Institute Press, 1989), 23; and Arquilla, 55–59.

[13] See Donald C.F. Daniel, *Antisubmarine Warfare and Superpower Strategic Stability* (London: Brassey's, 1986).

[14] William S. Cohen, *Annual Report to the President and the Congress 2000*, chapter 6, 2, accessed at <www.dtic.rnil/execsec/adr2000/chap6.html>.

[15] Also, a near-term reduction to 1,000 warheads, for example, could appear to place too many eggs in too few baskets since, at present, ballistic missile submarines deploy with as many as 192 warheads, but presumably a submarine would not have to deploy with that number under the 1,000 restriction. Alternatively, the nuclear deterrent might be placed on single-warhead, submarine-based cruise missiles, but their radius of attack would be much shorter. One of the best studies on the use of missiles to strike land targets from the sea is Owen R. Cote, Jr., *Precision Strike From the Sea: New Missions for a New Navy* (Cambridge, MA: Massachusetts Institute of Technology Security Studies Program, n.d.)

[16] But if the U.S. deploys an effective national defense system, it would certainly encourage a reduction in offensive weapons.

[17] See Richard J. Newman, "Shooting from the Ship," *U.S. News and World Report*, July 3, 2000, accessed at <http://ebird.dtic.mil/Jun 2000/e20000626shootingfrom.htm>.

[18] These numbers probably do not reflect ship movements (including by submarines in circumstances where stealth is a premium) that were never publicly acknowledged. On the Cold War years, see Edward A. Smith, Jr., ". . . From the Sea: The Process of Defining a New Role for Naval Forces in the Post-Cold War World," in *The Politics of Strategic Adjustment: Ideas, Institutions and Interests*, ed. Peter Trubowitz, Emily Goldman, and Edward Rhodes (New York: Columbia University Press, 1999), 288–289.

[19] For the 1990s, see Thomas P.M. Barnett and Henry H. Gaffney, Jr., "Top Ten Post-Cold War Myths," U.S. Naval Institute *Proceedings* 127, no. 2 (February 2001), 32–38. Counting responses is as much art as science. Barnett and Gaffney point out, for example, that their total of 81 reflects uncertainty about "how to *interpret* the lengthy *strings of* sequential operations clustered around Iraq, Somalia, Haiti, and Yugoslavia." See also Adam Siegel's discussion of "Methodological Issues" in *The Use of Naval Force in the Post-War Era: U.S. Navy and Marine Corps Crisis Response Activity, 1946–1990*, ed. Adam Siegel (Alexandria, VA: Center for Naval Analyses, February 1991), 5–6.

[20] This is not to say that navies can do without bases. See Barry M. Blechman and Robert G. Weinland, "Why Coaling Stations Are Necessary in the Nuclear Age," *International Security* (Summer 1977), 88–99.

[21] Thomas E. Ricks, "For Pentagon Asia Moving to the Forefront," *The Washington Post*, May 26, 2000, 1. The Australian defense analyst Paul Dibb united some of these themes in a conclusion to a recent paper: "Potential military operations in the Asia-Pacific region will be essentially maritime in nature. Apart from the Korean peninsula, U.S. military forces are not likely to be involved in large-scale, land forces operations. The dominant geopolitical change . . . has been the virtual elimination . . . of allied continental commitments. The emerging struggle for power in Asia will focus on fault lines that are maritime rather than continental in aspect. The development of China's military power, and the response by India and Japan, is likely to put pressure on the chain of America's friends and allies in the long littoral extending between South Korean and Taiwan in the north . . . to the ASEAN countries and Australia in the south." See Dibb, "Strategic Trends in the Asia-Pacific Region," Paper prepared for the Current Strategy Forum, U.S. Naval War College, Newport, RI, June 13, 2000, 16.

[22] Two anecdotes illustrate the second nature claim and associate it with aircraft carriers in particular. Former Secretary of Defense and now Vice President Dick Cheney has related that when he would meet with President George H.W. Bush to deal with a crisis, "literally the first thing he always [said was], 'How are we fixed for carriers?'" See Grant Willis, "Secretary Receives First-hand View of Carrier Operations," *Navy Times*, November 13, 1989, 4. Along the same lines, former Vice President Al Gore's chief national security advisor, Leon Fuerth, gave the following answer during the 2000 Presidential campaign when asked what Mr. Gore might do about defense strategy: "I think his view is that

the two major contingency strategies have served us very well, and it is possible to see exactly where the vice president has been in the Cabinet Room with the president and others when we had to ask ourselves whether if we move a carrier . . . we are opening ourselves up to adventures by one opponent or the next." See Elaine Sciolino, "A Gore Advisor Who Basks in the Shadows," *The New York Times*, April 25, 2000, A14.

[23] Jean-Marie Guehenno, "The Impact of Globalization on Strategy," *Survival* (Winter 1998–1999), 14.

[24] See discussion in Barnett and Gaffney, 32–33.

[25] See Donald C.F. Daniel, *Beyond the 600-Ship Navy*, Adelphi Paper 261 (London: Brassey's, 1991), 24–30.

[26] Dov Zakheim, et al., *Political and Economic Implications of Global Naval Presence*, Technical Report SPC Log No.: 96–0989 (Arlington, VA: System Planning Corporation, September 30, 1996), 12, 21 . The report, prepared for the Navy, is based on an unspecified number of interviews with "opinion leaders-government minister, senior officials, active and retired senior military officers, academics and businessmen" in each region as well as foreign officials visiting Washington.

[27] Colin Powell once praised this versatility of naval forces by remarking, "It's hard to lie offshore with a C–141 or C–130 [aircraft] full of airborne troops." See Jeffrey Record, "Strike from the Sea," *Baltimore Sun*, April 25, 1990, 17. A possible argument against reliance on naval forces is that, unless they are already on scene, they are too slow to respond, but a conclusion of an ongoing project by analysts at the Center for Naval Analyses (CNA) is that response time by deployed forces was generally not a problem because contingencies usually do not arise out of the blue, but rather consisted of situations that the United States had been tracking. The author is indebted to the CNA project leader, Henry H. Gaffney, Jr., for this point.

[28] A troubling counterpoint to the claim made in the text above about the Navy's relative independence from land bases is evidenced by the USS *Cole*'s need to refuel in Aden where it was attacked. It had to refuel there because of a reduction in the number of replenishment oilers. The issue is priorities: which ships get serviced by what oilers?

[29] Immediately after the USS *Cole* incident, the Navy ordered its 22 ships in the Persian Gulf area to deploy to sea. It then ordered three amphibious ships to Aden waters to provide marine protection and "hotel services" for civilian and military investigators sent to Aden. Robert Drogin and David Kelly, "3 Warships Head to Yemen to Bolster Investigative Team," *Los Angeles Times*, October 17, 2000, 8.

[30] Richard L. Kugler argues that there is a "trend toward an enlarging U.S. and Western operating perimeter in key regions" (to incorporate, for example, Eastern Europe, North Africa, the greater Middle East, and Southeast Asia) and that there is a concomitant need to transform U.S. forces and their global support structure. "U.S. forces now deployed" in Cold War-era bases, he adds, "would acquire an outward-looking mentality. Their current bases would become facilities for launching them on projection missions. . . . The U.S. Navy already thinks in these terms as a result of its maritime focus." See Kugler, *Changes Ahead: Future Direction for the U.S. Overseas Military Presence* (Santa Monica, CA: RAND, 1998), 75, 29.

[31] An important issue is the level of response most suited for naval forces. In a recent article, Eliot Cohen argues for the need for U.S. conventional dominance over any potential opponent. He also says that such "dominance, particularly against China, will involve long-range forces, primarily aerial and naval, that could cope with events such as an assault on Taiwan." See Cohen, "Defending America in the Twentieth Century," *Foreign Affairs* (November/December 2000), 48.

[32] Edward A Smith, Jr., was part of a group of 25 officers assembled from around the world for several months to consider a new strategic concept for the U.S. Navy after the end of the Cold War. He writes, "there was a vigorous debate even among the . . . officers . . . over how if at all, 'presence' contributed to deterring crises and conflicts." See Smith, ". . . *From the Sea*: The Process of Defining a New Role for Naval Forces in the Post-Cold War World," 288. Sam J. Tangredi argues persuasively that the Navy must prove the case for presence, although naval presence would intuitively appear to have some deterrent effects. See Tangredi, "The Fall and Rise of Naval Forward Presence," U.S. Naval Institute *Proceedings* 126, no. 5 (May 2000), 28–32.

[33] John R. Fisher, "A Tale of Two Centuries," *Seapower*, 2000 Almanac Issue (January 2000), 4.

[34] Ronald A. O'Rourke, "Gulf Ops," U.S. Naval Institute *Proceedings* (May 1989), 43.

[35] Trying to prove deterrence runs against the fallacy of proving a negative. Adam Siegel deals with this issue quite well in "To Deter, Compel, and Reassure in International Crises: The Role of U.S. Naval Forces," CRM 94–193 (Alexandria, VA: Center for Naval Analyses, February 1995).

[36] Arquilla, 143, 150.

[37] See discussion in Edward Rhodes, "Conventional Deterrence," *Comparative Strategy* (July-September 2000), 221–254.

[38] James McConnell contends, once a crisis had occurred involving U.S. and Soviet client states, that both navies operated according to "rules of the game" that contributed to deterring escalation between them. See McConnell, "The 'Rules of the Game': A Theory on the Practice of Superpower Naval Diplomacy," in Bradford Dismukes and James McConnell, *Soviet Naval Diplomacy* (New York: Pergamon Press, 1979), 240–280.

[39] Edward Rhodes, Jonathan DiCicco, Sarah Milburn Moore, and Tom Walker, "Forward Presence and Engagement: Historical Insights into the Problem of Shaping," *Naval War College Review* 53, no. 1 (Winter 2000), 45–49. The cases that the team drew on are broad, leading to questions about the strengths of the conclusions. For example, one particularly naval case concerns the British Royal Navy's presence in the Eastern Mediterranean Sea from 1816 to 1852. That presence was credited with deterring Egyptian attack on the Ottoman Empire, but the paucity of specific details makes it hard to credit the claim fully. Nevertheless, this remains an interesting article.

[40] Results of the country team interviews can be found in Bradford Dismukes, *National Security Strategy and Forward Presence: Implications for Acquisitions and Use of Naval Forces*, CRM 93–7 (Alexandria, VA: Center for Naval Analyses, March 1994), and Dismukes, *The Political-Strategic Case for Presence—Implications for Force Structure and Force Employment*, CAB 93–7 (Alexandria, VA: Center for Naval Analyses, June 1993). Results of the interviews of foreign leaders can be found in Zakheim, et al.

[41] Jay Johnson, "Anytime. Anywhere: A Navy for the 21st Century," U.S. Naval Institute *Proceedings* 123, no. 6 (November 1997), 50.

[42] See Donald C.F. Daniel, "The Evolution of Naval Power to the Year 2010," *Naval War College Review* 48, no. 3 (Summer 1995), 70–71.

[43] See Robert G. Weinland, *A Somewhat Different View of Optimal Naval Posture*, Center for Naval Analyses Professional Paper 214 (Arlington, VA: Center for Naval Analyses, 1978).

Chapter 28

A Naval Operational Architecture for Global Tactical Operations

J. Noel Williams and James S. O'Brasky

No naval policy can be wise unless it takes into very careful account the tactics that ought to be used in war.[1]

—Commander Bradley Fiske, USN, 1905

T he continuing effects of globalization on military and naval operations inevitably require the development of new tactics. This chapter describes an affordable, executable, naval operational architecture designed to carry out tactical operations successfully in an uncertain future characterized by globalization. The purpose of the architecture is to demonstrate how naval forces can be organized, trained, and equipped for tactical success in a balanced system that nests within the larger Department of Defense (DOD) system to create a *system of systems*.[2] Such a system of systems, approach is fully in consonance with *Joint Vision 2020*, the future warfare vision of the Chairman of the Joint Chief of Staff.

While more art than science in its execution, this architecture will delineate required capabilities with sufficient detail to articulate clearly its overall design and to provide a viable framework for implementation. Specifically, it will emphasize

J. Noel Williams recently retired as lieutenant colonel in the U.S. Marine Corps and is now associated with the Potomac Institute Center for Emerging Threats and Opportunities. His last military assignment was to the Strategic Initiatives Group, HQMC. A graduate of the Virginia Military Institute, he earned an M.A. in national security studies at Georgetown University, a Master of Military Studies from the Marine Corps University, an international relations secondary occupational specialty, and is also a graduate of the Marine Corps School of Advanced Warfighting. James S. O'Brasky is an expert in joint and naval force design and planning and in gaming advanced technology system designs. He recently retired from Government service after 32 years with the Naval Surface Warfare Center, Dahlgren Division.

expeditionary littoral operations as an illustrative example of one component of a larger naval operational concept.[3] Secondarily, it is another attempt to fulfill the challenge issued by Captain Wayne P. Hughes, USN (Ret.), in his seminal work *Fleet Tactics*, for a rebirth of tactical thought among naval officers.[4] In describing the intellectual environment at the turn of the last century, Hughes stated, "It was a time when naval officers aggressively asserted that policy and strategy were not to be unfounded wishes but plans that derived from a calculated capacity for tactical success."[5]

At the beginning of this global millennium, we must foster a similar intellectual environment within the naval services and acknowledge, along with Hughes, that "tactical and technological developments are inseparable."[6] While excellence in operational art and strategy are necessary conditions for victory, they are not sufficient conditions. Tactical success is the foundation upon which the higher military arts are based. Employment of tactical units in a complex and hostile operating environment is based upon a well-developed and executed set of tactics and doctrine that seeks either to produce decisive tactical advantage in each deliberately initiated engagement or to neutralize the effectiveness of any engagement initiated by the enemy.

The Systemic Challenge of Tactical Change

It is worth remembering the words of Alfred Thayer Mahan, who observed:

> Changes in tactics have only taken place after changes in weapons which is necessarily the case, but that the interval between such changes has been unduly long. This arises from the fact that an improvement of weapons is due to the energies of one or two, while changes in tactics have to overcome the inertia of a conservative class, but it is a great evil.[7]

He continues, "History shows that it is vain to hope that military men generally will be at the pain to do this, but that the one who does will go into battle with a great advantage."[8] These are strong, critical but insightful words—words no less relevant today than when they were written over a century ago. As noted in chapter 1, there is a relationship that we are only beginning to recognize between contemporary globalization and seapower. Mahan was the great prophet of seapower, but he was also a strong proponent of technological and tactical change, what might today be called *transformation*. In his view, such change should suit the strategic environment and circumstances of the nation.[9] Current circumstances are defined by globalization, including the proliferation of advanced military technology suitable for integration into antiaccess strategies. To achieve success in this environment requires an operational architecture that is more specifically tailored to the globalizing world, rather than simply retaining an architecture originally designed for the Cold War.

What follows is an operational architecture that optimizes existing and planned capabilities while encouraging the development of the doctrinal, cultural, and experiential foundation upon which the naval forces of this nation can go into battle in a globalizing world with great advantage.

Environment and Requirements

As noted in chapter 2, change and uncertainty are the dominant features of the future security environment. But this is nothing new. The end of the Cold War could be said to usher in a return to normalcy in international relations. Globalization, deferred by World War II and the Cold War, has once again taken the forefront of the international agenda. As also noted in chapter 2, there are differences between the *more typical* times before the Cold War and today, particularly the increasing connectedness of modern information technology, but many of the strategic principles—of which the foremost is to prepare for uncertainty—remain. This is a principle that guides the proposed architecture, which will articulate capabilities designed for a changing, uncertain world—a full-spectrum world.

As a maritime nation in a globalized world, the United States needs maritime forces capable of full-spectrum engagement and full-spectrum access assurance. In national security terms, *full spectrum* means the range of activities from peacetime training and engagement activities to theater warfighting campaigns—in short, the familiar low to high range of military training, peacekeeping, and warfighting operations. Agility and flexibility come to mind when thinking of characteristics necessary for forces to be effective in such a world.

Maritime forces, by their nature, are continuously engaged globally. As "permanent" overseas U.S. presence declines and as the interconnectedness of the world increases, the demand for maritime forces to remain active in the full spectrum of military activities will grow. Meaningful engagement in this type of world is hands-on, face-to-face, boots-on-the-ground, soles-on-the-deck-plates kind of work. Antiseptic, virtual presence will not do. Engagement is about people, not machines or technology, and being there is the sine qua non. Engagement is both physical and psychological— the act of conditioning a future battlespace involves developing detailed understanding of the political, military, and physical environment and shaping its future development to encourage allies, deter potential foes, and provide a state of assured coalition defense for U.S. interests.

Assuring geographic access is also a critical task for maritime forces. Technology is strengthening the hand of those smaller nations and actors who wish to deny access to regions vital to the economic and security interests of the Nation. There is an ever-present requirement to guarantee access to sea lines of communication and, should conflict arise, to defeat the opponent's area denial systems. Maritime forces are designed to assure access. The sustainable rapid response capabilities that maritime forces uniquely provide make them essential enablers of the joint fight.

Tasks for the Fleet

A forward-deployed peacetime fleet should provide three specific functional capabilities: peacetime naval functions, battlespace dominance, and power projection. These functions are further broken down into specific measurements of the required tasks in the table below.[10]

Peacetime Naval Functions

- Assure safe transit of naval, joint, and coalition forces and commercial shipping
- Conduct at least two simultaneous noncombatant evacuation operations (NEOs)
- Conduct theater engagement activities and other peacetime missions as required
- Develop situational awareness
- Provide theater-wide situational awareness

Battlespace Dominance

- Neutralize land-space denial system
    —Protect three critical theater complexes
    —Defeat a denial system consisting of 400 theater ballistic missiles (TBMs), 400 cruise missiles, 200 transporter-erector-launchers (TELs)
- Neutralize airspace denial system
    —Destroy 4 integrated air defense system (IADS) command centers, 12 radar sites, 100 TELs
    —Defeat a tactical air force of 200 planes (coordinated attack of 50 planes)
- Neutralize sea denial system
    —Destroy 4 command centers, 12 sensor sites, 100 TELs
    —Defeat a navy of 50 ships and 15 attack submarines
    —Neutralize up to 2,000 sea mines laid in multiple fields

Power Projection

- Halt a corps-sized ground force
- Defeat a brigade-sized ground force
- Neutralize 4 command centers and 100 TELs
- Neutralize complexes of 6 ports and 20 airfields

These tasks are notional and intended only to demonstrate the types of threats a fleet can be prepared to counter in the first 2 weeks of a zero-warning future conflict.

As noted in chapter 25 of the current volume, successful execution of such a wide variety of near simultaneous tasks with the limited assets available to a forward-deployed fleet is a daunting challenge. Success demands a high standard of tactical mastery employed to take full advantage of the battlespace conditioning that skillful and persistent peacetime forward engagement practice makes possible.[11]

Force Composition

Even in a network-centric combat environment, tactical groups (small, integrated systems of systems) will be required to cope with collapsed battlespace conditions and saturation raids.[12] These tactical groups constitute the elements of an operational architecture. The presence of these forward-deployed groups in peacetime operations will serve as a major deterrent, but should deterrence fail, their ability to defeat area denial systems, dominate the maritime battlespace, and support coalition forces ashore can provide a foundation of assured coalition defense upon which limited-objective offensive operations may be undertaken.[13]

The design and operation of these tactical groups will have a serious impact on current naval culture since the requirement to create tactical groups for specific combat tasks contrasts so sharply with the single multimission platform focus of the recent past. A single multimission platform tends to have a good but limited technical mission capability in several warfare areas, such as antisubmarine warfare (ASW), antiair warfare (AAW), and strike warfare, but maintenance and training demands tend to preclude development of sustained tactical competence in more than two disciplines simultaneously. Even if the technical potential of a single multimission platform could be fully realized, the limited magazine load-out would severely limit unit effectiveness in a high-intensity engagement. The classic solution to this problem is the formation of permanent tactical groups containing a mission-focused capability package surrounded by two layers of defensive capability in each applicable medium.[14] The aircraft carrier battlegroup (CVBG) is the classic naval exemplar of this sort of thinking.

Dispersed networked multimission platforms can constitute an effective force in the absence of threat but invite defeat in detail when a single platform can be exposed to a mass saturation attack or a stealth threat. In the presence of significant threats, the well-integrated tactical group can still exploit the benefits of theater-scale networking, while providing effective combined arms mutual support between elements.

A new feature in tactical group design is the deliberate attempt to correlate mission capability with group signature. A tactical group designed to operate in a collapsed battlespace or near the edge of a defended envelope should not present a cooperative target. Such a group should have comprehensive signature control and quiet operating modes (that is, it should be able to disappear into the environmental background at will) and have the situational awareness to know when to do so.

A group designed to execute a sustained mission that demands high-signature operations must operate well within a defended envelope and must be provided with effective multilayered defenses. Such a group may well be strategically or operationally significant. As a high-value, detectable target, it will attract enemy attention. An astute commander can employ camouflage, cover, and deception techniques to induce an enemy to commit and expose large resources to engage an enticing and exposed but *false* target.

Four new naval tactical groups should be formed to complement the aircraft carrier battlegroup:

- theater air and missile defense group (TAMDG)
- theater land attack group (TLAG)
- mine countermeasures group (MCMG)
- expeditionary littoral attack group (enhanced amphibious ready group/Marine expeditionary unit–special operations capable [ARG/MEU–SOC]).

These five standing tactical groups would be the basic building blocks for most naval operational forces. The four new groups would provide a sound foundation for a renaissance in expeditionary warfare and restore operational mobility to the carrier battlegroup as well. The following will describe these tactical groups using the force structure of 2015 to 2021 for convenience and simplicity. Some groups can be implemented today using program of record forces. Others, to achieve their full potential, must await the arrival of new capabilities in the 2010 to 2015 timeframe.

Aircraft Carrier Battlegroup

The redefined aircraft carrier battlegroup would consist of a nuclear powered carrier (CVN), a CG–52 class cruiser, 2 DDG–51 class destroyers, a nuclear powered attack submarine (SSN), and a logistics element consisting of a T–AO and T–AKE. The CVBG command element would manage the strike warfare assets of the fleet. This group is similar to but somewhat smaller than the traditional CVBG. It actually represents more air defense and strike capability and equal ASW capability than was present in a late Cold War CVBG. This CVBG is illustrated in figure 28–1.

Theater Air and Missile Defense Group (TAMDG)

The Navy theater-wide ballistic missile defense (TBMD) capability is scheduled for deployment in CG–52 class cruisers approximately in the year 2010. Deployment of this capability will make these ships high value strategic assets. If the CG–52 is to provide real protection, at least two and preferably three ships of this class must be kept forward deployed continuously in each of the high-threat theaters. The TAMDG would consist of two CG–52 ships for TBMD capability and would serve as host for the area air defense commander (AADC). These high-signature ships would

Figure 28–1. **Aircraft Carrier Battlegroup (CVBG)**

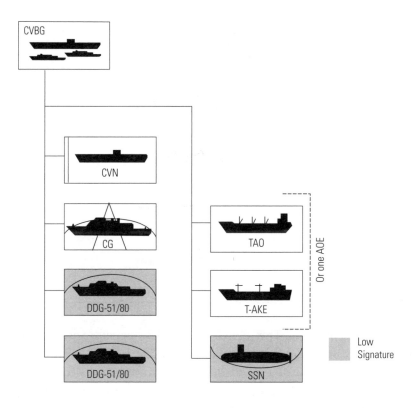

be positioned by the joint force commander (JFC), protected by a DDG–51 and an SSN, and generally stationed well within the defended envelope. Being forward deployed and continually on station, the TAMDG is well positioned to coordinate theater air and missile defenses. The AADC can marshal the resources of the fleet to provide a protective air and missile defense umbrella over the theater area of responsibility (AOR). The TAMDB is illustrated in figure 28–2.

Theater Land Attack Group (TLAG)

The Navy is scheduled to deploy an interim surface land attack capability in the CG–47, CG–52, and DDG–51 class ships by 2007, with a mature capability arriving in the DD(X) class starting in 2010. The TLAG of 2015 would consist of one DDG–51,

Figure 28–2. **Theater Air and Missile Defense Group (TAMDG)**

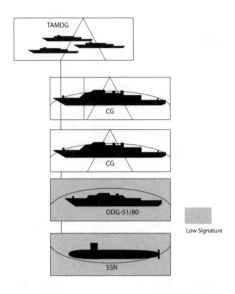

two DD(X), and one SSN. This TLAG will be a low-signature group capable of oper-ating at the edge of the defended envelope and will be capable of intervening decisively in corps-scale ground maneuver warfare. The forward-deployed TLAG will become another strategic asset. This group will be responsive to the JFC by maintaining a con-tinuous counterinvasion posture in peacetime. As additional TLAGs surge into theater, groups of this type become available to support forcible entry operations or to serve as a mobile naval firebase conducting deep interdiction operations. In the interim, the CG–52 and CG–47 could substitute for DD(X) starting in 2003. As NTW capability is deployed in the CG–52, they will no longer be available for this application. Nonethe-less, establishing interim TLAGs would allow early development of tactics and tactical doctrine for such a group, would firmly establish their role with the JFCs, and would provide an additional decade for the development of the naval fire support coordina-tion and command culture needed to turn this vital potential capability into a reality. Retaining the DD–963 and giving it the naval land-attack upgrade would be more log-ical than playing a shell game with the CG–52. But it would also be more costly than operating the FFG–31 that will be retained in its place pending the DD(X) arrival.[15] The TLAG is illustrated in figure 28–3.

Figure 28–3. **Theater Land Attack Group (TLAG)**

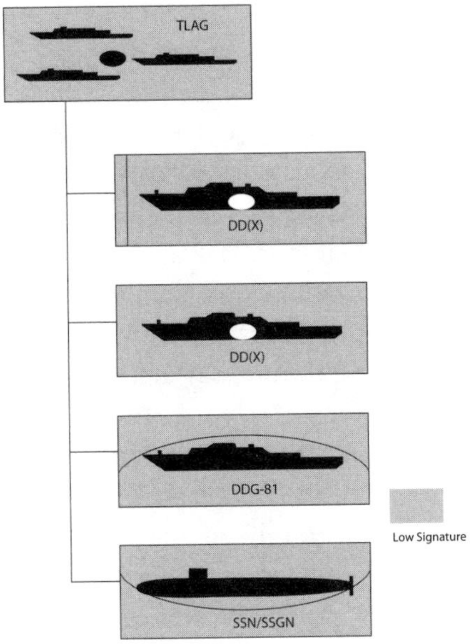

Mine Countermeasures Group (MCMG)

Naval mine warfare shapes the spatial and temporal dimensions of the littoral battlespace. A typical sea denial system consists of a regional ocean surveillance system, a command, control, communications, computers, and intelligence (C⁴I) element, a maritime strike element, a coastal defense element, a submarine warfare element, and a mine warfare element. As detailed in chapter 20, a properly integrated sea denial system can make maritime theater access quite difficult to assure. Over the next 20 years, we must expect to encounter some full-blown sea denial systems, a point well made in chapter 25. We are much more likely to face a light mine warfare threat in every operating area and a medium to heavy local mine warfare threat wherever an enemy nation deliberately plans aggression against our allies or our interests. We can no longer afford to wish away such threats. If we do not aggressively engage the mine warfare threat, we will find that our transoceanic power projection strategy becomes increasingly ineffective. This environment provides the strategic rationale for a major departure in our approach to mine warfare.

The Navy intends to distribute widely an organic mine countermeasure capability throughout the fleet. This capability should provide a sea mine reconnaissance and mine avoidance capability with a limited mine disposal capability. This approach provides for a reasonable mine threat characterization and the ability to operate the fleet with reasonable safety in areas of light mine threat. But it does not provide the capability to assure the safe and timely movement of shipping over sea lines of communication, nor does it provide the capability to open port approaches or to ensure safe operating areas for amphibious forcible entry operations in the face of a medium to heavy mine threat. A heavier, dedicated, forward-deployed MCM capability is required to deal with such threats in a timely manner. This would be combined with a comprehensive program to exploit organic MCM capabilities by conducting an extensive and sustained overt and covert mine reconnaissance/precision seabed mapping and surveillance program in peacetime to develop and sustain up-to-date databases for exploitation in crisis response and theater warfare. Every Navy ship in transit would thus become a data-gathering platform.

The mine countermeasures group is the embodiment of a dedicated MCM capability. It would consist of a mine countermeasures headquarters ship (MCS), an air MCM squadron equipped with modified Sea Hawk (CH–60) helicopters, a surface MCM squadron equipped with 4 Avenger-class mine countermeasures ships (MCM–1) and 3 Osprey-class mine hunter/coastal ships (MHC–51), a float-on/float-off (FLO/FLO) ship to provide high speed transport for the surface MCM squadron and a damaged ship evacuation capability, a sea barge ship (manned by Seabees, construction battalion personnel) to provide a magazine for assault MCM expendables and to transport eight landing craft air cushion vehicles modified for MCM duties (MCACs), and a SEAL team/underwater demolition team (UDT) group. This group would be complemented by an SSN for covert mine reconnaissance and a DDG–81 to provide area air defense and fire support for the MCM operation.

One mine countermeasures group should be forward deployed in Japan or prepositioned at Guam. This Western Pacific MCMG could be activated about the third day following notification, Day (N+3), and on station and fully effective by Day (N+7) in the Northeast Asia (NEA) region. We propose that a second MCMG be forward deployed in Southwest Asia (SWA) or prepositioned in Diego Garcia, Singapore, or Perth, Australia. This deployment gives a similar employment timeline in SWA to that defined for NEA. This group can also deploy to the Mediterranean AOR by Day (N+10). Thus, one-third of the U.S. MCM capability can be operational in either the SWA or NEA regions within 1 week and two-thirds within 10 days thereafter. The third MCMG would be based in Texas and would serve as an MCM training and experimental base. The third MCMG should also have a rapid deployment capability (a third FLO/FLO and Seabee barge would be needed).

Figure 28–4. **Mine Countermeasures Group (MCM)**

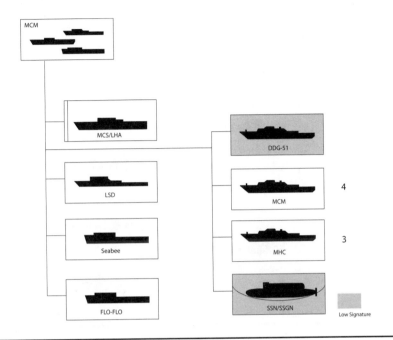

The mine countermeasures group is essential for ensuring theater access in the face of a sea denial system and provides a credible basis for reactive early forcible entry and deliberate forcible entry operations.

In addition to organic mine countermeasure capabilities, consisting largely of mine avoidance capabilities, a forward-deployed MCMG would be required to meet medium to high threat environments characteristic of forcible entry operations. The MCMG is illustrated in figure 28–4.

Expeditionary Littoral Attack Group[16]

The expeditionary littoral attack group (ELAG) of 2015–2021 would consist of four amphibious ships, a DDG–51, a special operations capable (SOC) SSN, and a DD(X) (DD[X] or Streetfighter). This configuration forms a complete group level system of systems, better allowing multiple tasking (split amphibious ready group operations), allows for increased combat vehicle embarkation, and provides space for rapid reconfiguration. The ELAG design provides full composite warfare commander battle management, two layers of AAW defense (JSF–M Marine version Joint Strike

Figure 28–5. **Expeditionary Land Attack Group (ELAG)**

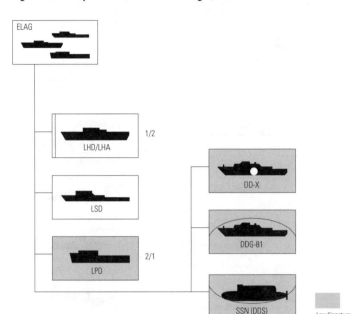

Fighters and SM–IIBK4 standard missiles for area air defense and ship self-defense system on all ships for local area and self-defense) and ASW defense (SSN for outer zone, the SH–60R from an amphibious assault ship [LHD] and destroyers for inner- and middle-zone ASW), substantial fire support capability, and covert intelligence, surveillance, and reconnaissance and special operations forces insertion/recovery capability. The ELAG command element would be fully capable of marshaling and directing the full resources of the fleet for intervention in ground maneuver combat. The Navy currently plans to support 36 amphibious warfare ships. The current Global Naval Force Presence Policy can be fully satisfied with 9 ELAGs using the current peacetime rotational cycle. While a standard ELAG composition containing two large deck amphibious ships would be ideal, the program of record will not support such a design. The actual force would contain two ELAG varieties. Three ELAG (H)s would each contain a LHD, a *Tarawa*-class amphibious assault ship (LHA), a *Whidbey Island*-class dock landing ship (LSD–41), and a *Harpers Ferry*-class (LSD–49) as their amphibious component. Six ELAG (M)s would each contain a LHD/LHA, two *San Antonio*-class amphibious transport docks (LPD–17s), and a LSD–41 or 49 in their amphibious component. The ELAG (H)s would be based to service the Northeast Asia and Mediterranean AORs where the experience of the last decade shows that split-ARG operations are most likely.

The ELAG, incorporating an enhanced four-ship ARG/MEU (SOC), would become the central building block for establishing amphibious forcible entry capabilities. This approach becomes possible because the ELAG has enough space to accommodate a complete battalion landing team (BLT) set of equipment with room in its lift print for reconfiguration afloat.[17]

The above naval operational architecture, consisting of five tactical groups, proposes a federated naval force operational architecture based on a small set of combined arms naval tactical groups. An operational concept is needed to animate this operational architecture. The naval operational concept would include a basing and deployment pattern that provides peacetime engagement forces for the joint force commanders and supports a crisis response pattern that sustains deterrence in the unengaged theaters while providing adequate and timely combat potential for employment in the engaged theater.[18] This early maritime forcible entry capability would be employable about Day (N+12) to (N+14). An operationally decisive deliberate maritime forcible entry capability may be rapidly concentrated for employment in major theater warfare about Day (N+30) to (N+35).

To have a credible maritime forcible entry capability, a naval force must be able to achieve and sustain air and sea dominance in the objective area, isolate the land battlespace from reinforcement, reduce resistance on the beach and inland landing zones to low levels, and rapidly breach or bypass all obstacles and barriers to ingress to and egress from the landing zones and landing force objectives. It must also be able to land rapidly and sustain a landing force of sufficient combat power to seize and hold its objectives.

A peacetime fleet between the years 2015 and 2021 would normally consist of a CVBG, a TAMDG, a TLAG, and an ELAG. By Day (N+10), this force level could be at least doubled. In addition, the forward-deployed/prepositioned MCMG and at least one maritime prepositioned squadron would have been activated and would have arrived on scene. This naval force constitutes a fairly large fleet. By Day (N+12), all of the preconditions for an early forcible entry (EFE) operation should have been achieved. We will now focus on how an amphibious task force with the mission payload for a Marine expeditionary brigade (MEB)—such as that detailed in chapter 23—can be rapidly formed from forward-deployed/forward-based forces and ready surge forces. The ELAG is illustrated in figure 28–5.

Early Forcible Entry Marine Expeditionary Brigade (MEB)

An amphibious advanced force would be formed from the regional MCMG, a TLAG, and an LHD from a forward-deployed ELAG (M) on or about Day (N+10). About the same time, a surging ELAG (H) and the remaining elements of the ELAG (M) would be concentrated in theater. The LHD of the ELAG (M) would be operated as a light aircraft carrier with a JSF–M air group. All surging and prepositioned shipping would sortie with a full personnel load. Other personnel would be flown to waypoints by commercial air transport to join ships in transit as they pass. Two composited enhanced MEUs represent the largest landing force reliably achievable on short notice with the existing program of record force. Some fairly minor modifications to the program of record open much broader horizons.

A service support package for fly-in Marine squadrons could be prepositioned on forward-deployed CVNs. The retirement of the Tomcat fighter (F–14) and Viking-ASW aircraft (S–3B) squadrons after 2006 will create enough space on the 2 CVNs of our notional force to accommodate the 3 Marine Corps fighter-attack squadrons and 1 reconnaissance-intelligence aircraft squadron of a Marine aircraft group (MAG). This action will allow the seabasing of a fixed wing MAG on the CVNs and LHD (which would function as a light aircraft carrier). We further propose stationing a large medium-speed roll-on/roll-off ship (LMSR) acquired as the third ship of maritime prepositioning force–enhanced (MPF–E) in Diego Garcia (designated T–AK). This T–AK would have about 250,000 square feet of excess space. We propose modifying this ship to accommodate a landing craft air cushion (LCAC) compatible side stage and provide personnel accommodations for 900 people (for example, tank battalion personnel plus naval support element detachment). The net result is that about 150,000 square feet of actual vehicle space would be available in this one ship. After unload, this T–AK would become a combat service support ship for the MEB. We would also propose that three LMSR variants be built (designated T–AKD). This class would have a 4 LCAC well deck, accommodations for 900 personnel, and 250,000 square feet of actual vehicle space. One of these three ships would also be prepositioned at Diego Garcia. The T–AK and T–AKD at Diego Garcia could support a forcible entry operation in the Mediterranean or Northeast Asia AORs by Day (N+12).

The landing force for our MEB can be a heavy brigade-sized ground combat element (GCE) with a substantial air combat element (ACE) and a lean combat service support element (CSSE) and at least 15 days of supply. The GCE could contain as many as one AAV mounted infantry battalion, one vertical assault battalion, a tank battalion (fly-in personnel, equipment aboard LMSR), and a light armored reconnaissance (LAR) battalion as its main close combat elements. Its ground fire support element would consist of one direct support artillery battalion and one high mobility artillery rocket (HIMAR) battery. The air transport component of the ACE is sufficient to deliver the vertical assault battalion in 2 lifts up to a 90 nautical mile radius in about 2 hours. The ATF surface assault can deliver 2 to 3 mechanized BLTs from about 20 nautical miles at sea in about 3 hours.

This EFE MEB (assault echelon [AE]) requires 315,000 square feet (350,000 square feet if we include the NSE with the MEB assault echelon). The combined gross vehicle space in the 2 ELAGs is 208,000 square feet. The LMSR (T–AK) as modified for MPF–E adds about a gross of 150,000 square feet. The T–AKD adds an additional gross of 250,000 square feet. The total gross vehicle square available in the early forcible entry ATF is thus 608,000 square-foot gross to house a 350,000 square-foot ATF. This yields a combat loading factor of ≈ 1.7. This extra space allows the landing force to reconfigure its load plan afloat if necessary.

The EFE ATF requires a well-designed deployment pattern controlled by a thoroughly professional joint maritime command element. This force could be the maritime component of a joint early entry task force that would resemble a small composite MEF. An Army airborne/air-landed brigade could provide a second ground combat element and an Air Force aerospace expeditionary force could reinforce the Marine ACE. Synchronization of the training, readiness, and deployment of the entire naval force will be required to ensure a responsive global surge capability, and a naval forces command (Navy/Marine Corps) could facilitate this essential task.

Deliberate Forcible Entry MEB

A deliberate forcible entry (DFE) force is another option available for military planners. A DFE force, available in the combat theater at Day (N+30), is a very large fleet including up to 5 CVBGs, 4 TAMDGs, 10 TLAGs, 2 MCMGs, and 1 expeditionary littoral attack force (ELAF) consisting of up to 2 MEB-size landing forces embarked on 2 ATFs. The MEB GCE is a heavy mechanized brigade with a robust ACE and a capable CSSE. Each MEB GCE is somewhat larger than that assigned to the EFE MEB. It has an additional mechanized BLT and artillery battalion. The DFE MEB can deliver 2 vertical assault BLTs up to 75 nautical miles inland in 2 lifts and can deliver 3 mechanized BLTs in 3 assault waves from about 20 nautical miles at sea in less than 2.5 hours. In this case, 2 ATFs with 32 of the planned 36 amphibious ships and 3 T–AKDs are committed to the operation. The DFE MEB GCE contains up to 3 AAV mounted infantry battalions, 1 LAR battalion, and a tank battalion as its main close combat elements. Its fire support element contains two direct support artillery battalions and a HIMAR battery. The corresponding ACE includes 32 Sea Stallion CH–53E, 48 Osprey MV–22, 24 Cobra AH–1 Z, and 12 Huey UH–1Y aircraft.

An MEB-sized amphibious task force contains 16 amphibious ships and 1 proposed T–AKD. The DFE MEB (AE) requires 365,000 square feet (about 410,000 square feet if the NSE is included with the MEB). The ATF is composed of one ELAG (H) and three ELAG (M)s. The total gross vehicle space in this force is 681,000 square feet (431,400 square feet in the ELAGs + 250,000 square feet in the AKD = 681,000 square feet). This yields a combat loading factor of 1.7. A combat loading factor of 1.3 represents a tight load with about 18 inches of space around each vehicle.[19]

The DFE ATF would be capable of delivering 4 mechanized BLTs ashore from about 20 nautical miles at sea in about 2 hours. It is also capable of delivering 2 air-mobile BLTs to landing zones at a radius of 100 nautical miles in about 2.5 hours.

In summary, a robust amphibious forcible entry capability could be employed at 35 days following conflict start (C+35). The planned 36 ship amphibious force is fully utilized in support of an ELAF and an advanced force; however, the planned lift fingerprint is much too tight to allow for load plan flexibility. As discussed, this deficiency can be corrected by acquisition of three LMSR variants. The fly-in of ACE elements to the forward-deployed carriers mentioned earlier would be essential to forcible entry operations. A substantial Marine SSP and personnel augmentation could also be accommodated. An SSP could be prepositioned on each of the three forward-deployed carriers.

Of note, the similarity between the two proposed forcible entry MEBs (EFE and DFE) and the MPF MEB design offers the possibility of standardizing the Marine Corps at the MEB level, which is discussed in chapter 22. A notional MEF would contain an MPF MEB and a DFE MEB.

Conclusion

The central feature of modern warfare is that a smaller, well-trained, well-balanced combined arms force is much more capable than a larger unbalanced force. The foregoing discussion is intended to provide a notional construct of how such a balanced naval force can be created with minor adjustments to the program of record. It is a compelling argument when one considers the emerging globalized security environment in which naval forces could be the primary means of establishing military access to areas of crisis.

Notes

[1] Bradley A. Fiske, "American Naval Policy," U.S. Naval Institute *Proceedings*, January 1905, 79.

[2] For a military perspective of the *systems of systems* concept, see William A. Owens with Edward Offley, *Lifting the Fog of War* (New York: Farrar, Straus and Giroux, 2000), 98–102, 224–225.

[3] The difference between an *operational architecture* and an *operational concept* is that the former documents how a naval force should be organized and the capabilities that it should possess, while an operational concept describes in more detail how the force expects to fight.

[4] Wayne P. Hughes, *Fleet Tactics: Theory and Practice* (Annapolis, MD: U.S. Naval Institute Press, 1986); and rev. ed., Hughes, *Fleet Tactics and Coastal Combat* (Annapolis, MD: U.S. Naval Institute Press, 2000).

[5] Hughes, *Fleet Tactics: Theory and Practice*, 1.

[6] Ibid., 25.

[7] Alfred Thayer Mahan, *The Influence of Seapower Upon History, 1660–1783* (New York: Dover Publications, 1987), 9–10.

[8] Ibid., 10.

[9] See, for example, Mahan's discussion in "Considerations Governing the Disposition of Navies," in *Mahan on Naval Strategy: Selections from the Writings of Rear Admiral Alfred Thayer Mahan* (Annapolis, MD: Naval Institute Press, 1991), 281–318.

[10] These are based on our own assessment of mission requirements in a globalized world and may not necessarily reflect current policy.

[11] The zero-warning condition is an essential force design assumption. As force designers, we are charged with providing the warfighter with a system that ensures a reasonable probability of success under plausible worst-case conditions. For the foreseeable future, the plausible worst-case condition is a zero-warning conflict in the presence of area denial systems armed with weapons of mass effect. Zero-warning conflicts can arise from the following conditions:

1. An enemy that attacks from an exercise posture without full force generation.
2. An enemy deployment pattern that gradually saturates the indication and warning indicators so that an attack-imminent condition becomes the routine situation leading to discounted warning.
3. An error in decisionmaking on the part of the President or the Secretary of Defense (for example, misinterpreting indications and warning).

[12] The dominant reference on network-centric warfare remains Arthur K. Cebrowski and John J. Gartska, "Network-Centric Warfare: Its Origin and Future," U.S. Naval Institute *Proceedings* 124, no. 1(January 1998), 28–35.

[13] Recognizing that both Clark A. Murdock (chapter 25) and Donald C.F. Daniel (chapter 27) argue that forward-deployed naval forces may not provide a significant deterrent, we have elected to focus on their capacity to support limited-objective offensive operations.

[14] Layered defenses are designed to provide multiple opportunities to intercept threats to the group. Optimally, a naval group should have both an area AAW defense and individual ship self-defense capabilities with a "depth of fire" that would allow for at least independent shots. A three-shot system reduces the possibility of a single missile leaking through to less than 3 percent. Likewise, the group should have an ASW outer zone, inner zone, and individual ship self-defense capabilities. In this regard, the group's acoustic and electronic operational signature largely determines the dimensions and location of safe operating areas.

[15] The FFG–31 class is the late construction product improvement of the FFG–7 design. Its combat system is more complete and better integrated than the earlier versions. An FFG–31 costs about half as much to operate as a DD–963 VLS.

[16] As noted in chapter 19 of the current volume, the Office of the Chief of Naval Operations has recently initiated development of a concept of an expeditionary assault group, consisting of Aegis DDGs, SSNs, and combat logistics ships attached to (and trained with) current amphibious ready groups (ARGs). However, similar proposals have been studied in the past without resulting in changes to the current ARGs. Our concept of expeditionary littoral attack groups is similar to the proposed expeditionary assault group but includes additional capabilities.

[17] A 60,000 square-foot enhanced MEU would be fitted into 104,000 square feet of actual space. This produces a combat loading factor of 1.7 versus the traditional 1.3. The current MEU lift print is ≈ 48,500 square feet.

[18] A full exploration of the future naval operational concept is beyond the scope of this chapter. We must settle for a short exposition on how our tactical groups may be orchestrated to create an early maritime forcible entry capability for joint decisive operations in smaller-scale contingencies and for tactically decisive forcible entry operations in the early stages of major theater warfare.

[19] The current lift print is even tighter because it includes vehicles preboated in the landing craft. A 1.7 combat loading factor eliminates the preboating and allows easy reconfiguration of the load plan afloat. A 2.0 combat loading factor would be needed if decontamination, container processing, and intermediate maintenance activity afloat were required.

Chapter 29

The Navy before and after September 11

Henry H. Gaffney

B efore September 11, the Navy was facing hard choices between maintaining force structure and transforming its forces, especially given resource constraints imposed by the Bush administration. After September 11, the Navy rose splendidly to support the campaign in Afghanistan. Two carriers were available in the Indian Ocean immediately, with two more joining within days. The Navy was also available for homeland defense of the United States, with carrier battlegroups deploying off the two coasts, and the USNS *Comfort* hospital ship and USNS *Denebola* supply ship deploying to New York.

Meanwhile, the United States has girded for more terrorist attacks at home. The intensive bombing campaign in Afghanistan to root out Osama bin Laden, demolish the al Qaeda training facilities, and bring down Taliban rule lasted 73 days, from October 7 to December 18.[1] Reportedly, 70 percent of the strikes in Afghanistan were by naval aircraft. Naval air continues to support the campaign. As of April 1, 2002, it was still necessary to strike al Qaeda regrouping facilities, and Omar and Osama still had not been captured.

Beyond the campaign in Afghanistan, the possibilities exist of similar follow-up campaigns to root out al Qaeda in Somalia, Yemen, and Indonesia (special forces are providing assistance in the Philippines and Yemen). Beyond these campaigns, it will take mostly police work and banking investigations to roll up al Qaeda. The Navy may be able to return to its normal operations by summer 2002, but for the foreseeable future, two carriers may be stationed in the Indian Ocean.

Henry H. Gaffney is a research manager at the CNA Corporation, serving as team leader for globalization research and as director of the Strategy and Concepts Group of the Center for Strategic Studies. He has conducted research for senior defense leaders and served in the U.S. Mission to NATO. He has authored numerous research studies, reports, and professional articles, particularly in the U.S. Naval Institute *Proceedings*. His latest article, "Globalization Gets a Bodyguard" (co-authored with Thomas P.M. Barnett), appeared in the November 2001 U.S. Naval Institute *Proceedings*.

The attacks on the United States came at a moment when the U.S. economy was entering recession. The attacks have reinforced that recession, although recent statistics indicate recovery may be sooner than expected. Yet the combination of budget increases and supplementals for the war have improved the Navy's budget. However, the combination of recession and extra expenses for rebuilding, homeland defense, the war, and stimuli for the economy is leading to a return to a deficit in the Federal budget. This in turn will eventually put a squeeze on the level of the defense budget, even though it is being increased in the near term. With only a vaguely defined role in homeland security, the Navy would then be back to making hard choices about its forces, operations, and modernization, subject to guidance from the administration—choices that may well lead to reductions in the number of ships. The Navy will then have to choose between several options—for example, shrinking the combat elements proportionately, emphasizing one over the other, or taking new paths that are not necessarily dependent on the number of ships to increase capabilities. Naval aviation, including the carriers, has made such a crucial contribution to the campaign in Afghanistan that cutting the number of carriers below 12 is hard to imagine, despite rumors to that effect.

The Navy before September 11

Programs and Force Structure. In its programs and budgets, the Navy and Marine Corps were slated for approximately $99 billion per annum of the overall Department of Defense funding profile of nearly $332 billion. Even at that level, the Congressional defense appropriation categories of *Ship Construction and Conversion, Navy* (SCN) and *Aviation Procurement, Navy* (APN) were underfunded. As a result, the Navy was finding it hard to sustain enough shipbuilding to maintain a force structure level of 312 ships. Indeed, both the guided missile destroyer (DDG–51) and amphibious transport dock (LPD–17) programs were experiencing cost overruns, taking even more funds than originally planned. One alternative that had been floated was to reduce the overall fleet to 11 carriers and 11 amphibious ready groups (ARGs) to fund the ship construction shortfall. However, the Defense Planning Guidance (issued before September 11) directed the services to maintain their current manpower and, by implication, total force structure. On the other hand, compensation and medical care had both been improved, and recruitment and retention were up.

Readiness was improving, especially for deploying ships. The F/A–18E/F Strike Hornet aircraft was in full production, and the Joint Strike Fighter (JSF) program source selection was drawing near. But production of MV–22 Osprey was set back by 2 more years for further development. The DD 21 Zumwalt-class land attack destroyer program source selection had been deferred since the last days of the Clinton administration, and it was in trouble with both the Bush administration and Congress. The submarine force used the conclusion of a recent Joint Chiefs of Staff study that 68 nu-clear-powered attack submarines (SSNs) were required to sustain a level of at least 55 in an operational status. A decision had not yet been made to proceed with the con-version of Trident nuclear-powered ballistic missile submarines (SSBNs) to nuclear-powered cruise missile attack submarines (SSGNs). The Navy was shifting from spe-cialized mine warfare forces to organic mine countermeasures throughout the fleet. Given that the Bush administration was directing that the services keep force struc-ture, the Office of the Secretary of Defense and the Secretary of the Navy were looking for efficiencies instead, including a targetting goal of up to $10 billion in savings a year for the Navy. As planned, these efficiencies would include base closures, but Congress has deferred their consideration to 2005.

Operations. In its forward deployments, the Navy was maintaining the deploy-ment of 2.5 carrier battlegroups and ARGs. With readiness improvements, the de-ploying ships were adequately supplied, although the problems with Vieques were threatening predeployment training. The Navy was continuing its role in Operation *Southern Watch*, which necessitated a 1.0 carrier presence in the Gulf, and had thus re-duced its Mediterranean carrier presence to 0.5 (while the western Pacific carrier pres-ence was around 1.4, counting USS *Kitty Hawk* in Japan). However, it no longer had a role in the Adriatic. Operations *Southern* and *Northern Watch* and drug patrols were keeping EA–6Bs and E–2Cs busy. The multinational interception operation (MIO) was maintained in the Gulf to prevent Iraq from smuggling oil. Turn-around ratios for vessel and deploying units had been growing somewhat longer—up toward 4.0 in the Atlantic Fleet—especially given the increasing number of nuclear carriers in the fleet and their longer maintenance needs. The interdeployment training cycle (IDTC) was thus being more carefully managed, and naval personnel were not as stressed during the IDTC as they had been earlier. After the bombing of the USS *Cole* in Aden, force protection measures had been stepped up, leading to even fewer in-port days in the Gulf. SSBNs continued their routine patrols. Goals for personnel tempo (PER-STEMPO), the amount of time personnel spent deployed as compared to time in homeport or training, had not been broken since Operation *Desert Storm.*

Future planning. In the defense debates about the future, the Navy continued to stress its unique contributions to forward presence, to engagement with countries, and to navy-to-navy contacts—altogether referred to as combat credible forward presence. The submarine force emphasized its value in gathering intelligence. The Navy contin-ued to be concerned with antiaccess—the threats from mines, diesel submarines, shore-based cruise missiles, and swarming small boats (but not particularly with com-bat aircraft flying out to sea; Aegis provides good protection, and few if any hostile countries train that way). For future capabilities, the Navy advocated netcentric war-fare, although it was not clear what it consisted of beyond the ongoing Cooperative

Engagement Capability (CEC) program. The Navy had gained enormous amounts of dedicated communication frequency bandwidth throughout the 1990s, which permitted it to install the IT–21 Internet system on ships, communicate better with airborne warning and control systems (AWACS), and receive joint air tasking orders electronically (which had been a problem during *Desert Storm*).

Together the Navy and Marine Corps had begun the Navy-Marine Corps Common Internet (NMCI) program to connect all Navy and Marine units at sea and ashore.[2] The Navy was acquiring more precision-guided munitions (PGMs). Tomahawk had already gained the surface combatant force an independent role. Vice Admiral Arthur Cebrowski—from his position as president of the Naval War College and immediate supervisor of the new Naval Warfare Development Command—pushed for the small littoral combatant concept called Streetfighter, although it had not yet received funding in the overall program.[3] CVNX and DD 21 represented the epitome of research and development (R&D) for ships—R&D directed at reducing manning, developing electric drive motors, and so forth. The prospect of a short take-off and landing version of the JSF meant that air-capable ship platforms might be multiplied.[4] The Navy was more timid about acquiring unmanned aerial vehicles (UAVs), though. The possibility of a near-amphibious family of maritime prepositioning force forward positioned (MPF[F]) ships was discussed, but it was not yet funded in the program. The last of 20 large roll-on/roll-off sealift ships had been launched. Discussion about stretching presence through the rotation of crews, double-crewing, or overseas homeporting (especially in Guam) kept coming up, but such programs have not been executed.

Upon September 11

The Navy responded quickly. For homeland defense, an aircraft carrier and several Aegis ships were deployed toward New York, and similar measures were taken on the West Coast. The hospital ship USNS *Comfort* was manned and got under way to help in New York in 24 hours rather than the 5 days planned for it. Some of the Navy's *Cyclone*-class patrol craft, originally built for special forces, augmented the Coast Guard. The aircraft carriers USS *Carl Vinson* and the USS *Enterprise* were already in the Indian Ocean, and the USS *Theodore Roosevelt* was deployed 6 weeks earlier than planned and eventually relieved the *Enterprise*. The USS *Kitty Hawk* was stripped of most of its air wing and sent from Japan to the Indian Ocean to serve as a staging base for Army Special Forces. Tomahawks were on station on surface combatants and SSNs. The carrier aircraft carrying out strike missions into Afghanistan were refueled by Navy carrier-based S–3s and Air Force land-based (and long-range) KC–10s and were directed in their attacks by AWACS as well as through tracking on laser guidance provided by special forces on the ground. Numerous surface combatants were in the area, including those involved in the ongoing MIO in the Gulf. Naval presence in the

Mediterranean and Western Pacific was reduced.[5] The political pressure on the controversy over the live-fire range at Vieques had receded into the background and the referendum in Puerto Rico postponed. Altogether, the Navy was in the vicinity of Afghanistan, highly ready and responsive, for any joint action to be executed. PERSTEMPO was (and is) being substantially broken for the first time since *Desert Storm*, but it may turn out to be necessary only for the crews of the carriers, not those of surface combatants and ARGs. The Marines were directed to set up a base south of Kandahar and later moved to Kandahar airport. Force protection measures that had been set in train after the *Cole* bombing were intensified.

Defense has been authorized $345 billion for fiscal year (FY) 2002, including the $332 billion originally planned plus the supplemental. The supplemental provides minimal additions for the Navy, however. Two Trident SSGN conversions have been funded (two more were added in the FY03 budget submission). PGM inventories are funded. The budget does not, however, solve the SCN and APN deficits, and the Navy planned to finance only five new ships with FY02 funds.

The new requirements for homeland defense were being studied intensively, but there remains considerable uncertainty as to what the role of the Navy may be. The Coast Guard is already taking much of the action to patrol harbors—witness their careful escorting of a natural gas tanker into Boston Harbor in October 2001.[6] The Coast Guard has had to give up other missions, such as drug patrols.[7] It is not clear whether the Coast Guard will be adequately funded for its new missions with the mere $203 million it has received in supplemental funding. Its Deepwater program may well be subject to new review.[8] The Navy is concerned with international airliner attacks, attacks on cruise ships à la the USS *Cole*, and rogue merchant ships. Better intelligence and intelligence coordination is the first need, for the problem of rogue merchant ships must be identified at the port of embarkation.

The Changed Long-Term Outlook for the Navy

Operations. For Navy deployments, the long-term outlook for the Navy will initially be driven by the intensity and length of the campaign in Afghanistan. The Navy would be under great strain if it were required to keep four (or even three) carriers on station in the Indian Ocean.[9] In *Desert Storm*, 6 carriers were present (and 2 more were being readied), but the war lasted only 45 days. If the Navy were to maintain four carriers on station, the IDTC would be greatly shrunk after a year, with consequent problems in training and maintenance. But the pace of strikes in Afghanistan hardly compares to *Desert Storm* or Kosovo, and two carriers in the Indian Ocean seem sufficient. A total of 2 can be sustained indefinitely with the current force of 12 carriers, although the carrier presence in the Mediterranean would go to near-zero, and in the Western Pacific the presence would be around 1.0 (the aircraft carrier homeported in

Japan.) If the United States were to establish substantial airbases and a fighter air-craft presence in Uzbekistan, Tajikistan, or Kyrgyzstan, the carriers might not be needed at all, and one of them could return to a resumed *Southern Watch* over Iraq (*Southern Watch* has been maintained minimally by the Air Force during the Afghanistan conflict).

It is of note that only a minimal number of Tomahawks were fired into Afghanistan so far, and few escort ships are accompanying the carriers, perhaps be-cause of the absence of any retaliatory threat. It may be that surface combatants can maintain their regular schedules and not even break PERSTEMPO. The same would apply to submarines. The Marine expeditionary unit special operations capable (MEU[SOC]) was deployed in December 2001 from the USS *Pelileu* ARG to Afghanistan, where it set up Camp Rhino southwest of Kandahar, later moved to Kan-dahar airport, and was replaced by units of the Army's 101st Airmobile Division in Jan-uary 2002. Another ARG/MEU(SOC) remains in the Indian Ocean. It was not so much Marine amphibious capability but rather its inherent expeditionary ability to sustain itself on the ground for 30 days with minimal resupply that counted on this occasion, though they were readily available to move from the sea to shore staging points.

If the war were extended to Iraq (while continuing in Afghanistan), the demands on the Navy would be huge. The consumption of munitions could be enormous, and the United States might have to go on some kind of wartime footing to produce the required ordnance and call up reservists. So far, Saddam Husayn has not provided the excuse for such a war, even though—according to the former two major theater war doctrine—opportunistic adversaries are expected to take advantage of U.S. distraction to attack their neighbors.

In March 2002, the campaign in Afghanistan renewed its intensity with the bat-tles near Gardez. However, the Taliban was out of power, and the previous operating and training bases of al Qaeda had been demolished. But Mohammed Omar and Osama bin Laden had escaped, along with much of the al Qaeda leadership. Some of the al Qaeda operatives in the 60 cells in countries around the world were in custody, but many were still at large, and the question remained open as to how loosely (versus centrally) directed al Qaeda really was, and how dependent on both the charisma and decisions of bin Laden. Some U.S. military attention was shifting to Somalia and the Philippines. Yemen was being watched, and U.S. Special Forces were sent to train its troops. The new homeland defense agency under former Governor Thomas Ridge was doing much in the way of planning for contingencies and for the reorganization of do-mestic security agencies. Warnings were frequent, but no new terrorist incidents had taken place.

Aside from the continuing campaign to round up al Qaeda operatives and break the organization, the world of conflicts and confrontations would probably revert to what it had been before September 11, but with some changed attitudes and per-spectives about what had previously been considered the threats to U.S. and world se-curity. The United States is already developing better relations with Russia, following President Vladimir Putin's initiatives to "join the West." The China-Taiwan con-frontation had been softening, with complicated politics in Taiwan and a recession in the Taiwanese economy. China is entering the World Trade Organization. North Korea and Iraq are still hostile, but the slow evolution of Iranian politics continues. Their minimal cooperation on Afghanistan, however minimal, lay in contrast to their shipping of arms to the Palestinians. The Israeli-Palestinian war continues. In Europe, the only current action is in the Balkans, where peacekeeping forces are still present in Bosnia and Kosovo, and a truce has been arranged in Macedonia. Naval forces are not needed in the Adriatic Sea for now. The Mediterranean region is otherwise quiet: Libya seems restrained of late; the Algerian civil war is quiet for the moment; and Greek-Turkish enmities, including those over Cyprus, are being handled by diplo-matic means.

Thus, the Persian Gulf and Indian Ocean area remain the priority for both joint forces and U.S. naval forces for the foreseeable future. The shift to an East Asian strat-egy with accompanying shifts of forces, which the administration indicated earlier might happen, seems to have been put aside for the duration. The future of an Asian strategy depends on whether the war on terror changes the otherwise confrontational relations between the United States and China.

The possibility exists for more Navy assets—for example, ships and patrol/early warning aircraft such as P–3s, E–2Cs—to be devoted to patrolling home waters. As noted, the Coast Guard has had to give priority to homeland defense measures over patrolling for drug traffic. The Navy may be affected as well. There is also a question of the extent to which budget resources will be devoted to force protection; the amounts might seem marginal, but all current programs operate on a tight margin in any case. Force protection is yet another burden on the Department of the Navy's budget. As for the need for coastal patrols, it appears that gathering intelligence and tips would be more important to the interception of the great threats—rogue mer-chant ships—with the consequent need to be able to vector an intercepting ship or air-craft out quickly. In the longer term, homeland defense might involve having surface combatants contribute to national missile defense and thus not be available for over-seas deployments. The decisions on the naval contribution to missile defense depend on the success of R&D and thus lie years in the future.

Future planning. As for future naval programs, the United States and the world are in an economic slump approaching a recession. The time and path of economic recovery is uncertain. Together with tax cuts, the U.S. economic slowdown will lead to a renewed Federal Government deficit. The deficit, combined with measures for homeland defense, will put a new squeeze on the defense budget. Initially for the FY03 program and budget submission, the Navy proposed to retire the rest of the *Spruance*-class destroyers, thus going down to 98 surface combatants, and to reduce to 286 total ships. New guidance for the preparation of the FY03 budget, with the possibility of a 15 percent budget increase, may allow the Navy to increase SCN and keep anywhere from 305 to 325 ships. It is hard to believe that such an increase will in fact be realized before the economy shows growth again, but the FY03 budget deliberations in Congress will provide the answer.

Since September 11, Lockheed-Martin was chosen in the JSF source selection, so a program that some thought to be a candidate for cancellation proceeds (toward an initial operational capability of 2008, presumably for the Air Force version). In the meantime, production of F/A–18E/F is to proceed at a full 48 aircraft a year. The DD 21 program is to be restructured to be the DD(X), a multipurpose platform rather than one mostly dedicated to shore bombardment. Smaller and more modular versions were under discussion. In addition, a new air defense cruiser class built on the same hull as the DD(X) has been proposed. In the meanwhile, service life extension of the 22 CG–47 class ships with the vertical launch system (VLS) has been initially funded. They would eventually be missile defense ships; however, the Navy Area Defense program has been cancelled and the Navy Theater Wide missile defense lies well into the future. The Navy's programmed budget for FY03 (PR03) proposes to slip CVNX funding one year, from FY06 to FY07. Although it looked like four Tridents would be converted to SSGNs, the submarine construction program still did not have room to ramp up to funding of two SSN–774s a year. Not included in the PR03 submission was funding for a proposed littoral combat ship (LCS) as a spin-off of the DD(X) program. LCS would be essentially a mission-limited version of Cebrowski's Streetfighter concept.

Otherwise, replacements for amphibious assault ships (LHA follow-ons, including funding for LHD–8), P–3 maritime patrol aircraft (the proposed multipurpose maritime aircraft), new maritime prepositioning ships, LCC command ships (the JCC(X) joint command ship program), and EA–6B (possibly replaced by the F/A–18G[10]) were still in the analysis-of-alternatives stage, with no places yet in the actual program of record.

So far, we see an emerging Navy that generally looks like the pre-September 11 Navy of the 1990s. A struggle has been occurring between the Office of the Secretary of Defense, which wants transformation, and the services, which seek to keep force structure in the numbers and shapes they have had. But much transformation takes place *on* the platforms rather than through creating new platforms—such as all the PGMs entering the force (including Tactical Tomahawk), the interconnections (IT–21, NMCI, and CEC), and the upgrading and evolution of Aegis and Standard missiles for missile defense. The Navy still struggles with mine warfare and cruise missile defenses—the main (and old) instruments of antiaccess. And it worries about diesel submarines in the littoral warfare context.

Alternatives for a Future Navy

There is a lot of discussion about futuristic concepts: Streetfighter (will the LCS version of DD[X] suffice?); space warfare; netcentric warfare; big shifts to UAVs; fast transport with *Jervis Bay*-type ships, etc.[11] None of these have acquired a place in prospective force structures as yet. More important for the allocation of resources would be progress on missile defense, both for homeland defense and tactical and theater defense in combat zones overseas.

Uncertainty about the duration of the war in Afghanistan would tend to postpone any radical thinking or changes in Navy deployments or training. The aircraft carriers are in the limelight and are likely to be tied down in the Indian Ocean for the foreseeable future. The Navy can sustain two carriers on station in the Indian Ocean indefinitely with its current force structure and deployment schedules. The operational need is less for surface combatants, submarines, and amphibious ships, so they can presumably stick more closely to normal rotations. In any case, the Persian Gulf and Indian Ocean area is pegged as the cockpit of the world for the foreseeable future, and a "carrier-centric" Navy has proven its worth.

If indeed carriers and naval aviation are the wave of the future (and noting how dependent they are in functioning within a joint structure, for target selection, refueling, and target direction on the scene), one might well imagine an even greater shift to carriers—but the ability to ramp up carrier construction is severely constrained, as is aircraft production. But that would be only one model of the possible future Navy.

The big questions affecting future overall U.S. defense efforts would be the shape of the world, the incidence of conflict in that world, and how U.S. foreign policy reacts to and engages in the world—in other words, the particulars of globalization. Since the other chapters have discussed these topics and they are too complex to detail here, I will confine this discussion to variations of the current Navy. In any case, it is my view that the triad of world evolution/globalization, U.S. foreign policy, and the evolution of U.S. forces is only loosely connected. But in that series of loose connections lie flexibility and adaptability for the appropriate evolution of the forces and their uses by U.S. political authorities.

Persistent constraints on the configuration of naval forces will continue to exist. These constraints will include tighter budgets, which lead to the inevitable long-term trend of the decline of numbers as the capabilities get more sophisticated. Fortunately, no country is exempt from such trends—unlike during the Cold War, when the Soviet Union defied economics for 45 years and paid the price with its total collapse. The second constraint is the legacy forces—past investments that are still useful—such as aircraft carriers and supposedly range-limited F/A–18s. Third is the fact that there are no competing global navies out there. The Navy is more worried about opposition from the shore, a situation that is effectively a "constraint" that shapes the sort of Navy to be built.[12]

A final constraint is the fact that every future campaign the United States commits its military forces to will be joint, with only trivial exceptions. The United States likes to use as many tools in the tool box as it can lay its hands on; however, arguably, the Navy is most likely to be used when it provides unique rather than simply complementary capabilities.

How the Navy stands now. The Navy had the capabilities on hand that were appropriate for the campaign in Afghanistan. The carriers were quickly on hand, and F–14s and F/A–18s conducted strikes with PGMs. Some Tomahawks were also fired. The strikes were conducted in a joint operation: they were generally directed from the air headquarters at Prince Sultan Air Force Base in Saudi Arabia. They were responsive to special forces spotters on the ground. They were refueled by U.S. Air Force and Royal Air Force tankers as well as their own S–3 Viking aircraft. The USS *Kitty Hawk* provided a mobile staging base for special forces helicopters. The Marines were offshore, ready to be moved into Afghanistan. These same forces would be appropriate to similar operations in Somalia or Yemen (which are even more accessible from the ocean), or to strike Iraq. The Navy's homeland defense roles remain to be determined. It is likely to be used more as a response force than a routine patrol force. The indefiniteness of the operations off Afghanistan may eventually strain the forces.

Beyond these operations, the Navy will look again to the future. The future will remain constrained by the defense budget, which is not likely to be generous if the economy continues to have difficulties, the Federal budget is in deficit, and tax cuts maintain their priority.

However, the Navy has realized numerous improvements in its programs, even despite the constant use of the *Weapons Procurement, Navy* (WPN) and *Other Procurement, Navy* (OPN) accounts as bill-payers. The platforms themselves are slowly evolving. There is a strong emphasis on littoral warfare. The force is becoming more joint. Missile defense, however, is likely to continue in development for some years to come.

Alternative evolutions. Several major directions can be postulated for the future Navy. These alternatives revolve around the five major combatant platforms: aircraft carriers and naval aviation, surface combatants, amphibious ships, attack submarines (SSNs and SSGNs), and SSBNs. Whatever the talk about netcentric warfare, the Navy will remain platform-centric if it is to continue to be a navy, that is, if it is to be at sea and afloat. Any network must have nodes, and ships are the maritime nodes. What is done off these platforms, and how they are connected, especially in joint operations, is nonetheless important and most improvements are directed to these ends. Four alternatives for the composition of the Navy can be set forth:

- Evolution of the current five platforms *versus* the development of radically different maritime platforms.
- A naval fleet that becomes more joint in its ability to transport and sustain Army and Air Force units *versus* a focus on improving the support of a independent littoral operation by the Marine Corps.
- The current fleet balance of the same five combat platforms *versus* a drastic rebalancing based on a different concept and operational architecture for naval platforms.
- A continuation of the post-Cold War evolution toward greater reach in littoral operations (that is, forward-deployed strike against land targets) *versus* a navy focused primarily on sea control and homeland defense.

In light of the sunk costs of legacy forces—and because even these legacy forces are better than those of any other country in the world—and given that carriers have proven so valuable in *Desert Storm, Southern Watch,* Kosovo, and Afghanistan, an evolutionary force dominated by carriers and naval aviation is most likely.[13] This force would probably remain at 12 carriers, despite competing arguments about why it should be 10 or 15. However, keeping 12 carriers and equipping them with new aircraft in the future almost inevitably would squeeze the numbers of surface combatants and submarines. The Navy had already planned to reduce the amphibious force to 36 ships with the introduction of the LPD–17 *San Antonio*-class. But the LPD–17 construction program is taking longer than expected, and the Navy could decide to retire aging amphibious dock land ships and LPDs earlier than planned. If this evolutionary process to maintain some balance among the platforms continues, the future MPF(F) program as currently conceived is unlikely to find a place in the budget. F/A–18E/F aircraft constitute a successful program, and their production would continue until JSF became available—providing JSF is actually brought to completion (remembering the experience with prototypes of the F–22). Decisions on the replacement of P–3s may drag on for some time. SH–60s would continue as mainstay helicopters, but the fate of the MV–22 becomes uncertain at this juncture. The Trident SSBNs would likely remain at 14 for the indefinite future. Whatever the minor changes in the balances among the five platforms, this evolutionary process would nonetheless provide a versatile toolbox.

The other alternatives are unlikely to be chosen for political and industrial base reasons, but they illustrate choices that might have to be made. Some of the more likely arguments include:

Retention of current warfare communities. There are thresholds below which any of the Navy communities might not survive. The greatest flexibility lies in the number of surface combatants. Submarines could be reduced—but to what level? One Navy study of force alternatives thought the lowest number of submarines was 38, but the British sustain a community with 16 SSBNs and SSNs. The issue of what force levels are required to justify the existence of a specialized warfare community is contentious.[14]

Survival of the Marine Corps. If all major operations are to be joint, as has been increasingly the case over the past 3 decades, it is unlikely the future Navy would be re-configured solely to support Marine Corps amphibious landings. The MV–22 is now in trouble, and the Marines were transported into Afghanistan without it. As noted, MPF(F) may not find a place in the budget—though how to extend the capability rep-resented by the present "black hulls" of the Maritime Prepositioning Squadron to the Army would have to be examined. And the precision aviation drops demonstrated in Afghanistan would seem to reduce the necessity of long-range guns.

Diversion of resources to homeland defense. Homeland defense could conceivably pose serious constraints on the numbers of naval ships that could deploy overseas. Be-fore September 11, the dilemma of diverting a major part of the cruiser force to mis-sile defense was being contemplated. Surface combatants could be placed in a new ver-sion of the distant early warning line extension of the 1950s, but that is unlikely.[15] The patrol craft (PCs) have taken on a new utility in homeland waters and might not be re-tired.[16] An increase in the Coast Guard might come at the cost of the Navy (but is highly unlikely to, given the committee structure in Congress). A new emphasis on SSBNs might even come into play down the road, depending on intercontinental bal-listic missile threats to the United States.

What Will Future Evolutions of the Navy Have to Do with Globalization?

How appropriate are these evolutionary naval forces for the foreseeable future? It is very important that such issues are addressed in the context of globalization.

Globalization, a dynamic process, is a current characterization of the world sys-tem that is expressed in economic, social, and cultural terms, with governments and politics in mediating roles. It is not a system expressed in military terms—unlike the Cold War, the military balance of power thinking of the 19th century, or the theoreti-cal bipolarity or multipolarity concepts in international relations. Basing our concep-tion of the international system on an exclusively military focus leads to zero-sum arms races, confrontations, and posturing. Basing the system on the economic focus of globalization is non-zero-sum—everybody gains—with governments in mediating, rule-setting roles rather than in directing roles. Since military establishments are in turn instruments of governments, they do not have (despite the arguments of many chapters in this volume) any obvious direct roles in economic matters.

Looking at the U.S. military establishment in this globalization context, we can note—consistent with the Quadrennial Defense Review 2001—that its effects on economic development lie in deep historical background to the globalizing world that evolved out of the Cold War world (and before that, World War II). As the sole surviving *superforce* (following the collapse of the Soviet military), the U.S. military establishment saves most other countries of the world from having to build their own superforces, or even much of any kind of forces at all. That in itself is worth our military investment during this current era of globalization.

Continuing technological improvements in our military forces—as demonstrated in the chain from *Desert Storm* through Kosovo to Afghanistan—dissuade other countries from making investments in the technological improvements heralded by the revolution in military affairs.[17] Beyond that, our high-technology military specifically deters what were previously referred to as the four rogue states (Libya, Iraq, Iran, and North Korea)—and now the axis of evil (plus Libya)—from aggression against their neighbors. And beyond that, our extensive forces have been available to intervene along the fringes of the functioning globalized economy in those mostly internal conflicts that arise but are not necessarily threatening to the overall economics of the globalization process. In other words, they are sometimes the enabler of our humanitarian instincts in a chaotic Third World. In deep background to all this is the general deterrent of U.S. strategic nuclear forces.

What roles do U.S. naval forces play in this? In sustaining the largest and most capable blue-water navy in the world, the U.S. Navy is part of the global historical background to the current general peace that has permitted globalization to proceed. The United States has discouraged and dissuaded other navies from building up, especially with carriers (not counting vertical or short take-off and land [V/STOL] aircraft carriers). They are a major deterrent to three of the four rogues (Iraq and Iran—especially, and also Libya; the major deterrent to North Korea is South Korean forces, backed by U.S. nuclear weapons). They are a deterrent to Chinese threats (if not attacks) on Taiwan. In interventions, they are a crucial part of U.S. joint forces, providing offshore bases—such as during operations in Afghanistan (they were less essential for the Kosovo war where land bases were available). Despite the concerns expressed in chapter 8, they do not need to patrol the sea lines of communication and straits (with the exception of the Strait of Hormuz) because the ocean threats are practically nonexistent—unless an actual rogue terrorist merchant ship threat to the U.S. homeland were to materialize. U.S. Navy SSBNs will soon be providing 73 percent of U.S. strategic nuclear missile warheads in that deep background role.

These roles within the globalization context do not in themselves provide very specific guidance on how to configure U.S. naval forces. It is not clear how numbers of ships count in this context, given the lack of threats at sea and the fact that in the global economy, every other country operates under the same kind of budget constraints as the United States, although more so. The U.S. Navy is conducting far more innovation in platforms, technology, communications, and weapons than any other navy, so this dissuasion function can continue to be served. The U.S. Navy practice of deployments and associated readiness means that it can continue to sustain a substantial presence in the most distant waters, that is, the Persian Gulf. As noted in chapter 6, this in turn provides a major stabilization of the oil market.

In a globalizing world, it may be that the worse threat to the U.S. Navy is the fact that it is taken for granted. Evolutionary developments conducted in the background are easily ignored, or worse yet, put off or underfunded. There will always be a per-suasive advocate of the latest strategic buzzword or hottest weapon system who will be able to attract public attention away from the dissuasive function, even though dis-suasion may be the most important way that U.S. military forces can assist globaliza-tion. If you want effective dissuasion in a globalizing world, you need an effective, overwhelming, global navy.

Notes

[1] Coincidentally, Operation *Allied Force* in Kosovo and Serbia lasted 78 days, but it was toward a definite end (Milosevic's capitulation). The end in Afghanistan is not in sight.

[2] A good summary of Navy-Marine Corps Common Internet implementation is Bill Murray, "Joining Forces," *Government Executive*, December 2000, 42–46.

[3] See, for example, Greg Jaffe, "Debate Surrounding Small Ship Poses Fundamental Questions For U.S. Navy," *The Wall Street Journal*, July 11, 2001, 1.

[4] For a discussion of Navy views on vertical short take-off and landing and short take-off and vertical landing, see Charles H. Brown, "Up, Up and Away," U.S. Naval Institute *Proceedings* 127, no. 8 (August 2001), 36–40.

[5] In 1999, during Operation *Allied Force* in Kosovo and Serbia, the USS *Kitty Hawk* was sent to the Gulf to cover for the USS *Theodore Roosevelt*, which had been diverted to the Adriatic. There was then a public controversy in the United States concerning the fact that the Western Pacific had been left uncovered. No such hue and cry was raised in 2001 when the *Kitty Hawk* was deployed to the Indian Ocean.

[6] Pressure by Boston officials to stop or escort liquid natural gas (LNG) tankers had been intense. See "Coast Guard Revokes Ban on Natural-Gas Shipments," The *Wall Street Journal*, October 17, 2001, B6B; William B. Cassidy, "USCG lifts Boston LNG blockade," *Traffic World*, November 5, 2001, 31.

[7] See, for example, Robert S. Boyd, " Coast Guard's Focus Has Shifted Since 9/11," *Philadelphia Inquirer*, February 18, 2002, 1; Matthew Weinstock, "Changing Course," *Government Executive*, December 2001, 55–57.

[8] See discussion in Vago Muradian, "Deepwater More Important Ever For Coast Guard, Requirements Un-changed," *Defense Daily*, December 7, 2001, 1.

[9] In the event, four carriers were present together for only about a week. USS *Theodore Roosevelt* relieved *En-terprise*, and *Kitty Hawk* returned to Japan in December once special forces had bases on land adjacent to Afghanistan.

[10] See Allan J. Assel, "Airborne Electronic Attack: What's Next," U.S. Naval Institute *Proceedings* 126, no. 2 (Feb-ruary 2001), 52–55.

[11] The original articles on Streetfighter include: Arthur K. Cebrowski and Wayne P. Hughes, "Rebalancing the Fleet," U.S. Naval Institute *Proceedings* 124, no. 11 (November 1999), 31–34; Wayne P. Hughes, "22 Questions for

Streetfighter," U.S. Naval Institute *Proceedings* 125, no. 2 (February 2000), 46–49. On naval space warfare, see Randall G. Bowdish and Bruce Woodyard, "A Naval Concepts-Based Vision for Space," U.S. Naval Institute *Proceedings* 124, no. 1 (January 1999), 50–53; Sam J. Tangredi, "Space is an Ocean," U.S. Naval Institute *Proceedings* 124, no. 1 (January 1999), 52–53; Rand H. Fisher, and Kent B. Pelot, "The Navy Has a Stake in Space," U.S. Naval Institute *Proceedings* 126, no. 10 (October 2001), 58–62. The definitive article on netcentric warfare remains Arthur K. Cebrowski and John J. Gartska, "Network-Centric Warfare: Its Origin and Future," U.S. Naval Institute *Proceedings* 123, no. 1 (January 1998), 28–35. On developments in naval UAVs, see Kevin P. Miller, "UAVs Hold Promise for No-Fly Zone Enforcement," U.S. Naval Institute *Proceedings* 126, no. 9 (September 2001), 38–41. On *Jervis Bay*-type high-speed vessels, see Robert Morrison, Vaughn Rixon, and John Dudley, "Chartering and HMAS Jervis Bay," U.S. Naval Institute *Proceedings* 125, no. 9 (September 2000), 75–77.

[12] The editor makes this case forcefully in (amoung other sources) Sam J. Tangredi, "Beyond the Sea and Jointness," U.S. Naval Institute *Proceedings* 126, no. 9 (September 2001), 60–63.

[13] One of the best arguments for the value of carriers is David A. Perin, "Are Big Decks Still the Answer?" U.S. Naval Institute *Proceedings* 126, no. 6 (June 2001), 30–33.

[14] An interesting discussion on the reorganization of the Navy helicopter community in light of its reduction in platforms is Frederick Latrash, "Reorganizing the Navy Helo Force," U.S. Naval Institute *Proceedings* 126, no. 1 (January 2001), 46–51.

[15] For a discussion of how the U.S. Navy conducted that mission in the 1950s and 1960s, see Joseph F. Bouchard, "Guarding the Cold War Ramparts: The U.S. Navy's Role in Continental Air Defense," *Naval War College Review* 52, no. 3 (Summer 1999), 111–135.

[16] See, for example, Jack Dorsey and Dale Eisman, "Navy May Help Bail Out Mission-Swamped Coast Guard," *Norfolk Virginian-Pilot*, October 17, 2001, 1; Thomas B. Hunter, "The Need for Speed," U.S. Naval Institute *Proceedings* 126, no. 1 (January 2001), 76–79.

[17] Among the first to discuss this dissuasion function was then-Secretary of the Navy Richard Danzig, *The Big Three: Our Greatest Security Threats and How to Address Them* (Washington, DC: National Defense University Press, 1999).

Chapter 30

Will Globalization Sink the Navy?

James J. Wirtz

T he September 11 attacks against the World Trade Center and the Pentagon have provided a new context for reassessing the relationship between globalization, naval strategy, and U.S. foreign and defense policy. This reassessment suggests that despite the opportunities created by globalization for the U.S. Navy, strategic thinking became moribund, or at best focused on simply preserving funding and force structure, in the aftermath of the Cold War. September 11, however, suggests that globalization and the information revolution have produced more than prosperity and democratization. The same trends that have empowered people of good will also have empowered global actors with sinister ambitions and objectives. The rise of a new transnational threat to the United States has created the need for new thinking about how the Navy can better protect America. There is a need for a new vision of the Navy role in homeland defense. National security requirements have created a real demand for naval strategy—not simply the budget and program-justifying briefings that have passed for official naval thought in recent years.[1]

To explain why the need for naval strategy now exists, this chapter first describes the opportunities and challenges that shaped U.S. Navy policy and planning during the last decade. It then explains why much current thinking about Navy strategy has been overtaken by recent events. The chapter also identifies the forces that have conspired to challenge Navy dominance of the world's oceans. It then suggests several ideas that Navy strategists might consider as they respond to the challenges posed by the emergence of new global mediums of communication.

James J. Wirtz is chairman and professor in the Department of National Security Affairs at the Naval Postgraduate School, Monterey, California. He is the author of *The Tet Offensive: Intelligence Failure in War* (Ithaca, NY: Cornell University Press, 1991), and the coeditor of numerous volumes, most recently of which include (with Jeffrey A. Larsen) *Rocket's Red Glare: Missile Defense and the Future of World Politics* (Boulder, CO: Westview Press, 2001) and (with John Baylis, Eliot Cohen, and Colin S. Gray) *Strategy in the Contemporary World* (New York: Oxford University Press, 2002).

A View from the Roaring '90s

Our global age is a naval age. Previous chapters have provided ample evidence of that. But instead of pleasing Navy officers, this bumper sticker statement and the ideas behind it often made these officers uneasy during the 1990s. Globalization complicated their attempts to explain the Navy contribution toward preserving American security in the aftermath of the Cold War. Globalization implies peace, or at least a set of market and strategic conditions that allows trade, commerce, and travel to proceed without fear of war or a nagging apprehension about what might happen next.[2] Globalization also implies an absence of a blue-water naval threat; for the indefinite future there is no prospect of a grand engagement such as the battles of Midway, Jutland, or Trafalgar. In an age of globalization, traditional methods of justifying naval force structure based on numbers of capital ships, or the potential air, naval, and land threat posed by competing great powers, are useless. New measures of effectiveness and depictions of the threat have to be devised to generate public and legislative support for what is in fact an extraordinarily expensive and ambitious enterprise: maintenance of a global and dominant naval presence.

Depicting a threat in the age of globalization, however, is no small matter, especially for an organization that relies on tradition as a guide to its operations, planning, and procurement.[3] Globalization itself implies that security threats are relatively minor and are receding. If prosperity leads to peace and if peace is the natural order of things, as many people mistakenly believe, what role does a global navy play in maintaining the status quo? Is a global navy sailing the seven seas simply a vestige of the bad old past? Would it be better for the Navy to abandon the wear and tear involved in maintaining forward presence and spend more time tied up to the dock?[4]

The effort to answer these questions created a great deal of heartburn for admirals and their staffs, especially as defense budgets remained stagnant after a sharp decline at the end of the Cold War. A variety of studies were launched to demonstrate how forward-deployed naval forces contributed to U.S. political and economic objectives.[5] The strategy of forward presence itself became a centerpiece of naval strategy not only because it made sense (a navy tied up to the dock is not much good to anyone) but also because it helped justify force structure (it takes at least three ships in the pipeline to maintain one operating forward).[6] Many strategists, however, also recognized that the organizational, doctrinal, and political problems that globalization created for the Navy were only part of the story. Globalization has produced real strategic opportunities during what amounts to a golden age for naval power. A global age is a naval age because the threats to U.S. security are relatively small, difficult to predict, and materialize quickly.[7] In other words, the kinds of military threats encountered in a naval age are right-sized for a forward-deployed carrier battlegroup or Marine amphibious ready group. Also, if naval units happen not to be in the right spot at the right time, they can probably arrive faster on the scene of a crisis than significant Army or Air Force combat units—particularly, as we have seen in Afghanistan, in the absence of available land bases.

Of course, the Navy and Marines needed to continue to engage in technological and doctrinal transformation to increase the firepower, accuracy, and range of their weapons in order to project power ashore. But in a global age, a carrier battlegroup combined with Marine units that can operate virtually anywhere while using organic logistics can have a major influence on most events on land. If these forward-deployed naval units cannot bring a conflict to a speedy conclusion, then they can contain the situation until the rest of the Navy, Army, and Air Force arrive.

Even more important than the apparent fit between naval capabilities and conventional threats is the link between globalization, economic prosperity, and the U.S. Navy. As discussed in the first chapter and elsewhere in the current volume, globalization and the strategic thinking articulated by Alfred Thayer Mahan go hand in hand.[8] Mahan's vision of a United States growing rich from its ability to use the seas as a means of communication fits well with contemporary thinking about how the information revolution has facilitated international commerce, contacts among individuals, and cultural exchange. The Navy plays a critical role in the process of globalization because it controls access to the world's primary means of communication (ocean transportation) and, by implication, access to global resources and markets. The Navy guarantees that the United States, its allies, and its friends will have access to the wealth produced by global trade among market economies. The Navy helps to create and maintain the political, commercial, and security conditions necessary for globalization to occur. The Navy patrols and protects the sea lines of communication/commerce that spread democracy and create global markets.

Despite plenty of hand wringing about the proliferation of antiaccess technologies and strategies, the greatest challenges that faced the U.S. Navy at the turn of the 21st century appeared to be a disinterested American public and a new Republican administration that sought to shed what it saw as its predecessor's excessive overseas commitments. Navy strategy documents in this period thus dwelled not on issues of true strategy, but instead upon reiterating basic ideas about what a navy can do (for example, navies are more useful at sea, not in port; the United States depends upon maritime trade; forward-deployed forces can respond quickly to crises).[9] To preserve its force structure in an age of globalization, the overriding goal of naval strategy was to win the hearts and minds of the American public and Congress. In terms of military threats, there was a general expectation that the Navy would be able to defeat any challenge from the land or sea.

The Return of Naval Strategy

The September attacks on the World Trade Center and the Pentagon showed Americans what can happen when forward presence fails to deter or defeat attacks upon the United States. The U.S. military, including forward-deployed naval forces, did not place the slightest impediment in the path of the terrorists. In the parlance of the Cold War, al Qaeda was able to engage in the diplomacy of violence by directly attacking countervalue targets in the United States without first defeating the U.S. defense establishment.[10] At the price of a few hundred thousand dollars and 19 lives, al Qaeda killed thousands of people, inflicted billions of dollars worth of property damage, and negatively affected the national economy.

Senior Navy officers no longer have to worry about public disinterest in international affairs or a lack of support for a strong Navy. But they do need to develop a new naval strategy to defeat the challenge posed by the emergence of hostile nonstate actors and a variety of asymmetric threats to U.S. security. As events would play out, the Navy did deliver on a decade's worth of promises: Navy carrier battlegroups and Marine amphibious ready groups quickly took the fight to al Qaeda in Afghanistan. Given the distances involved, this was no small accomplishment; one would hazard to guess that before September 2001, most observers would have estimated that Afghanistan was beyond the reach of the Navy. But because they are little more than the statement of the obvious, strategies that simply extol the importance of forward presence have been rendered obsolete by the events of September 11. Everyone now recognizes that it is important to deal with the bad guys *over there* before they get *over here*. It is up to naval officers to decide exactly where and how they intend to use existing and planned forces to defend their fellow citizens and family members against real threats to the security of the United States.

The idea that September 11 should force a complete overhaul of naval strategy, however, would probably be viewed by senior Navy officers as alarmist or at best counterproductive. Some might dismiss the terrorist attacks launched by al Qaeda as a bizarre or anomalous event. Why change everything because of the actions of a bunch of fanatics? Given the devastating attacks inflicted on terrorists as they ran for their lives in the hills and deserts of Afghanistan, the Navy also has helped reduce the likelihood that similar attacks will occur in the future. Terrorists, rogue states, or groups of lunatics can act up, but some officer might argue that the real-time global surveillance and precision-guided munitions incorporated in Navy operations will guarantee that they will not act up for long.

Yet the September attacks marked a new kind of warfare that is not only a response to globalization but also is itself facilitated by globalization. Globalization instills in people the idea that they should take their destiny into their own hands. It also empowers and equips them to shape that destiny by affecting world events. In an ironic twist, globalization has not only produced a dangerous political backlash, but it has also produced a new actor—a syndicate of religious fanatics, revolutionaries, and anarchists—to threaten directly U.S. security. The fact that the Navy dominates the world's oceans did not matter September 11. That data point alone should cause a re-assessment of naval strategy.

Origins of the New Challenges

The September attacks have cast the relationship between naval strategy and globalization in a new light. While naval strategists focused on the diplomatic, military, and economic implications of globalization, the information revolution was producing a profound social transformation and skill revolution among individuals who were lucky enough to gain access to the new information technologies. Bill Gates, for instance, has not hidden his hope that individuals will be empowered when they gain access to computers and the Internet. He suggested that the Internet would give individuals capabilities only possessed by bureaucracies less than a generation ago, thereby transforming the world.[11] In a series of analyses written over the last decade, James Rosenau also has identified "four flows of influence" that are transforming social and political relationships:

> (1) a technological revolution has facilitated the rapid flow of ideas, information, pictures, and money across continents; (2) a transportation revolution has hastened the boundary-spanning flow of elites, ordinary folk, and whole populations; (3) an organizational revolution has shifted the flow of authority, influence, and power beyond traditional boundaries; and (4) an economic revolution has redirected the flow of goods, services and capital, and ownership among countries.[12]

Naval strategy has responded to Rosenau's fourth flow of influence: forward presence was often justified as a way to facilitate the flow of goods, services, and capital among countries. Naval doctrine also was intended to capitalize on the technological revolution: Net-Centric Operations and FORCEnet concepts will integrate new technologies into existing ships and aircraft.[13] Planners and strategists, however, paid little attention to the second and third influence flows mentioned by Rosenau, the ones that had the greatest impact on individuals. Globalization and the information revolution had combined to give average individuals the ability to become actors on the world stage, a role once reserved for the brilliant, rich, fortunate, or truly evil.

Evidence of the transportation revolution and the breakdown of traditional authority relationships is everywhere, but it never received much attention from Navy planners. The decrease in the cost and increase in the availability of intercontinental jet transportation might pose a problem for customs officers or health officials, but it was not a matter of strategic consequence for the Navy. Similarly, the Navy, when compared to other sectors of American society, was probably less affected by the breakdown in traditional authority and the way new computer and communication technology empowered individuals. Senior officers had staff that could shield them from the leveling effects produced by the availability of e-mail and the Internet. Navy tradition produced important continuities in shipboard life, despite the introduction of co-ed crews and the ability of individual sailors to maintain private global communication networks while at sea. Throughout the rest of society, by contrast, leaders in business, education, or government lacked the resources or traditions needed to shield them from the direct communications and increased scrutiny of their employees or constituents. As the distance between the leaders and the led shrinks, officials find it increasingly difficult to use their bureaucratic position to justify their decisions or to deflect criticism. The mystique of leadership is undermined by accessibility and transparency. E-mail facilitates networks, not hierarchical communications. We are all on a first name basis on the Internet.

Navy officers along with most individuals failed to recognize that there is an ideology (or a logic, so to speak) embedded in every technology. This ideology affects the way individuals are likely to employ a given technology and the long-term effects a new technology is likely to have on society.[14] Sometimes the inventor of the technology recognizes and understands this ideology: Bill Gates hoped that his work would have a revolutionary impact on society. More often, the inventor of a machine is unaware of the logic inherent in the technology he or she is creating. Gutenberg was a Catholic, but his printing press made the Protestant Reformation possible because printing facilitates the dissemination of competing ideas (that is, heresy).[15] The automobile transformed America—dispersing extended families, creating suburbs and new American cultures.[16] But the automobile's effects were perceived only when the transformation of society was under way.

The Internet and the personal computer empower people by giving them the ability to process data and communicate globally at virtually no cost, capabilities that only states or enormous bureaucracies (for example, the Internal Revenue Service) possessed as late as the 1980s. The fact that people, not just states, have the technology needed to begin to overcome time and distance in communication will have a profound effect on international relations. Access to the Internet allows people to coordinate activities globally, to gather detailed information about local conditions and infrastructure for just about anywhere on the planet, and to move financial resources at virtually no cost. Powerful tools have been placed in the hands of individuals, and as September 11 demonstrated, they will not necessarily be put to good use.

Globalization and the information revolution have produced two profound changes in the international security environment. First, they have created new mediums of global communication. The Internet, global satellite television, transnational financial flows, international jet travel, and a host of grassroots organizations and informal networks of individuals have emerged to link people together in faraway places. Although the world's oceans remain as the dominant means of communication in terms of the flow of goods and trade, they no longer are the dominant way in which people, ideas, or even wealth move across borders.[17] Unlike maritime communications, which are best exploited by nations or large corporations (oceangoing vessels constitute a significant capital investment), nonstate actors and individuals can easily exploit these new methods of communication. Globalization itself suggests that nation states and their military instruments no longer dominate emerging transnational networks.

Second, people have come to believe that they *ought* to make use of these new technologies to take matters into their own hands. The ideology embodied in the new communication and data processing tools shapes individual and collective behavior in a way that empowers individuals and groups at the expense of governments or bureaucracies. Rosenau, for example, has written extensively about how the information revolution and globalization have produced a global authority crisis as traditional institutions are now undermined by the changing behavior and expectations of individuals. From Madison Avenue comes the message that the information revolution not only can be used to empower the consumer, but it can also level the playing field between the corporation and the individual when it comes to investing on Wall Street, buying a car, or shopping for a home mortgage.

These empowered individuals and groups create a new challenge for naval strategists. As chapter 1 notes, while armies control territory, navies control access to territory and communications. Navies, according to Tangredi, are the portions of military forces that operate "in the fluid mediums that humans use for information, transportation, and exchange but cannot normally inhabit. Its prime purpose is to ensure or deny access."[18] Prior to September 11, the Navy failed to deny access to these new mediums of communication and al Qaeda took advantage of that opening. Globalization and the information revolution have created new kinds of electronic oceans, and millions of individuals, groups, and organizations have moved quickly to exploit them for their own purposes.

Defending America

Homeland defense strikes fear in the hearts of naval officers everywhere, conjuring up images of maritime patrols along America's coasts, ships' crews being turned out to form naval infantry, and the transformation of the Navy into a Coast Guard auxiliary. Admittedly, the clamor for homeland defense casts doubt on much of the naval strategy of the 1990s because the political and military basis for strategy has changed in the aftermath of September 11. Before the tragedy, Navy strategists were forced constantly to explain fundamental maritime concepts to a disinterested public and Congress. After the tragedy, Navy strategists now face a far more difficult problem; they must explain to an alarmed U.S. public and Congress how they intend to protect average Americans from the murderous assaults of fanatics. They must devise a way of patrolling and protecting, so to speak, the new mediums of communication that were exploited with devastating effect by al Qaeda.

How can a carrier battlegroup steaming across the Pacific Ocean affect the way someone in Paris, Kabul, or Hong Kong uses a computer? How can the Navy decrease the appeal of millenarians who preach salvation through violence? How can the Navy disrupt and destroy shadowy networks of state and nonstate actors who conspire to kill Americans and discredit the United States? These are important questions, but there are no readily available answers. It will take time and some creative thinking to bring to bear existing Navy assets to counter emerging transnational threats. But U.S. sailors and marines have accomplished extraordinarily difficult missions—such as storming heavily defended beaches, tracking hostile submarines, and landing on pitching flight decks—that are considered nearly impossible (or prohibitively dangerous) by other navies. What is needed is an honest appraisal of the threat facing the United States and a sustained effort to devise ways to direct naval power against America's enemies.

In bringing naval power to bear against emerging threats, planners would do well to keep several principles in mind as they contemplate future strategy. First, it makes no sense for naval strategists to ignore the events of September 2001 by simply restating the benefits provided by forward presence. Suggestions that the Navy "does not do homeland defense" or that the Navy should concentrate on the "away game" will only generate public and Congressional hostility. Instead, senior officers and officials must state repeatedly that the primary mission of the U.S. Navy and Marine Corps is to protect America, its allies, and its interests overseas. People are less interested in how the Navy accomplishes this primary mission than in the fact that the Navy and Marines are doing everything in their power to keep fellow citizens and friends safe. Strategists should avoid highlighting the particular military benefits provided by global maritime dominance (a theme repeatedly stated during the 1990s) and concentrate instead on specific missions that the Navy can undertake to protect the United States.[19]

Second, the ability of the U.S. Navy and Marine Corps to project power on short notice to distant parts of the planet was demonstrated clearly in the war against the Taliban and al Qaeda. Navy ability to conduct and support joint operations (here the use of the USS *Kitty Hawk* as a special operations platform comes to mind) was evident during the battle in Afghanistan. The Navy also demonstrated an outstanding ability to make use of real-time intelligence and to employ extensively precision-guided weapons. But all of these capabilities need to be enhanced greatly so that naval forces can more effectively and quickly attack a vast array of targets.

If Navy officers and Marines want to continue to provide the primary short-notice strike capability available to the United States (a primary mission in the war against terrorism), they need to exploit new technologies (to improve networks, sensors, weapons, and platforms), strategies, and tactics, especially in the effort to attack very small targets at great distances. For example, aircraft carriers should be supplied with long-range unmanned aerial vehicles (UAVs) that can linger over a target for hours or days, looking for targets of opportunity. New long-range precision strike weapons—such as missiles, cruise missiles, or perhaps even UAVs—need to be developed for surface combatants and submarines so that they too can take advantage of real-time intelligence and support ground operations. In other words, the Navy already possesses a significant capability to deliver sustained precision strikes against large target sets given a few weeks notice. What it needs to develop now is a capability to deliver limited long-range strikes (against a manufacturing complex, a terrorist cell meeting in a specific location, or even a lone individual) in real time.

Third, to combat the rise of nonstate opponents, the Navy needs to exploit weapons and technologies that are not painted gray and offer no opportunity for command at sea. Coast Guard captain Stephen Flynn in a recent article in *Foreign Affairs*, for example, has identified a relatively inexpensive method to identify suspicious containers among the millions of containers annually carried by ship into the United States. According to Flynn, if the world's shipping megaports (Long Beach, Los Angeles, Hong Kong, Singapore, Hamburg, Antwerp, and Rotterdam[20]) implemented a standard security and tracking system, smaller port facilities would be forced to adopt the system. It then would be relatively easy to use computers, global positioning system (GPS) transponders, and electronic tags to track containers. Possible instances of tampering or shipments from shadowy locations could be identified. Navy warships could then target suspicious vessels far from America's shores.[21] This sort of system would actually constitute a naval presence in the specific portion of cyberspace that controls the commercial movement of goods around the globe. Both state and nonstate actors are making use of off-the-shelf technologies to achieve objectives. Navy planners must make use of the same technologies to develop a presence in the same mediums of communication exploited by America's enemies.

Fourth, Navy planners should stop to consider an important counterfactual question: what would have happened if the terrorists had struck the three carriers docked in Norfolk, Virginia, on September 11, 2001? They must consider the threat of asymmetric attacks intended to cripple U.S. military capabilities before they can be brought to battle. There is little that nonstate actors can do to stop a carrier battlegroup as it moves across the Pacific Ocean, but there are many ways terrorists armed with chemical, biological, or radiological weapons might achieve a mission kill against vital assets. In fact, scholars have recently called attention to the fact that surprise and asymmetric strategies hold an often exaggerated and unrealistic appeal to weaker parties in a conflict who hope, by striking a critical node, they can attack the will of their stronger opponents.[22] Navy officers also must embrace the fundamental idea behind force protection: the distinction between the threat involved in combat operations and peacetime is vanishing. Navy officers died at their desks in the Pentagon during peacetime; by contrast, combat operations over the skies of Afghanistan mercifully proved to be less lethal for the Navy. Al Qaeda sought to target the Navy in Singapore, a place that appeared to be a safe haven as carrier battlegroups transited to the war zone. For the moment, at least, America's enemies intend to engage U.S. military forces not on some recognized battlefield, but when and where we least expect it.

Conclusion

Will globalization sink the Navy? The answer to the question is *no*, but globalization and the information revolution have produced a challenging set of circumstances. Like the rise of aviation, new mediums of communication have emerged over the last 20 years that have complicated the ability of navies to control access to a country's shores. The terrorist attacks launched against the United States in the fall of 2001 demonstrated that nonstate actors are willing to make use of these mediums to achieve their objectives. The opportunities and trends unleashed by the information revolution and globalization will only multiply and accelerate in the years ahead. Navy planners must devise ways to respond to the real security challenges that are now clearly on America's strategic horizon.

Notes

[1] This is evident through the contrast between the vibrant concept development effort of the U.S. Marine Corps and a fragmented Navy effort. A significant part of the problem is that senior leadership has consistently avoided identifying which Navy organization among the centers of policy analysis and development—OPNAV N3/5, N513 Strategy and Concepts Branch, OPNAV N7, Naval War College, Naval Warfare Development Command, CNO Executive Panel, CNO Strategic Studies Group, the VCNO Long Range Planners, OPNAV QDR Cell (now Naval Operations Group), or the Center for Naval Analyses (now CNA Corporation)—has *the* lead in developing the future Navy vision. Whichever organization has the lead should be given the power to task and coordinate the active support of the other organizations in order to generate an efficient, thoughtful, and comprehensive product. In contrast, the Marine Corps Doctrine Command, supported by other Marine elements, appears to have led the efforts for new strategic and operational concepts in the Corps. On June 11, 2002, Chief of Naval Operations Admiral Vernon E. Clark announced a new "concept" of naval operations called Sea Power 21 at the annual Current Strategy Forum Conference at the Naval War College. This concept immediately received negative media coverage as "old wine in a new bottle" and lacking a transformational vision. One critic described it as a "vision of the 21st century Navy you would expect from a 19th century officer." See Gopal Ratnam, "Critics Question Depth of Navy's Sea Power Vision," *Defense News*, June 24–30, 2002, 12. It is unclear which policy analysis and development centers participated in drafting the Sea Power 21 concept.

[2] According to Ellen L. Frost, "A fundamental enabler of globalization in most regions of the world is the absence of a major war or major internal strife. A stable, secure environment is often taken for granted, but it is the underpinning of growth. Since sound business decisions require a degree of stability, investments tend to be postponed when nations are at war or on the brink of war." Frost, "Globalization and National Security: A Strategic Agenda," in

The Global Century: Globalization and National Security, ed. Richard L. Kugler and Ellen L. Frost (Washington, DC: National Defense University Press, 2001), 42.

[3] Adversity produces inertia in naval strategy. This is not surprising, given the role played by tradition in the Navy. According to Carl Builder, "In tradition, the Navy finds a secure anchor for the institution against the dangers it must face. If in doubt, or if confronted with a changing environment, the Navy looks to its traditions to keep it safe." See Builder, *The Masks of War* (Baltimore: Johns Hopkins University Press, 1989), 18.

[4] Daniel Goure, "The Tyranny of Forward Presence," *Naval War College Review* 54, no. 3 (Summer 2001), 11–24.

[5] Robert Looney, David Schrady, and Ronald Brown, "Estimating the Economic Benefits Engaged Naval Forces," *Interfaces*, July/August 2001, 74–86; Dov S. Zakheim, et al., *The Political and Economic Implications of Global Naval Presence* (Arlington, VA: System Planning Corporation, 1996); Daniel J. Whiteneck, *Naval Forward Presence and Regional Stability* (Alexandria, VA: Center For Naval Analyses, 2001); and Edward Rhodes, et al., "Forward Presence and Engagement: Historical Insights into the Problem of 'Shaping,'" *Naval War College Review*, Winter 2000, 25–61.

[6] For an explanation of both the advantages and disadvantages of a strategy based on naval forward presence, see Sam J. Tangredi, "The Fall and Rise of Naval Forward Presence," U.S. Naval Institute *Proceedings* 126, no. 5 (May 2000), 28–32.

[7] James J. Wirtz, "QDR 2001: The Navy and the Revolution in Military Affairs," *National Security Studies Quarterly*, Autumn 1999, 43–60.

[8] Sam J. Tangredi, "Security from the Oceans," in *Global Century*, 475–496.

[9] *Forward . . . From the Sea* is the title of a U.S. Navy document, produced in the 1990s, that outlines policy and strategy for the sea services. The title captures the mood at the time; it could be interpreted to mean "let's go boating." Notice that what is going to be done with, from, or to the boat, is captured by the inherently vacuous ellipse.

[10] Thomas Schelling, *Arms and Influence* (New Haven: Yale University Press, 1966).

[11] Bill Gates, *The Road Ahead* (New York: Penguin, 1996).

[12] James N. Rosenau, "Stability, Stasis, and Change: A *Fragmegrating* World," in *Global Century*, 137.

[13] The definitive sources on network-centric operations remain Arthur K. Cebrowski and John J. Gartska, "Network-Centric Warfare: Its Origin and Future," U.S. Naval Institute *Proceedings* 124, no. 1 (January 1998), 28–35; and David S. Alperts, John J. Gartska, and Frederick P. Stein, *Network Centric Warfare: Developing and Leveraging Information Superiority*, 2d ed. (Washington, DC: DoD C4ISR Cooperative Research Program, February 2000). FORCEnet is a study concept of the CNO Strategic Study Group that is defined in their various papers as "the architecture and building bloc of sensors, networks, decision aids, weapons, warriors, and supporting systems integrated into a highly adaptive, human-centric, comprehensive systems [sic] that operates from seabed to space, from sea to land."

[14] There is a rich literature on the effect of the information revolution on society. Several critics are especially provocative. See Gene I. Rochlin, *Trapped in the Net: The Unanticipated Consequences of Computerization* (Princeton: Princeton University Press, 1997); Theodore Roszak, *The Cult of Information* (Berkeley: University of California Press, 1986); and Neil Postman, *Technopoly: The Surrender of Culture to Technology* (New York: Vintage Books, 1993).

[15] Printing increased literacy because it provided common people with something to read. Without printing, Martin Luther could not have encouraged people to read the Bible themselves.

[16] George F. Kennan, *Around the Cragged Hill* (New York: Norton, 1994).

[17] The Introduction and chapter 1 of the current volume point out that ultimately ideas and wealth are translated into goods, which do require oceanic transportation. However, I consider the phenomenon of global flows of people, ideas, and wealth as having even more significant effects in themselves.

[18] Tangredi, "Security from the Oceans," 473.

[19] One source that does so, albeit at a high level of abstraction, is Sam J. Tangredi and Randall G. Bowdish, "Core of Naval Operations: Strategic and Operational Concepts of the U.S. Navy, *Submarine Review*, January 1999, 11–23.

[20] Contrast Flynn's list with Donna J. Nincic's list in chapter 8 of the current volume.

[21] Stephen E. Flynn, "America the Vulnerable," *Foreign Affairs*, January/February 2002, 60–74.

[22] Thomas J. Christensen, "Posing Problems without Catching Up: China's Rise and Challenges for U.S. Security Policy," *International Security*, Spring 2001, 5–40. See the thorough discussion of asymmetric strategies and their appeal to weaker states in Kenneth F. McKenzie, Jr., *The Revenge of the Melians: Asymmetric Threats and the Next QDR* (Washington, DC: National Defense University Press, 2000).

Conclusion: An Agenda for Research, a Menu for Choice

Sam J. Tangredi

U ltimately, the purpose of identifying the effects of globalization on maritime forces is to help determine the best ways to deal with a globalized future—how to shape it, defend against its threats, and maximize its benefits.

Maritime forces, as all other aspects of national security—including economic security as well as military defense—are but a portion of the capabilities that American society has at its disposal in dealing with globalization. They also represent only one area of society in which globalization has considerable effects. Yet, hopefully, the contributors to this volume have collectively presented an effective case as to the great importance of maritime forces for our future and the unique relationship that they have with globalization. One does not have to buy a "Globalization Begins at Sea" bumper sticker to accept the fact that without open seas there would be limited open trade—and without open trade it is hard to see how globalization could begin at all.

Globalization and Maritime Power aims to provide policy recommendations that derive from contributor research. Each chapter holds recommendations for policy, some of which may conflict with other chapters. We make no apology for this; all policymaking consists of tying together potentially conflicting objectives within a confusing, cluttered framework of facts. Our objective has been to cut away the clutter on a topic-by-topic basis. When viewed from a distance, the mosaic argues for the increasing relevance of global naval power. But on an individual issue basis, it seems appropriate to paraphrase the words of Lord Horatio Nelson: no naval analyst or policymaker can do very wrong if he places current preconceptions alongside the thoughts of the relevant chapter. Our aim has been to give a full intellectual broadside.

The contributors to this volume argue passionately that having effective, globally capable naval forces is critical to maintaining free and open seas and trade. This would indeed appear the verdict of history, and history, by its very nature, consists of the forces that shape the present and future. It is obvious that this age of globalization—the *global century*—is not starting off as the unprecedented era of peace and global prosperity for which we might have hoped. Interconnectedness does not in itself bring

563

peaceful relations. We have been shocked by global terrorism, much of it facilitated by the tools that allow for a global economy. Furthermore, at the time this book goes to print, two peoples with the most intertwined economics in the world—the Israelis and Palestinians—are in a bloody standoff. One does not have to pick sides in order to recognize the dangers that lurk in the international system, dangers against which prudent nations defend themselves, dangers which are inherent in human freedom and allow some to make evil choices. Naval forces are intended to defend against the consequences of such choices.

Blessed by its maritime geography and a fortuitous history, the United States has developed into a great maritime power. Such power is the least threatening and the most reassuring to other nations that desire peace. It also has the potential to support the most beneficial aspects of globalization and to thwart some of the most harmful. Oceans no longer seem like impenetrable lines of defense perhaps once envisioned, but they do remain the great common and physical "Internet" on which the *things* of the world must flow, and above which people and ideas may pass. Homeland security blends with forward security, which blends with global security. Global navies are the prime means of projecting sustained yet unobtrusive power across the great common and into regions of potential crisis. Under such circumstances, is there any force more globalized than an oceangoing navy?

All of this points to the need for a continuing research agenda in the relationship between maritime power and globalization. This volume is only the beginning, and if it convinces others to do their own research in this area—if only to challenge our present conclusions—it will have fulfilled part of its purpose.

Bibliography

"A Former U.S. Envoy Links Greek Politicians to Assassin Group." *The New York Times,* November 8, 2001, 9.

A.T. Kearney, Inc./*Foreign Policy* Magazine. "Measuring Globalization." *Foreign Policy,* no. 122 (January/February 2001): 56–65.

Adams, David. "We Are Not Invincible." U.S. Naval Institute *Proceedings* 123, no. 5 (May 1997): 35–39.

Adams, Thomas K. "Radical Destabilizing Effects of New Technologies." *Parameters* 28, no. 3 (Autumn 1998): 99–111.

Advisory Panel to Assess Domestic Response Capabilities For Terrorism Involving Weapons of Mass Destruction. *First Annual Report: Assessing the Threat,* Washington, DC: RAND, December 15, 1999.

Afkhami, Gholam R. *The Iranian Revolution: Thanatos on a National Scale.* Washington, DC: Middle East Institute, 1985.

Alderson, Kai, and Andrew Hurrell. *Hedley Bull on International Society.* New York: Palgrave, 2000.

Allen, Thomas B. "Run Silent, Run Deep." *Smithsonian Magazine* 31, no. 12 (March 2001): 50–61.

Alperts, David S., John J. Gartska, and Frederick P. Stein. *Network Centric Warfare: Developing and Leveraging Information Superiority.* 2d ed. Washington, DC: DoD C4ISR Cooperative Research Program, August 1999.

Anand, Vinod. "Evolution of a Joint Doctrine for Indian Armed Forces." *Strategic Analysis* 25 (July 2000): 733–750.

Anderson, Jennifer. *The Limits to Sino-Russian Strategic Partnership.* International Institute for Strategic Studies Adelphi Paper 315. Oxford: Oxford University Press, December 1997.

Anderson, John R. "Multi-National Naval Cooperation into the 21st Century." Halifax Maritime Symposium, Halifax, Nova Scotia, May 22–23, 1996; accessed at <http://www.dal.ca/~centre/cfps.html>.

Angell, Sir Norman. *The Great Illusion*. London: W. Heinemann, 1913.

—————. *The World's Highway: Some Notes on America's Relation to Sea Power and Non-Military Sanctions For the Law of Nations*. New York: George H. Doran Company, 1915.

Arctic Council/Arctic Monitoring and Assessment Programme. *Arctic Pollution Issues: A State of the Arctic Environment Report*, June 1997; accessed at <http://www.amap.no/assess/soaer10.htm>.

Arctic Council/Protection of the Arctic Marine Environment. *Arctic Environmental Protection Strategy: Arctic Offshore Oil & Gas Guidelines*, June 13, 1997.

Arquilla, John. *Dubious Battles*. Washington, DC: Crane Russak, 1992.

Arthur, Stanley R. Interview, *Desert Shield/ Desert Storm*: The 10th Anniversary of the Gulf War. Tampa, FL: Faircloth LLC, January 2001, 113.

Assel, Allan J. "Airborne Electronic Attack: What's Next." U.S. Naval Institute *Proceedings* 127, no. 2 (February 2001): 52–55.

Associated Press. "Italian Leader Says West Can 'Conquer' Islam." *The Washington Post*, September 27, 2001, A15.

Axelson, Mattias, with Andrew James. *The Defense Industry and Globalization*. Stockholm: Division of Defence Analysis, Defence Research Establishment, 2000.

Bacevich, Andrew J. "Policing Utopia: The Military Imperative of Globalization." *The National Interest*, no. 56 (Summer 1999): 5–13.

Bakoyannis, Dora. "Terrorism in Greece: Revisiting an Issue." *Mediterranean Quarterly* 12, no. 3 (Summer 2001): 1–7.

Balmer, Crispian. "Muslims Call Italians' Take on Islam 'Racist'." *The Washington Post*, September 28, 2001, A26.

Barber, Benjamin R. *Jihad Versus McWorld: How Globalism and Tribalism are Reshaping the World*. New York: Times Books, 1996.

Barbier, Edward B. *Economics, Natural-Resource Scarcity and Development: Conventional and Alternative Views*. London: Earthscan Publications Limited, 1989.

Barnett, Thomas P.M. "Asia: The Military-Market Link." U.S. Naval Institute *Proceedings* 127, no. 10 (January 2002): 53–56.

—————. "Globalization is Tested." U.S. Naval Institute *Proceedings* 127, no. 10 (October 2001): 57.

—————. "Top Ten Post-Cold War Myths." U.S. Naval Institute *Proceedings* 128, no. 2 (February 2001): 32–38.

—————, and Henry H. Gaffney, Jr. "Globalization Gets a Bodyguard." U.S. Naval Institute *Proceedings* 127, no. 11 (November 2001): 50–53.

—————, and Linda D. Lancaster. *Answering the 9–1–1 Call: U.S. Military and Naval Crisis Response Activity, 1977–1991*. Center for Naval Analyses Information Memorandum 229. Alexandria, VA: Center for Naval Analyses, August 1992.

Batchelor, Charles. "Choppy Waters Ahead: Declining Returns on Container Operations are behind Recent Spate of Mergers." *The Financial Times*, April 25, 1997, 21.

Battilega, John A. *Transformation in Defense Markets and Industries: Implications for the Future of Warfare, Volume 1: The Emerging Global Armament Systems and the Future of Warfare.* Greenwood Village, CO: Science Application International Corporation, February 1, 2001.

Baylis, John, and Steve Smith, eds. *The Globalization of World Politics.* Oxford: Oxford University Press, 1997.

Benedick, Richard E. "Human Population and Environmental Stresses in the Twenty-first Century." *Environmental Change & Security Project Report No. 6* (Summer 2000): 11–20.

Bennett, Drew A. "Military Presence in Asia is Key." U.S. Naval Institute *Proceedings* 128, no. 1 (January 2002): 57–60.

Bentley, J.H. "AHR Forum: Cross-Cultural Interaction and Periodization in World History." *American Historical Review* 101 (June 1996): 749–770.

Bergeron, James Henry. "An Ever Whiter Myth: The Colonization of Modernity in European Community Law." In *Europe's Other: European Law between Modernity and Postmodernity*, ed. Peter Fitzpatrick and James Henry Bergeron, 3–26. Aldershot, UK: Ashgate, 1998.

———. "Europe's Emprise: Symbolic Economy and the Postmodern Condition." In *Europe's Other: European Law between Modernity and Postmodernity*, ed. Peter Fitzpatrick and James Henry Bergeron, 67–92. Aldershot, UK: Ashgate, 1998.

Bergsten, Fred. "America's Two Front Economic Conflict." *Foreign Affairs* 80, no. 2 (March/April 2001): 16–28.

Bernstein, Richard, and Ross H. Munro. *The Coming Conflict with China.* New York: Random House, 1998.

Binnendijk, Hans. "How to Build an International Consensus for Missile Defense." *International Herald Tribune*, March 7, 2001.

Blechman, Barry M., and Robert G. Weinland. "Why Coaling Stations Are Necessary in the Nuclear Age." *International Security* 2, no. 1 (Summer 1977): 88–99.

———, and Stephen S. Kaplan. *Force Without War: US Armed Forces as a Political Instrument.* Washington, DC: The Brookings Institution, 1978.

Bloom, D. and Jeffrey Sachs. "Geography, Democracy, and Economic Growth in Africa." *Brookings Papers on Economic Activity*, no. 2, 1998, 207–289.

Bloom, Howard. *The Lucifer Principle: A Scientific Expedition into the Forces of History.* New York: Atlantic Monthly Press, 1995.

Blouet, Brian. *Globalization and Geopolitics.* London: Reaktion Books, 2001.

Boadle, Anthony. "Senators Worry Pentagon May Retreat in Drug War." Reuters, May 15, 2001.

Boop, Anthony E., and George M. Lady. "A Comparison of Petroleum Futures versus Spot Prices as Predictors of Prices in the Future." *Energy Economics* (October 1991): 274–282.

Boot, Max. "Vietnam's Lessons on How to Fight Globo-Guerrillas." *The Wall Street Journal*, October 2, 2001, A18.

Borgese, Elisabeth Mann. "Law of the Sea: The Next Phase." *Third World Quarterly* (October 1982): 698–718.

Bouchard, Joseph F. "Guarding the Cold War Ramparts: The U.S. Navy's Role in Continental Air Defense." *Naval War College Review* 52, no. 3 (Summer 1999): 111–135.

Bowdish, Randall G. "Information Age Psychological Operations." *Military Review* 78, no. 6 (December 1998/January-February 1999): 29–37.

———. "Psychological Operations . . . From the Sea." U.S. Naval Institute *Proceedings* 124, no. 2 (February 1998): 70–72.

———, and Bruce Woodyard. "A Naval Concepts-Based Vision for Space." U.S. Naval Institute *Proceedings* 125, no. 1 (January 1999): 50–53.

Boyd, Robert S. " Coast Guard's Focus Has Shifted Since 9/11." *Philadelphia Inquirer*, February 18, 2002, 1.

Boyle, Richard. "Waldo Lyon: A Legacy of Dedication." *Submarine Review* (July 1998): 115–117.

Bracken, Paul. "The Second Nuclear Age." *Foreign Affairs* 79, no. 1 (January/February 2000): 146–157.

———. *Fire in the East: The Rise of Asian Military Power and the Second Nuclear Age*. New York: HarperCollins, 1999.

Brass, G.W., ed. *The Arctic Ocean and Climate Change: A Scenario for the U.S. Navy, U.S. Arctic Research Commission Special Report*. Arlington, VA: U.S. Arctic Research Commission, 2001.

Brewer, James. "Internet: Malacca Break Reveals New Web of Demands." *Lloyd's List*, December 5, 2000, 2.

Brigham, Lawson W. "An International Polar Navigation Code for the Twenty-First Century." *Polar Record* 33 (1997): 283–284.

———. "The Northern Sea Route, 1998." *Polar Record* 36 (2000): 19–24.

———. "The Northern Sea Route: Soviet Legacy and Uncertain Future." *British East-West Journal* (September 1998): 3–4.

Brimelow, Peter. "The Silent Boom." *Forbes Magazine*, July 7, 1997, 170–171.

Bristow, Damon. "Weighing the Balance of Power: Aircraft Acquisition on the Up in East Asia." Global Defence Review 1999; accessed at <http://www.global-defence.com/99/1998/SeaSystems/weigh.htm>.

Broadus, James, and Raphael V. Vartanov, eds. *The Oceans and Environmental Security: Shared U.S. and Russian Perspectives.* Washington, DC: Island Press, 1994.

Brooke, James. "Through the Northwest Passage in a Month, Ice-Free." *The New York Times,* September 5, 2002, A3.

Brown, Charles H. "Up, Up and Away." U.S. Naval Institute *Proceedings* 127, no. 8 (August 2001): 36–40.

Brown, Christopher E. "The 'Q' Transition." U.S. Naval Institute *Proceedings* 123, no. 2 (February 1997): 57–61.

Brownlie, Ian. *Principles of Public International Law.* 5th ed., rev. New York: Oxford, 1998.

Brubaker, R. Douglas. "The Legal Status of the Russian Baselines in the Arctic." *Ocean Development & International Law* 30, 1999, 209–210.

———, and Willy Østreng. "The Northern Sea Route Regime: Exquisite Superpower Subterfuge?" *Ocean Development & International Law* 30 (1999): 320–330.

Brush, Peter. "The War's 'Constructive Component'." *Vietnam,* February 1997; accessed at <http://www.shss.montclair.edu/english/furr/pbvietnam0297.html>.

Brzezinski, Zbigniew. *The Strategic Triad: Living with China, Europe and Russia.* Washington, DC: Center for Strategic and International Studies, 2001.

Buchanan, Pat. *How American Sovereignty and Social Justice Are Being Sacrificed to the Gods of the Global Economy.* New York: Little, Brown and Company, 1998.

Buchner, Gerold. "What is Security." *Berliner Zeitung,* February 4, 2002; accessed at <http://www.berlinonline.de/suche.bin/>.

Builder, Carl. *The Masks of War.* Baltimore: Johns Hopkins University Press, 1989.

Bulloch, Gavin. "Military Doctrine and Counterinsurgency: A British Perspective." *Parameters* 26, no. 4 (Summer 1996): 4–16.

Burns, Robert. "Warships on Guard Amid High Alert." *Hampton-Newport News Daily Press,* September 13, 2001, A4.

Cagle, Malcolm W., and Frank A. Manson. *The Sea War in Korea.* Annapolis, MD: Naval Institute Press, 1957.

Caminos, Hugo, and Michael R. Molitor. "Progressive Development of International Law and the Package Deal." *American Journal of International Law* 79, no. 4 (October 1985): 871–890.

Campbell, Kurt M. "Globalization at War." *The Washington Post,* October 22, 2001, A19.

Canadian Directorate of Defense. *Arctic Capabilities Study,* June 2000; accessed at <http://12.1.239.251/arctic/Arctic%20Study%20Final%20-%20Canada1.htm>.

Canahute, Tom. "U.S. Coast Guard Tweaks Requirements For Deepwater Program." *Defense News*, December 17, 2001; accessed at <http://www.defensenews.com>.

"Can't Get There From Here." *Armed Forces Journal International* 137, no. 2 (September 2000): 4–5.

Carlucci, Frank, Robert Hunter, and Zalmay Khalilzad. *Taking Charge: A Bipartisan Report to the President Elect on Foreign Policy and National Security—Discussion Papers*. RAND, MR1306/1–RC, 2000.

Carter, Ashton B., and William J. Perry. *Preventive Defense: A New Security Strategy for America*. Washington, DC: The Brookings Institution, 1999.

Cassidy, William B. "USCG Lifts Boston LNG Blockade." *Traffic World*, November 5, 2001, 31.

Cebrowski, Arthur K., and Wayne P. Hughes. "Rebalancing the Fleet." U.S. Naval Institute *Proceedings* 125, no. 11 (November 1999): 31–34.

———, and John J. Gartska. "Network-Centric Warfare: Its Origin and Future." U.S. Naval Institute *Proceedings* 124, no. 1 (January 1998): 28–35.

Chandler, Clay. "GM's China Bet Hits Snag: WTO (Car Shoppers Await Discount From Trade Deal)." *The Washington Post*, May 10, 2000, E1.

Chase, John. "The Function of the Navy." U.S. Naval Institute *Proceedings* 95, no. 10 (October 1969): 27–33.

Chen, Lung Chu. *An Introduction to Contemporary International Law: A Policy-Oriented Perspective*. 2d ed. New Haven: Yale University Press, 2000.

Chivers, C.J. "Long Before War, Green Berets Built Military Ties to Uzbekistan." *The New York Times*, October 25, 2001, 1.

Chong, Florence. "Kobe's Dogged Hop, Step, and Jump." *Business Times*, July 14, 1995, 6.

Choucri, Nazli, and Robert North. *Nations in Conflict: National Growth and International Violence*. San Francisco: Freeman, 1975.

Christensen, Clayton M. *The Innovator's Dilemma: When New Technologies Cause Great Firms to Fail*. Cambridge, MA: Harvard Business School, 1997.

———, Thomas Craig, and Stuart Hart. "The Great Disruption." *Foreign Affairs* 80, no. 2 (March/April 2001): 80–95.

Christensen, Thomas J. "Posing Problems Without Catching Up: China's Rise and Challenges for U.S. Security Policy." *International Security* 25, no. 4 (Spring 2001): 5–40.

Chu, Henry, and Richard C. Paddock. "Russia Looks to China as an Ally Amid West's Ire." *Los Angeles Times*, December 8, 1999, 1.

Clark, Wesley K. *Waging Modern War: Bosnia, Kosovo and the Future of Combat*. New York: Public Affairs Press, 2001.

Clements, Michael. "GM Strike Snowballs: Local Labor Dispute Out of Control." *USA Today*, March 14, 1996, 1B.

Cliff, Roger, Sam J. Tangredi, and Christine E. Wormuth. "The Future of U.S. Overseas Presence." In *QDR 2001: Strategy-Driven Choices for America's Security*, ed. Michèle Flournoy, 235–262. Washington, DC: National Defense University Press, 2001.

"Coast Guard Revokes Ban on Natural-Gas Shipments." *The Wall Street Journal*, October 17, 2001, B6.

"Cohen Sends Navy Shipbuilding Report To Congress." *Inside the Navy*, July 3, 2000, 6–7.

Cohen, Eliot A. "Defending America in the Twentieth Century." *Foreign Affairs* 79, no. 6 (November/December 2000): 40–56.

———. "A Revolution in Warfare." *Foreign Affairs* 75, no. 2 (March/April 1996): 37–54.

Cohen, Saul B. "Geopolitics in the New World Era: A New Perspective on an Old Discipline." In *Reordering the World: Geopolitical Perspectives on the 21st. Century*, ed. George J. Demko and William B. Wood, 40–68. 2ᵈ ed. Boulder: Westview, 1999.

Cohen, William S., Secretary of Defense. *Annual Report to the President and the Congress 2000*. Washington, DC: Department of Defense, 2000.

Coombs, Barry, and Les Sim. "The Russians Are Here." U.S. Naval Institute *Proceedings* 121, no. 3 (March 1995): 68–69.

Coons, Ken. "Coast Guard Stretches to Expand Mission," October 4, 2001; accessed at <http://www.seafood.com>.

Cooper, Henry F. "New Life for Sea-Based Defense." *National Review Online*, January 30, 2002; accessed at <http://www.nationalreview.com/comment/ comment-cooper013002.html>.

Cooper, Richard N. "The Gulf Bottleneck: Middle East Stability and World Oil Supply." *Harvard International Review* 20, no. 1 (Summer 1997): 20–21.

Cordesman, Anthony H. "Compensating for Smaller Forces: Adjusting Ways and Means Through Technology." In *Strategy and Technology*. Carlisle Barracks, PA: Strategic Studies Institute, Army War College, April 1, 1992, 16–19.

———. "The Military in a New Era: Living with Complexity." In *The Global Century: Globalization and National Security*, ed. Richard L. Kugler and Ellen L. Frost, 389–422. Washington, DC: National Defense University Press, 2001.

———. "The Lessons and Non-Lessons of the Air and Missile War in Kosovo." Center for Strategic and International Studies, September 29, 1999; accessed at <http://www.csis.org/kosovo/Lessons.html>.

Corless, Joshua. "Fresh Approach to Submarine Upgrades." Global Defence Review 1999; accessed at <http://www.global-defence.com/99/seasys/sea1.htm>.

Corum, James. "A Comprehensive Approach to Change: Reform in the German Army in the Interwar Period." In *The Challenge of Change: Military Institutions and New Realities, 1918–1941*, ed. Harold R. Winton and David R. Mets, Lincoln, NE: Nebraska University Press, 2000, 35–73.

Cote, Owen, Jr. "Buying '. . . From the Sea': A Defense Budget for a Maritime Strategy." In *Holding the Line: U.S. Defense Alternatives for the Early 21st Century*, ed. Cindy Williams. Cambridge, MA: MIT Press, 2001.

———. *Precision Strike from the Sea: New Missions for a New Navy*. Cambridge, MA: Security Studies Program, Massachusetts Institute of Technology, August 1998.

Coward, Brian. "Ireland's New Duties in a Changing Europe." *Irish Times*, November 18, 2000.

Cox, Gregory V. *Keeping Carriers Forward Deployed: Harder Than It Seems*. Alexandria, VA: Center for Naval Analyses, 2000.

Cox, Kenneth M., and Thomas P. Maloney. "Applied Submarine Technology for the 1990s." *Proceedings of the Submarine Technical Symposium*, The Johns Hopkins University Applied Physics Laboratory, May 1993.

Crickard, Fred W. and Richard H. Cimblett. "The Navy as an Instrument of Middle Power Foreign Policy: Canada in Korea 1950 and the Persian Gulf 1990." *Maritime Forces in Global Security*, proceedings of a colloquium in June 1994, Halifax, NS, Canada: Centre for Foreign Policy Studies, Dalhousie University, 1995.

Critchon, John. "Ford—the Global Shipping Shopper."*Containerisation International*, February 1997, 33.

Crowl, Phillip A. "Alfred Thayer Mahan: The Naval Historian." In *Makers of Modern Strategy*, ed. Peter Paret, 444–477. Princeton, NJ: Princeton University Press, 1986.

Cusack, Jim. "Infantry Battalion will be Irish RRF Contribution." *Irish Times*, November 21, 2000.

Daniel, Donald C.F. "The Evolution of Naval Power to the Year 2010." *Naval War College Review* 48, no. 3 (Summer 1995): 62–71.

———. *Beyond the 600-Ship Navy*. Adelphi Paper 261. London: Brassey's/International Institute for Strategic Studies, 1991.

———. *Antisubmarine Warfare and Superpower Strategic Stability*. London: Brassey's/International Institute for Strategic Studies, 1986.

———. "Antisubmarine Warfare in the Nuclear Age," *Orbis* (Fall 1984): 549–555.

Danzig, Richard. *The Big Three: Our Greatest Security Threats and How to Address Them*. Washington, DC: National Defense University Press, 1999.

David, Dominique. "The First Strategic Lessons to be Drawn from September 11." *Paris Politique Etrangere*, October-December 2001, 766–775.

Davis, Ralph. *The Rise of the English Shipping Industry in the Seventeenth and Eighteenth Centuries*. London: David and Charles, 1962.

Davis, Zachary S. *Weapons of Mass Destruction: New Terrorist Threat?* Washington, DC: Congressional Research Service, January 8, 1997.

De Bendern, Paul. "Booming World Trade Threatens Panama Canal Status." Reuters, September 23, 1997; accessed at <http://www.infoseek.com>.

De Santis, Hugh. *Mutualism: An American Strategy for the Next Century*. Strategic Forum No. 162. Washington, DC: Institute for National Strategic Studies, National Defense University, May 1999.

DeKay, James Tertius. *The Battle of Stonington: Torpedoes, Submarines and Rockets in the War of 1812*. Annapolis, MD: Naval Institute Press, 1990.

Desch, Michael C. *When the Third World Matters: Latin America and United States Grand Strategy*. Baltimore: Johns Hopkins University Press, 1993.

Dillon, Dana R. "Piracy in Asia: A Growing Barrier to Maritime Trade." *The Heritage Foundation Backgrounder*, June 22, 2000; accessed at <http://www.heritage.org>.

Dionne, E.J., Jr. "The "Glocalization" Problem." *The Washington Post*, June 6, 2000, A27.

Dobson, William J., and M. Taylor Fravel. "Red Herring Hegemon: China in the South China Sea." *Current History* (September 1997): 258–263.

Donnelly, Thomas. *Rebuilding America's Defenses: Strategy, Forces, and Resources For a New Century*. Washington, DC: Project for the New American Century, 2000.

Dorsey, Jack, and Dale Eisman. " Navy May Help Bail Out Mission-Swamped Coast Guard." *Norfolk Virginian-Pilot*, October 17, 2001, 1.

Drogin, Bob, and David Kelly. "3 Warships Head to Yemen to Bolster Investigative Team." *Los Angeles Times*, October 17, 2000, 8.

DuBois, W.E.B. *The Suppression of the African Slave-Trade to the United States 1638–1870*. Boston: Harvard University Press, 1896, reprinted Williamstown, MA: Corner House Publishers, 1970.

Dugger, Celia W. "High-Stakes Showdown: Enron's Right Over Power Plant Reverberates Beyond India." *The New York Times*, March 20, 2001, C1.

Duignan Peter, and L.H. Gann. *The United States and Africa: A History*. New York: Cambridge University Press, 1984.

Dunlap, Charles J., Jr. "21st Century Land Warfare: Four Dangerous Myths." *Parameters* 27, no. 3 (Autumn 1997): 27–37.

———. "How We Lost the High Tech War of 2007." *The Weekly Standard* 1, no. 19 (January 29, 1996): 22–28.

Dunn, Robert M., Jr. "Has the U.S. Economy Really Been Globalized?" *Washington Quarterly* 24, no. 1 (Winter 2001): 53–64.

Dur, Philip A. "Presence: Forward, Ready, Engaged." In *Strategy and Force Planning*, ed. Naval War College Strategy and Force Planning Faculty, 469–479. 3d ed. Newport: Naval War College Press, 2000.

Eisman, Dale. "Navy Moves to Develop a Novel Type of Warship." *The Virginian-Pilot*, February 4, 2002; accessed at <http://www.hamptonroads.com>.

Elliot-Meisel, Elizabeth B. "Still Unresolved after Fifty Years: The Northwest Passage in Canadian-American Relations, 1946–1998." *American Review of Canadian Studies* 29, no. 3 (Autumn 1999): 407–430.

Eltis, David, and Stanley L. Engerman. "The Importance of Slavery and the Slave Trade to Industrializing Britain." *Journal of Economic History* 60, no. 1 (March 2000): 123–144.

Elwell, Craig. *Global Markets: Evaluating Some Risks the U.S. May Face.* Washington, DC: Congressional Research Service, February 11, 2001.

Emerson, Mike. "Coast Guard Helos: A Call to Arms." U.S. Naval Institute *Proceedings* 125, no. 10 (October 1999): 30–33.

EQE. *The January 17, 1995 Kobe Earthquake: An EQE Summary Report,* April 1995, 2; accessed at <http://www.eqe.com/publications/kobe/economic.htm>.

Ercan, Ersoy. "Chevron Talks Straits, Pipeline with Turkey." *Turkish Daily News,* May 17, 1996, 1.

Evans, David C., and Mark R. Peattie. *Kaigun: Strategy, Tactics, and Technology in the Imperial Japanese Navy, 1887–1941.* Annapolis, MD: Naval Institute Press, 1997.

Fabey, Michael. "Northrop to Bid on Subs for Taiwan: NNS Yard's Expertise Gives it an Advantage." *Newport News Daily Press,* January 24, 2002, A1.

Falkenrath, Richard, Robert D. Newman, and Bradley A. Thayer. *America's Achilles' Heel: NBC Terrorism and Covert Attack.* Cambridge, MA: MIT Press, 1998.

Fargo, Thomas, and Ernest Riutta. "A 'National Fleet' for America." U.S. Naval Institute *Proceedings* 125, no. 4 (April 1999): 48–53.

Fesharaki, Fereidun. "Energy and Asian Security Nexus." *Journal of International Affairs* 53, no. 1 (Fall 1999): 85–99.

Feshbach, Murray. "Dead Souls." *The Atlantic Monthly* (January 1999): 26–27.

Fielding, Lois E. *Maritime Interception and U.N. Sanctions.* Bethesda, MD: Austin and Winfield Publishers, 1997.

Finnegan, Philip. "Defense News Top 1000: Europeans Make Great Strides Against U.S. Megafirms." *Defense News,* August 7, 2000, 1.

Fisher, John R. "A Tale of Two Centuries." *Seapower,* 2000 Almanac Issue, January 2000, 4.

Fisher, Rand H., and Kent B. Pelot. "The Navy Has a Stake in Space." U.S. Naval Institute *Proceedings* 127, no. 10 (October 2001): 58–62.

Fiske, Bradley A. "American Naval Policy." U.S. Naval Institute *Proceedings* (January 1905): 79.

FitzSimonds, James R., and Jan M. van Tol. "Revolutions in Military Affairs." *Joint Force Quarterly,* no. 4 (Spring 1994): 24–31.

Flanagan, Stephen J. "Meeting the Challenges of the Global Century." In *The Global Century: Globalization and National Security,* ed. Richard L. Kugler and Ellen L. Frost, 7–32. Washington, DC: National Defense University Press, 2001.

———, Ellen L. Frost, and Richard L. Kugler. *Challenges of the Global Century: Report of the Project on Globalization and National Security*. Washington, DC: National Defense University Press, 2001.

Flynn, Stephen E. "America the Vulnerable." *Foreign Affairs* 81, no. 1 (January/February 2002): 60–74.

Fournier, Ron. "U.S. Freezes Terror Network Assets." Associated Press, November 7, 2001; accessed at <http://www.firstcoastnews.com/news/2001–11–07/usw_assets.asp>.

Frank, Andre Gunder. *ReOrient: Global Economy in the Asian Age*. Berkeley: University of California Press, 1998.

Friedberg, Aaron L. *In the Shadow of the Garrison State: America's Anti-Statism and Its Cold War Grand Strategy*. Princeton, NJ: Princeton University Press, 2000.

Friedman, Norman. *Seapower and Space: From the Dawn of the Missile Age to Net-Centric Warfare*. Annapolis, MD: Naval Institute Press, 2000.

———. *The Fifty-Year War: Conflict and Strategy in the Cold War*. Annapolis, MD: Naval Institute Press, 1999.

———. *World Naval Weapons Systems 1997–1998*. Annapolis, MD: Naval Institute Press, 1997.

———. *The U.S. Maritime Strategy*. New York: Jane's Publishing Company, 1988.

Friedman, Thomas L. "Altered States." *The New York Times*, October 1, 2000, A17.

———. "Was Kosovo World War III?" *The New York Times*, July 2, 1999, A17.

———. *The Lexus and the Olive Tree*. Rev. ed. New York: Anchor Books, 2000.

Fritz, Alarik, et al. *Navy Role in Homeland Defense Against Asymmetric Threats, Volume One: Summary Report*. Alexandria, VA: Center for Naval Analyses, September 2001.

Frost, Ellen L. "Globalization and National Security: A Strategic Agenda." In *The Global Century: Globalization and National Security*, ed. Richard L. Kugler and Ellen L. Frost, 35–74. Washington, DC: National Defense University Press, 2000.

Fulghum, David A., Robert Wall, and John D. Morrocco. "Strikes Hit Old Targets, Reveal New Problems." *Aviation Week*, February 23, 2001.

Gaffney, Frank J., Jr. "Defense Fire Sale Redux." *The Washington Times*, April 3, 2001, 15.

Gaffney, Henry H., Jr., et al. *U.S. Naval Responses to Situations, 1970–1999*. Alexandria, VA: Center for Naval Analyses, December 2000.

Galdorisi, George V. "Navy Theater Missile Defense." *Shipmate* (July/August 2000): 43.

———, and Kevin R. Vienna. *Beyond the Law of the Sea: New Directions of U.S. Oceans Policy*. Westport, CT: Praeger, 1997.

Gates, Bill. *The Road Ahead*. New York: Penguin, 1996.

Gattuso, Joseph A., Jr. "Naval Force in the New Century." *Naval War College Review* 54, no. 1 (Winter 2001): 129–138.

Gilpin, Robert, and Jean Millis Gilpin. *The Challenge of Global Capitalism: The World Economy in the 21st Century*. Princeton, NJ: Princeton University Press, 2000.

Glasser, Susan. "Russian, Iran Renew Alliance Meant to Boost Arms Trade." *The Washington Post*, March 13, 2001, A14.

Goldman, Emily O. "Mission Possible, Organizational Learning in Peacetime." In *The Politics of Strategic Adjustment: Ideas, Institutions, and Interests*, ed. Peter Turbowitz, Emily Goldman, and Edward Rhodes, New York : Columbia University Press, 1999, 243–247.

Goure, Daniel. "The Tyranny of Forward Presence." *Naval War College Review* 54, no. 3 (Summer 2001): 11–24.

Graham, Bradley. "Rise and Fall of a Navy Missile." *The Washington Post*, March 28, 2002, A3.

Granberg, Alexander G. "The Northern Sea Route: Trends and Prospects of Commercial Use." *Ocean and Coastal Management* 41 (1998): 183–198.

Gray, Colin S. "The Coast Guard and Navy: It's Time for a 'National Fleet'." *Naval War College Review* (Summer 2001): 112–138.

———. *The Leverage of Sea Power: The Strategic Advantage of Navies in Wa.*, New York, NY: Free Press, 1992.

———. The *Navy in the Post-Cold War Period: The Uses and Value of Strategic Sea Power*. University Park, PA: Pennsylvania State University Press, 1992.

———. *The Geopolitics of Superpower*. Lexington: University of Kentucky Press, 1988.

———, and Roger Barnett, eds. *Seapower and Strategy*. Annapolis, MD: Naval Institute Press, 1989.

Green, Jerrold M. *Revolution in Iran: The Politics of Countermobilization*. New York: Praeger, 1982.

"Greenpeace's Risky Tactics." *St. Louis Post-Dispatch*, December 7, 1989, 35.

Griffiths, Franklyn. "Environment in the U.S. Security Debate: The Case of the Missing Arctic Waters." *Environmental Change and Security Project Report* (Spring 1997): 22.

Grossman, Elaine M. "Defense Officials Close to naming New Homeland Security Command." *Inside the Pentagon*, December 6, 2001, 1.

Grove, Eric. *The Future of Sea Power*. Annapolis, MD: Naval Institute Press, 1990.

Guehenno, Jean Marie. "The Impact of Globalisation on Strategy." *Survival* 40, no. 4 (Winter 1998/1999): 5–19.

Hagan, Kenneth J. *This People's Navy: The Making of American Sea Power*. New York: Free Press, 1991.

Halliday, James. *Scotland: A Concise History*. 2ᵈ ed. Edinburgh: Gordon Wright Publishing, 1990.

Hamilton, George K. "Foreign Cooperation Is Essential for Force Protection." U.S. Naval Institute *Proceedings* 125, no. 7 (July 1999): 44–45.

Hanson, Victor Davis. *Culture and Carnage: Landmark Battles in the Rise of Western Power.* New York: Doubleday, 2001.

Harrison, Pete. "Container Ships Could Be Used as Bombs by Terrorists." *The Irish Examiner,* October 30, 2001.

Hartmann, Gregory K. *Weapons That Wait.* Annapolis, MD: Naval Institute Press, 1979, 55.

Havely, Joe. "World: Asia-Pacific Analysis: Flashpoint Spratly." BBC News On-line, February 14, 1999; accessed at <http://news.bbc.co.uk/>.

Held, David, Anthony McGrew, David Goldblatt, and Jonathan Perraton. *Global Transformations: Politics, Economics and Culture.* Stanford, CA: Stanford University Press, 1999.

Henley, Lonnie. "The RMA After Next." *Parameters* 29, no. 4 (Winter 1999–2000): 46–57.

"Herding Pariahs: Russia's Dangerous Games." Stratfor.com, February 8, 2000; accessed at <http://www.stratfor.com>.

Heston, Alan W., and Neil A. Weiner, eds. *Dimensions of Globalization* [*The Annals of the American Academy of Political and Social Science*, vol. 570]. London: Sage Publications, 2000.

Heymann, Philip B. *Terrorism and America: A Commonsense Strategy for a Democratic Society.* Cambridge, MA: MIT Press, 1998.

Higgins, Joshua S. "Anti-Terrorism Unit Set for Activation." *Marine Corps News*, October 17, 2001; accessed at <http://www.usmc.mil/marinelink/mcn2000.nsf/ac95bc775efc34 c685256ab50049d458>.

Hill, J.R. *Maritime Strategy for Medium Powers.* Annapolis, MD: Naval Institute Press, 1986.

Hirschkorn, Phil, Rohan Gunaratna, Ed Blanche, and Stefan Leader. "Blowback." *Jane's Intelligence Review*, August 2001, 42–45.

Hodge, Nathan. "Admiral Sees Stiff Competition For New Surface Combatant." *Defense Week*, February 4, 2002, 2.

Hoffman, Frank G. *Decisive Force: A New American Way of War.* Westport, CT: Praeger, 1996.

———. "Strategic Concepts and Marine Corps Force Structure in the 21st Century." *Marine Corps Gazette*, December 1993, 70–75.

Holland, W.J., Jr. "A Fleet to Fight in the Littorals." *Submarine Review* (April 2001): 33–44.

———. "Battling Battery Boats." U.S. Naval Institute *Proceedings* 123, no. 6 (June 1997): 30–33.

———. "ASW is Still Job One." U.S. Naval Institute *Proceedings* 118, no. 8 (August 1992): 30–34.

———. "How Many SSBNs Are Enough?" *Submarine Review* (July 1989).

Holley, I.B. "Doctrine on the Wrong Foot." *Naval War College Review* 49, no. 1 (Winter 1996): 117–118.

Holzer, Robert. "Rumsfeld Directs DSB To Assess Future Role of U.S. Aircraft Carriers." DefenseNews.com, August 29, 2001; accessed at <http://www.paxriver.org/news/010829.htm>.

Homer-Dixon, Thomas F. "Environmental Scarcities and Violent Conflict: Evidence from Cases." *International Security* 19, no. 1 (Summer 1994): 5–40.

———. "On the Threshold: Environmental Changes As Causes of Acute Conflict." *International Security* 16, no. 2 (Fall 1991): 76–116.

"Hong Kong Retains Top Box Slot." *Fairplay*, January 11, 2001, 11.

Hook, Steven W., and John Spanier. *American Foreign Policy Since World War II*. 15th ed. Washington, DC: CQ Press, 2000.

Howard, Michael. *The Invention of Peace: Reflections on War and International Order*. New Haven: Yale University Press, 2000.

———. *War and the Liberal Conscience*. New Brunswick, NJ: Rutgers University Press, 1986.

Howe, Jonathan T. "A Global Agenda for Foreign and Defense Policy." In *The Global Century: Globalization and National Security*, ed. Richard L. Kugler and Ellen L. Frost, 179–195. Washington, DC: National Defense University Press, 2001.

Huebert, Rob. "Polar Vision or Tunnel Vision: The Making of Canadian Arctic Waters Policy." *Marine Policy* 19 (1995): 343.

Hughes, Wayne P., Jr. *Fleet Tactics and Coastal Combat*. Annapolis, MD: Naval Institute Press, 2000.

———. "22 Questions for Streetfighter." U.S. Naval Institute *Proceedings* 126, no. 2 (February 2000): 46–49.

———. "The Power in Doctrine." *Naval War College Review* 48, no. 3 (Summer 1995): 9–31.

———. *Fleet Tactics: Theory and Practice*. Annapolis, MD: Naval Institute Press, 1986.

———, and Mike Bowman. "Doctrine on the Wrong Foot." *Naval War College Review* 49, no. 2 (Spring 1996): 108–112.

Hunter, Thomas B. "The Need for Speed." U.S. Naval Institute *Proceedings* 127, no. 1 (January 2001): 76–79.

Huntington, Samuel P. *The Clash of Civilizations and the Remaking of World Order*. 2d ed. New York: Touchstone Books, 1997.

———. "The Clash of Civilizations." *Foreign Affairs* 72, no. 3 (Summer 1993): 22–60.

———. "National Policy and Transoceanic Navy." U.S. Naval Institute *Proceedings* 80, no. 5 (May 1954): 483–493.

Ignatieff, Michael. *Virtual War: Kosovo and Beyond*. New York: Metropolitan Books, 2000.

Ikenberry, G. John. *After Victory: Institutions, Strategic Restraint and the Rebuilding of Order after Major Wars*. Princeton, NJ: Princeton University Press, 2001.

Inan, Yüksel. "The Current Regime of the Turkish Straits." *Perceptions: Journal of International Affairs* 6, no. 1 (March–May 2001); accessed at <http://www.mfa.gov.tr/grupa/percept/VI-1/default.htm>.

Independent World Commission on the Oceans. *The Ocean, Our Future. . . . The Report of the Independent World Commission on the Oceans.* Cambridge: Cambridge University Press, 1998.

Intergovernmental Panel on Climate Change (IPCC). *Special Report—The Regional Impacts of Climate Change: An Assessment of Vulnerability, Summary for Policymakers* (November 1997); accessed at <http://www.grida.no/climate/ipcc/regional/054.htm>.

———. IPCC Working Group 1. *Contribution to the Third Assessment Report of the IPCC, Climate Change, 2001: The Scientific Basis (Draft), Summary for Policymakers* (January 21, 2001).

———. IPCC Working Group 2. *Contribution to the Third Assessment Report of the IPCC, Climate Change 2001: Impacts, Adaptation, and Vulnerability (Draft), Summary for Policymakers* (February 19, 2001).

International Campaign to Ban Landmines. *Landmine Monitor Report: Toward a Mine Free World* (September 2001); accessed at <http://www.icbl.org/lm2001/exec/hma.html#Heading680>.

International Chamber of Commerce, Crime Services. *Weekly Piracy Report*, May 22–28, 2001, 1.

"Iran Ends Naval Exercises: Oil Shipments Resume Through Strait of Hormuz." *Digital News Network*, April 14, 1996; accessed at <http://www.pres96.com/nwi10s5.htm>.

Jaffe, Greg. "Debate Surrounding Small Ship Poses Fundamental Questions For U.S. Navy." *The Wall Street Journal*, July 11, 2001, 1.

Jervis, Robert. *Systems Effects: Complexity in Political and Social Life.* Princeton: Princeton University Press, 1997.

Joergensen, Tim Sloth. "U.S. Navy Operations in Littoral Waters: 2000 and Beyond." *Naval War College Review* 51, no. 2 (Spring 1998): 20–29.

Johnson, Jay. "Anytime. Anywhere: A Navy for the 21st Century." *U.S. Naval Institute Proceedings* 123, no. 11 (November 1997): 48–50.

Johnson, Tim. "Drug-Policing Efforts May Suffer." *Miami Herald*, October 18, 2001.

Jones, Peter. "Multi-National Operations: Their Demands and Impact on Medium Power Navies." *Maritime Security Working Papers*, no. 3. Halifax, NS, Canada: Centre for Foreign Policy Studies, Dalhousie University, May 1996.

Jones, James L. *Expeditionary Maneuver Warfare.* Washington, DC: Headquarters, U.S. Marine Corps, November 10, 2001.

———. *Marine Corps Strategy 21.* Washington, DC: Department of the Navy, November 3, 2000.

Joy, Bill. "Why the Future Doesn't Need Us." *Wired*, April 2000, 238–262.

Kagan, Donald. *On The Origins of War and the Preservation of Peace*. New York: Doubleday, 1995.

Kaldor, Mary. "Wanted: Global Politics." *The Nation*, November 5, 2001, 15–17.

Kant, Immanuel. *Perpetual Peace: A Philosophical Essay*. Trans. M. Campbell Smith. New York: Garland, 1972.

Kaplan, Robert D. "The Coming Anarchy." In *Strategy and Force Planning*, ed. Naval War College Strategy and Force Planning Faculty. 3ᵈ ed. Newport: Naval War College Press, 2000, 381–409.

———. *The Coming Anarchy: Shattering the Dreams of the Post Cold War*. New York: Random House, 2000.

Kapteyn, Paul. *The Stateless Market*. London: Routledge, 1996.

Kauai Economic Development Board. "Navy Establishes Missile Defense Office." *Kauai Now*, July 5, 2000; accessed at <http://www.kedb.com/news/navy-missile-office.html>.

Kaufmann, Chaim D., and Robert A. Pape. "Explaining Costly International Moral Action: Britain's Sixty-Year Campaign Against the Atlantic Slave Trade." *International Organization* 53, no. 4 (Autumn 1999): 631–668.

Keaney, Thomas. "Globalization, National Security and the Role of the Military." *SAISphere*, Winter 2000; accessed at <http://www.sais-jhu.edu/pubs/saisphere/winter00/indexkk.html>.

Keating, Thomas. "Naval Power is Vital." U.S. Naval Institute *Proceedings* 127, no. 7 (July 2001): 46–49.

Keegan, John. *The Price of Admiralty: The Evolution of Naval Warfare*. New York: Penguin Books, 1988.

Kellerhals, Merle D. "U.S. Will Withdraw From 1972 Anti-Ballistic Missile Treaty." U.S. Department of State, International Information Programs, December 13, 2001; accessed at <http://usinfo.state.gov/topical/pol/arms/stories/01121301.htm>.

Kellerman, David N. *Worldwide Maritime Piracy*. Special Ops Associates, June 1999; accessed at <http://www.specialopsassociates.com>.

Kelly, Michael R. "The Shoal Water of Homeland Defense." U.S. Naval Institute *Proceedings* 128, no. 5 (May 2002): 65–70.

Kennan, George F. *Around the Cragged Hill*. New York: W.W. Norton and Company, 1994.

———. "The Origins of Containment." In *Containment: Concept and Policy*, ed. Terry L. Deibel and John Lewis Gaddis, 23–32. Washington, DC: National Defense University Press, 1985.

Kennedy, Paul M. "The Eagle Has Landed," *The Financial Times*, February 1, 2002; accessed at <http://globalarchive.ft.com/globalarchieve/article.htm?id=020201011552&query=NATO+>.

———. *The Rise and Fall of the Great Powers.* New York: Random House, 1987.

———. *The Rise and Fall of British Naval Mastery.* London: Ashfield Press, 1976.

Keogh, Dermot. "The Diplomacy of 'Dignified Calm': An Analysis of Ireland's Application for Membership in the EEC, 1961–1963." *Chronicon* 1, no. 4 (1997): 1–68.

Keohane, Robert O., and Joseph S. Nye, Jr. "Introduction." In *Governance in a Globalizing World,* ed. Joseph S. Nye and John D. Donahue. Washington, DC: Brookings Institution Press, 2000.

King, Admiral, Ernest J., USN, Commander-in-Chief, United States Fleet and Chief of Naval Operations. *War Instructions: United States Navy, 1944,* F.T.P. 143(A). Washington, DC: Government Printing Office, November 1944.

Klare, Michael. "The New Geography of Conflict." *Foreign Affairs* 80, no. 3 (May/June 2001): 49–61.

Koch, Andrew. "USN Pushes Littoral Combat Ship." *Jane's Defence Weekly,* January 23, 2002, 6.

Kosiak, Steven, Andrew F. Krepinevich, and Michael Vickers. *A Strategy for a Long Peace.* Washington, DC: Center for Strategic and Budgetary Assessments, January 2001.

Kosnick, Mark E. "The Military Response to Terrorism." *Naval War College Review* 53, no. 2 (Spring 2000): 13–39.

Krauthammer, Charles. "The Unipolar Moment." *Foreign Affairs* 70, no. 1 (America and the World 1990/1991 Issue): 23–33.

Krepinevich, Andrew F. "Calvary to Computer: The Patterns of Military Revolutions." *The National Interest,* no. 37 (Fall 1994): 30–42.

Kristof, Nicholas D. "Search for the Sorcerer." In *Thunder from the East: Portrait of a Rising Asia,* ed. Nicholas D. Kristof and Sheryl WuDunn, 5–23. New York: Alfred A. Knopf, 2000.

Kryukov, Valery, Valery Shmat, and Arild Moe. "West Siberian Oil and the Northern Sea Route: Current Situation and Future Potential." *Polar Geography,* no.19 (1995): 234.

Kugler, Richard L. *Changes Ahead: Future Direction for the US Overseas Military Presence.* Santa Monica, CA: RAND, 1998.

———, and Ellen L. Frost, eds. *The Global Century: Globalization and National Security.* Washington, DC: National Defense University Press, 2001.

Kurtz, Howard. "Journalists Worry About Limits on Information Access." *The Washington Post,* September 24, 2001, A5.

Kuzik, B., N. Novichkov, V. Shvarev, M. Kenshetaev, and A. Simakov. *Rossiia na mirovom rynke oruzhiia: Analiz i perspektivy* [Russia on the Global Arms Market: Analysis and Perspectives]. Moscow: Voennyi Parad, 2001.

Lacey, Marc. "Hunting For Elusive Terrorists Off Somalia's Coast." *The New York Times,* April 2, 2002, A13.

LaFeber, Walter. *Inevitable Revolutions: The United States in Central America.* New York: W.W. Norton, 1984.

———. *The New Empire: An Interpretation of American Expansionism, 1860–1898.* Ithaca, NY: Cornell University Press, 1963.

LaFleur, Timothy. "Taking Defense Littorally." *The Washington Times*, August 5, 2001, B5.

Langhorne, Richard. *The Coming of Globalization.* New York: Palgrave, 2001.

Lasswell, James A. "Assessing Hunter Warrior." *Armed Forces Journal International*, May 1997, 14–15.

Latrash, Fredrick. "Reorganizing the Navy Helo Force." U.S. Naval Institute *Proceedings* 127, no. 1 (January 2001): 46–51.

Lawrence, Bruce B. *Defenders of God: The Fundamentalist Revolts Against the Modern Age.* San Francisco: Harper and Row, 1989.

Lehman, John. *Command of the Seas.* New York: Charles Scribners' Sons, 1988.

Lieven, Anatol. "Nasty Little Wars." *The National Interest*, no. 62 (Winter 2000/2001): 65–76.

Lindert, Peter H., and Jeffrey G. Williamson. *Does Globalization Make the World More Unequal?* National Bureau of Economic Research Working Paper 8228. Cambridge, MA: MIT Press, 2001.

"Linkages versus Size Effects." *Economia Internazionale* (July/August 1991): 228–243.

Lockwood, Ben. *A Note on the Robustness of the Kearney/Foreign Policy Globalization Index.* GSR, University of Warwick Working Paper No. 79.01, August 2001.

Loeb, Vernon. "For Jones, Marines, Time for a Change." *The Washington Post*, September 4, 2001, 17.

———. "Planned Jan. 2000 Attacks Failed or Were Thwarted." *The Washington Post*, December 24, 2000, A2.

Lok, Joris Janssen. "Promoting a European Maritime Initiative." *Jane's Navy International* (Web version), December 12, 2001; accessed at <http:/jni.janes.com/docs/jni/ search/shtml>.

———, and Richard Scott. "Amphibious Lift Bound by a Common Thread." *Jane's Navy International*, January/February 2002, 16–21.

Long, Robert L.J. "Foreword." *The Role of Seapower in U.S. National Security in the 21st Century.* Washington, DC: Center for Strategic and International Studies, March 1998.

Looney, Robert E. "Real or Illusionary Growth in an Oil Based Economy: Government Expenditures and Private Sector Investment in Saudi Arabia." *World Development*, September 1992, 1367–1376.

———. "Oil Revenues and the Dutch Disease in Saudi Arabia: Differential Impacts on Sectoral Growth." *Canadian Journal of Development Studies* 11, no.1 (1990): 119–133.

———, David A. Schrady, and Ronald L. Brown. "Estimating the Economic Benefits of Forward-Engaged Naval Forces." *Interfaces*, July 2001, 74–86.

———, David Schrady, and Douglas Porch. *Economic Impact of Naval Forward Presence: Benefits, Linkage, and Future Prospects as Modified by Trends in Globalization.* Monterey, CA: Naval Postgraduate School, December 2001.

Lucas, Robert. "On the Mechanics of Economic Development." *Journal of Monetary Economics* 22, no. 1 (July 1988): 3–42.

Luttwak, Edward. "From Geopolitics to Geo-Economics." *The National Interest*, no. 20 (Summer 1990): 17–23.

Macdonald, Scott B. "The New Bad Guys: Exploring the Parameters of the Violent New World Order." In *Gray Area Phenomena: Confronting the New World Disorder*, ed. Max G. Manwaring. Boulder, CO: Westview, 1993.

Macgregor, Douglas A. *Breaking the Phalanx: A New Design for Landpower in the 21st Century.* Westport, CT: Praeger, 1997.

MacKinder, Halford J. *Democratic Ideas and Reality.* London: Henry Holt and Co., 1919. Reprint. Washington, DC: National Defense University Press, 1996.

Maddison, G.R. "Operations in the Adriatic." In *Multinational Naval Forces*, ed. Peter T. Haydon and Ann L. Griffiths, 198–199. Proceedings of a workshop held July 13–15, 1995, Halifax, NS, Canada: Centre for Foreign Policy Studies, Dalhousie University, 1996.

Mahan, Alfred Thayer. "Considerations Governing the Disposition of Navies." *National Review*, July 1902, 701–719.

———. *Mahan on Naval Strategy.* Ed. John B. Hattendorf. Annapolis, MD: Naval Institute Press, 1991.

———. *The Influence of Sea Power Upon History 1660–1783.* Boston: Little, Brown, 1890. Reprint. New York: Dover Publications, 1987.

Mahnken, Thomas G. "Deny U.S. Access?" U.S. Naval Institute *Proceedings* 124, no. 9 (September 1998): 36–39.

———. "America's Next War." *The Washington Quarterly* 16, no. 3 (Summer 1993): 171–184.

Malik, Yogendra, and V.B. Singh. *Hindus Nationalists in India: Rise of the Bharatiya Janata Party.* Boulder, CO: Westview, 1994.

Mann, Stephanie. "Maritime Piracy Increasing Dramatically," *VOA News*, July 8, 2001.

Mansfield, Edward D., and Helen Milner. "The New Wave of Regionalism." *International Organization* 53, no. 3 (Summer 1999): 589–627.

———, and Jack Snyder. "Democratization and War." *Foreign Affairs* 74, no. 3 (May/June 1995): 79–97.

Manvel, J. Talbot. "The Next-Generation Aircraft Carrier." U.S. Naval Institute *Proceedings* 126, no. 6 (June 2000): 70–72.

"Marines Getting Good Results with Australian High Speed Vessel." *Inside the Navy*, October 15, 2001, 9.

Markusen, Ann. "The Rise of World Weapons." *Foreign Policy*, no. 114 (Spring 1999): 40.

Marolda, Edward J., and Robert J. Schneller, Jr. *Shield and Sword: The United States Navy and the Persian Gulf War*. Annapolis, MD: Naval Institute Press, 2001.

Marotte, Bertrand. "GM Strike Will Be Brutal for Economy." *Vancouver Sun*, October 4, 1996, D6.

May, Keith W. "Building on A Proven Record." U.S. Naval Institute *Proceedings* 127, no. 7 (July 2001): 64–67.

McCain, John, and Evan Bayh. "A New Start for National Service." *The* New *York Times*, November 6, 2001, A23.

McConnell, James. "The 'Rules of the Game': A Theory on the Practice of Superpower Naval Diplomacy." In *Soviet Naval Diplomacy*, ed. Bradford Dismukes and James McConnell, 240–280. New York: Pergamon Press, 1979.

McKenzie, Kenneth F. *The Revenge of the Melians, Asymmetric Threats and the 2001 QDR*. McNair Paper 62. Washington, DC: National Defense University Press, 2000.

McNeil, William H. "Navy On Lookout For Pirates In Indonesia." *Navy Times*, January 24, 2002, 10.

"Mega Boxships Loom: Ships of 13,000 TEU Possible." *Fairplay*, July 10, 1997, 38.

Menard, Russell. "Transport Costs and Long-Range Trade, 1300–1800: Was There a European 'Transport Revolution' in the Early Modern Era?" In *The Political Economy of Merchant Empires*, ed. James D. Tracy, 228–275. Cambridge: Cambridge University Press, 1991.

Micklethwait, John, and Adrian Wooldridge. "The Globalization Backlash." *Foreign Policy*, no. 126 (September/October 2001): 16–26.

Milani, Mohsen M. *The Making of Iran's Islamic Revolution: From Monarchy to Islamic Republic*. Boulder, CO: Westview, 1988.

Milbank, Dana. "Professor Shapes Bush Rhetoric." *The Washington Post*, September 26, 2001, A6.

Miller, Jerry. *Nuclear Weapons and Aircraft Carriers*. Washington, DC: Smithsonian Institution Press, 2001.

Miller, Kevin P. "UAVs Hold Promise for No-Fly Zone Enforcement." U.S. Naval Institute *Proceedings* 127, no. 9 (September 2001): 38–41.

Miller, Paul David. "A New Mission for Atlantic Command." *Joint Force Quarterly*, no. 1 (Summer 1993): 80–87.

Modelski, George, and William R. Thompson. *Seapower in Global Politics, 1494–1993*. Seattle: University of Washington Press, 1988.

Moens, Alexander, and Rafal Domisiewicz. *European and North American Trends in Defence Industry: Problems and Prospects of a Cross Atlantic Defence Market.* Ottawa, Canada: Department of Foreign Affairs and International Trade, April 2001.

Montesquieu, Baron de (Charles de Secondat). *Spirit of Laws.* Trans. Thomas Nugent, rev. J.V. Prichard, vol. 35 of *The Great Books of the Western World*, ed. Mortimer Adler. Chicago: Encyclopedia Britannica, 1990.

Morrison, Robert, Vaughn Rixon, and John Dudley."Chartering and HMAS Jervis Bay." U.S. Naval Institute *Proceedings* 127, no. 9 (September 2000): 75–77.

Muradian, Vago. "Deepwater More Important Ever For Coast Guard, Requirements Unchanged." *Defense Daily*, December 7, 2001, 1.

———. "Camus Hopes EADS Can Crack U.S. Defense Market Within Four Years." *Defense Daily*, April 23, 2001, 8.

———. "Canada to Buy British Upholder Subs in $525 Million Deal." *Defense Daily*, April 7, 1998, 1.

Murray, Bill. "Joining Forces." *Government Executive* 32, no. 14 (December 2000): 42–46.

Murray, Williamson, and Allan R. Millett. *Military Innovation in the Interwar Period.* Cambridge: Cambridge University Press, 1996.

Naegele, Jolyon. "Turkey: Caspian Oil Presents Challenge to the Straits." Radio Free Europe/Radio Liberty, June 23, 1998; accessed at <http://www.rferl.org>.

Naim, Moises. "Al Qaeda, the NGO." *Foreign Policy*, no. 129 (March/April 2002): 99–100.

National Research Council, Naval Studies Board. *Network-Centric Naval Forces: A Transition Strategy for Enhancing Operational Capabilities.* Washington, DC: National Academy Press, 2000.

Neves, Juan Carlos. "Interoperability in Multinational Coalitions: Lessons from the Persian Gulf War." *Naval War College Review* 48, no. 1 (Winter 1995): 50–62.

"New US Fleet Defies Iran's Terror." *Minnesota Daily Online*, April 22, 1996; accessed at <http://www.daily.umn.edu/daily/1996/04/22/editorial_opiniions/ofleet.col/index.html>.

Newman, Richard J. "Shooting from the Ship." *US News and World Report*, July 3, 2000.

Newman, Sally. "Political and Economic Implications of Global Naval Presence." In *Naval Forward Presence: Present Status, Future Prospects*, ed. Dan Goure and Dewey Mauldin, 47–59. Washington, DC: Center for Strategic and International Studies, November 1997.

Newton, George B. "Don't Forget the Arctic." *Submarine Review* (April 2001): 91–100.

Nikolskiy, Aleksey. "Russia has Overtaken France in Military-Technical Cooperation." *Moscow Vedimosti*, January 14, 2002. FBIS translated text, document ID: CEP20020114000328.

Nimitz, Chester W. *Principles and Applications of Naval Warfare: United States Fleets, 1947*, USF–1. Washington, DC: Office of the Chief of Naval Operations, May 1947.

Nincic, Miroslav. *How War Might Spread to Europe*. London: Taylor and Francis, 1985.

————, Roger Rose, and Gerard Gorski. "The Social Foundations of Strategic Adjustment." In *The Politics of Strategic Adjustment: Ideas, Institutions and Interests*, ed. Peter Trubowitz, Emily O. Goldman, and Edward Rhodes, 176–212. New York: Columbia University Press, 1998

Noer, John H., and David Gregory. *Chokepoints: Maritime Economic Concerns in Southeast Asia*. Washington, DC: National Defense University Press, 1996.

Nordquist, Myron H., ed. *United Nations Convention on the Law of the Sea: A Commentary*. Boston: Martinus Nijhoff, 1985.

Norris, Pippa. "Global Governance and Cosmopolitan Citizens." In *Governance in a Globalizing World*, ed. Joseph S. Nye and John D. Donahue, 155–177. Washington, DC: Brookings Institution Press.

North Atlantic Treaty Organization, Military Agency for Standardization. *NATO Glossary of Terms and Definitions (English and French)*, AAP–6(V) modified version 2, August 7, 2000, 2–D–6.

Notestein, Frank W., et al. *The Future Population of Europe and the Soviet Union: Population Projections, 1940–1970*. Geneva: League of Nations, 1944.

"NRDC Nuclear Notebook." *Bulletin of the Atomic Scientists* (November/December 2000): 78–79.

Nye, Jr., Joseph S. "Globalization's Democratic Deficit." *Foreign Affairs* 80, no. 4 (July/August 2001): 2–6.

Office of Naval Intelligence. *Challenges to Naval Expeditionary Warfare*. Washington, DC: Office of Naval Intelligence, 1997.

Office of the Secretary of Defense, Defense Science Board Task Force on Globalization and Security. *Report of the Task Force on Globalization and Security*. Washington, DC: Department of Defense, December 1999.

————, Defense Science Board. *Report of the Defense Science Board Task Force on The Creation and Dissemination of All Forms of Information in Support of Psychological Operations (PSYOP) in Time of Military Conflict*. Washington, DC: Department of Defense, May 2000.

————, National Defense Panel. *Transforming Defense: National Security in the 21st Century*. Washington, DC: Department of Defense, December 1997.

O'Hanlon, Michael. E. "Coming Conflicts: Interstate War in the New Millennium." *Harvard International Review* 23, no. 2 (Summer 2001): 42–46.

————. *Defense Policy Choices for the Bush Administration 2001–2005*. Washington, DC: Brookings Institution Press, 2001.

————. *Technological Change and the Future of Warfare*. Washington, DC: Brookings Institution Press, 2000.

———. "Can High Technology Bring U.S. Troops Home?" *Foreign Policy*, no. 113 (Winter 1998–1999): 72–86.

"Opening up the Northern Sea Route." *The Naval Architect* (November 2000): 6–8.

O'Rourke, Briffni. "EU: Prodi Seeks to Reassure Candidates on Security." *Radio Free Europe/Radio Liberty*, September 6, 2001; accessed at <www.rferl.org/nca/features/ 2001/09/06092001114157.asp>.

O'Rourke, Kevin H., and Jeffrey G. Williamson. *After Columbus: Explaining the Global Trade Boom, 1500–1800*. National Bureau of Economic Research Working Paper 8186. Cambridge, MA: MIT Press, 2001.

———. *Globalization and History: The Evolution of a Nineteenth-Century Atlantic Economy*. Cambridge, MA: MIT Press, 1999.

———. *When Did Globalization Begin?* National Bureau of Economic Research Working Paper 7632. Cambridge, MA: MIT Press, 2001.

———. *Globalization and Inequality: Historical Trends*. National Bureau of Economic Research Working Paper 8339. Cambridge, MA: MIT Press, 2001.

O'Rourke, Ronald. *Navy Ship Procurement Rate and the Planned Size of the Navy: Background and Issues for Congress*. Washington, DC: Congressional Research Service, April 4, 2000.

———. *Navy Ship Procurement Rate and the Planned Size of the Navy: Background and Issues for Congress*. Washington, DC: Congressional Research Service, August 28, 2001, 1–6.

———. *Statement before the Senate Armed Services Committee, Subcommittee on Seapower, Hearing on Ship Procurement and Research and Development Programs*. March 2, 2000.

———. "Gulf Ops." U.S. Naval Institute *Proceedings* (May 1989): 43.

Owen, Richard, and Daniel McGrory. "Business-Class Suspect Caught in Container." *The Times* (London), October 26, 2001; accessed at <http://www.thetimes.co.uk/article/ 0,,2001350024–2001371211,00.html>.

Owens, William A., with Edward Offley. *Lifting the Fog of War*. New York: Farrar, Straus and Giroux, 2000.

Owens, Mackubin Thomas Owens. "In Defense of Classical Geopolitics." *Naval War College Review* 52, no. 4 (Autumn 1999): 59–76.

———. "The Case For Ground Troops." *The Wall Street Journal*, October 31, 2001, A24.

"Paris Declaration Respecting Maritime Law." In *Documents on the Laws of War*, ed. Robert Adams and Richard Guelff, 3ᵈ ed., rev. New York: Oxford University Press, 2000.

Parker, Geoffrey. *Geopolitics: Past, Present, and Future*. London: Pinter, 1998.

Patton, James H. "Coping With ASW Minefields." *Defense Science* (March 1988): 25–30.

———. "Submarines versus Mines." *Submarine Review* (April 1995): 23–26.

————. "Impact of Weapons Proliferation on Naval Forces." In *Naval Forward Presence and the National Military Strategy*, ed. Robert L. Pfaltzgraf, Jr., and Robert H. Schultz, Jr. Annapolis, MD: U.S. Naval Institute Press, 1993, 133–142.

Pearlstein, Steven. "Globalization Regaining Impetus." *The Washington Post*, December 7, 2001, A12–13.

"Pentagon Proposal for Foreign Build Navy Ships is Killed." *American Shipbuilder*, October 2000, 2; accessed at <http://www.americanshipbuilding.com/news-oct00.htm>.

Perin, David A. "Are Big Decks Still the Answer?" U.S. Naval Institute *Proceedings* 127, no. 6 (June 2001): 30–33.

Pesaran, M. Hashem, and Bahram Pesaran. *Working With Microfit 4.0: Interactive Econometric Analysis*. Cambridge: Camfit Data, 1997.

Peters, Ralph. *Fighting for the Future: Will America Triumph?* Mechanicsburg, PA: Stackpole Books, 1999.

————. "Constant Conflict," *Parameters* 27, no. 2 (Summer 1997): 4–14.

Pettis, Michael. "Will Globalization Go Bankrupt?" *Foreign Policy*, no. 126 (September/October 2001): 2–59.

Pierce, Terry C. "Sunk Costs Sinks Innovation." U.S. Naval Institute *Proceedings* 127, no. 4 (April 2001): 4–6.

"Piloting: Chemical-laden Tanker's Hair-Raising Close Call at the Golden Gate." *Marine Watch Institute*; accessed at <http://www.marinewatch.com>.

Polmar, Norman. "A Problem with Precision?" U.S. Naval Institute *Proceedings* 127, no. 4 (April 2001): 4–6.

"Possible Sale of Perry Class Frigates to Turkey." *Defense Systems Daily*, January 25, 2002; accessed at <http://defense-data.com/current/page133373.htm>.

Postman, Neil. *Technopoly: The Surrender of Culture to Technology*. New York: Vintage Books, 1993.

Priest, Dana. "A Four-Star Foreign Policy? U.S. Commanders Wield Rising Clout, Autonomy." *The Washington Post*, 28 September 2000, A1.

Quinliven, James T. "Flexible Ground Forces." In *Holding the Line: U.S. Defense Alternatives for the Early 21st Century*, ed. Cindy Williams, 181–204. Cambridge, MA: MIT Press, 2001.

"RAM Passes OpEval." U.S. Naval Institute *Proceedings* 126, no. 4 (April 2000): 6.

Reeve, Henry. "The Orders in Council on Trade During War." *Edinburgh Review*, July 1854, 221–222.

Reich, Robert. "A Proper Global Agenda." *The American Prospect*, September 24, 2001.

Renner, Michael. "Alternative Futures in War and Conflict." *Naval War College Review* 53, no. 4 (Autumn 2000): 45–56.

Reppy, Judith, ed. *The Place of the Defense Industry in National Systems of Innovation.* Occasional Paper No. 25. Ithaca, NY: Cornell University Peace Studies Program, April 2000.

Ressa, Maria. "Indonesian War Games on Oil-Rich Island Sends Message." CNN, September 22, 1996; accessed at <http://cnn.com/WORLD/9609/22/indonesia/index.html>.

Rhodes, Edward. "Conventional Deterrence." *Comparative Strategy* 19, no. 3 (July–September 2000): 221–254.

———. "Conventional Deterrence: Review of Empirical Literature." *Second Navy RMA Round Table*, SAIC, Tysons Corner, VA, June 4, 1997.

———, Jonathan DiCicco, Sarah Milburn Moore, and Tom Walker. "Forward Presence and Engagement: Historical Insights into the Problem of 'Shaping.'" *Naval War College Review* 53, no. 1 (Winter 2000): 25–61.

Ricks, Thomas E. "For Pentagon, Asia Moving to the Forefront." *The Washington Post*, May 26, 2000, 1.

Robins, Robert S., and Jerrold M. Post. *Political Paranoia: The Psychopolitics of Hatred.* New Haven: Yale University Press, 1997.

Rochlin, Gene I. *Trapped in the Net: The Unanticipated Consequences of Computerization.* Princeton: Princeton University Press, 1997.

Romer, Paul. "Endogenous Technical Change." *Journal of Political Economy* 98, no. 5 (October 1990): s71–s102.

———. "Increasing Returns and Long Run Growth." *Journal of Political Economy* 94, no. 5 (October 1986): 1002–1037.

Ronzitti, Natalino, ed. *Maritime Terrorism and International Law.* Boston: Martinus Nijhoff/Kluwer Academic Publishers, 1990.

Rosen, Stephen Peter. *Winning the Next War: Innovation and the Modern Military.* Ithaca: Cornell University Press, 1991.

Rosenau, James N. "Stability, Stasis, and Change: A Fragmegrating World." In *The Global Century: Globalization and National Security*, ed. Richard L. Kugler and Ellen L. Frost, 127–153. Washington, DC: National Defense University Press, 2000.

———. "The Dynamics of Globalization: Toward an Operational Formulation." *Security Dialogue* (September 1996): 247–262.

———. *Turbulence in World Politics: A Theory of Change and Continuity.* Princeton, NJ: Princeton University Press, 1990.

Roskill, Stephen W. *The Strategy of Sea Power.* London: Collin's, 1962.

Roszak, Theodore. *The Cult of Information.* Berkeley: University of California Press, 1986.

Rothrock, D.A., Y. Yu, and G. A. Maykut. "Thinning of the Arctic Sea-Ice Cover." *Geophysical Research Letters*, December 1, 1999, 3469–3472.

Royal Australian Navy. *Australian Maritime Doctrine*, R[oyal] A[ustralian] N[avy] Doctrine 1. October 5, 2000. Canberra ACT: Defence Publishing Service, 2000.

"Running the Fleet Ragged—Duct Tape Aviation." *Navy Times*, September 10, 2001, 12–14.

Ryn, Claes G. *The New Jacobinism: Can Democracy Survive?* Washington, DC: National Humanities Institute, 1991.

Sachs, Jeffrey D. "Globalization and Patterns of Economic Development." *Weltwirtschaftliches Archiv* 136, no. 4 (2001).

———. "The Geography of Economic Development." *Naval War College Review* 53, no. 4 (Autumn 2000): 93–105.

———. "The Limits of Convergence: Nature, Nurture, and Growth." *The Economist*, June 14, 1997, 19.

Salpukas, Agis. "Quake in Japan: Commerce: Kobe Earthquake Disrupts the Flow of Global Trade." *The New York Times*, January 21, 1995, 1.

Scales, Robert H., Jr. "The Indirect Approach: How U.S. Military Forces Can Avoid the Pitfalls of Future Urban Warfare." *Armed Forces Journal International* (October 1998): 68–74.

Schelling, Thomas. *Arms and Influence.* New Haven: Yale University Press, 1966.

Schmalz, Jeffrey. "After Skirmish with Protestors, Navy Tests Missile." *The New York Times*, December 5, 1989, A1.

Schmidt, John F. "A Critique of the Hunter Warrior Concept." *Marine Corps Gazette*, June 1998, 13–19.

Schneider, Greg. "Scuttled By the Process: Navy Likes Md. Firm's Ideas for Battle System—but Won't Use Them." *The Washington Post*, August 29, 2001, E1.

Scholte, Jan Aart. *Globalization: A Critical Introduction.* New York: St. Martin's Press, 2000.

Schroeder, Paul. *The Transformation of European Politics, 1763–1848.* New York: Oxford University Press, 1994.

Sciolino, Elaine. "A Gore Advisor Who Basks in the Shadows." *The New York Times*, April 25, 2000, A14.

Scully-Power, Paul, and Richard J. Stevenson. "Swallowing the Transparency Pill." U.S. Naval Institute *Proceedings* 113, no. 21 (December 1987): 149–152.

Semmel, Bernard. *Liberalism and Naval Strategy: Ideology, Interest, and Sea Power during the Pax Britannica.* Boston: Allen and Unwin, 1986.

Sen, Amartya. "If It's Fair, It's Good: 10 Truths About Globalization." *International Herald Tribune*, July 14, 2001.

Sharp, Richard G. Foreword. *Jane's Fighting Ships 1989–1990* (rpt. in SEAPOWER, Arlington, Virginia, July 1989, 37–47).

"Ship Rams Greenpeace; Sub Unleashes Trident 2." *San Diego Union Tribune*, December 5, 1989, A10.

Siegel, Adam B. "International Naval Cooperation during the Spanish Civil War." *Joint Force Quarterly,* no. 29 (Autumn/Winter 2001–2002): 82–90.

———. *The Use of Naval Force in the Post-War Era: U.S. Navy and Marine Corps Crisis Response Activity, 1946–1990.* Alexandria, VA: Center for Naval Analyses, February 1991.

Simpson, Glenn R. "Pentagon Moves to Postpone Dutch Deal for Silicon Valley Group." *The Wall Street Journal,* March 8, 2001, B6.

———. "Treasury Interpretation of Law Lets Bush Delay Taking Sides in Dutch-U.S. Merger." *The Wall Street Journal,* April 27, 2001, A20.

Sims, C. "Large Scale Econometric Models." *Econometrica* (January 1980): 1–48.

Small, Christopher, and Joel Cohen. "Continental Physiography, Climate, and the Global Distribution of Human Population." *Proceedings of the International Symposium on Digital Earth,* 1999; accessed at <http:/www.ldeo.columbia.edu/-small/pdf/isde_mallcohen.pdf>.

Smith, Adam. *The Wealth of Nations.* Vol. 2. London, 1776, reprinted 1791.

Smith, Alan, and Michael Meese with Hartmut Spieker. *Defense Economics: Reform, Restructuring, Realignment.* George C. Marshall European Center for Security Studies; accessed at <http://www.marshallcenter.org/Conference%20Center/Conference%20Reports.htm>.

Smith, Edward A. Jr. "Network Centric Warfare: What's the Point?" *Naval War College Review* 54, no. 1 (Winter 2001): 59–75.

———. ". . . *From the Sea:* The Process of Defining a New Role for Naval Forces in the Post-Cold War World." In *The Politics of Strategic Adjustment: Ideas, Institutions and Interests,* ed. Peter Trubowitz, Emily Goldman, and Edward Rhodes, 267–304. New York: Columbia University Press, 1999.

Sokolsky, Joe J. "NATO's New Maritime Role: The Sea Power Solution or Allies Adrift?" In *Maritime Forces in Global Security,* ed. Ann L. Griffiths and Peter T. Haydon. Proceedings of a colloquium in June 1994, Halifax, NS, Canada: Centre for Foreign Policy Studies, Dalhousie University, 1995.

Soulsby, H.G. *The Right of Search and the Slave Trade in Anglo-American Relations, 1814–1862.* Baltimore: Johns Hopkins University Press, 1933.

Spencer, Jack, and Joe Dougherty. "The Quickest Way to Global Missile Defense: First From the Sea." *The Heritage Foundation Backgrounder,* no. 1384, July 13, 2000.

Sprinzak, Ehud. "The Great Superterrorism Scare." *Foreign Policy,* no. 112 (Fall 1998): 110–119.

Spykman, Nicholas. *The Geography of the Peace.* Ed. Helen R. Nicholl. New York: Harcourt, Brace and Company, 1944.

"Stars Raise $150 Million." ABCNews.com, September 25, 2001; accessed at <http://more.abcnews.go.com/sections/entertainment/DailyNews/tribute010925.html>.

"State Minister Mirzaoglu Says Maritime Traffic Capacity in Turkish Straits Has Reached Its Limits." Turkish Maritime Pilot's Association, March 28, 2001; accessed at <http://www.turkishpilots.org>.

Steele, George P. "Killing Nuclear Submarines." U.S. Naval Institute *Proceedings* 86, no. 12 (November 1960): 45–51.

Stelzer, Irwin. "Oil Loses Power to Drive Boom off Course." *London Times*, January 23, 2000.

Stone, Andrea. "Soldiers Deploy on Mental Terrain." *USA Today*, October 3, 2001, 7.

Stone, Norman. *Europe Transformed, 1878–1919*. Cambridge, MA: Harvard University Press, 1983.

Strassler, Robert R., and Victor Davis Hanson. *The Landmark Thucydides: A Comprehensive Guide to the Peloponnesian War*. New York: Free Press, 1996.

Strausz-Hupé, Robert. "Population as an Element of National Power." *Foundations of National Power: Readings in World Politics and American Security*. 2ᵈ ed. New York: Van Nostrand, 1951.

———. *The Balance of Tomorrow*. New York: Putnam, 1945

———. *Geopolitics: The Struggle for Space and Power*. New York: Harcourt Brace, 1942.

Strickland, C. Frank. "It's Not About Mousetraps—Measuring the Value of Knowledge for Operators." *Joint Force Quarterly*, no. 13 (Autumn 1996): 90–96.

Stubbs, Bruce. "Whither the National Fleet?" U.S. Naval Institute *Proceedings* 127, no. 5 (May 2001): 72–73.

———. "The U.S. Coast Guard: A Unique Instrument of U.S. National Security." *Marine Policy*, June 18, 1994, 513.

Sumida, Jon Tetsuro. *Inventing Grand Strategy and Teaching Command: The Classic Works of Alfred Thayer Mahan Reconsidered*. Baltimore: Johns Hopkins University Press, 1997.

Swartz, Peter M. "Classic Roles and Future Challenges: The Navy After Next." In *Strategic Transformations and Naval Power in the 21st Century*, ed. Pelham G. Boyer and Robert S. Wood, 273–305. Newport: Naval War College Press.

System Planning Corporation. *Political and Economic Implications of Global Naval Presence*. Report for the Office of the Deputy Chief of Naval Operations (N81), September 30, 1996.

Talmon, J. L. *Origins of Totalitarian Democracy*. New York: W.W. Norton, 1970.

"Tamil Suicide Boat Rams Oil Tanker." BBC News On-line, October 30, 2001; accessed at <news.bbc.co.uk>.

Tangredi, Sam J. "Sea Power—Theory and Practice." In *Strategy in the Contemporary World*, ed. John Baylis, James Wirtz, Eliot Cohen, and Colin S. Gray, 111–136. New York: Oxford University Press, 2002.

———. "Beyond Sea and Jointness." U.S. Naval Institute *Proceedings* 127, no. 9 (September 2001): 60–63.

————. "Security from the Oceans." In *The Global Century: Globalization and National Security*, ed. Richard L. Kugler and Ellen L. Frost, 471–492. Washington, DC: National Defense University Press, 2001.

————. *All Possible Wars? Toward A Consensus View of the Future Security Environment.* Washington, DC; National Defense University Press, 2000.

————. "The Fall and Rise of Naval Forward Presence." U.S. Naval Institute *Proceedings* 126, no. 5 (May 2000): 28–32.

————. "A Ship for All Reasons." U.S. Naval Institute *Proceedings* 125, no. 9 (September 1999): 92–95.

————. "Space is an Ocean." U.S. Naval Institute *Proceedings* 125, no. 1 (January 1999): 52–53.

————. "Are We Firing Tomahawks Too Easily?" U.S. Naval Institute *Proceedings* 10, no. 12 (December 1996): 8–10.

————, and Randall G. Bowdish. "Core of Naval Operations: Strategic and Operational Concepts of the U.S. Navy." *Submarine Review* (January 1999): 11–23.

"Telethon Audience is Bigger Than Bush's." *Los Angeles Times*, September 23, 2001; accessed at <http://www.latimes.com/news/nationworld/nation/la-092301tele.story>.

Tellis, Ashley J., Janice Bially, Christopher Layne, and Melissa McPherson. *Measuring National Power in the Postindustrial Age.* Washington, DC: RAND, 2000.

Thach, James B. "USCG's Urgent Need for Deepwater Replacements." *Sea Power* 41, no. 4 (April 1998): 82.

Thucydides. *History of the Peloponnesian War*. Trans. Rex Warner. New York: Penguin, 1972.

Thunman, Nils. "Diesel Submarines of the U.S. Navy?" U.S. Naval Institute *Proceedings* 111, no. 8 (August 1985): 136–137.

Tomisek, Steven J. *Homeland Security: The New Role for Defense.* Strategic Forum No. 189. Washington, DC: National Defense University Press, February 2002.

Tonelson, Alan. *The Race to the Bottom: Why a Worldwide Worker Surplus and Uncontrolled Free Trade Are Sinking American Living Standards.* Boulder, CO: Westview, 2000.

Trebilcock, Craig T. "The Myth of Posse Comitatus." *Homeland Security Journal*, October 2000; accessed at <http://www.homelandsecurity.org/journal/Articles/Trebilcock.htm>.

Tritten, James J., and Paul N. Stockton, eds. *Reconstituting America's Defense: The New U.S. National Security Strategy.* New York: Praeger Publishers, 1992.

————. *Our New National Security Strategy: America Promises to Come Back.* New York: Praeger, 1992.

Trofimenko, Genrikh. *The U.S. Military Doctrine.* Moscow: Progress Publishers, 1986.

Truver, Scott C. "The U.S. Navy in Review." U.S. Naval Institute *Proceedings* 126, no. 5 (May 2000): 76, 78.

————. "Tomorrow's U.S. Fleet." U.S. Naval Institute *Proceedings* 126, no. 3 (March 2000): 107–109.

Turbowitz, Peter, Emily Goldman, and Edward Rhodes, eds. *The Politics of Strategic Adjustment: Ideas, Institutions, and Interests.* New York: Columbia University Press, 1999.

Ullman, Harlan K. "Influencing Events Ashore." In *The Global Century: Globalization and National Security*, ed. Richard L. Kugler and Ellen L. Frost, 493–520. Washington, DC: National Defense University Press, 2001.

United Nations. *1982 United Nations Convention on the Law of the Sea.* United Nations Publication 1261 (1982), reproduced from UN Document/CONF.62/122 of October 7, 1982.

"U.S. Air Force to Test Navy's CEC." *Jane's Defence Weekly*, August 1, 2001, 6.

U.S. Chairman, Joint Chiefs of Staff. *Joint Vision 2020: America's Military—Preparing for Tomorrow.* Washington, DC: Government Printing Office, June 2000.

————. *Shape, Respond, Prepare Now: A Military Strategy for a New Era.* Washington, DC: Government Printing Office, 1997.

————. *National Military Strategy of the United States of America.* Washington, DC: Government Printing Office, February 1995.

U.S. Coast Guard. "Polar Class Icebreakers (WAGB)." January 19, 2001; accessed at <http://www.uscg.mil/datasheet/icepolr.htm>.

————. *Threats and Challenges to Maritime Security 2020.* Accessed at <http://www.uscg.mil>.

————. "USCGC Healy." March 13, 2001; accessed at <http://www.uscg.mil/pacarea/healy/>.

U.S. Commission on National Security in the 21st Century. *Road Map for National Security: Imperative for Change, Phase III Report on a U.S. National Security Strategy for the 21st Century.* Washington, DC: Government Printing Office, March 2001.

————. *Seeking a National Strategy: A Concert for Preserving Security and Promoting Freedom, Phase II Report on a U.S. National Security Strategy for the 21st Century.* Washington, DC: Government Printing Office, April 2000.

————. *New World Coming: American Security in the 21st Century, Supporting Research and Analysis, Phase I Report on the Emerging Global Security Environment for the First Quarter of the 21st Century.* Washington, DC: Government Printing Office, September 1999.

————. *New World Coming: American Security in the 21st Century, Major Themes and Implications, Phase I Report on the Emerging Global Security Environment for the First Quarter of the 21st Century.* Washington, DC: Government Printing Office, September 1999.

U.S. Congress. Hearings on the National Defense Authorization Act for Fiscal Year 2002: H.R. 2586 and Oversight Previously Authorized Programs before the Committee on Armed Services House of Representatives, One Hundred Seventh Congress, First Session, July 12, 2001; accessed at <http://www.house.gov/hasc/openingstatementsandpressreleases/ 107thcongress/01-07-12clark.html>.

U.S. Congressional Budget Office. *Budgeting for Naval Forces: Structuring Tomorrow's Navy at Today's Funding Level.* Washington, DC: Government Printing Office, October 2000.

U.S. Department of Defense. "Navy Area Missile Defense Program Cancelled." News Release 637–01, December 2001; accessed at <www.defenselink.mil/news/Dec2001>.

———. *Quadrennial Defense Review Report.* Washington, DC: Department of Defense, September 2001.

———. *Department of Defense Dictionary of Military and Associated Terms,* Joint Publication 1–02. Washington, DC: Department of Defense, April 2001.

———. *Proliferation: Threat and Response.* Washington, DC: Department of Defense, January 2001; accessed at <http://www.defenselink.mil/pubs/ptr20010110.pdf>.

———. *Final Report to Congress: Conduct of the Persian Gulf War.* Washington, DC: Department of Defense, April 1992, 200–208.

U.S. Department of Energy. *International Energy Outlook 2001.* Washington, DC; accessed at <http://www.eia.doe.gov/analysis/2001anal02.html>.

———, Energy Information Administration. *International Energy Outlook 2000: With Projections to 2020.* Washington, DC: Government Printing Office, March 2000; accessed at <http://www.eia.doe.gov/oiaf/ieo/index.html>.

———, Energy Information Administration. *Chokepoints.* Accessed at <http://www.eia.doe.gov>.

U.S. Department of Justice, Counterterrorism Threat Assessment and Warning Unit, Counterterrorism Division, Federal Bureau of Investigation. *Terrorism in the United States, 1999.* Washington, DC: Government Printing Office, 1999; accessed at <http://www.fbi.gov/publications/terror/terror99.pdf>.

U.S. Department of the Navy. *Lessons of the Falklands, Summary Report.* Washington, DC: Department of the Navy, February 1983.

U.S. Department of State. *Background Information on Foreign Terrorist Organizations.* Washington, DC: Department of State, October 8, 1999.

———. *Foreign Terrorist Organizations,* Designations by Secretary of State Madeleine K. Albright, 1999 Report. Washington, DC: Department of State, October 8, 1999; accessed at <http://www.state.gov/www/global/terrorism/fto_1999.html>.

———. *Patterns of Global Terrorism: 1999.* Washington, DC: Department of State, April 2000, 1.

————. Foreign Service Institute, Center for the Study of Foreign Affairs. *Thinking About World Change*. Washington, DC: Department of State, 1990.

U.S. General Accounting Office. *Kosovo Air Operations: Need to Maintain Alliance Cohesion Resulted in Doctrinal Departures*. Washington, DC: Government Printing Office, July 2001.

————. *Tactical Aircraft: Modernization Plans Will Not Reduce Average Age of Aircraft*. Washington, DC: Government Printing Office, February 16, 2001; accessed at <http://commdocs.house.gov/committees/security/has193000.000/has193000_0f.htm>.

U.S. Government Interagency Working Group. *International Crime Threat Assessment*. Washington, DC: Government Printing Office, 2000, 32.

U.S. Joint Chiefs of Staff, *Joint Warfare of the Armed Forces of the United States*, Joint Publication 1, Washington, DC: Government Printing Office, November 2000.

————. *Joint Doctrine for Multinational Operations*, Joint Publication 3–16. Washington, DC: Government Printing Office, April 2000.

————. *Joint Tactics, Techniques, and Procedures for Antiterrorism*, Joint Publication 3–07.2. Washington, DC: Government Printing Office, March 1998.

U.S. Marine Corps. MCDP 1, *Warfighting*. Washington, DC: Department of the Navy, June 1997, 37.

U.S. National Intelligence Council. *Growing Global Migration and its Implications for the United States*. Washington, DC: Government Printing Office, March 2001.

————. *Global Trends 2015*. Washington, DC: Government Printing Office, January 2001.

————. *Global Trends 2015: A Dialog about the Future with Nongovernment Experts*. Washington, DC: Government Printing Office, December 2000.

U.S. Navy, Chief of Naval Operations. *Navy Strategic Planning Guidance with Long Range Planning Objectives*. Washington, DC: Department of the Navy, April 2000, 36.

————, Naval Doctrine Command. *Naval Warfare*, NDP–1. Washington, DC: Government Printing Office, March 1994.

————, Naval Doctrine Command. *Multinational Maritime Operations*. Washington, DC: Government Printing Office, September 1996.

————. "Navy Intercepts Ballistic Missile; Accelerates TBMD Program." January 24, 2002; accessed at <http://www.chinfo.navy.mil/navpalib/weapons/ missiles/standard/ standard.html>.

————, Navy Inspector General. *Final Report of Naval Aviation Spares and Readiness*. Washington, DC: Department of the Navy, April 2000.

————. *The Commander's Handbook on the Law of Naval Operations*, Naval Warfare Publication 7, chapter 5; accessed at <http://www.cpf.navy.mil/pages/legal/ NWP%201–14/NWPCH5.htm>.

———. *Network Centric Operations: A Capstone Concept for Naval Operations in the Information Age.* Draft report. Newport: Navy Warfare Development Command, 2001.

U.S. Office of the National Drug Control Policy Coordinator. *The National Drug Control Strategy 2001 Annual Report.*Washington, DC: Government Printing Office, 2001.

"U.S. Ready to Go It Alone." BBC News, February 2, 2002; accessed at <http://news.bbc.co. uk/hi/ english/world/europe/newsid_1798000/1798132.stm>.

U.S. Special Operations Command. *U.S. Special Operations Forces Posture Statement 2000.* Washington, DC: Department of Defense, 1–9.

Vagg, Jon. "Rough Seas? Contemporary Piracy in South East Asia." *British Journal of Criminology* (Winter 1995): 63–80.

Vego, Milan N. *Naval Strategy and Operations in Narrow Seas.* Portland, OR: Frank Cass Publishers, 1999.

———. *Soviet Naval Tactics.* Annapolis, MD: Naval Institute Press, 1992.

Visser, Dean. "U.S. Helping Asia Combat Sea Piracy." Associated Press, July 5, 2001; accessed at <http://wire.ap.org/public_pages/WirePortal.pcgi/ us_portal.html>.

Von Clausewitz, Carl. *On War.* Ed. and trans. Michael Howard and Peter Paret. Princeton: Princeton University Press, 1976.

Wadhams, P., and N. Davis. "Further Evidence of Ice Thinning in the Arctic Ocean." *Geophysical Research Letters,* December 15, 2000, 3973–3975.

Walker, Ruth. "Arctic Thaw Opening up Lucrative Shipping Route." *The Christian Science Monitor,* June 7, 2000, 1.

Walker, Tom. "Coast Guard Expects Smuggling to Increase." *Daily Citizen* (Key West, FL), March 24, 2001, 1.

Wall, Robert, and David A. Fulgham. "What's Next For Navy Missile Defense." *Aviation Week & Space Technology,* December 24, 2001; accessed at <www.aviationnow.com/ content/publication/awst/20011224/aw43b.htm>.

Wallerstein, Immanuel. *The Modern World System: Capitalist Agriculture and the Origins of the European World-Economy in the Sixteenth Century.* New York: Academic Press, 1974.

Waltz, Kenneth N. "Structural Realism after the Cold War." *International Security* 25, no.1 (Summer 2000), 5–41.

———. "Globalization and American Power." *The National Interest,* no. 59 (Spring 2000): 46–56.

Wayman, C. Mullins. *Terrorist Organizations in the United States: An Analysis of Issues, Organizations, Tactics and Responses.* Springfield, IL: Charles C. Thomas Publisher, 1988, 95.

Weinland, Robert G. *A Somewhat Different View of Optimal Naval Posture.* CNA Professional Paper 214. Alexandria, VA: Center for Naval Analyses, 1978.

Weinstock, Matthew. "Changing Course." *Government Executive,* December 2001, 55–57.

"Western European Industry Ownership Jigsaw Puzzle." *Defence Systems Daily*, accessed at <http://defence-data/current/pagerip1.htm>.

Westing, Arthur H. *Global Resources and International Conflict: Environmental Factors in Strategic Policy and Action*. Oxford: Oxford University Press, 1986.

The White House. Office of the Press Secretary. "Remarks by the President on National Missile Defense." December 13, 2001, accessed at <http://usinfo.state.gov/topical/pol/arms/stories/01121302.htm>.

———. *A National Security Strategy for a New Century*. Washington, DC: The White House, December 1999.

———. *International Crime Control Strategy*. Washington, DC: The White House, May 1998.

Whiteman, Marjorie M. *Digest of International Law*. Washington, DC: Department of State, 1963–1973.

Whiteneck, Daniel J. *Naval Forward Presence and Regional Stability*, Alexandria, VA: Center for Naval Analyses, September 2001.

Wijnolst, Niko. "Malacca-Max-2." *Lloyd's List*, November 28, 2000, 7.

Willett, Lee. "Global Submarines." Global Defence Review; accessed at <http://www.global-defence.com/pages/subs.html>.

Williamson, Jeffrey G. "Globalization, Convergence, and History." *Journal of Economic History* 56, no. 2 (June 1996): 1–30.

Willis, Grant. "Secretary Receives First-hand View of Carrier Operations." *Navy Times*, November 13, 1989, 4

Winton, Harold R. "Introduction on Military Change." In *The Challenge of Change: Military Institutions and New Realities, 1918–1941*, ed. Harold R. Winton and David R. Mets. Lincoln, NE: Nebraska University Press, 2000.

Wirtz, James J. "QDR 2001: The Navy and the Revolution in Military Affairs." *National Security Studies Quarterly* (Autumn 1999): 43–60.

Wolf, Martin. "Will the Nation-State Survive Globalization." *Foreign Affairs* 80, no. 1 (January/February 2001): 178–190.

Wolfe, Frank. "Marine Officials Ride Australian-Built High Speed Vessel." *Defense Daily*, November 20, 2001, 4.

Wood, Adrian. *North-South Trade, Employment, and Inequality: Changing Fortunes in a Skill-Driven World*. New York: Oxford, 1994.

Woodward, Bob. "In Hijacker's Bags, a Call to Planning, Prayer, and Death." *The Washington Post*, September 28, 2001, A1.

World Bank. *World Development Indicators 2000*. Washington, DC: World Bank, 2000.

Ya'ari, Yeddia. "A Case for Maneuverability." *Naval War College Review* 50, no. 4 (Autumn 1997): 125–132.

Yergin, Daniel, Dennis Eklof, and Jefferson Edwards. "Fueling Asia's Recovery." *Foreign Affairs* 77, no. 2 (March/April 1998): 34–50.

Zakheim, Dov S., et al. *The Political and Economic Implications of Global Naval Presence.* Arlington, VA: System Planning Corporation, 1996.

Zink, Jeffrey A. "The End of the Triad: Morality, Reality, and the Ideal Deterrent." *Naval War College Review* 47, no. 3 (Summer 1994): 51–66.

Index

About the Editor

Captain Sam J. Tangredi, USN, is a senior military fellow in the Institute for National Strategic Studies at the National Defense University. His most recent previous assignments were as commanding officer of USS *Harpers Ferry* (LSD–49) and as Head of the Strategy and Concepts Branch of the Office of the Chief of Naval Operations. Author of *All Possible Wars? Toward a Consensus View of the Future Security Environment, 2001–2025* (Washington, DC: National Defense University Press, 2000) and numerous articles, reviews, and book chapters on defense and foreign policy issues, Captain Tangredi has won nine literary awards, including the U.S. Naval Institute's prestigious Arleigh Burke prize. A graduate of the U.S. Naval Academy and distinguished graduate of the Naval Postgraduate School, he earned a Ph.D. in international relations from the University of Southern California and was a Federal executive fellow in the Hoover Institution at Stanford University. He has appeared in The History Channel's *The Great Ships* series and in the documentary movie *At Sea*. He is married to Reverend Deborah L.H. Mariya, a United Methodist minister and former U.S. Navy chaplain.